Microsoft

Microsoft® Office Excel 2003 Programming Inside Out

Curtis Frye
Award-winning author of books
and online courses

Wayne Freeze
Computer consultant, author,
and programmer

Felicia Buckingham
Principal of FKB Consulting,
and Office VBA expert

PUBLISHED BY
Microsoft Press
A Division of Microsoft Corporation
One Microsoft Way
Redmond, Washington 98052-6399

Library of Congress Cataloging-in-Publication Data
Frye, Curtis, 1968-
    Microsoft Office Excel 2003 Programming Inside Out / Curtis Frye, Wayne S. Freeze, Felicia K.
    Buckingham.
        p. cm.
    Includes index.
    ISBN 0-7356-1985-9
    1. Microsoft Excel (Computer file)   2. Business--Computer programs.   3. Electronic
    spreadsheets.   I. Title.

    HF5548.4.M523F792 2003
    005.54--dc22   2003064850

Printed and bound in the United States of America.

3 4 5 6 7 8 9   QWT   8 7

Distributed in Canada by H.B. Fenn and Company Ltd.

A CIP catalogue record for this book is available from the British Library.

Microsoft Press books are available through booksellers and distributors worldwide. For further information about international editions, contact your local Microsoft Corporation office or contact Microsoft Press International directly at fax (425) 936-7329. Visit our Web site at www.microsoft.com/mspress. Send comments to *mspinput@microsoft.com*.

Acquisitions Editor: Juliana Aldous
Project Editor: Dick Brown
Technical Reviewer: Mark Dodge
Indexer: Richard Shrout

Body Part No. X10-09355

To our families

Contents at a Glance

Part 1
Preliminaries   1

Chapter 1
What's New in Excel 2003 3

Chapter 2
Exploring Excel 13

Part 2
Visual Basic
for Applications   23

Chapter 3
**Exploring Visual Basic
for Applications** 25

Chapter 4
VBA Programming Starter Kit 41

Chapter 5
**Creating Sub and
Function Procedures**. 85

Part 3
The Excel
Object Model   105

Chapter 6
The *Application* Object 107

Chapter 7
Workbooks and Worksheets 129

Chapter 8
Ranges and Cells 161

Part 4
Advanced VBA   191

Chapter 9
Manipulating Data with VBA. . . . 193

Chapter 10
Formatting Excel Objects. 219

Chapter 11
**Creating Add-Ins and
COM Add-Ins** 239

Chapter 12
**Understanding and
Using Events** 265

Chapter 13
Manipulating Files 281

Chapter 14
Developing Class Modules 299

Part 5
Manipulating
Excel Objects   319

Chapter 15
Charts. 321

Chapter 16
PivotTables and PivotCharts. . . . 341

Chapter 17
Command Bars 365

Chapter 18
Customizing Dialog Boxes 383

Contents At A Glance

Chapter 19
Creating User Forms 395

Chapter 20
**Creating Advanced
User Forms.** 419

Part 6
**Excel and the
Outside World:
Collaborating
Made Easy   443**

Chapter 21
**Excel and Other Office
Applications** 445

Chapter 22
**Excel and the
Structured Query Language** 467

Chapter 23
Introducing ADO 481

Chapter 24
Excel Query Program 497

Chapter 25
Excel and the Web 519

Chapter 26
**Excel and the Extensible
Markup Language (XML)** 539

Table of Contents

Acknowledgments . . . . **xix**
We'd Like to Hear from You . . . . **xxi**
About the CD . . . . **xxiii**
    What's on the CD xxiii
    Using the CD xxiii
    System Requirements xxiv
    Support Information xxiv
Conventions and Features Used in this Book . . . . **xxv**
    Text Conventions xxv
    Design Conventions xxv

Part 1
Preliminaries

Chapter 1
What's New in Excel 2003   3

    Using Improved Statistical Functions 3
    Creating Smart Documents 6
    Creating Document Workspaces 6
    Implementing Information Rights Management 7
    Comparing Workbooks Side By Side 7
    Getting Information with the Research Task Pane 8
    Using Extended XML Capabilities 8
        Creating Excel Lists 9
        Mapping Excel Data to XML Schemas 10
        Publishing Spreadsheets with Web Components 11

Chapter 2
Exploring Excel   13

    Workbooks 13
    Worksheets 14
    Cells and Ranges 15
    The Excel Interface 18
    Formulas 21

Part 2
Visual Basic for Applications

Chapter 3
Exploring Visual Basic for Applications   **25**

An Overview of Object-Oriented Programming 25
    Properties 26
    Methods 27
    Events. 27
    Collections 28
Working with Macros 29
    Recording and Viewing Macros 29
    Running a Macro 31
    Debugging a Macro 34
    Implementing Macro Security and Digital Signatures 36

Chapter 4
VBA Programming Starter Kit   **41**

Introducing the Visual Basic Editor 41
    Opening the Visual Basic Editor. 41
    Recognizing Parts of the Visual Basic Editor. 41
    Customizing the Visual Basic Editor. 49
Managing Code Windows 53
    Handling Windows 53
    Adding Code 53
    Notes on Programming Style and Code Readability 54
Developing Projects with the Project Explorer 55
    Creating VBA Modules 55
    Deleting VBA Modules 56
    Copying Modules Between Projects 57
Declaring Variables, Constants, and Data Types 57
    Declaring Variables. 58
    Defining Data Types 58
    Defining Constants. 59
    Handling Strings. 59
    Handling Dates and Times 60
    Handling Variants and Data Type Conversions. 61
    Understanding Variable Scope and Lifetimes 62
Assigning Values to Variables 64
Working with Arrays 64
    Creating an Array 65
    Creating Multidimensional Arrays. 65
Creating Dynamic Arrays 66

Writing to the Screen and Accepting Input 67
  Creating a Message Box. 67
  Creating an Input Box 71
Defining Object Variables 72
Creating Custom Data Types 72
  With...End With Command 73
Controlling Program Flow. 73
  Selection Statements. 74
  Loops 77
  GoTo Statement. 82
Error Handling 82

Chapter 5
Creating Sub and Function Procedures 85

Defining Sub Procedures. 85
  Defining the Scope of a Sub Procedure 90
  Running a Sub Procedure from Within Another Procedure 93
  Retaining Values Between Procedure Calls. 98
Defining Function Procedures 98
  Creating a Function Procedure. 100
  Running Function Procedures 101
  Passing Arguments to Procedures 101
  Passing Named Arguments 103
Organizing for Success 104

Part 3
The Excel Object Model

Chapter 6
The *Application* Object 107

Introducing the *Application* Object 108
  Properties 108
  Methods 119

Chapter 7
Workbooks and Worksheets 129

The *Workbooks* Collection 129
  Creating New Workbooks 129
  Opening Workbooks 130
  Workbook Properties 138
  Workbook Methods 145
  Printing and Previewing Workbooks 147

The *Sheets* and *Worksheets* Collections 149
    Properties 149
    Methods 150
    Worksheet Methods 156

Chapter 8
Ranges and Cells 161

Basic Range Manipulations 161
    Finding the Active Range 161
    Selecting a Range 162
Referring to Ranges 166
    Referencing Ranges on the Active Worksheet 166
    Referencing Ranges on an Inactive Worksheet 167
    Referencing Cells in a Range 167
    Referencing Cells Using the *Offset* Property 167
    Defining a Range Using the *Cells* Property 172
    Referencing Columns and Rows 172
    Referencing Non-Contiguous Groups of Cells 172
Manipulating Groups of Cells 172
    Resizing Cells Programmatically 172
    Joining Two Ranges Together 173
    Detecting Empty Cells 176
Using Named Ranges 177
    Defining a Named Range 177
    Changing Notation Styles 179
    Reserved Range Names 182
    Copying Data Between Ranges and Arrays 185
Getting Data Entry Right the First Time 187

Part 4
Advanced VBA

Chapter 9
Manipulating Data with VBA 193

Manipulating Text 193
    Determining if the Value in a Cell Is Text 193
    Preparing String Data for Processing 195
    Determining the Number of Characters in a String 197
    Concatenating Text from Two or More Cells or Variables 198
    Returning the First or Last Several Characters from a String 200
    Returning Characters from Arbitrary Positions in a String 202
    Finding a String Within Another String 202
Manipulating Numbers 206
    Performing Summary Calculations 206
    Performing Financial Calculations 208

Manipulating Dates and Times 213
 Time and Date Serial Numbers 213
 Date and Time Functions 213

Chapter 10
Formatting Excel Objects   **219**

Using Excel Color Constants and the Color Palette 219
 Manipulating the Current Excel Color Palette 223
 Using the Excel Color Palette on the Web 226
Formatting Worksheet Elements 230
Formatting Fonts 231
Formatting Cells 233
Formatting Borders 236

Chapter 11
Creating Add-Ins and COM Add-Ins   **239**

Introducing Add-Ins 239
Using the Add-Ins dialog box 240
 Installing an Add-In 241
 Unloading an Add-In 241
Creating Excel Add-Ins 241
 Creating an Add-In 241
 Saving the Add-In 242
 Installing the Add-In 243
Using the *AddIns* Collection 244
 AddIns Collection 244
 AddIn Object 245
Creating Automation and COM Add-Ins 247
 Using the *IDTExtensibility2* Interface 248
 Registry Keys 250
Building an Automation Add-In with Visual Basic 6 250
 Designing the Add-In 250
 Registry Entries 256
Building a COM Add-In with Visual Basic .NET 256
 Running the Shared Add-In Wizard 257
 Modifying the Template 259
 Installing the Add-In 261

Chapter 12
Understanding and Using Events   **265**

Enabling and Disabling Events 266
Workbook Events 267
 Open Event 269
 Activate Event 270
 SheetActivate Event 270

Table of Contents

NewSheet Event 270
BeforeSave Event 271
Deactivate Event 271
BeforePrint Event 271
BeforeClose Event 272
Worksheet Events 273
Change Event. 275
SelectionChange Event 276
BeforeRightClick Event 276
Application Events 276
Turning on Application Event Monitoring 278
Detecting When a Workbook Is Opened 279

Chapter 13
Manipulating Files   **281**

Locating External Files 281
Returning All Files 282
Limiting the File Search 285
Finding Files with the FileDialog Dialog Box 291
Writing to an External File 295
Reading from an External File 296
Searching a File for a Value. 298

Chapter 14
Developing Class Modules   **299**

What Is an Object?. 299
What Is a Class? 299
What Are Properties? 299
What Are Methods? 300
What Are Events?. 300
Introducing Class Modules 300
Accessing Objects 301
Declaring Objects. 302
Objects and *Nothing*. 302
Objects with Multiple Object Variables 303
Properties, Methods, and Events. 303
Public vs. *Private* Properties, Methods, and Events 303
Properties 304
Methods 304
Events. 304
Building a Class. 305
Creating a Class Module. 305
Defining Simple Properties 305
Defining Property Routines 306
Defining Methods. 309

Defining Events 310
Defining Private Variables, Subroutines, and Functions 310
Special Events for Classes 311
Resolving References 311
Practical Class Design 312
A Simple Class 312
Extending a Simple Class 313
A *Collection* Class 313
A Class with Business Rules 317

Part 5
Manipulating Excel Objects

Chapter 15
Charts   321

Introducing Charts 321
Creating Embedded Charts or Chart Sheets 322
Defining the Chart Object Model 326
Manipulating Charts 327
Activating a Chart 327
Deactivating a Chart 330
Modifying a Chart's Data Series 331
Modifying a Chart to Use Data from Arrays 333
Defining a Chart's Labels 335
Formatting a Chart 336
Modifying All Charts in a Workbook 338
Printing Charts 339
Final Thoughts on Programming Charts 339

Chapter 16
PivotTables and PivotCharts   341

PivotTables and PivotCharts 341
Introducing PivotTables 341
Creating a PivotTable with the PivotTable Wizard 343
Introducing PivotCharts 346
Creating a PivotChart with the PivotTable Wizard 346
Online Analytical Processing (OLAP) Issues 347
PivotTable Objects 348
PivotTables Collection 349
PivotTable Object 349
PivotCaches Collection 351
PivotCache Object 352
PivotField Objects 353
PivotItem Object 356

Programming PivotTables 356
    Creating a PivotTable 357
    Creating a PivotChart 358
Manipulating PivotTables Programmatically. 359
    Pivoting a PivotTable Programmatically 359
    Resetting a PivotTable to Its Original Position 361
    Recording and Restoring Arbitrary PivotTable Positions 361

Chapter 17
Command Bars

365

Identifying Parts of the Menu System. 365
    CommandBars Collection 366
    CommandBar Objects 367
    Listing *CommandBar* Objects. 369
    Adding a Floating Command Bar 370
    Deleting a Command Bar 371
Command Bar Controls. 371
    CommandBarControls Collection 371
    CommandBarControl Object. 373
    Button Controls 375
    Creating Toolbars 377
    Combo Box Controls. 378
    Using a Combo Box 379
    Pop-Up Controls 380
    Displaying a Pop-Up 380
    Adding Items to an Existing Menu 382

Chapter 18
Customizing Dialog Boxes

383

Displaying Existing Dialog Boxes 384
Modifying Existing Dialog Boxes. 388
    Exploring the *Dialogs* Collection 389
    Passing Arguments to Existing Dialog Boxes. 393
Planning with Dialog Boxes 394

Chapter 19
Creating User Forms

395

Creating a *UserForm*. 395
    Adding a *UserForm* 395
    Designing a *UserForm*. 396
    Modifying a *UserForm* 397
    Properties of a *UserForm* 398
    Displaying a *UserForm* 399

UserForm Controls 401
   Programming Controls 401
   Common Properties, Methods, and Events. 402
   The *Label* Control 404
   The *CommandButton* Control. 404
   The *TextBox* Control 405
   The *CheckBox* Control. 406
   The *ToggleButton* Control 407
   The *SpinButton* Control. 407
   The *Frame* Control 408
   The *OptionButton* Control 409
   The *Image* Control 410
   The *ScrollBar* Control 411
   The *ListBox* Control. 412
   The *ComboBox* Control 414
   The *RefEdit* Control. 415
   The *TabStrip* Control 415
   The *MultiPage* Control. 417

Chapter 20

Creating Advanced User Forms   419

Capturing Information. 419
   Form Application Overview 419
   Designing a Form 420
   Displaying Data 422
   Navigating the Worksheet 425
   Editing Data. 427
   Adding Data. 428
   Validating Data. 429
   Displaying the User Form 430
Building a Multi-Step Wizard 431
   Wizard Application Overview 431
   Handling Menus. 433
   Building the *UserForm*. 434
   Navigating the Pages 435
   Collecting Options for the Wizard. 438
   Summarizing the Options 440
   Running the Wizard 441

Part 6
Excel and the Outside World: Collaborating Made Easy

Chapter 21
Excel and Other Office Applications   445

Starting Another Application 445
Activating Another Application 449
Binding 449
  Late Binding 450
  Early Binding 452
Interacting with Other Office Applications 455
  Opening a Document in Word 457
  Accessing an Active Word Document 460
  Creating a New Word Document 461
  Controlling Excel from Other Office Applications 462
Working with Multiple Applications to Get the Job Done 465

Chapter 22
Excel and the Structured Query Language   467

Comparing Spreadsheets and Databases. 467
  Fundamental Database Concepts 467
  Database Keys. 469
  Accessing Databases from Excel. 470
Manipulating Databases with SQL 471
The *Select* Statement 471
  Simple *Select* Statements. 472
  Retrieving Rows 473
  Sorting Rows 475
  Using Multiple Tables 476
  Using Functions 477
The *Insert* Statement 478
  Using the *Insert* Statement 478
The *Update* Statement 479
The *Delete* Statement. 479

Chapter 23
Introducing ADO   481

The ADO Object Model 482
  Using the ADO Object Model 483
The *Connection* Object 483
  Key Properties and Methods of the *Connection* Object. 484
  Connecting to Different Database Management Systems 485
  Using the *Errors* Collection 486
  Using the *Error* Object 487

The *Command* Object 487
   Key Properties and Methods of the *Command* Object 488
   Using the *Parameters* Collection 489
   Using the *Parameter* Object. 490
The *Recordset* Object 491
   Key Properties and Methods of the *Recordset* Object 491
   Using the *Fields* Collection 494
   Using the *Field* Object. 494

Chapter 24
Excel Query Program   497

Excel Query Program Overview. 497
Setting Up the Project. 498
Initializing the Program 499
Ending the Program 500
Connecting to a Database. 501
   Initializing the DBInfo *UserForm* 502
   Changing Database Providers 503
   Selecting Windows Authentication 504
   Saving the Database Info 504
Editing a Query 505
Executing a Database Query 508
   Getting the Information to Run the Query 508
   Building a Connection String 509
   Getting the Query. 512
   Running a Query. 512
   Copying Rows 514
Using the Excel Query Program 515
   Configure the Connection Information 516
   Enter a Query. 516
   Run the Query 517

Chapter 25
Excel and the Web   519

HTML 520
   Saving a Worksheet as a Web Page 520
   Publishing a Worksheet to the Web 523
   Making Web-Based Worksheets Interactive. 525
Using the Internet as a Data Source 527
   Opening Web Pages as Workbooks 528
   Using Web Queries. 529
   Parsing Web Pages for Specific Information 532
Using the Internet to Publish Results. 533
   Setting Up a Web Server. 533
   Saving Worksheets as Web Pages 534

Table of Contents

Adding Interactivity with the Web Components 534
Communicating with a Web Server. 536
Using Internet Solutions with Excel 537

Chapter 26

Excel and the Extensible Markup Language (XML)   539

Introducing Data Lists. 539
Creating Data Lists Programmatically. 541
Creating XML Schemas. 546
Creating XML Data Files 549
Adding XML to a Workbook Manually 550
Importing XML Data Manually 552
Adding XML to a Worksheet Programmatically. 553
Mapping a Schema to a Worksheet Programmatically 553
Mapping Schema Elements to Cells Using XPath 557

Acknowledgments

From Curtis Frye:

First and foremost I'd like to thank my co-authors, Wayne Freeze and Felicia Buckingham, for their knowledge and skill at presenting a series of complex topics so effectively. Westley Annis pitched in on several chapters as well, for which I am grateful.

I value my relationship with Microsoft Press for many reasons, but right up there on the list is the terrific working relationship I have with everyone there. I'm happy to say our relationship survived intact despite many changes in all of our lives that transpired during this project. Juliana Aldous Atkinson invited me to submit an outline and shepherded the proposal through the review process. Sandra Haynes was the first project editor, and Dick Brown took over when Sandra assumed different duties within Press. Wendy Zucker stepped in to help during the revision process when Dick went on vacation for a week. The phrase "team effort" doesn't begin to describe the sort of support they provided.

I was also very fortunate to have Mark Dodge, co-author of *Microsoft Office Excel 2003 Inside Out*, as my technical editor. His knowledge of both the series and Excel gave him the perspective to make many terrific recommendations. Lisa Pawlewicz, ably assisted by Jaime Odell, performed what was probably one of the more involved copy edits that has passed over their desks in a while. Page proofs were handled by Sandi Resnick at Microsoft and the nSight team of Joe Armstrong, Steve Boudreault, Catherine Cooker, Beth Lew, Katie O'Connell, Dan Shaw, Asa Tomash, and Melissa von Tschudi-Sutton. Barbara Levy and Carl Diltz turned my Word files into the beautiful pages you see before you, William Teel got the graphics ready for production, Joel Panchot created the original art, and Richard Shrout created a thorough index. Tess McMillan heads the team that created the Companion CD.

Finally, I'd like to thank my agent, Neil Salkind of StudioB, for introducing me to Microsoft back in December of 2000. He was concerned about recommending a relatively new author to such an important publisher, but I'd say things have turned out pretty well.

From Wayne Freeze:

Curt: thanks for putting up with me while writing this book. I valued your patience, especially when I was running behind schedule as usual. *Laura:* thank you for making my first year at StudioB a very worthwhile experience. *Steve:* thank you for the opportunities and challenges you tossed my way this year and I have even higher expectations for the next. *Christopher and Samantha:* thanks for tolerating the long hours I've spent working on this book alongside my other projects. *Jill:* thank you for being you—I love you.

From Felicia Buckingham:

Thanks to everyone from Microsoft Press for their work on the project, and thanks to Curt for the opportunity to co-author my first book.

We'd Like to Hear from You

Our goal at Microsoft Press is to create books that help you find the information you need to get the most out of your software.

The *Inside Out* series was created with you in mind. As part of our ongoing effort to ensure that we're creating the books that meet your learning needs, we'd like to hear from you. Let us know what you think. Tell us what you like about this book and what we can do to make it better. When you write, please include the title and author of this book in your e-mail message, as well as your name and contact information. We look forward to hearing from you!

How to Reach Us

E-Mail: nsideout@microsoft.com
Mail: Inside Out Series Editor
         Microsoft Press
         One Microsoft Way
         Redmond, WA 98052

Note: Unfortunately, we can't provide support for any software problems you might experience. Please go to http://support.microsoft.com *for help with any software issues.*

About the CD

The Companion CD that ships with this book contains many tools and resources to help you get the most out of your *Inside Out* book.

What's on the CD

Your *Inside Out* CD includes the following:

- **Complete eBook.** In this section, you'll find an electronic version of *Microsoft Office Excel 2003 Programming Inside Out*. The eBook is in PDF format.
- **Computer Dictionary, Fifth Edition eBook.** Here you'll find the full electronic version of the *Microsoft Computer Dictionary, Fifth Edition*. Suitable for home and office, the dictionary contains more than 10,000 entries.
- **Insider Extras.** This section includes the sample files used in the book.
- **Microsoft Resources.** In this section, you'll find information about additional resources from Microsoft that will help you get the most out of Microsoft Office Excel 2003 and other business software from Microsoft.
- **Extending Excel.** In this section, you'll find great information about third-party utilities and tools you use to further enhance your experience with Microsoft Office Excel 2003.

The Companion CD provides detailed information about the files on this CD, and links to Microsoft and third-party sites on the Internet. All the files on this CD are designed to be accessed through Microsoft Internet Explorer (version 5.01 or later).

> **Note** The links to third-party sites are not under the control of Microsoft Corporation, and Microsoft is therefore not responsible for their content, nor should their inclusion on this CD be construed as an endorsement of the product or the site. Software provided on this CD is in English language only and may be incompatible with non-English language operating systems and software.

Using the CD

To use this Companion CD, insert it into your CD-ROM drive. If AutoRun is not enabled on your computer, click on Index.htm in the WebSite folder in the root of the CD.

System Requirements

Following are the minimum system requirements necessary to run the CD:

- Microsoft Windows XP or later or Windows 2000 Professional with Service Pack 3 or later.
- 266-MHz or higher Pentium-compatible CPU
- 64 megabytes (MB) RAM
- 8X CD-ROM drive or faster
- Microsoft Windows–compatible sound card and speakers
- Microsoft Internet Explorer 5.01 or later
- Microsoft Mouse or compatible pointing device

Note System requirements may be higher for the add-ins available via links on the CD. Individual add-in system requirements are specified at the sites listed. An Internet connection is necessary to access some of the hyperlinks. Connect time charges may apply.

Support Information

Every effort has been made to ensure the accuracy of the book and the contents of this Companion CD. For feedback on the book content or this Companion CD, please contact us by using any of the addresses listed in the "We'd Like to Hear From You" section.

Microsoft Press provides corrections for books through the World Wide Web at *http://www.microsoft.com/mspress/support/*. To connect directly to the Microsoft Press Knowledge Base and enter a query regarding a question or issue that you may have, go to *http://www.microsoft.com/mspress/support/search.asp*.

For support information regarding Windows XP, you can connect to Microsoft Technical Support on the Web at *http://support.microsoft.com/*.

Conventions and Features Used in this Book

This book uses special text and design conventions to make it easier for you to find the information you need.

Text Conventions

Convention	Meaning
Abbreviated menu commands	For your convenience, this book uses abbreviated menu commands. For example, "Click Tools, Track Changes, Highlight Changes" means that you should click the Tools menu, point to Track Changes, and click the Highlight Changes command.
Boldface type	**Boldface** type is used to indicate text that you enter or type.
Initial Capital Letters	The first letters of the names of menus, dialog boxes, dialog box elements, and commands are capitalized. Example: the Save As dialog box.
Italicized type	*Italicized* type is used to indicate new terms.
Plus sign (+) in text	Keyboard shortcuts are indicated by a plus sign (+) separating two key names. For example, Ctrl+Alt+Delete means that you press the Ctrl, Alt, and Delete keys at the same time.

Design Conventions

 This icon identifies a new or significantly updated feature in this version of the software.

 Inside Out

This statement illustrates an example of an "Inside Out" problem statement

These are the book's signature tips. In these tips, you'll get the straight scoop on what's going on with the software—inside information about why a feature works the way it does. You'll also find handy workarounds to deal with software problems.

Tip   Tips provide helpful hints, timesaving tricks, or alternative procedures related to the task being discussed.

Troubleshooting

This statement illustrates an example of a "Troubleshooting" problem statement

Look for these sidebars to find solutions to common problems you might encounter. Troubleshooting sidebars appear next to related information in the chapters. You can also use the Troubleshooting Topics index at the back of the book to look up problems by topic.

Cross-references point you to other locations in the book that offer additional information about the topic being discussed.

 This icon indicates information or text found on the companion CD.

Caution   Cautions identify potential problems that you should look out for when you're completing a task or problems that you must address before you can complete a task.

Note   Notes offer additional information related to the task being discussed.

Sidebars

The sidebars sprinkled throughout these chapters provide ancillary information on the topic being discussed. Go to sidebars to learn more about the technology or a feature.

Part 1

Preliminaries

1   What's New in Excel 2003   3

2   Exploring Excel   13

What's New in Excel 2003

Using Improved Statistical Functions 3

Creating Smart Documents 6

Creating Document Workspaces 6

Implementing Information Rights Management. 7

Comparing Workbooks Side By Side 7

Getting Information with the Research Task Pane. 8

Using Extended XML Capabilities. 8

Microsoft Excel has been around since 1985, so it's no surprise that the basic spreadsheet elements of the program have remained fairly constant for quite some time. That said, there is always room for improvement, and Microsoft Office Excel 2003 has a bunch of new features that make data gathering, collaboration, and data transfer much more effective than in previous versions. The bulk of the improvements in Excel 2003 revolve around the use of *Extensible Markup Language*, or XML, which is a flexible, text-based markup system that lets you describe the contents of a spreadsheet so that the data it contains can be handled automatically instead of manually, saving time and reducing the possibility of errors introduced from re-keying or copying the data. Excel 2003 also comes with a suite of improved statistical functions, which are far more precise than in previous versions of the program.

Using Improved Statistical Functions

Most Excel users will never go beyond the relatively simple formulas and formatting tasks used to track business and financial data, but scientific and advanced business or academic users who take advantage of the advanced statistical functions available in Excel need great precision from those functions. The Excel programming team changed how the program calculates the results of quite a few statistical functions, improving the accuracy of those results and making them much more useful to advanced users. Table 1-1 lists the enhanced functions and describes each one.

Table 1-1. Improved Statistical Functions

BINOMDIST	Determines the probability that a set number of true/false trials, where each trial has a consistent chance of generating a true or false result, will result in exactly a specified number of successes (for example, exactly five out of ten coin flips will end up heads).
CHIINV	Finds a value that best fits a result in a *chi*-squared distribution.
CONFIDENCE	Returns a value you can use to construct a confidence interval for a population mean.
CRITBINOM	Determines when the number of failures in a series of true/false trials exceeds a criterion (for example, more than 5 percent of light bulbs in a production run fail to light).
DSTDEV	Estimates the standard deviation of values in a column by considering only those values that meet a criterion.
DSTDEVP	Calculates the standard deviation of values in a column based on every value in the column.
DVAR	Estimates the variance of values in a column or list by considering only those values that meet a criterion.
DVARP	Calculates the variance of values in a column or list based on every value in the column.
FINV	Returns the value that would generate a target result from an F-test (a test of variability between two data sets).
FORECAST	Calculates future values based on an existing time series of values.
GAMMAINV	Returns the value that would generate a given result from a gamma-distributed (that is, skewed) data set.
GROWTH	Predicts the exponential growth of a data series.
HYPGEOMDIST	Returns the probability of selecting an exact number of a single type of item from a mixed set of objects. For example, a jar holds 20 marbles, 6 of which are red. If you choose three marbles, what is the probability you will pick exactly one red marble?
INTERCEPT	Calculates the point at which a line will intersect the *y*-axis.
LINEST	Generates a line that best fits a data set by generating a two-dimensional array of values to describe the line.
LOGEST	Generates a curve that best fits a data set by generating a two-dimensional array of values to describe the curve.
LOGINV	Returns the inverse logarithm of a value in a distribution.
LOGNORMDIST	Returns the number of standard deviations a value is away from the mean in a lognormal distribution.
NEGBINOMDIST	Returns the probability that there will be a given number of failures before a given number of successes in a binomial distribution.

Table 1-1. Improved Statistical Functions

NORMDIST	Returns the number of standard deviations a value is away from the mean in a normal distribution.
NORMINV	Returns a value that reflects the probability a random value selected from a distribution will be above it in the distribution.
NORMSDIST	Returns a standard normal distribution, with a mean of 0 and a standard deviation of 1.
NORMSINV	Returns a value that reflects the probability a random value selected from the standard normal distribution will be above it in the distribution.
PEARSON	Returns a value that reflects the strength of the linear relationship between two data sets.
POISSON	Returns the probability of a number of events happening, given the Poisson distribution of events.
RAND	Generates a random value.
RSQ	Returns the square of the Pearson coefficient of two sets of values.
SLOPE	Returns the slope of a line.
STDEV	Estimates the standard deviation of a numerical data set based on a sample of the data.
STDEVA	Estimates the standard deviation of a data set (which can include text and true/false values) based on a sample of the data.
STDEVP	Calculates the standard deviation of a numerical data set.
STDEVPA	Calculates the standard deviation of a data set (which can include text and true/false values).
STEYX	Returns the predicted standard error for the y value for each x value in a regression.
TINV	Returns a t value based on a stated probability and degrees of freedom.
TREND	Returns values along a trend line.
VAR	Estimates the variance of a data sample.
VARA	Estimates the variance of a data set (which can include text and true/false values) based on a sample of the data.
VARP	Calculates the variance of a data population.
VARPA	Calculates the variance of a data population, which can include text and true/false values.
ZTEST	Returns the probability that the mean of a data sample would be greater than the observed mean of data in the set.

Creating Smart Documents

Excel workbooks have always been able to interact with other Office documents, but those interactions have been somewhat limited. Creating links to data on the Web, in a database, or in another Office document are all valuable abilities, but the workbook was simply a stand-alone collection of bits. In Office 2003, *smart documents* are Office documents that have *metadata* (that is, data that tells the document about itself) with information regarding how they fit within a business process, allowing the documents to take programmed actions based on that context.

As an example, if you work at a technical services firm that uses an Excel-based template to track the time you spend on various projects, you probably create a new workbook (with one worksheet) at the beginning of every week, save it with your identifying information, and fill in your time at the end of each day. Then, at the end of the week, you either save the workbook to a network folder or e-mail the workbook to your administrative contact. Smart documents, by contrast, have programming that fills in the details about how your timecard fits in the business process. When you create a new timecard workbook, Excel recognizes who you are and fills in your personal data (name, employee number, projects, etc.). Then, when you're ready to leave for the week, the smart document displays a button that lets you send the workbook to the next stage in the process. And as far as you're concerned, it doesn't matter what mechanism is used to send the data along; it could be written to a database, saved as a worksheet in a workbook elsewhere on the network, incorporated into data on a BizTalk server tracking workflow issues, or attached to a Microsoft Outlook e-mail message and sent to your administrative contact.

Creating Document Workspaces

An increasing number of documents require input from more than one person. When you estimate the cost of a large project, for example, you will probably require input from every member of your team to determine which products and components should be considered and ultimately used in the project, not to mention the amount of labor and corporate overhead spending required to support the project internally. Sharing and merging workbooks is one way to get the information out there, but the process is filled with pitfalls. If one of your colleagues adds or changes a password for their copy of the workbook, for example, you won't be able to include their changes in the merge.

When you use Excel 2003 in conjunction with Microsoft Windows SharePoint Services, however, you can streamline the process of collaborating, editing, and reviewing workbooks by creating a document workspace. A *document workspace* is a virtual work area set up on a SharePoint site that lets individuals with access to the workbook modify the copy on the SharePoint server or work with a local copy, which they can update by adding changes from the master copy in the document workspace. After you establish the document workspace and give each of your team members access to that portion of the site, your colleagues will be able to work on the same copy of the workbook. Any changes saved to any copy of the document become available for every member of the team; if the changes conflict, you as the administrator are able to choose which changes will be adopted. You can also use the controls on the Shared Workspace task pane to create and manage a document workspace.

> **Note** Document workspaces are available for Microsoft Office Word 2003, Excel 2003, PowerPoint 2003, and Visio 2003.

Implementing Information Rights Management

One of the hardest problems to solve in the digital domain is limiting access to information. You can use passwords, accounts, and other access restrictions to limit who can view files on a computer or network, but once an unprotected file is out in the open it can be copied and distributed easily. The new Information Rights Management (IRM) capabilities in Office 2003 help maintain the confidentiality and integrity of your information by limiting who is able to view and edit your files. Specifically, network administrators can create policies that allow you to set user-level permissions to limit access to the material. Users who somehow get their hands on unauthorized copies of the files will not be able to peek at your company's budget for the next year. Users who are authorized recipients of the file but don't have Office 2003 or later installed on their computer will be able to use file viewers that let them examine the files, but not edit them.

> **Note** Information Rights Management is only available in Microsoft Office Professional Edition 2003, Word 2003, Excel 2003, and PowerPoint 2003.

Comparing Workbooks Side By Side

Another useful new capability in Excel 2003 is the ability to scroll through two windows at the same time so that you can compare the contents. Cell data forms patterns as it scrolls by, and you can often pick out differences visually. The differences are even more pronounced when you use conditional formats or change tracking to display cell data in a format that's different than the main body of data. To turn on simultaneous scrolling, open the two workbooks you want to compare and choose Window, Compare Side By Side With.

One of the enhancements in Excel 2003 is the set of additional research tools you can use to get information from a number of sources. You can display the Research task pane by choosing View, Task Pane and, if necessary, clicking the Other Task Panes bar at the top of the task pane and clicking Research. Once you have displayed the Research task pane, you can type a word or phrase in the Search For box, select the reference works you want to search, and click the Start Searching button (the arrow to the right of the Search For box) to get more information. Figure 1-1 shows the Research task pane and a selection of the reference materials available for you.

Getting Information with the Research Task Pane

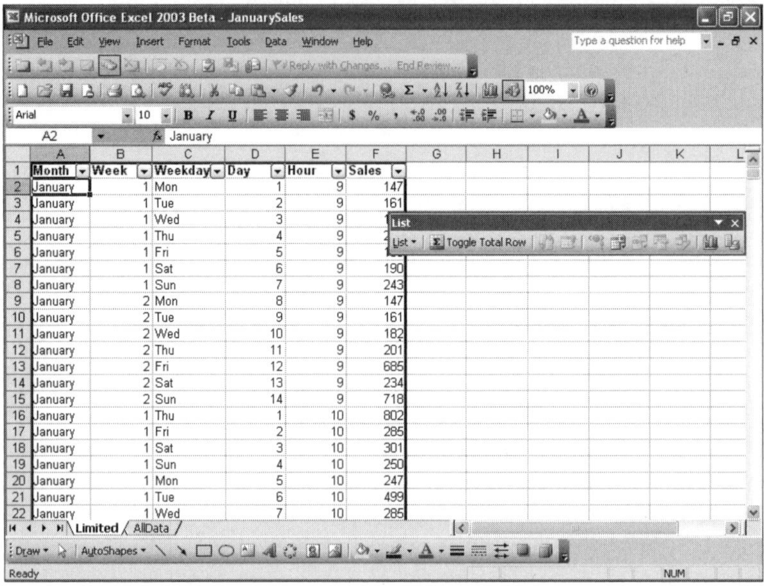

Figure 1-1. You can find synonyms, look up words in encyclopedias, and translate words into foreign languages using the tools on the Research task pane.

Tip   Research the contents of a cell

You can research the contents of a cell using the reference books in the Research task pane by holding down the Alt key and clicking the cell containing the text you want to research.

At the bottom of the Research task pane are links you can click to update the research tools installed on your computer, such as the thesauruses and dictionaries, and a link to the Office Marketplace. The Office Marketplace is a resource on the Microsoft Web site that lists sub-scription services you can use when the basic tools at your disposal in the Research task pane don't give you all of the information you need. Two such resources are the eLibrary, which provides access to 13 million multimedia documents, including photographs and maps, that are collected from periodicals published around the world, and more than 450,000 corporate profiles from the Thomson Profiles collection. The collection includes information on 300,000 U.S. companies and includes industry comparisons, market share information, rankings, and news stories from a collection of 2,500 journals.

Using Extended XML Capabilities

Probably the most dramatic change in Excel 2003 is the enhanced support for documents using *Extensible Markup Language* (XML). Unlike Hypertext Markup Language (HTML), which is used to describe the appearance of data on the Web, XML is used to describe the structure of data. For example, an HTML table containing a company's sales data would be understood perfectly by any human viewing the page, but the server presenting the data and the client receiving the data on behalf of its user would have no idea as to what sort of data was transmitted. If the file were an XML file, on the other hand, the machines involved could recognize the data as sales data and handle it appropriately. XML support was introduced in Excel 2002, but you were limited to opening and saving workbooks in the XML Spreadsheet Schema, which was a useful but far from comprehensive ability.

Note All new XML capabilities described in this section are only available in the Microsoft Office 2003 Professional Edition. Users with other editions will still be able to save and open XML workbooks as in Excel 2002.

Creating Excel Lists

Many of the advanced data tools in Excel operate on a *list*, which is a range of cells consisting of one or more columns where each column has a label at the top. In Excel 2002 and earlier, lists were a bit haphazard; when you wanted to create a PivotTable, sort data, or create an AutoFilter, you clicked any cell in the range and selected the menu item to perform the command you wanted. If Excel couldn't determine the boundaries of the range, such as by being unable to find a heading for one or more columns, the process would come to a grinding halt. In Excel 2003, lists are well-defined entities that you create by choosing Data, List, Create List, and using the controls in the Create List dialog box to define the area comprising the list.

Note If you select the cells in your list before you choose Data, List, Create List, the range appears in the Create List dialog box.

When you create a list, several things happen.

- A border appears around the list's edges. You can drag the edges of the border to resize your list.
- AutoFilter controls appear in the heading cells, which you can use to limit the data that is displayed within the list.
- An *insert row*, designated by an asterisk, appears. Just as in an Access table or an Excel data entry form, you can fill in the insert row and press Enter to add the row of data to the list and create a new insert row.
- The List toolbar appears, containing helpful list-management buttons.
- You have the option to display a *total row* at the bottom of the list by choosing the Toggle Total Row button on the List toolbar. The default operation in the total row is to sum the contents of a column, but you can click any cell in the total row to display a list of other summary operations available for use in the row.

After you create a list (one example of which is shown in Figure 1-2), you can work with the list as a separate entity within your worksheet. For example, you can filter the data, create a PivotTable, or add new rows to the list. Whichever task you perform, Excel will shift the worksheet contents around the list to reflect the new entry (such as by adding a blank row when you add data to a list). If you are working on a network equipped with SharePoint Services, you can publish the list to the server, update the list's data using the copy of the list on the SharePoint site, or edit a copy of the list on a computer away from the network and integrate your changes when you return. You can also use the more advanced data validation tools available through SharePoint to limit the types of data you and your colleagues can enter into the lists. In Excel, you can require users to enter numerical values, but on a SharePoint server you can be more specific as to data type, such as by requiring users to enter integer values.

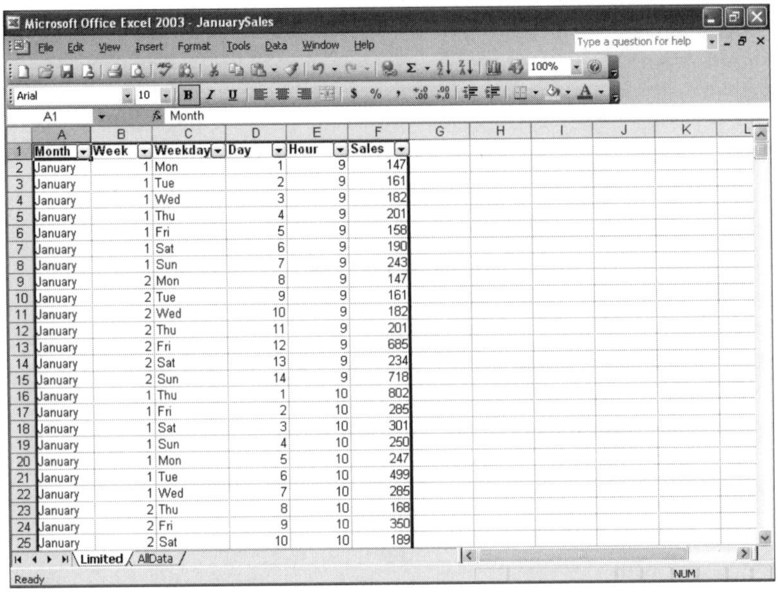

Figure 1-2. Data lists enhance your ability to create and display data collections in Excel 2003.

Mapping Excel Data to XML Schemas

XML data structures are defined in a *schema*, which in Excel is stored in a .xsd file. The following XML code listing shows how you might construct part of a schema to store data about a product.

> This XML code isn't a macro you can run using the Microsoft Visual Basic Editor. Instead, the code describes a product with three attributes.

```
<xs:complexType name="productType">
    <xs:sequence>
        <xs:element name="productId" type="xs:string" />
        <xs:element name="productName" type="xs:string" />
        <xs:element name="priceEach" type="xs:decimal" />
    </xs:sequence>
</xs:complexType>
```

This schema tells Excel to expect three data elements for a data structure named *productType*: *productId*, *productName*, and *priceEach*. The *complexType* statement names the data structure, whereas element definition statements give you the name of the element and the expected data type (in this case, either a string or a decimal value), while the `<xs:sequence>` statement tells Excel to expect the elements in exactly that order every time.

Publishing Spreadsheets with Web Components

Technically part of the Microsoft Office program suite, rather than Excel, the Office Web Components available for your use in Excel 2003 offer updated functionality that make it possible for you to publish Web pages that behave like spreadsheets. There are three Web components available in Office 2003: PivotTable Lists, Spreadsheets, and Charts. A fourth component, the *Data Source Component*, provides database access for Web-based PivotTable lists.

Exploring Excel

Workbooks 13
Worksheets 14
Cells and Ranges 15

The Excel Interface 18
Formulas 21

If you're interested in programming Microsoft Office Excel 2003, you're probably pretty familiar with the basic layout of an Excel workbook and have a good handle on how to manipulate workbooks, worksheets, data, and formulas. Even if you are familiar with Excel, you should at least skim this chapter to see if there are any interesting tidbits that you can use to make your life easier. But, if you're comfortable creating scenarios, know how many colors can be used in an Excel workbook, and have a good handle on how Excel helps you create formulas, feel free to skip right to the next chapter.

Workbooks

The basic unit of organization in Excel is the *workbook*. In the Microsoft Office hierarchy, an Excel workbook is at the same level as a Microsoft Word document, a Microsoft Access database, and a Microsoft PowerPoint presentation. And, just as documents contain sections, databases are built around tables, and presentations contain slides, Excel workbooks contain a set of sheets that actually hold the data and other Excel objects. Excel 2003 supports the following four types of sheets, but you will probably just use the first two of them:

- Worksheets
- Chart sheets
- Excel 4.0 macro sheets (also known as XLM files)
- Excel 5.0 dialog sheets (a way to create a custom dialog box)

While you can no longer create XLM files or dialog sheets, Excel 2003 does let you open files from Excel 4.0 or Excel 5.0 without losing any of the workbooks' functionality. If you're working in a company that has used the same basic workbooks for quite some time, the ability of Excel 2003 to work with the older files allows a straightforward transition from old to new.

New Excel workbooks come with three worksheets by default, but you can change that value by clicking Tools, Options, General and typing the desired number of worksheets in the Sheets In New Workbook box.

> **Tip**   **Limit the number of worksheets to one**
> If you plan to create a lot of templates, which requires saving a workbook that contains a single worksheet, you could save a few steps by changing the default number of worksheets to one until you are done creating templates.

You navigate among worksheets in a workbook using the controls on the tab bar at the bottom left corner of the Excel window. Each worksheet has its own sheet tab (named Sheet1, Sheet2, and Sheet3 by default); clicking a sheet tab displays the corresponding sheet, while right-clicking a sheet tab displays a shortcut menu with commands to insert a new sheet, rename or delete the selected sheet, move or copy sheets, or change the color of the sheet tab of the selected sheet. The ability to change the color of a sheet tab was introduced in Excel 2002 and is a handy technique you can use to indicate where you made changes in a workbook, emphasize one sheet over another (such as if you create a summary worksheet), and facilitate workbook navigation.

> **Important**   One little-known limitation in Excel is that you may use up to only 56 colors in a workbook. The limitation doesn't include the colors depicted in graphics you embed or link to in a workbook, so if you need to display a complex chart with more than 56 colors you will need to create the chart, export the chart and its legend to a graphics program, edit the chart and legend, and either display the chart and legend as a separate graphics file or embed the new file in your workbook.

Worksheets

Of the four basic types of sheets you'll work with in Excel, *worksheets* are by far the most common. Worksheets contain cells, which are arranged in rows and columns, where you store data and create formulas to summarize that data. As noted in Table 2-1, Excel worksheets have a maximum of 256 columns and 65,536 rows. If you're working with larger data sets, such as those generated by scientific experiments or a transaction tracking system in a busy sales organization, you should probably write the data to a text file and either process it in manageable chunks or use a more powerful, enterprise-worthy application to analyze the data.

Table 2-1. Excel Worksheets Can Hold a Lot of Data but Have Their Limits

Attribute	Limit
Maximum rows	65,536
Maximum columns	256
Column width	255 characters
Row height	409 points
Maximum number of page breaks	1000

Table 2-1. Excel Worksheets Can Hold a Lot of Data but Have Their Limits

Attribute	Limit
Maximum number of scenarios	No maximum, but only 251 will be displayed in a scenario summary
Maximum number of changing cells in a scenario	32
Maximum number of changing cells in Solver	200

One of the most underused capabilities in Excel is the *scenario*, which lets you define alternative data sets for a worksheet. As noted in Table 2-1, each scenario can contain up to 32 changes. The advantages of scenarios are that you can define them quickly (by clicking Tools, Scenarios and using the controls in the Scenario Manager dialog box, shown in Figure 2-1), and you're able to switch between alternative data sets without having to create a new worksheet to contain the speculative data. If you're creating one new worksheet that contains 12 values, 3 of which change, scenarios probably won't save you that much time. However, if you have a broad range of values (and combinations of values) that could change and you don't want to keep track of separate worksheets for each possible combination, you can create a scenario for each combination and switch within the same worksheet.

Figure 2-1. The Scenario Manager dialog box helps you manage and present alternative data sets.

If you need to create a scenario with more than 32 changes, you should probably ceate a new worksheet to hold the data.

Cells and Ranges

At the bottom of the organizational hierarchy in Excel is the *cell*, which is formed by the intersection of a column and a row in a worksheet. A cell can contain a value or a formula. By default, Excel displays the result of a formula in its cell, but you can change that setting by clicking Tools, Options, clicking the View tab, and selecting Formulas. What's interesting is that the formula in a cell is always displayed in the formula bar, regardless of whether or not you have formulas displayed in the cells. You might expect Excel to toggle between showing the formula result or the formula based on what was shown in the body of the worksheet.

> **Note** Displaying formulas instead of the formulas' results in a worksheet's cells displays the Formula Auditing toolbar, which has buttons you can use to identify cells used in your formulas, watch how the values in specific cells change, and step through formulas one calculation at a time to zero in on errors.

After you have your data, you can choose how to display it. The Formatting toolbar, which is displayed by default, has a range of buttons you can use to make basic changes to the appearance of your data, such as displaying the cell's contents in bold type or in a different font, but if you want fine control over your data's appearance you need to click Format, Cells to display the dialog box shown in Figure 2-2. From within the Format Cells dialog box, you can change the direction of the text in a cell, cause the contents of a cell to shrink to fit the existing size of the cell without wrapping, or add borders to a cell. It can be easy to go overboard with the formatting, so you should always keep in mind that the objective of an Excel worksheet is to make the data easy to read, not to display it as a work of art.

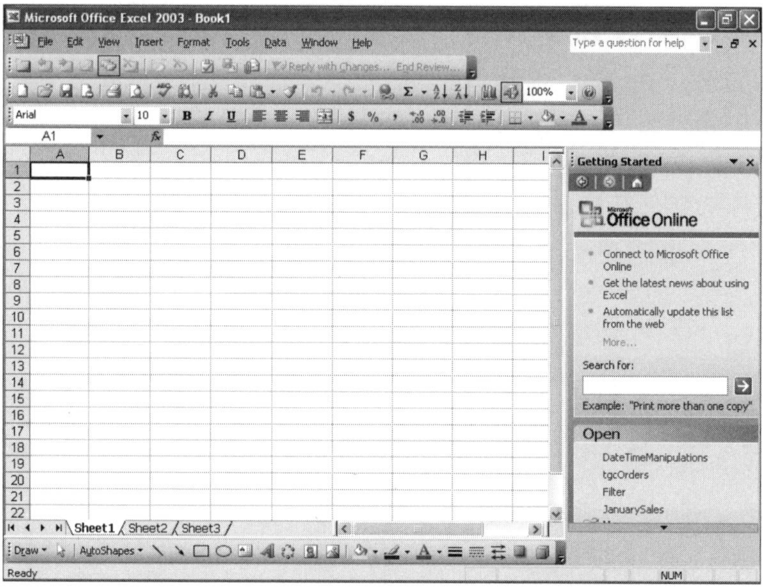

Figure 2-2. Use the controls in the Format Cells dialog box to present your data effectively.

You can deal with cells individually or in groups. When you want to change the formatting of a group of cells, you can select the cells and make any changes you desire. If you want to use the values from a group of cells in a formula, you can do much the same thing. For example, you could type a formula such as =SUM() into a cell, set the insertion point between the parentheses, and then select the cells you want to be used in the formula. As you select cells, the cell references are inserted into the formula. In this instance, selecting the cells from C3 to C24 would result in the formula =SUM(C3:C24). And, as of Excel 2002, you are able to select discontiguous groups of cells by holding down the Ctrl key. For example, typing =SUM() into a cell, positioning the insertion point between the parentheses, selecting cells C3 to C24, and then holding down the Ctrl key while you select cell C26, would result in the formula =SUM(C3:C24,C26).

> **Important** When creating a formula, pressing the Enter key before you complete the formula will result in an error. You need to type **=SUM(** and then select the cells you want to include, before you type the closing parenthesis.

When you work with a lot of worksheets and formulas, or if you need to pass a workbook you created to a colleague, just using cell references to designate the values used in a formula can lead to a lot of confusion. Rather than stay with the simple but somewhat cryptic cell references, you can create *named ranges* (often just called *names*) to make your formulas easier to read. For example, if you had a worksheet with sales for several different product categories, you could create a named range for each category and create a formula such as =SUM(**MachineTools,Software,Consulting**) instead of =SUM(**C3:C24,D3:D24,E3:E24**).

The quickest way to create a named range is to select the cells you want in the range, click in the Name box at the left edge of the formula bar, and type the name for the range. (The Name box is the area in the formula bar that displays the address of the currently selected cell.)

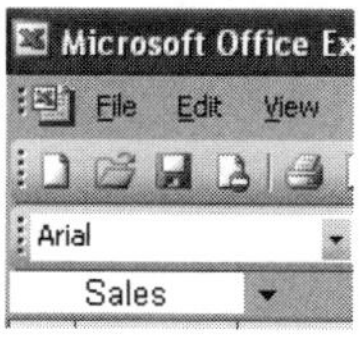

If you want to work with existing ranges, you can click Insert, Name, Define to display the Define Name dialog box, shown in Figure 2-3. From there, you can add or delete ranges.

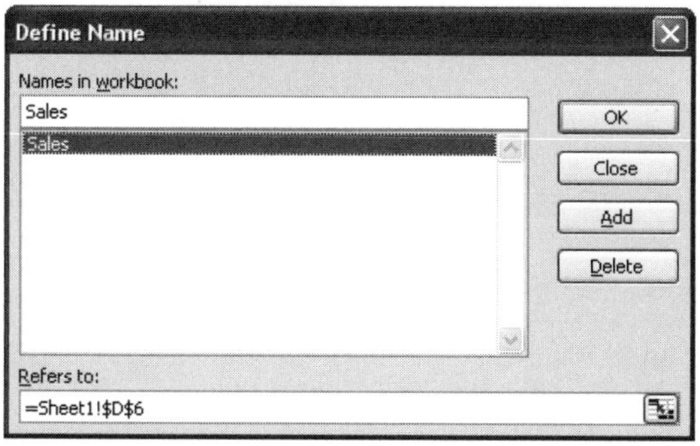

Figure 2-3. Use the Define Name dialog box to manage your named ranges.

You can have Excel show which cells comprise a named range by clicking the down arrow at the right edge of the Name box and clicking the name of the range you want to see.

The Excel Interface

Having a powerful spreadsheet program at your fingertips doesn't do you any good if you're not able to find what you're looking for, so the Excel designers spent a lot of time working on the organization and appearance of the Excel interface to make it easier for users to get the most out of their workbooks. Figure 2-4 shows the Excel window in all its glory, with callouts for the elements most commonly used in using and programming Excel.

Inside Out

Starting with Excel 2002, the program came with an adaptive menu system that just displayed the most basic commands, requiring you to hover the mouse pointer over the bottom of a menu to expand the menu. It's a great idea in theory, but for most users, who don't have thorough knowledge of the program, it's quite a hindrance. You can, and should, turn off the adaptive menu system by clicking Tools, Customize, Always Show Full Menus.

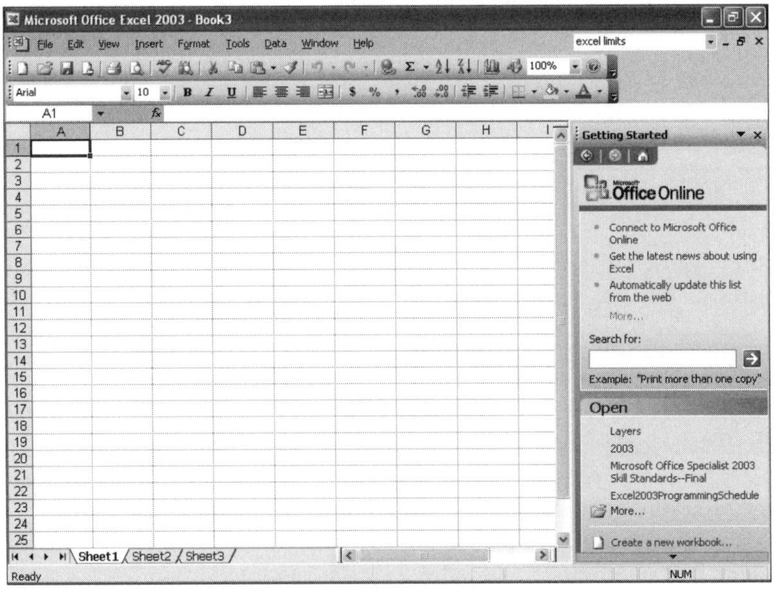

Figure 2-4. The Excel interface offers quick access to the program's diverse capabilities.

Title Bar. The title bar is at the top of the Excel window and displays the name of the program (Microsoft Office Excel 2003) followed by the name of the active workbook, if any. If the active workbook has any access restrictions or is shared, the workbook name will be followed by a designation in brackets. If you've opened more than one copy of the same workbook, the first name will be followed by *:1*, the second by *:2*, and so on.

Select All Button. The Select All button is the bare piece of real estate to the left of the Column A header and above the Row 1 header; clicking it selects every cell in a worksheet.

Command Bars. Menu bars and toolbars might look different, but underneath they work exactly the same way. Clicking File, Save is no different from clicking the Save toolbar button, so why have both systems, plus the Ctrl+S keyboard shortcut, in place? Because different users prefer different methods.

Formula Bar. The formula bar, the long, white strip just above the column headers in a worksheet, is where Excel displays the formula in the active cell. If there is no formula in the active cell, the cell's value appears on the formula bar. You can hide the formula bar by clicking View, Formula Bar, which is a *toggle* (that means you click the bar to turn it off, and click again to turn it back on).

Name Box. The name box is in the running as the most versatile element in the Excel interface. If you have created a named range, as described earlier in this chapter, you can select a range by clicking the down arrow to the right of the name box and clicking the name you want to select (thereby outlining the cells in the named range). When you don't have a named range selected, the name box displays the reference of the active cell (for example, A1), or the area selected while dragging. For instance, if you select an area three rows high by ten columns wide, the name box displays 3R × 10C until you release the mouse button, and then the name box displays the reference of the cell in the upper-left corner of the selected range.

> **Note** Knowing the precise dimensions of the area you've selected is helpful if you need to paste a group of cells from another worksheet into the active worksheet.

Program Window Controls. The standard Windows program controls are positioned at the top right of the Excel window: the Minimize button, the Restore button, the Maximize button (which appears when the program window has been resized), and the Close button.

Workbook Window Controls. These buttons operate in exactly the same manner as the program window controls, but they affect only the active workbook. (The Excel window stays the same size it was when the buttons were clicked.)

Ask A Question Box. The Ask A Question box is the quickest way to look up topics in the Excel help system. You type a word or phrase in the Ask A Question box, press Enter, and a list of available help topics appears in the Search Results task pane at the right edge of the workbook. Clicking the name of the help topic displays that topic.

Task Pane. Introduced in Excel 2002, task panes are interface objects with links to perform common tasks in a number of subject areas. The task panes appear at the right edge of the Excel window when you perform certain tasks (for example, clicking File, New displays the New Workbook task pane). You can also display the task panes by clicking View, Task Pane. The following task panes are available to you in Excel 2003:

- **Clip Art.** The Clip Art task pane gives you links you click to search for clip art in the Office gallery, to organize clips you have saved, and to get help on topics related to clip art.

- **Clipboard.** The Clipboard task pane is the new home for the Office Clipboard. The Office Clipboard can hold up to 24 items you have copied or cut to the clipboard.

- **Document Recovery.** If Excel crashes while you have a workbook open, the Document Recovery task pane appears when you re-open Excel. You'll have the chance to choose whether you want to revert to the most recently saved version of the workbook or to recover the workbook using the last AutoRecover file.

- **Document Updates.** Used with SharePoint Services, the Document Updates task pane gives you the ability to monitor workbooks you have placed in a shared workspace for changes.

- **Getting Started.** The Getting Started task pane contains links for opening a recently used file, creating a new workbook, or connecting to the Microsoft Office Web site.

- **Help.** The Help task pane has links to Microsoft support newsgroups, to information about assistance and training for Microsoft Office, and find out what's new in Excel 2003.

- **New Workbook.** The New Workbook task pane lets you use templates to create a new workbook, search for workbook templates on your computer or on the Microsoft Office site, or create a blank workbook.

- **Research.** The Research task pane has links to a range of tools you can use to look up words and phrases. There are dictionaries and thesauruses available in several languages, and there is a "translation" utility you can use to find corresponding terms in French, Portuguese, Italian, and other languages.

- **Search Results.** The Search Results task pane lets you search the Help system, Microsoft.com, the Office Support site, or online research tools for a word or phrase you type in the Search box.

- **Shared Workspace.** Also part of the new Excel 2003 support for SharePoint Services, the Shared Workspace task pane contains a set of hyperlinks you can use to create and manage workspaces where you and your colleagues can collaborate on a shared document.

- **XML Source.** The XML Source task pane contains a set of tools that let you assign XML structure to a worksheet so that you can exchange XML-formatted data with colleagues and clients.

Tab Bar. The tab bar displays a sheet tab for each worksheet in a workbook. You can navigate from sheet to sheet using the arrows on the tab bar, click the sheet tab of a worksheet to display that sheet, or change the color of the sheet tab.

Status Bar. As the name implies, the Excel status bar displays the program's status. The status bar indicates whether a save or AutoRecover save is in progress, displays the running total of values in selected cells, and tells you, among other things, if your keyboard has caps lock, scroll lock, and/or number lock turned on.

Inside Out

The running total feature is a little-known but very handy way to quickly summarize a few cells of data in Excel. When you select more than one cell, a summary of the data appears on the status bar a bit to the left of the number lock indicator. The default summary operation is to find the sum of the data, but you can right-click the pane where the summary appears and, from the shortcut menu, click Average, Count, Count Nums (that is, the number of cells in the selection that contain a numeric value), Maximum, Minimum, or Sum. If you want to turn the feature off, you click None. To turn it back on, just right-click the same area of the status bar and select the new summary operation.

Formulas

Excel is a terrific program for storing data, but the real power in a spreadsheet comes from the ability to summarize that data. To that end, Excel lets you create formulas to manipulate and summarize the values in your workbooks. The formulas can be as simple as displaying a value from one cell in another cell (for example, =**A1** would display the value from cell A1 in the cell where the formula resides) to advanced statistical functions that comprehend data from thousands of cells.

In Excel 2003, you're not left to your own devices when you begin typing a formula into a cell. Instead, when Excel recognizes the function you are typing, the program displays the expected parameters for the formula as a tool tip. For example, when you type =**VLOOKUP(**, Excel displays *VLOOKUP(lookup_value, table_array, col_index_num, [range_lookup])* in a tool tip. The first parameter to enter, the cell designation or value that is the *lookup_value*, is displayed in bold type until you type in the parameter, followed by a comma. After you type the comma, which indicates that you are done entering the value for that parameter, the name of the next parameter is displayed in bold type.

Tip In the tool tip that appears when you type in a formula, you can click the name of any parameter for which you have already entered a value to edit that value.

There's even more help available for creating formulas, though. If you're not sure which function you need to use to generate a result, you can click Insert, Function or click the Insert Function button at the left edge of the formula bar to display the Insert Function dialog box, which is shown in Figure 2-5. The Insert Function dialog box lists all of the available functions by category and, when you click a function, a description of what it does and the arguments it expects appear in the Insert Function dialog box. When you double-click the formula name, a secondary dialog box appears to help you create the formula piece by piece.

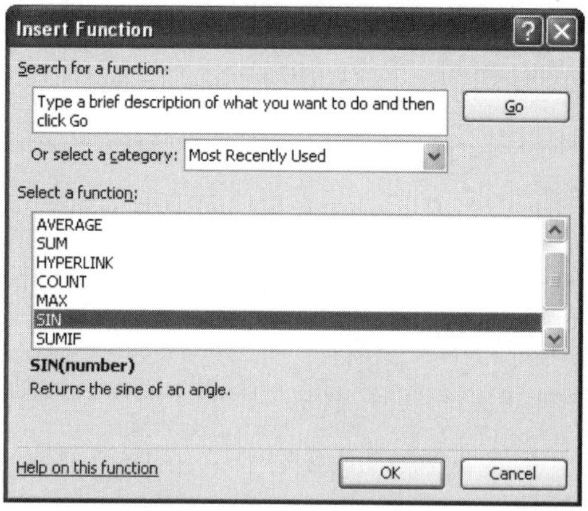

Figure 2-5. The Insert Function dialog box helps you find the function you want and guides you through the creation process.

Part 2

Visual Basic for Applications

3 Exploring Visual Basic for Applications   **25**

4 VBA Programming Starter Kit   **41**

5 Creating Sub and Function Procedures   **85**

Exploring Visual Basic for Applications

An Overview of Object-Oriented
Programming 25

Working with Macros 29

This chapter provides an overview of how macros work in the context of Microsoft Office Excel 2003. The second part of the chapter covers macro recording and other related topics, but the first part steps back and gives you some perspective on what is happening when you create a macro. The quick version of that story is that Visual Basic for Applications (VBA) sees Excel as a series of objects that have attributes to describe them and actions those objects "know" how to take. Chapter 1, "What's New in Microsoft Office Excel 2003," showed you some of the basic elements you'll encounter when using and programming Excel; this chapter takes that analysis a few steps further by showing you how object-oriented programming languages represent those elements, and how to manipulate those objects using the macro recorder.

An Overview of Object-Oriented Programming

A computer program is, at its base, nothing more than a set of instructions the computer executes in a specified order. In Excel, that order may change based on the contents of the worksheet the program is working with, but one fundamental principle behind programming languages is that if you give a program an identical data set to work with you will get the same result every time.

The first generation of popular programming languages were *procedural* languages, which meant that programmers designed an algorithm, or procedure, for the program to follow and defined *variables* (placeholders for values) as the program developed. As programs became increasingly complex, the need for descriptive variable names increased in importance. While it's easy to create a variable named *price* to store the price of a product you offer for sale in a store, it's difficult to write an expandable program that can keep track of all of the prices in an ever-changing product inventory. Every time you wanted to add a product to your store, you would need to create a new variable. Doing that once or twice is no big deal, but if you write a lot of programs and want to save time and effort by reusing your code, you need some way of organizing your program around the *things* in your environment.

Procedural programmers attempted to solve the problem by representing the things in their environment using an *abstract data type*, which is a collection of characteristics and operations that reflect the values and actions associated with something you need to represent in a program (such as a product). For example, a garden supply store could have both an indoor sales area and a greenhouse, with products associated with each location. The abstract data type *product* might have values reflecting the name of the product, the category to which the product belongs, the product's price, the product's supplier, a description, and so on. It's important to note, however, that defining an abstract data type for a product doesn't create a place to hold the values and actions associated with that product. Instead, you would need to create an *instance* of the product abstract data type to store the data and actions associated with the new brand of potting soil you just started offering for sale in your garden supply store. The instance would have a unique identifier within the system, such as *product001*, and the program would know that the product name, category, price, description, and supplier would all refer to that particular product.

While abstract data types are a handy way to define sets of variables in a program, the underlying structure of the programming languages that use abstract data types is still procedural because there can be routines that exist outside of the abstract data types. In an object-oriented programming language, every aspect of your computer code is based around the things in your environment. Those "things," not surprisingly, are represented as *objects*, and all actions and data are *encapsulated* within those objects. In Excel, those objects could be workbooks, worksheets, ranges of cells, or external files. In general, there are four aspects of objects you can use to flesh out a program:

- Properties
- Methods
- Events
- Collections

Properties

In brief (actually, in total as well), *properties* are variables that describe some aspect of the object in which they are included. A common property for objects in Excel is *Name*, which holds the identifying value you or Excel assigned to the workbook, worksheet, cell range, or other object to which you're referring. If you change the worksheet's name, whether by using VBA code or by right-clicking the worksheet's tab on the tab bar, clicking Rename, and editing the value, you change the value that is stored in the *Name* property. You can set new values for some worksheet properties (such as *Name*) directly, but to change other workbook properties you need to either take action using the Excel interface (such as by protecting a cell range) or a *method* (described in the next subsection).

In VBA, properties are referred to in a program using *dot notation*, where the object name is written first, the property name is written second, and the two elements are separated by a period. For example, to change the name of a worksheet, you would use the *Worksheet.Name* property. Changing the name of a worksheet when you've edited or updated the values in one or more worksheet cells lets you and your colleagues know that the data on that sheet is new and should be checked before the worksheet is included in any final written products.

Methods

A *method* is an action that an object "knows" how to perform. For example, you probably know that the worksheet displayed in the Excel window is referred to as the *active worksheet*. In Excel VBA, you can change the worksheet you're affecting with your VBA code by calling the target worksheet's *Activate* method. After the *Activate* method runs, the worksheet to which it is attached moves to the front of the worksheets in the Excel window and becomes available for editing. As with properties, methods are called using dot notation. To recalculate all of the formulas in a worksheet, for example, you would call the *Worksheet.Calculate* method.

Events

Just as a property is a quantifiable attribute of an object and a method is an action an object knows how to take, an *event* is an action an object recognizes as having happened. For example, Excel 2003 knows about the following events (among many others):

- A workbook is opened or closed.
- A worksheet is activated or deactivated.
- A workbook is saved.
- A chart is clicked.
- A key (or combination of keys) is pressed.
- Data is typed into a cell.
- The formulas in a worksheet are recalculated.
- A hyperlink is followed.

Excel comes with a number of *event handlers*, or code routines that watch for particular actions to occur. When one of those actions does occur, and you've told Excel what you want it to do when the event happens, Excel will run the code in your event handler. For example, if after creating a new workbook you want Excel to display all open workbooks as a cascaded set of windows, you could create the following event handler:

```
Private Sub App_NewWorkbook(ByVal Wb As Workbook)
Application.Windows.Arrange xlArrangeStyleCascade
End Sub
```

Don't worry if you're not sure what each and every element of the event handler routine does; for now you can concentrate on the middle line of code, which tells the Excel application to arrange its windows using the cascade style. It's the same result that would occur if you clicked Window, Arrange, Cascade in the Excel menu system, but if it's an action you want to happen every time a particular event occurs, you can use VBA to make it happen and save you the trouble.

Collections

The final element of object-oriented programming with which you should be familiar is the *collection*. As the name implies, a collection is a group of objects of the same type that are contained within another object. For example, a workbook contains a collection of one or more worksheets. If you wanted to make a change to every worksheet in a workbook, you could step through every worksheet in the collection and make the change programmatically.

If you've programmed before, you've probably run into the *For...Next* loop, which lets you repeat a set of instructions a number of times using something like the following sequence, which adds the directory path of the active workbook to the right section of the footer on the first three worksheets:

```
For i = 1 to 3
Worksheets(i).PageSetup.RightFooter = Path
Next i
```

The problem with hard-coding (that is, assigning a set value to) the upper limit of a *For...Next* loop is that you would need to change the code every time you added or deleted a worksheet. That's no big deal once or twice, but if you're managing a lot of code you'll inevitably forget to change it in a few places, causing errors you'll have to fix. Worse yet, those errors might not be noticed until the proofreader discovers that the first 500 printed copies of your annual report aren't formatted correctly and you've turned off your wireless phone as you while away your time on the beach. Yes, you can use a bit of code to discover the number of worksheets in your workbook, but there's a simpler way to do it: use a *For Each...Next* loop instead. *For Each...Next* loops find the number of objects in a collection, such as worksheets in a workbook, and step through each occurrence. In this example, the preceding code would be written this way.

```
For Each Wksht in Worksheets
Wksht.PageSetup.RightFooter = Path
Next Wksht
```

Instead of incrementing the value in a standard *For...Next* loop, the *For Each...Next* loop simply looks for the next member of the *Worksheets* collection and stops when it doesn't find one.

For more information on *For...Next* and *For Each...Next* loops, see "Controlling Program Flow" in Chapter 4, "VBA Programming Starter Kit."

Working with Macros

The most obvious benefit to creating macros in Excel is that you can automate repetitive tasks. While there's a lot more to macros and Visual Basic for Applications than repeating a series of actions without the need for human intervention, it's a great place to start. This section shows you how to record macros, run them using the method you find easiest, and use the built-in macro security capabilities to guard against viruses.

Recording and Viewing Macros

Recording a macro in Excel 2003 is a straightforward process: you click Tools, Macro, Record New Macro to display the Record Macro dialog box (depicted in Figure 3-1).

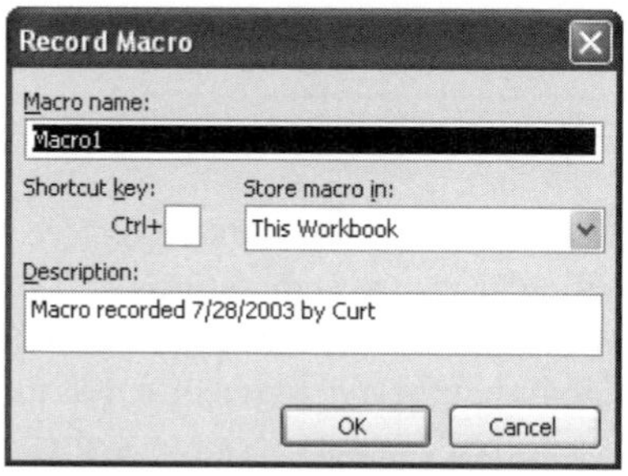

Figure 3-6. The Record Macro dialog box provides an interface for managing the macros in your workbook.

Type the name of the macro you want to create into the Macro Name box, and click OK. The Record Macro dialog box will go away, to be replaced by the Stop Recording toolbar.

You're recording! Perform the actions you want to be included in your macro, click the Stop Recording button on the Stop Recording toolbar, and your macro is ready for use. As with any programming effort, you should plan what you want to do so you can do it as quickly and efficiently as possible. You should also practice the macro a few times so you are sure your actions generate the desired result.

When you're done recording a macro, you can view the VBA code Excel created by clicking Tools, Macro, Macros, <*macro_name*>, Edit. Your macro will appear in the Visual Basic Editor, as shown in Figure 3-2.

> **Note** You'll see a lot more of the Visual Basic Editor in Chapter 4, "VBA Programming Starter Kit."

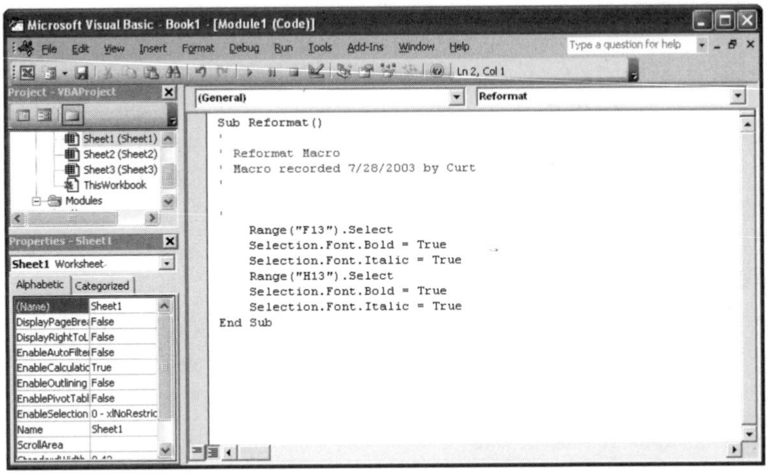

Figure 3-7. You can view the code behind a macro in the Visual Basic Editor.

This macro applies bold and italic formatting to the contents of the selected cell and to the contents of cell H13. Another aspect of this particular macro is that it was supposed to work for the active cell and the cell two columns to its right, but instead affects the active cell and cell H13. The reason that happened for this macro is that the macro recorder was using *absolute references*, which reflect the names of the cells selected during macro recording, instead of *relative references*, which reflect the positions of the selected cells in relation to the active cell when you start recording the macro. You can change your macro from absolute references to relative references by clicking the Relative References button on the Stop Recording toolbar. Figure 3-3 shows the same macro recorded using relative references.

Figure 3-8. A more flexible macro that works on any set of cells, not just the cells selected when the macro was recorded.

> For more information on creating relative references using the Offset property, see "Referring to Ranges" in Chapter 8: "Ranges and Cells".

Running a Macro

Once you've created a macro, you can run it at any time by clicking Tools, Macro, Macros, *<macro_name>*, Run. Also, in the Macro dialog box, you can display the macros available in other workbooks by clicking the arrow next to the Macros In box and selecting a workbook by name or by selecting All Open Workbooks, which will display every macro in any open workbook. If you select either of those choices, the macro names displayed will include the name of the workbook in which the macro is stored.

> **Tip** Running Macros Automatically
>
> If you want to have a macro run every time a particular workbook is opened, name the macro *Auto_Open*.

There are several other ways you can run a macro in Excel, though they require you to assign the macro to an action a user can take. Those actions are:

- Pressing a key sequence.
- Linking a macro to a toolbar button.
- Linking a macro to a menu item.

Assigning a Macro to a Key Sequence

For readers who prefer to use keyboard shortcuts such as Ctrl+C (for copying) when you use Excel, you can assign macros to key sequences. It's important to remember that if you assign a macro to a key sequence that's already taken (for example, Ctrl+S, which saves a workbook), the new assignment will take precedence over the default behavior in the workbook where the assignment was made.

To assign a key sequence to a macro, follow these steps:

1. Click Tools, Macro, Macros.
2. In the Macro name box, select the name of the macro to which you want to assign to a keyboard shortcut key.
3. Click Options.
4. Type a letter in the Shortcut key box. Typing a lowercase letter lets you use Ctrl+*letter*, while typing an uppercase letter lets you use Ctrl+Shift+*letter* as the shortcut.

> **Note** The shortcut key must be a letter; you can't pick a number or special character such as the dollar sign ($) or ampersand (&).

5 Type a description for your macro in the Description box.

6 Click OK.

7 Click Cancel.

Assigning a Macro to a Toolbar Button

Running a macro from inside the Macros dialog box is the easy "built-in" way to do it, but when you're moving quickly through a worksheet, the last thing you want to do is dig through the menu system to open a dialog box, remember the name of the macro you want to run, and run it. It's much simpler to assign the macro to a toolbar button so you can run the macro with a single click of the mouse. You can add a new toolbar button to an existing toolbar, but it usually makes more sense to create a new toolbar to hold the buttons for your macros. If you have your monitor set at a relatively low screen resolution to avoid eyestrain, for example, there won't be much room on any of the standard toolbars for another button. Also, if you have toolbar buttons for more than one macro, it might be difficult to pick the button out of a crowd on a densely populated toolbar. If you put your macro toolbar buttons on a toolbar clearly labeled as your custom macro toolbar, you'll have a much easier time finding your macros and remembering which button is which.

To create a new toolbar, add a button to it, and assign a macro to the button, follow these steps:

1 Click Tools, Customize. Then, if necessary, click the Toolbars tab to display the Toolbars tab page of the Customize dialog box.

2 Click New. Then, in the Toolbar Name box, type the name of the new toolbar and then click OK to create the toolbar.

3 In the Customize dialog box, click the Commands tab.

4 In the Categories list, click Macros.

5 Drag the Custom Button command to your new toolbar.

6 On the new toolbar, right-click the button you just added, click Name, type a name for the button, and press Enter.

7 On the Custom Macros toolbar, right-click the new button and click Assign Macro.

Assign Macro

Macro name:

Reformat
Reformat2

Macros in: All Open Workbooks

Description

OK

Cancel

Edit

Record...

8 Select the macro you want to assign to the toolbar button and click OK.

9 In the Customize dialog box, click Close.

Assigning a Macro to a Menu Item

Just as you can create toolbars to hold toolbar buttons that run your macros, you can create custom menus to serve the same purpose. While toolbars and menus are functionally equivalent, there are two possible arguments in favor of adding a macro to a menu instead of a toolbar. The first argument is that there is usually room to add a new menu to the main menu bar. Also, because menus don't display their full contents until you open them, menu items don't take up valuable real estate on a toolbar in the Excel window. The second argument in favor of using menus over toolbars comes down to personal preference. If you like using the menu system, assign your macros to menu items; if you prefer to use toolbar buttons, create a new toolbar.

To assign a macro to a menu item, follow these steps:

1 Click Tools, Customize. If necessary, click the Commands tab.

2 In the Categories list, click New Menu and drag the new menu to the right end of the main menu bar.

3 Right-click the new menu, and click Name. Type your new menu name, and press Enter.

4 In the Categories pane of the Customize dialog box, click Macros.

5 In the Command list, drag the Custom Menu Item command to the head of your new menu. When a box appears under the new menu head, drag Custom Menu Item onto it.

6 On the new menu, right-click Custom Menu Item and then click Name.

7 Type a new name for the menu, and press Enter.

Chapter 3

8 On the new menu, right-click the menu item you just renamed and click Assign Macro. Then, in the Assign Macro dialog box, click the name of the macro you want to assign to the menu item and click OK.

9 Click Close.

Debugging a Macro

Part of the art of writing and recording macros is *debugging*, or the process of discovering why your VBA code isn't working the way it should. The Visual Basic Editor provides quite a few tools for you to use in testing a macro you've recorded or written. One interesting technique you can use to debug your code is to step through the code one instruction at a time.

1 To start the process, click Tools, Macro, Macros, *<macro_name>*, Step Into to display the macro in the Visual Basic Editor.

2 From within the editor, press F8 to execute the next macro instruction. As shown in Figure 3-4, an arrow will appear beside the next instruction to be executed, and the instruction itself will be highlighted.

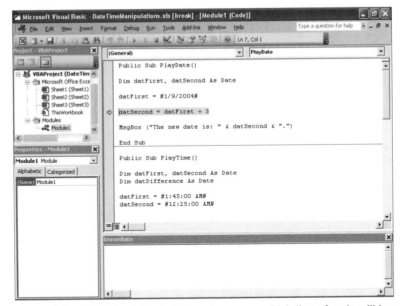

Figure 3-9. The Visual Basic Editor shows you which line of code will be executed next.

Subsequent presses of F8 will execute the highlighted step in the macro and highlight the next step, if any. There are a number of other ways you can control how your macro executes. Table 3-1 lists those keyboard shortcuts and offers a brief description of what each shortcut does.

Table 3-2. Keyboard Shortcuts for Executing Macro Steps in the Visual Basic Editor

Sequence	Result
F5	Runs the macro code.
F8	Executes the highlighted step in the macro code and moves the highlight to the next step in the code.
Shift+F8	Skips the highlighted step and moves the highlight to the next step in the code.
Ctrl+Shift+F8	Stops executing the macro code.
Ctrl+F8	Positions the cursor in the macro code; pressing Ctrl+F8 causes the editor to run the code until it reaches the cursor.
Shift+F9	Sets a quick watch to follow the value of a selected variable in the code.
F9	Inserts a breakpoint at the cursor, which will allow the code to execute to that point but then stop.
Ctrl+Shift+F9	Clears all breakpoints.
Ctrl+F9	Identifies the selected statement as the next statement to execute.

When your macro runs but doesn't produce the result you're expecting, it makes the most sense to have your macro code in one window and your worksheet in another, and to step through the macro one line at a time using F8. Skipping steps with Shift+F8 lets you bypass any instructions that you know aren't operating correctly, and if things aren't going right at all and you want to stop before anyone gets hurt, Ctrl+Shift+F8 lets you *stop* the whole process. You don't undo any of the steps that occurred before you pressed Ctrl+Shift+F8, but you do prevent any additional code from running.

Caution When you're running and re-running a macro, don't forget to undo the changes the macro made to your worksheet. If you don't, you won't see any changes the next time you run it.

A *breakpoint*, by contrast, is a set stopping point that lets you run the code up to the breakpoint. You can continue past the breakpoint by pressing F5. As shown in Figure 3-10, the Visual Basic Editor indicates the presence of a breakpoint by putting a dot in the vertical bar at the left edge of the code window, and displaying the code in reverse video.

Chapter 3

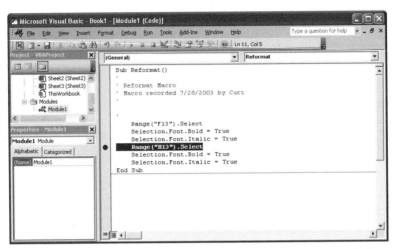

Figure 3-10. Breakpoints let you run your code to a specific point before you step through it line by line.

Implementing Macro Security and Digital Signatures

Viruses and other forms of harmful software (sometimes called *malware*) are a fact of life you have to deal with when you work with a powerful and flexible programming language such as VBA. You should already have a virus checking program or two installed on each of your computers to act as the first line of defense against *macro viruses* (viruses written using a macro programming language), but new viruses pop up all the time and it's possible that your detection programs won't recognize newer threats. After your second line of defense, which is you casting a critical eye on every file you receive, expected or not, you have the Excel macro security settings.

> **Tip Avoid Running Auto Macros**
> If you want Excel to start without running an Auto_Open macro, hold down the Shift key when you start the program.

The Excel macro security settings determine how permissive Excel should be about allowing macros to be run on your computer. There are three macro security settings: High, Medium, and Low, which you can control by clicking Tools, Options, Security, Macro Security to display the Security dialog box.

You should cross the *Low* option off your list of acceptable macro security settings; even if you have an all-but-foolproof virus scanner, allowing even one virus to get through is one too many. No software can know what files you are or aren't expecting, so you need to make sure there's an active human in the security loop. That human is you.

Chapter 3

The next-higher security level is *Medium*, which means Excel will display a dialog box asking if you want to enable macros whenever you try to open a workbook that contains macros. Clicking Enable Macros will open the workbook and allow you to run the macros in the workbook, clicking Disable Macros will open the workbook but prevent the macros from being run, and clicking Cancel will prevent the workbook from being opened. If you work with a lot of macros, are the only person who uses your computer, and you are confident you will remember not to click Enable Macros if an unexpected file, or a file you didn't expect to contain macros, appears in your e-mail In box or a shared folder, you can use the Medium setting. If you share your computer with other users, or if you go away on vacation and want to be a bit cautious about what can and can't be done on your computer, you should strongly consider changing the macro security level to High. You can always switch back to Medium when you return.

Introducing Digital Signatures

The mechanics of the High security setting relies in part on the use of *digital signatures* to verify the source of the VBA code in a workbook. A digital signature is the result of an operation using the principles of public-key encryption techniques to create a unique combination of the signed material and a file that is known only to you, but the result of which can be verified as having been signed by you. The mathematics are quite complex, relying on group theory and other disciplines only a handful of researchers really understand, but here's a synopsis of how it works.

The first step is for you to generate a key that will be used to encrypt your data by adding the values in the key to the values in the text. A simple example would be if your key were *a* and the word to be encrypted were *kazoo*. If you "add" *a*, the first letter in the alphabet, to each letter in *kazoo*, you will increment the letter by one place, resulting in the encrypted word *lbapp*. The key you'll actually generate is much, much longer, and it's split into two pieces: a public half and a private half. The private half, called your *private key*, is to be kept secret; you don't need to share it with anyone else, and anyone who asks you to do so does not have your best interests at heart. You can and should distribute the public half, called the *public key*, to anyone with whom you will exchange digitally signed files. The trick behind public-key encryption is that anyone who has a copy of your public key can verify that a document you signed using your private key is from you and is unchanged since you signed it. It's important to note that anyone who attempts to sign a file using your public key will *not* appear to be you.

Depending on the encryption software package you use, you might be able to use your public-key and private-key pair to digitally sign workbooks and macro code that you distribute over your internal network. The problem with using keys that aren't distributed outside your organization is that no one outside your network will have any idea whether your signature is valid or not. If you need to work with individuals outside your corporate network, you can obtain a *digital certificate* from a trusted third-party vendor. A digital certificate is an electronic file that identifies you, and contains information such as your organization name, the certificate's issuing authority, your e-mail address and country, and the certificate's expiration date, and it has a copy of your public key. After you sign a document using a digital certificate, anyone who wants to verify that the certificate used to sign the document belongs to you can go to the *key server* maintained by the issuing authority and match the signature to your public key.

Inside Out

Digital Certificates: You Can Even Create Your Own

There was a lot of competition in the digital certificate market in the latter half of the 1990s, as various companies vied for a share of the trusted authority pie. At the end of the decade, two companies stood out: VeriSign, and Thawte Consulting. In December 1999, VeriSign ended the competition by buying Thawte, consolidating the two largest digital certificate providers under a single corporate umbrella. You can visit the companies at *http://www.verisign.com/* or *http://www.thawte.com/* to get a feel for the products and services they offer.

While Thawte and VeriSign are the leaders in the digital certificate market, you should pay close attention to the disclaimers they have in their standard contract. While they make their best effort to verify the identity of the individuals and organizations that purchase digital certificates, they do not warrant that their methods are infallible and, in fact, require you to hold them harmless should someone evade their verification procedures and assume a false digital identity.

Digitally Signing Workbooks and Macros

After you have acquired a digital certificate, you can sign a workbook by clicking Tools, Options, Security, Digital Signatures, Add, *<certificate_name>*, OK. After you click Add, the Select Certificate dialog box (shown in Figure 3-6) appears with a list of unexpired certificates available on your computer. You can then click the name of the certificate with which you want to sign your workbook (or click View Certificate if you want to view the details of the certificate in case some of your certificates have similar names) and click OK to sign your workbook.

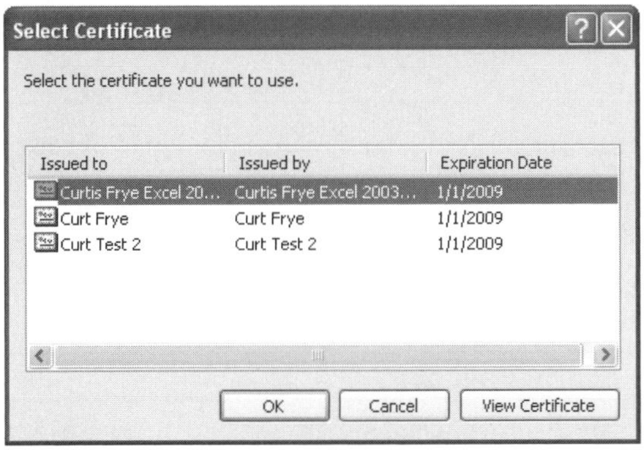

Figure 3-11. The Select Certificate dialog box lists the certificates available for digitally signing a workbook.

The process for signing code in the Visual Basic Editor is similar to signing a workbook. To sign the VBA code associated with a workbook, you click Tools, Macro, Visual Basic Editor. In the Visual Basic Editor, click Tools, Digital Signature, Choose, select a *<certificate_name>*, and click OK. Unlike the Select Certificate dialog box that appears when you sign a workbook, the Select Certificate dialog box that appears when you sign your VBA code lets you use a certificate that has expired. Listing expired certificates is an odd choice because, as you'll see in the next section, signing a macro with an expired certificate is equivalent to not signing it at all.

> **Note** After the author of this chapter (Curt Frye) signed a macro using an expired certificate, a warning box appeared about two minutes later indicating there was a problem with the digital certificate and that the signature would be discarded. It would be better not to list expired certificates at all, but detecting the problem before the code could be sent out is an acceptable workaround.

Using Digital Signatures with the High Macro Security Setting

The preceding discussion of digital signatures sets the stage for discussing the *High* macro security level. When you have your macro security level set to High, Excel is extremely cautious about allowing any macros to run. If Excel doesn't recognize the source that signed

39

the macros in the workbook you're trying to open, the security routine will either require your permission to trust the source that signed the macro or will disable macros entirely.

You can add a trusted source to Excel by opening the file that contains the digitally signed macros from the developer that you want to add to the list. A Security Warning box will appear, indicating the publisher is not on the trusted list. To add the publisher to the list of trusted sources, select the Always Trust Macros from this Publisher check box and click Enable Macros.

> **Note** Your network administrator can prevent users from adding sources to the list of trusted sources, so you might need to ask your administrator to add new developers to the list.

There are a number of scenarios under which digital signatures and macros can interact with Excel when the macro security level is set to High; Table 3-2 summarizes those situations and the effect of the High security setting.

Table 3-3. How Excel Reacts to Various Digital Signature Scenarios When Macro Security Is Set to High

Circumstance	Reaction
The macro does not have a digital signature.	Excel disables macros and opens the workbook.
The macro has a valid signature from a trusted source.	Excel enables macros and opens the workbook.
The macro has a valid signature from an unknown source.	Excel displays information about the certificate used to sign the macro and, if not disabled by a network administrator, asks if you want to trust the source and the certification authority.
The macro has an invalid signature, indicating the file might have been corrupted by a virus.	Excel disables macros and warns you there might be a virus.
The signature can't be verified because the public key is missing or can't be found on a key server.	Excel disables macros and indicates it was unable to verify the signature.
The macro was signed with a certificate that has either expired or has been revoked.	Excel disables macros and indicates the certificate is invalid.

VBA Programming Starter Kit

Introducing the Visual Basic Editor 41
Managing Code Windows 53
Developing Projects with the
Project Explorer. 55
Declaring Variables, Constants, and
Data Types 57
Assigning Values to Variables 64
Working with Arrays 64

Creating Dynamic Arrays 66
Writing to the Screen and
Accepting Input 67
Defining Object Variables. 72
Creating Custom Data Types 72
Controlling Program Flow. 73
Error Handling .82

Introducing the Visual Basic Editor

The Visual Basic Editor is a powerful tool that lets you extend the power and versatility of macros beyond anything that can be done through recording alone. So that you can fully understand how to use the Visual Basic Editor, this chapter examines all facets of the Visual Basic Editor: what the various components are, what they do, and how to use them. With that purpose stated, it's time to examine the Visual Basic for Applications language, which is used to program all macros.

If you have never worked with the Visual Basic Editor before, you might find it more convenient to work through this chapter from start to finish. If you've worked with the Visual Basic Editor before, jumping to specific sections will allow you to quickly find the information you are seeking.

Opening the Visual Basic Editor

As with most Microsoft Windows–based applications, there are several methods for opening the Visual Basic Editor. You can select Tools, Macro, Visual Basic Editor from the menu bar or press Alt+F11. If there is a specific macro that you want to edit or view, you can select Tools, Macro, Macros to bring up the Macro dialog box. From there, you can highlight the macro you want to work with and select the Edit button. You can also open the Macro dialog box by pressing Alt+F8.

Recognizing Parts of the Visual Basic Editor

When you open the Visual Basic Editor directly, you use the Project Explorer window to select the macro you want to work on. The Project Explorer presents all *projects* (groupings of code) and the macros they contain in a tree view that works the same as the tree view in

Windows Explorer. The *root object*, or base object of the tree, is the current workbook that you are working in, along with any other workbooks and Add-Ins that might be open.

The main elements utilized by VBA projects are each stored in a separate folder within the project. Those elements include objects, which were introduced in Chapter 3; modules, which contain the macro code associated with a worksheet; class modules, which are definitions of user-defined objects you've created for your workbook (described in more detail in Chapter 14); and user forms, which are described in Chapter 19.

In the example shown in Figure 4-1, the current workbook is identified as VBAProject (DateTimeManipulations.xls). The three worksheets included in the workbook (Sheet1, Sheet2, Sheet3), along with the entire workbook (ThisWorkbook), are inside the Microsoft Office Excel Objects folder. Any macros programmed in VBA or recorded also appear in the Modules folder. Any class modules or user forms would appear in a Class Modules or a Forms folder, respectively.

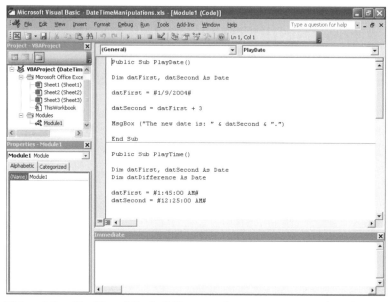

Figure 4-1. The Visual Basic Editor organizes your programming elements to make them easier to manage.

Directly below the Project Explorer window is the Properties window, which is used to examine and change the various properties associated with the selected object. For modules and worksheets, usually the *Name* property is the only one available, although worksheets do have additional properties that can be changed. Working with properties is most often done when working with user forms.

> **Caution**   The value in the Name property of a worksheet or workbook is not necessarily the same as the name of the same object inside of Excel. Although the two names might appear to be similar because of default naming rules that the Visual Basic Editor uses, the names might be different but could be linked together internally to ensure the proper object is referenced. Object names are more restrictive because they must follow the Visual Basic for Applications naming rules (no spaces, must begin with a letter, can't be a reserved word, and no more than 31 characters in length).

The Code window is the largest window within the Visual Basic Editor and is topped with two drop-down boxes, as shown in Figure 4-2. The drop-down box on the left, the Object box, is used to select an object to work on. When working with code only, the box will display the default *General* object. The second drop-down box, the Procedure box, is used to select individual macros within the current module. As macros are added and deleted from the module, they are also added and deleted from the Procedure box.

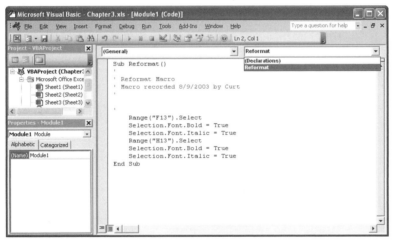

Figure 4-2.   The Visual Basic Editor Code Window lets you pick objects and procedures to work on.

Besides using the Procedure box to select a macro, you can also use the up and down arrow keys to scroll through the code listings until you reach the macro you want. As you scroll through each macro, the Procedure box is updated to reflect the macro the insertion point is in.

The Code window is replaced by the Form Editor when you click Insert, user form, as shown in Figure 4-3.

> For more information about user forms, refer to Chapter 19, "Creating User Forms."

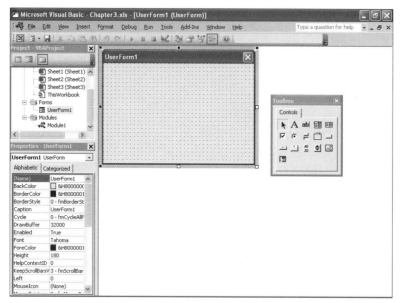

Figure 4-3. The Visual Basic Editor Form Editor takes over when you move from writing VBA code to creating user forms.

Just like every other Windows-based application, the Visual Basic Editor has a menu bar and tool bar providing access to many other features. Most of the menu options available on the File, Edit, Window, and Help menus reflect the same options available in other Windows-based applications. The rest of the menus, however, contain valuable capabilities that you'll use frequently while working with the Visual Basic Editor.

The View Menu

The View menu lets you open and/or jump to specific windows within the Visual Basic Editor; through it you can open windows that aren't currently visible or even return to Excel without closing the Visual Basic Editor. Table 4-1 summarizes the items available on the View menu.

Table 4-1. **Menu Items Available on the View Menu in the Visual Basic Editor**

Item	Description
Code	Displays or activates the Code window for the currently selected item within the Project Explorer.
Object	Displays or activates the object currently selected within the Project Explorer.
Definition	Displays or activates the Object Browser window showing the entry for the currently selected item within the Code window. If the item is a procedure or function, it displays the code for that procedure or function.

Table 4-1. Menu Items Available on the View Menu in the Visual Basic Editor

Item	Description
Last Position	Returns the cursor to the beginning of the last line of code edited.
Object Browser	Displays or activates the Object Browser window.
Immediate Window	Displays or activates the Immediate window.
Locals Window	Displays or activates the Locals window.
Watch Window	Displays or activates the Watch window.
Call Stack	Displays or activates the Call Stack dialog box.
Project Explorer	Displays or activates the Project Explorer window.
Properties Window	Displays or activates the Properties window.
Toolbox	Displays or activates the Toolbox, which contains objects used to design user forms.
Tab Order	Displays or activates the Tab Order dialog box.
Toolbars	Lets you turn on and off the various toolbars available within the Visual Basic Editor as well as customize them.
Microsoft Office Excel	Switches to the active workbook, restoring the display if it is minimized.

The Insert Menu

The Insert menu lets you insert new procedures, modules, or user forms into your project. Table 4-2 summarizes the items available on the Insert menu in the Visual Basic Editor.

Table 4-2. Menu Items Available on the Insert Menu in the Visual Basic Editor

Item	Description
Procedure	Displays the Add Procedure dialog box to help you build the declaration statement for a new procedure inside the current module.
UserForm	Inserts a new user form into the current project.
Module	Inserts a new module into the current project.
Class Module	Inserts a new class module into the current project.
File	Displays the File Open dialog box to allow you to import a text file (*.txt), a Basic file (*.bas), or a class file (*.cls). Text files will be inserted into the current Code window, whereas Basic or class files will be inserted into the current project as separate modules or class modules.

Chapter 4

45

The Format Menu

The Format menu contains commands to assist with the placement and formatting of objects on user forms. Table 4-3 lists the items available on the Format menu.

Table 4-3. Menu Items Available on the Format Menu in the Visual Basic Editor

Item	Description
Align	Displays the Align submenu, which lets you line up two or more objects along a common border
Make Same Size	Displays the Make Same Size submenu, which lets you make two or more objects the same size in width, in height, or both
Size to Fit	Resizes an object's height and width so that its contents fit exactly
Size to Grid	Resizes an object's height and width so that its borders rest upon the nearest grid lines shown on the user form
Horizontal Spacing	Displays the Horizontal Spacing submenu, which lets you adjust the horizontal spacing among two or more objects
Vertical Spacing	Displays the Vertical Spacing submenu, which allows you to adjust the vertical spacing among two or more objects
Center in Form	Displays the Center in Form submenu, which lets you center an object either horizontally or vertically on a form
Arrange Buttons	Displays the Arrange Buttons submenu, which allows you to arrange button objects evenly along the bottom or right side of the user form.
Group	Creates a group out of selected objects so that they can be manipulated together
Ungroup	Removes the grouping of objects
Order	Displays the Order submenu, which lets you rearrange the order in which objects are layered on the user form

The Debug Menu

The Debug menu provides several tools to assist with debugging (testing) the execution of procedures. Table 4-4 lists the items available on the Debug menu.

Table 4-4. **Menu Items Available on the Debug Menu in the Visual Basic Editor**

Item	Description
Compile	Compiles the code for the currently selected project. Identified on the menu as *Compile <ProjectName>*.
Step Into	Lets you step through your code one line at a time. Each line is highlighted before being executed.
Step Over	Allows you execute an entire procedure at once. This is useful if the current procedure calls a second procedure and you don't need to step through the second procedure.
Step Out	Lets you execute all remaining code within the current procedure, stopping when all lines have been executed.
Run to Cursor	Lets you run all code up to the line where the cursor is currently residing.
Add Watch	Displays the Add Watch dialog box, which you use to add any variables or expressions you want to keep an eye on.
Edit Watch	Displays the Edit Watch dialog box, which you can use to modify any variables or expressions you're currently watching.
Quick Watch	Displays the Quick Watch dialog box, which displays the value of the current variable or expression selected in the Code window. You can also hover the mouse over a variable or expression and have the value displayed in a ToolTip.
Toggle Breakpoint	Lets you create a breakpoint on the current line of code. Execution will pause whenever a breakpoint is encountered. If the current line already contains a breakpoint, selecting this command will clear it. You can also create and clear breakpoints by placing the mouse along the left border of the code (so that the mouse pointer changes to an arrow pointing to the top-right) and double-clicking.
Clear All Breakpoints	Lets you clear all breakpoints within the current code module.
Set Next Statement	Lets you set the next line of code that will be executed, skipping other lines if necessary.
Show Next Statement	Lets you quickly jump to the next line of code that will be executed. This is helpful when you have scrolled through the code listing and want to quickly return to the next executable line of code.

Chapter 4

The Run Menu

The Run menu contains several commands that allow execution of program code and the display of user forms. Table 4-5 lists the items available on the Run menu.

Table 4-5. Menu Items Available on the Run Menu in the Visual Basic Editor

Item	Description
Run Sub/UserForm	Start executing the current procedure or user form. If none is selected, the Run Macro dialog box is displayed, allowing you to select a procedure to run. When a procedure is running and in Break mode, this command will change to Continue to allow you to continue normal execution of the procedure.
Break	Lets you stop execution of the procedure and places the code in Break mode.
Reset	Lets you reset all module-level variables and clear the Call Stack.
Design Mode	Lets you toggle Design mode on and off for the selected procedure.

The Tools Menu

The Tools menu gives you commands to run procedures, add references to external procedures, set options for the Visual Basic Editor, set properties for the current project, and digitally sign the project. Table 4-6 lists the items available on the Tools menu.

Table 4-6. Menu Items Available on the Tools Menu in the Visual Basic Editor

Item	Description
References	Displays the References dialog box for the current project, which lets you specify which object libraries and other VBA projects the project should be able to access.
Additional Controls	Displays the Additional Controls dialog box, which lets you add more controls to the Toolbox.
Macros	Displays the Macros dialog box, which lets you quickly select and execute a macro from all open projects.
Options	Displays the Options dialog box, which lets you set different options for the Visual Basic Editor itself.
Properties	Displays the Project Properties dialog box, which lets you set several properties for the current project. The current project is identified on the Menu as ProjectName Properties.
Digital Signature	Displays the Digital Signatures dialog box, which allows you to digitally sign your code using any digital signature you have installed on your PC.

Customizing the Visual Basic Editor

The Visual Basic Editor is fully customizable and can be configured to fit your own personal work style. The various windows can be undocked from their default positions and placed anywhere on the screen, including along a different edge of the window. Also, as discussed in Chapter 3, you can move, hide, and display any of the available toolbars, in addition to adding or removing toolbar buttons from any toolbar.

All of the ancillary windows within the Visual Basic Editor have a default docked location. To move a window, place the mouse pointer inside the title bar for the window and drag it to its desired location. An outline box will appear to show you where the window will be located when you release the mouse, as shown in Figure 4-4.

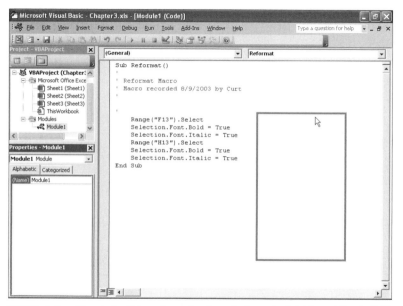

Figure 4-4. The default locations for the windows in the Visual Basic Editor appear here, but you can move the windows around to optimize your working environment.

Tip A quick way to swap between a docked window and the last undocked position is to double-click the Title bar of the window. This trick is especially handy when trying to return to the docked position because it can be hard at times to get the Visual Basic Editor to recognize that you want to return the window to a docked position.

Customizing the toolbars requires the same procedures as in other Windows-based applications. To move a toolbar, simply click within a blank area of the toolbar and drag it to the desired location. Click the Toolbar Options button (located in the lower right corner of the toolbar) or right-click a blank area of the toolbar and click Customize to display the Customize dialog box, from which you can add or remove buttons from the visible toolbars. By right-clicking any of the toolbars, you can also show or hide any available toolbar.

Chapter 4

The Options dialog box within the Visual Basic Editor also has several options that affect the Visual Basic Editor environment. The controls in the Options dialog box are organized on four tabs: Editor, Editor Format, General, and Docking.

The Editor tab, shown in Figure 4-5, is further divided into two sets of options. The first set, Code Settings, controls the display of IntelliSense tool tips, code formatting, variable declaration, and syntax errors. Auto Quick Info provides information on functions and their parameters as you type them, as well as applicable intrinsic constants during design mode. In run-time mode, Auto Data Tips provide the value of a variable when the mouse is hovered over it. Code formatting options include Auto Indent, which indents new lines to the same position as the line above it, and Tab Width, which sets the number of spaces one tab will occupy. Turning on the Require Variable Declaration option will prevent you from attempting to use a value in a variable you haven't defined yet, and the Auto Syntax Check option will check each line of code for syntax errors as it is entered. Finally, selecting the Auto List Members check box causes the Visual Basic Editor to display information that could be used to complete a statement you're typing.

![Options dialog box showing the Editor tab with Code Settings and Window Settings sections. Code Settings includes checked boxes for Auto Syntax Check, Auto List Members, Auto Quick Info, Auto Data Tips, and Auto Indent, with Require Variable Declaration unchecked. Tab Width is set to 4. Window Settings includes checked boxes for Drag-and-Drop Text Editing, Default to Full Module View, and Procedure Separator.]

Figure 4-5. The Editor tab of the Options dialog box gives you the tools to change how code, errors, and tips are displayed in the Visual Basic Editor.

Inside Out

Avoiding Errors Through Declarations

Requiring yourself to define a variable before you use it might be annoying, but it can prevent one of the most mysterious errors in programming: the *divide by zero* error. A simple case of attempting to divide by zero would be if you want to find the average temperature for a week. If you try to divide the sum of the temperatures by a new variable named *intNumDays*, to which you have not assigned a value, the program will assume the value is zero and generate the error.

The second set of options, Window Settings, controls how the Code window displays multiple procedures and determines how you may move code using the mouse. By enabling the Drag-and-Drop-Text option, you can drag and drop elements within the current code and from the Code window to and from the Immediate and/or Watch windows. Turning on the Default to Full Module View sets the view for new module windows to either a scrollable window or a single procedure view, while turning on the Procedure Separator option will draw a line separating procedures.

The controls on the Editor Format tab of the Options dialog box, shown in Figure 4-6, let you control the font style that is used to display code. From the color of different code elements (keywords, comments, syntax errors, selected elements, and so on) to the typeface and the size of the font, the code window can be customized to fit your particular needs. You can also turn the Margin Indicator Bar on and off, though you should probably leave it on because it provides a quick way to turn Break Points on and off.

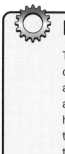

Figure 4-6. The Editor Format tab lets you determine everything from the font in which your code is displayed to the text color used to highlight important program elements.

Inside Out

The General tab, shown in Figure 4-7, provides options for Form Grid Settings, the display of ToolTips, the automatic closing of Form and Module windows, warning before variables are reset, error trapping, and determining when code is compiled. The Form Grid Settings allow you turn the grid dots on and off when designing user forms; you can also change the horizontal and vertical distance between grid dots and opt to have new controls aligned to the grid as they are added. You can also turn the ToolTips that help explain what each button on a toolbar does on and off.

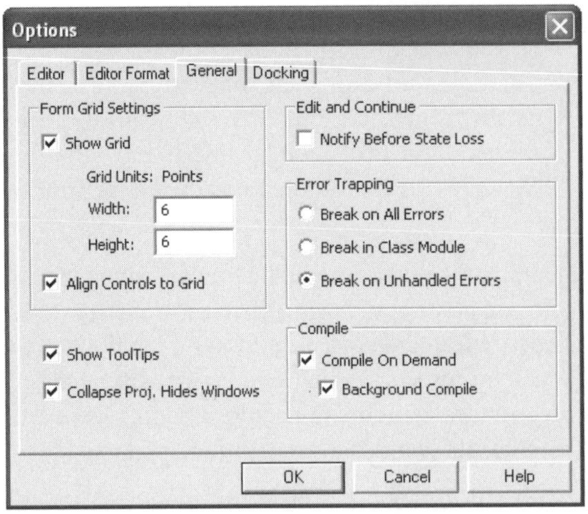

Figure 4-7. The General tab of the Options dialog box contains the controls that don't fit well into the other tab pages in the dialog box.

Selecting the Collapse Proj. Hides Windows option will automatically close module and user form windows when the project is collapsed in the Project Explorer window. Selecting the Notify Before State Loss option informs you when performing a specific action will reset all variables.

There are three options available for Error Trapping. Selecting the Break on All Errors option will force the Visual Basic Editor to enter Break mode on all errors, regardless of whether there are any error traps within the running procedures; selecting Break in Class Module will enter Break mode on an untrapped error, highlighting the line of code within the class module that produced the error; and selecting Break on Unhandled Errors will enter Break mode only if there is no error handler active. If the untrapped error occurred within a class module, the line of code within the calling procedure is highlighted instead of the code within the class module.

The last two options available on the General tab specify when the procedures are compiled. For fastest execution, both Compile on Demand and Background Compile should be selected. The first option allows faster application execution by compiling code on the fly rather than all at once, and the second determines if idle processing time is used to finish compiling the project during run-time mode.

The fourth and final tab available in the Options dialog lets you specify whether any of the ancillary windows within the Visual Basic Editor are dockable. By default, all windows are dockable with the exception of the Object Browser window.

Chapter 4

Managing Code Windows

Keeping code organized and easy to find is just as important within an Excel project as keeping the files located on your hard drive organized. Fortunately, the Visual Basic Editor Project Explorer presents the elements of a project in the same tree view that is used by Windows Explorer. The Project Explorer is not as flexible as Windows Explorer, but it does keep similar elements of a project grouped together within a common folder. This familiar organization makes it easier to find a particular module, class module, user form, or other Excel object when needed.

Handling Windows

Each individual module, class module, or user form will be displayed within its own code window, which means that as you add more modules, the number of windows needed to work with them will grow. Regardless of the number of modules a project contains, you do not need to open them all to be able to work with the project. Only the module or user form you want to edit needs to be opened.

To assist you with navigating the various windows, the Visual Basic Editor provides some tools to open, switch, and close windows. Opening a module can be accomplished by double-clicking the module from within the Project Explorer window. You can also use this method to switch to a module if it has already been opened.

To switch among the various open windows, you can use the Window menu to select the desired window. You can also scroll forward through the various windows by pressing Ctrl+F6 or backward by pressing Shift+Ctrl+F6. When you're done working with the contents of a window, you can close it by clicking the Close Window button or pressing Ctrl+F4.

Each of the windows can also be minimized or resized within the parent Visual Basic Editor window, allowing you to view more than one module window at a time. The Window menu provides commands to tile the open windows horizontally or vertically or to cascade them. If you need to view two different sections of the same module, you can split the module window by using the split window handle or **Split** command from the Window menu.

Chapter 4

Adding Code

Adding code to a project can be done several ways, but the first consideration is to have a container to hold the code, such as a code module, a class module, or a user form. The container you use depends upon the tasks that will be performed by the code you intend to add. Although it is possible to keep all of your code within one module, it is best to keep your code separated into different modules grouped by tasks. To add a new module, select the type of module (module, class module, or user form) needed from the Insert menu or the Insert button on the Standard toolbar.

To add a new procedure to a module or class module, you can type directly into the code window of the module. You can also click Insert, Procedure to open the Add Procedure dialog box, shown in Figure 4-8, which will prompt you for the minimum information needed to create a procedure.

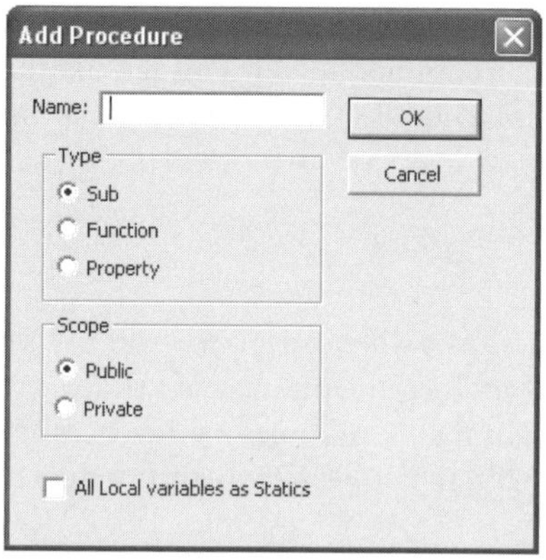

Figure 4-8. The Add Procedure dialog box lets you determine the basic outline of your procedure.

Note You can find more information on the options available in the Add Procedure dialog box later in this chapter.

Notes on Programming Style and Code Readability

Programmers come from many different backgrounds, and each has their own style of writing code. Programmers who work for or have worked for large software companies might follow a strict format specified by the company, while solo programmers might follow no set format. While neither the company nor the solo programmer is necessarily right or wrong, it is absolutely vital that you write code that is easy to read and understand. Even if you understand the code you write today, you or another programmer might need to modify it in the future. Unless you have a photographic memory, you might have difficulties understanding the logic you wrote earlier and find it that much harder to make your changes.

There are several steps you can take to make your code as readable as possible.

- Keep your procedures as short as possible. If you need a macro that will open a workbook, ask the user for information, make changes to the workbook, then save and close the workbook, and then break the macro up into several procedures: one procedure for each task. Then have one main procedure to call the other procedures. This format of constructing a series of subprocedures that are called by a main procedure will also make finding and correcting programming errors (debugging) easier because you will be able to narrow it down to a much smaller section of code.

- If a line of code goes beyond the edge of the Code window, you can type a space followed by an underscore to indicate that the code on the following line belongs with the code on the current line. *The PermissionLoop* procedure on page 81 is the first of many procedures that use this convention.

- Pick a naming convention, and stick with it. Projects, procedures, variables, and other programming elements all need names. The name should be something meaningful that conveys what the element is used for. There are a number of naming conventions that you could choose from, and most are usually some form of Hungarian notation.

> **Note** Hungarian notation is named after the native country of Dr. Charles Simonyi, the inventor of this naming style. Dr. Simonyi was Chief Architect at Microsoft when he designed the convention. The original chapter of *Programming Windows* that described how to use it can be found by going to *http://msdn.microsoft.com/* and typing **Simonyi Hungarian Notation** in the Search box.

- Choose names that are as concise as possible. While descriptive names are desired, names greater than 10 to 15 characters become cumbersome to type. Use abbreviations where they make sense to keep names short. Remember: The longer the name, the greater the likelihood of it being mistyped.

Developing Projects with the Project Explorer

You use the Project Explorer to manage your projects and modules within the Visual Basic Editor. It lets you create new modules, delete modules, and copy modules from one project to another. About the only thing you can't do in the Project Explorer is create a new project (for that, you need to create a new workbook), but you can use the Project Explorer to manage the contents of the project.

Creating VBA Modules

All macros and procedures are stored within a VBA module. You can have more than one module within a project, and that might even be necessary depending upon the complexity of your project.

To create a new module, click Insert and then click Module, Class Module, or UserForm, depending on the type of module you want to create. Figure 4-9 shows a recently created blank module in a project. Once you've created the module, you can begin adding procedures or designing the user form. Another option is to import a module from a text file. By clicking File, Import File, you can select a text file that includes the code to be used in other modules or user forms. The Visual Basic Editor creates a new module, so unless the code you import is a complete procedure it won't run until you add the *Sub...End Sub* notation.

55

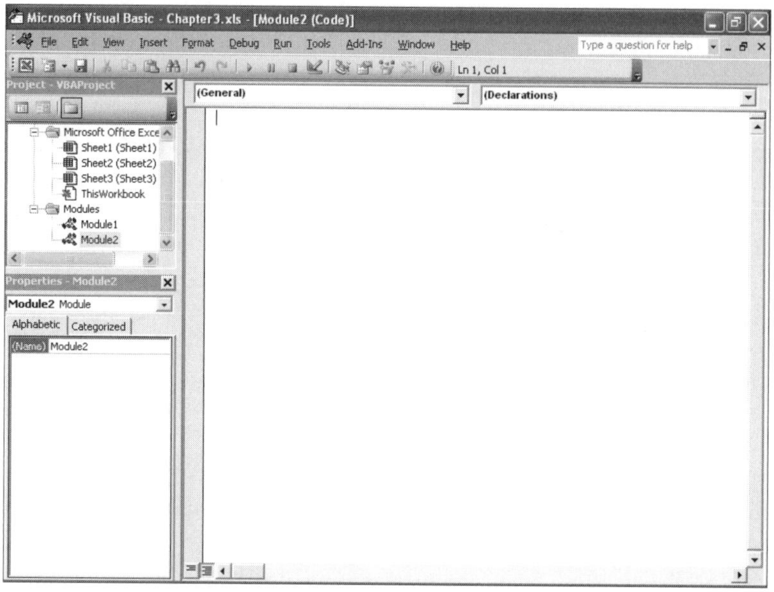

Figure 4-9. Creating a new module gives you a place to put your code.

Deleting VBA Modules

If a module is no longer needed within a project, you can delete it. Select the module you want to remove from within the Project Explorer, and then click File, Remove Module Name. Module Name will change to reflect the name of the module that is currently selected. Before deleting the module, the Visual Basic Editor will ask if you want to export the module to a text file, as shown in Figure 4-10. This gives you an opportunity to backup a module before it is completely removed.

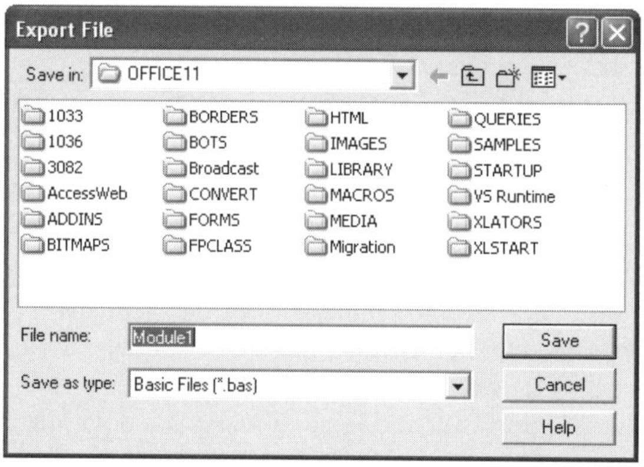

Figure 4-10. It's probably a good idea to take the opportunity presented by the Export File dialog box to save deleted code in a text file, just in case.

You can export a module at any time by clicking File, Export.

Copying Modules Between Projects

The Project Explorer provides an easy method for copying modules from one project to another. To do so, open the source project and the destination project and then, from within the Project Explorer window, click the module you want to copy from the source project and drag it to the destination module. Once the mouse pointer is within the destination project, it will change appearance from a circle with a line through it to an arrow with an outline box and plus sign beneath it, as shown in Figure 4-11.

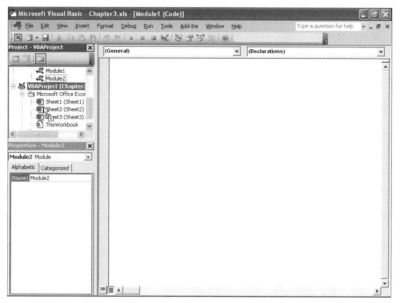

Figure 4-11. The mouse pointer changes to indicate a valid drop-off point when copying modules.

If you copy a module into a project that already has a module of the same name, the Visual Basic Editor will rename the module by adding a number behind the name, starting with *1* and incrementing each time a module of the same name is copied. Also, if there are no modules of the type you're moving, the Visual Basic Editor will create a module and the appropriate folder to hold it.

Declaring Variables, Constants, and Data Types

Most procedures will need some type of temporary storage area to manipulate data and hold it for later use. VBA stores this data in memory using a *variable*. It is also possible to store in memory a value that is not going to change; these values are called *constants*. Variables can hold values of different data types, which are specified when the variable is named, or declared. Variables should always be declared to reduce the chance of introducing bugs in the procedure and to properly allocate the amount of storage needed to hold the variable.

Declaring Variables

Variables are declared within a procedure by using the *Dim*, or dimension, statement. The most common usage of the *Dim* statement is

```
Dim varname as type
```

This statement explicitly declares a variable named *varname* as a variable of *type*. Multiple variables can be declared on one line by separating them with a comma, like this:

```
Dim varname1 as type, varname2 as type, ...
```

Defining Data Types

When variables are declared, they should be declared as a specific data type. This data type determines the values that can be stored within the variable and how much memory is required to store the value. VBA provides different data types to handle numbers, strings, dates and times, Boolean values, and objects. You can even declare your own data type when needed.

The majority of the data types available in VBA are numeric types, each of which handles a different range of values with varying amounts of precision. The numeric data types along with their specifications are listed in Table 4-7.

Table 4-7. **Numeric Data Types**

Type	Range	Description	Storage Requirements
Byte	0 to 255	Unsigned, integer number	1 byte
Currency	-922,337,203,685,477.5808 to 922,337,203,685,477.5807	A signed, fixed-point number with up to 15 digits to the left of the decimal and 4 digits to the right; used for financial or other calculations requiring a high degree of precision	8 bytes
Decimal	+/- 79,228,162,514,264,337,593,543,950,335 with no decimal point and +/- 7.9228162514264337593543950335 with 28 digits behind the decimal point.	Can't be directly declared in VBA; requires the use of a Variant data type	12 bytes

Table 4-7. Numeric Data Types

Type	Range	Description	Storage Requirements
Double	Negative values: -1.79769313486231E308 to -4.94065645841247E-324 Positive values: 4.94065645841247E-324 to 1.79769313486231E308	Signed double-precision floating-point number	8 bytes
Integer	-32,768 to 32,767	Signed integer number	2 bytes
Long	-2,147,483,648 to 2,147,483,647	Signed integer number	4 bytes
Single	Negative values: -3.402823E38 to -1.401298E-45 Positive values: 1.401298E-45 to 3.402823E38	Signed single-precision floating-point number	4 bytes

Defining Constants

Some procedures will require a reference to a particular value that rarely, if ever, changes. Rather than repeatedly entering the same value, you can create a reference, called a *constant*, for it. Defining a constant lets you specify the actual value only once in your code and use the reference whenever you need it.

VBA itself has many built-in constants, called *intrinsic constants*, designed to make it easier for you to work with the many functions available. For example, if you had a procedure to create a line chart, you could use the intrinsic constant *xlDot* to make the line dotted in appearance.

> **Note** You can display a list of the available intrinsic constants by typing **intrinsic constants** in the Help box in the Visual Basic Editor.

You specify your own constants by using the *Const* statement, which works the same as the *Dim* statement with the exceptions that you must supply the value of the constant and only one constant can be declared on a line. The following lines declare two constants, the first a byte value with the number of days in December and the second a *Single* variable with an accepted value for *pi*.

```
Const conDaysDec as Byte = 31
Const conPi as Single = 3.1415929
```

Handling Strings

As mentioned earlier, there are other data types besides numeric ones. Variables can also hold text values using the *String* data type. Strings can be either variable-length or fixed-length.

Variable-length strings can hold approximately 2 billion (2 ^ 31) characters, subject to available memory, and fixed-length strings can hold about 65,000 characters (2 ^ 16).

Both types of strings are declared similarly using the *Dim* statement just as was done with the numeric types. Fixed-length strings add extra code to specify the length of the string. The first line in the following code fragment specifies a variable-length string, and the second line specifies a fixed-length string of 25 characters:

```
Dim MyString as String
Dim MyFixedString as String * 25
```

Strings that have been declared but have not yet had a value assigned to them are known as *empty strings*. To assign a value to a string variable, it needs to be enclosed within double quotation marks. The following lines are examples of assigning values to strings:

```
MyString = "Hello world."
MyFixedString = "This is a fixed string."
MyEmptyString = ""
```

> **Note** Fixed strings must be exactly 25 characters in length; therefore, the Visual Basic Editor will either add spaces or truncate the string so it is the proper length.

Handling Dates and Times

Dates and times are stored within the *Date* data type. The range of dates that can be stored is from January 1, 100, to December 31, 9999, with all times from 0:00:00 to 23:59:59. Although a *Date* variable can hold both a date and time, if you need only one element, only that element needs to be assigned to the variable; the other will be omitted from the variable.

You can assign values to a date variable by enclosing a recognizable literal string within number signs (#). VBA can recognize dates and times in just about any format, but you should always be as explicit as possible to ensure the correct value is being used. Here are some examples of dates and times VBA can recognize.

```
MyDate = #15 July 1999#
StartDate = #April 8, 2001#
MyTime = #8:47 PM#
StartingDateTime = #05/07/1992 15:56#
```

The Visual Basic Editor might change the dates and times that you type to reflect your computer's date and time settings. For example, #15 July 1999# might become #7/15/1999#.

> **Note** When entering dates, VBA will recognize two-digit years and uses 2029 as the cutoff year. All two-digit years from 00 to 29 are recognized as being a part of the 2000s. The remaining years, 30 to 99, are considered part of the 1900s. It is best to always include the full four-digit year to remove any ambiguities.

Handling Variants and Data Type Conversions

Variants are the catchall data type of VBA. If a variable is declared but not typed, it will be cast as a *Variant* data type. Variants can hold any type of data except for fixed-length strings and must be used for certain data types, such as *Currency*.

When working with variants, VBA will attempt to use it as the data type that best fits the data being stored in the variable, but it might not always pick the right type. Assigning a variant the value of 64 * 1024 produces an error message. Because both operands, 64 and 1024, are considered *Integer* data types by VBA, it tries to store the result as an *Integer*. The actual result, 65536, is too large for an *Integer* data type and produces the error message.

To avoid having VBA pick the wrong data type, you can convert values to a specific data type. In the preceding example, by explicitly converting one of the values to the *Long* data type, VBA will cast the result as a *Long* also and avoid the error.

VBA provides functions to convert values to any numeric data type. When converting from one data type to another, keep in mind the level of precision that is used by each type and the limitations of each data type. For example, converting a *Single* variable, which has a decimal component, to a *Long*, which does not, will result in losing the decimal portion of the value, and converting the variable back to a *Single* will not restore the decimal portion of the original value.

```
lngOffset = CLong(sngOffset)
```

A list of the conversion functions along with the type of data returned and rounding rules is provided in Table 4-8. The expression argument provided to the functions can be any numeric or string expression. String expressions need to be in a format that can be recognized as a numeric value, but the specific format varies from region to region.

Table 4-8. Data Type Conversion Functions

Function	Result	Remarks
CBool(expression)	True/False (-1/0)	Any non-zero expression will result in *True* (-1).
CByte(expression)	Byte	.5 will round to the nearest even integer.
CCur(expression)	Currency	Rounding to four decimal places. Five decimals and greater is undocumented and might return unexpected results.
CDate(expression)	Date/Time	Numeric expressions will return a date matching number of days from January 1, 100. String expressions will return an interpreted date.
CDbl(expression)	Double	Rounding to the nearest floating-point number within range.
CDec(expression)	Decimal	Rounding to a variable number of decimal places dependent upon size of number.

continued

61

Chapter 4

Table 4-8. Data Type Conversion Functions   *(continued)*

Function	Result	Remarks
CInt(expression)	Integer	.5 will round to the nearest even integer.
CLng(expression)	Long Integer	.5 will round to the nearest even integer.
CSng(expression)	Single	Rounding to the nearest floating-point number within the range.
CVar(expression)	Variant	Numeric expressions convert to a *Variant Double*. Expressions enclosed within # convert to a *Variant Date*. All others convert to string.

Understanding Variable Scope and Lifetimes

Variables have a set lifetime and visibility within modules and procedures. A variable lifetime begins when the variable is declared and lasts until the procedure or module that declared the variable has completed execution. If a procedure calls a second procedure, the variables of the first procedure remain alive and retain their values during the execution of the second procedure.

> **Note** Although only the term *variable* is used in this section regarding *Scope* and *Lifetime*, the same rules apply to constants also.

A variable can also have a virtually unlimited lifetime if it's declared as a *static* variable. Static variables within a procedure will retain their values from one call to the containing procedure to the next so long as the module containing the procedure has not been stopped or reset. Static variables are declared using the same syntax as normal variables, replacing the statement *Dim* with *Static*.

Besides having a set lifetime, variables also have a certain visibility. Variables declared within a procedure can be used only within that procedure; other procedures within the same module can't see them. This means that two procedures within the same module can each declare a variable using the same name, but the two variables will be separate entities and visible only by the procedure that declared them. Consider the following code as an example:

```
Sub Procedure1()
Dim intCounter as Integer, intResult as Integer
    intCounter = 87
    intResult = intCounter * 74
End Sub

Sub Procedure2()
Dim intCounter as Integer, intResult
    intResult = intCounter * 74
End Sub
```

In the preceding procedures, both Procedure1 and Procedure2 have declared a variable named *intCounter*. In Procedure1, *intCounter* has been set to 87, this means *intResult* will be set to 6438 when the third line is executed. In Procedure2, *intCounter* has not been set to a specific value so it retains the initialized value for an *Integer*, which is 0. Then the second line is executed, and *intResult* is given a value of 0 also (0 * 74 = 0).

To use a variable in more than one procedure, it needs to be declared at the module level. Variables declared at the module level can be used by any procedure that is within the same module. To declare a module variable, the declaration statement for the variable needs to be entered in the *Declaration* section of the module (following any *Option* statements and before any procedures), as shown in Figure 4-12.

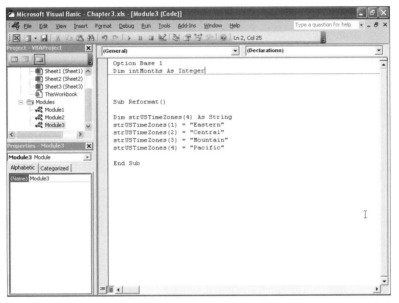

Figure 4-12. If you want a variable to be available to all procedures in a module, you need to declare the variable in the declaration section for modules.

Module variables can be exposed to other modules by using the *Public* modifier. When a variable is declared *Public*, it becomes visible to all other modules, not just the module it is declared in.

Although all module variables are private by default, for clarity it is better to declare them using *Private* instead of *Dim*. Variables that are to be visible to all modules are declared using the *Public* statement. The following two declarations illustrate the difference between a *Public* and a *Private* declaration:

```
Private intThisModuleOnly as Integer
Public intAllModules as Integer
```

Assigning Values to Variables

A variable is useless if you aren't able to assign a value to it. Assigning a value to a variable is done using an equal sign (=), which is also known as the *assignment operator*. The name of the variable is given first, followed by the assignment operator, and then an expression of the value that you wish to assign to the variable. The value expression could be a literal value, or it could be something more complicated, such as a mathematical equation.

```
MyNumber = 23
YourNumber = 16 + 85
MyString = "This is a literal string."
TwoStrings = "This is the first part." + "This is the second part."
MyDate = #05/07/1992#
```

You can also assign the value from one variable to another variable, or you can reference the same variable you are assigning a value to. For example, if you are keeping a running total of hours worked, you can update the total hours worked by adding the number of hours worked during the current day.

```
TotalLaps = LapCounter
TotalHoursWorked = TotalHoursWorked + HoursWorkedToday
```

Working with Arrays

An *array* is a group of values that are of the same data type. Although an array contains multiple values, VBA treats the array as one variable, which offers some flexibility when working with arrays. You can work with the entire array at once or just one element in the array at a time. To work with an individual element of an array, you specify the element's *index number*, which represents the element's position within the array. If you visualize an array as a list, the index number is the element's position in the list.

Arrays have two boundaries, a lower and an upper. The default lower boundary for arrays is 0, which can lead to a bit of confusion at times. With a starting index number of 0, the first element in the list would be at position 0. This means you are always working with an index number that is actually one less than the actual position in the array.

If you prefer to start counting from 1, you can change the lower boundary of an array using the *Option Base* statement. The *Option Base* statement must be placed in the declarations section of a module before any arrays are defined and before any procedures. The *Option Base* statement can take only an argument of 0 or 1, as shown in this example:

```
Option Base 1
```

Creating an Array

You create an array using the same procedure you use to define a variable. Use a *Dim*, a *Private*, a *Public*, or a *Static* statement followed by the array name and the date type that is to be stored in the array. The only difference between creating an array and creating a variable is that you must define at least an upper boundary in the array declaration. (You can also specify a lower boundary, as you'll see shortly.) To create a string array that could hold the names of the 12 months, for example, you would use the following statement:

```
Dim strMonths(11) as String
```

Remember, unless specified otherwise, arrays start with a default lower boundary of 0. Therefore, to hold the twelve months, you set an upper boundary of 11 (0 to 11 provides you with twelve elements). If you had included the *Option Base 1* statement in the declarations section then you could declare the array like this:

```
Dim strMonths(12) as String
```

Besides using the *Option Base* statement, you can also set the lower boundary of an array to a value other than 0 or 1 by explicitly declaring it when you create the array using a *To* clause. For example, if you wanted to declare an array that included only the three months of summer, you could use the following statement:

```
Dim strSummerMonths(6 To 8) as String
```

Creating Multidimensional Arrays

All the arrays we have talked about so far have been simple, single-dimensional arrays. You can also create multidimensional arrays with up to 60 dimensions, although you will probably never find a reason to use more than 3 or 4 dimensions.

To declare a multidimensional array, you separate the boundaries of each dimension by commas. A two-dimensional array that could hold a value for each month over 10 years could be declared with the following statement:

```
Dim intDecadeArray(9, 11) as Integer
```

Visualizing multidimensional arrays might seem daunting, but some could be straightforward. For example, one use of a two-dimensional array would be as a table, where the first dimension represents the rows of the table while the second dimension represents the columns, much like the appearance of a worksheet in Excel.

Expanding to a third dimension is not much harder. Continuing with the table or worksheet example, you could use a third dimension to keep track of multiple tables or worksheets. For example, if a garden supply store were open sixteen hours a day, you could create an array such as the following:

```
Dim curHourlySales(12, 31, 16) as Currency
```

Chapter 4

Creating Dynamic Arrays

The preceding examples of declaring arrays are all *fixed* arrays, meaning that each array has a set size that can't be changed. *Dynamic* arrays have the ability to increase in size as needed. This expansion doesn't happen automatically; rather, you make it happen with commands you add to your procedures.

To declare a dynamic array, you omit the boundary from the declaration statement. If you wanted to create a test dynamic array, you could use the following statement:

```
Dim intTestArray() as Integer.
```

Before using a dynamic array, you do need to set the number of elements it will contain by using the *ReDim* statement. *ReDim* lets you reset, or *redimension*, an array to the number of elements that are needed. The *ReDim* statement requires only the name of the array and the number of elements that it can now contain, as in the following command:

```
ReDim intTestArray(365)
```

The *ReDim* statement reinitializes the array, which causes the array to lose all data that is contained within its elements. To increase the number of elements an array can hold without losing the data it contains, you need to add the *Preserve* keyword to the command, as in the following example:

```
ReDim Preserve intTestArray(730)
```

Caution There is no way to decrease the size of an array without losing the data it contains.

You can store data in an array by specifying the index number of the element to which you want to assign the value. The following code fragments create an array to hold the names of the four major time zones within the continental United States and assign those names to the array:

```
Option Base 1
Dim strUSTimeZones(4) as String
strUSTimeZones(1) = "Eastern"
strUSTimeZones(2) = "Central"
strUSTimeZones(3) = "Mountain"
strUSTimeZones(4) = "Pacific"
```

Retrieving a value from an array works the same way: you specify the index number of the element you want to use. The following statement retrieves the fourth element from the third dimension of a two-dimensional array:

```
intValue = intMyArray(3,4)
```

Chapter 4

Writing to the Screen and Accepting Input

Accepting input from users and providing status messages are common tasks that you'll use within many procedures. VBA lets you use two common Windows methods of displaying and asking for information from a user, which makes your macros easier to use because they present a familiar interface to the user.

Creating a Message Box

When small informational messages or simple questions need to be asked, the *MsgBox* (message box) function can be used. Message boxes are useful for a number of reasons. Besides being familiar aspects of just about any Windows application, they are extremely simple and easy to use. Here is a list of some common tasks for which you can use message boxes.

- Inform the user of an action that is about to take place, and possibly allow them the option to cancel the action or choose a different action.

- Inform the user of an error condition that has occurred, and allow them to take corrective actions.

- Inform the user that a particular task has been completed successfully or not. The message box can inform the user exactly what was done to perform the task.

A primary advantage of using a message box is that it lets you present a message to the user that can't be ignored. It's even possible to force the user to react to the message box by not allowing them to switch to or open any other application.

As useful as message boxes are, they do have several limitations, such as the following:

- A message box can present only one, two, or three buttons for users to choose from, which means a limited number of options for the user.

- The buttons are available only in predefined sets—you can't place a custom button into a message box.

- No other features are available in a message box. You can't add additional controls to present more information/options to a user.

Despite these limitations, the message box is a very handy tool for any programmer. The syntax of a message box statement is shown here.

```
MsgBox(prompt[, buttons] [, title][, helpfile, context]) as Integer
```

- *prompt*   A required argument for the *MsgBox* function that contains the text that is displayed within the message box. The text can be no longer than about 1024 characters, depending upon the width of the characters. If the text contains multiple lines, you can specify the line breaks by including a carriage return with the constant vbCr, (*Chr$(13)*), linefeed with the vbLf constant, (*Chr$(10)*), or carriage return/linefeed combination with the vbCrLf constant.

Chapter 4

> **Note** While it's easier to use the intrinsic constants for a carriage return and a line feed, you might see (*Chr$(13)*) for a carriage return, (*Chr$(10)*) for a line feed, and (*Chr$(13)* & *Chr$(10)*) for both.

- *buttons* Optional numerical argument used to specify the buttons and the icon that is to be displayed within the message box. By adding the value of the selected options together, you can specify not only which buttons and icon to display, but also which button is the default button and the modality of the message box. You can use the Visual Basic intrinsic constants to specify options. See Table 4-9 for a complete list of options available. The default button is selected if the user presses the Enter key. If *buttons* is not given, the default value of 0 is used.

- *title* Optional string argument used to specify the text to be displayed within the message boxes title bar. If omitted, "Microsoft Office Excel" is displayed.

- *helpfile* Optional string argument used to specify the help file used to provide context-sensitive help. If *helpfile* is specified, *context* must also be specified.

- *context* Optional numerical argument that is the Help context number assigned to the appropriate Help topic. If *context* is provided, *helpfile* must also be provided.

The *MsgBox* function returns an integer value that indicates which button was clicked by the user. These values are listed in Table 4-10.

Table 4-9. **Button Options for Message Boxes**

Intrinsic Constant	Value	Description
Buttons		
vbOkOnly	0	Displays an OK button only.
vbOkCancel	1	Displays an OK and a Cancel button.
vbAbortRetryIgnore	2	Displays three buttons labeled *Abort*, *Retry*, and *Ignore*.
vbYesNoCancel	3	Displays three buttons labeled *Yes*, *No*, and *Cancel*.
vbYesNo	4	Displays buttons labeled *Yes* and *No*.
vbRetryCancel	5	Displays buttons labeled *Retry* and *Cancel*.
Icons		
vbCritical	16	Displays a solid red circle enclosing a white X.
vbQuestion	32	Displays a cartoon balloon enclosing a question mark.
vbExclamation	48	Displays a yellow triangle enclosing an exclamation point.
vbInformation	64	Displays a cartoon balloon enclosing a lowercase letter *i*.

Table 4-9. Button Options for Message Boxes

Intrinsic Constant	Value	Description
Default Button		
vbDefaultButton1	0	Sets the first button as the default button.
vbDefaultButton2	256	Sets the second button as the default button.
vbDefaultButton3	512	Sets the third button as the default button.
vbDefaultButton4	768	Sets the fourth button (such as a Help button) as the default button.
Modality		
vbApplicationModal	0	Marks the message box as application modal. Stops all processing of the current application until the message box is dismissed. Does not interfere with any other applications.
vbSystemModal	4096	Marks the message box as system modal; it will always appear as the topmost window regardless of which application the user switches to.
vbMsgBoxHelpButton	16384	Adds a Help button to the message box.
vbMsgBoxSetForeground	65536	Causes the message box to be displayed in the foreground.
vbMsgBoxRight	524288	Causes the text in the message box to be right-aligned.
vbMsgBoxRtlReading	1048576	Causes the text to be displayed right-to-left on Hebrew and Arabic systems.

Table 4-10. Values Returned by a Message Box

Intrinsic Constant	Value
vbOk	1
vbCancel	2
vbAbort	3
vbRetry	4
vbIgnore	5
vbYes	6
vbNo	7

If a Cancel button is displayed in the message box, pressing Esc has the same effect as clicking it. You should select exactly one option from each group; if more than one is selected, Excel will use the option with the highest value.

You can display a simple message box just by providing the *title* argument.

Chapter 4

69

```
Sub Welcome()
    MsgBox "Welcome to Excel."
End Sub
```

The preceding procedure produces a simple message box with only the text and an OK button displayed. Because the statement doesn't include a value for the message box title, the title defaults to the name of the application (as you can see in Figure 4-13).

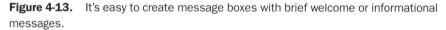

Figure 4-13. It's easy to create message boxes with brief welcome or informational messages.

Besides using literal strings to display messages, you can also use string variables. The following code fragment displays a message box with two lines of text in the message, an information icon, and a title in the title bar, with the result shown in Figure 4-14.

```
Sub Travel()
    strPrompt = "Welcome!" & vbCrLf & "Enter your travel data below."
    MsgBox strPrompt, vbInformation, "Travel Voucher Records"
End Sub
```

Figure 4-14. It's not that much harder to create a simple message box with two lines of text.

When choosing an icon to display in the message box, you can use the following guidelines, provided by Microsoft in the Windows User Interface guidelines:

- The information icon should be used to provide results to the user of a command previously issued. No choices should be offered, and only the OK button should ever be displayed with the information icon.

- The exclamation icon should be used to warn the user of a problem or situation that requires a decision from the user before continuing. This is especially true of situations where data might be irreversibly changed or erased.

- The critical icon should be used to inform the user of a critical error or problem that needs to be corrected before further processing can be done.

- The question icon should not be used in any instance and is provided only for backward compatibility.

Creating an Input Box

An *input box* is similar to a message box in that it displays text, but it has the additional functionality of being able to accept text responses from users. Instead of presenting the user with a few buttons that can be clicked in response to messages displayed in the window, input boxes contain a text box where the user can type in responses. The input box displays a prompt and title just as a message box does, but no icons are displayed and an OK and a Cancel button are always present. An input box that asks for a user's name would look similar to Figure 4-15.

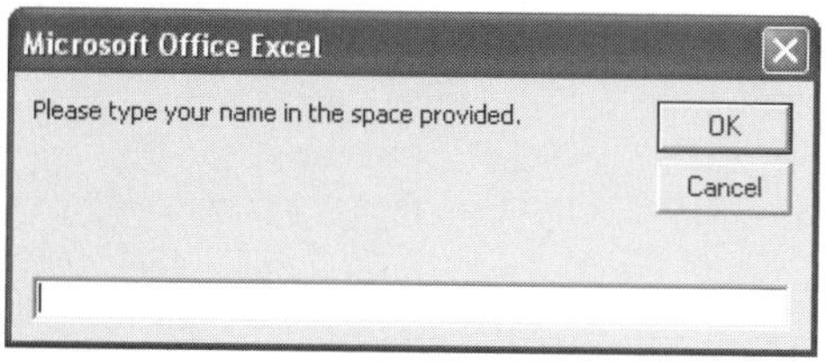

Figure 4-15. Creating an input box would allow users to enter personal information, such as their name.

The syntax for an input box is shown here.

```
InputBox (prompt [, title][, default][, xpos][, ypos][, helpfile, context]) as
String
```

- *prompt*   Required argument for the *InputBox* function that contains the text that is displayed within the input box. The text can be no longer than about 1024 characters, depending upon the width of the characters. If the text contains multiple lines, you can specify the line breaks by including a carriage return with vbCr, a linefeed with vbLf, or a carriage return/linefeed combination with vbCrLf. You can also use the Visual Basic intrinsic constants *vbCr*, *vbLf*, and *vbCrLf* to represent the characters.

- *title*   Optional string argument used to specify the text to be displayed within the input boxes title bar. If omitted, "Microsoft Office Excel" is displayed.

- *default*   Optional string value that is displayed within the text box as the default value if no other information is entered. The user can erase or modify the default answer.

- *xpos*   Optional numeric expression that represents the number of twips from the left edge of the screen to the left edge of the input box. If *xpos* is omitted, the input box is centered horizontally.

Note   A *twip* (twentieth of a point) is 1/1440th of an inch or 1/567th of a centimeter. So, to start an input box half an inch in from the left edge of the screen, you would assign an *xpos* value of 720.

- *ypos*   Optional numeric expression that represents the number of twips from the top edge of the screen to the top edge of the input box. If *ypos* is omitted, the input box is centered vertically.

71

- *helpfile*   Optional string argument used to specify the help file used to provide context-sensitive help. If *helpfile* is specified, *context* must also be specified.

- *context*   Optional numerical argument that is the Help context number assigned to the appropriate Help topic. If *context* is provided, *helpfile* must also be provided.

The *InputBox* function returns a string value, so if the text box is blank or the Cancel button pressed, the returned string is empty.

The returned value from an input box is usually stored within a string variable so that it can be processed further. The following code fragment displays a message box asking for the user's place of birth. All parameters are entered as variables, although literals or constants could have also been used.

```
Sub BirthCity()
Dim strResponse as String, strPrompt as String, strTitle as String
strResponse = "New Orleans"
strPrompt = "Please enter your city of birth."
strTitle = "My InputBox"
strResponse = InputBox(strPrompt, strTitle, strResponse)
End Sub
```

Defining Object Variables

One of the strengths of VBA is that you are not limited to creating simple variables that hold data assigned from another variable or derived from a calculation. In fact, if you want to create a new worksheet, a chart, or any other "thing" in Excel that is represented as an object in the Excel VBA object model, you can do so by declaring an *object variable*. Using the *Dim* statement, you provide a name for the variable and then indicate the type of object you wish to create, as in the following code fragment, which creates a reference to a worksheet:

```
Dim myObj as Worksheet
```

Using the object variable is very different from using normal variables, mainly because object variables are pointers to an object, not the object itself. That is, you haven't actually created a new worksheet yet—all you've done is tell VBA that you want the *myObj* variable to hold a Worksheet object. Therefore, you need to actually provide the object you want assigned to the variable, which you accomplish using the **Set** command. The following command sets the object variable *myObj* to point to the first worksheet:

```
Set myObj = Worksheets(1)
```

Creating Custom Data Types

VBA provides all of the simple data types that you will ever need when writing macros for Excel. In some instances, you might need a data type that is more complex. For example, if you wanted to create a custom data type that would hold both the horizontal and vertical

Chapter 4

coordinates for a point on a map, you could do so and avoid storing the values in separate variables. Using the *Type* statement, you can define a new data type to hold both coordinates.

```
Private Type MapLocation
    sglHorizontal as Single
    sglVertical as Single
End Type
```

With the new type defined, you then use it as you would any other variable type, using a period (.) to reference the subelements of your new type.

```
Dim myMapLocation as MapLocation
myMapPoint.sglHorizontal = 29.57
myMapPoint.sglVertical = 90
```

Custom data types have to be defined within the declarations section of a module. They can be marked as *Public* or *Private*.

With...End With Command

One useful shorthand notation you can use to make your code more readable, and shorter, is the **With...End With** command. The **With...End With** command defines an object that the VBA compiler will assume is being referenced by every property, method, and event called in the procedure. Once you define the object in the *With* line of code, you can use a period followed by the name of the property that you want to set. The following procedure, for example, changes the top and bottom margins of a worksheet to two inches, and changes the orientation of the worksheet from *portrait* (with the column headers running parallel to the short edge of the paper) to *landscape* (with the column headers running parallel to the long edge of the paper).

```
Sub PageSetup()
    With ActiveSheet.PageSetup
        .TopMargin = Application.InchesToPoints(2)
        .BottomMargin = Application.InchesToPoints(2)
        .Orientation = xlLandscape
    End With
End Sub
```

Controlling Program Flow

VBA, as a derivative of Visual Basic, is an *event-driven language*, which means that the code you write is executed as a response to something that has happened, such as a button being clicked or a workbook being opened. Program execution normally flows from the first line of code down to the last line within a procedure, but there are times when this top-down flow of execution needs to be broken. VBA provides several methods for repeating certain sections of code, skipping some sections of code, and making decisions about which sections of code to execute.

Chapter 4

Selection Statements

A key facet of most applications is the ability to make decisions. This ability allows the application to make decisions about input received from the user and any values that might be calculated.

If...Then...Else **Statement**

The simplest form of decision making is performed with the *If...Then...Else* statement. It examines an expression to see if it is true or not. If the expression is *True*, the code performs one set of actions; otherwise, it performs a different set of actions.

If...Then...Else statements can take two forms, either single-line or multi-line. The syntax of both forms is shown here.

```
If condition Then statements Else elsestatements
```

or

```
If condition Then
    [ statements ]
[ ElseIf elseifcondition [ Then ]
    [ elseifstatements ] ]
[ Else
    [Else elsestatements] ]
End If
```

- *condition*   A required expression that must evaluate to a *True* or *False* Boolean value
- *statements*   Optional block of one or more statements that are to be executed when the *condition* is *True*
- *elseifcondition*   A required expression if *ElseIf* is present that must evaluate to a *True* or *False* Boolean value
- *elseifstatements*   Optional block of one or more statements that are to be executed when the *elseifcondition* is *True*
- *elsestatements*   Optional block of one or more statements that are to be executed if no previous *condition* or *elseifcondition* is *True*
- *End If*   A required element in multi-line form and terminates the *If...Then* block

Using the *If...Then...Else* statements requires the use of comparison operators to build the needed *condition* statements. The comparison operators compare two or more values and decide if the values are equal to each other or if one is greater than the other; then the operators return a True or False answer. The six comparison operators are listed in Table 4-11.

Chapter 4

Table 4-11. Comparison Operators

Operator	Description
=	Determines if two values are equal
<	Determines if value on left side of operand is less than value on right side
>	Determines if value on left side of operand is greater than value on right side
<=	Determines if value on left side of operand is less than or equal to value on right side
>=	Determines if value on left side of operand is greater than or equal to value on right side
<>	Determines if two values are not equal to each other

The following code fragments show examples of using the *If…Then…Else* statement to determine if a person's age allows them to vote:

```
If intAge >= 18 Then
    boolAllowVote = True
Else
    boolAllowVote = False
End If

If boolAllowVote Then
    [Display ballot and record vote]
End If

intReturn = MsgBox("Do you wish to continue?", vbYesNo + vbExclamation, "My App")
If intReturn = vbYes Then
    [Continue processing]
Else
    [Exit Procedure]
End If
```

Select Case Statements

Select Case statements allow you to check for multiple values at once. Suppose you had to calculate different values depending upon what month it was. You would need to write eleven *If…Then…Else* statements to check for all twelve months, but using a *Select Case* statement lets you drop the number of conditional statements to one, making your code easier to read and maintain.

The syntax of the *Select Case* statement is shown here.

```
Select [Case] testcondition
    [Case expressionlist
        [statements] ]
    [Case Else
        elsestatements
End Select
```

Chapter 4

- *testcondition*   Required expression that must evaluate to one of the basic data types, such as *Boolean, Integer, String*, and so on.

- *expressionlist*   A list of expression clauses representing values for *testexpression*. Multiple expression clauses are separated by commas and can take one of the following forms:

- *Expression1 To Expression2*   Used to represent a range of values from *Expression1* to *Expression2*. *Expression1* must be less than *Expression2*.

- *[Is] comparisonoperator Expression*   *comparisonoperator* is used to specify a restriction on the value of *Expression*.

- *Expression*   The expressions in expressionlist can be any data type so long as they are implicitly convertible to the type of *test condition*.

- *Statements*   One or more statements that are executed if the *testexpression* matches any clause in *expressionlist*.

- *else statements*   One or more statements that are executed if the *testexpression* does not match any clause in *expressionlist*.

- *End Select*   Required to mark the end of the *Select Case* block.

The following code fragment demonstrates using the *Select Case* statement to set a variable to the number of days in each month.

```
Select Case strMonth
    Case "February"
        intDays = 28

    Case "April", "June", "September", "November"
        intDays = 30

    Case "January", "March", "May", "July", "August", "October", "December"
        intDays = 31

End Select
```

This preceding code is just a simple example of specifying the number of days in a month, but does not make any provisions for leap years. More code can be added to the "February" clause to properly set the number of days in February, as in the following code:

```
Case "February"
    If (intYear Mod 100) = 0 Then
        If (intYear Mod 400) = 0 Then
            intDays = 29
        Else
            intDays = 28
        End If
    Else
        If (intYear Mod 4) = 0 Then
            intDays = 29
```

```
        Else
            intDays = 28
        End If
    End If
```

This example also shows how you can mix *If...Then...Else* statements inside a *Select Case* statement.

Loops

There will be numerous times when you'll need to perform a certain task several times, so VBA provides several methods of creating loops. Loops can be divided into two categories: *iteration* loops and *logical* loops.

Iteration Loops

Iteration loops, which are used to ensure that a specific number of repetitions have occurred, have a definitive starting point and ending point. There are two iteration loops, both similar in style and syntax.

The first type of iteration loop, the *For...Next* loop, is normally used for counting and is particularly useful with arrays. The syntax of a *For...Next* loop is shown here.

```
For counter = start To end [Step step]
    [statements]
    [Exit For]
    [statements]
Next counter
```

- **counter**   Required numeric variable that is used as a counter. It can't be a Boolean or member of an array.
- **start**   Required value used as the starting point of the array.
- **end**   Required value used as the ending point of the array.
- **step**   Optional value by which the counter should be incremented during each iteration of the loop. Step value can be a positive or negative value. Default value is 1.
- **statements**   One or more optional statement lines that are executed during each iteration of the loop.
- **Exit For**   Optional statement used to exit the loop prematurely. Code execution resumes at the first line following the *Next counter* statement.
- **Next counter**   Required statement marking the end of the *For...Next* loop.

You can omit the counter variable used within the *Next* statement, but it isn't recommended. By including the counter, you add an extra level of protection against programming errors.

As stated earlier, a *For...Next* loop ensures that a specific number of repetitions are performed. Suppose you had an array of 26 elements, and you wanted to set each one to its corresponding letter of the alphabet. A *For...Next* loop provides the perfect means to accomplish this. The following code creates a 26-member array, assigns a letter of the alphabet to each element, and then builds a message box to display those elements.

```
Sub AlphabetArray()
Dim strABC(1 To 26) as String
Dim intCounter as Integer
Dim strPrompt as String
For intCounter = 1 to 26
    strABC(intCounter) = Chr$(intCounter + 64)
Next intCounter
strPrompt = "The strABC array contains the following values:" & vbCrLf
For intCounter = 1 to 26
    strPrompt = strPrompt & strABC(intCounter)
Next intCounter
MsgBox strPrompt
End Sub
```

For...Next loops can be nested inside one another, so you can build even more complex iterations. The following example modifies the previous example by building a two-dimensional array and displaying the elements of the array backward:

```
Dim strABC(100 To 101, 1 To 26) As String
Dim intCounter1 As Integer, intCounter2 As Integer
Dim strPrompt As String
For intCounter1 = 100 To 101
    For intCounter2 = 1 To 26
        strABC(intCounter1, intCounter2) = Chr$(intCounter2 + 64)
    Next intCounter2
Next intCounter1
strPrompt = "The strABC array contains the following values:"

For intCounter1 = 100 To 101
    strPrompt = strPrompt & vbCrLf & "Dimension" & Str$(intCounter1) & ": "
    For intCounter2 = 26 To 1 Step -1
        strPrompt = strPrompt & strABC(intCounter1, intCounter2)
    Next
Next intCounter1
MsgBox strPrompt
```

The other iteration loop, the *For Each...Next* loop, is used with collections of objects or arrays, ensuring that each member of the group is touched upon. It has syntax very similar to the *For...Next* loop.

```
For Each element In group
    [statements]
    [Exit For]
    [statements]
Next element
```

- *element*   Required object or variant variable that is used to point to each member of the group. Array loops require a variant variable regardless of the data type of the array.
- *group*   Required collection of objects or array containing the elements that will be affected by the loop.
- *statements*   One or more optional statement lines that are executed during each iteration of the loop.
- *Exit For*   Optional statement used to exit the loop prematurely. Code execution resumes at the first line following the *Next counter* statement.
- *Next element*   Required statement marking the end of the *For…Next* loop.

The *For Each…Next* loop is a handy method of performing the same action to a collection of objects. (You will learn more about object collections and how to work with them in Chapter 6, Chapter 7, and Chapter 8.) If you wanted, for example, to rename all the worksheets in a workbook, you could use a *For Each…Next* loop to ask the user for a name for each worksheet, rename it, and continue on to the next one until all of the worksheets were renamed.

```
Sub RenameAllWorksheets()
Dim myWorksheet As Worksheet
Dim strPrompt As String, strResult As String
Dim intCounter As Integer

intCounter = 0
strPrompt = "Please enter the new name for worksheet "
For Each myWorksheet In Application.Worksheets
    strResult = InputBox(strPrompt & myWorksheet.Name)
    myWorksheet.Name = strResult
    intCounter = intCounter + 1
Next myWorksheet
strPrompt = "Total worksheets renamed =" & Str$(intCounter)
MsgBox strPrompt
End Sub
```

Logical Loops

Logical loops have no predetermined number of iterations. Instead, they rely on a logical expression that tests for a particular condition and then repeat the loop until the condition is either met or cleared, depending upon the type of loop.

Although there are four forms of logical loops, they can be simplified into two styles: those that test the condition before performing an action and those that test the condition after performing an action. Within each style, the two loops differ in that one loops when the condition is true and the other loops when the condition is false.

The *Do While…Loop* and *Do Until…Loop* both test the condition before performing the action within the loop. The difference between the two is that *Do While* loops perform the action when the condition is true and *Do Until* loops perform the action while the condition is false. To decide which one to use, you need to find the simplest way to express the condition and then pick the loop that will best match the condition.

As you can see in the following code, the syntax for the two loops is straightforward:

```
Do While condition
[statement]
[Exit Do]
[statement]
Loop
```

and

```
Do Until condition
[statement]
[Exit Do]
[statement]
Loop
```

- *condition*   A required numeric or string expression that must evaluate to True or False
- *statement*   One or more optional statement lines that are executed during the loop
- *Exit Do*   Optional statement to exit the loop prematurely
- *Loop*   Required statement to mark the end of the *Do While* or *Do Until* statement block

The *Do While* loop tests the condition first, before entering the loop, and executes while the condition is true. This example performs a simple counting loop, similar to a *For...Next* statement:

```
Dim intCounter as Integer
intCounter = 1
Do While intCounter <= 10
    intCounter = intCounter + 1
Loop
```

The following *Do Until* loop performs the same actions as the *Do While* loop, but notice how the condition expression has changed:

```
Dim intCounter as Integer
intCounter = 1
Do Until intCounter = 11
    intCounter = intCounter + 1
Loop
```

Both examples run a simple counting loop from 1 to 10. In these two examples, it is easier to figure out that the *Do While* loop is counting from 1 to 10. The *Do Until* loop appears to be counting to 11, but the action is not performed once the counter reaches 11. It is last performed with a value of 10.

The *Do...Loop While* and *Do...Loop Until* loops are similar to each other, just as they are similar to the *Do While* and *Do Until* loops mentioned earlier. Both check the conditional expression at the end of the loop, guaranteeing at least one pass through the loop. Again, *Do...Loop While* loops while the condition is true, and *Do...Loop Until* loops while the condition is false. The syntax declarations for them are shown here:

```
Do
[statement]
[Exit Do]
[statement]
Loop While condition
```

and

```
Do
[statement]
[Exit Do]
[statement]
Loop Until condition
```

- *condition*   Required expression that must evaluate to True or False
- *statement*   One or more optional statement lines that are executed during the loop
- *Exit Do*   Optional statement to exit the loop prematurely
- *Loop*   Required statement to mark the end of the *Do While* or *Do Until* statement block

The following example increments a counter during each pass through the loop and uses a message box to ask the user if they wish to continue:

```
Sub PermissionLoop()
Dim intCounter As Integer, strPrompt As String
Dim intResult As Integer

intCounter = 0
Do
    intCounter = intCounter + 1
    strPrompt = "You have looped" & Str$(intCounter) & " times." _
        & vbCrLf & "Do you wish to continue?"
    intResult = MsgBox(strPrompt, vbYesNo + vbExclamation)
Loop While intResult = vbYes
End Sub
```

And here is the same example, using the *Do…Loop Until* statement:

```
Sub PermissionLoop2()
Dim intCounter As Integer, strPrompt As String
Dim intResult As Integer

intCounter = 0
Do
    intCounter = intCounter + 1
    strPrompt = "You have looped" & Str$(intCounter) & " times." _
        & vbCrLf & "Do you wish to continue?"
    intResult = MsgBox(strPrompt, vbYesNo + vbExclamation)
Loop Until intResult = vbNo
End Sub
```

Chapter 4

GoTo Statement

The *GoTo* statement forces the procedure to change immediately to another section of the procedure unconditionally. The section of code that is to be branched to needs to be marked with either a line number or a line label, allowing the program to jump either forward or backward within the procedure. Using the *GoTo* statement is discouraged because it can cause procedures to become more difficult to understand and debug.

The syntax for the *GoTo* statement is shown here:

```
GoTo line
```

In the preceding code, *line* is a required line label that must be a line number or a line label that is defined within the same procedure. Line numbers can be any series of digits and must begin in the first column. Line labels can be any series of characters that starts with a letter and ends with a colon (:). Line labels are not case sensitive and must begin in the first column.

Because *GoTo* statements can lead to unstructured code, using them is strongly discouraged. If used sparingly, they can be very useful. The following section on error handling offers better understanding of when and how to use the *GoTo* statement and line labels.

Error Handling

Every procedure should have some form of error-handling abilities, even if it does no more than inform the user of what caused the error and then exits. Procedures that are meant to be called from other procedures and not necessarily invoked by the user, for example, should return to the calling procedure some type of indication that it was able to complete successfully.

Consider the *Select Case* example covered earlier in the chapter that calculated the number of days in a month. It specifically checked whether or not the variable *intMonth* matched any of the expected clauses. If *intMonth* contained any value outside of the 1 to 12 range, the *Select Case* statement returned a -1.

By returning a value that is outside the realm of expected values, it allows any statement that depended upon the value of *intMonth* to confirm that it was a legal value.

Besides adding data validation code to check your own code, VBA also allows you to trap errors that it detects. By trapping the errors that VBA detects, your procedure might be able to correct them and continue executing.

To trap VBA errors, you use the **On Error** command. It takes the basic form

```
On Error Goto line label
```

In this line of code, *line label* specifies the section of code you have written to handle errors.

The following code fragment shows how you could trap errors and branch to a label named *ErrorHandler*:

```
On Error GoTo ErrorHandler
    [statements]
ErrorHandler:
    [error handler statements]
```

Because you would want to start trapping errors as quickly as possible, the *On Error* statement should be at the beginning of the procedure. Also, you are not limited to only a single error handler per procedure; you could specify different error handlers as the procedure progresses, even returning to earlier error handlers. The following code fragment illustrates one way to construct a series of error- handling routines:

```
On Error GoTo ErrorHandler1
    [statements]
On Error GoTo ErrorHandler2
    [statements]
On Error GoTo ErrorHandler1
    [statements]
ErrorHandler1:
    [errorhandler1 statements]
ErrorHandler2:
    [errorhandler2 statements]
```

Because VBA will execute an entire procedure until the end is reached, it is necessary to include instructions so that VBA will skip any error handlers you have written if no error has been trapped. The most common way to cause VBA to avoid executing error-handling code is to place all error-handling code at the end of a procedure and then, in the line immediately before the error handler, placing the *Exit Sub* or *Exit Function* statement to exit the procedure.

> **For more information about the two types of procedures (Sub procedures and Function procedures), see Chapter 5, "Creating Sub and Function Procedures."**

Once an error has been trapped, how can you tell what the error was and take corrective actions if possible? VBA sets various properties of the *Err* object to describe the error. Two of the properties, *Number* and *Description*, provide a numerical error code and a string description, respectively, of the error. You can use the error code to recognize and correct common or expected errors.

Error handlers work only for the procedure in which they appear; once the procedure has ended, the error trap is disabled. You can also disable the error handler yourself by using the following statement:

```
On Error GoTo 0
```

If your error handler is able to fix the problem that raised the error to begin with, you will want to resume execution of your procedure. That is done by using the **Resume** command. Placed inside of an error handler, it resumes execution with the statement that generated the error originally.

At times, the error handler might not be able to correct the problem, but if the error itself was not fatal to the execution, the error would not cause the rest of the procedure to fail. If that's the case, you can resume execution of the procedure by using the *Resume Next* statement. This continues execution with the statement immediately after the statement that raised the error. You can also specify execution to resume at a specific statement by using the *Resume line* statement. This will continue execution at the statement named by *line*.

The following code fragment illustrates a common method of using error handlers:

```
On Error Goto ErrorHandler
    [statements]
FinishedSub:
Exit Sub
ErrorHandler:
MsgBox(str$(Err) & ": " & Err.Description, vbInformation, "Error Handler")
Resume FinishedSub
```

This rather lengthy, though hopefully complete, chapter has covered all of the basic skills you need to begin creating VBA macros. You've learned how to define and assign values to variables, to control the flow of your programs using loops and tests, and to handle any errors that come along. In Chapter 5, you'll learn how to create and use procedures that contain your VBA code.

Creating Sub and Function Procedures

Defining Sub Procedures 85   Organizing for Success. 104
Defining Function Procedures. 98

The first several chapters of this book, but particularly Chapter 4, used sample procedures to illustrate how you can use Visual Basic for Applications (VBA) to make Microsoft Excel do your bidding. The goal in Chapter 4 was to introduce the programming constructs you can use to create and control how your VBA code operates, whether that means repeating a bit of code a set number of times using a *For…Next* loop, operating on every member of a collection using a *For Each…Next* loop, or repeating the code until a condition is met. There was a lot of hand waving at that stage when it came to putting your code into a usable package, but now it's time to get down to specifics.

In this chapter, you'll learn how to add Sub and Function procedures to your code modules, determine whether the procedures will be available from other workbooks, control whether Excel remembers the values generated by a procedure until the Excel program is closed, and learn how to transfer values to and from procedures so you can use the results elsewhere in your programs.

Defining Sub Procedures

There are two types of procedures you can create in Excel VBA: a Sub procedure and a Function procedure. What's the difference between the two types of procedures? It's whether or not the procedure returns a value you can use elsewhere in the program. For example, a Sub procedure set up to check whether a given purchase would put a customer over their credit limit might look like the following:

```
Private Sub CheckCreditLimit()
    If ActiveCell.Value + Range ("C3").Value > Range ("C2").Value Then
        MsgBox("The purchase would exceed the customer's credit limit.")
    End If
End Sub
```

85

When you read through the procedure, you'll notice that there is no statement that sends any value to any outside procedure. As mentioned in Chapter 4, the message box is used only to send some output to the screen; no value is passed to any other procedures.

> For more information on passing values between procedures, see "Passing Arguments to Procedures" later in this chapter.

With the overview out of the way, it's time to offer a more formal description of what constitutes a Sub procedure.

```
[Private | Public] [Static] Sub name [(arglist)]
[statements]
[Exit Sub]
[statements]
End Sub
```

Table 5-1 describes the elements of a Sub procedure.

Table 5-1. Elements of a Sub Procedure

Element	Description
Public	An optional element that indicates the Sub procedure is accessible to all other procedures in all modules. If used in a module that contains an *Option Private* statement, the procedure is not available outside the project.
Private	An optional element that indicates the Sub procedure is accessible only to other procedures in the module where it is declared.
Static	An optional element that indicates the Sub procedure's local variables are preserved between calls. The *Static* attribute doesn't affect variables that are declared outside the Sub procedure, even if they are used in the procedure.
name	A required element that indicates the name of the Sub (for example, *Sub AvailableCredit*). The name does need to follow the standard variable naming conventions.
arglist	An optional list of variables representing arguments that are passed to the Sub procedure when it is called. Multiple variables are separated by commas.
statements	An optional group of statements to be executed within the Sub procedure.

To add a procedure to a code module, follow these steps:

1 Click Tools, Macro, Visual Basic Editor to display the Visual Basic Editor.

2 If necessary, click Insert, Module to create a new code module (or if you want to create a new module for organizational purposes).

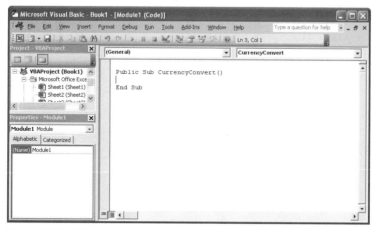

3 Click Insert, Procedure to display the Add Procedure dialog box.

4 Type the name of your procedure in the Name box.

5 Select the Sub option button.

6 Click OK.

Note There are other options available to you in the Add Procedure dialog box—you'll learn about those possibilities a little later in this chapter.

After you finish the preceding procedure, the outline of a procedure appears in the active code module, as shown in Figure 5-1.

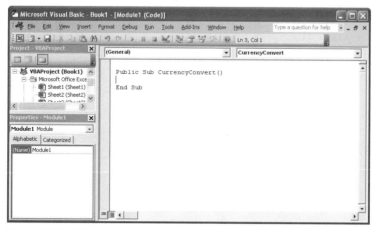

Figure 5-1. As soon as you click OK in the Add Procedure dialog box, the skeleton of your new procedure appears in the active code module.

Chapter 5

You can then fill in the details of your procedure using the Visual Basic Editor to pick objects, built-in functions, properties, events, and so on using the Object Browser. The following code listing contains a procedure that checks the contents of the active cell and, when the value matches any of the tests in the *If...Then* statement, changes the cell's font color to the named color.

```
Sub AvailableCredit()
    With ActiveCell
        If .Value = "" Then Exit Sub
        If .Value <= 1000 Then .Font.Color = vbRed
        If .Value > 1000 Then .Font.Color = vbBlack
        If .Value > 4999 Then .Font.Color = vbBlue
        If .Value > 9999 Then .Font.Color = vbGreen
    End With
End Sub
```

The colors listed in the preceding code are represented by VBA constants, but there are many millions of specific colors available to you. For more information on using colors to format the contents of items in your workbook, see Chapter 10, "Formatting, Excel Objects."

It's interesting to notice that the seemingly equivalent procedure that follows, which uses a *Select Case* statement to test the values in the active cell, actually generates an incorrect result.

```
Sub AvailableCreditCase()
Remaining = ActiveCell.Value
Select Case Remaining
Case ""
            Exit Sub
    Case Is >= 10000
            ActiveCell.Font.Color = vbGreen
    Case Is <= 9999
    ActiveCell.Font.Color = vbBlue
Case Is <= 4999
ActiveCell.Font.Color = vbBlack
Case Is <= 1000
            ActiveCell.Font.Color = vbRed
    End Select
End Sub
```

Inside Out

The Pitfalls of *Case* Statements and Conditional Formats

If you compare the *If...Then* and *Select Case* versions of the AvailableCredit routines side by side, you might notice that the *If...Then* statements check for values greater than some other value (for example, `If .Value > 5000 Then .Font.Color = vbBlue`), whereas all but the last *Case* statement checks for values in a definite range. You should use definitive rules in a *Select Case* statement because *the instant Excel finds a case that's true, it exits the Select Case statement*. So, if you were to evaluate a cell value of 5500 using the *If...Then* statement listed in the preceding example, the procedure would go through the following steps:

1 Is the cell blank? No, so take no action.

2 Is the value less than 1000? No, so take no action.

3 Is the value greater than 1000? Yes, so change the font color to black.

4 Is the value greater than 5000? Yes, so change the font color to blue.

5 Is the value greater than 10,000? No, so take no action.

The routine changed the font color an extra time (first to black, and then to blue), but you got the right result and the extra step is not a problem for a simple program on a computer that can perform millions of calculations per second. However, because the rules in the following *Select Case* statement are constructed in the same order, the cell's contents would be displayed in black type, not blue.

```
Select Case Remaining
Case ""
            Exit Sub
Case Is < 1000
            ActiveCell.Font.Color = vbRed
Case Is >= 1000
ActiveCell.Font.Color = vbBlack
    Case Is >= 5000
        ActiveCell.Font.Color = vbBlue
Case Is >= 10000
            ActiveCell.Font.Color = vbGreen
    End Select
```

You get incorrect results because the routine quits when it finds the cell value is less than or equal to 9999. You'll run into the same problem when you create conditional formats, which you do by clicking Format, Conditional Formatting and using the controls in the Conditional Formatting dialog box to create your rules. The rules in the following graphic correspond to the incorrect order noted earlier and would also result in an improperly formatted cell value.

continued

Chapter 5

Conditional Formatting ☒

Condition 1
| Cell Value Is ▾ | greater than or equal to ▾ | 10000 | 🔣 |

Preview of format to use
when condition is true: | AaBbCcYyZz | Format... |

Condition 2
| Cell Value Is ▾ | less than or equal to ▾ | 9999 | 🔣 |

Preview of format to use
when condition is true: | AaBbCcYyZz | Format... |

Condition 3
| Cell Value Is ▾ | less than or equal to ▾ | 4999 | 🔣 |

Preview of format to use
when condition is true: | AaBbCcYyZz | Format... |

Add >>   Delete...   OK   Cancel

Tip   You're limited to three conditions for conditional formatting
The conditional format in the graphic also points out one of the advantages of VBA: you are allowed only three conditions in the Conditional Formatting dialog box.

Of course, if you were to reverse the order of the *Case* statements (ignoring the first case, which checks for a blank cell), the most restrictive case would come first, the second most restrictive next, and so on. And that's the trick to creating effective *Select Case* and *If...Then* statements: after you check for a blank cell, you should always check for the most restrictive set of values. Also bear in mind that the comparison operator and the statement you use determine the order in which the sets become more or less restrictive. In a *Select Case* statement, if you want to check whether values are greater than other values, you need to check for the higher values first (for example, you ask "is the value greater than 10,000" before asking "is the value greater than 5000"); if you check whether values are less than other values, you need to check for the lower values first (for example, you ask "is the values less than 1000" before asking "is the value less than 5000").

Defining the Scope of a Sub Procedure

The first element of a Sub procedure, the optional *Public* or *Private* declaration, determines the scope of the procedure. Simply put, a procedure with a Private scope can be referred to only by other procedures in the same module, whereas procedures with a Public scope can be referred to by any procedure in any module.

Note   Unless otherwise stated, every procedure is a Public procedure.

Creating Sub and Function Procedures

As an example, consider the code module from CreditLineInfo.xls, displayed in Figure 5-2, which contains one Private procedure and one Public procedure.

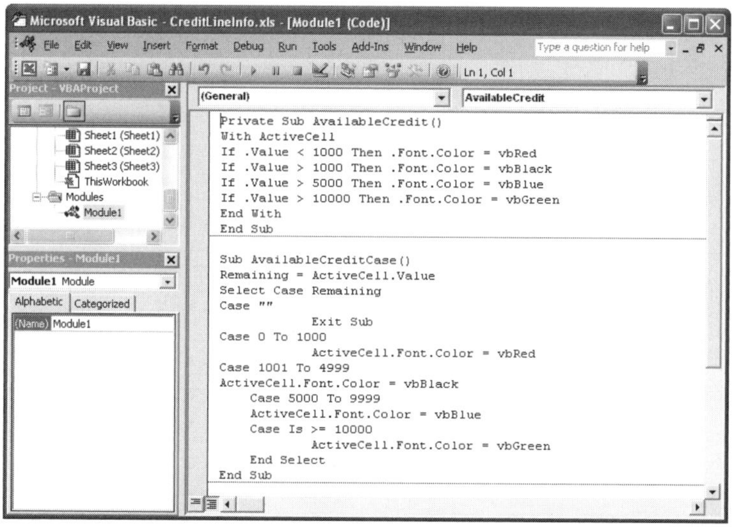

Figure 5-2. Using the *Public* and *Private* keywords helps limit the availability of your macros when appropriate.

When you click Tools, Macro, Macros to open the Macro dialog box from within any workbook, you will only be able to view, run, or edit the AvailableCreditCase procedure. You could, however, run the AvailableCredit procedure from another procedure in the same code module (but not from a procedure in another module, even if that module is attached to the same workbook).

> **Note**   You'll learn more about running procedures from within other procedures later in this chapter.

If you're writing a set of macros you don't want to be seen (or run) by anyone who knows how to open the Macro dialog box, you can put an *Option Private Module* statement in the declarations section at the top of the code module to make every procedure, even those that use the *Public* keyword, private. The macros will still be available in the code module, however.

For example, one procedure in Figure 5-3 has the *Public* keyword in the *Sub* statement, but the *Option Private Module* line in the declarations section at the top of the module takes precedence.

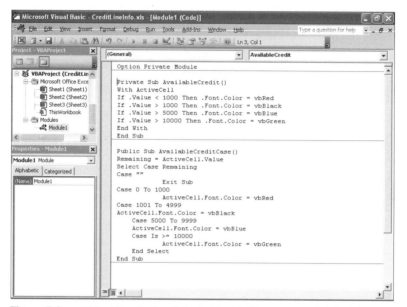

```
Microsoft Visual Basic - CreditLineInfo.xls - [Module1 (Code)]

File  Edit  View  Insert  Format  Debug  Run  Tools  Add-Ins  Window  Help          Type a question for help

                                                                    Ln 3, Col 1

Project - VBAProject                (General)                    AvailableCredit

VBAProject (CreditLin              Option Private Module
  Microsoft Office Exce
    Sheet1 (Sheet1)               Private Sub AvailableCredit()
    Sheet2 (Sheet2)               With ActiveCell
    Sheet3 (Sheet3)               If .Value < 1000 Then .Font.Color = vbRed
    ThisWorkbook                  If .Value > 1000 Then .Font.Color = vbBlack
  Modules                         If .Value > 5000 Then .Font.Color = vbBlue
    Module1                       If .Value > 10000 Then .Font.Color = vbGreen
                                  End With
                                  End Sub
Properties - Module1
Module1 Module                    Public Sub AvailableCreditCase()
                                  Remaining = ActiveCell.Value
Alphabetic  Categorized           Select Case Remaining
(Name)  Module1                   Case ""
                                          Exit Sub
                                  Case 0 To 1000
                                          ActiveCell.Font.Color = vbRed
                                  Case 1001 To 4999
                                  ActiveCell.Font.Color = vbBlack
                                      Case 5000 To 9999
                                      ActiveCell.Font.Color = vbBlue
                                      Case Is >= 10000
                                          ActiveCell.Font.Color = vbGreen
                                      End Select
                                  End Sub
```

Figure 5-3. Adding the *Option Private Module* line to a module's declaration section hides all procedures in a module from view.

To display the declarations section of a code module, you click the down arrow at the right edge of the Procedure list box and click Declarations. When you do, a new section, delineated by a line, will appear in your code module.

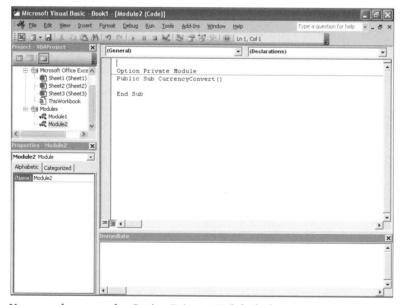

```
Microsoft Visual Basic - Book1 - [Module2 (Code)]

File  Edit  View  Insert  Format  Debug  Run  Tools  Add-Ins  Window  Help          Type a question for help

                                                                    Ln 1, Col 1

Project - VBAProject                (General)                    (Declarations)

  Microsoft Office Exce              Option Private Module
    Sheet1 (Sheet1)                 Public Sub CurrencyConvert()
    Sheet2 (Sheet2)
    Sheet3 (Sheet3)                 End Sub
    ThisWorkbook
  Modules
    Module1
    Module2

Properties - Module2
Module2 Module

Alphabetic  Categorized
(Name)  Module2




Immediate
```

You may then type the *Option Private Module* declaration in the proper section.

Chapter 5

Tip   Use the keyboard to enter the declarations section

You can also enter the declarations section of a code module by moving the insertion point to the left of the first line of code in the module, pressing Enter, and moving back up to the newly blank first line. When you do, the value in the Procedure list box changes to Declarations and you can begin typing the declaration. You can also start typing the declaration in the first position of the first line of the module and press Enter. When the Visual Basic Editor recognizes you put a declaration on the first line, it will create a Declarations section and put in a line marking the end of the section.

Inside Out

The Good News Is That You Didn't Break It...

There might be times when you want to change the scope of a procedure from Public to Private, perhaps after you've finished testing the procedure and you don't need to run it from the Macro dialog box any more. Another situation where you might want to make a procedure private is if you attached the macro to a toolbar button or menu item and, while you still want to allow your colleagues to run the macro from the custom button or menu item, you don't want just anyone who knows how to use the Customize dialog box to assign the macro to another button or, worse, edit it in the Visual Basic Editor. If someone is determined to get into the code and you don't have the workbook password-protected, you can't really stop them, but you can make it more difficult by taking the procedure Private. And, as the title of this Inside Out sidebar implies, making a Public procedure Private doesn't break the link between the toolbar button, menu item, or object to which you assigned the macro. Clicking the macro trigger, whatever it is, will still run the macro.

Running a Sub Procedure from Within Another Procedure

After you have created a Sub procedure, you will want to run it. As mentioned before, you can run the procedure by linking the macro to a trigger, but you can also run the macro by calling it from within another macro. For example, if you want to run an existing procedure, such as NOW, which returns the current date and time, you can do so.

```
Sub ShowTheTime
    MsgBox (NOW())
End Sub
```

The same mechanism works for running a Sub procedure.

To call a Sub procedure from another procedure, type the name of the procedure and include values for any required arguments. The *Call* statement is not required, but if you use it, you must enclose any arguments in parentheses.

93

With the definition in mind, take a look at the following Sub procedure, which converts a quantity of American dollars into Swedish krona at the current exchange rate, as drawn from the Microsoft Money Central Web site and stored in cell C35:

```
Sub Krona()
    sngInKrona = ActiveCell.Value * Range("C35").Value
    MsgBox("The value of $" & ActiveCell.Value & " is " _
    & sngInKrona & " krona.")
End Sub
```

> You can find currency quotes on the Web by visiting *http://moneycentral.msn.com/* and typing "currency rates" into the Search box. For more information on getting information from the Web into your Excel worksheets, see Chapter 24, "Excel and the Web."

If you want to run this Sub procedure from another procedure, you could do so using one of these three techniques:

- Type the name of the procedure and any arguments it takes. (If there are no arguments, type an empty pair of parentheses.)
- Type the *Call* keyword, and then type the name of the procedure and any arguments it takes. (If there are no arguments, type an empty pair of parentheses.)
- Use the Application object's *Run* method to run the macro. This method is useful if you want to use your VBA code to determine which of several macros to run, and to assign the name of the macro you decide upon to a variable.

You've already seen the first technique in action, but it's actually the same as the second technique. When Excel encounters an unfamiliar word followed by a set of open and close parentheses, it searches the available modules for Public procedures of the same name. You used to be required to put the *Call* keyword before the procedure name, but that's no longer mandatory. Even so, some programmers choose to put the *Call* keyword in front of procedures they have created to ensure that they (and anyone else who examines the code in the module) will understand that the procedure is not part of the standard Excel library.

As you might expect, you're not limited to calling procedures from within the same code module or even the same workbook. If you want to reach out to use procedures in other modules, you can do so. In fact, if the Excel VBA engine doesn't find the procedure you call in the same module as the calling procedure, it will search the other modules in the active workbook and, if it still hasn't found the procedure you called, will go on to all other open workbooks in an attempt to find the code.

When you know the name of the module that contains the procedure you want to run and the module is in the active workbook, you can put the name of the module in front of the procedure name using *dot notation*, as in the following brief Sub procedure:

```
Sub CallOut()
    Call CurrencyModule.Krona()
End Sub
```

Creating Sub and Function Procedures

When you create a new code module, the Visual Basic Editor gives it the name Module1, Module2, and so on. You should strongly consider renaming the modules in your projects to make their contents more obvious.

To rename a module, follow these steps:

1 Open the workbook to which the module is attached, and click Tools, Macro, Visual Basic Editor.

2 In the Project window, click the name of the module you want to rename.

3 In the Properties window, select the existing module name next to the *Name* property, type the new module name, and then press Enter.

> **Caution**   You can run into trouble if you have procedures with the same name in two or more workbooks. You can't have two procedures with the same name in a module, but because you can use dot notation to specify which module's procedure you want, you can avoid any problems. That said, if you have several procedures with the same name in different modules and you attempt to call one of them without specifying the module that contains the procedure (for example, CurrencyModule.Krona), the Visual Basic Editor will display an *Ambiguous name detected* error and halt the execution of the code that attempted to call the procedure.

If you know that the procedure you want to run is available in a module attached to another workbook and for some reason don't want to copy the code to your current workbook, you can call the procedure from the other workbook in one of two ways: by using the *Application.Run* method and specifying the name of the workbook, or by creating a reference to the workbook that contains the procedure.

Using the *Application.Run* method to run a procedure in another workbook requires you to name only the other workbook and the procedure you want to run. You name the workbook and procedure using a syntax that looks a lot like the reference you create when you link from a worksheet cell to a cell in another workbook.

If you wanted to call the *ConvertToKrona* procedure from the workbook ExchangeRates.xls, you would use the following statement:

```
Application.Run "'ExchangeRates.xls'!ConvertToKrona"
```

One limitation of the *Application.Run* method is that the workbook that contains the called procedure must be open to allow Excel to look into it to see what procedures are available. That requirement is the reason that the Macros dialog box can display macros in the current workbook, any open workbook, or all open workbooks: the program designers chose not to let Excel reach into workbooks unless they were already open and ready for use.

You can, however, make it possible to call procedures in any workbook, open or not, by creating a *reference* to the procedure. Just as using the *Application.Run* method to call a procedure from another workbook is similar to creating a link from a worksheet cell to a cell in another workbook, creating a reference to a procedure in another workbook is very similar to linking or embedding an outside file in an Excel workbook. But, instead of using the Insert Object dialog box in Excel, you use the Tools, References dialog box in the Visual Basic Editor (shown in Figure 5-4).

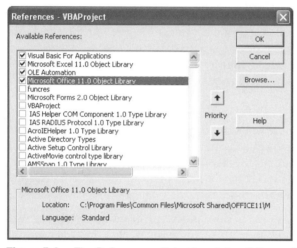

Figure 5-4. The References dialog box lists all the available resources to which you can link and subsequently call procedures.

When you first display the References dialog box, it doesn't list the projects available in the Excel workbooks on your computer (and any network drives to which you have access), but you can go looking for them using the Add Reference dialog box.

To add a reference to an Excel workbook to the list in the References dialog box, follow these steps:

1 Click Tools, References.

2 Click Browse.

3 Click the Files of Type down arrow, Microsoft Office Excel Files (*.xls;*.xla).

4 Navigate to the directory containing the workbook, click the workbook, and click Open.

After you create the reference, the name of the project in the workbook you just selected appears in the References dialog box. What's interesting about the creation process is that most projects are named *VBAProject* (the default). And, just as you should change the name of your code modules so that they are more descriptive than Module1, you should also change the name of your projects so that they give you some clue as to their contents. One possibility would be to change the project name so that it's the same (or close to the same) as the workbook name. If you don't, you'll see a list of VBAProject references in your list and will have no idea which one is which. The procedure for renaming a project is similar to that of renaming a module: in the Project window, click the name of the project and then change the *Name* property in the Properties window.

Inside Out

Recursion and Public Use: Two Procedural Pitfalls

When you call a procedure from within the same procedure, the procedure is said to be *recursive*. For example, if you do any work with probability and statistics you know about FACT, which finds the factorial of a number (for example, 3! = 3 * 2 * 1 = 6, 5! = 5 * 4 * 3 * 2 * 1 = 120, and so on). The programmer who wrote the FACT function put in a test to ensure the procedure didn't continue to call itself after it reached 1, and it's a good thing. If the procedure didn't check its progress, it would continue to churn through multiplications by 0, -1, -2, and so on, until the computer ran out of memory and crashed. If you should need to write a procedure that calls itself, be sure to add some logical test in an *If...Then* or *Do...While* loop to prevent any sort of infinite mischief.

Another interesting procedural pitfall could happen if you use the *Static* keyword to preserve the values of the variables in a procedure between calls. Assume you're working with a worksheet that keeps track of your daily sales, and the workbook has the macro described earlier in this chapter that maintains a running total of your sales. What happens if one of your colleagues examines another workbook that calls the same procedure? For example, you might have given your colleague one of last month's workbooks to learn how you set up the office before you go on a much-deserved vacation away from e-mail messages and wireless phones. If that colleague examines the workbook, sees what the macro code does, types a large negative value into a cell and runs the procedure, the next update on your computer will not reflect the true value of sales. Now, it's good to note that this sort of error would be of minimal harm if you didn't do anything other than monitor the values to keep an eye on things. Also, if the sales total were far smaller than you remembered, you would probably realize that the lack of a large negative value in your copy of the worksheet indicated that something odd was happening in another copy of the workbook.

That said, if you use any sort of running total or other static variables as an integral part of your business, you should strongly consider putting the update procedures in a module with *Option Private Module* featured prominently at the top.

Retaining Values Between Procedure Calls

The second optional element in a procedure declaration is whether or not to make the procedure retain the values generated by previous executions of the procedure. One example of a procedure where you might want to keep a running total for a value is a procedure that wrote sales for a day into a worksheet. Sure, you could write the values for a day to a file or an array and add up the totals, but it's much simpler to display the running total for a day by ensuring the procedure remembers the values that came before.

As you probably guessed from the available keywords in the Sub procedure definition statement, the keyword you want to use is *Static*. As an example, consider the following procedure, which attempts to maintain a running total of a day's sales using the *intTotal* variable:

```
Sub RunningTotal()
    intTotal = intTotal + ActiveCell.Value
    Range("B10").Value = intTotal
End Sub
```

The benefit of this procedure, if it were working properly, is that you wouldn't need to run a query or even some sort of fancy refreshable summation formula in cell B10 to update the sales total in your worksheet. But, the procedure as written always generates the same answer: the value in the active cell. The problem is that the variable *intTotal* is re-created every time you run the procedure, so its value is set to 0 every time. How do you fix the procedure so that it keeps a real running total? By adding the *Static* keyword in front of the *Sub* statement, as in the following listing:

```
Static Sub RunningTotal()
    intTotal = intTotal + ActiveCell.Value
    Range("B10").Value = intTotal
End Sub
```

When you add the *Static* keyword to the *Sub* statement, Excel knows to create a durable storage space for each variable and to maintain that space and its contents until you close the workbook.

> **Note** You can also reset the value of the variables in a static procedure by displaying the procedure in the Visual Basic Editor and clicking Run, Reset.

Defining Function Procedures

A Function procedure is similar to a Sub procedure, but a function can also return a value. A Function procedure can take arguments, such as constants, variables, or expressions that are passed to it by a calling procedure. As an example, consider the SUM function you most likely use all the time when you create formulas in an Excel worksheet. The following example formula finds the sum of the values in cells C14 to H14, J14 and adds 100:

=SUM(C14:H14, J14, 100)

The SUM function adds everything in the statement that calls it; if it can't make sense of its input, such as when it tries to add a non-numerical value, it will return an error message and display an error code. If a Function procedure has no arguments, its *Function* statement must include an empty set of parentheses.

```
[Private | Public] [Static] Function name [(arglist)] [As type]
[statements]
[name = expression]
[Exit Function]
[statements]
[name = expression]
End Function
```

Table 5-2 describes the elements of a Function procedure, many of which will be familiar from the description of a Sub procedure.

Table 5-2. Elements of a Function Procedure

Element	Description
Public	An optional element that indicates the Function procedure is accessible to all other procedures in all modules. If used in a module that contains an *Option Private* statement, the procedure is not available outside the project.
Private	An optional element that indicates the Function procedure is accessible only to other procedures in the module where it is declared.
Static	An optional element that indicates the Function procedure's local variables are preserved between calls. The *Static* attribute doesn't affect variables that are declared outside the Function procedure, even if they are used in the procedure.
name	A required element that indicates the name of the Function (for example, *Function InterestDue*). The name does need to follow the standard variable naming conventions.
arglist	An optional list of variables representing arguments that are passed to the Function procedure when it is called. Multiple variables are separated by commas.
type	An optional statement that specifies the data type of the result returned by the Function procedure. For example, a function returning an integer value would have *As Integer* in this space.
statements	An optional group of statements to be executed within the Function procedure.

Chapter 5

Creating a Function Procedure

You can create a Function procedure in an existing code module by opening the module in the Visual Basic Editor by typing the following:

```
Function name()
...
End Function
```

You will need to name the function and put instructions in the middle where the ellipsis is now, but you can do it much more quickly using the Add Procedure dialog box.

To add a Function procedure to a code module, follow these steps:

1 Click Tools, Macro, Visual Basic Editor to display the Visual Basic Editor.

2 If necessary, click Insert, Module to create a new code module (or if you want to create a new module for organizational purposes).

3 Click Insert, Procedure to display the Add Procedure dialog box.

4 Type the name of your procedure in the Name box.

5 Select the Function option button.

6 Click OK.

Note As with Sub procedures, you can make your Function procedures available to procedures in every other workbook by putting the *Public* keyword in front of the declaration. The *Public* keyword is added by default when you add a procedure using the Insert Procedure dialog box.

Running Function Procedures

If you want to run a Function procedure, you can do so using one of the following methods:

- Use the Function procedure in a formula.
- Call the Function procedure from within another procedure.
- Call the Function procedure from a cell on a worksheet.

> **Important**   Your Function procedures don't appear in the Macros dialog box.

You've already seen the first technique several times in the preceding two chapters, and you've no doubt used functions many times in your worksheets. One example of an existing function you might use in a worksheet would be =**NOW**(), which returns the current date and time. The third way to run a Function procedure is to call it from a cell on a worksheet. To do so, you can call it the same way you would call any other function (for example, =**Amortize(ActiveCell.Value)**).

So, when might you want to use a function procedure instead of a Sub procedure to operate on a value? There are two such times: when you want to use the result of the function in an expression in your VBA code, or when you want to use the result in a formula in one of your worksheets. For example, if The Garden Company repackaged potting soil from 25-pound bags into 5-pound bags, you could create a function that multiplied the number of 25-pound bags by five to generate the total number of small bags. Then you could create a function such as this one:

```
Function SmallBags(intLargeBags as Integer) as Integer
    SmallBags = intLargeBags * 5
End Function
```

Once created, you could call the function from within a cell using the formula =**SmallBags(C16)** to convert the number of large bags of potting soil in an order, which was stored in cell C16, into the number of small bags of potting soil that order will produce.

Passing Arguments to Procedures

So far in this chapter, you've seen procedures that operate on fixed values, such as the contents of a cell, and procedures that don't operate on any values at all, such as the NOW function. When you write a procedure that operates on a value from a cell by calling the cell's value from inside the procedure using the *ActiveCell.Value* property or the *Range(<cell>).Value* property, you don't need to worry about passing values from variables. Unfortunately, the situation won't always be so straightforward. There might be times where you want to operate on a value that's stored in a variable in a procedure, not in a worksheet cell. That's when you need to tell the procedure the values on which you want it to operate; those values are called *arguments*.

You probably noticed that the first line of the *SmallBags* function looked different from most of the other procedures you'd seen earlier in the chapter. The following function, which recommends a retail price of an item that's 180 percent of the item's wholesale price, also takes an argument:

```
Function MarkupPrice(curItemPrice as Currency) as Currency
    MarkupPrice = curItemPrice * 1.8
End Function
```

Let's take a moment to break down the first line in the function. The *Function* keyword is familiar, as is the function name that follows it, but the next two elements are new. The element in the parentheses, `curItemPrice as Currency`, is the name and data type of the variable that's being passed to the function. In other words, regardless of how the function gets its variable, it knows to treat the value it receives as a variable of type *Currency*.

> **Caution**   As with other functions, if the data the function receives is of the incorrect type, the function will return a #VALUE! error message in the worksheet cell where the function is called.

The last element of the first Function procedure statement is the second occurrence of `as Currency`. That element tells the function the data type of the value it returns to the formula or procedure that called it. Most of the time the result of the procedure will be returned as the same data type as the value passed to the procedure, but you might want to divide a single by an integer and return an integer value. One situation where that would be the case would be if you have 22.3 pounds of potting soil and want to see how many full 5-pound bags you could make out of it.

So where is the value calculated by the procedure stored? It's stored in a variable with the same name as the Function procedure. In the code listed earlier, the second line executes the arithmetic.

```
    MarkupPrice = intLargeBags * 1.8
```

The *MarkupPrice* variable is created using the data type named at the end of the first statement in the procedure.

If you need to pass more than one argument to a procedure, you do so by separating the arguments by commas, as in the following example:

```
Function ConvertMultiple (sngKrona as Single, sngEuro as Single) as Single
```

Inside Out

Protecting Your Original Cell Data

One of the dangers of programming is that you can inadvertently change the original values in your worksheet. For example, if you create a Sub procedure that assigns some value to the active cell, you'll end up destroying your original data. So, in addition to always creating backup copies of all your data, you can consider using the *ByVal* keyword to have the procedure use a copy of the data and not the original cell value (or array, or object, or whatever) itself. A Sub procedure to calculate the number of small bags of soil to be created from a number of large bags would be written the following way:

```
Sub SmallBags(byVal intLargeBags)
    MsgBox("The number of large bags is " & intLargeBags * 5).
End Sub
```

Passing Named Arguments

All the procedures in this chapter that have called a procedure have passed the arguments the procedure requires in an order the procedure expects. For example, when you type **MsgBox** to begin a statement to create a message box, the Visual Basic Editor displays a ToolTip indicating the expected arguments, as shown in Figure 5-5.

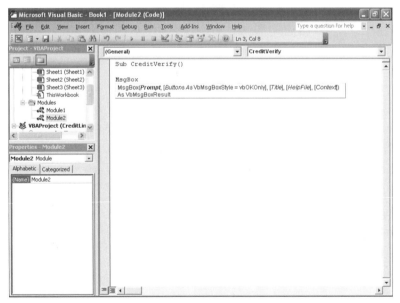

Figure 5-5. The Visual Basic Editor helps you create effective procedures by listing the expected arguments.

Chapter 5

If you want to make the arguments you pass to a procedure easier to read, if a bit more verbose, you can use *named arguments*. A named argument consists of the name of the argument followed by a colon and an equal sign (:=) and the value assigned to the argument. For example, the MsgBox procedure has the following syntax:

```
MsgBox(prompt[, buttons] [, title] [, helpfile, context])
```

If you wanted to create a message box with a specific title and prompt (two of the arguments listed earlier), you could do so with the following statement:

```
MsgBox Title:="Status Report", Prompt:="Order Accepted"
```

> For more information on creating message boxes, see Chapter 4, "VBA Programming Starter Kit."

Organizing for Success

It can be tempting to throw every bit of code you need to complete a series of tasks into a single procedure, but it's much more efficient and effective to write bite-sized procedures that do one task and then call the individual tasks from within a single main procedure. For example, if you wanted to create a program that wrote the contents of your daily sales worksheet to a database, saved the current file under a new name based on the date, deleted the contents of the sales worksheet, and saved and closed all open files, you might have a main program that looks like the following code:

```
Sub Main()
    Call UpdateSQL()
    Call ResaveWorkbook()
    Call DeleteData()
    Call SaveAndClose()
End Sub
```

The contents of the individual procedures are not a concern to the Main procedure. In fact, you can change them as often as you like without having to go in and mess around with all the code in the Main procedure. This type of routine has been a hallmark of programming for years, and it's a practice you would do well to adopt.

In this chapter, you learned how to create Sub and Function procedures, the containers for your VBA code. Remember the big difference between the two: Sub procedures don't return a result to the main program, but Function procedures do. And now that you know how to create those containers, you're ready to start affecting Excel workbooks with your code. Chapter 6 starts you on your way by introducing the *Application* object.

Chapter 5

Part 3

The Excel Object Model

6   The *Application* Object   107

7   Workbooks and Worksheets   129

8   Ranges and Cells   161

Chapter 6

The *Application* Object

Introducing the *Application* Object 108

Visual Basic for Applications (VBA) uses *objects* to control Microsoft Excel. Whether you are working with the Excel application (*Application* object), workbooks (*Workbook* object), or individual cells (*Cell* object), you do everything by manipulating an object. All of the objects either contain other objects or are part of a larger object. For example, the *Workbook* object contains *Worksheets* objects, which in turn contain *Cell* objects.

When working with an object, either a property is being set or read, or the object is told to perform an action, called a method. If you wanted to select a worksheet named *Sheet2* in the active workbook, you would use the *Select* method of the *Worksheet* object, *Worksheets("Sheet2").Select*.

The *object model* (shown in Figure 6-1) is used to describe how each object within Excel relates to other objects. When you view the object model, you can see how one object contains other objects, which contain other objects, which can contain even more objects. An object might even contain multiple objects of the same type. For example, a workbook can contain multiple worksheets.

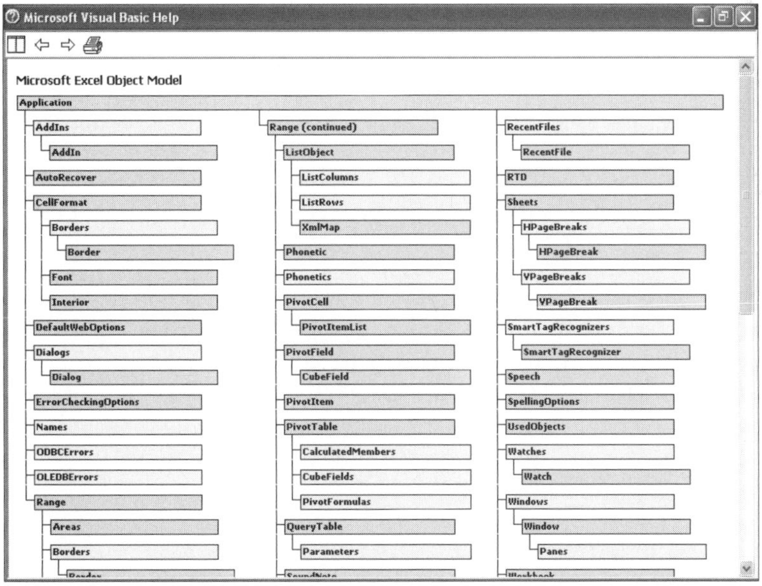

Figure 6-1. The Microsoft Office 2003 Excel Object Model is the repository of all knowledge in Excel.

An object that contains multiple objects of the same type is a *collection*, and each object within the collection is a *member* of the collection. To refer to a particular member of a collection, you can use either its index number or its name. In the preceding example, we used the *Worksheets* collection and referred to the particular worksheet named *Sheet2*.

Introducing the *Application* Object

The *Application* object is the highest object within the Microsoft Excel Object Model. The *Application* object contains all of the properties and methods to fully manipulate the Excel application, along with the objects that represent individual workbooks and the data they contain.

Because it is the topmost object within the object model, logically you would need to begin all references with the *Application* object. To refer to the first cell in a worksheet (A1), you would need to start at the *Application* object, go to the *Worksheet* object, and then select the *Cell* object. To set the first cell equal to 100, the VBA code would be as follows:

```
Application.Workbooks(1).Worksheets(1).Cells(1,1) = 100
```

Lengthy sequences in dot notation are cumbersome to use, so the Excel programmers did expose some of the more common objects directly, such as workbooks, worksheets, and cells, without the code having to go through the *Application* object. Care must be taken, especially when working with cells directly, that you have selected the proper workbook and worksheet. If you're sure you have selected the proper workbook and worksheet, such as by using the *Worksheet* object's *Activate* method described in the next section of this chapter, you could abbreviate the previous command to `Cells(1,1) = 100`.

Properties

Working with the *Application* object will usually involve reading or setting one of its many properties. The *Application* object contains more than 170 properties that let you control every aspect of the Excel application. From workbooks and worksheets to columns and rows, the *Application* object provides access to practically every element of Excel and Excel workbooks.

With so many properties, it is impossible to know every available property, and it's not necessary to do so. There is a short list of about 10 properties that are the most common properties and should be learned to fully work with Excel using VBA. The other properties can be learned as you need them. The important thing is to know that they are there for future exploration.

The *Application* Object

The following *Application* object properties are the most used:

- *ActiveCell*
- *ActiveChart*
- *ActiveSheet*
- *ActiveWindow*
- *ActiveWorkbook*
- *RangeSelection*
- *Selection*
- *ScreenUpdating*
- *StatusBar*
- *ThisWorkbook*

> You can get information on every element of the Excel object model in the Visual Basic Editor help system by typing **object model** in the Ask A Question box and viewing the Microsoft Excel Object Model help topic.

The short list of *Application* properties contains the most common objects that are used within Excel. Most have been exposed directly by the Excel programming team so that an explicit reference to the application object isn't needed. These properties are described in the following sections in alphabetical order.

ActiveCell Property

The *ActiveCell* property is exactly what its name implies: a reference to the currently active cell on the active work sheet on the active workbook. When called, the *ActiveCell* property returns a *Range* object that can be used to set the value or formula of the cell along with any formatting changes you might want to make (font style, borders, format of numbers, and so on).

The following example uses the CellBorder procedure to examine the value of a cell and change the border around the cell if it has a value between 500 and 1000. The ApplyBorders procedure loops through all of the specified data cells within the Y2001ByMonth.xls workbook, shown in Figure 6-2, and then calls the CellBorder procedure for each cell.

```
Sub ApplyBorders()
Dim MyCell As Range
    For Each MyCell In _
        ActiveSheet.Range(D6:O36").Cells
        MyCell.Select
        If ActiveCell > 500 And ActiveCell < 1000 Then
          With ActiveCell.Borders
            .Weight = xlThick
            .Color = vbBlue
          End With
        End If
    Next MyCell
End Sub
```

Chapter 6

109

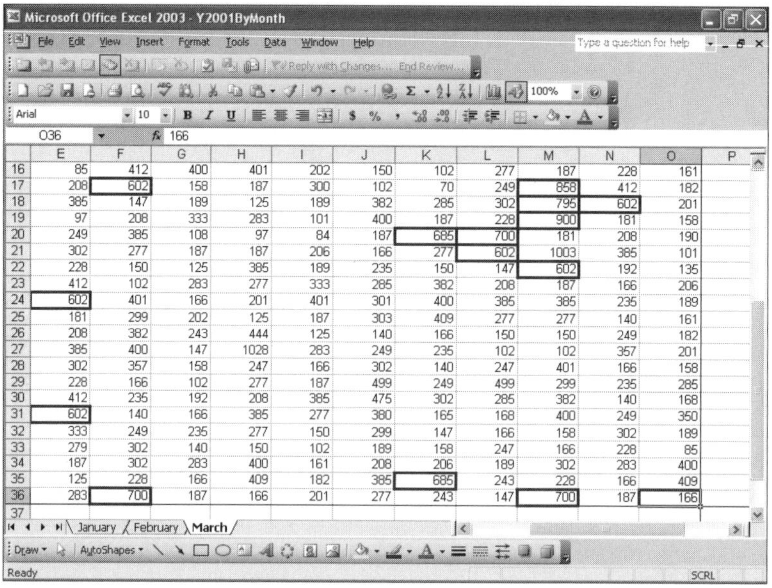

Figure 6-2. The *ActiveCell* property lets you make changes to the active cell without writing a specific cell or range reference.

It is important to remember that the value of the *ActiveCell* property is different from the value of the *Selection* property. A *Selection* can return a range of multiple cells, but only one cell within the selection can be the active cell. When you look at a worksheet where more than one cell is selected, the *active* cell is the cell with the border around it and no highlight; the other cells in the selection are highlighted. (The default highlight color is a grayish blue.)

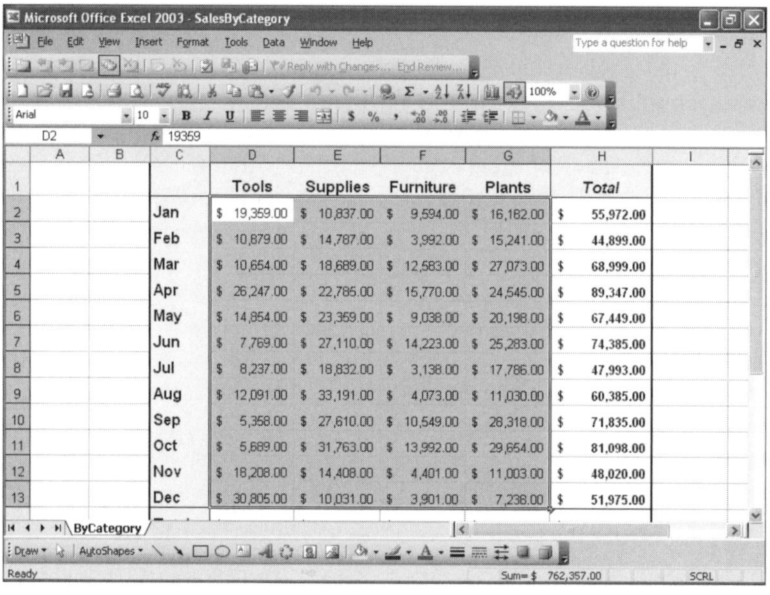

Chapter 6

ActiveChart Property

The *ActiveChart* property lets you manipulate the currently selected chart, whether it is an embedded chart or a chart sheet. All of the properties of the chart are available, which means you can change the data points on the chart, the format of the chart, and other attributes.

The following example automatically builds a three-dimensional column chart in the SalesByCategory.xls workbook using the existing data and positions it beneath the data source, as shown in Figure 6-3.

```
Sub BuildChart()
    Charts.Add     'Add a new chart object
    ActiveChart.ChartType = xl3DColumn     'Set the Chart type to 3D Column
    ActiveChart.SetSourceData _
        Source:=Sheets("ByCategory").Range("C1:G13"), _
            PlotBy:=xlColumns     'Set the data source
    ActiveChart.Location Where:=xlLocationAsObject, Name:="ByCategory"
    With ActiveChart     'Format the chart
        .HasTitle = True
        .ChartTitle.Characters.Text = "Monthly Sales by Category"
        .Axes(xlCategory).HasTitle = True
        .Axes(xlCategory).AxisTitle.Characters.Text = "Month"
        .Axes(xlSeries).HasTitle = True
        .Axes(xlSeries).AxisTitle.Characters.Text = "Category"
        .Axes(xlValue).HasTitle = True
        .Axes(xlValue).AxisTitle.Characters.Text = "Sales"
    End With
    ActiveSheet.Shapes(1).IncrementLeft -133.5     'Position the chart
    ActiveSheet.Shapes(1).IncrementTop 214.5
    ActiveSheet.Shapes(1).ScaleWidth 1.77, msoFalse, msoScaleFromTopLeft
    ActiveSheet.Shapes(1).ScaleHeight 1.35, msoFalse, msoScaleFromTopLeft
End Sub
```

> For more information on charts and how to change them programmatically, see Chapter 15, "Charts."

Microsoft Office Excel 2003 Programming Inside Out

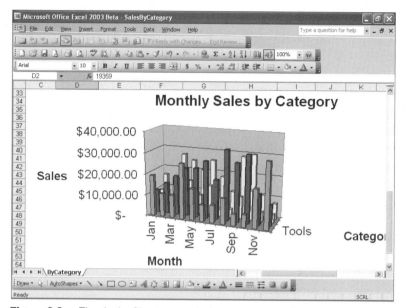

Figure 6-3. The *ActiveChart* property lets you streamline your chart creation and manipulation.

ActiveSheet Property

The *ActiveSheet* property returns a worksheet object that represents the currently selected worksheet. You can perform all worksheet manipulations using this object. For example, if you created a workbook where each worksheet recorded hourly sales figures for every day in a month, you could write a macro to create a new sheet with the name of the next month and the correct weekday next to the date. Figure 6-4 shows the results of this macro, which uses the January worksheet of the Y2004ByMonth.xls workbook as its model.

```
Sub CopySheet()

    Sheets("January").Select      'Select sheet to copy
    ActiveSheet.Copy After:=Sheets(Sheets.Count)      'Copy sheet to last position
    Sheets(Sheets.Count).Select      'Select new sheet
    ActiveSheet.Name = Format(Str$(Sheets.Count) & "/01/03", "MMMM")
    'Rename to latest month
    Range("D6:O36").Select      'Select data cells and erase
    Selection.ClearContents
    Range("C6").Select      'Start at first day, set day of week for first 3 days
    ActiveCell.FormulaR1C1 = Format(Str$(Sheets.Count) & "/01/" & _
    Str$(Year(Now())), "ddd")
    Range("C7").Select
    ActiveCell.FormulaR1C1 = Format(Str$(Sheets.Count) & "/02/" & _
    Str$(Year(Now())), "ddd")
    Range("C8").Select
    ActiveCell.FormulaR1C1 = Format(Str$(Sheets.Count) & "/03/" & _
```

```
Str$(Year(Now())), "ddd")
    Range("C6:C8").Select
    Selection.AutoFill Destination:=Range("C6:C36"), Type:=xlFillDefault
    'Autofill remaining days
    Range("C6:C36").Select    'Correct borders
    With Selection.Borders(xlEdgeRight)
        .LineStyle = xlContinuous
        .Weight = xlThin
    End With
    Range("C36").Select
    With Selection.Borders(xlEdgeBottom)
        .LineStyle = xlContinuous
        .Weight = xlThin
    End With

End Sub
```

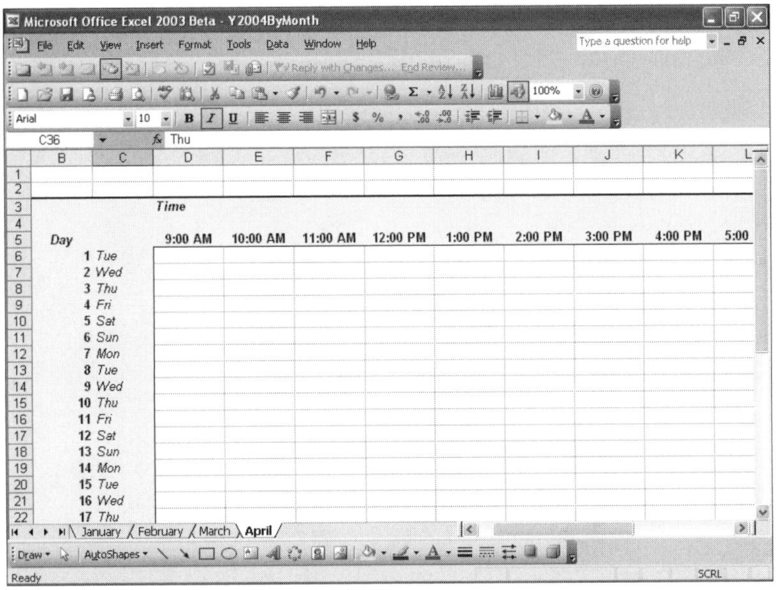

Figure 6-4. This macro creates a new worksheet based on an existing template but adds the correct weekday and date for the upcoming month as well as the unchanging hour column headings.

ActiveWindow Property

The *ActiveWindow* property returns a *Windows* object that represents the currently selected window within the Excel application. The *ActiveWindow* is always the topmost window within an application.

The *Caption* property of a *Window* object also doubles as a *Name* property. When you assign a value to the *Caption* property, you make it possible to refer to a particular window in the

Microsoft Office Excel 2003 Programming Inside Out

Windows collection by using the *Caption* value instead of an index number. The following code fragment assigns the string "My Window" to the *Caption* property of the active window, and then invokes the *ActiveSheet* object's *Calculate* method to recalculate all of the formulas on the active sheet in *MyWindow*.

```
ActiveWindow.Caption = "My Window"
Application.Windows("My Window").ActiveSheet.Calculate
```

The best use of the *ActiveWindow* object is to control the zoom level of the window or move the window to display a particular cell. The *ScrollRow* and *ScrollColumn* properties provide the cell that's in the upper-left corner.

The following example illustrates how to use the *ScrollColumn*, *ScrollRow*, and *Zoom* properties. The example enters text into cell H18 using a 4-point font size, too small to read at Zoom levels below 200 percent. The macro then increases the Zoom level to the maximum of 400% and positions the window so that cell H18 is in the upper-left corner.

```
Sub ZoomScrollSample()
    Range("H18").Select
    ActiveCell.Font.Size = 4
    ActiveCell.Value = "This text is very small and hard to read."
    ActiveWindow.ScrollColumn = 6
    ActiveWindow.ScrollRow = 16
    ActiveWindow.Zoom = 100
    MsgBox "Click OK to zoom in to read", vbOKOnly + vbInformation, _
        "Programming Microsoft Excel Inside Out"
    ActiveWindow.Zoom = 400
    ActiveWindow.ScrollColumn = 8
    ActiveWindow.ScrollRow = 18
End Sub
```

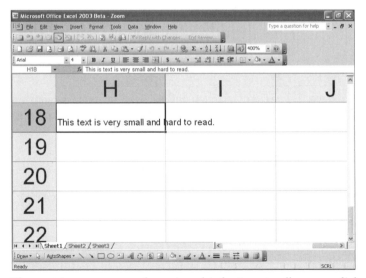

The next two macros can be assigned to buttons to allow one-click access to zoom in or out.

Chapter 6

The *Application* Object

```
Sub ZoomIn()
Dim intZoom As Integer

    intZoom = ActiveWindow.Zoom + 50
    If intZoom > 400 Then intZoom = 400
    ActiveWindow.Zoom = intZoom
End Sub

Sub ZoomOut()
Dim intZoom As Integer

    intZoom = ActiveWindow.Zoom - 50
    If intZoom < 50 Then intZoom = 50
    ActiveWindow.Zoom = intZoom
End Sub
```

ActiveWorkbook **Property**

The *ActiveWorkbook* property returns a *Workbook* object that references the currently selected workbook. If the clipboard window is active, the *ActiveWorkbook* property returns *Nothing*.

> **Note**   The *ActiveWorkbook* property also returns *Nothing* if the only open workbook is hidden.

The following example builds a new quarterly workbook by extracting the desired sheets out of the annual workbook:

```
Sub ExtractQuarterlyFigures()
Dim szMyName As String, szQuarter As String, intCount As Integer
Dim szSheetName As String, szName As String

    szMyName = ActiveWorkbook.Name
    szQuarter = InputBox("Which quarter to extract (1,2,3, or 4)?", _
        " Microsoft Office Excel 2003 Programming Inside Out", "1")
    Application.Workbooks.Add
    Select Case szQuarter
        Case 1: szName = "1st Quarter.xls"
        Case 2: szName = "2nd Quarter.xls"
        Case 3: szName = "3rd Quarter.xls"
        Case 4: szName = "4th Quarter.xls"
        Case Else
            MsgBox "Invalid entry ('" & szQuarter & "').", vbOKOnly + _
            vbInformation, " Microsoft Office Excel 2003 Programming Inside Out"
            Exit Sub
    End Select
    Workbooks(Workbooks.Count).SaveAs szName
    For intCount = 1 To 3
        Workbooks(szMyName).Activate
        ActiveWorkbook.Sheets(intCount * Val(szQuarter)).Activate
        Range("A1", ActiveCell.SpecialCells(xlLastCell)).Select
        szSheetName = ActiveSheet.Name
```

continued

Chapter 6

```
        Selection.Copy
        Workbooks(szName).Activate
        Sheets(intCount).Select
        ActiveSheet.Paste
        ActiveSheet.Name = szSheetName
    Next intCount
End Sub
```

DisplayAlerts **Property**

The *DisplayAlerts* property determines if Microsoft Excel will display alerts while a macro is running. By changing the value to *False*, Excel will choose the default response for all alerts that would have been displayed; the one exception is when using the *SaveAs* method for workbooks. When *DisplayAlerts* is *True*, the OverWrite alert has a default response of Yes, but Excel will use *No* as a response when *DisplayAlerts* is *False*.

Excel will reset the *DisplayAlerts* property to the default value of *True* when the macro completes.

The following macro, which removes all unused worksheets from a workbook, sets the *DisplayAlerts* property to False so that the user isn't prompted every time the macro attempts to delete a worksheet:

> **Warning** You must run this workbook on a workbook that contains some data. If you run this on a new workbook with nothing but empty sheets, you get VB runtime error 1004: "A workbook must contain at least one visible sheet."

```
Sub RemoveEmptySheets()
Dim intCount As Integer

    Application.DisplayAlerts = False
    For intCount = Sheets.Count To 1 Step -1
        Sheets(intCount).Select
        Range("A1", ActiveCell.SpecialCells(xlLastCell)).Select
        If Selection.Address() = "$A$1" And ActiveCell = "" Then
            Sheets(intCount).Delete
            intCount = Sheets.Count + 1
        End If
    Next intCount

End Sub
```

RangeSelection **Property**

The *RangeSelection* property returns a *Range* object that represents the selected cells on the selected workbook. Even when a graphic object is selected, the *RangeSelection* property will return a range of cells, returning the last cells that were selected.

When cells are selected, the *RangeSelection* property and the *Selection* object both represent the same cells. When a graphic object is selected, the *RangeSelection* property will still return the last cells that were selected.

The *Application* Object

The following example displays the address of the cells currently selected:

```
MsgBox ActiveWindow.RangeSelection.Address
```

Selection Property

The *Selection* property returns an object type of whatever the current selection happens to be. For cells, it will return a *Range* object; for charts, it will return a *Chart* object.

Assuming the current selection is a range of cells, this example will clear all values and formulas.

```
Selection.Clear
```

StatusBar Property

The *StatusBar* property allows you to change the current message displayed on the Status Bar at the bottom of the Excel window. This message can be helpful when you have a procedure that will take some time to complete because it allows you to keep the user informed that something is happening. To disable any message you might have placed on the status bar, set it to *False*.

This example is a modified version of the BuildChart procedure that was used previously to demonstrate the *ActiveChart* property. Several lines of code were added to display messages to the user on the Status Bar about what the macro was currently doing.

Inside Out

Pausing a Macro

One of the features of Excel is the ability to pull in data from outside sources. Suppose the flower shop has decided to expand and now has multiple stores. As the owner, you want to build a report that examines the sales data from each of the different stores every day. However, the macro to build the report takes some time to compile all the information and present in the manner you desire, so you'd like it to run overnight so that the report is waiting for you in the morning.

Rather than having to wait until all stores have submitted their data to the main server and then running your macro, you can use the *Wait* method to pause the macro until a specific time. Using the code `Application.Wait "20:00:00"` instructs the macro to wait until 8:00 P.M. before continuing to execute. To pause for a specific time interval and not a specific time, you can add the time interval to the current time.

Careful testing should be done before setting too great of an interval for pausing. The *Wait* method will halt all activity within Microsoft Excel and also has the potential to prevent you from using any other application on your computer.

ScreenUpdating Property

VBA macros execute very quickly, especially when compared with the speed at which a human could perform the same steps. As Excel performs the different actions programmed in the macro, the screen changes to reflect those actions. Enough actions could happen fast enough that the screen updates aren't processed as quickly as the actions in the macro and it appears as if the screen is flashing as it attempts to reflect the different steps performed. These screen updates also require some processing time, which will slow down the execution of the macro.

To minimize the screen flashing and also maybe to gain a few seconds in processing time, especially on macros that require a lot of processing time, you can disable screen updates using the *ScreenUpdating* property.

Setting the *ScreenUpdating* property to *False* at the start of a macro instructs Excel not to update the screen during execution until the property has been reset to *True*. It is very important to fully test a macro for errors and add some type of error trapping when turning off screen updates so that the user does not think the macro or Excel has crashed when there is actually an error condition that's not being displayed to the user. It's also important to set *ScreenUpdating* to *True*, the default value, when the procedure has executed so that any other procedure that might have called the one that turns the screen updating off doesn't have to be concerned with whether or not the screen updates were turned on or off outside its own scope.

The following procedure creates a new chart based on the data in the SalesByCategory.xls workbook and then waits three seconds before terminating the procedure.

```
Sub BuildChart()
    Application.StatusBar = "Adding new chart..."
    Application.Wait (Now + TimeValue("0:00:03"))
    Application.ScreenUpdating = False
    Charts.Add    'Add a new chart object
    ActiveChart.ChartType = xl3DColumn    'Set the Chart type to #D Column
    ActiveChart.SetSourceData Source:=Sheets("ByCategory").Range("C1:G13"), _
        PlotBy:=xlColumns    'Set the data source
    ActiveChart.Location Where:=xlLocationAsObject, Name:="ByCategory"
    Application.StatusBar = "Configuring new chart..."
    With ActiveChart    'Format the chart
        .HasTitle = True
        .ChartTitle.Characters.Text = "Monthly Sales by Category"
        .Axes(xlCategory).HasTitle = True
        .Axes(xlCategory).AxisTitle.Characters.Text = "Month"
        .Axes(xlSeries).HasTitle = True
        .Axes(xlSeries).AxisTitle.Characters.Text = "Category"
        .Axes(xlValue).HasTitle = True
        .Axes(xlValue).AxisTitle.Characters.Text = "Sales"
    End With
    ActiveSheet.Shapes(1).IncrementLeft -133.5    'Position the chart
    ActiveSheet.Shapes(1).IncrementTop 214.5
    ActiveSheet.Shapes(1).ScaleWidth 1.77, msoFalse, msoScaleFromTopLeft
    ActiveSheet.Shapes(1).ScaleHeight 1.35, msoFalse, msoScaleFromTopLeft
    Application.Wait (Now + TimeValue("0:00:03"))
    Application.StatusBar = False
    Application.ScreenUpdating = True
End Sub
```

The *Application* Object

ThisWorkbook Property

ThisWorkbook returns a *Workbook* object that refers to the workbook that contains the macro that's currently running. This property lets Add-Ins refer to the workbook that contains the code. *ActiveWorkbook* will not work because it refers to the currently active workbook and not the workbook that actually contains the code being executed.

The following example demonstrates the *ThisWorkbook* property by displaying a message box with the name of the active workbook and the name of the workbook the macro is being executed from:

```
Sub TestThisWorkbook()
Dim strMessage As String

    strMessage = "Active Workbook = " & ActiveWorkbook.Name & vbCrLf
    strMessage = strMessage & "This Workbook = " & ThisWorkbook.Name

    MsgBox strMessage, vbOKOnly + vbInformation, _
        "Microsoft Office Excel 2003 Programming Inside Out"

End Sub
```

Methods

Methods are the actions that objects can perform. They allow the contents of the object container to be processed. You can think of it as a kitchen blender. The blender is the object container. The food placed inside the blender is the contents. Each of the individual buttons, stir, chop, liquefy, and so on, is a different method.

Calculate Method

Calculate forces all open workbooks to recalculate all cells that contain new, changed, or volatile cells and their dependents. Using this method is similar to pressing the F9 key, and it is used to force Excel to recalculate a workbook when the Calculation option in the Tools, Options dialog box has been set to manual. This example recalculates all open workbooks if the Calculation option is not set to automatic.

```
Sub RecalcAll()
    If Application.Calculation <> xlCalculationAutomatic Then
        Calculate
    End If
End Sub
```

Chapter 6

119

Inside Out

Limiting the Calculations

The *Calculate* method can also be used on *Worksheet* and *Range* objects, and it allows you to narrow down the number of calculations that are performed. Using a *Worksheet* object will perform all needed calculations on the specified worksheet. The following example calculates the active sheet:

```
Sub RecalcSheet()
    If Application.Calculation <> xlCalculationAutomatic Then
        ActiveSheet.Calculate
    End If
End Sub
```

To calculate a limited number of cells, use a *Range* object to specify the cells you want to recalculate. This example recalculates the formulas for all cells in the range C1:G13:

```
Sub Recalc()
    ActiveSheet.Range("C1:G13").Cells.Calculate
End Sub
```

CalculateFull Method

CalculateFull forces all open workbooks to recalculate all cells regardless of the contents. The following example recalculates all open workbooks:

```
Sub ReCalcFull()
    Application.CalculateFull
End Sub
```

FindFile Method

The *FindFile* method displays the Open dialog box and opens the file selected by the user. It returns a *True* value if a file was successfully opened or a *False* if the user clicked the Cancel button. The following example prompts the user to locate the ProductList.xls file:

```
Sub FindProductList()
Dim bReturn As Boolean, strPrompt As String

    strPrompt = "Please locate the ProductList.xls file."
    MsgBox strPrompt, vbOKOnly + vbInformation, " Microsoft Office Excel 2003 _
        Programming Inside Out"

    bReturn = Application.FindFile
    If Not bReturn Then
        strPrompt = "File not opened."
```

```
MsgBox strPrompt, vbOKOnly + vbInformation, " Microsoft Office Excel 2003 _
    Programming Inside Out"
  End If

End Sub
```

InputBox Method

The *InputBox* method is very similar to the *InputBox* function in that both the method and function display a simple dialog box that allows the user to enter information to be manipulated within your macro. The difference between the two is the *InputBox* method can perform selective validation of the user's input and can be used with other Excel objects, error values, and formulas. The *InputBox* function, by contrast, just returns a value you can work with in a macro.

> For more information on creating input boxes, see Chapter 4, "VBA Programming Starter Kit."

As with the *InputBox* function, you can specify a prompt to tell the user what type of value you are looking for, a title to appear within the title bar of the dialog box, a default value, where on the screen the dialog box should appear, and a link to a Help file. Additionally, you can specify the type of value the *InputBox* should accept. The choices are shown in Table 6-1, along with usage notes. You can add the values together to specify more than one type. For example, you could add the value for number (1) and the value for text (2) together and use the sum of 3 to allow the *InputBox* to accept both numbers and text. When no type is specified, the default value for text is used.

The full syntax for using the *InputBox* method is

```
expression.InputBox(Prompt, Title, Default, Left, Top, HelpFile,
    HelpContextID, Type)
```

Expression, an *Application* object, and *Prompt*, a string value, are both required elements for calling the *InputBox* method. The other parameters are optional, but placeholders must be used when calling the method in standard form. To avoid placeholders, you can name the parameters you are supplying, such as the following:

```
Application.InputBox(Prompt:="My Prompt", Type:=8)
```

The *InputBox* allows the user to use the mouse to select a cell or range of cells from any open workbook. The *Set* statement must be used to assign the selected cells to a *Range* object; otherwise, the value of the selected cells is used.

You need to use a *Set* statement whenever you want to assign a specific instance of an object to a variable. For example, you can create a variable to point to a *Worksheet* object using the following statement:

```
Dim wksNewSheet As Worksheet
```

There is one more step to go, though; merely creating a variable to point to an object neither creates a new object nor points to an existing instance of the object. To have the *wksNewSheet* variable point to a worksheet named January, you would use the following statement:

```
Set wksNewSheet = Worksheets("January")
```

Now that the variable *wksNewSheet* is assigned to the worksheet named January, you can use the variable name as a pointer to the January worksheet. These two lines of code are equivalent.

```
wksNewSheet.Name = "January2"
Worksheets("January").Name = "January2"
```

The following example uses the *InputBox* method to ask the user to specify a range of cells to use for the monthly totals and then prompts the user for the values needed:

```
Sub InputMonthlyTotals()
Dim strPrompt As String, rgeMonth As Range, sglTotal As Single
Dim intColumn As Integer

    strPrompt = "Please select cells to place monthly totals in."
    Set rgeMonth = Application.InputBox(Prompt:=strPrompt, Title:=" Microsoft _
        Office Excel 2003 Programming Inside Out", Type:=8)
    strPrompt = "Please enter the total sales."
    For intColumn = 1 To rgeMonth.Columns.Count
        sglTotal = Application.InputBox(Prompt:=strPrompt, Title:=" Microsoft _
            Office Excel 2003 Programming Inside Out", Type:=1)
        rgeMonth(1, intColumn) = sglTotal
    Next intColumn

End Sub
```

The *Application* Object

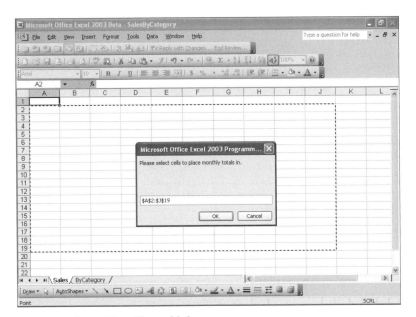

Table 6-1. *InputBox* Type Values

Value	Meaning	Notes
0	A formula	Any valid Excel formula is returned as a text string. You must use the *FormulaLocal* property to assign the formula to a *Range* object. Cell references are returned in A1-style and use the *ConvertFormula* function to switch to R1C1-style if needed.
1	A number	Will also calculate a formula, if entered, to return a number. For example, if **=8*8** is entered, the *InputBox* will return 64.
2	Text	Accepts a text (string) value.
4	A logical value (True/False)	Accepts any variant that can be converted to a logical value.
8	A cell reference, as a *Range* object	The *Set* statement must be used to assign the result to a *Range* object.
16	An error value, such as #NULL!	Returns a string value consisting of the word "Error" and the error number associated with the error value. (See Table 6-2 for a list of error values.) Any non-error value entered returns "Error 2015".
64	An array of values	Accepts a list of values.

Inside Out

The *FormulaLocal* Property and Local Settings

The *FormulaLocal* property returns or sets a formula in the language specified in the active Windows user's regional settings. For example, if a user types the formula **=SOMME(B3:B15)** into an input box (*SOMME* is the French version of *SUM*), you can assign the formula to cell B16 on the first worksheet in your workbook using the following statement:

```
Range(B16).FormulaLocal = InputBox("Enter a formula.")
```

Table 6-2. **Cell Error Values**

Error Value	Return
#####	Error 2015
#DIV/0!	Error 2007
#N/A	Error 2042
#NAME?	Error 2029
#NULL!	Error 2000
#NUM!	Error 2036
#REF!	Error 2023
#VALUE!	Error 2015

Intersect Method

The *Intersect* method compares two or more ranges to determine if they overlap or share any common cells. Figure 6-5 shows one range bounded at B3:E6 and a second range bounded at D5:G8. The intersection of the two would be the range D5:E6 as illustrated in the following example:

```
Sub DisplayIntersection()
    Range("B3:E6").BorderAround Color:=vbBlack, Weight:=xlThick
    Range("B3:E6").Select
    Set rge1 = Selection
    Range("D5:E8").BorderAround Color:=vbYellow, Weight:=xlThick
    Range("D5:E8").Select
    Set rge2 = Selection
    Set myRange = Application.Intersect(rge1, rge2)
    Range(myRange.Address).Select
    Selection.Interior.Color = vbBlue
End Sub
```

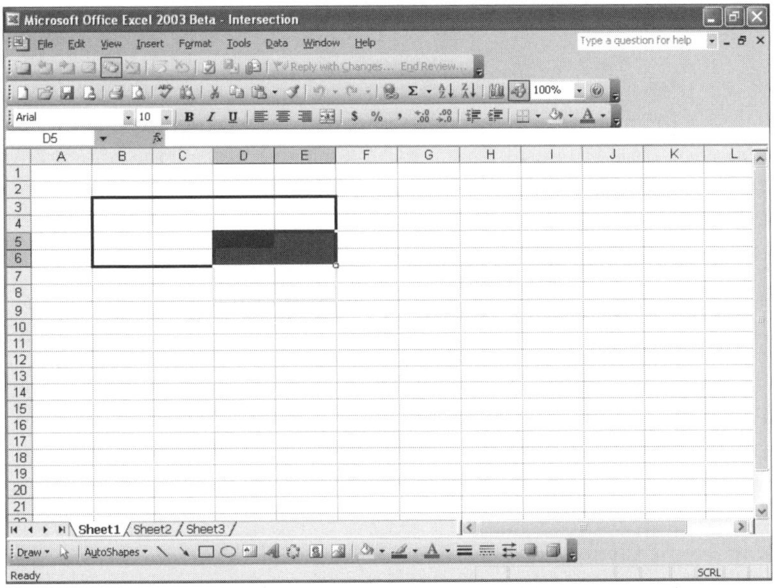

The *Application* Object

Figure 6-5. The *Intersect* method finds the cells representing the intersection of two ranges.

A popular use of the *Intersect* method is to determine if a cell selected by the user is within a specific range. The TestPlants procedure prompts the user to select the largest monthly total for Plants in the SalesByCategory.xls file and displays an error message if a cell is selected that is not one of the monthly plant totals.

```
Sub TestPlants()
Dim strPrompt As String, rgePlants As Range, rgeIntersect As Range

    strPrompt = "Please select the highest monthly total for Plants."
    Set rgePlants = Application.InputBox(Prompt:=strPrompt, Title:=" Microsoft _
        Office Excel 2003 Programming Inside Out", Type:=8)
    Set rgeIntersect = Application.Intersect(Range("G2:G13"), rgePlants)
    If rgeIntersect Is Nothing Then
        strPrompt = "You did not select a Plant value".
        MsgBox strPrompt, vbOKOnly + vbInformation
    End If

End Sub
```

OnKey Method

The *OnKey* method allows you to create hotkeys that will run a particular routine when pressed or block Excel from behaving normally when the key combination is pressed. The syntax for the *OnKey* method is

```
Application.OnKey(Key, Prodecure)
```

Key is a string value representing the key combination to be assigned; see Table 6-3 for a list of special key codes.

Procedure is a string value representing the name of the procedure to be invoked. If *Procedure* is blank (that is, the parameter is set to the empty string by assigning it the value " "), the key combination performs no action, even if Excel normally reacts to the key combination. If the *Procedure* argument is omitted entirely (that is, there is nothing after the comma), the key combination is reset to normal, default actions.

You can combine a key with one or more of the key modifiers (Shift, Ctrl, and/or Alt) to create key combinations as needed. The following example runs a procedure when Alt+H is pressed:

```
Application.OnKey "%h", "MyProcedure"
```

The following example takes the key combination that normally opens the Excel Find and Replace (Ctrl+H) dialog box and uses it to invoke a custom procedure:

```
Application.OnKey "^h", "MyProcedure"
```

This example stops any code from running when Ctrl+H is pressed.

```
Application.OnKey "^h", ""
```

This last example resets Ctrl+H to the default action in Excel (Find and Replace).

```
Application.OnKey "^h"
```

The most common usage of the *OnKey* method would be to set hot keys when a workbook is opened or closed. This allows the workbook to provide hot keys that are specific to the workbook and resets the keys to their default values when closed. The two following procedures, when placed inside the Y2001ByMonth.xls file, assign the hot key of Alt+C to the CopySheet procedure to add a new worksheet to the workbook:

```
Sub Auto_Open()
    Application.OnKey "%c", "CopySheet"
End Sub

Sub Auto_Exit()
    Application.OnKey "%c"
End Sub
```

Table 6-3. **Key Codes**

Key	Key Code
Backspace	{Backspace} or {BS}
Break	{Break}
Caps Lock	{CapsLock}
Clear	{Clear}

Table 6-3. Key Codes

Key	Key Code
Delete or Del	{Delete} or {Del}
Down Arrow	{Down}
End	{End}
Enter	~ (Tilde)
Enter (Numeric Keypad)	{Enter}
F1 through F15	{F1} through {F15}
Help	{Help}
Home	{Home}
Insert or Ins	{Insert}
Left Arrow	{Left}
Num Lock	{NumLock}
Page Down	{PGDN}
Page Up	{PGUP}
Return	{Return}
Right Arrow	{Right}
Scroll Lock	{ScrollLock}
Tab	{Tab}
Up Arrow	{Up}
Key Modifier	Key Code
Shift	+ (Plus Sign)
Ctrl	^ (Caret)
Alt	% (Percent Sign)

SendKeys Method

The *SendKeys* method allows you to send keystrokes to the keyboard buffer for when you need to send keystrokes to the current application. This can be especially useful if you know your procedure will cause a dialog box to open and there is no method to prevent the dialog box from appearing and waiting on user input.

The syntax for the *SendKeys* method is

```
expression.SendKeys (Keys, Wait)
```

- *expression*   is an optional expression that returns an *Application* object.
- *Keys*   is a required variant expression, usually expressed as a string, that contains the key codes you want to send. (See Table 6-3 for a list of key codes for special keys.)

Microsoft Office Excel 2003 Programming Inside Out

- *Wait* is an optional variant expression, usually expressed as a *True* or *False* Boolean value that specifies if the procedure should halt further execution until the keys have been processed. When *True*, the procedure will pause until all keys sent have been processed. When *False* or omitted, the procedure continues execution without regard to whether or not the keys have been processed.

The keys are placed into a key buffer first until an application calls for keys from the buffer. This means the keys need to placed into the buffer before you call a method that will require the keystrokes.

This example goes through a list of customers and generates a personalized e-mail message for each customer. The *SendKeys* method is used to pass an Alt+S keystroke to the default e-mail program to actually send the e-mail message. The *Wait* method is used to allow the e-mail program time to generate the e-mail message before trying to send it.

```
Sub SendEmail()
Dim strLink As String, rgeEmail As Range
Dim strMsg As String

    strMsg = "%0A%0AThis month save $10 off all orders over $100.%0A "
    strMsg = strMsg & "Visit The Garden Company for all your gardening needs."
    For Each rgeEmail In Range(Cells(2, 1), Cells(7, 1))
        strLink = "Mailto:" & rgeEmail.Offset(0, 1).Value & "?subject="
        strLink = strLink & "Monthly Special%0A&body="
        strLink = strLink & "Dear " & rgeEmail.Value & ",%0A"
        strLink = strLink & strMsg
        ActiveWorkbook.FollowHyperlink (strLink)
        Application.Wait (Now + TimeValue("0:00:02"))
        SendKeys "%s", True
    Next rgeEmail

End Sub
```

This chapter introduced the *Application* object, which contains a number of useful properties and methods that let you affect how Excel functions at its highest levels. You can assign new procedures to control key combinations, prevent the screen from flashing as a procedure makes multiple changes to a workbook, and work with the active window, workbook, chart, sheet, or cell with the *ActiveWindow*, *ActiveWorkbook*, *ActiveChart*, *ActiveSheet*, and *ActiveCell* properties. Chapter 7 moves to the next level of detail, introducing you to the *Workbook* and *Worksheet* objects.

Workbooks and Worksheets

The *Workbooks* Collection 129

The *Sheets* and *Worksheets*
Collections 149

The workbook is the highest level of organization within Microsoft Excel, so you might think that there aren't a whole lot of actions you can take on a workbook beyond creating new workbooks, saving changes, closing workbooks, or deleting workbooks you no longer need. While it is true that most "workbook" manipulations actually occur at the worksheet and cell level, you'll still find plenty to do with workbooks. This chapter also discusses worksheets, both as worksheets and as members of the *Sheets* collection, so you'll find the resources you need to create workbooks and set them up the way you want them (in terms of password protection, the number of worksheets, and the names of those worksheets) before you start manipulating the values contained in them.

The *Workbooks* Collection

The *Workbooks* collection contains references to every workbook that you have open in your copy of Excel. If there's some change you want to make to every open workbook, you can use a *For Each…Next* loop to move through the collection and make those changes. The *Workbooks* collection contains a number of other useful methods that you can use to manipulate your existing workbooks, but the most basic ability is that of creation—you need to be able to create a new workbook before you can manipulate it.

Creating New Workbooks

One of the basic tasks you'll want to complete when you program Excel is to create a new workbook. New workbooks can be the repository of new information or the target of worksheets copied from existing workbooks. Regardless of what you want to use the new workbook for, you can create the workbook using the following code:

```
Workbooks.Add
```

If you want to create a workbook that's a copy of an existing workbook, you can do so by setting the *Add* method's *Template* parameter, as in the following procedure:

```
Sub AddNewWorkbook()
    Dim NewWbk As Workbook
    Set NewWkbk = Workbooks.Add(Template:="C:\ExcelProg\MonthlySales.xls")
End Sub
```

Opening Workbooks

After you've created one or more workbooks, you'll probably want to open them at some point with the *Workbooks* collection's *Open* method, which, in its simplest form, appears as follows:

```
Workbooks.Open (FileName:="MonthlySales.xls")
```

You do have plenty more options when you open a workbook, however. The *Open* method has the following full syntax:

```
expression.Open(FileName, UpdateLinks, ReadOnly, Format,Password,WriteResPassword,
IgnoreReadOnlyRecommended, Origin, Delimiter, Editable, Notify,
Converter,AddToMru, Local, CorruptLoad)
```

Table 7-1 describes the parameters available for use with the *Workbooks.Open* method. Of particular interest are the *ReadOnly* parameter, which requires that the user running your macro open the workbook in read-only mode; the *Password* parameter, which need only be set if the workbook is password protected; and the *Delimiter* parameter, which specifies the character used to separate fields if the file the user is opening is a text file.

> **Note** You'll learn more about opening text files later in this section.

Table 7-1. **The Parameters Associated with the *Workbooks.Open* Method**

Parameter	Description
FileName	Required string specifying the name and path of the file to open.
UpdateLinks	Tells Excel how to handle any links from the workbook to other workbooks. 0 means no updates, 1 means update external references, 2 means update remote references, and 3 means update both external and remote references.
ReadOnly	When set to *True*, opens the workbook in read-only mode.
Password	A string that contains the password required to open the workbook. If you omit the argument, the regular Excel password protection routine will take over.
WriteResPassword	A string that contains the password required to write to a write-reserved workbook. If you omit the argument, the regular Excel password protection routine will take over.
IgnoreReadOnly Recommended	If the workbook was saved with the Read-Only Recommended option turned on, setting this parameter to *True* causes Excel to skip showing the Read-Only Recommended message box when the workbook is opened.
Origin	Indicates the operating system used to create the file. The three constants are *xlWindows*, *xlMacintosh*, and *xlMSDOS*. If this parameter isn't specified, Excel uses the current operating system.

Table 7-1. The Parameters Associated with the *Workbooks.Open* Method *(continued)*

Parameter	Description
Format	Specifies the character used to separate one cell's value from the next cell's value. 1 means tab, 2 means comma, 3 means space, 4 means semicolon, 5 means there is no delimiter, and 6 indicates another character specified in the *Delimiter* parameter.
Delimiter	Contains the delimiter character indicated by a *Format* parameter value of 6.
Editable	If the file is an Excel 4 add-in, setting this argument to *True* opens the add-in as a visible window. If the argument is *False* or omitted, the add-in will be hidden and not able to be unhidden. This option doesn't apply to add-ins created with Excel version 5.0 or later. If the file is an Excel template (*.xlt file), setting the argument to *True* opens the template for editing, whereas setting it to *False* or omitting it creates a new workbook based on the template.
Notify	If the file is in use, setting this parameter to *True* means Excel will open the file in read-only mode, keep checking for the file's availability, and let the user know when the file can be opened in read-write mode.
Converter	An Excel constant indicating the first converter to try when the file is opened. These converters are additional files that let you convert files to Excel from programs Excel doesn't already know how to open. You will usually need to get the converter from the other software vendor, but some converters are available on the Microsoft Office Web site.
AddToMru	When set to *True*, adds the workbook to the recently used file list.
Local	A Boolean variable that indicates whether to use the local language set in Excel or the local language set in VBA (if different).
CorruptLoad	When set to *xlNormalLoad*, opens the file normally. When set to *xlRepairFile*, attempts to repair the file. When set to *xlExtractData*, attempts to extract the data into a recovery file.

One of the most useful and versatile file formats is the text format. Regardless of the program you use to create a spreadsheet or database table, you can usually save it as text and then open it in Excel. For example, if you are working with a colleague at another company who uses a spreadsheet or database program that doesn't read or create Excel-compatible files, you can always write the data to a text file, which can then be read into Excel. You lose any formatting or formulas from the original file when you go the text route, but getting the data from one place to another is an ability worth knowing about.

The key to using a text file to represent spreadsheet data is in creating a clear division between cells. Many programs use the comma as a *delimiter*, or character that represents the boundary between two cells. For example, Figure 7-1 displays a worksheet as a table with three rows of data and three cells per row.

```
10345,5738,6029
24082,7459,3108
5119,8003,14972
```

	A	B	C
1	10,345	5,738	6,029
2	24,082	7,459	3,108
3	5,119	8,003	14,972

Figure 7-1. You can open a file that contains comma-delimited data directly into Excel.

It would be incorrect, however, to write the data to a text file with comma delimiters while using a comma as a thousands separator (in the United States) or decimal separator (in Europe). Figure 7-2 shows what would happen if the same data list were written using commas both as thousands separators and as delimiters:

```
10,345,5,738,6,029
24,082,7,459,3,108
5,119,8,003,14,972
```

Instead of the expected three rows of three cells, the above data file would produce a worksheet with three rows and four cells per row.

	A	B	C	D	E	F
1	10	345	5	738	6	29
2	24	82	7	459	3	108
3	5	119	8	3	14	972

Figure 7-2. When delimiters appear in unexpected places, data chaos ensues.

You can use characters other than commas as delimiters if you need to bring in data that includes commas, such as text or numbers with thousands separators. In the Text Import Wizard, you can select an option button indicating which delimiter your file uses (comma, space, tab, semicolon, or another character you type in yourself). You can do the same thing in Visual Basic for Applications (VBA) by setting the parameters of the *Workbooks.OpenText* method. The *OpenText* method has the following full syntax:

```
expression.OpenText(FileName, Origin, StartRow, DataType, TextQualifier,
ConsecutiveDelimiter, Tab, Semicolon, Comma, Space, Other, OtherChar,
FieldInfo, TextVisualLayout, DecimalSeparator, ThousandsSeparator,
TrailingMinusNumbers, Local)
```

Table 7-2 lists and describes the available parameters.

Workbooks and Worksheets

Table 7-2. Parameters Available with the *Workbooks.OpenText* Method

Parameter	Description
FileName	Required string specifying the name and path of the file.
Origin	Indicates the operating system used to create the file. The three constants are *xlWindows*, *xlMacintosh*, and *xlMSDOS*. If this parameter isn't specified, Excel uses the current operating system.
StartRow	The number of the row from which Excel should begin reading data into the worksheet.
DataType	Specifies the column format of the data in the file using one of the following *XlTextParsingType* constants: *xlDelimited*, which indicates there is a delimiting character, or *xlFixedWidth*, which indicates each field is of a fixed length. If this argument is not specified, Excel attempts to determine the column format when it opens the file.
TextQualifier	Uses an *XlTextQualifier* constant to indicate the character used to indicate that a field contains a text value. The available constants are *xlTextQualifierDoubleQuote* (double quotes, the default), *xlTextQualifierNone* (no character indicates a field contains text), and *xlTextQualifierSingleQuote* (single quotes).
ConsecutiveDelimiter	Set these parameters to *True* if you want to treat two or more consecutive delimiter characters as a single cell boundary.
Tab, *Semicolon*, *Comma*, *Space*	Set this parameter to *True* if the named character is the delimiter used in the text file.
FieldInfo	An array containing parse information for individual columns of data. When the data is delimited, this argument is an array of two-element arrays, with each two-element array specifying the conversion options for a particular column. The first element is the column number (1-based), and the second element is one of the *xlColumnDataType* constants specifying how the column is parsed. Those constants are *xlGeneralFormat* (a General value), *xlTextFormat* (a Text value), *xlMDYFormat* (an MDY date), *xlDMYFormat* (a DMY date), *xlYMDFormat* (a YMD date), *xlMYDFormat* (an MYD date), *xlDYMFormat* (a DYM date), *xlYDMFormat* (a YDM date), *xlEMDFormat* (an EMD date), and *xlSkipColumn*. (Do not import the column.) You can use *xlEMDFormat* only if you have installed and selected Taiwanese language support. The *xlEMDFormat* constant specifies that Taiwanese era dates are being used.
TextVisualLayout	A variant, not used in the American English version of Excel, that controls how the workbook is displayed within the Excel interface.

continued

Table 7-2. Parameters Available with the *Workbooks.OpenText* Method *(continued)*

Parameter	Description
Other	Set this parameter to *True* if you use *OtherChar* to define a non-standard delimiter character.
OtherChar	The character used as the delimiter in the file to be opened. If there is more than one character in the string, Excel uses the first character.
DecimalSeparator, ThousandsSeparator	The characters assigned to these two arguments indicate the decimal separator (a period in the United States) and the thousands separator (a comma in the United States).
TrailingMinusNumbers	A value that indicates whether a number comes after the minus sign (*True*, the default value) or if the minus sign comes after a negative number (*False*, almost never used). Unless you have a specific reason to set this parameter to *False*, you should never include it in the *OpenText* method's call.
Local	A Boolean variable that indicates whether to use the local language set in Excel or the local language set in VBA (if different).

A routine to open a text file named SalesExport.txt that uses semicolons as its delimiter characters would look like this:

```
Sub BringInText()
    Workbooks.OpenText Filename:="SalesExport.txt", Semicolon:=True
End Sub
```

When you write a program that changes other files, it's important to remember that you're assuming you have complete control over the files and that they're not open. The best-written code in the universe is little good to you if you try to open a file but get a read-only copy of the file because one of your co-workers opened it to fill in some numbers for a project briefing.

The following procedure lets you avoid those problems by checking to see if a particular workbook is open:

```
Sub CheckIfOpen()
Dim Wkbk As Workbook
Dim Filename As String
Filename = InputBox("Type the name of the file you want to check.")
For Each Wkbk in Application.Workbooks
    If Wkbk.Name = Filename Then
        MsgBox (Filename & " is open; changes may result in errors.")
    End If
    Next Wkbk
End Sub
```

> **Caution**   Remember that the name of a file is case-sensitive and includes the file extension, which is usually .xls for Excel files. Typing **SalesSummary** or **salessummary.xls** into this procedure's *InputBox* wouldn't indicate that the file SalesSummary.xls was open!

Saving Workbooks

Just as it's important to save your workbooks when you enter data or change formatting manually, it's vital that you save your workbooks when you make significant changes using VBA. One scenario where it's possible for things to go wrong is if you were to import data into a workbook but close the workbook before you save the new data. If the source file is on another computer and you aren't able to re-establish your connection to it for some reason, it would be as if you hadn't run the macro at all.

There is a property of the *Application* object that comes in handy when you want to save the workbook that contains your macro code. That property is the *ThisWorkbook* property, which returns a *Workbook* object representing the workbook that contains the VBA code you're running. With the new *Workbook* object in hand, you can call the *Save* method to save a copy of your workbook.

The code to save the workbook containing the code is simply this:

```
ThisWorkbook.Save
```

> **Note**   If you use the *ThisWorkbook.Save* method to save a workbook for the first time, Excel attempts to save the workbook using its current name. If it's the first workbook you've created in this Excel session, its name will be Book1. If there is another workbook in the same directory with the same name, a message box will appear offering you the opportunity to overwrite the existing file by clicking Yes or to abort the operation by clicking No or Cancel. If you decide not to overwrite the existing file, a Microsoft Visual Basic run-time error message box appears, indicating that the method failed (error 1004).

If you want to save a workbook with a new name or in a new location, you can use the *SaveAs* method of the *ThisWorkbook* property. However, just as clicking the Save toolbar button is much less complicated than clicking File, Save As to open the Save As dialog box and all of its possibilities, so is using the *ThisWorkbook.Save* method much less complicated than using the *ThisWorkbook.SaveAs* method. But, truth to tell, using the *ThisWorkbook.SaveAs* method is fairly straightforward. The *SaveAs* method has the following full syntax:

```
expression.SaveAs(FileName, FileFormat, Password, WriteResPassword,
ReadOnlyRecommended, CreateBackup, AccessMode, ConflictResolution, AddToMru,
TextCodePage, TextVisualLayout, Local)
```

The parameters are listed in Table 7-3 for your convenience.

Table 7-3. **The *ThisWorkbook.SaveAs* Parameters**

Parameter	Description
FileName	The name and path of the file to be saved.
FileFormat	The Excel constant representing the file format in which to save the file. There are 44 Excel file format constants, which you can look up in the Visual Basic Editor help system by typing **xlFileFormat** in the Ask A Question box.
Password	Sets a password for the file. The password must be 15 characters or fewer.
WriteResPassword	Sets a password for restricting who may write changes to the file, while still allowing the file to be opened as read-only.
ReadOnlyRecommended	When set to *True*, displays a dialog box recommending the user open the file in read-only mode.
CreateBackup	When set to *True*, creates a backup copy of the workbook.
AccessMode	Indicates whether the file is saved in exclusive mode (*xlExclusive*), in no changes mode (*xlNoChange*), or as a shared file (*xlShared*). In exclusive mode, only one user may have the workbook open and make changes at a time. Saving a file with no changes leaves the access mode unchanged, while saving a file as a shared file lets more than one user have read/write access to the file at a time.
ConflictResolution	Indicates how Excel should handle conflicting changes in a shared workbook by setting *ConflictResolution* to one of these *XlSaveConflictResolution* constants: *xlUserResolution*, the default, which displays the Conflict Resolution dialog box; *xlLocalSessionChanges*, which causes Excel to automatically accept the local user's changes; or *xlOtherSessionChanges*, which causes Excel to accept other changes instead of the local user's changes.
AddToMru	When set to *True*, adds the file name to the list of most recently used files on the File menu.
TextCodePage	A variant, not used in the American English version of Excel, that controls how the characters in a workbook are interpreted and displayed.
TextVisualLayout	A variant, not used in the American English version of Excel, that controls how the workbook is displayed within the Excel interface.
Local	A Boolean variable that indicates whether to use the local language set in Excel or the local language set in VBA (if different).

The properties you'll probably use the most in your work are *FileName* and *AddToMru*, with *FileFormat* and *Password* in the running for third place in your heart. The *AddToMru* property, which puts a file on the recently used files list that appears on the File menu, might seem to be an odd choice, but you can use that property to remind yourself which workbooks you need to work with the next time you or one of your colleagues run Excel. For example, if you wrote a macro that updated the values in a series of workbooks that would later need to be reviewed by the president of your company, adding the names of the updated workbooks to the most recently used files list would make it easy for your boss to find the files that need a look.

If you want to save every open workbook, you can write a macro to do just that using a *For Each…Next* loop, as in the following procedure:

```
Sub SaveThemAll()
    Dim Wkbk as Workbook
    For Each Wkbk in Workbooks
        If Wkbk.Path <> "" Then Wkbk.Save
    Next Wkbk
End Sub
```

The *If…Then* statement in the *For Each…Next* loop checks whether a workbook has an undefined path, meaning that the workbook in question has never been saved. This check is important if you want the procedure to run without human intervention; if someone needs to be on hand to save the workbooks, you might as well save them manually.

A related method that's available for use with workbooks is the *SaveCopyAs* method, which saves a copy of the current workbook under a new name. The *SaveCopyAs* method is a great way to make backup copies of a workbook during a lengthy procedure to guard against data loss, and as part of a general backup and file maintenance policy. The syntax of the procedure is simply this:

```
ThisWorkbook.SaveCopyAs "path\filename.xls"
```

Warning   If you use the *SaveCopyAs* method to save a file using an existing file name, the macro will overwrite the existing file without asking permission.

Activating Workbooks

In the *Save* and *SaveAs* property discussions, you noticed that the code used the *ThisWorkbook* object, which refers to the workbook to which the VBA code is attached. The *ActiveWorkbook* object is related to the *ThisWorkbook* object in that it refers to a workbook (obviously), but it refers to the workbook you have chosen to act on, not the workbook to which the code is attached. You can change the active workbook by calling the *Workbooks* collection's *Activate* method, as in the following line of code:

```
Workbooks("2004Q3sales.xls").Activate
```

Closing Workbooks

When you're done changing a workbook, it's a good idea to close it, both to save system resources and to reduce the likelihood that something will happen to the file while it's open. After all, all it takes is a stray keystroke here or there and the best data can become a meaningless jumble. As with the *Save* and *SaveAs* techniques you saw earlier in this section, you can use the *ThisWorkbook* property of the *Application* object to invoke the *Close* method, as in the following statement:

```
ThisWorkbook.Close
```

If you want to close another workbook from within a procedure, you can use this type of statement:

```
Workbooks("name").Close
```

When you've reached the end of a macro and want to clean up by saving and closing every open workbook, you can use the following procedure:

```
Sub CloseAll()
    Dim Wkbk as Workbook
    For Each Wkbk in Workbooks
        If Wkbk.Name <> ThisWorkbook.Name Then
            Wkbk.Close SaveChanges:=True
        End If
    Next Wkbk
    ThisWorkbook.Close SaveChanges:=True
End Sub
```

This procedure checks each workbook to ensure it isn't the workbook containing the VBA code. If the code were to close its own workbook while any other workbooks were open, any remaining open workbooks wouldn't be affected because the code would stop running.

> **Caution** The procedure does display a Save As dialog box if any of the open workbooks are new.

Workbook Properties

Even though workbooks are the focal point of Excel, you'll actually spend less time manipulating workbooks than working with worksheets and cell ranges. Even so, there are a number of workbook properties you can use to help you and your colleagues work with Excel effectively.

Using the *ActiveChart* Property

Charts are great for visually summarizing data, but if you're constrained to displaying a chart within a relatively small area and don't have the room to include a legend or other information, you can use message boxes to display information about the chart that's selected. The following macro might be attached to a command button on a worksheet offering help to the user on the information in the active chart.

```
Sub ChartHelp()
  ChartChosen = ActiveChart.Name
    Select Case ChartChosen
      Case "": Exit Sub
      Case "Sheet1 Chart 1": MsgBox "This chart shows the sales for 2000-2004."
      Case "Sheet1 Chart 2": MsgBox "This chart shows the profits for 2000-2004."
    End Select
End Sub
```

For more information on creating and manipulating charts in VBA, see Chapter 15, "Charts."

Displaying Drawing Objects

Workbooks are full of data and, regardless of how well you structure the data, it might not always be easy to follow what's going on. Adding drawing objects, such as text boxes and arrows, lets you call out special features of your worksheets and provide helpful information to your users. If you use drawing objects to provide that sort of information, you also have the option to hide or display the objects at will by using the *DisplayDrawingObjects* method. The following code assumes you have a series of drawing objects that might obscure your data if left on the worksheet, but would help explain what's going on if the user could turn them on and off as desired. Figure 7-3 shows the message box produced by the procedure: clicking OK hides the drawing objects, whereas clicking Cancel leaves the objects visible.

```
Public Sub ShowObjects()
    ThisWorkbook.DisplayDrawingObjects = xlDisplayShapes
    Answer = MsgBox(Prompt:="Click OK to hide the drawing _
      objects.", Buttons:=vbOKCancel + vbQuestion)
    If Answer = vbCancel Then
        Exit Sub
    Else
      ThisWorkbook.DisplayDrawingObjects = xlHide
    End If
End Sub
```

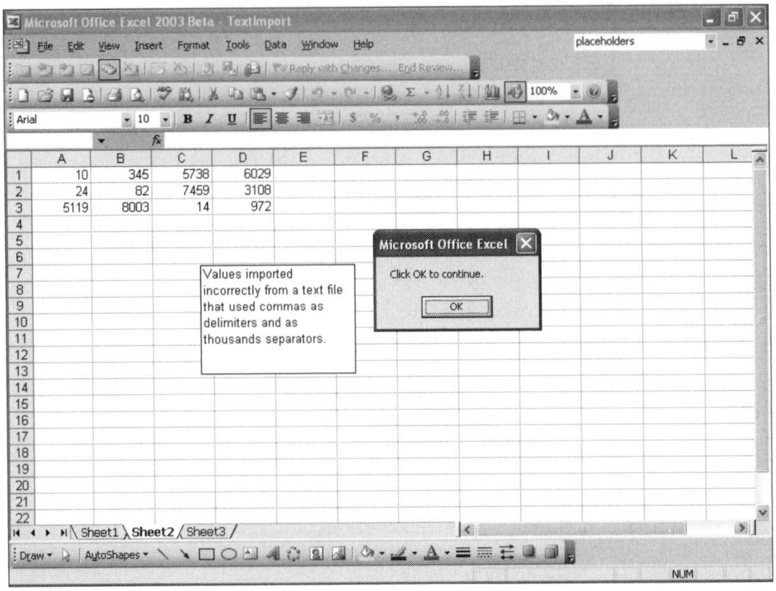

Figure 7-3. You can create procedures that let your users decide whether to hide drawing objects or leave them visible.

There are three available Excel constants that can be used as values for the *DisplayDrawing-Objects* property. They are *xlDisplayShapes*, which shows all shapes in their full glory; *xlHide*, which hides all shapes; and *xlPlaceHolders*, which causes Excel to print just the objects on your worksheet.

Managing File Settings

There are two aspects of a workbook's information you can use when you manipulate the workbook: the workbook's path and the workbook's full name. A path is the complete directory listing for a file, such as *C:\Excel\Data*, while a workbook's full name would include the workbook's file name, such as *C:\Excel\Data\Q12004.xls*. You can refer to these properties of the workbook that contains your macro code using these two methods:

```
ThisWorkbook.Path
ThisWorkbook.FullName
```

When you're working in the Visual Basic Editor and want to add the full name or path of the workbook to which you're adding code, you can click View, Immediate Window to open the Immediate Window and type **MsgBox (ThisWorkbook.FullName)** or **MsgBox (ThisWorkbook.Path)** to find the directory and file name information for your procedures. This information isn't of great importance if you don't plan to transfer your code outside of the current workbook, but if you need to refer to this particular workbook from elsewhere, you will need to use the full name of the file. And, while you could get the same information by trying to save the file and clicking the Save In down arrow to find the folder in which your workbook is stored, using the Immediate Window means you don't have to leave the Visual Basic Editor, which should help you keep your work flowing.

> **Note** The full name of a file includes a path, but the path will be blank if the file hasn't been saved yet.

Earlier in this chapter you used the *Save* and *SaveAs* methods of the *ThisWorkbook* property to save the files you change using VBA. Excel keeps track of whether a workbook has unsaved changes, which is helpful if you want to check the workbook and save it every time you run a procedure that affects the workbook's contents, or if you want to close a workbook without saving any of the changes you've made (such as when you run a series of formatting routines to highlight different aspects of your data but want everything reset when you're done). The following code fragment would have Excel close the active workbook without saving any unsaved changes:

```
ThisWorkbook.Saved = True
ThisWorkbook.Close
```

Another aspect of saving values in a workbook relates to how extensively you use links to external data sources. For example, if you were part of an enterprise that made a lot of individual sales that you tracked in a Microsoft Access database, you might want to create links from each cell in the workbook to the corresponding cell in the database table. If you had Excel continue its default behavior of recalculating the workbook by checking the values in the database table, you could have a long wait on your hands every time you open the workbook.

The code you use to save the link values is

```
ThisWorkbook.SaveLinkValues = True
```

Setting the *SaveLinkValues* property to *False* would cause Excel to re-check the values every time the workbook is opened and, if the values were not available, would generate an error.

Requiring a Password to Open a Workbook

Figuring out ways to maintain the integrity of your data in a corporate environment is one of the most important parts of working in the information industry. While you certainly need to protect your data against snoopers who get into your system from the outside or from internal users who gain extra privileges and browse through the intranet, you can also grant anyone access to one of your workbooks but still require them to provide the proper password when they try to save any changes to the workbook.

The following code listing lets a user set a password that will be required to open the workbook. Once someone opens the workbook, they'll be able to make any changes they want, but only if they know the password!

```
Sub SetPassword()
Dim strPassword1 As String
Dim strPassword2 As String
strPassword1 = InputBox ("Type a password for the workbook.")
strPassword2 = InputBox ("Re-type the password.")
    If strPassword1 <> strPassword2 Then
        MsgBox ("The passwords don't match. Please try again.")
    Else
        ThisWorkbook.Password = strPassword1
        MsgBox ("The password is set.")
    End If
End Sub
```

Important   You probably noticed that the SetPassword procedure required the user to type in the same password twice to set the password for the workbook. When you build routines that restrict access to data, you should always make sure to verify the password is what the user intended it to be. Remember, if the data is important enough to protect, it's worth it to add extra measures to safeguard the password.

Another way you can protect a workbook is to prevent users from saving changes unless the user knows the password used to protect the workbook. When a workbook is write-protected, the *WriteReserved* property is set to *True*. Writing code to change a write-protect password on the fly is messy, because the user would need to type in the current password and then set a new one, so the following routine checks to make sure the active workbook is not write-protected before allowing the user to set a password users must enter before being allowed to save changes:

```
Sub SetWritePassword()
Dim strPassword1 As String
Dim strPassword2 As String
strPassword1 = InputBox ("Type a password for changes to be saved.")
strPassword2 = InputBox ("Re-type the password.")
    If strPassword1 <> strPassword2 Then
        MsgBox ("The passwords don't match. Please try again.")
    Else
        If ActiveWorkbook.WriteReserved = False Then
          ActiveWorkbook.WritePassword = strPassword1
        Else MsgBox ("The workbook is already write protected.")
        End If
        MsgBox ("The password is set.")
    End If
End Sub
```

Protecting Workbooks from Changes

When you use the *WritePassword* method to protect your workbook, you're requiring users to know a password so they can open the workbook. Of course, once they have opened the workbook, they can make any changes they like to it. If you want to add a second layer of protection, you can do so by setting a separate password that must be entered before users would be able to make any changes to your workbook. By using the *Protect* method, you can prevent users from

Workbooks and Worksheets

changing the workbook by adding worksheets, deleting worksheets, displaying hidden worksheets (that is, changing the workbook's *structure*), and also prevent users from changing the sizes or positions of the windows in your workbook (changing the workbook's *windows*).

> **Note** When you use the *Protect* method attached to a *Workbook* object, the protections you set will apply to the entire workbook.

The *Workbook* object's *Protect* method has the following syntax:

```
Protect[Password], [Structure], [Windows]
```

No need for a table this time! The *Password* parameter is the password (that's required), but the *Structure* and *Windows* parameters are optional. By default they're set to *False*, but if you set them to *True*, as in the following code example, then the structure and windows layout of the workbook will be protected.

```
Sub SetProtection()
Dim strPassword1 As String
Dim strPassword2 As String
'First, check to be sure the workbook isn't protected already.
    If (ActiveWorkbook.ProtectStructure <> True And _
        ActiveWorkbook.ProtectWindows <> True) Then
            strPassword1 = InputBox("Type a password to protect the workbook.")
            strPassword2 = InputBox("Re-type the password.")
'Verify the passwords are the same
        If strPassword1 <> strPassword2 Then
            MsgBox ("The passwords don't match. Please try again.")
        Else
          ActiveWorkbook.Protect Password:=strPassword1, Structure:=True, _
            Windows:=True
         MsgBox ("The password is set.")
        End If
'Back in the part of the routine that checks for protection.
  Else
    MsgBox ("The workbook is already protected.")
  End If
End Sub
```

Inside Out

When Is an Error Not an Error?

It's interesting to note that attempts to protect a workbook that's already protected don't generate an error message: they just fail. An earlier version of the Sub SetProtection procedure just shown checked for errors and, rather than stopping when the procedure was run against a protected workbook, the routine blithely continued to the end without notifying the user that anything was wrong. The only reliable way to check for protection is to query the *ProtectStructure* and *ProtectWindows* properties.

If you want to remove the protection from a workbook, you can do so through the *Unprotect* method. The *Unprotect* method has a single parameter, the password required to unprotect the workbook.

```
ActiveWorkbook.Unprotect Password:=password
```

The following procedure lets the user attempt to unprotect a workbook:

```
Sub UnprotectThisWkbk()
Dim strPassword As String
    If (ActiveWorkbook.ProtectStructure = True Or _
        ActiveWorkbook.ProtectWindows = True) Then
        strPassword = InputBox ("Type the password to remove protection from _
            this workbook.")
        ActiveWorkbook.Unprotect Password:=strPassword
    Else
        MsgBox ("The workbook is not protected.")
    End If
End Sub
```

The UnprotectThisWkbk procedure checks to see if either the *ProtectStructure* or the *ProtectWindows* property is set to *True* because it's possible to protect one aspect of your workbook and not the other.

Inside Out

Creating Passwords That Will Stand the Test of Time

The best passwords are random strings of characters, but random characters are hard to remember. One good method of creating hard-to-guess passwords is to combine elements of two words with a number in between. For example, you might have a password *prog#2003exce*, which could be read as "programming version 2003 of Excel." In any event, avoid dictionary words in English or any other language, as they can be found easily by password-guessing programs available on the Internet. The Excel encryption algorithm is strong enough to force a cracker to spend around 30 days on average to find the key that unlocks a workbook, but sensitive financial data has a significantly longer shelf life than a month, so if your data is truly sensitive and you want to guard against theft or accidental disclosure, you should use a stronger commercial encryption program.

Workbook Methods

Workbooks are the basic document in Excel, so it's not surprising that there are a lot of methods you can invoke to take action in your workbooks. You can add a workbook to your list of favorite files and URLs, activate a workbook so you can work with it without naming the workbook in every command, or preview a workbook before you print it.

Activate Method

When you first start writing macros, it's likely that you'll work within a single workbook most of the time. The simpler macros you create for tasks such as manipulating the values in a worksheet or backing up a workbook by saving a copy of the file using the *SaveCopyAs* method all use properties and methods within the active workbook. When you want to start working on several workbooks from within the same macro, however, you need to let the VBA engine know that you're changing gears. To do so, you use the *Workbook* object's *Activate* method. As an example, the following code snippet would make the workbook named *Q42003Sales.xls* the active workbook:

```
Workbooks ("Q42003Sales.xls").Activate
```

Caution   It's important to remember that the *ThisWorkbook* property and the *ActiveWorkbook* property might refer to different workbooks. *ThisWorkbook* always refers to the workbook that contains the module with the code you're executing, but the file referred to by the *ActiveWorkbook* property can be changed.

Once you change the active workbook, every method you call using the *ActiveWorkbook* property will affect the active workbook. For example, if you are working with five workbooks but have just made changes to two of them, you could activate the workbooks in turn, save them, and return to the original workbook, as in the following procedure:

```
Sub SaveAfterChange()
    Workbooks("Q4SalesSummary.xls").Activate
    ActiveWorkbook.Save
    Workbooks("2004SalesSummary.xls").Activate
    ActiveWorkbook.Save
    Workbooks("Q42004Sales.xls").Activate
End Sub
```

AddToFavorites Method

Earlier in this chapter you saw how setting the *AddToMru* property caused the name of a saved file to be added to the recently used file list at the bottom of the File menu. You can also add a file to the list of Favorites that shows up in Internet Explorer, My Computer (as shown in Figure 7-4), or on the Web toolbar in Excel.

Chapter 7

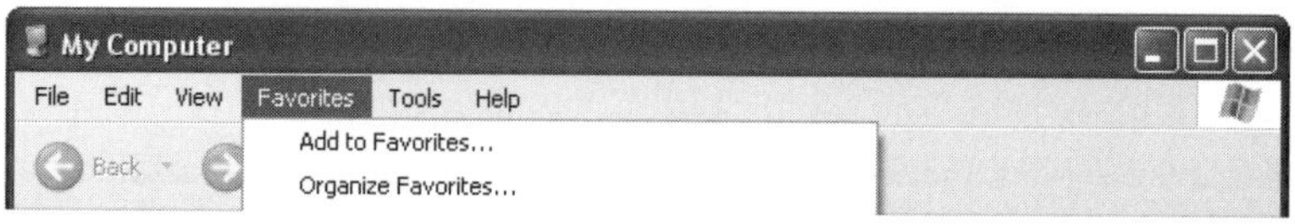

Figure 7-4. The Favorites list contains links to files and hyperlinks you want to remember and access quickly.

Tip Make Your Favorites Easy to Find

Of course, you can add the Favorites toolbar button to any toolbar by clicking Tools, Customize, Commands to display the Commands page of the Customize dialog box. Then, in the Categories pane, click Web and drag Favorites from the Commands pane to the toolbar where you want the Favorites list to reside.

You invoke the *AddToFavorites* method to add a workbook to the Favorites list using any method attached to an object that references a workbook object, as in the following two code fragments:

```
ActiveWorkbook.AddToFavorites
ThisWorkbook.AddToFavorites
```

FollowHyperlink Method

One useful way to create help and informational files for the Excel applications you create is to save them as Web pages, which lets you set up a series of hyperlinks users can click to get help on using a form or other object. The following code listing presents the basic syntax of the FollowHyperlink method, with Table 7-4 fleshing out the details of the most-used parameter.

```
expression.FollowHyperlink(Address, SubAddress, NewWindow, ExtraInfo, Method,
HeaderInfo)
```

Table 7-4. The Parameters of the *FollowHyperlink* Method

Parameter	Type	Description
Expression	Required	An expression that returns a *Workbook* object.
Address	Required String	The address of the target document.
SubAddress	Optional Variant	The location within the target document. The default value is the empty string.
NewWindow	Optional Variant	*True* to display the target application in a new window. The default value is *False*.

You won't need to set most of these parameters when you use the *FollowHyperlink* method, but the *NewWindow* parameter does come in handy when you want to be sure that the document you open appears in a separate window and doesn't overwrite any existing information. The parameters that are listed in the code but not in the table are only used if you need to call the Web page using specific Hypertext Transfer Protocol (HTTP) instructions. You'll need to check with your network administrator for the proper settings.

The following example displays the Web page at *http://example.microsoft.com* in a new window:

```
ActiveWorkbook.FollowHyperlink Address:="http:
//example.microsoft.com", _ NewWindow:=True
```

> For more information on using hyperlinks and the Web, see Chapter 25, "Excel and the Web."

Printing and Previewing Workbooks

Printing workbooks is one of the most valuable tasks you can perform because it lets you communicate your data to other individuals in a fixed form that isn't dependent on a computer. The venerable device from which you read these words (a book) is one implementation of that concept. When you want to give your colleagues the ability to print a copy of a workbook, you use the *PrintOut* method.

```
expression.PrintOut(From, To, Copies, Preview, ActivePrinter, PrintToFile,
Collate, PrToFileName)
```

> **Note** The *PrintOut* method is also available for sheets, charts, objects, and cell ranges.

The parameters of the *PrintOut* method correspond to most of the controls in the Print dialog box, shown in Figure 7-5. The only exceptions are the Properties button, which displays the control program for the active printer, and the Find Printer button, which uses the Directory Service (if available) to display the available printers on the network, but neither of those facilities are vital to printing a workbook on a known network configuration.

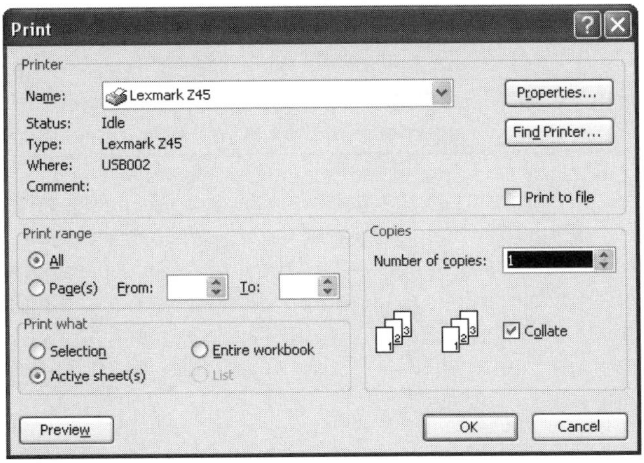

Figure 7-5. The *PrintOut* method includes all of the important controls from the Print dialog box.

> **Note** You should have an error-handling routine in place to inform the user if the workbook fails to print. If possible, you should also write a routine to print the workbook on another printer and, in any case, inform the user on which printer the procedure printed the workbook.

Table 7-5 lists and describes the parameters available for use with the *PrintOut* method. The settings and descriptions are straightforward, with one exception. When you set the *Preview* parameter to *True*, Excel displays the workbook in Print Preview mode, within which the user must click the Print button to begin printing.

Table 7-5. The Parameters of the *PrintOut* Method

Parameter	Type	Description
Expression	Required	An expression that refers to a workbook, a worksheet, a chart, an object, or a cell range.
From	Optional Variant	The number of the page at which to start printing. If this argument is omitted, printing starts at the beginning.
To	Optional Variant	The number of the last page to print. If this argument is omitted, printing ends with the last page.
Copies	Optional Variant	The number of copies to print. If this argument is omitted, one copy is printed.
Preview	Optional Variant	*True* to have Excel invoke print preview before printing the object. *False* (or omitted) to print the object immediately.
ActivePrinter	Optional Variant	Sets the name of the active printer.
PrintToFile	Optional Variant	*True* to print to a file. If *PrToFileName* isn't specified, Excel prompts the user to enter the name of the output file.
Collate	Optional Variant	*True* to collate multiple copies.
PrToFileName	Optional Variant	If *PrintToFile* is set to *True*, this argument specifies the name of the file you want to print to.

If you want to take a user directly to Print Preview, you can do so using the *PrintPreview* method. The *PrintPreview* method, which also applies to sheets, charts, objects, and cell ranges, has a single parameter: *EnableChanges*. When the *EnableChanges* parameter is set to *True* (the default), the user is able to change the workbook's page setup and margin settings before printing. When *EnableChanges* is set to *False*, the Page Setup and Margins buttons are disabled, but the user can still choose whether to print (by clicking the Print button) or not (by clicking the Close button).

The *Sheets* and *Worksheets* Collections

When most users think of a "sheet" in a workbook, they think of a worksheet, with rows, columns, cells, data, and formulas. However, there are several types of sheets you can have in a workbook. There is the worksheet, of course, but there is also a *chart sheet*. It's a bit confusing that a worksheet can contain a chart, but when you go through the Chart Wizard, you get the option to put the chart on a separate chart sheet. The other two types of sheets are meant to handle Excel 4 macros; there is one sheet for U.S. macros and another for international macros.

Properties

The *Sheets* and *Worksheets* collections have a number of properties in common, but there are a few things you have to watch out for when you work with every sheet in a workbook. Those issues are most pronounced with regard to the *Count* property, which is the first property you'll encounter in this section.

Count Property

The *Count* property of the *Worksheets* collection looks through the named workbook and counts the number of worksheets in the workbook, while the *Count* property of the *Sheets* collection reflects the combined number of chart sheets and worksheets in your workbook. You can use the *Count* property of the *Sheets* and *Worksheets* collections to check your workbooks' structure for accuracy before you pass the workbook to another procedure for additional processing.

```
Sub CheckWorkbooks()
    Do While Worksheets.Count < 12
        ThisWorkbook.Sheets.Add
    Loop
End Sub
```

You'll find the remainder of this procedure below in the discussion of the *Workbook* object's *Add* method.

Name Property

Part of a sheet's public face is its name, which is how the sheet is identified on the tab bar and one way you can identify the sheet in your VBA code. If you want to change the name of a worksheet, you can do that by setting the *Name* property. For example, if you copy the weekly sales totals to a worksheet at the end of a workbook, you can change the name of that worksheet to *Summary* using this procedure:

```
Sub ChangeName()
    Dim strWkshtName As String
    strWkshtName = "Summary"
    Sheets(Sheets.Count).Name = strWkshtName
End Sub
```

Visible **Property**

The other frequently used property in the *Worksheets* and *Sheets* collections is the *Visible* property, which reflects whether a particular sheet is displayed on the sheet tab within a workbook. There are three possible values for the *Visible* property: the *xlSheetVisible*, *xlSheetHidden*, and *xlSheetVeryHidden* Excel constants. When the *Visible* property is set to *xlSheetVisible*, the sheet appears on the tab bar and can be edited directly by the user. When the *Visible* property is set to *xlSheetHidden*, the sheet isn't represented on the tab bar but the user can display it by clicking Format, Sheet, Unhide and then clicking the name of the sheet in the Unhide dialog box.

Setting the *Visible* property to *xlSheetVeryHidden* means that the hidden sheet doesn't appear in the Unhide dialog box and can only be made accessible by using VBA code to change the *Visible* property to either *xlSheetHidden* or *xlSheetVisible*.

Methods

The *Sheets* collection is home to a wide variety of methods you can use to add, delete, move, copy, and set the sheet's page setup options (margins, headers, footers, and so on).

Add **Method**

Whenever you want to bring data in from an outside file, you should consider storing the imported data in a new worksheet. To create a new worksheet in an existing workbook, you use the *Add* method, which has the following syntax:

```
Sheets.Add(Before, After, Count, Type)
```

The *Before* and *After* parameters are mutually exclusive—which one you use depends on where you want to place the new worksheet in the workbook. The *Before* and *After* parameters can take an index value that reflects the position of the sheet in the workbook, a sheet name, or the active sheet (using the *ActiveSheet* property as the value for the parameter).

For example, if you wanted to place the added worksheet at the front of the workbook, you would set the *Before* parameter using any of the following statements:

```
ThisWorkbook.Sheets.Add Before:=Worksheets(1)
ThisWorkbook.Sheets.Add Before:=Sheet1
ThisWorkbook.Sheets.Add Before:=ActiveSheet
```

The last statement does assume that Sheet1 is the active sheet.

> **Note** Unlike normal arrays, which start with an index value of 0 by default, the *Sheets* and *Worksheets* collections begin with an index value of 1. Go figure.

If you want to add more than one worksheet to a workbook, the Visual Basic Editor help system indicates you can set the *Count* parameter to reflect the number of sheets you want to add. For example, if you wanted to add three sheets after a sheet named *March*, you would use the following command:

```
ThisWorkbook.Sheets.Add After:=March, Count:=3
```

The last parameter you can use with the *Add* method is the *Type* parameter, which determines the type of sheet that's added to the workbook. You can use the following four constants:

- *xlWorksheet*, which adds a worksheet (the default)
- *xlChart*, which adds a chart
- *xlExcel4MacroSheet*, which adds an Excel 4 macro sheet
- *xlExcel4IntMacroSheet*, which adds an international Excel 4 macro sheet

The *xlExcel4MacroSheet* and *xlExcel4IntMacroSheet* constants are included to ensure Excel 2003 is backward compatible with Excel 4.

You might have noticed that there's no direct way to add a sheet to the end of a workbook; however, you can use the *Count* property of the *Sheets* or (if there are no other types of sheets in your workbook) *Worksheets* collection to determine how many sheets are in the workbook and add the worksheet after it. The following code shows one way to do just that:

```
ThisWorkbook.Sheets.Add After:=Sheets(Sheets.Count)
```

> **Tip** **Start with the Right Number of Sheets**
> If you know how many total worksheets you will need in a given workbook, you should probably create the workbook with the required number of worksheets rather than adding them later. You should create the workbook with the proper number of worksheets so that you avoid any problems accessing the workbook, whether the difficulties are from another user having the workbook open or a network problem if you're trying to change a workbook on another computer.

Delete **Method**

The *Delete* method is complementary to the *Add* method; rather than putting additional sheets in your workbook, you can delete any sheet from a workbook. When you use the *Delete* method from the *Sheets* collection, you can delete any sheet in the workbook, but if you use the *Delete* method from the *Worksheets* collection, you'll be assured of not deleting a chart sheet by accident (and the same is true if you try to delete a worksheet using the *Charts* collection's *Delete* method).

The syntax for deleting a sheet follows the familiar pattern of naming the collection from which you want to delete the sheet, naming the sheet using either the sheet's name or its position in the collection, and then invoking the *Delete* method. As an example, any of the following lines of code would delete the worksheet named *Summary*, provided it was the fourth sheet of a workbook:

```
Worksheets("Summary").Delete
Sheets("Summary").Delete
Worksheets(4).Delete
Sheets(4).Delete
```

You could also delete the active sheet using the *ActiveSheet* property, as in this statement:

```
ActiveSheet.Delete
```

One thing that's important to notice, however, is that the last of the four lines of code listed in the preceding example wouldn't delete the correct sheet if there were a chart sheet anywhere among the first four sheets of the workbook. As an illustration, consider a workbook created for The Garden Company with five sheets, the fourth of which is a chart sheet.

In this workbook, the fourth member of the *Worksheets* collection is the *Summary* worksheet, but the fourth member of the *Sheets* collection is the *Q1Sales* chart sheet.

> **Tip** Delete by Name, Not Position
>
> When possible, you should always refer to sheets by name to ensure you delete the correct ones. The exception to that guideline would be when you're deleting all but one sheet in a workbook and that sheet is in a known position or it has a known name (for example, you moved it to the front or the back of the workbook or gave it a specific name that's hard-coded into your procedure). If that's the case, you can use a *For Each...Next* loop to delete all but the first or last sheet, or to skip over a sheet with a specific name. Be sure to test your code on dummy workbooks before putting it to work on real data, though.

When you invoke the *Delete* method, Excel displays an alert box asking if you're sure you want to delete the worksheet. Of course, the last thing you want to see when you're using an automated procedure is an alert box that requires human intervention for the procedure to continue. You can use the *Application* object's *DisplayAlerts* property to turn off alert boxes, however, so you can keep the expected alert box from appearing during a known operation. It's usually a good idea to turn alerts back on, though, so that if something unexpected happens, your procedure won't proceed without you or a colleague ensuring no harm will be done.

```
Sub DeleteSheet()
    Application.DisplayAlerts = False
    Sheets(1).Delete
    Application.DisplayAlerts = True
End Sub
```

Move and *Copy* Methods

Another handy skill when manipulating workbooks with VBA code is to change the position of sheets in a workbook, or to move or copy a sheet to a new workbook. One example of when moving sheets within a workbook would be handy is when you are creating a workbook that will be used in an annual report or another type of presentation. Because those types of reports often have strict formatting guidelines, you might end up moving sheets around to fit the format. You also might need to move or copy a sheet from a workbook into a summary workbook. For example, if a project manager summarized labor and equipment expenditures on a sheet with a known name, you could copy that sheet into a target workbook and use that sheet, not the original, for any processing you needed to do.

Whether you move or copy a sheet depends on whether or not you want to keep the original sheet. Copying a sheet is a nondestructive operation in that the sheet being copied isn't deleted, but moving a sheet does cause the sheet to be deleted from its original location.

The *Move* and *Copy* methods let you set the target position of your moved worksheet using either the *Before* or the *After* parameter. (If for some reason you try to use both, you'll get an "expected end of line" error.) For example, the following procedure counts the number of sheets in the existing workbook and moves the sheet named *Summary* to the end of the workbook:

```
Sub MoveToEnd()
    Sheets("Summary").Move After:=Sheets(Sheets.Count)
End Sub
```

If you want to move or copy more than one sheet in a workbook, you can specify an array in the *Sheets* collection. For example, the following procedure moves the sheets named *Summary* and *PivotTable* to the beginning of the workbook:

```
Sheets(Array("Summary", "PivotTable")).Move Before:=Sheets(1)
```

If you move or copy a sheet without specifying a *Before* or *After* parameter, Excel will create a new workbook where the copied sheet is the only sheet in the workbook, regardless of the default number of worksheets included in new workbooks.

PageSetup Object

Regardless of whether you work in Excel through the user interface or using VBA code, the one thing you need to remember is that the data in your workbooks is the most important element of your workbook. Once you're sure the data is entered and summarized correctly, you can focus on how it looks. You'll learn a lot more about formatting data and worksheets in Chapter 10, "Formatting Excel Objects," but it makes sense to discuss how to change the layout of your worksheets on the page by using the *PageSetup* property of the *Worksheet* object.

The *PageSetup* property of the *Worksheet* object actually returns a *PageSetup* object, which in turn contains a series of properties reflecting the worksheet's positioning, orientation, margins, and level of detail when viewed. Table 7-6 lists a number of the more important properties of the *PageSetup* object, but you can find a complete listing in the Visual Basic Editor help system.

Table 7-6. Selected Properties of the *PageSetup* Object

Property	Description
BlackAndWhite	When set to *True*, forces a sheet to be printed in black and white.
BottomMargin	Determines the distance, in points, between the top of the footer and the bottom of the worksheet.
CenterHorizontally	When set to *True*, centers the worksheet horizontally on the printed page.
CenterVertically	When set to *True*, centers the worksheet vertically on the printed page.
FirstPageNumber	Sets the page number assigned to the first printed page.
FitToPagesTall	Sets the number of vertical pages on which the worksheet will be printed. Useful for shrinking a too-large worksheet onto a specific number of pages.
FitToPagesWide	Sets the number of horizontal pages on which the worksheet will be printed. Useful for shrinking a too-large worksheet onto a specific number of pages.
FooterMargin	Determines the distance, in points, between the top of the footer and the bottom of the printed page.
HeaderMargin	Determines the distance, in points, between the bottom of the header and the top of the printed page.
LeftMargin	Determines the amount of white space to remain between the edge of the page and the leftmost element of the worksheet.
Orientation	Determines whether a worksheet is in landscape mode (*xlLandscape*) or portrait mode (*xlPortrait*).
RightMargin	Determines the amount of white space to remain between the edge of the page and the rightmost element of the worksheet.
TopMargin	Determines the amount of white space to remain between the bottom of the header and the topmost element of the worksheet.
Zoom	Determines the magnification level of the worksheet view between 10 percent and 400 percent.

It should be noted that the values for the margin settings are all expressed in terms of points (there being 72 points per inch). You probably don't want to keep that number in your head and perform conversions all the time, so you will want to use the *Application.InchesToPoints* method to make the conversion for you. All you need to do is put the number of inches in the parentheses of the method and assign that value to the appropriate property. For example, you could set a top margin of three-quarters of an inch using the following code:

```
ActiveSheet.PageSetup.TopMargin = Application.InchesToPoints(0.75)
```

Another important aspect of changing how a worksheet is printed is in the proper placement of page breaks. A page break represents the last row or column that will be printed on a page; in most cases, you can let Excel set the page breaks automatically, moving a row or column to the next page only when it would encroach on a margin. If you'd rather specify where page breaks should occur, you can do so by specifying the column to the right of where you want the page break, or the row below where you want the page break.

> **Note** Yes, referencing rows and columns is more like the topics you'll find in Chapter 8, "Ranges and Cells," but it also makes sense to cover page breaks here with the rest of the printing topics.

The syntax for setting a manual page break requires you to specify the row or column below or to the right of where you want the break to be placed. For example, if you wanted to set a manual page break above row 30 on *Sheet2*, you would use the following line of code:

```
Worksheets("Sheet2").Rows(30).PageBreak = xlPageBreakManual
```

Setting a manual page break to the left of column D on *Sheet1*, however, would use this code:

```
Worksheets("Sheet1").Columns("D").PageBreak = xlPageBreakManual
```

To delete a page break, you set the *PageBreak* property to either of the Excel constants *xlPageBreakNone* or *xlNone*, as in the following examples:

```
Worksheets("Sheet2").Rows(30).PageBreak = xlPageBreakNone
Worksheets("Sheet1").Columns("D").PageBreak = xlNone
```

You can remove all of the page breaks on a worksheet using the worksheet's *ResetAllPageBreaks* method:

```
Worksheets("Sheet1").ResetAllPageBreaks
```

> **Tip**   **Print to Your Specification**
> Remember that you can force a worksheet to print on a specified number of pages by setting the *FitToPagesTall* and *FitToPagesWide* properties of a worksheet's *PageSetup* object.

Worksheet Methods

Worksheets are the lifeblood of a workbook, and there are a number of methods you can call to get the most out of your worksheets. Some of these methods are similar to those you'll find with the workbooks, but with subtle distinctions that make them unique to the worksheet. In this section, you'll learn about the following methods:

- *Calculate*, which recalculates the results of all formulas in a worksheet
- *Protect*, which lets you require users to enter a password to modify specified elements of a worksheet
- *SaveAs*, which saves a worksheet as a new workbook
- *Select*, which lets you work on more than one worksheet at a time

Calculate Method

The *Worksheet* object's *Calculate* method is used to recalculate all of the formulas in a worksheet, which is handy if those formulas draw on data that might have changed since the last time you opened the workbook containing those formulas. The *Calculate* method's syntax is straightforward; all you need to do is name the worksheet you want to calculate and append the *Calculate* method, as in the following examples:

```
Worksheets(1).Calculate
Worksheets("Summary").Calculate
```

If you want to update the result of every formula in every open workbook, you can add the single method *Calculate* (short for *Application.Calculate*) to your VBA code to have Excel recalculate each of those values.

Normally Excel recalculates your formulas whenever you make a change, so you might want to change when Excel recalculates your formulas. Choosing when to recalculate the values of formulas in your worksheets is an inexact science; if you always need the more recent results from formulas that could change from moment to moment, it makes sense to recalculate every time your worksheet changes. Another approach would be to place a command button on a worksheet that your users could click to recalculate the formulas whenever they needed up to date values to make a decision. The difficulty with that approach is when you have a large worksheet that draws data from several other sources. If your network is busy, or if you have literally hundreds of formulas that need to be updated, you might want to create a process that updates the formulas once overnight, bearing in mind that you would want to update each of the source worksheets first to avoid any potential inconsistencies caused by updating the summary worksheet before updating the source worksheets.

You can change when Excel recalculates a worksheet by setting the *Application* object's *Calculate* property (yes, it has the same name) to one of the *XlCalculate* constants. Those constants are:

- *xlCalculationAutomatic,* the default value, which causes Excel to recalculate your formulas every time a change is made.

- *xlCalculationManual,* which requires a user to press Shift+F9 to recalculate the formulas in the active worksheet.

- *xlCalculationSemiautomatic,* which recalculates all formulas in a worksheet, except for those formulas in a table.

If you only want to calculate formulas just before you save a workbook, you can set recalculation to manual and then set the *Application* object's *CalculateBeforeSave* property to *True,* as in the following code:

```
Application.Calculation = xlCalculationManual
Application.CalculateBeforeSave = True
```

Protect Method

The first line of defense against changes to a worksheet starts with requiring users to enter a password before they are allowed to open the workbook. The *Workbook* object's *Protect* method is somewhat limited, allowing you to protect against unauthorized access to the workbook, to protect against changes to the workbook's structure, or to protect against changes to the size and placement of the workbook's windows. There's quite a bit more going on at the worksheet level, however, and the *Sheet* and *Worksheet* objects' *Protect* methods have correspondingly more options available.

```
expression.Protect(Password, DrawingObjects, Contents, Scenarios,
UserInterfaceOnly, AllowFormattingCells, AllowFormattingColumns,
AllowFormattingRows, AllowInsertingColumns, AllowInsertingRows,
AllowInsertingHyperlinks, AllowDeletingColumns, AllowDeletingRows,
AllowSorting, AllowFiltering, AllowUsingPivotTables)
```

Table 7-7 provides the default values for each of these parameters and describes what is or is not allowed when the options are set to *True* or *False.*

Table 7-7. Parameters of the *Worksheet.Protect* Method

Parameter	Default	Description
Expression	n/a	A required expression that returns a *Worksheet* object.
Password	n/a	A string that specifies a case-sensitive password for the worksheet or workbook. If this argument is omitted, you can unprotect the worksheet or workbook without using a password.
DrawingObjects	False	When set to *True,* this parameter protects drawing objects from changes.

continued

Table 7-7. Parameters of the *Worksheet.Protect* Method *(continued)*

Parameter	Default	Description
Contents	True	When set to *True*, protecting the contents of a worksheet protects any locked cells from changes.
Scenarios	True	When set to *True*, the user cannot make changes to scenarios.
UserInterfaceOnly	False	When set to *True*, the user interface is protected, but the user can edit macros. When left blank or set to *False*, both the user interface and macros are protected.
AllowFormattingCells	False	When set to *True*, users can format any cell on a protected worksheet.
AllowFormattingColumns	False	When set to *True*, users can format any column on a protected worksheet.
AllowFormattingRows	False	When set to *True*, users can format any row on a protected worksheet.
AllowInsertingColumns	False	When set to *True*, users can insert columns into the protected worksheet.
AllowInsertingRows	False	When set to *True*, users can insert rows into the protected worksheet.
AllowInsertingHyperlinks	False	When set to *True*, users can add hyperlinks to a protected worksheet.
AllowDeletingColumns	False	When set to *True*, users can delete columns on the protected worksheet, provided every cell in the column to be deleted is unlocked.
AllowDeletingRows	False	When set to *True*, users can delete rows on the protected worksheet, provided every cell in the row to be deleted is unlocked.
AllowSorting	False	When set to *True*, users can sort the data on the protected worksheet, provided every cell in the sort range is unlocked or unprotected.
AllowFiltering	False	When set to *True*, users can set filters on the protected worksheet and change filter criteria but can't enable or disable an auto filter.
AllowUsingPivotTables	False	When set to *True*, users can use PivotTables on the protected worksheet.

Another way you can extend a worksheet's protection is to limit which cells the user can select by assigning a value to the *EnableSelection* property. After you protect a worksheet, you can set the *EnableSelection* property to any of the following Excel constants:

- *xlNoSelection*, which prevents the user from selecting any cells on the sheet
- *xlUnlockedCells*, which allows the user to select only those cells whose *Locked* property is set to *False*
- *xlNoRestrictions*, the default value, which allows the user to select any value

The following code snippet prevents users from selecting any cells on the protected January worksheet:

```
Worksheets("January").EnableSelection = xlNoSelection
```

Important Setting the *EnableSelection* property has an effect only if the worksheet is protected.

As with a workbook, you can allow a user to unprotect a worksheet by providing the password. The line of code you use is simply this:

```
ActiveWorksheet. Unprotect
```

Excel displays an input box to accept the password for you, so you don't even have to write any additional code to handle the entry.

SaveAs Method

Just as you can save a workbook under a different name or to a different location, you can save an individual worksheet as a separate file using the *Worksheet* method's *SaveAs* method.

```
expression.SaveAs(FileName, FileFormat, Password, WriteResPassword,
ReadOnlyRecommended, CreateBackup, AddToMru, TextCodepage, TextVisualLayout,
Local)
```

The *SaveAs* method of the *Worksheet* object is very similar to the same method of the *Workbook* object, so you can refer to Table 7-3 for details on most of the parameters of the *Worksheet* object's *SaveAs* method.

Select Method

At first glance the *Select* method seems to be the same as the *Activate* method. The difference between the two methods is that the *Activate* method only works on one worksheet at a time, whereas the *Select* method lets you operate on more than one worksheet at a time. As an example using the user interface, you can move two worksheets at a time by clicking the sheet tab of the first worksheet, shift-clicking the second sheet tab, and dragging the sheets as a unit to their new position in the workbook.

> **Note** In the case just mentioned, the first worksheet you click would be considered the active worksheet.

The following code snippet selects the worksheet named *Sheet1*:

```
Worksheets("Sheet1").Select
```

If you'd like to select more than one worksheet at a time, you can use an array as the argument for the *Select* method, as in the following example:

```
Worksheets (Array ("Sheet1", "Sheet2")).Select
```

In this chapter, you've encountered the most important properties and methods you will use to manipulate Excel workbooks and worksheets. Whether you want to save your workbooks programmatically, change when your formulas are recalculated, or protect your workbooks and worksheets by requiring users to know the password to gain access, you can make your workbooks and worksheets behave as you want them to behave. In Chapter 8, you'll learn how to perform similar tasks with ranges and cells.

Ranges and Cells

Basic Range Manipulations 161

Referring to Ranges 166

Manipulating Groups of Cells 172

Using Named Ranges. 177

Getting Data Entry Right
the First Time. 187

Before any work can be done with the information inside a workbook, you need to be able to access it. You've already looked at accessing the larger elements of the Excel Object Model, namely the Microsoft Excel application itself and workbooks and worksheets. In this chapter, you will learn how to work with cells and ranges of cells.

Basic Range Manipulations

A *cell* is the basic working unit inside an Excel worksheet, but within the Excel Object Model, a *Range* object is the basic working unit. You use a *Range* object to work with either groups of cells or an individual cell.

Finding the Active Range

Although there is no *ActiveRange* object to use, there are other ways of working with the currently selected range. The most common method is to use the *Selection* object. The *Selection* object will return whatever the current selected object is, whether it is a range of cells or a chart. Most often it will refer to a cell or range of cells. Manipulating the *Selection* object lets you control the actions within a cell as if you were actually performing them step by step using the keyboard or mouse. For example, you could use the following code to display the values in the selected cells in bold type:

```
Selection.Font.Bold = True
```

> **Note** Remember that *active* is not synonymous with *selected*. You can select every cell in a worksheet by pressing Ctrl+A, but only one cell (usually A1 if you press Ctrl+A) is the active cell.

Selecting a Range

The *Select* method of a *Range* object provides various ways to select a range of cells. Many of the procedures are similar to selecting cells using the keyboard, making it very easy to emulate the way you would work if you were actually typing in the keystrokes needed to select the cells.

The following example uses the *CurrentRegion* property of the *ActiveCell* object to select the range of cells that are currently being used within the worksheet. The range is copied to the clipboard, pasted onto a new worksheet, and then necessary formatting is applied and the value contents are erased, leaving blank cells for a new year's worth of information in the SalesByCategory.xls workbook.

```
Sub InsertNewSheet()

    Range("C1").Activate
    ActiveCell.CurrentRegion.Select
    Selection.Copy
    Sheets.Add After:=Sheets(Sheets.Count)
    Sheets(Sheets.Count).Name = "New Year"
    Sheets("New Year").Select
    Range("C1").Activate
    ActiveSheet.Paste
    Columns("C:H").EntireColumn.AutoFit
    Range("D2:G13").Select
    Selection.ClearContents

End Sub
```

Besides using the *CurrentRegion* property of the *ActiveCell*, you can also use the *End* method to extend a range beyond the *ActiveCell*. When used with one of the values listed in Table 8-1, Excel will extend a range using the same rules as when you use the End key combined with one of the arrow keys to move to the end of a row or column.

The following example searches all of the time entries for one month in the Y2001ByMonth.xls workbook for the highest entry. Once the highest entry is found, Excel extends the range upwards and downwards to include all entries for that time period and changes the fill color of the cells to blue.

```
Sub HighLightTimeFrame()
Dim MyCell As Range, strAddress As String
Dim sngMaximum As Single

    sngMaximum = 0
    For Each MyCell In Range("D6:O36").Cells
        If MyCell > sngMaximum Then
            sngMaximum = MyCell
            strAddress = MyCell.Address
        End If
    Next MyCell

    Range(strAddress).Activate
    Range(ActiveCell.End(xlUp), ActiveCell.End(xlDown)).Select
    Selection.Cells.Interior.ColorIndex = 41
End Sub
```

Table 8-1 lists the methods available to the *Range* object and describes how the method affects which cells are selected.

Table 8-1. Range Selection Methods

Method	Action Performed
.End(xlDown)	Extends range downward.
.End(xlUp)	Extends range upward.
.End(xlToRight)	Extends range to the right.
.End(xlToLeft)	Extends range to the left.
.SpecialCells(xlCellTypeAllFormatConditions)	Extends range to include cells with any formatting changes applied. Excel begins searching from cell A1, not from the ActiveCell.
.SpecialCells(xlCellTypeAllValidation)	Extends range to first cell containing validation rules.
.SpecialCells(xlCellTypeBlanks)	Extends range to first blank cell.
.SpecialCells(xlCellTypeComments)	Extends range to first cell containing a comment.
.SpecialCells(xlCellTypeConstants)	Extends range to first cell containing a constant.
.SpecialCells(xlCellTypeFormulas)	Extends range to first cell containing a formula.
.SpecialCells(xlCellTypeLastCell)	Extends range to the left and downward to the cell last used.
.SpecialCells(xlCellTypeSameFormatConditions)	Extends range to first cell containing the same formatting conditions.
.SpecialCells(xlCellTypeSameValidtion)	Extends range to first cell containing the same validation rules.
.SpecialCells(xlCellTypeVisible)	Extends range to all visible cells.
.EntireColumn	Extends range to entire column.
.EntireRow	Extends range to entire row.

Inside Out

How Excel Extends a Range

When searching for a cell that matches one of the special cell types listed in Table 8-1, Excel begins searching at the active cell. From there, it searches to the right and downward, performing a *greedy search*, selecting as many cells as needed to reach the farthest cell that meets the criteria. If no cells are found, Excel changes the search direction and switches to a *lazy search*, returning the first cell that matches.

Excel will continue searching to the right, looking upward instead of downward for a match. If no matching cells are found, Excel will then search to the left. Again, Excel searches downward first and then upward.

To figure out which cells Excel will select, remember the following rules:

- Right first, left second.
- Down first, up second.
- Right-down is a greedy search; all others are lazy searches.

Referring to Ranges

The versatility of ranges is manifested in the number of ways you can refer to a range. Whether directly by cell address, as an offset from another cell, by name, or by using the current selection, referring to a range has many useful options. The *Range* property allows several methods of referring to a range. The syntax for the *Range* property is

```
expression.Range(Cell1, Cell2)
```

expression is a required element that should return either an *Application*, a *Range*, or a *Worksheet* object. If *expression* is omitted, *ActiveSheet* is implied.

Cell1 is a required variant that supplies the A1-reference to a cell or range of cells. If you use the *Cell1* parameter to refer to a range of cells, the variant can include the range operator (a colon), the intersection operator (a space) or the union operator (a comma). Dollar signs ($) can be included, but they are ignored. A locally defined name can also be supplied.

Cell2 is an optional variant that, when paired with *Cell1*, specifies the cell in the lower-right corner of the range.

As the property description implies, there are many ways you can specify which cells to include. You can use absolute references by using the *ActiveSheet* as the base object (*expression*), or you can use relative references by using the *ActiveCell* or other range object as the base object. You can specify a single cell, a group of continuous cells, a group of intermittent cells, or entire rows or columns.

Referencing Ranges on the Active Worksheet

Referring to a range on the active worksheet is the most common method, and the majority of range references in VBA are geared toward using the active worksheet. You can refer to a range on the *ActiveSheet* by simply using the *Range* property. For example, to refer to cell D6 on the active worksheet, you could use the following code: `Range("D6").Select`.

⚙ Inside Out

Staying Away from Select

Although the tendency is to always select a range first, it's not necessary to do so and it will put a performance hit on your procedure. (See "Copying Data Between Ranges and Arrays" later in this chapter for more information.) If you have to use only a single formatting command, specify the range and the formatting all in one line, rather than selecting the range first and then doing the formatting.

As an example, to highlight the entire list of 6:00 P.M. entries in the Y2001ByMonth.xls workbook and make the font color blue, you would use the following command:

```
Range("M6:M36").Font.ColorIndex = 41
```

Referencing Ranges on an Inactive Worksheet

The number of worksheets in an Excel workbook is limited only by the amount of available memory. Information can be spread across any number of worksheets, not just the active worksheet. To reference a range on an inactive worksheet, you need to specify the worksheet that contains the range.

Using the *Range* property on an inactive worksheet is no different from using it on the *ActiveSheet*. When the worksheet object is not specified, the active worksheet in implied. Going back to previous example of reference cell D6, on an inactive worksheet it would be referenced using code similar to the following:

```
Worksheets(2).Range("D6").Select.
```

It is possible to reference a range on an inactive worksheet without specifying the worksheet, but only if the range is named. (See "Using Named Ranges" later in this chapter.) By using the statement `Range("Frequency").Select` the named range *Frequency* is selected, regardless of whether it is on the active worksheet or not.

Referencing Cells in a Range

Referencing an individual cell within a range works the same as referencing a cell within the entire workbook. The cell in the top-left corner of the range would be addressed as "A1". The cell three rows down and four columns to the right would be cell "D3". As an example, in the workbook Y2001ByMonth.xls, you could assign the range D6:O36 to a range object. To reference the 9:00 A.M. entry on the first day (cell D6 in the worksheet), you would use cell A1 of the range object. Likewise, the 7:00 P.M. of the sixteenth day (cell N21 in the worksheet) would be cell K16 of the range object.

Referencing Cells Using the *Offset* Property

If the information you need to use is located in a particular location away from a known cell, you can use the *Offset* property to reference the cell. By specifying the number of rows and columns from a set location, you can reference the cell. It's similar to giving driving directions where you tell someone to start at a particular location. The person you're giving directions to needs to get to the starting spot on their own, but once there, they can follow your directions to reach the final destination.

The *Offset* property works by moving the number of rows and columns specified. Positive numbers move down and to the right while negative numbers move up and to the left. A zero maintains the current row or column. The *Calculate_Table* routine inside the Loan Calculation.xls workbook, shown in Figure 8-1, uses the *Offset* property to set the formula for the Present Value and Interest Paid columns.

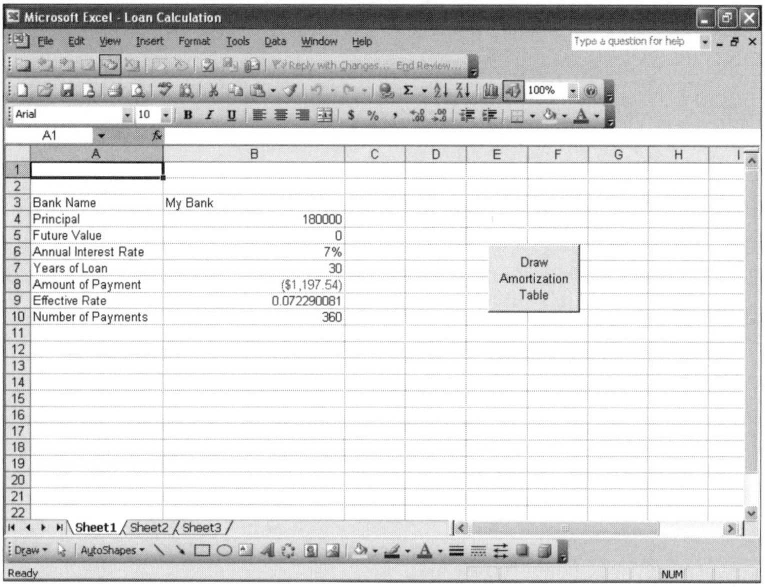

Figure 8-1. This sample worksheet lets you calculate the components of a mortgage loan.

```
Sub Calculate_Table()
Dim counter As Integer, Payments As Integer, Frequency As Integer
Dim Temp As String, intRow As Integer, intColumn As Integer
Dim intOffset As Integer, strR1C1Address As String, strA1Address As String

    ActiveWorkbook.Sheets.Add After:=Worksheets(Worksheets.Count)
    Sheets(Sheets.Count).Select
    ActiveSheet.Name = Range("Name")
    Payments = Range("Payments")
    Frequency = 12

    ' Set headers
    Range("A5") = "Payment"
    Range("B5") = "Principal"
    Range("C5") = "Interest"
    Range("D5") = "Present Value"
    Range("E5") = "Interest Paid"

    ' Loop through number of payments and insert formulas
    ' Use various methods of referencing a range
    For counter = 1 To Payments
        intRow = 5 + counter
        intColumn = 1
```

```
        strR1C1Address = "R" & Format(intRow, "#0") & "C" & _
            Format(intColumn, "#0")
        strA1Address = Application.ConvertFormula(strR1C1Address, _
            xlR1C1, xlA1)
        Range(strA1Address) = "Payment:" + Str$(counter)
        Range(strA1Address).Range("B1") = "=PPMT(APR/" & _
            Str$(Frequency) & "," & Str$(counter) & _
            ",Payments,Principal, Future_Value)"
        Range(strA1Address).Select
        Selection.Range("C1") = "=IPMT(APR/" & Str$(Frequency) _
            & "," & Str$(counter) & ",Payments,Principal," _
            & " Future_Value)"
        Selection.Offset(0, 3) = "=R[-1]C+RC[-2]"
        Selection.Offset(0, 4) = "=RC[-2]+r[-1]c"
    Next counter

    ' Reset "Present Value" and "Interest Paid" formulas for
    ' first payment
    Range("D6").Formula = "=Principal+B6"
    Range("E6").Formula = "=C6"

    ' Autosize columns to necessary width
    Columns("A:E").Select
    Columns.EntireColumn.AutoFit

    ' Set Titles
    Range("A1").Value = ActiveSheet.Name
    Range("A1:E1").Select
    Selection.Merge
    Range("A2").Value = "Amortization Chart"
    Range("A2:E2").Merge
    With Range("A1")
        .HorizontalAlignment = xlCenter
        .Font.Bold = True
    End With
    With Range("A2")
        .HorizontalAlignment = xlCenter
        .Font.Bold = True
    End With

End Sub
```

Building a Version of the Loan Calculation Workbook

The *Calculate_Table* macro relies upon several features in Excel to work, such as named ranges (discussed later in this chapter), form controls, and command buttons. To build the workbook yourself, follow these steps.

1   Open a blank workbook by clicking the New button on the Standard toolbar or selecting Blank workbook from the New Workbook Task Pane.

2   In column A, type the following descriptions, one per line. You can use Figure 8-2 as a guide:

- Bank Name
- Principal
- Future Value
- Annual Interest Rate
- Years of Loan
- Amount of Payment
- Effective Rate
- Number of Payments

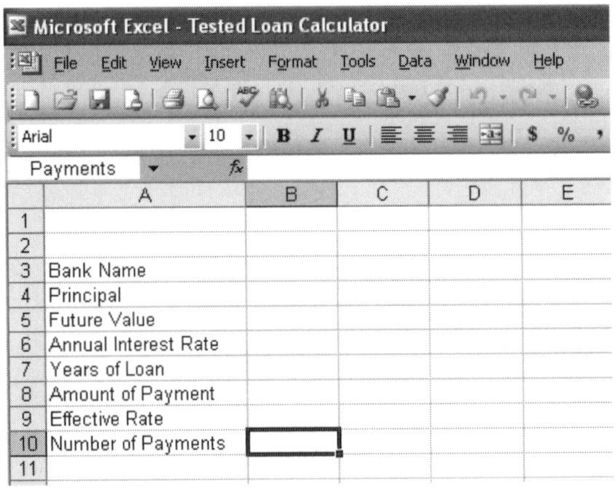

Figure 8-2.   The Loan Calculator requires a number of specific inputs—here are those descriptions.

3   In column B, assign names to the cells alongside the description. Match the cell name in column B to the description in column A: **Name**, **Principal**, **Future_Value**, **APR**, **Years**, **Payment**. Skip the cell for Effective Rate, and name the last cell **Payments**.

4   Select the field cell for Amount of Payment, and type the following formula:
=PMT(APR/12,Payments,Principal, Future_Value)

> **Note**   When you first enter this formula, a #DIV/0 error will appear in the cell because there are no values in the cells used in the formula. Once you enter those values, the error will disappear.

5   Select the field cell for Effective Rate, and type in the following formula:
=EFFECT(APR,12)

> **Note**   When you first enter this formula, a #NUM! error will appear in the cell because there is no value in the Years cell. Once you enter a value in that cell, the error will disappear.

6   Select the field cell for Number of Payments, and type the following formula:
=Years*12

7   After you have typed in the *Calculate_Table* macro, select the Button button on the Forms tool bar and draw a button on the worksheet, as shown in Figure 8-3. The Assign Macro dialog box will appear, allowing you to choose the *Calculate_Table* macro.

8   With the button still selected, select the text in the button and type in the following: **Draw Amortization Table**.

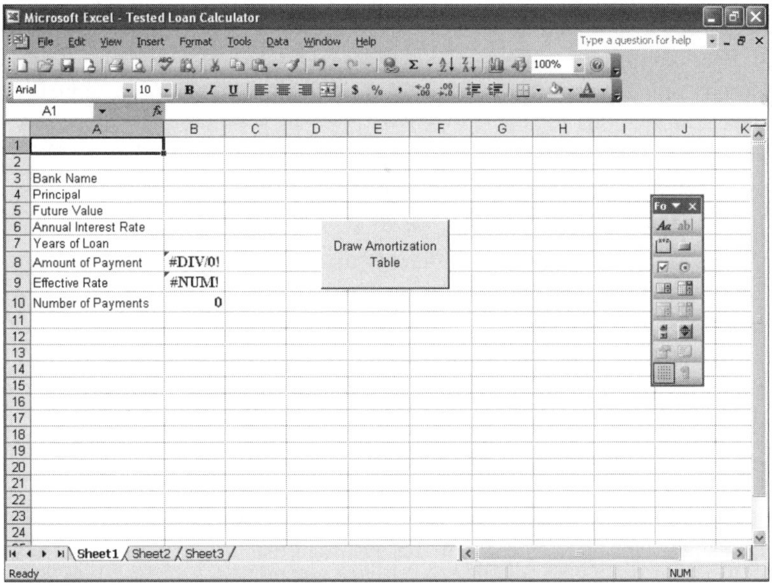

Figure 8-3.   Adding the Button Control to the form.

Once you type information in the fields, you can click the Draw Amortization Table button to have the *Calculate_Table* macro executed. If you want to run the macro again, you need to change the name of your bank, which is used as the name of the new worksheet. If you try to create a worksheet with a duplicate name, the macro will generate an error.

Chapter 8

Defining a Range Using the *Cells* Property

Another method of referencing the same cell would be to specify the cell using the *Cells* method. To do so, you would have to specify the row and column numbers of the cells in opposite corners of the range you want to specify. For a single cell, you have to specify the same cell twice; after all, it's the same cell in opposite corners. For example, to select cell D6, you would use the following code:

```
Range(Cells(4,6), Cells(4,6)).Select
```

Referencing Columns and Rows

Referring to an entire column or row is done using the *Columns* or the *Rows* property. You can select a single column or row or multiple columns or rows. This code snippet from the *Calculate_Table* routine selects columns A through E and resizes them to fit the contents of the cells.

```
Columns("A:E").Select
Columns.EntireColumn.AutoFit
```

Referencing Non-Contiguous Groups of Cells

Not all ranges you need to work with will be contiguous. You can specify non-contiguous cells by separating the ranges with commas. For example, to select all of the sales data for Mondays in January in the Y2001ByMonth.xls workbook, you could use the following code:

```
Range("D6:O6, D13:O13, D20:O20, D27:O27, D34:O34").Select.
```

Manipulating Groups of Cells

One reason for using a range of cells is to manipulate all of the cells within the range together as one group rather than having to work with each cell individually. There are numerous things that can be done to a group of cells collectively, such as resizing them, adding borders, or changing the format of how the contents appear. You can even work with two groups of cells together to generate either the union of the two groups or find where the two groups intersect.

Resizing Cells Programmatically

The default size for a cell has a width of 8.43 points and a height of 12.73 points. These settings usually work just fine if you are working on a simple worksheet that's not going to be shared with anyone else. With a worksheet that is to be shared or that contains a good bit of data, however, you might need to resize some of your cells.

To begin with, it is not possible to resize one particular cell. Any changes in width will affect the entire column, and any changes in height will affect the entire row. Therefore, make any changes done within a macro using either the *Width* property of the *Column* object or the *Height* property of the *Row* object. You can set the *Width* and *Height* properties explicitly, if you have a predetermined size to use. You can also instruct Excel to calculate the proper size by using the *AutoFit* method.

Joining Two Ranges Together

It might not always be desirable to create a range of non-contiguous cells when defining ranges. You might need to keep the ranges separate for tracking purposes. In the Y2001ByMonth.xls workbook, the values are stored by date, but some analysis might need to be done based on the day of the week. Naturally, each individual weekday is separated from its kin by the other days of the week. We can pull all the same weekday ranges together using the *Application* object's *Union* method.

For more information on the *Application* object, see Chapter 6, "The *Application* Object."

The *Union* method takes two or more ranges and combines them into one range. The syntax is

```
expression.Union(Arg1 as Range, Arg2 as Range, …)
```

- *expression*   is an optional *Application* object.
- *Arg1, Arg2, …*   are range objects of which at least two must be specified.

The following procedure calculates the average sales for each day of the week by hour:

```
Sub CalcWeeklyAverages()
Dim intDayOfWeek As Integer, intWeeks As Integer, intHours As Integer
Dim rgeWeek As Range, rgeMonth As Range, rgeDay As Range
Dim sglTotal As Single
Dim strRow As String, intWeek As Integer

    'Loop through each day of the week
    For intDayOfWeek = 1 To 7

        'Find first day of month
        Set rgeDay = Range("D6", Range("D6").End(xlDown))
        Set rgeMonth = Nothing
        intWeeks = 0

        'Loop through each week
        For intWeek = intDayOfWeek To _
            rgeDay.Cells(rgeDay.Cells.count, -1) Step 7

            'Calculate row number
            strRow = Format(intWeek + 5, "#0")
            Set rgeWeek = Range("D" & strRow & ":O" & strRow)
            If intWeek = intDayOfWeek Then 'Adjust for first week
                Set rgeMonth = rgeWeek
            Else
                Set rgeMonth = Union(rgeMonth, rgeWeek)
            End If

            'Count number of times weekday occurs
            intWeeks = intWeeks + 1
        Next intWeek
```

```
'Calculate row number
strRow = Format(intDayOfWeek + 41, "00")

'Set title column
With Range("C" & strRow)
    .Formula = rgeDay(intDayOfWeek, 0)
    .Interior.ColorIndex = 36
    .Font.Italic = True
End With

'Loop through each time period
For intHours = 1 To 12
    sglTotal = 0
    For intWeek = 1 To intWeeks
        sglTotal = sglTotal + rgeMonth(intWeek, intHours)
    Next intWeek

    'Set average and format
    With Range(Chr$(Asc("C") + intHours) & strRow)
        .Formula = sglTotal / intWeeks
        .NumberFormat = "_($* #,##0.00_);_($* (#,##0.00)"
    End With
Next intHours

'Add average total for weekday
With rgeMonth(1, 1).Offset(36, 13)
    .Formula = "=Sum(R[0]C[-13]:R[0]C[-2])"
    .NumberFormat = "_($* #,##0.00_);_($* (#,##0.00)"
End With
Next intDayOfWeek

End Sub
```

Inside Out

Measuring the Dimensions of a Cell

Change the dimensions of a cell, either by adjusting the width or the height, by using the Format, Column, Width or the Format, Row, Height commands. Both commands display a dialog box that shows the current value and lets you enter a new value. What neither box explains is the unit of measurement being used to determine the size.

For row height, it's fairly simple. By default all rows are set to *AutoFit*. This setting means the row will increase in size to match either the largest-size font that's entered on that row or all the lines of a multi-line entry. Row height is measured in points (1 point = 1/72 inches), the same as font size. The *AutoFit* option will add a couple of points as padding to help ensure the entire text is visible.

Because there is no standard method of measuring width, Microsoft had to devise its own method. The width of a cell within Excel is done by calculating the average number of digits 0 through 9 that will fit in the cell using the standard font (usually 10 point Arial). Unfortunately, it is not an exact measurement. The number of digits that are visible will vary depending upon the Zoom level of the worksheet. Figure 8-4 shows a worksheet with the

Zoom level set at 100%. Just about nine complete digits are visible, slightly more than the "8.43" default column width. Adjusting the Zoom level to 200%, as displayed in Figure 8-5, barely shows any features of the ninth digit, not even coming close to the "8.43" specified in the column width.

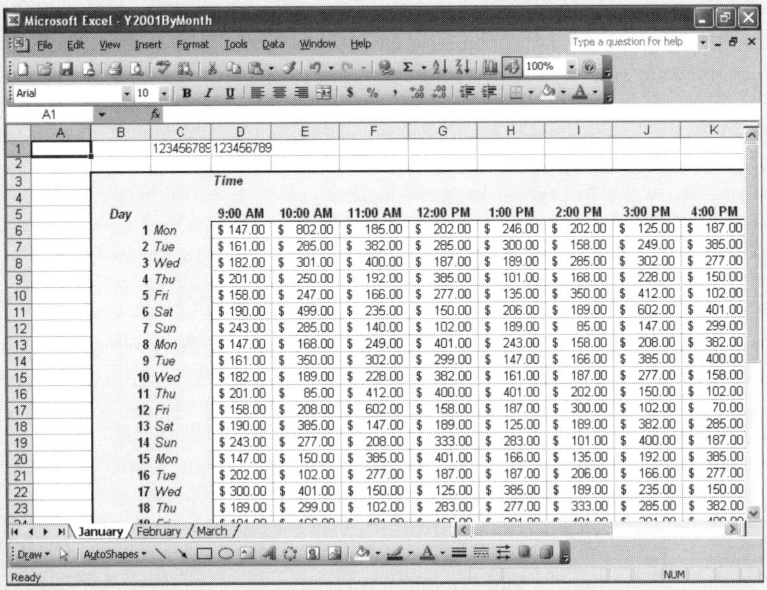

Figure 8-4. The number of digits visible at 100% Zoom…

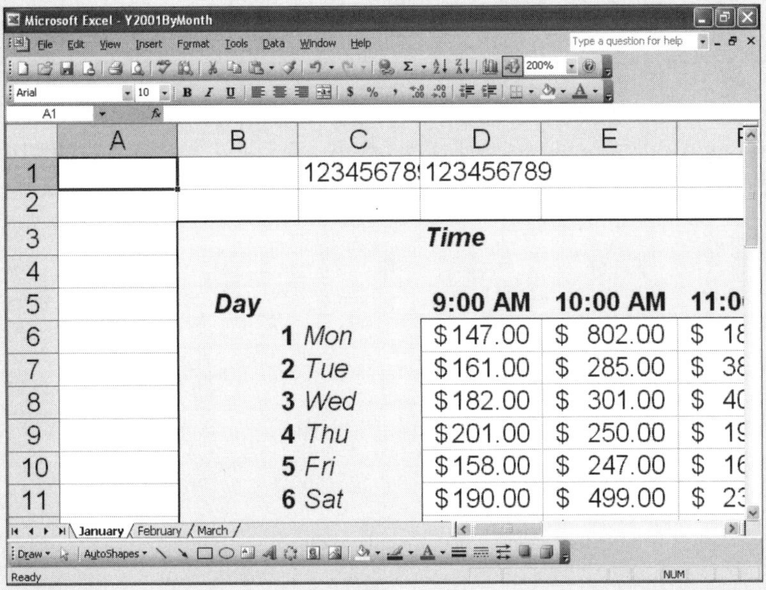

Figure 8-5. …might not be the same as the number of digits visible at 200% Zoom

Detecting Empty Cells

An infamous saying among computer programmers is "garbage in, garbage out." What this means is that if bad data is fed into a procedure, it will generate a bad answer. To guard against this, the integrity of the data needs to be verified.

One element you should check before relying on the totals within the Y2001ByMonth.xls workbook is that all values have been entered. You can do so by searching for empty cells and prompting the user for a value to be entered into the cell. Searching for empty cells is accomplished by using the *Range* object's *SpecialCells* method. The syntax for the *SpecialCells* method is

`expression.SpecialCells(`*Type, Value*`)`

expression is a required range object.

Type is a required value that should match one of the *xlCellType* constants, listed in Table 8-1.

Value is an optional variant. If *Type* is *xlCellTypeConstants* or *xlCellTypeFormulas*, *Value* is used to determine which type of cells to include in the result. The numeric values that correspond to the *xlSpecialCellsValues* constants, listed in Table 8-2, can be added together to return more than one type of special cell.

Table 8-2. *xlSpecialCellsValue* Constants

Constant	Description	Numeric Value
xlErrors	Returns cells that contain errors	16
xlLogical	Returns cells that contain a logical (that is, Boolean) value	4
xlNumbers	Returns cells that contain numerical values	1
xlTextValues	Returns cells that contain text	2

This FindEmptyCells procedure searches for empty cells in the data areas of Y2001ByMonth.xls and prompts the user for a value to enter into each empty cell found.

```
Sub FindEmptyCells()   '
Dim rgeSearch As Range, rgeEmpties As Range, rgeCurrent As Range
Dim strPrompt As String, strTitle As String, strReturn As String
Dim strRow As String, strAddress As String, strColumn As String

    strTitle = "Microsoft Office Excel 2003 Programming Inside Out"

    'Select proper range based on days in month
    Set rgeSearch = Range("D6", Range("D6").End(xlDown))
    Set rgeSearch = Range(rgeSearch, rgeSearch.End(xlToRight))

    'Find Empties - End if none found
    'Set Error trap for no cells found
    On Error Resume Next
```

Chapter 8

```
    Set rgeEmpties = rgeSearch.SpecialCells(xlCellTypeBlanks)
    If Err.Number = 1004 Then
        strPrompt = "No empty cells found!"
        MsgBox strPrompt, vbOKOnly + vbInformation, strTitle
        Exit Sub
    Else
        strPrompt = "Unexpected error - " & Str$(Err.Number) & _
            vbCrLf & Err.Description
        MsgBox strPrompt, vbOKOnly + vbExclamation, strTitle
    End If

    'Reset error handler
    On Error GoTo 0

    'Loop through empties prompting for new values
    For Each rgeCurrent In rgeEmpties

        'Calculate time period
        strAddress = "R5C" & Format(rgeCurrent.Column, "#0")
        strAddress = Application.ConvertFormula(strAddress, xlR1C1, xlA1)
        strPrompt = "Value missing for " & Format(Range(strAddress), _
            "h:mm AM/PM")

        'Calculate day
        strAddress = "R" & Format(rgeCurrent.Row, "#0") & "C2"
        strAddress = Application.ConvertFormula(strAddress, xlR1C1, xlA1)
        strPrompt = strPrompt & " on " & ActiveSheet.Name & " " & _
            Range(strAddress)
        strReturn = InputBox(strPrompt, strTitle)
        rgeCurrent = CSng(strReturn)
    Next rgeCurrent
End Sub
```

Using Named Ranges

You might already know that you can select a range of cells on a worksheet and give it a name by typing it in the Name Box. This lets you quickly select the range by choosing its name from the drop-down list provided in the Name Box. These same names are available to you within a macro. Instead of providing the cell coordinates for a range, you can use the name of the range instead.

Defining a Named Range

Excel stores the names of defined ranges within the *Names* collection, which is a property of the *Workbook* object. Using the *Add* method, you can create a *Named* range within the workbook by specifying the name you want to use and the range it should point to.

If you wanted to do some analysis of the sales data for each hourly time period within the Y2001ByQuarter.xls workbook, you could make your formulas easier to read by defining each time period as a range. Rather than manually selecting the range and typing a name, you can use a macro to do the work for you. The following *CreateNames* routine will build a named range for each of the time periods on the current worksheet and name it based on the name of the worksheet and the time period. The basic syntax is **expression**.Add(*Name, RefersTo, Visible, MacroType, ShortcutKey, Category, NameLocal, RefersToLocal, CategoryLocal, RefersToR1C1, RefersToR1C1Local*).

Of the various parameters that are passed to the method, only four of them are of importance.

- *Name*   A variant value that specifies the name that is to be given to the range.
- *RefersTo*   A variant value that specifies the cells to be included in the range using A1 notation. Required if *RefersToR1C1* is not used.
- *RefersToR1C1*   A variant value that specifies the cells to be included in the range using R1C1-style notation. Required if *RefersTo* is not used.
- *Visible*   An optional variant value that determines whether the *Name* is visible or not. Setting the property to *True* (the default) means the *Name* will appear in the Define Name, Paste Name, and Goto dialog boxes, while setting the property to *False* means the *Name* won't appear in those three dialog boxes (although you may still refer to the *Name* in formulas and VBA code).

Inside Out

Naming Ranges

There are a few guidelines to follow when naming a range:

- A name must start with a letter or an underscore (_) character. The rest of the name can contain any combination of letters, digits, periods (.), or underscores.
- A name cannot be the same as an existing cell reference (B22, CB76, R2C20, and so on).
- A name cannot contain spaces or other special characters, curly braces, square brackets, or parentheses.
- A name cannot exceed 255 characters. Also, names over 253 characters are not selectable from the drop-down list.
- Names are not case sensitive. MyRange is the same as myrange.
- A name must be unique to workbook; you can't use the same name to refer to ranges on different worksheets.

The following sample macro, *CreateNames*, works by looping through each of the columns that contains entries based on time. On each pass of the loop, the name of the current worksheet and the label of the column being marked are used to generate the name of the range in the format MonthHourAMPM, as shown in Figure 8-6. (The 1:00 P.M. entries on the February worksheet would be named as February1PM.)

```
Sub CreateNames()
Dim strRangeName As String, strWorksheetName As String
Dim intCounter As Integer, strRangeFormula As String
Dim strColumn As String, strR1C1Formula As String
Dim strA1Formula As String

    For intCounter = 1 To 12
        strWorksheetName = ActiveSheet.Name

        'Calculate proper column name (D-O) by converting
        'from R1C2 notation to A1 notation
        strR1C1Formula = "R5C" & Format(intCounter + 3, "#0")
        strA1Formula = Application.ConvertFormula(Formula:=strR1C1Formula, _
            FromReferenceStyle:=xlR1C1, ToReferenceStyle:=xlA1)
        strRangeName = strWorksheetName & Format(Range(strA1Formula), "hAMPM")

        'Format column portion of range formula
        strColumn = "C" & Format(intCounter + 3, "#0")
        strRangeFormula = "=" & strWorksheetName & "!R6" & _
            strColumn & ":R36" & strColumn

        'Add new range and continue
        ActiveWorkbook.Names.Add Name:=strRangeName, _
            RefersToR1C1:=strRangeFormula
    Next intCounter
End Sub
```

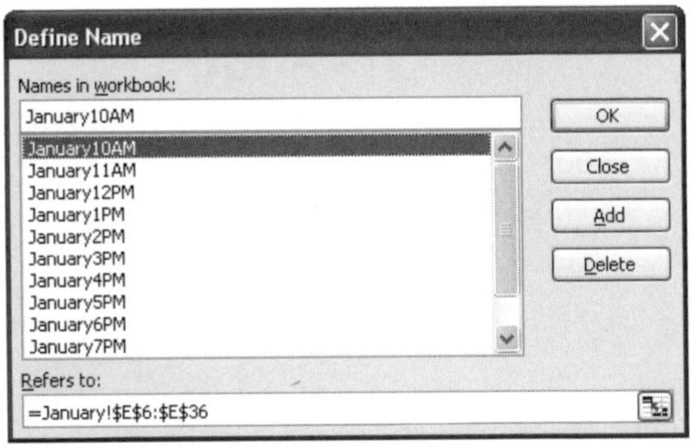

Figure 8-6. This procedure creates names in the Y2001ByQuarter.xls workbook.

Changing Notation Styles

The *CreateNames* routine uses the *ConvertFormula* method of the *Application* object to facilitate the use of a counter to specify the column being referenced. Using a counter or any numeric variable to point to a specific column makes it very easy to move left or right among the columns. Using a value of 4 to point to column D, 6 can be added to point to column J or 2 can be subtracted to point to column B.

However, the *Range* object will take cell pointers only by using the A1 style of notation or the *Cells* method. Rather than use the *Cells* method, the procedure takes advantage of the *ConvertFormula* method to build a reference in R1C1 notation and convert it to A1 notation.

The *ConvertFormula* method also lets you convert from the A1 notation to the R1C1 notation. It will also allow you to change a formula's reference type from absolute to relative or vice versa.

In the *CreateNames* routine, the *ConvertFormula* method converts a simple cell address from one reference type to another. As the name implies, you can pass a more complex formula for conversion, such as this example, which computes the daily average for the first two Mondays in January using the Y2001ByQuarters workbook.

```
strA1Formula = Application.ConvertFormula( _
    Formula:=" =AVERAGE(R5C2:R5C13, _
    R12C2:R12C13), fromReferenceStyle:=xlR1C1, _
    toReferenceStyle:=xlA1)
```

The *ConvertFormula* method has the following syntax:

```
expression.ConvertFormula(Formula, FromReferenceStyle, ToReferenceStyle,
ToAbsolute, RelativeTo)
```

- **Expression**   A required expression that returns an *Application* object.
- **Formula**   A required variant that provides the formula to be converted as a string.
- **FromReferenceStyle**   A required integer that matches one of the two *xlReferenceStyle* constants.
- **ToReferenceStyle**   An optional integer that matches one of the two *xlReferenceStyle* constants. If not supplied, the reference style is not changed.
- **ToAbsolute**   An optional integer that matches one of the *xlReferenceType* constants. If omitted, the reference type is not changed.
- **RelativeTo**   An optional variant that returns a range object that points to a single cell. Relative references relate to this cell.

Table 8-3 lists the available *xlReferenceStyle* and *xlReferenceType* constants you can use with the *ConvertFormula* method.

Table 8-3. Constants Used with the *ConvertFormula* Method

Constant	Integer
xlReferenceStyle	
xlA1	1
xlR1C1	-4150
xlReferenceType	
alAbsolute	1
xlAbsRowRelColumn	2
xlRelRowAbsColumn	3
xlRelative	4

Inside Out

Names as Formulas

Excel actually stores the names of ranges as a formula. You can take advantage of this handling in several ways to enhance the shortcuts you use in your spreadsheets. Ordinarily, you cannot use a name more than once within a single workbook, but what if you have a workbook with multiple sheets that are all similar, such as the Y2001ByMonth.xls workbook? It would be handy to be able to use the same name to refer to the same area of a worksheet regardless of which worksheet it is. You can do this by specifying the name to be specific to the worksheet and not available to the entire workbook.

Select the cells you want to name as you usually would, and click in the name box to type a name. This time, instead of just typing the name, type the name of the worksheet first, followed by an exclamation point (!), and then the name of the range. (You must still follow normal naming rules behind the exclamation point.)

The exclamation point serves as a separator between the sheet name and the range name. When Excel sees a sheet name, it knows to define the name as being specific to the worksheet.

You can also expand names even further by using relative references. Names will use an absolute reference by default, but if you enter the range that the name refers to manually by clicking Insert, Name, Define, you can use a relative reference. As an example, open the Y2001ByMonth.xls workbook, display the January worksheet, and follow these steps:

1 Select any cell in column A.

2 Click Insert, Name, Define.

3 In the Name box, type **DailyValues**.

4 In the Refers To box, type **=A$6:A$36**.

5 Click the Add button and then the OK button.

6 Select cell D38.

7 Type in **=Sum(DailyValues)** and press Enter.

continued

Chapter 8

The total that appears in the cell should be the same, $5,571.00. Examine the definition of the DailyValues name. Go back into the Define Name dialog, and select DailyValues from the Names list box. The Refers To box will show **=January!D$6:D$36**. The column names are relative, but the rows are absolute. You can use the name DailyValues within a formula if you need to reference the entire range of values entered within that column, from row 6 through row 36.

> **Warning** You can use the names you create in any row except rows 6 through 36; if you use the names in a formula in those rows, you create a circular reference that invalidates your formula.

Reserved Range Names

There are a few reserved names that Excel uses for internal purposes and that can't be used when defining your own ranges. However, knowing what the names are used for and how to apply them lets you extend the usability of your macros further. The reserved names are *Consolidate_Area*, *Criteria*, *Database*, *Data_Form*, *Extract*, *Print_Area*, *Print_Titles*, and a collection of others that begin with the prefix *Auto_*.

The *Print_Area* name is perhaps the most useful; it lets you set the range of cells that will be printed. Although this task can also be done using the *PrintArea* property of *Worksheet.PageSetup* object, using the *Print_Area* range is more flexible. The *PrintArea* property lets you set only the range of cells to print using A1 style notation or other range names. Furthermore, any examination of the property will reveal the range in A1 notation, even if you used the name of a range.

Ranges and Cells

The *Print_Area* range lets you set the range of cells using your choice of A1 notation, R1C1 notation, or range names. Examination of the *Print_Area* range properties will show you the range in the style that was used to set it.

The following *SelectPrint* routine allows the user to choose between printing the entire sheet or just the evening values from the Y2001ByMonth workbook. The *Print_Area* range is used to inform Excel what values to print.

```
Sub SelectPrint()
Dim intReturn As Integer, strPrompt As String, strTitle As String
Dim strRange As String, objName As Name, intCounter As Integer

    'Call CreateNames subroutine to ensure properly named ranges
    'are available
    CreateNames

    'Prompt for values to print out
    strPrompt = "Click Yes to print only the evenint values " _
    & "and click No to print all values."
    strTitle = "Microsoft Office Excel 2003 Programming Inside Out"
    intReturn = MsgBox(strPrompt, vbYesNoCancel, strTitle)

    'Check response from user
    Select Case intReturn
        Case vbNo 'Print full chart
            strRange = "=" & ActiveSheet.Name & "!" & _
                ActiveSheet.Name & "AllValues"
        Case vbYes 'Print evening times only
            strRange = "=" & ActiveSheet.Name & "!" & _
                ActiveSheet.Name & "1PM:" & _
                ActiveSheet.Name & "8PM"
        Case vbCancel 'Cancel completely
            Exit Sub
    End Select

    'Loop through Names collection. Delete Print_Area or
    'Print_Titles if found.
    intCounter = ActiveSheet.Names.count
    While (intCounter > 0)
        If ActiveSheet.Names(intCounter).Name = ActiveSheet.Name _
```

```
          & "!Print_Area" Then
          ActiveSheet.Names(intCounter).Delete
          intCounter = ActiveSheet.Names.count
      ElseIf ActiveSheet.Names(intCounter).Name = ActiveSheet.Name _
          & "!Print_Titles" Then
          ActiveSheet.Names(intCounter).Delete
          intCounter = ActiveSheet.Names.count
      End If
      intCounter = intCounter - 1
    Wend

    'Set print area
    ActiveWorkbook.Names.Add Name:=ActiveSheet.Name & _
        "!Print_Area", RefersTo:=strRange
    'Set titles if needed
    If vbYes Then
        ActiveSheet.PageSetup.PrintTitleColumns = _
            ActiveSheet.Columns("B:C").Address
        ActiveSheet.PageSetup.PrintTitleRows = _
            ActiveSheet.Rows("5:5").Address
    End If
    'Print worksheet
    ActiveWorkbook.PrintPreview
End Sub
```

Copying Data Between Ranges and Arrays

All of the information within a workbook is easily available for manipulation through a VBA macro. Why would you want to copy that information to someplace else before working with it? Speed. It's a very time-consuming process for VBA to read or write information to a worksheet. By minimizing the number of times that VBA needs to read or write to the worksheet, you can greatly reduce the amount of time needed for your procedure to operate.

How can you reduce the number of read and writes to the worksheet? By reading or writing a range of cells at a time. It's the setup time that VBA needs to access a worksheet that takes time. Unfortunately, VBA goes through the same setup process every time it needs to read or write another range, whether the range consists of only one cell or several hundred cells.

> **Warning** As with most things, there is a point of diminishing returns or outright failure. VBA cannot transfer more than about 3000 cells at one time. As long as you stay well below that number, you should have no problems.

So the question now becomes how can you read or write to multiple cells at one time? Transferring multiple cells between a workbook and VBA is done through the use of variant arrays. A variant data type can hold any other data type, including arrays. More importantly, the variant variable does not have to be declared as an array to hold an array. In fact, for the purposes of copying data to and from a worksheet, the variant variable cannot be declared as an array. The variable needs to be declared as a simple variant type, as in the following statement.

```
Dim varA As Variant
```

Reading the cells into a variant variable is done through an assignment statement, that is, `varA = Range("January1PM")` or `varA = Range("H6:H36")`. These two examples would read the same range into the variable *varA*, with the individual cells accessed the same as a single element of an array. Once you have assigned values to the variant, you can use the variable as a reference to the range. For example, you could use this code to display a message box containing just the sum of the values in cells E12:E15.

```
Sub VariantSum()
Dim varA As Variant, intSum As Integer
varA = Range("E12:E15")
intSum = WorksheetFunction.Sum(varA)
MsgBox (intSum)
End Sub
```

> **Note** A range will always return a multi-dimensional array, usually two dimensions, regardless of the number of columns. The second dimension will contain at least one element but could have more depending upon the number of columns within the range.

If you need to determine the size of an array, you can use the *LBound* and *UBound* functions to give you the lower and upper boundaries of the array. *LBound(var)* returns the lower boundary, usually a 0 or 1, whereas *UBound(var)* will return the upper boundary.

To determine the boundaries of all dimensions in a multi-dimensional array, specify the dimension you want the boundary of. For example, using the statement varA = Range("JanuaryAllValues") in the Y2001ByMonth.xls workbook would read all the cells from B3:Q38. To find the number of rows, you could use UBound(varA, 1) or simply UBound(varA). Retrieving the number of columns would use the command UBound(varA, 2).

When reading the values from a named range, you can also shrink or expand the number of cells being read by using the *Resize* method. As an example, to read only the first seven rows of data, but three hours worth of data from 1:00 P.M. in the Y2001ByQuarter.xls workbook, you could use the following statement:

```
varA = Range("January1PM").Resize(7, 3)
```

Writing information back into the range is a simple reversal of the statement, Range("January1PM") = varA. However, some care should be taken when writing information back into the cells. You should ensure that the range is the same size as the array to prevent overwriting the wrong cells. This is to preserve data integrity and is easily done by combining the *UBound* function with the *Resize* method, as follows:

```
Range("January1PM").Resize(UBound(varA, 1), UBound(varA, 2)) = varA.
```

A simpler method of ensuring the integrity of your data is to fill the array with the values from the range first. This method will actually serve two purposes: it will size the array to match the range, and it will fill the array with the current values contained within the range so that when the data is written back Excel will maintain the values that have not been changed within the procedure.

The following procedure helps illustrate the difference in processing times between using direct access to the cells and copying the cells to an array first. (Each method is repeated 50 times so that the time needed to perform the reads is high enough to measure.)

```
Sub ProcessTime()
Dim rgeCells As Range, intCount As Integer
Dim strPrompt As String, strTitle As String
Dim sglStart As Single, sglEnd As Single
Dim rgeCell As Range, varCells As Variant
Dim intRows As Integer, intColumns As Integer
Dim intLoop As Integer

    intCount = 0
    strTitle = "Microsoft Office Excel 2003 Programming Inside Out"
    sglStart = Timer
    Debug.Print sglStart
    For intLoop = 1 To 50
        For Each rgeCell In Range("JanuaryAllValues")
            intCount = intCount + 1
        Next rgeCell
```

```
Next intLoop
sglEnd = Timer
Debug.Print sglEnd
strPrompt = "Processing time range method: " & _
    Format(sglEnd - sglStart, "#0.00000") & _
    "   Total Cells:" & Str$(intCount) & vbCrLf

sglStart = Timer
intCount = 0
For intLoop = 1 To 50
    varCells = Range("JanuaryAllValues")
    For intRows = 1 To UBound(varCells)
        For intColumns = 1 To UBound(varCells, 2)
            intCount = intCount + 1
        Next intColumns
    Next intRows
Next intLoop
sglEnd = Timer

strPrompt = strPrompt & "Processing time array method: " & _
    Format(sglEnd - sglStart, "#0.00000") & _
    "   Total Cells:" & Str$(intCount)
MsgBox strPrompt, vbOKOnly + vbInformation, strTitle

End Sub
```

Getting Data Entry Right the First Time

Typing data into a worksheet or form is one of the most tedious activities known to humanity. If you've ever typed ISBNs into a database eight hours a day and five days a week for two months, you can begin to get an appreciation for what data entry clerks go through. Columns of numbers transpose in front of your eyes, books you've already entered find their way onto your "to do" pile, and you change hands to avoid the worst effects of repetitive stress disorders. Add in the potential for typographical errors, and you can understand why electronic data collections are so notoriously inaccurate.

You can help catch data entry errors at the source by setting *validation rules* for cells in your worksheets. As the name implies, a validation rule is a criterion that cell data must meet in order to ensure that only meaningful information is added to your data collection. You get to choose whether the invalid data is accepted as input or whether the user has to re-type the data before being allowed to go on to the next cell. You can also specify whether to allow users entering data to leave cells blank.

The key to creating validation rules for your cells is, as you probably guessed, the *Range* object's *Validation* property. The *Validation* property, which returns a *Validation* object, gives you the tools to set the validation rules and notification styles for your cell ranges. Table 8-4 lists the *Validation* object's useful properties and methods.

Table 8-4. The Properties and Methods of the *Validation* Object

Attribute	Description
Properties	
AlertStyle	This property can be set to one of three Excel constants: *xlValidAlertInformation* (which displays an information box), *xlValidAlertStop* (which displays a stop box), *xlValidAlertWarning* (which displays a warning box).
ErrorMessage	This property contains the user-defined message that appears in the alert box after a user enters invalid data.
ErrorTitle	This property contains the user-defined value that appears on the title bar of the alert box that appears after a user enters invalid data.
Formula1	This property contains the first (and possibly the only) value used in a criterion (for example, between 5 and 10 or less than 10).
Formula2	This property contains the second of two values used in a criterion (for example, between 5 and 10).
IgnoreBlank	Setting this Boolean property to *True* allows a user to leave a cell blank.
InCellDropdown	This property determines whether the cell contains a down arrow with a list of values from which a user must pick.
InputMessage	This property contains the message that appears in the input box into which a user enters cell data.
InputTitle	This property contains the value that appears on the title bar of the input box into which a user enters cell data.
Operator	This property contains the operator of a criterion, which may be one of the following Excel constants: *xlBetween*, *xlEqual*, *xlGreater*, *xlGreaterEqual*, *xlLess*, *xlLessEqual*, *xlNotBetween*, and *xlNotEqual*.
ShowError	A Boolean property that, when set to *True*, causes Excel to display a message indicating the user entered invalid data.
ShowInput	A Boolean property that, when set to *True*, causes Excel to display the contents of the *InputMessage* property whenever the cell is activated.
Type	A property that determines the type of value you will be validating. The available data types are *xlValidateCustom*, *xlValidateDate*, *xlValidateDecimal*, *xlValidateInputOnly*, *xlValidateList*, *xlValidateTextLength*, *xlValidateTime*, and *xlValidateWholeNumber*.
Value	A Boolean property set to *True* if all validation rules are satisfied, or *False* if at least one rule is not satisfied.

Table 8-4. The Properties and Methods of the *Validation* Object

Attribute	Description
Method	
Add	A method to create a validation rule for a range of cells. Table 8-5 gives you more information on which parameters you need to set.
Delete	A method that deletes a *Validation* object.
Modify	A method that changes the validation rules for a range of cells. The *Modify* method uses the same parameter rules listed in Table 8-5.

Which parameters of the *Add* and *Modify* methods you use depends on the type of value you want to validate. The corresponding values for each validation type are shown in Table 8-5.

Table 8-5. The List of Parameters Used in an *Add* or *Modify* Statement

Validation Type	Parameters
xlValidateCustom	*Formula1* is required, whereas *Formula2* is never used. (Any value assigned to *Formula2* is ignored.) *Formula1* must contain an expression that evaluates to *True* when data entry is valid and *False* when data entry is invalid.
xlInputOnly	*AlertStyle*, *Formula1*, or *Formula2* are used.
xlValidateList	*Formula1* is required, but *Formula2* is never used. (Any value assigned to *Formula2* is ignored.) *Formula1* must contain either a comma-delimited list of values or a worksheet reference to this list.
xlValidateWholeNumber, xlValidateDate, xlValidateDecimal, xlValidateTextLength, or *xlValidateTime*	One of either *Formula1* or *Formula2* must be specified, or both may be specified.

If you wanted to set validation criteria for 600 cells in the H column of a worksheet, you could use the following code to do so.

```
With Range("H6, H606").Validation
    .Add Type:=xlValidateWholeNumber, AlertStyle:=xlValidAlertStop, _
        Operator:=xlLessEqual, Formula1:="5000"
    .InputTitle = "Credit Limit"
    .ErrorTitle = "Credit Limit Too High"
    .InputMessage = "Enter the customer's credit limit."
    .ErrorMessage = "The credit limit must be less than $5,000."
End With
```

Chapter 8

In this chapter, you've learned how to refer to and manipulate ranges and individual cells in your worksheets. The fundamental concept to remember is that, while you can refer to individual cells within a range, even single cells are called using the *Range* object (for example, `Range("A16")`. Once you've specified the range you want to work with, you can use the range's values in formulas, define a name to allow more streamlined and user friendly references to the range, and validate the data entered into the range.

Part 4

Advanced VBA

9   **Manipulating Data with VBA**   **193**

10 **Formatting Excel Objects**   **219**

11 **Creating Add-Ins and COM Add-Ins**   **239**

12 **Understanding and Using Events**   **265**

13 **Manipulating Files**   **281**

14 **Developing Class Modules**   **299**

Manipulating Data with VBA

Manipulating Text 193   Manipulating Dates and Times 213
Manipulating Numbers 206

When you're given a workbook filled with data, you're going to want to ask questions about the data. What is the sum of the sales for a day? Or a month? Or a year? How much time elapsed between a customer's orders? And is the data you're about to write to a text file in the proper format to be read into a database? You can answer all of these questions, and many more, using the text, number, and date/time processing functions available to you in Excel VBA.

In this chapter, you will learn how to do the following:

- Prepare text strings for processing.
- Concatenate, find, and modify strings.
- Perform summary calculations on numerical data.
- Make financial decisions using Excel calculations.
- Work with dates and times in Excel.

Manipulating Text

Although you might normally think of Excel as a number crunching financial application, it's actually quite a versatile program. Not only can you perform myriad calculations on your numerical data, but you can also handle any text that comes along with that data. Whether you want to perform a simple task such as displaying a welcome message after a user opens a workbook or import data from a text file into an Excel worksheet, you can do so using the text-handling procedures available to you in Excel VBA and as worksheet formulas.

Determining if the Value in a Cell Is Text

The first step in manipulating a text value without generating an error is determining whether the variable or cell value you want to work with is, in fact, a text value. You can determine whether the value in a cell, a variable, or the value typed into an input box, is text by processing the string with the ISTEXT function. For example, you can use the ISTEXT function to guard against data entry errors, such as when someone types the wrong sort of data into a cell or a UserForm. This sort of problem often occurs after you've changed a procedure or put a new form into use—the data entry folks (and it could be you) get so used to typing a customer's identification code first that they forget they're supposed to start with the company name now.

> ISTEXT is shown in all capital letters because it is one of many worksheet functions you can call using VBA code. For more information on calling worksheet functions such as ISTEXT in your VBA code, see the Inside Out titled "Is a Function Built into VBA or Not?" later in this chapter.

You can also use the ISTEXT function to ensure that data imported from an external source is formatted as you expected it to be before you run a set of procedures. If you've ever run a text-processing routine on non-text data, you know precisely the type of chaos a little checking can prevent. You can also use ISTEXT as a basic function when you might not be sure precisely what sort of text data you'll receive, but so long as you do know it's text you can write a procedure to cycle through the non-empty cells in a worksheet and perform at least this rudimentary check.

So what do you do if the data you want to work with as a string is actually a number? In that case, you can use the STR function to represent the number as a string. The STR function's syntax is minimal: *STR(number)*, where number is the variable name or address of the cell that contains the number you're changing to text.

> For more information on validating cell data, see "Getting Data Entry Right the First Time" on page 187.

ISTEXT is not the only function available in the IS family; Table 9-1 lists the worksheet functions you can use to determine whether a value fits a given category.

Table 9-1. The IS Family of Functions

Function	Returns *True* If This Condition Is Met
ISBLANK	The value refers to an empty cell.
ISERR	The value refers to any error value except #N/A (value not available).
ISERROR	The value refers to any error value (#N/A, #VALUE!, #REF!, #DIV/0!, #NUM!, #NAME?, or #NULL!).
ISLOGICAL	The value refers to a logical value.
ISNA	The value refers to the #N/A (value not available) error value.
ISNONTEXT	The value refers to any item that is not text. (Note that this function returns TRUE if value refers to a blank cell.)
ISNUMBER	The value refers to a number.
ISREF	The value refers to a reference.
ISTEXT	The value refers to text.

When you're ready to write your string data to a cell, you need to be sure the cell is prepared to accept text data. For example, if the cells are formatted using the *General* number format (the default) and you try to write a string that appears to be a number (for example,

0000097239) to the cell, the leading zeros will be deleted. You can ensure Excel will treat your input as a string by changing the cell's number format to *Text*. You would perform this action in the Excel interface by clicking Format, Cells, displaying the Number tab page, and clicking Text. You can do the same thing using the *Range* object's *NumberFormat* property.

For example, if you wanted to change the number format of the active cell (which is considered a range in this context) to *Text*, you would use the following line of code:

```
ActiveCell.NumberFormat = "@"
```

You can change the number format of a range to any of the values displayed in the list of Custom number formats available in the Format Cells dialog box (shown in Figure 9-1). If you're not sure which format to use, assign the format to a cell using the Format Cells dialog box, and then click Custom to display the code. Be sure to enclose the code in quotes!

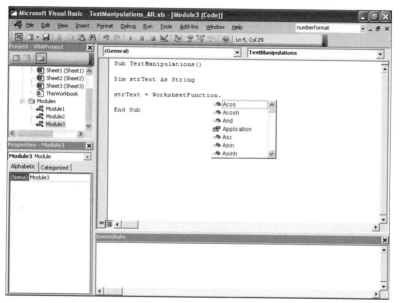

Figure 9-1. You can change the format of your cell to any of the formats in the Custom list.

Preparing String Data for Processing

Once you've determined that the data you're about to perform text operations on is, in fact, text, you can take additional steps to ensure that the data will look its best when you process it. There are two functions you can use to process your data: CLEAN and TRIM. The CLEAN function strips out any *nonprinting characters* from a string. Nonprinting characters are also known as *control characters*, because they're usually entered by pressing the Ctrl key while typing another key sequence. Nonprinting characters don't often show up in text files or worksheets, but if you import data from another program into Excel you might find them sneaking in as interpretations of formatting or data structure instructions that weren't stripped out when the original data was saved.

Inside Out

Is a Function Built into VBA or Not?

Remember that the default behavior of the Visual Basic Editor is to display the required arguments for a function and the available properties, methods, and events of an object after you've typed the name of the object and a trailing period. You can usually figure out whether you need to use the *Application.WorksheetFunction* object by trying to type the function in without the object and seeing if a ToolTip listing the required arguments appears. If the ToolTip appears, you can use the function as a function; if not, try typing **Application.WorksheetFunction.** (there is a period after *WorksheetFunction* there) and see if the worksheet function you want to use appears in the list of available properties for the object.

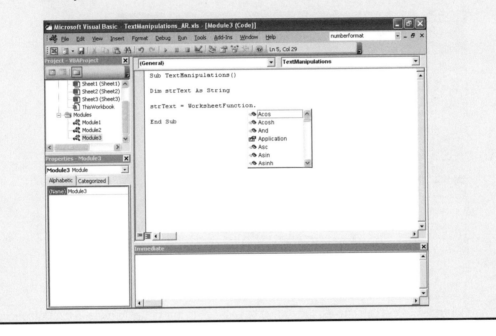

Note The following line consists entirely of nonprinting characters:

The TRIM function is similar to the CLEAN function in that both functions get rid of unwanted characters, but the TRIM function strips away unwanted white space (spaces, tabs, carriage returns, line breaks, and so on) before the first alphanumeric character and after the last alphanumeric character in the string. The TRIM function also strips away all but one space between words. Again, these extraneous characters can sneak in as an artifact of untranslated formatting instructions, or the extra space might have been added because the fields in the file had fixed lengths and the originating program padded the string with spaces to make up the difference.

Because CLEAN and TRIM are useful *worksheet* functions, the fine minds at Microsoft decided to let you use them in Excel VBA. You can call the CLEAN and TRIM functions, plus a host of other useful worksheet functions, by adding the name of the desired function as a property of the *Application.WorksheetFunction* object. Such calls would look like this:

```
ActiveCell.Value = Application.WorksheetFunction.Clean(ActiveCell.Value)
ActiveCell.Value = Application.WorksheetFunction.Trim(ActiveCell.Value)
```

Determining the Number of Characters in a String

Another of the basic text-processing operations that you can perform in Excel VBA is to determine the number of characters in a string, which you do using the LEN function. And, just as the ISTEXT function is useful for validating data, you can use the LEN function to ensure the data you're inputting, importing, or exporting is of the expected length. One example of an occasion when determining that data is of a particular length is if you're typing in International Standard Book Numbers (ISBNs), which are used to identify books. An ISBN is exactly 10 characters long, so if you or a colleague is typing in the title, the authors, the ISBN, and the price of every book in your company's library, you should make sure the ISBNs are of the correct length. Although ISBNs are one example when verifying the length of worksheet or UserForm data would come in handy, the applications are nearly infinite. If your order or customer numbers are all of a specified length, if your product codes are eight characters long but your customer codes are nine characters long, or if you want to make sure no stray digits were mistakenly added to a phone number, you can use the LEN function to verify that your rules are being followed.

The following code verifies the value in the active cell to ensure the product code contained in the cell is exactly 10 characters in length:

```
If LEN(ActiveCell.Value) <> 10 Then
    MsgBox ("The product code in this cell is not of the required length.")
    ActiveCell.Value = "Error"
End If
```

If you work with older database management systems, or with a database that has set character lengths for each of its fields, you should be sure to add a validation rule to a column so that you can ensure every entry was read in correctly. And, although many databases are small enough that you can waste a bit of storage by allocating more space than is strictly necessary to hold the field's value, it's a good idea to limit the size of every field (with the possible exception of a comment field) to the minimum possible number of characters.

Another good use for the LEN function is to guarantee that the passwords your colleagues assign to workbooks and worksheets are of a minimum length. As mentioned in Chapter 7, the Excel password protection scheme won't prevent your data from being compromised, but you can make an attacker's job much more time-consuming by assigning longer passwords.

Chapter 9

An Excel password can be up to 15 characters in length, but it's a good idea to require users to use passwords that are at least 8 characters long.

> For more information on using the LEN to verify that a password contains at least one non-alphanumeric character, see "Returning Characters from Arbitrary Positions in a String" later in this chapter.

Inside Out

When to Validate, and When to Use an *If...Then* Statement

When you're working with values that need to be a certain length, you have a choice of methods to make certain everything falls into line. Way back in Chapter 8, you learned how to use the *Range* object's *Validation* property to establish criteria that a cell's value must meet before being accepted. You can set the *Validation* object's *Type* parameter to *xlValidateTextLength* to have Excel check a cell's value to ensure it is of the proper length. Of course, you can use an *If...Then* rule to the same effect. So why would you choose one method over the other?

● **You should use a *Range* object's *Validation* property when** You want to create a single rule that is easily expressed using the *Validation* property's parameters.

● You want the input box to have a specific title and to be grouped with the validation rules.

● You want to display a specific type of message box (information, warning, or stop) and have the behavior (whether to move to the next cell or not) programmed as part of the message box type.

● You want to have all the criteria stored in a single object.

● **You should use an *If...Then...Else* statement when** You want to have multiple criteria and find that using multiple *If...Then...Else* constructions is easier than using the *Validation* object's *Modify* method.

● You want to have conditional criteria that change depending on a set of circumstances. For example, the maximum credit limit an employee can assign to a customer could vary by employee.

Concatenating Text from Two or More Cells or Variables

Some of the procedures you've encountered so far in this book have generated message boxes using the text from one or more variables or worksheet cells as part of the message box's prompt. The authors of this book admit to playing a bit fast and loose with the order of topics, but now is the time to bring everything up to date by showing you how to add text from a cell, a variable, or a literal into a single output. You use the & operator.

There is a potential trap here, mainly because many readers will be familiar with the ampersand character, &, as the equivalent of the word *and*. Also, if you have previous programming experience, you might have used the & operator to indicate a logical "and" in expressions such as

```
If ((Range("C5").Value >= 1000) & (Range("D5")<=10)) Then…
```

Don't fall into that trap! The VBA concatenation operator & is not the same as the logical *And* operator, the latter of which is spelled out as the word *And*. The previous *If* condition statement is properly written as

```
If ((Range("C5").Value >= 1000) And (Range("D5")<=10)) Then…
```

The concatenation operator is fairly straightforward to use. For example, you could use the concatenation operator in conjunction with the LEN function described earlier to indicate why the data typed into a cell is invalid.

```
Public Sub VerifyLength()
If Len(ActiveCell.Value) <> 10 Then
    MsgBox ("The product code entered is " & LEN(ActiveCell.Value) & _ "
characters, not 10.")
    ActiveCell.Value = ""
End If
End Sub
```

The LEN function and the & operator are also useful if you need to add characters to a cell value or a variable so the text is the expected length for export to a program that requires fixed-length data. To add characters to the beginning or end of a string, you use the REPT function in combination with the & operator. The REPT function has the following syntax:

```
Application.WorksheetFunction.REPT(string, times)
```

The *string* parameter provides the string to be repeated, and *times* indicates the number of times the character should be repeated. For example, if you worked for a fast-growing company that used a variable-length order code to track orders, you might need to change the 5-character code to a 10-character code. That's no problem in Excel—all you need to do is repeat a zero at the front of each order code to bring the length up to 10 characters. The following procedure checks the length of the order code string in the cells the user identifies and adds enough *x*'s to make the string 10 characters long:

```
Public Sub MakeTen()

Dim strFirst, strLast, strAllCells, strPadding, strContents As String
Dim intPadding As Integer

strFirst = InputBox("Enter the address of the first cell.")
strLast = InputBox("Enter the address of the last cell.")
strAllCells = strFirst & ":" & strLast
```

```
For Each MyCell In Range(strAllCells).Cells

If Len(MyCell.Value) < 10 Then
    Range(MyCell.Address).Select
    strContents = MyCell.Value

    intPadding = 10 - Len(MyCell.Value)
    strPadding = Application.WorksheetFunction.Rept("0", intPadding)
    MyCell.NumberFormat = "@"
    MyCell.Value = strPadding & strContents
End If

    MyCell.NumberFormat = "@"

Next MyCell

End Sub
```

> **Caution** You need to make sure that the order code you're changing is stored as a string, not as a number. If you add a string of zeros to the beginning of a cell value that Excel translates as a number (which includes a cell with a General format), Excel will discard the zeros as meaningless. For a worksheet cell, change the cell's format to Text.

Returning the First or Last Several Characters from a String

When you work with spreadsheet data, it's likely that you'll find patterns in the data, perhaps patterns that you yourself program in. Although it's certainly possible that every character in a string will serve a known purpose, you might just need to read in the first or last few characters of a string to derive the information that you need for a particular task. For example, if the first five digits of a book's ISBN tell you the book's publisher (and they do), you could read those digits into memory, look up the publisher's identity in a database or worksheet table, and write the data into another cell programmatically.

To return the first or last several characters in a string, you use the *Left* function, which returns characters from the beginning of a string, or the *Right* function, which returns characters from the end of the string. The syntax of the two functions, with the exception of the function name, of course, is identical.

```
Left(string, length)
Right(string, length)
```

For these functions, *string* is the variable or range that contains the string you want to process and *length* is the number of characters you want to return. As an example, consider a worksheet where the items included in orders placed with The Garden Company are stored as a collection of worksheet rows.

Because The Garden Company uses a consistent naming system for its products, you can create a procedure to determine the category of each product ordered. In this naming system, the first two characters of an item's identification code indicate to which category the item belongs (*TL* for Tools, *SP* for Supplies, and *FN* for Furniture). So, rather than require a user to enter the category, the procedure could do it for them.

Note The data in the worksheet has all uppercase letters, so the entries in the procedure's *Case* statements look for uppercase-only category codes.

```
Public Sub NoteCategory()

Dim MyCell As Range
Dim strFirst, strLast, strAllCells, strCategory As String

strFirst = InputBox("Enter the address of the first cell in the OrderItem
column.")
strLast = InputBox("Enter the address of the last cell in the OrderItem column.")
strAllCells = strFirst & ":" & strLast

For Each MyCell In Range(strAllCells).Cells

    Range(MyCell.Address).Select
    strCategory = Left(MyCell.Value, 2)

    Select Case strCategory
    Case "TL"
        ActiveCell.Offset(0, 1).Value = "Tools"
```

```
        Case "FN"
            ActiveCell.Offset(0, 1).Value = "Furniture"
        Case "SP"
            ActiveCell.Offset(0, 1).Value = "Supplies"
        Case Else
            ActiveCell.Offset(0, 1).Value = "Error"
        End Select

    Next MyCell

End Sub
```

> For more information on and a practical example of looking up values from existing lists, including those stored in databases, see Chapter 22: "Excel and ADO Data Sources."

Returning Characters from Arbitrary Positions in a String

Life is so much easier when you know what's coming, and working with spreadsheet data is no exception. Well-ordered data streaming in from outside sources is one of the little joys in an Excel programmer's life, because it means you can reach into the data string and pull out what you need. One such example in the United States is the Vehicle Identification Number (VIN). VINs are 17 characters long and encode all of the pertinent information about a car: the make, the model, the color, the year manufactured, the plant where the car was manufactured, and so on. When you have a known data structure, you can use the MID function to pull out just the characters you need for a procedure.

Unlike the *Left* and *Right* functions, which pull data from the beginning or end of a string, the MID function pulls a set number of characters from the body of the string. The MID function's syntax is similar to both the *Left* and *Right* functions, with the only difference being that you define the position of the first character to return and the number of characters to be returned.

```
MID(string, start, length)
```

To pull characters in positions 4 through 8 (a total of five characters) from the value in cell D5, you would use the following code (which assumes you created the variables *strCode* and *strDetails* earlier):

```
strCode = Range("D5").Value
strDetails = MID(strCode, 4, 5)
```

Finding a String Within Another String

You might have read the heading for this section and wondered why in the world someone would want to find a string within another string. In the world of genetics, you could search for a specific protein sequence to locate a chromosome, but if you're doing that you most likely won't be working through an Excel worksheet to find that substring. Instead, you might have received rows of data that, through no fault of your own, were imported in Excel as a single cell per row. What's worse, the data fields aren't of a fixed length, so you can't use the MID function without a bit of tweaking. However, even if you are ever unfortunate enough to see data such as OI1800230IT7801CI486SPFX2D in a single worksheet cell, you can still find a way to read it if you're clever.

Rather than keep you in suspense, you should know that the data actually breaks out this way: `OrderID OI1800230, Item IT7801, CustomerID CI486, Shipping FedEx Second Day`. But how to you find that out? The method is equal parts cleverness and skill. The cleverness comes from marking the beginning of each field with a distinct code. In the example string just shown, the first seven characters represent the *OrderID*, OI1800230. The *OrderID* begins with the letters *OI*, which you can assume for the purposes of this example won't occur anywhere else in the string. The same marking technique is used to call out the *Item* number (*IT*), the *CustomerID* (*CI*), and the *Shipping* method (*SP*).

> **Note** You could guard against any stray occurrences of the marker sequences by putting brackets around the marker, such as *<OI>* or *<IT>*. It's the same sort of markup system used in the Hypertext Markup Language (HTML) and the Extensible Markup Language (XML), and it works well for other systems that don't need to encode brackets as values.

When it comes to locating strings within other strings, having skill is operationally defined as knowing about the SEARCH and FIND functions. Both functions return the number of the character within a string at which a specific character or text string is found, but there are minor but important differences in how the functions operate. Here are the functions' syntaxes:

```
SEARCH(find_text, within_text, start_num)
FIND(find_text, within_text, start_num)
```

find_text is the text you want to find. If you use the SEARCH function, you can use the wildcard characters, question mark (?) and asterisk (*), in *find_text*. A question mark matches any single character, whereas an asterisk matches any sequence of characters. If you want to find an actual question mark or asterisk, type a tilde (~) before the character. The SEARCH function isn't case-sensitive, so searching for *e* will also find *E*. The FIND function is case-sensitive and doesn't allow wildcards—you can think of it as a more precise version of the SEARCH function. With FIND, searching for *e* will not find *E*.

- *within_text* is the text in which you want to search for *find_text*.
- *start_num* is the character number in *within_text* at which you want to start searching. If you leave this parameter blank, the search will start from the beginning of the string (that is, `start_num = 1`).

The benefit of the SEARCH and FIND functions really comes to the fore when you combine them with the MID function. Once you've used the SEARCH or FIND function to locate the start of two consecutive fields, you can use the MID function to draw in the part of the string you want. There is one more subtlety of which you need to be aware. Although the MID function is part of the standard VBA package, the SEARCH and FIND functions are not, so you'll once again need to use the *Application.WorksheetFunction* object to call the functions, as in the following example:

```
Application.WorksheetFunction.Search("IT", ActiveCell.Value)
```

Note The VBA function INSTR also returns the position of the character where a string begins within another string, but the function is the equivalent of the FIND function in that the INSTR function is case-sensitive.

If you reconsider the nightmare scenario where order item records were imported incorrectly, you could use the SEARCH and the MID functions to find the beginning and the end of each field's values and write the values into a cell, as in the following procedure:

```
Public Sub SeparateValues()

Dim MyCell As Range
Dim intIT, intCI, intSP As Integer
Dim strFirst, strLast, strAllCells As String

strFirst = InputBox("Enter the address of the first cell.")
strLast = InputBox("Enter the address of the last cell.")
strAllCells = strFirst & ":" & strLast

For Each MyCell In Range(strAllCells).Cells

    Range(MyCell.Address).Select

    intIT = Application.WorksheetFunction.Search("IT", MyCell.Value)
    intCI = Application.WorksheetFunction.Search("CI", MyCell.Value)
    intSP = Application.WorksheetFunction.Search("SP", MyCell.Value)

    ActiveCell.Offset(0, 2).Value = Mid(MyCell.Value, 1, intIT - 1)
    ActiveCell.Offset(0, 3).Value = Mid(MyCell.Value, intIT, intCI - intIT)
    ActiveCell.Offset(0, 4).Value = Mid(MyCell.Value, intCI, intSP - intCI)
    ActiveCell.Offset(0, 5).Value = Mid(MyCell.Value, intSP)

Next MyCell

End Sub
```

This procedure would take the strings in cells in the range entered by a user (A2:A21 in this example) and write the component values into the cells to the right, as shown in Figure 9-2.

Chapter 9

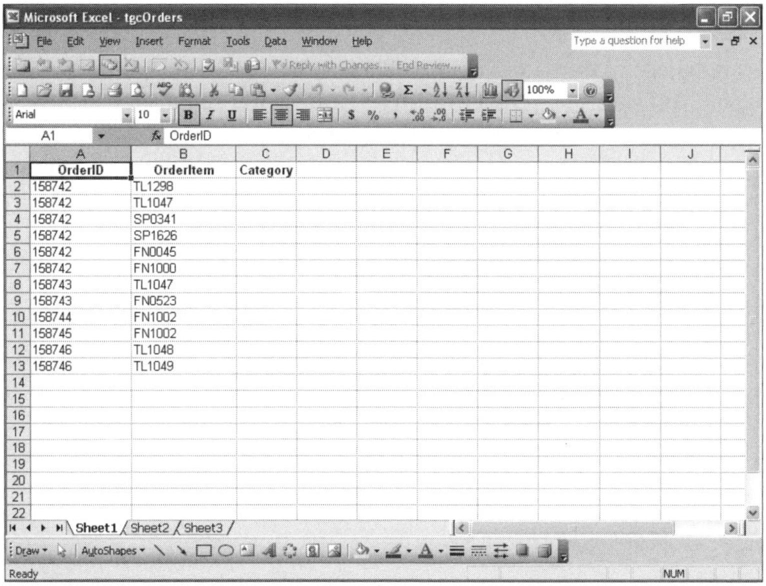

Figure 9-2. The SEARCH and MID functions, among others, let you reach into lengthy text strings to extract the interesting parts.

Note If you are working with data where each field or cell is of a known length, you can dispense with the calculations to determine where each substring starts.

Inside Out

Text Processing and Browser Cookies

Running a complex corporate Web site means a lot of work for the administrators and, more often than not, a substantial cash outlay on the part of a company to get everything looking and performing just so. Part of the administrator's job, like it or not, is justifying the money and time being spent on the site. And if your site doesn't use a lot of programming, and you're the person who administers the site without doing a lot of programming, you probably live in dread of being asked to process the information stored in cookies that your Web server places on your visitors' computers. Although programming cookies is beyond the scope of this book, you might find a cookie with a single string where a user's activities are encoded in much the same manner as the order strings shown earlier in the chapter. For example, the text of a cookie might be the string UI007589TM37900.77589, where 007589 is the visitor's user identification and 37900.77589 is the date/time string representing the user's last visit (which, in this case, was 10/6/2003 6:37 P.M.).

Manipulating Numbers

The topics discussed in the following section are, strictly speaking, part of the standard functioning of an Excel worksheet and not VBA programming. That being said, there are a number of financial calculations that you perform frequently in business settings, so they're included in this book. These functions are discussed in the context of VBA routines, but there will be enough examples of how to use the financial functions in your worksheets so that you'll learn how to use them as formulas, too.

Performing Summary Calculations

One of the strengths of the Excel spreadsheet program is that you can summarize worksheet data in many different ways, but one of its weaknesses, at least in terms of relatively new users taking advantage of those features, is that you need to know they're there. Table 9-2 lists the mathematical operations (and a few other operations) that you can use to summarize the data in a worksheet.

Table 9-2. The Most Common Summary Calculations You'll Perform in Excel

Function	Description
AVERAGE	Finds the arithmetic average (mean) of a data set
COUNT	Counts the number of cells in a range
COUNTA	Counts the number of non-blank cells in a range
COUNTBLANK	Counts the number of blank cells in a range
COUNTIF (range, criteria)	Counts the number of cells in a range that match a given criteria
MAX	Finds the largest value in a range
MEDIAN	Finds the median value or values (the value or the value pair closest to the average) of a range
MIN	Finds the smallest value in a range
MODE	Finds the most common value in a range
STDEV	Finds the standard deviation of the values in a range
SUM	Finds the arithmetic sum of the values in a range
SUMIF(range, criteria)	Finds the arithmetic sum of the values in a range that meet a given criteria

So now you know what the basic summary functions are, but how will your colleagues know which operations they can use? Simple: you tell them. You can list the available operations in a cell, a comment, or a text box that you place beside the data.

The following procedure is an example of how you might go about allowing your colleagues to identify which data to summarize and to select which summary operation to perform.

206

> **Note** Although this version of the procedure uses a *Select Case* statement with included code to perform each summary calculation, you could choose to create a function for each summary operation and call the function from within the corresponding *Case* statement. You might also choose to let the user type in the number of the summary operation they want to perform instead of the name. (To avoid spelling and capitalization errors, the values must match exactly.)

```
Public Sub Summarize()
    Dim intColNumber As Integer
    Dim strOperation, strCriteria As String
    Dim sngResult As Single

    MsgBox ("Select a cell within the table you want to summarize." _
    & "Type the number, not the letter, representing the column of the " _
    & "cells you want to summarize.")

    intColNumber = InputBox("Which column do you want to summarize?")
    strOperation = InputBox("Which summary operation do you want to perform?" _
& " The options are Sum, SumIF, Max, Min, Count, CountA, CountBlank, " _
& "CountIF, Average, Mode, StDev. (Type them exactly as they appear.)")
    With ActiveCell.CurrentRegion.Columns(intColNumber)
    Select Case strOperation
    Case "Sum"
    sngResult = Application.WorksheetFunction.Sum(.Cells)
    MsgBox ("The sum of the column is " & sngResult & ".")
    Case "SumIF"
    strCriteria = InputBox("Type a criteria for the method by " _
& "typing a number alone or preceded by one of the operators " _
& ">, <, or =.")
    sngResult = Application.WorksheetFunction.SumIf(.Cells, strCriteria)
    MsgBox ("The sum of the values is " & sngResult & ".")
    Case "Max"
    sngResult = Application.WorksheetFunction.Max(Cells)
    MsgBox ("The maximum value in the column is " & sngResult & ".")
    Case "Min"
    sngResult = Application.WorksheetFunction.Min(.Cells)
    MsgBox ("The minimum value in the column is " & sngResult & ".")
    Case "Count"
    sngResult = Application.WorksheetFunction.Count(.Cells)
    MsgBox ("The number of cells is " & sngResult & ".")
    Case "CountA"
    sngResult = Application.WorksheetFunction.CountA(Cells)
    MsgBox ("The number of non-blank cells is " & sngResult & ".")
    Case "CountBlank"
    sngResult = Application.WorksheetFunction.CountBlank(.Cells)
    MsgBox ("The number of blank cells is " & sngResult & ".")
    Case "CountIF"
    strCriteria = InputBox("Type a criteria for the method by " _
& "typing a number alone or preceded by one of the operators " _
& ">, <, or =.")
```

```
        sngResult = Application.WorksheetFunction.CountIf(.Cells, strCriteria)
        MsgBox ("The number of cells that meet the criteria is " & sngResult & ".")
        Case "Average"
        sngResult = Application.WorksheetFunction.Average(.Cells)
        MsgBox ("The average of the values is " & sngResult & ".")
        Case "Mode"
        sngResult = Application.WorksheetFunction.Mode(.Cells)
        MsgBox ("The mode of the values is " & sngResult & ".")
        Case "StDev"
        sngResult = Application.WorksheetFunction.StDev(.Cells)
        MsgBox ("The standard deviation of the values is " & _
        sngResult & ".")
        Case Else
        MsgBox ("Unrecognized operation; please try again.")
        End Select
        End With
    End Sub
```

> **Note** You probably noticed how much work the `With ActiveCell.CurrentRegion.Columns(intColNumber)` statement saved in the *Summarize* procedure. If it weren't for the *With* statement, the range reference code would have wrapped around every line, making the code extremely hard to read. Always look for such opportunities to simplify your code.

Performing Financial Calculations

One of the most common financial calculations you'll be asked to perform is to determine the monthly payment on a loan. For that calculation you use the PMT function, which has the syntax:

`PMT(rate, nper, pv, fv, type)`

Table 9-3 describes the five arguments used with the PMT function.

Table 9-3. An In-Depth Look at the PMT Function's Arguments

Argument	Description
rate	The interest rate, to be divided by 12 for a loan with monthly payments
nper	The total number of payments for the loan
pv	The amount loaned (*pv* is short for present value, or principal)
fv	The amount to be left over at the end of the payment cycle (usually left blank, which indicates 0)
type	0 or 1, indicating whether payments are made at the beginning or at the end of the month (usually left blank, which indicates 0, or the end of the month)

If you wanted to borrow $20,000 at an 8 percent interest rate and pay the loan back over 24 months, you could write the formula in a worksheet cell as =**PMT(8%/12, 24, 20000)**, which results in a monthly payment of $904.55. In Excel VBA, you would once again use the *Application.WorksheetFunction* object to call the PMT function within a VBA function procedure. The sample procedure assumes the rate is in cell B2, the number of payments is in cell B3, the amount borrowed is in cell B4, the amount owed at the end of the loan (always 0) is in cell B5, and the time when a payment is made (leave blank to use the default value) is in cell B6.

```
Public Function MonthlyPayment(rate, nper, pv, fv, when) As Currency
    With Application.WorksheetFunction
        MonthlyPayment = .Pmt(rate / 12, nper, pv, fv, when)
    End With
End Function

Public Sub Payment()
    MsgBox (MonthlyPayment(Range("B2"), Range("B3"), Range("B4"), _
        Range("B5"), Range("B6")))
End Sub
```

Warning   You might have noticed that in the *MonthlyPayment* function the *type* argument is replaced with *when*—it's because *type* is a reserved word in VBA and Excel generates an error when the compiler encounters it.

There are also Excel worksheet functions that you can use to determine the amount of a payment devoted to interest and to the loan's principal. These calculations are important for tax reasons. For example, if the interest on your home loan is tax-deductible, it helps to know exactly how much of each monthly payment represents interest and how much pays down the principal. The IPMT worksheet function lets you calculate how much of a payment goes toward interest. The syntax of the IPMT function is similar to the PMT function's syntax, but there are some key differences.

```
IPMT(rate,per,nper,pv,fv,type)
```

The *rate*, *pv*, *fv*, and *type* arguments all mean the same as they do in the PMT function, but the *per* argument is new. The *per* argument represents the period for which you want to find the interest and must be somwhere between 1 and *nper*. For example, if you wanted to determine how much of each month's payment is devoted to interest, you could do so using the following procedure, which places the resulting value in the active cell:

```
Public Sub DetermineInterest()
    Dim intRate, intPer, intNper As Integer
    Dim curPv, curInterest As Currency
```

```
intRate = InputBox("What is the interest rate (as an integer)?")
intPer = InputBox("For which month do you want to find the interest?")
intNper = InputBox("How many payments will you make on the loan?")
curPv = InputBox("How much did you borrow?")

With Application.WorksheetFunction
    curInterest = -1 *(.IPmt(intRate / 1200, intPer, intNper, curPv))
End With

ActiveCell.Value = curInterest
End Sub
```

> **Note**   This procedure multiplies *curInterest* by -1 to produce a positive result. It's true that your cash flow is negative, but most folks like to think of payments in positive numbers (if not positive terms).

You can list how much each payment contributes to interest by adding a *For...Next* loop around the periodic interest calculation, which places the resulting values in a column starting with the active cell.

```
Public Sub DetermineAllInterest()
Dim intRate, intPer, intNper, intPayment As Integer
Dim curPv, curInterest As Currency

    intRate = InputBox("What is the interest rate (integer number only)?")
    intNper = InputBox("How many payments will you make on the loan?")
    curPv = InputBox("How much did you borrow?")

    For intPer = 1 To intNper
        With Application.WorksheetFunction
        curInterest = -1 * (.IPmt(intRate / 1200, intPer, intNper, curPv))
        'Divide by 1200 to get a monthly percentage (12 months * 100 per cent)
    End With

    ActiveCell.Value = curInterest
    ActiveCell.Offset(1, 0).Activate
    Next intPer

End Sub
```

The complementary function of IPMT is PPMT, which determines the amount of a payment that is devoted to the loan's principal. The PPMT function's syntax is exactly the same as that of IPMT, but the result is the dollar amount of a payment that is applied to the principal.

Now that you've seen the functions you use to determine your payments, and what share of those payments go toward interest and principal, it's time to show you how to reverse engineer an interest rate from a known payment schedule. Yes, it's rare that you would need to figure out your interest rate for a home loan (because it's something few folks forget, and it'll be right there on the loan papers), but just in case you need to, here it is.

The syntax of the RATE function is similar to those of the PMT family of functions.

```
RATE(nper,pmt,pv,fv,type,guess)
```

Because there are some differences between RATE and the other PMT functions, Table 9-4 summarizes the RATE function's arguments for you.

Table 9-4. The Rate Function's Arguments

Argument	Description
Nper	The total number of payment periods in an annuity.
Pmt	The payment made each period. This value can't change over the life of the annuity. If *pmt* is omitted, you must include the *fv* argument.
Pv	The present value of the annuity—the total amount that a series of future payments is worth now.
Fv	The future value, or a cash balance that you want to attain after the last payment is made. If *fv* is omitted, it's assumed to be 0. (The future value of a loan, for example, is 0.)
Type	The number 0 or 1, indicating when payments are due. (0 is the default, which means payments are due at the end of the month.)
Guess	Your guess for what the rate will be. If you omit guess, it's assumed to be 10 percent. If RATE doesn't converge, try different values for *Guess*. RATE usually converges if *Guess* is between 0 and 1.

So, if you wanted to figure out the interest rate on a $150,000 home loan that you were paying back at $1,186.19 a month over 15 years, you would use the following formula to determine the annual percentage rate of the loan:

```
=RATE(180,-1186.19,150000)*12
```

It's important to enter the payment (the second parameter) as a negative number. It might make it easier to remember this requirement if you think of the payment as money that's leaving your bank account.

Determining the Present Value of an Investment

The PV, or *present value*, function returns the present value of an investment, which is finance-speak for the total amount of money that a series of equal-value future payments is worth now. When you borrow money, the loan amount is the present value to the lender. For example, if you wanted to calculate the present value of a $150,000 loan with 5 percent interest to be paid back monthly over 15 years, you would use the following formula:

```
PV(rate,nper,pmt,fv,type)
```

Chapter 9

In the preceding formula, once again, *rate* is the interest rate per period (usually an annual rate divided by 12), *nper* is the total number of payment periods (in this case, 12 * 15, or 180), *pmt* is the payment made each period (1186.19 in this case), *fv* is the future value, or a cash balance you want to attain after the last payment is made (the future value of a loan is 0), and *type* indicates if a payment is due at the end of the month (0, the default, means you pay at the end of the month, and 1 means you pay at the beginning of the month). So, for the loan described above, you would create this formula:

```
=PV(5%/12, 180, -1186.19)
```

The preceding formula generates a present value of $150,000, the total amount of the loan. The sum total of the payments is actually $213,514.20, but the present value of the loan is lower because, when the loan is made, the interest hasn't had time to compound. After 10 years of payments, for example, a homeowner would have paid $142,342.80 but would still be facing another 60 payments!

Determining the Net Present Value of an Investment

A function that's related to PV is NPV, which calculates the *net present value* of an investment. The primary difference between present value and net present value is that net present value assumes the value of investment decreases over time due to inflation or another discount rate. That assumption is reflected in the NPV function's syntax.

```
NPV(rate, value1, value2, value3…)
```

Another difference between present value and net present value calculations is that the values in an NPV formula can vary, but in a PV calculation the payments must be constant over the life of the annuity. For example, you might consider making a $5,000 investment in a security that would pay you $1,000 after the first year, $1,500 after the second year, $2,000 after the third year, and $2,500 after the fourth year. Assuming 4 percent inflation, you would create the following formula to evaluate the investment:

=NPV(4%, -5000, 1000, 1500, 2000, 2500)

The preceding formula generates a result of $1,214.78. There's no magical threshold where the net present value of an investment makes it worthwhile; you need to compare the return of several investments to determine whether and how to invest your money.

> For more information on using Excel to perform in-depth financial analysis, see *Data Analysis and Business Modeling with Microsoft Excel*, by Wayne L. Winston (Microsoft Press, 2004).

Manipulating Dates and Times

As with the number and text functions described earlier in this chapter, manipulating dates and times is more in the realm of the Excel formula than something that, strictly speaking, you need VBA to accomplish. However, it's important to be able to work with dates and times when you're doing advanced work in Excel, so it seems right to include these functions.

Time and Date Serial Numbers

If you've ever typed a date into a worksheet cell and then changed the cell's format to General or Number, you've seen the date change into a number. For example, if you type the date **October 6, 2003** into a cell and then change the cell's format to General, the cell's value changes to 37900. The reason for the change in value is that Excel treats dates and times as numbers, not strings. In Excel, the default behavior for the program is to begin counting from January 1, 1900. So January 1, 1900, was day 1, January 2, 1900, was day 2, and so on. Representing a date as a number makes it easy to determine the number of days between two events. For example, if a company were founded on August 2, 1998, and first became profitable on January 9, 2004, you would know the number of days it took to attain profitability was 1986.

> **Important** Dates prior to January 1, 1900, are treated as strings. You can't manipulate them using the date functions covered in the next section, but they are accepted as valid input.

Date and Time Functions

There are many instances when the date or time of an event would be important to you. If you use Excel to track orders placed with your business, you can enter the date and time of an order into your worksheet using the following VBA code:

```
ActiveCell.Value = Now
```

Yes, you could also enter the current date and time into a worksheet cell using the Excel formula =**NOW**, which returns the current date and time, but if you didn't take the time to replace the formula with its value by clicking the Copy button, clicking the Paste Options button (the arrow next to the button), and then selecting Values, Excel will recalculate the formula whenever you open the workbook and replace the time of the order with the current time. You can avoid that problem by creating a macro that assigns the value of *Now* to the active cell.

Now is not the only date or time function available to you in Excel VBA. Table 9-5 lists the functions available to you and describes them.

Table 9-5. Useful Functions for Finding All or Part of a Date or Time

Function	Description
Date	Returns the current date.
Time	Returns the current time.
Now	Returns the current date and time.
Timer	Returns the number of seconds since midnight.
DateValue	Given a character string, such as "August 2, 2004", returns a date (for example, 8/2/2004).
TimeValue	Given a character string, such as "19:30", returns a time (for example, 7:30:00 P.M.)
DateSerial (year, month, day)	Given a year, month, and day (for example, *DateSerial*(2004, 8, 2) returns the date (8/2/2004).
TimeSerial (hour, minute, second)	Given an hour, minute, and second, (for example, *TimeSerial*(19, 30, 24), returns the time (7:30:24 PM).
Hour, Minute, Second	Given a time, returns the hour, minute, or second component of that time.
Year, Month, Day	Given a date, returns the year, month, or day component of that date.
Weekday	Given a date, returns the weekday (**Sunday = 1**, **Monday = 2**, and so on) of that date.
MonthName	Given an integer, returns the month corresponding to that integer (for example, 8 returns August).

With the exception of the *Weekday* and *MonthName* functions, writing the result of any of the mentioned date and time functions to a worksheet cell means that Excel will format the cell with its default Date format.

There are a number of other date-related and time-related functions that you can use to perform calculations in your Excel VBA code. The two most useful functions are *DateAdd* and *DateDiff. DateAdd*, as the name implies, lets you add a time period to a date or time. Yes, you can add three days to a date with simple addition, as in the following procedure:

```
Public Sub AddDays()

    Dim datFirst, datSecond As Date
    datFirst = #1/9/2004#
    datSecond = datFirst + 3
    MsgBox ("The new date is: " & datSecond & ".")

End Sub
```

Chapter 9

But what if you want to add a month to *datFirst*? Depending on the month, you would need to add either 28, 30, or 31 days. The *DateAdd* procedure lets you add a variety of time increments to a date or time through the use of an ingenious syntax

```
DateAdd("interval", number, date)
```

in which *interval* is the code (in quotes) of the time unit, *number* is the number of times to increment the date or time by the *interval,* and *date* is the date or time to which you want to add the time. Table 9-6 lists the available units and their corresponding codes.

Table 9-6. Codes for Intervals Used in the *DateAdd* Function

Unit	Code
yyyy	Year
q	Quarter (three months)
m	Month
ww	Week
y	Day of year
d	Day
W	Weekday
h	Hour
n	Minute
s	Seconds

For example, if you wanted to use a message box to display the date nine weeks from today, you would use the following function:

```
MsgBox (DateAdd("ww", 9, DATE))
```

You can also use negative values within the *DateAdd* function to move backward in time. For example, the function to return the time eight hours ago (reckoning from the current time on your computer clock) would be

```
DateAdd("h", -8, NOW)
```

> **Note** You can also use negative values in the *DateSerial* and *TimeSerial* functions, described earlier, but the *DateAdd* function gives you more flexibility by letting you use different time units.

The *DateDiff* function, as the name implies, lets you find the number of time units (that is, months, years, minutes, and so on) between two dates or times. The syntax is similar to that of the *DateAdd* function, but instead of using a base date and an increment to determine an end date, the *DateDiff* function uses two dates to determine the difference in interval between them.

Chapter 9

```
DateDiff ("interval", date1, date2, firstdayofweek, firstweekofyear)
```

The arguments of the *DateDiff* function are listed in Table 9-7.

Table 9-7. The *DateDiff* Function's Arguments

Argument	Description
Interval	An interval value listed in Table 9-6.
Date1	The first date to use in the calculation.
Date2	The second date to use in the calculation.
firstdayofweek	A constant that specifies the first day of the week. If not specified, Sunday is assumed. The available constants are *vbUseSystem* (use the system setting), *vbSunday*, *vbMonday*, *vbTuesday*, *vbWednesday*, *vbThursday*, *vbFriday*, and *vbSaturday*.
firstweekofyear	A constant that specifies the first week of the year. The available constants are *vbUseSystem* (use the system setting), *vbFirstJan1* (the default, which uses the week that contains January 1), *vbFirstFourDays* (uses the first week with at least four days in the new year), *vbFirstFullWeek* (uses the first seven-day week in the new year).

For example, the following function returns the number of days between the current date and August 2, 2005 (remember that the date needs to be enclosed by pound signs):

```
DateDiff("d", NOW, #8/2/2005#)
```

When you subtract times, you don't need to use a special operator—the subtraction operator works, but you can run into problems if you cross midnight. For example, if you work from 9:00 P.M. to 6:00 A.M. you have worked nine hours, but subtracting .875 (the time serial of 9:00 P.M.) from .25 (the time serial of 6:00 A.M.) results in a negative number, which you can't have when working with time serials. The trick is to add a day to the smaller value to make the subtraction work. Adding 1 to the time serial for 6:00 A.M. results in the equation 1.25 − .875, which equals .375 (nine hours, or 9:00 A.M.). Here's how you implement this check in VBA:

```
'datTime1 is the start time, datTime2 is the finishing time
If datTime1 > datTime2 Then
datTime2 = datTime2 + 1
End If
datDifference = datTime2 - datTime 1
```

Inside Out

Working with Times That Exceed 24 Hours

If you've ever tried to add two times together in an Excel worksheet, you've probably found that the program doesn't handle results of more than 24 hours gracefully. In fact, if you were to add 8:00 (8 hours), 7:00 (7 hours), and 10:00 (10 hours) together, the worksheet cell with the formula displays 1:00 (1 hour)! In other words, Excel disregards the first 24 hours and just shows the number of hours beyond the first 24. The same thing happens if you add two instances of 12:00 (12 hours) to the formula—even though the total number of hours is 49:00, the worksheet cell displays 1:00.

You can overcome this difficulty by formatting the cell in which you want to display the results with one of the custom data formats available in the Format Cell dialog box, which you open by clicking Format, Cells. Within the Format Cell dialog box, click the Custom category and scroll down until you see this time format: *[h]:mm:ss*.

The square brackets ([]) around the hour symbol mean that the normal limit of 24 hours no longer applies, so the cell will display time increments such as 25:00 correctly. You can do the same thing if you want to display more than 60 minutes ([mm]:ss) or more than 60 seconds ([ss]), although you'd have to create your own custom format by typing it into the Type box. Do remember that Excel won't let you create a format such as [h]:[mm]:ss— because there's no limit on the number of minutes, the number of hours would always be 0. Also, you should be aware that you can't put square brackets around a day indicator or a month indicator.

In this chapter, you've learned how to manipulate the data in your Excel workbooks. Whether you want to summarize the data using mathematical functions, concatenate the values from two or more cells to create detailed message boxes, or work with dates and times effectively, you can find those functions in Excel VBA. And if the functions aren't available in Excel VBA, there's a good chance you can call them from the main Excel program using the *Application* object's *WorksheetFunction* property.

Formatting Excel Objects

Using Excel Color Constants and the
Color Palette 219
Formatting Worksheet Elements 230

Formatting Fonts 231
Formatting Cells 233
Formatting Borders 236

If left in their original condition, Microsoft Excel worksheets are fairly plain to look at. Black text on a white background, with gray gridlines indicating cell barriers, is a functional way to present data, but it's not the most exciting presentation imaginable. Not to mention the fact that if all of your data looks the same, there's nothing to distinguish one cell from another except for the value. And, yes, the values are the most important part of a worksheet, but presentation does count for something.

In this chapter you'll learn how to use Excel color constants and the Excel color palette, modify the existing color palette, find out how to get around the 56-color limit in Excel, and format cells by changing their interior, font, and border colors.

Using Excel Color Constants and the Color Palette

Although there are a lot of ways you can reformat the elements of a worksheet, one great way to call attention to an element is by changing that element's color. Whether you change the color of text in a cell to reflect the cell's value, change the color of a sheet tab to indicate there was a change made to the worksheet's data, or make a cell's background yellow to emphasize that it is the active cell, you can use colors to make your data stand out and your sheets easier to use.

The simplest way to assign a color to a worksheet element is to use one of the Microsoft Visual Basic for Applications color constants, which represent the eight basic colors available on a computer. The constants and the colors they represent are listed in Table 10-1.

Table 10-1. The RGB Values of the VBA Color Constants

Constant	Description	Constant	Description
vbBlack	Black	vbRed	Red
vbGreen	Green	vbYellow	Yellow
vbBlue	Blue	vbMagenta	Magenta
vbCyan	Cyan	vbWhite	White

Why are these colors the only ones with constants assigned to them? The reason lies in how colors are created on a computer. You probably encountered the *color wheel* sometime, probably in school, and you learned that you can combine red, blue, and yellow pigments to create any color you want. That's true for pigments (usually paint or ink), but it's not true when you're working with light. When you want to create colors using light, you operate with these three primary colors: red, green, and blue.

The difference between working with pigments and working with light is captured in the names of the two color systems: *subtractive color*, which refers to pigments, and *additive color*, which refers to light. In the subtractive color system, you begin with white (the absence of *color*) and, through the use of pigments, "subtract" colors by blocking them out with your paint. If you mix equal amounts of the primary colors (red, yellow, and blue) you'll get black because you've subtracted all of the colors. In the additive color system, by contrast, you start with black (the absence of *light*) and add colors to the mix. In the additive color system, adding full-intensity red, green, and blue light, you get white light.

Just as you can mix differing amounts of paint to produce unique colors (for example, mixing equal amounts of red and yellow makes true orange, whereas putting in more red than yellow makes a red-orange), you can mix differing amounts of light to create distinct colors on your computer. The Microsoft Windows operating system recognizes 256 intensities for each primary color (red, green, and blue). An intensity of 0 means that none of that light is added to the color of a *pixel* (a dot on your monitor screen), and an intensity of 255 means that the maximum amount of that color is added.

> **Note** A pixel is actually made up of three dots: one that emits red light, one that emits green light, and one that emits blue light.

To define a color using a mixture of red, green, and blue light, you use the Visual Basic RGB function, which has this syntax:

```
RGB(red, green, blue)
```

In this function, *red* is the amount of red light to be used, *green* is the amount of green light to be used, and *blue* is the amount of blue light to be used. (Any value over 255 is assumed to be 255.) Table 10-2 lists the RGB values for the eight colors assigned to the VBA color constants.

Table 10-2. The RGB Values of the VBA Color Constants

Constant	R	G	B
vbBlack	0	0	0
vbRed	255	0	0
vbGreen	0	255	0
vbYellow	255	255	0
vbBlue	0	0	255

Table 10-2. The RGB Values of the VBA Color Constants

Constant	R	G	B
vbMagenta	255	0	255
vbCyan	0	255	255
vbWhite	255	255	255

> **Note** There are 16,777,216 possible RGB color combinations, but the eight colors in Table 10-2 have variable names assigned to them because they are the simplest colors, representing the eight combinations available when the individual pixel lights are either on at full intensity or off.

You can use the RGB function to apply a color directly to an element of your worksheet, but there is an important limitation you need to know about in Excel: the program can only display 56 colors at a time, and Excel keeps track of those 56 colors in the Excel color palette. If the color you attempt to assign to the element isn't in the color palette, Excel displays the closest color that is in the palette.

Table 10-3 lists the RGB values of the colors assigned to each of the entries in the standard Excel color palette, along with the name of that color.

Table 10-3. The RGB Values of the Standard Excel Colors

Name	R	G	B
Black (Color 1)	0	0	0
White (Color 2)	255	255	255
Red (Color 3)	255	0	0
Green (Color 4)	0	255	0
Blue (Color 5)	0	0	255
Yellow (Color 6)	255	255	0
Magenta (Color 7)	255	0	255
Cyan (Color 8)	0	255	255
Color 9	128	0	0
Color 10	0	128	0
Color 11	0	0	128
Color 12	128	128	0
Color 13	128	0	128
Color 14	0	128	128
Color 15	192	192	192
Color 16	128	128	128

continued

Chapter 10

Table 10-3. **The RGB Values of the Standard Excel Colors** *(continued)*

Name	R	G	B
Color 17	153	153	255
Color 18	153	51	102
Color 19	255	255	204
Color 20	204	255	255
Color 21	102	0	102
Color 22	255	128	128
Color 23	0	102	204
Color 24	204	204	255
Color 25	0	0	128
Color 26	255	0	255
Color 27	255	255	0
Color 28	0	255	255
Color 29	128	0	128
Color 30	128	0	0
Color 31	0	128	128
Color 32	0	0	255
Color 33	0	204	255
Color 34	204	255	255
Color 35	204	255	204
Color 36	255	255	153
Color 37	153	204	255
Color 38	255	153	204
Color 39	204	153	255
Color 40	255	204	153
Color 41	51	102	255
Color 42	51	204	204
Color 43	153	204	0
Color 44	255	204	0
Color 45	255	153	0
Color 46	255	102	0
Color 47	102	102	153
Color 48	150	150	150
Color 49	0	51	102
Color 50	51	153	102

Table 10-3. **The RGB Values of the Standard Excel Colors**   *(continued)*

Name	R	G	B
Color 51	0	51	0
Color 52	51	51	0
Color 53	153	51	0
Color 54	153	51	102
Color 55	51	51	153
Color 56	51	51	51

Yes, once you get beyond the eight colors that are assigned to Visual Basic constants, the names of the colors reflect the color's position in the palette's index. That decision makes sense, though, once you realize that you as a programmer (or as a user of the main Excel program) can assign new RGB values to any of the slots in the palette.

> **Note**   The color palette, as referred to here, isn't the same as the palette displayed in the main Excel program. It's strictly used as an internal representation of the colors.

You can assign a color to a worksheet element by referring to a position in the Excel color palette. To do so, you use the *Workbook* object's *Colors* property, which has this syntax:

```
Workbook.Colors (index)
```

In the preceding code, *index* is any number from 1 to 56. If you have a pie chart with divisions for all 100 products sold by your company, you'll get some repeat colors. That's not such a bad thing…the colors should be far enough apart on the chart so that your colleagues won't have any trouble distinguishing the divisions. As an alternative, you can always create a chart in which you display the proportion of sales attributed to the top 50 products (with a single wedge for the other 50 products), and then break out the sales of the remaining products on a separate chart.

Manipulating the Current Excel Color Palette

Realizing that you're limited to using the colors in the color palette for a given workbook, you'd probably be interested in a procedure that lets you display the colors in the current palette. The DisplayPalette procedure does just that.

```
Sub DisplayPalette()
    Range("A1").Select
    ActiveCell.Formula = "Color"
    ActiveCell.Offset(0, 1).Formula = "Index"
    ActiveCell.Offset(1, 0).Activate
    For NumColor = 1 To 56
        With ActiveCell.Interior
            .ColorIndex = NumColor
            .Pattern = xlSolid
```

Chapter 10

```
        .PatternColorIndex = xlAutomatic
      End With
      ActiveCell.Offset(0, 1).Formula = NumColor
      ActiveCell.Offset(1, 0).Activate
   Next NumColor
End Sub
```

> **Caution** A version of this procedure was originally published on the Microsoft Knowledge Base at *http://support.microsoft.com/support/kb/articles/q149/1/70.asp*, but that version of the program has a variable naming error that causes it to repeat the same color in all 56 cells. For debugging practice, run the code, find out what happens, and see if you can spot the error (provided the MSDN folks haven't corrected it).

But what if the colors in the palette aren't what you need for your designs? Many organizations have policies regarding the specific colors used in and appearance of their logos and official documents. Rather than be forced to work with colors that might not be exactly right, you can substitute a custom color for an existing color in the palette.

To assign a new color to a slot in the Excel color palette from within the Excel program, follow these steps:

1 Click Tools, Options, and then click the Color tab in the Options dialog box.

2 Click the square of the color you want to replace, and then click Modify. If you see the color you want in the Colors dialog box that appears, click it and then click OK. If you don't see the color you want, click the Custom tab.

3 Verify that RGB is selected in the Color Model list box.

4 Type the red, blue, and green components of your color in the appropriate boxes.

Assigning a color to a position in the color palette takes a single line of code in Excel VBA.

```
ActiveWorkbook.Colors (index) = RGB (red, green, blue)
```

But which colors should you substitute? Any you won't use, of course, but there are actually a number of duplicate colors in the standard palette. Why? No clue. But here are the repeats:

- Color 5 (Blue) is repeated by Color 32.
- Color 6 (Yellow) is repeated by Color 27.
- Color 7 (Magenta) is repeated by Color 26.
- Color 8 (Cyan) is repeated by Color 28.
- Color 9 is repeated by Color 30.
- Color 13 is repeated by Color 29.
- Color 14 is repeated by Color 31.
- Color 18 is repeated by Color 54.
- Color 20 is repeated by Color 34.

You should probably replace the higher-numbered color first, especially if you're replacing a color that is named by one of the VBA color constants. The following procedure adds a new set of colors to the active workbook's palette using colors 26, 27, 28, 29, and 30:

```
Sub CustomColors()
    ActiveWorkbook.Colors(26) = RGB(240, 248, 255)
    ActiveWorkbook.Colors(27) = RGB(138, 43, 226)
    ActiveWorkbook.Colors(28) = RGB(165, 42, 42)
    ActiveWorkbook.Colors(29) = RGB(255, 250, 205)
    ActiveWorkbook.Colors(30) = RGB(199, 21, 133)
End Sub
```

Now when you run the DisplayPalette procedure listed earlier in this chapter, you will see your new colors in positions 26, 27, 28, 29, and 30.

Tip **Getting Around the Color Limit**

If you run into the 56-color barrier and don't have room to add colors for a corporate logo, you should insert the logo as a graphic. The colors in graphics don't count against the 56-color limit.

Changing the color palette of a workbook is relatively straightforward, but doing it for every workbook you create can be a pain if you try to do it by hand. However, you can write a short macro that copies the color palette from another workbook to the active workbook. Aside from the standard *Sub* and *End Sub* statements, you use the *Workbooks* collection's *Colors* property to copy the color palette from a workbook to the active workbook. If the workbook with the desired palette were named OurColors.xls, you would use the following procedure to copy the color palette over:

```
Sub GetOurColors()
    ActiveWorkbook.Colors = Workbooks("OurColors.xls").Colors
End Sub
```

To copy a color palette from another workbook using the Excel interface, follow these steps:

1 Open the workbook from which you want to copy the color palette.
2 In the workbook to which you want to copy the color palette, click Tools, Options.
3 Click the Color tab in the Options dialog box.
4 Click the Copy Colors From down arrow, and then click the name of the workbook from which you want to copy the color palette.

If you've changed the default Excel color palette, you can change it back to the default by calling the *Workbook* object's *ResetColors* method, as in the following procedure:

```
Sub NormalColors()
ActiveWorkbook.ResetColors
End Sub
```

To change the color palette back to the default using the Excel interface, follow these steps:

1 Click Tools, Options.
2 Click the Color tab in the Options dialog box.
3 Click Reset.

Using the Excel Color Palette on the Web

If you've used the Web a lot, you've probably found that some pages that appear perfectly normal in one browser are a mess in another browser. Whether the spacing is off, the text is larger in some paragraphs than in others, or the colors are different, you just don't get what you expect. Part of the difficulty can be traced to older Web browsers that don't understand the newer markup tags, but another reason is that some programs, such as Microsoft FrontPage, tend to create code that is interpreted perfectly by Microsoft Internet Explorer but less well by other browsers. Colors are no different from other HTML formatting instructions, so you need to know what can cause the errors and how to avoid them.

Beginning with Internet Explorer 4.0, there has been a list of named colors with associated RGB color values that the browser knows how to interpret. Not all browsers know how to interpret the names of the colors, but every major browser is able to interpret RGB color values. Table 10-4 lists the standard HTML colors and their associated RGB values so that you can add them to your Excel color palette if you want to create a workbook that looks good both in print and on the Web.

> For more information on how these colors will look on your monitor, see the full-color table on MSDN, the Microsoft Developer Network site, at: *http://msdn.microsoft.com/workshop/author/dhtml/reference /colors/colors.asp.*

Table 10-4. The RGB Values of Standard HTML Colors

Color	R	G	B	Color	R	G	B
aliceblue	240	248	255	antiquewhite	250	235	215
aqua	0	255	255	aquamarine	127	255	212
azure	240	255	255	beige	245	245	220
bisque	255	228	196	black	0	0	0
blanchedalmond	255	235	205	blue	0	0	255
blueviolet	138	43	226	brown	165	42	42
burlywood	222	184	135	cadetblue	95	158	160
chartreuse	127	255	0	chocolate	210	105	30
coral	255	127	80	cornflowerblue	100	149	237
cornsilk	255	248	220	crimson	220	20	60
cyan	0	255	255	darkblue	0	0	139
darkcyan	0	139	139	darkgoldenrod	184	134	11
darkgray	169	169	169	darkgreen	0	100	0
darkkhaki	189	183	107	darkmagenta	139	0	139
darkolivegreen	85	107	47	darkorange	255	140	0
darkorchid	153	50	204	darkred	139	0	0
darksalmon	233	150	122	darkseagreen	143	188	139
darkslateblue	72	61	139	darkslategray	47	79	79
darkturquoise	0	206	209	darkviolet	148	0	211
deeppink	255	20	147	deepskyblue	0	191	255
dimgray	105	105	105	dodgerblue	30	144	255
firebrick	178	34	34	floralwhite	255	250	240
forestgreen	34	139	34	fuchsia	255	0	255
gainsboro	220	220	220	ghostwhite	248	248	255
gold	255	215	0	goldenrod	218	165	32
gray	128	128	128	green	0	128	0
greenyellow	173	255	47	honeydew	240	255	240
hotpink	255	105	180	indianred	205	92	92
indigo	75	0	130	ivory	255	255	240
khaki	240	230	140	lavender	230	230	250
lavenderblush	255	240	245	lawngreen	124	252	0
lemonchiffon	255	250	205	lightblue	173	216	230
lightcoral	240	128	128	lightcyan	224	255	255

continued

Chapter 10

Table 10-4. **The RGB Values of Standard HTML Colors**   *(continued)*

Color	R	G	B	Color	R	G	B
lightgoldenrodyellow	250	250	210	lightgreen	144	238	144
lightgrey	211	211	211	lightpink	255	182	193
lightsalmon	255	160	122	lightseagreen	32	178	170
lightskyblue	135	206	250	lightslategray	119	136	153
lightsteelblue	176	196	222	lightyellow	255	255	224
lime	0	255	0	limegreen	50	205	50
linen	250	240	230	magenta	255	0	255
maroon	128	0	0	mediumaquamarine	102	205	170
mediumblue	0	0	205	mediumorchid	186	85	211
mediumpurple	147	112	219	mediumseagreen	60	179	113
mediumslateblue	123	104	238	mediumspringgreen	0	250	154
mediumturquoise	72	209	204	mediumvioletred	199	21	133
midnightblue	25	25	112	mintcream	245	255	250
mistyrose	255	228	225	moccasin	255	228	181
navajowhite	255	222	173	navy	0	0	128
oldlace	253	245	230	olive	128	128	0
olivedrab	107	142	35	orange	255	165	0
orangered	255	69	0	orchid	218	112	214
palegoldenrod	238	232	170	palegreen	152	251	152
paleturquoise	175	238	238	palevioletred	219	112	147
papayawhip	255	239	213	peachpuff	255	218	185
peru	205	133	63	pink	255	192	203
plum	221	160	221	powderblue	176	224	230
purple	128	0	128	red	255	0	0
rosybrown	188	143	143	royalblue	65	105	225
saddlebrown	139	69	19	salmon	250	128	114
sandybrown	244	164	96	seagreen	46	139	87
seashell	255	245	238	sienna	160	82	45
silver	192	192	192	skyblue	135	206	235
slateblue	106	90	205	slategray	112	128	144
snow	255	250	250	springgreen	0	255	127
steelblue	70	130	180	tan	210	180	140
teal	0	128	128	thistle	216	191	216
tomato	255	99	71	turquoise	64	224	208

Table 10-4. The RGB Values of Standard HTML Colors *(continued)*

Color	R	G	B	Color	R	G	B
violet	238	130	238	wheat	245	222	179
white	255	255	255	whitesmoke	245	245	245
yellow	255	255	0	yellowgreen	154	205	50

> **For more information on how to publish Excel worksheets and workbooks to the Web, see Chapter 25, "Excel and the Web."**

Some of the work of matching colors from the Excel palette to the Web has been done for you. Table 10-5 lists the colors in the Excel palette that closely correspond to the standard HTML colors.

Table 10-5. Excel Palette Colors That Correspond to HTML Colors

Excel Color	HTML Color	R	G	B
Color 1 (Black)	black	0	0	0
Color 2 (White)	white	255	255	255
Color 3 (Red)	red	255	0	0
Color 4 (Green)	lime	0	255	0
Color 5 (Blue)	blue	0	0	255
Color 6, 27 (Yellow)	yellow	255	255	0
Color 7, 26 (Magenta)	fuschia	255	0	255
Color 8, 28 (Cyan)	aqua	0	255	255
Color 9, 30	maroon	128	0	0
Color 10	green	0	128	0
Color 11, 25	navy	0	0	128
Color 12	olive	128	128	0
Color 13, 29	purple	128	0	128
Color 14, 31	teal	0	128	128
Color 15	silver	192	192	192
Color 16	gray	128	128	128
Color 19	lightyellow	255	255	204
Color 44	gold	255	204	0
Color 45	darkorange	255	153	0

Chapter 10

> **Caution** Some of the Excel palette and HTML colors in this list actually differ by a small amount, but the colors are practically identical to the human eye.

Formatting Worksheet Elements

Now that you have the Excel color system well in hand, you can get to work changing the appearance of the elements of your worksheet elements. There are two elements you can change at the window and worksheet level: gridlines and sheet tabs. In the default Excel workbook configuration, the gridlines are a medium gray. If you want to change that color to better fit your design, you can do so by setting the color to a custom RGB value or a color constant using the *ActiveWindow.GridlineColor* property or, if you want to assign a color from the Excel color palette, the *ActiveWindow.GridlineColorIndex* property. A benefit of using the *GridlineColorIndex* property is that you will have the ability to change the gridlines back to the default color by setting the property's value to the VBA constant *xlColorIndexAutomatic*.

As an example, the following procedure changes the gridlines to blue, then to white (which makes the gridlines invisible), and then changes them back to the automatic color:

```
Sub CycleGridlines()
    MsgBox ("Changing the gridline color to blue.")
    ActiveWindow.GridlineColorIndex = 5
    MsgBox ("Changing the gridline color to white.")
    ActiveWindow.GridlineColor = RGB (255, 255, 255)
    MsgBox ("Changing the gridline color back to the default color.")
    ActiveWindow.GridlineColorIndex = xlColorIndexAutomatic
    MsgBox ("Ending the procedure.")
End Sub
```

> **Note** The *GridlineColorIndex* property Help topic displays the default colors of the Excel color palette.

The other worksheet-level element you can change is the sheet tab. The sheet tabs appear on the tab bar at the bottom left of the Excel window. The tabs are normally white with black lettering when active and a neutral gray color when inactive, but you can highlight one or more of them by changing their color using either the *Worksheet.Tab.ColorIndex* or *Worksheet.Tab.Color* property. For example, if you wanted to change the tab of any worksheet where a user changes the existing data, you could do so by placing the following event procedure in the code module associated with each worksheet you want to monitor:

```
Private Sub Worksheet_Change(ByVal Target As Excel.Range)
    ActiveWorkbook.ActiveSheet.Tab.ColorIndex = 5
End Sub
```

> For more information on Excel events in general, and what does or does not trigger the *Worksheet_Change* event in particular, see Chapter 12, "Understanding and Using Events."

Figure 10-1 shows two worksheets with sheet tabs that were changed using the *Worksheet_Change* event procedure. The worksheet on the left is active, so Excel displays a line of the tab's color below the worksheet name, but notice that Excel displays the worksheet's name in black type on a white background so that the name can be read easily. The inactive sheet to the right displays the tab with a full blue background and black text, indicating it was also changed.

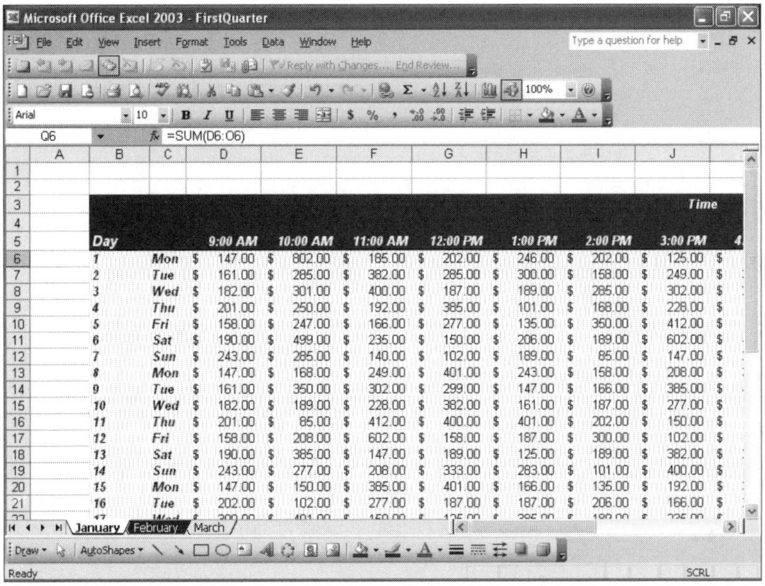

Figure 10-1. The active sheet's name is displayed with a view to readability, whereas inactive sheet tabs let the tab's color take precedence.

> **Important** You need to be sure to put the code for a worksheet event, such as *Worksheet_Change*, in the code module associated with the worksheet you want to monitor.

Formatting Fonts

When you program Excel using VBA, it can be easy to forget that the most important part of your worksheet is the data. The easier your data is to understand, the more effective your presentation will be. Figure 10-2 on page 234 offers a somewhat extreme example of the difference between a well-formatted worksheet and a worksheet with no distinction between headings and data.

Most Excel users learn how to use the controls on the Formatting toolbar and in the Format Cells dialog box very early in their Excel careers. In a similar vein, you should make the *Font* object part of your basic VBA repertoire. Table 10-6 lists and describes the properties of the Font object.

Table 10-6. **The *Font* Object's Properties**

Property	Description
Background	The *Background* property, which is only used for text on charts, can take one of three Excel constants: *xlBackgroundAutomatic* (which defaults to the chart element's setting), *xlBackgroundOpaque* (which makes the text box's background appear over other chart elements), or *xlBackgroundTransparent* (which lets other chart element colors show through).
Bold	Set to *True* or *False*, this property determines whether the font will be displayed in bold type.
Color	Uses the RGB property to return or set the font's color.
ColorIndex	Returns or sets a font color to a color in the Excel color palette.
FontStyle	Contains a string that is used to return or set the font style (for example, "Bold Italic" or "Regular"). The available styles differ depending on the font.
Italic	Set to *True* or *False*, this property determines whether the text will be displayed in italics.
Name	Contains a string that is used to return or set the name of the font in which the text is displayed.
Size	Returns or sets the size of the font, in points.
Strikethrough	Set to *True* or *False*, this property determines whether the text will have a horizontal line through the middle of the text.
Subscript	Set to *True* or *False*, this property determines whether the text will be formatted as subscript.
Superscript	Set to *True* or *False*, this property determines whether the text will be formatted as superscript.
Underline	Returns or sets the type of underlining for the selected text. The style of underlining is represented by one of these Excel constants: *xlUnderlineStyleNone*, *xlUnderlineStyleSingle*, *xlUnderlineStyleDouble*, *xlUnderlineStyleSingleAccounting*, or *xlUnderlineStyleDoubleAccounting*.

One of the fundamental strengths of Excel is the ability to create conditional formats, or formats that reflect the value of the data in a cell. As an example, consider the series of *If...Then* statements introduced in Chapter 5 to change the color of the active cell's contents based on the cell's value.

```
Sub AvailableCredit()
    With ActiveCell
    If .Value = "" Then Exit Sub
```

Chapter 10

```
      If .Value <= 1000 Then .Font.Color = vbRed
      If .Value > 1000 Then .Font.Color = vbBlack
      If .Value > 4999 Then .Font.Color = vbBlue
      If .Value > 9999 Then .Font.Color = vbGreen
      End With
End Sub
```

If you don't want to change the color of a cell's entire contents, you can use the *Range* object's *Characters* property to format some part of a cell's value. The *Characters* property uses the following syntax to indicate which characters in the cell's value to change:

```
Characters (start, length)
```

The *start* argument represents the character with which you want to begin your reformatting, and *length* indicates the number of characters (including the first) to reformat. Once you've identified the characters, you use the *Character* object's *Font* property to change the appearance of the characters. For example, if you knew that the fourth through eighth characters of an order tracking string identified the sales agent, you could display those characters in bold type.

```
Sub HighlightAgent()
Dim MyCell As Range
Dim strFirst, strLast, strAllCells, strCategory As String

strFirst = InputBox("Enter the first cell.")
strLast = InputBox("Enter the last cell.")
strAllCells = strFirst & ":" & strLast

For Each MyCell In Range(strAllCells).Cells
    Range(MyCell.Address).Select
    MyCell.Characters(4, 5).Font.Bold = True
Next MyCell
End Sub
```

> For more information on manipulating text strings and other cell values, and for finding the beginning and ending of substrings that match a given pattern, see Chapter 9, "Manipulating Data with VBA."

Formatting Cells

For the purposes of formatting, cells are divided into two sections: the interior and the border. And, just as you can change the appearance of the gridlines and sheet tabs of a workbook, you can change the color and fill pattern of the interior of a cell. Changing the fill color of a cell to yellow or light orange can help set off the values in the formatted cells. In fact, as seen in Figure 10-2, many of the Excel AutoFormats use colored cell interiors to set a worksheet's data labels apart from the data itself.

Chapter 10

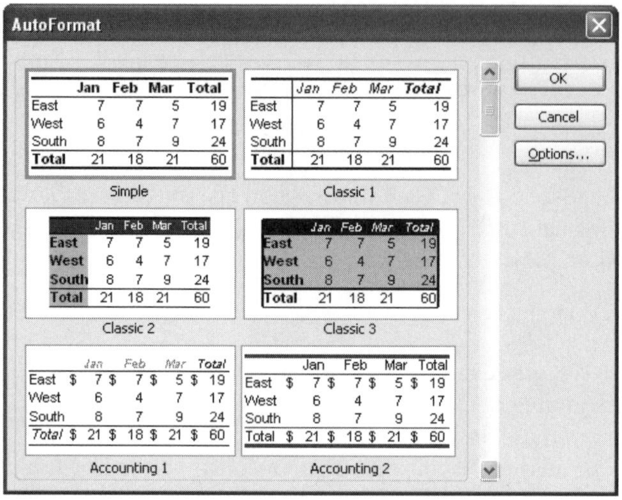

Figure 10-2. AutoFormats make data labels stand out so your worksheet data is easier to read.

You change the color and fill pattern of a cell by setting the properties of the *Interior* object, which is referenced by the *Interior* property of a cell. Table 10-7 lists the properties of the *Interior* object.

Table 10-7. The *Interior* Object's Properties for Formatting a Cell

Property	Description
Color	Determines the fill color of the interior of a cell using an Excel color constant or an RGB function value
ColorIndex	Determines the fill color of the interior of a cell using an index value that refers to the Excel color palette
Pattern	Determines the pattern used to fill the interior of a cell using one of the *XlPattern* Excel constants: *xlPatternAutomatic*, *xlPatternChecker*, *xlPatternCrissCross*, *xlPatternDown*, *xlPatternGray16*, *xlPatternGray25*, *xlPatternGray50*, *xlPatternGray75*, *xlPatternGray8*, *xlPatternGrid*, *xlPatternHorizontal*, *xlPatternLightDown*, *xlPatternLightHorizontal*, *xlPatternLightUp*, *xlPatternLightVertical*, *xlPatternNone*, *xlPatternSemiGray75*, *xlPatternSolid*, *xlPatternUp*, or *xlPatternVertical*
PatternColor	Determines the color of any fill pattern in the interior of a cell using an Excel color constant or an RGB function value
PatternColorIndex	Determines the color of any fill pattern in the interior of a cell using an index value that refers to the Excel color palette

Formatting Excel Objects

The array of patterns available to you, represented by the Excel constants in the *Pattern* property's description in the preceding table, are available for viewing by clicking Format, Cells, clicking the Patterns tab, and clicking the Pattern down arrow.

One important thing to know about the *Color* and *ColorIndex* properties is that they affect a different aspect of the cell's interior than do the *PatternColor* and *PatternColorIndex* properties. The default color for either the *PatternColor* or *PatternColorIndex* properties is black (represented in the *PatternColorIndex* property as the index number 1), but you can change the color of the pattern.

The following procedure changes the fill color of the active cell to blue, adds a pattern of thin, black, horizontal lines, and then changes the color of the fill pattern to white:

```
Sub ChangePattern()
With ActiveCell
 .Interior.ColorIndex = 5
 MsgBox ("OK to add the horizontal pattern?")
 .Interior.Pattern = xlPatternLightHorizontal
 MsgBox ("OK to change the pattern's color?")
 .Interior.PatternColorIndex = 2
End With
End Sub
```

Formatting Borders

As you would expect, the *Range* object's *Interior* property deals with the inside of a cell. To affect the outside of a cell, you use the *Borders* property. Yes, the property *Borders* is plural. The reason the property name is plural is because each cell actually has six (yes, six) borders. When you change a border, you need to use one of the *XlBordersIndex* constants to identify which element of the border you want to change. Those elements are *xlDiagonalDown*, *xlDiagonalUp*, *xlEdgeBottom*, *xlEdgeLeft*, *xlEdgeRight*, and *xlEdgeTop*.

> **Note** The *xlDiagonalDown* and *xlDiagonalUp* constants aren't what you would normally think of as borders; instead, they either draw a line from the top left corner to the bottom right corner of the cell (*xlDiagonalDown*) or from the bottom left corner to the top right corner of the cell (*xlDiagonalUp*).

When you reference the *Borders* property in your VBA code, Excel creates a *Borders* object. The *Borders* object's properties are listed in Table 10-8.

Table 10-8. The *Borders* Object's Properties

Property	Description
Color	Either sets or returns the color of a border using the RGB function
ColorIndex	Either sets or returns the color of a border using a reference to a position in the Excel color palette or either of the constants *xlColorIndexAutomatic* (sets the color to the default color) or *xlColorIndexNone* (formats the border with no color)
LineStyle	Sets the style of a line using one of the *xlLineStyle* constants: *xlContinuous*, *xlDash*, *xlDashDot*, *xlDashDotDot*, *xlDot*, *xlDouble*, *xlLineStyleNone*, or *xlSlantDashDot*
Weight	Sets the weight of the line using one of the *xlBorderWeight* constants: *xlHairline*, *xlMedium*, *xlThick*, or *xlThin*

You indicate which border you want to set by putting the appropriate *xlBordersIndex* constant in parentheses after the *Borders* property is called. For example, the following procedure puts a thin blue border on the bottom edge of cells in the range A1:D1:

```
Sub BlueBorder()
    With Worksheets("Sheet1").Range("A1:D1").Borders(xlEdgeBottom)
        .LineStyle = xlContinuous
        .Weight = xlThin
        .Color = vbBlue
    End With
End Sub
```

Using the *Borders* property for formatting the borders of your cells is fairly straightforward, but if you want to add a single border around a range of cells, you can use the *Range* object's *BorderAround* method to draw an outline around the range. The *BorderAround* method has the following syntax:

```
BorderAround(LineStyle, Weight, ColorIndex, Color)
```

The arguments *LineStyle*, *Weight*, *ColorIndex*, and *Color* all serve the purposes listed in Table 10-8, but you need to call them as parameters. For example, if you wanted to draw a thin, dashed, red border around the range B1:E1, you would do so using the following procedure:

```
Sub RedBorder()
Range("B1:E1").BorderAround LineStyle := xlDash, Weight := xlThin, _
    Color := vbRed
End Sub
```

In this chapter, you've learned how Excel manages colors, how to display the colors in the Excel color palette, and how to change those colors to meet your formatting needs. You've also been introduced to available formatting properties that let you make your headings stand out and your data easier to read and even highlight worksheets that have been changed since the last time they were saved.

Chapter 10

Creating Add-Ins and COM Add-Ins

Introducing Add-Ins. 239
Using the Add-Ins dialog box. 240
Creating Excel Add-Ins 241
Using the *AddIns* Collection 244
Creating Automation and COM Add-Ins 247

Building an Automation Add-In with
Visual Basic 6. 250
Building a COM Add-In with
Visual Basic .NET 256

This chapter introduces the concept of *add-ins*. In this chapter, you'll learn what an add-in is, how to load and unload add-ins from Microsoft Excel, some common add-ins supplied with Excel, and how to create your own Excel add-in.

Introducing Add-Ins

Add-ins allow you to extend Excel by adding commands and features to those normally found in Excel. These commands and features can be found in many different places, including files that were installed with Excel, the Microsoft Office Web site (*http://office.microsoft.com*), and programs that you develop yourself. Once installed, an add-in works like any other menu command or function.

There are three main types of add-ins: Excel add-ins, COM add-ins, and automation add-ins. *Excel* add-ins are based on macros that are written in Microsoft Visual Basic for Applications (VBA) and stored in a special type of workbook, called a Microsoft Office Excel Add-in, that has a file type of .xla. *COM* and *automation* add-ins are created using a compiled language such as Visual Basic or Visual C++.

There are two main reasons add-ins are used. First, an add-in provides a way to easily extend the capabilities of Excel in such a way as to make it appear to the user that the capability was originally included in Excel. This means that programmers and third-party developers can provide easy-to-use tools that can simplify the life of the average user.

Second, add-ins don't use any system resources until they are explicitly loaded into Excel. This improves the overall performance of Excel for users who don't need the extra capabilities, while making it easy for those individuals who want the extra capabilities to access them.

Using the Add-Ins dialog box

To use an add-in, it must be loaded into Excel. The Add-Ins dialog box (accessed by choosing Tools, Add-ins from the main menu) controls what add-ins are loaded when Excel starts. (See Figure 11-1.)

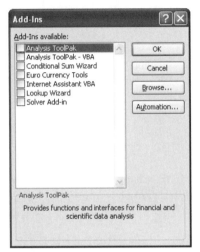

Figure 11-1. The Add-Ins dialog box dialog box controls which add-ins are loaded into Excel.

By default, the Add-Ins dialog box displays add-ins that have been installed with Excel. A check mark next to the add-in's name indicates that the add-in is currently loaded. Table 11-1 includes a list of add-ins that are typically installed with Excel.

Table 11-1. Add-Ins Supplied with Excel

Add-In	Description
Analysis ToolPak	Includes financial, statistical, and engineering analysis tools and functions
Analysis ToolPak VBA	Includes financial, statistical, and engineering analysis tools that can be accessed by Visual Basic for Applications programs
Conditional Sum Wizard	Creates a formula that computes the sum for data that matches the specified criteria
Euro Currency Tools	Includes tools to format values as euros and add the EUROCONVERT function to simplify currency conversion
Internet Assistant VBA	Includes developer tools that assist with publishing information from Excel to the Internet
Lookup Wizard	Creates a formula that looks up data in a range using another value from the range
Solver Add-In	Includes tools that compute solutions for what-if scenarios using adjustable cells and constraints

Chapter 11

Installing an Add-In

To install an add-in, simply place a check mark next to the add-in you wish to use in the Add-in Manager and click OK. The add-in will be immediately loaded and will be available for your use.

> **Note** Other Microsoft products such as Microsoft MapPoint might install add-ins that you can load into Excel.

If the add-in you wish to use isn't listed in the Add-Ins dialog box, press the Browse button to locate the add-in you wish to use. By default, user-created add-ins are stored in the \Documents and Settings\User\Application Data\Microsoft\AddIns folder; however, they may be located in any folder you choose.

> **Note** If any of the add-ins supplied with Excel aren't shown in the Add-Ins dialog box, use the setup disk to install the add-in you wish to use.

Unloading an Add-In

Once an add-in is loaded, it remains loaded until you explicitly unload it with the Add-Ins dialog box. To unload an add-in, simply uncheck the check box next to the name of the add-in that you wish to unload and press OK. The next time Excel is started, the add-in won't be loaded.

> **Note** If you remove an add-in, any formulas that reference functions in the add-in will be updated to reflect the file name of the workbook containing the add-in. If you reload the same add-in, the formulas will be restored to their original form.

Creating Excel Add-Ins

An Excel add-in is merely a special type of workbook that includes a set of macros and functions that perform whatever tasks you want.

Creating an Add-In

Suppose you have a worksheet that computes a discounted value based on the list price and the discount. It might look something like the following code:

```
Public Function DiscountedPrice(ListPrice, Discount) As Currency

If Discount <= 1 And Discount >= 0 Then
    DiscountedPrice = ListPrice * (1 - Discount)
```

```
Else
    DiscountedPrice = 0

End If

End Function
```

Before saving the add-in, you should update the properties of the workbook (by choosing File, Properties from the main menu). At a minimum, you should enter a meaningful value for the title property on the Summary tab. (See Figure 11-2.) This value will be used to identify the add-in in the Add-Ins dialog box. By default, Excel will store add-ins in the Application Data\Microsoft\AddIns directory in the user's Documents and Settings directory.

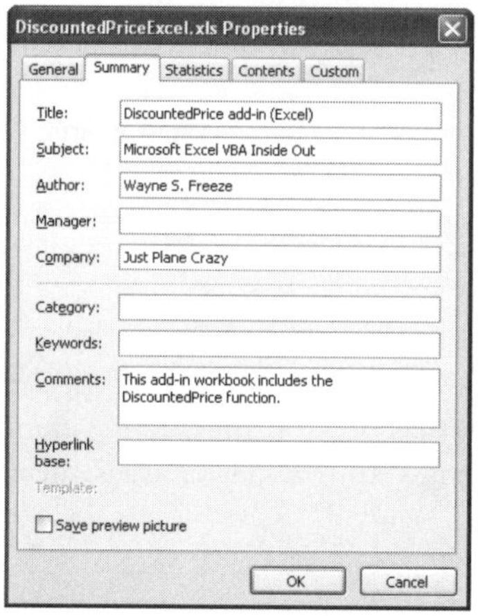

Figure 11-2. The title of the add-in should be specified along with any other properties of the workbook.

Saving the Add-In

To save the workbook as an add-in, choose File, Save As from the main menu. This will display the Save As dialog box. (See Figure 11-3.) Choose the folder where you want to save the file, and then select Microsoft Office Excel Add-In (*.xla) as the file type. Pressing the Save button will create your Excel add-in.

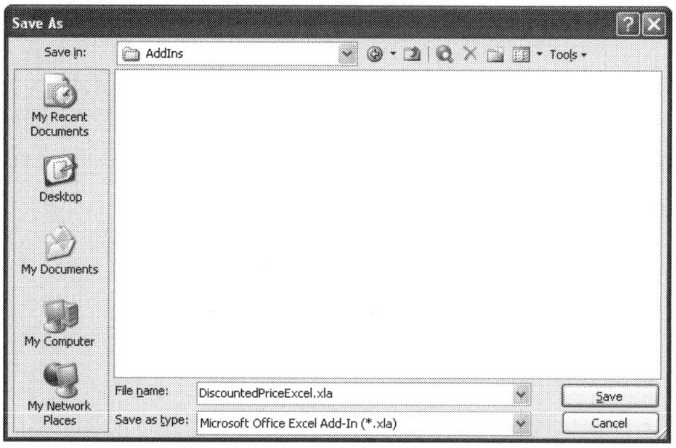

Figure 11-3. Selecting Microsoft Office Excel Add-In (*.xla) as the file type allows you to save the workbook as an add-in.

Installing the Add-In

Once the add-in has been saved, you can install it by using the Add-Ins dialog box (by choosing Tools, Add-ins from the main menu). When the Add-Ins dialog box is displayed, press the Browse button to locate your newly created add-in. Place a check mark next to the add-in name and press OK to include the add-in in the current workbook. (See Figure 11-4.)

Figure 11-4. Locate your new add-in by looking for the value you specified for the title of the workbook.

Then you can use it in a cell's formula like this:

```
=DiscountedPrice(D2, E2)
```

Chapter 11

Using the *AddIns* Collection

The *AddIns* collection contains the set of add-ins available whether or not they have been installed. The entries in this collection correspond to the add-ins listed in the Add-Ins dialog box. Through the *AddIns* collection, you can browse the add-ins available to Excel, add new add-ins, and install and remove add-ins from your program.

AddIns Collection

The *AddIns* collection is a typical collection object having the properties shown in Table 11-2.

Table 11-2. Properties

Property	Type	Description
Application	Object	Returns the *Application* object representing the creator of the add-in.
Count	Long	Returns the total number of *AddIn* objects in the collection.
Creator	Long	Returns a 32-bit integer containing the binary value XCEL.
Item(Index)	String	Returns the *AddIn* object associated with *Index*. If *Index* is numeric, it refers to the relative position of the object in the collection. If *Index* is a string, the *Item* property returns an object reference to the *AddIn* object whose *Name* property matches the value in *Index*.
Parent	Object	Returns the parent object associated with the add-in.

The *AddIns* collection includes a single method, *Add*. The *Add* method takes one or two parameters and returns an object reference to the new *AddIn* object. The syntax of the *Add* method as it applies to the *AddIns* object is

```
expression.Add(FileName, CopyFile)
```

The *FileName* parameter is required and specifies the full path and file name of the add-in. The *CopyFile* parameter is optional and applies only when the file is stored on a removable drive (that is, a floppy or a CD-ROM drive). When the second parameter is *True*, the add-in is copied to a hard disk, whereas *False* means that the file remains on the removable drive. If the second parameter isn't specified and the file resides on a removable drive, Excel will prompt the user to choose whether the file should be copied or not.

This code fragment shows you how you can use the *Add* method to include a new add-in workbook in the *AddIns* collection:

```
NewAddIn = Application.AddIns.Add("c:\Chapter11.xla")
```

AddIn Object

The *AddIn* object represents a single add-in that's available to Excel. Table 11-3 contains a list of the properties associated with a single add-in.

Table 11-3. *AddIn* **Properties**

Property	Type	Description
Application	Object	Returns the *Application* object representing the creator of the add-in
CLSID	String	Returns the CLSID of the add-in
Creator	Long	Returns a 32-bit integer containing the binary value XCEL
FullName	String	Returns the full path and file name to the workbook containing the add-in
Installed	Boolean	When *True*, means that the add-in is installed
Name	String	Returns the file name of the add-in
Parent	Object	Returns the parent object associated with the add-in
Path	String	Returns the path to the directory containing the add-in
ProgId	String	Returns the program identifier associated with the object

The *Application* and *Parent* properties can simplify referencing the application object that created the add-in and the parent object of the add-in.

The *Creator* property returns a *Long* value corresponding to the four characters XCEL. This property is useful when you wish to verify that the add-in was created for Excel.

The *ProgId* and *CLSID* properties only apply when using COM or automation-based add-ins. These properties will return an empty string for Excel add-ins.

The *Name*, *Path*, and *FullName* properties contain information about the file name of the add-in's workbook. *Name* contains only the file name, whereas *Path* indicates which directory contains the add-in file. As you might expect, *FullName* combines the *Path* and *Name* properties with a directory separator.

The *Installed* property controls whether that add-in is currently installed into Excel. Setting this property to *True* installs the add-in and triggers the *Workbook_AddinInstall* event. Setting this property to *False* removes the add-in and fires the *Workbook_AddinUninstall* event.

Chapter 11

Auto Routines

In versions of Excel prior to Excel 97, special macros such as *Auto_Add* and *Auto_Remove* were called when an add-in was installed or removed. These macros are stored in a module associated with the workbook rather than in the *ThisWorkbook* object. Although these macros continue to work even in this version of Excel, you should use the corresponding *Workbook* events.

Other auto routines you might encounter when working with older Excel applications are *Auto_Open* and *Auto_Close*, which correspond to *Workbook_Open* and *Workbook_Close*, and *Auto_Activate* and *Auto_Deactivate*, which correspond to *Workbook_Activate* and *Workbook_Deactivate*.

You can see the values stored in the *AddIn* object by writing a macro similar to the one shown in the following program listing. This macro uses a *For Each* statement to loop through each *AddIn* object in the *AddIns* collection and then insert the value into the current worksheet.

```
Sub GetAddIns()

Dim a As AddIn
Dim i As Long

i = 1
For Each a In Application.AddIns
    i = i + 1
    Cells(i, 1) = i - 1
    Cells(i, 2) = a.Application.Name
    Cells(i, 3) = a.CLSID
    Cells(i, 4) = a.Creator
    Cells(i, 5) = a.FullName
    Cells(i, 6) = a.Installed
    Cells(i, 7) = a.Name
    Cells(i, 8) = a.Parent.Name
    Cells(i, 9) = a.Path
    Cells(i, 10) = a.progID

Next a

End Sub
```

Because the *Application* and *Parent* properties return object references that can't be displayed in a cell, the *Name* property associated with each of those objects is displayed. Figure 11-5 shows the worksheet after running the *GetAddIns* macro.

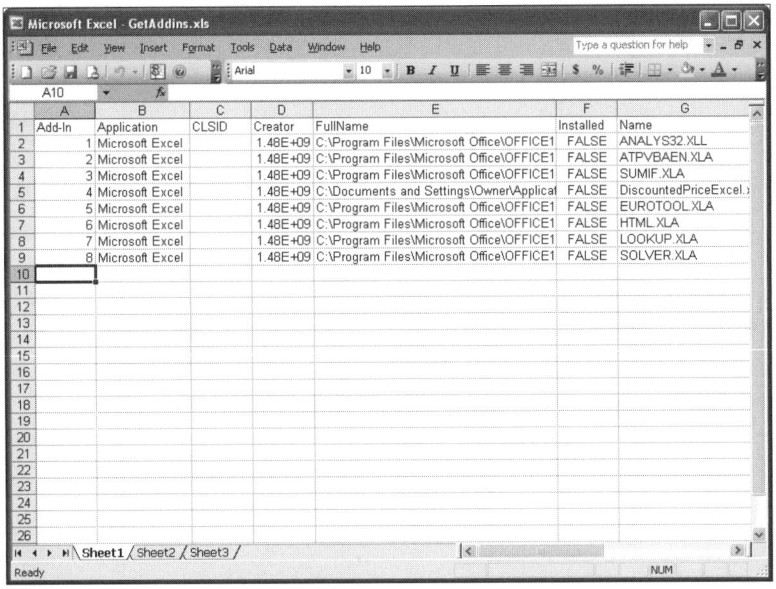

Figure 11-5. The *AddIns* collection contains information about each add-in known to Excel.

Creating Automation and COM Add-Ins

There are times when it isn't desirable to create an add-in using Visual Basic for Applications. Because VBA macros are interpreted, they execute slower than compiled code, which can seriously affect the performance of computation-intensive add-ins. Also, some functions aren't easily implemented using VBA, such as image processing or specialized networking applications.

To address this limitation, all Office applications including Excel have the ability to access an add-in stored in an external DLL or EXE file. Although there are two different techniques used to access the external add-ins, both are created with similar programming techniques.

COM add-ins are typically used to respond to clicking a command button or to some other Excel event such as opening or closing a workbook. Unlike Excel add-ins, you can't create a COM add-in that can be used as part of a cell's formula. Automation add-ins are less restricted and can be used to respond to Excel events as well as to provide functions that can be used in a formula.

COM add-ins are defined only through the COM Add-Ins dialog box on the toolbar, whereas automation add-ins can be defined through the COM Add-Ins dialog box, the Add-Ins dialog box, or both.

Chapter 11

247

EXE or DLL?

COM add-ins can be created as either a DLL or an EXE file. Both have their advantages and disadvantages. Generally, a DLL component will perform better than an EXE component because the DLL is run in-process, which avoids the extra overhead associated with calling an out-of-process component.

However, a DLL component can't include a main program, which can be a serious limitation if you have a utility that you want to access either as a stand-alone program or as an Office add-in. An EXE component also has the advantage of isolating the add-in's execution from that of the host application.

So, unless you really need either the isolation or main program feature of an EXE component, you should develop your add-in as a DLL component.

Another difference between a COM add-in and an automation add-in is that COM add-ins *must* support the *IDTExtensibility2* interface, whereas automation add-ins might or might not use this interface.

> **Tip**   **Displaying the COM Add-ins dialog box**
> Accessing the COM Add-ins dialog box can be tricky because the only way to access this dialog box is by adding the COM Add-Ins button to the toolbar. Right-click a toolbar, and choose the Customize command (lists at the bottom of the context menu). Click the Commands tab. Select Tools in the Category list, and then drag COM Add-Ins from the Commands list to a toolbar. Then click the COM Add-Ins button to display the COM Add-Ins dialog box.

Using the *IDTExtensibility2* Interface

The *IDTExtensibility2* interface is a general interface that's shared by many products besides Microsoft Office. This interface represents a standard way for an application to communicate with an add-in. Any COM add-in must implement each of the methods listed in Table 11-4.

Table 11-4. *IDTExtensibility2* Interface Methods

Method	Description
OnAddInsUpdate	Called when a change occurs to the list of add-ins, such as an add-in being loaded or unloaded.
OnBeginShutdown	Called when the application is being shut down. Remember that this method will be called only if the add-in is loaded.
OnConnection	Called when the add-in is loaded into the application. This can occur when the add-in is loaded through the Add-Ins dialog box or if the add-in is automatically loaded when the application starts.

Table 11-4. *IDTExtensibility2* **Interface Methods**

Method	Description
OnDisconnection	Called when the add-in is unloaded from the application.
OnStartupComplete	Called when the application has completed the startup process.

The *OnConnection* method is called when an add-in is loaded into the application. The add-in receives information about the environment it's running in through a set of parameters. The two key parameters are an object reference to the application object associated with the application and information about how the add-in was started (that is, was the add-in started from the COM Add-Ins dialog box or when the application was first started).

If the *OnConnection* method returns successfully, the add-in is considered by the application to be loaded. If it returns an error message, the application destroys the object associated with the add-in.

Tip **Initializing the Add-In**
You should use the *OnConnection* method to initialize the add-in and acquire any resources needed by the add-in. Then these resources can be released in the *OnDisconnection* method.

The *OnDisconnection* method is called when the application wants the add-in to unload itself. The application informs the add-in why the application is being unloaded (that is, the add-in was unloaded via the COM Add-Ins dialog box or the application itself is shutting down).

The *OnStartupComplete* and *OnBeginShutdown* methods are called just before the application is ready to accept user input and just after the user has requested the application to close.

Tip **Making Changes to Excel**
You should use the *OnStartupComplete* method to make any changes to the application, such as adding new menu items or toolbar buttons. Then you can undo these changes in the *OnBeginShutdown* method.

The *OnAddInsUpdate* method is called whenever the list of add-ins changes.

Warning You should be extremely careful about making changes to Excel when loading an add-in because Excel has the ability to dynamically load an add-in while in cell edit mode. Displaying a form or dialog box, changing the current selection, calling a property or method in the *Windows* collection, or changing some Excel settings could cause Excel to fail.

Chapter 11

Registry Keys

COM add-ins are required to provide certain entries in the Windows registry. All registry entries are stored using the following key, where *App* is the name of the Office application (such as Excel) and *ProgID* is the *ProgID* value associated with the add-in. Typically, these entries are made by the add-in's installation program.

```
HKEY_CURRENT_USER\Software\Microsoft\Office\App\Addins\ProgID
```

> **Warning** Manually changing the Windows registry can be dangerous. If you don't have a lot of experience editing the Windows registry, you should look but don't touch, and rely on the setup program for the add-in to make the proper changes. Should you wish to view and/or change registry entries, you can use the RegEdit program. (Click the Start button, click Run, type **RegEdit**, and click OK.)

Underneath the key specified above are a series of subkeys that contain specific information about the add-in. The *LoadBehavior* subkey is a *DWORD* value that determines when an add-in is loaded by the Office application. A value of 0 means that the add-in is not loaded. A value of 3 means that the add-in should be loaded when the application starts. A value of 9 means that the add-in is loaded when requested by the user. A value of 16 means that the add-in is loaded once, the next time the application starts.

The *Description* subkey is a *String* value that's displayed in the COM Add-Ins dialog box, whereas the *FriendlyName* subkey is a *String* value that's returned by the add-in's *Description* property.

Add-ins that use the *IDTExtensibility2* interface also should have a registry entry named *CommandLineSafe*. This is a *DWORD* value that marks an add-in as safe to use in applications that don't support a user interface. A value of 0x00 means that the add-in needs a user interface, whereas a value of 0x01 means that the add-in doesn't rely on a user interface.

Building an Automation Add-In with Visual Basic 6

Visual Basic 6 includes a template that simplifies creating add-ins that use the *IDTExtensibility2* interface, which you can use to create an automation add-in that implements the same *DiscountPrice* function that was built for the Excel add-in.

Designing the Add-In

The code for the automation add-in is shown on the next page. The module begins by defining a public variable that will hold the reference to the *Excel.Application* object. The rest of the code implements the five methods required to handle the *IDTExtensibility2* interface, along with one additional function that implements the same *DiscountPrice* function that was used in the Excel add-in earlier in this chapter.

```vb
Option Explicit

Public ExcelApp As Excel.Application

Private Sub AddinInstance_OnAddInsUpdate(custom() As Variant)

'Called when an add-in is changed

End Sub

Private Sub AddinInstance_OnBeginShutdown(custom() As Variant)

'Called when Excel is in the process of shutting down

End Sub

Private Sub AddinInstance_OnConnection(ByVal Application As Object, _
    ByVal ConnectMode As AddInDesignerObjects.ext_ConnectMode, _
    ByVal AddInInst As Object, custom() As Variant)

Set ExcelApp = Application

End Sub

Private Sub AddinInstance_OnDisconnection( _
    ByVal RemoveMode As AddInDesignerObjects.ext_DisconnectMode, _
    custom() As Variant)

Set ExcelApp = Nothing

End Sub

Private Sub AddinInstance_OnStartupComplete(custom() As Variant)

'Called when Excel is ready to use

End Sub

Public Function DiscountedPrice(ListPrice, Discount) As Currency

If Discount <= 1 And Discount >= 0 Then
    DiscountedPrice = ListPrice * (1 - Discount)

Else
    DiscountedPrice = 0

End If

End Function
```

Chapter 11

Of the five methods associated with the *IDTExtensibility2* interface, only two do any work in this example. The *AddinInstance_OnConnection* method saves an object reference to the Excel application that was passed using the *Application* parameter. This object is necessary for the add-in to access the information stored in the Excel application.

The *AddinInstance_OnDisconnection* method releases the object reference to the Excel object. Besides being a good programming practice, releasing the object helps to ensure the stability of the add-in.

To create a new add-in in Visual Basic 6, follow these steps:

1   Start Visual Basic 6. Then choose the AddIn project template in the New Project dialog box by selecting AddIn and pressing the Open button.

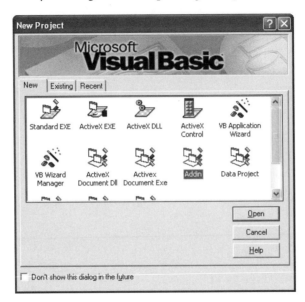

2   When Visual Basic 6 starts, go to the Project Explorer window. Right-click frmAddIn, and choose Remove frmAddIn from the popup menu because this form won't be needed in this project.

3   Choose Project, MyAddIn Properties from the main menu to display the Properties dialog box. Change MyAddIn in the Project Name field to something more meaningful. (See Figure 11-6.)

4   Next double-click the Connect item under the Designers icon in the Project Explorer. This will open the AddInDesigner. Go to the Properties window, and change the *Name* property from Connect to a more appropriate description.

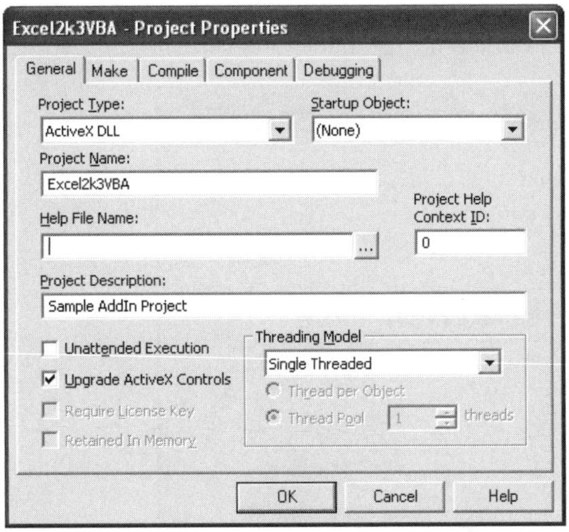

Figure 11-6. Choose a meaningful name for your add-in project.

5 Return to the AddInDesigner (shown in Figure 11-7) and update the Display Name and Addin Description fields as needed. Choose Microsoft Excel in the Application drop-down box, and select the desired version (if you have more than one version of Excel installed on your machine). Also, choose how the add-in will be initially loaded by selecting an entry from the Initial Load Behavior drop-down box.

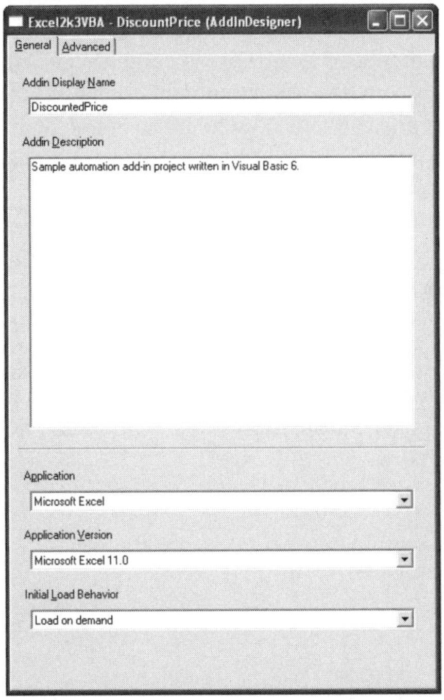

Figure 11-7. Fill in the proper information for your add-in.

Chapter 11

6 Choose Project, References from Visual Basic's main menu, and add the Microsoft Excel 11.0 Object Library to the list of references in this application.

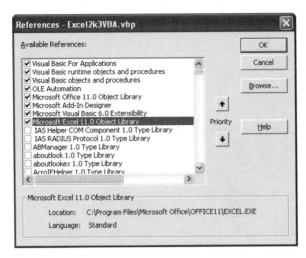

7 View the code associated with the designer by pressing the View Code icon in the Project Explorer or by right-clicking the designer's name and choosing the View Code command. Because the add-in template is geared toward developing add-ins for Visual Basic, you can delete almost all the code in the module. (See the following tip.)

Tip   Using Option Explicit

Don't delete the *Option Explicit* statement at the start of the code. *Option Explicit* forces you to define a variable with a *Dim*, a *Public*, or a *Private* statement before you use it. This helps you track down misspelled variables and variables that forgot to define at the module level. It's definitely a timesaver, and I strongly recommend that every Visual Basic module you write should include *Option Explicit* as its first statement.

---

8 Add the code found on page 251. Select File, Make Project from Visual Basic's main menu. This will create the DLL file containing the automation add-in. Then start Excel, and choose Tools, Add-Ins to display the Add-Ins dialog box. After that, press the Automation button to display the list of automation servers available on the system. Look for the project name in the list of automation servers to find the one you just created. Select the appropriate automation server, and press OK.

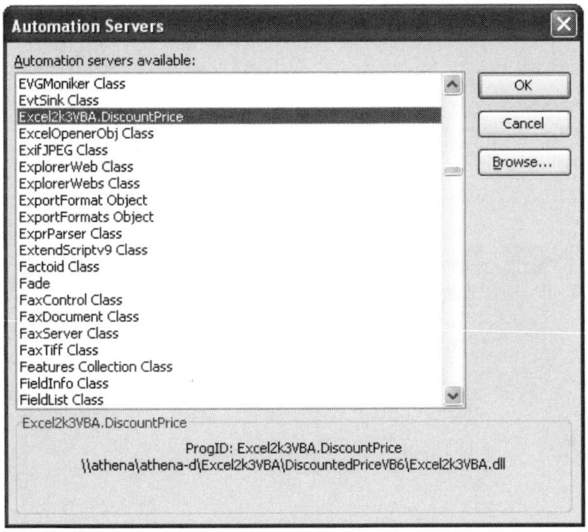

9   Create a worksheet that uses the *DiscountedPrice* function like the one shown in Figure 11-8.

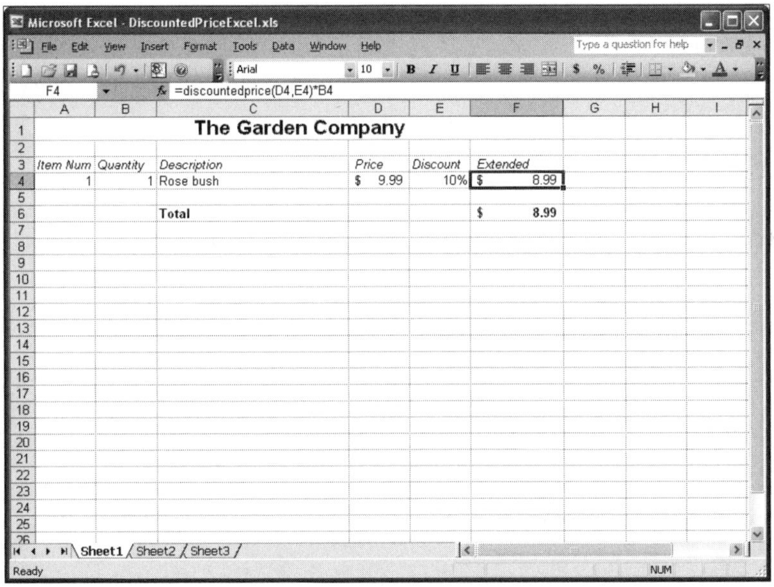

Figure 11-8. The *DiscountedPrice* function in the automation add-in works exactly as the one created for the Excel add-in.

Registry Entries

Although it seems like extra work to create an add-in using the Visual Basic 6 AddIn template and then to delete most of the default code, the AddInDesigner simplifies the amount of work needed by making all the appropriate entries in the Windows registry for you. (See Figure 11-9.) You can verify the entries in the registry by running RegEdit. (Click the Start button, then choose Run, type **RegEdit** and press OK.)

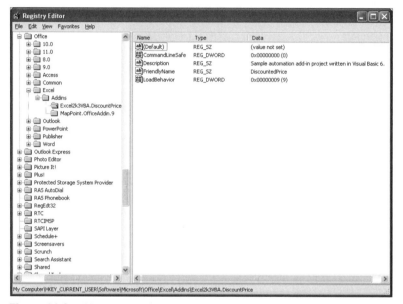

Figure 11-9. You can verify the entries made in the Windows registry by using the RegEdit utility.

Building a COM Add-In with Visual Basic .NET

Just because Visual Basic .NET doesn't have native support for COM components doesn't mean that you can't build COM add-ins with it. Like Visual Basic 6, Visual Basic .NET includes templates that help you to create your own add-ins.

The goal of this add-in is to put a new button on the Excel Standard toolbar (the one with the New, Open, Save, Print, and so on, buttons) and have it respond to a click with a message box.

Running the Shared Add-In Wizard

The easiest way to create an add-in is to use the Microsoft Visual Studio .NET Shared Add-in Wizard. This will create a new solution for you that includes all the pieces needed to run your add-in, including the logic to automatically add the registry keys.

The solution consists of two projects. The first project contains the code necessary to interact with the application, which you can use as a basis for building the add-in itself. The second project is an installation project, which will install the add-in including any necessary changes to the registry.

Follow these steps to create a new add-in solution:

1   Create a New Project in Visual Studio .NET. When prompted to choose the type of project, expand the Other Projects icon and select Extensibility Projects as the Project Type and then select the Shared Add-In template. Enter values for the project's Name and Location. Press the OK button to start the wizard.

2   The wizard will prompt you to choose which language you want to use. You can choose from Microsoft Visual C#, Visual Basic, or Visual C++/ATL. Select Visual Basic, and press the Next button.

3   On Page 2 of the wizard, you'll be prompted to choose which applications will host the add-in.

4   Step 3 of the wizard prompts you to enter the name of your add-in, along with the add-in's description. This information will be displayed to users when they select the add-in from the COM Add-Ins dialog box.

5   Step 4 prompts you to select whether or not you would like your add-in to load whenever the host application loads and whether or not the add-in should be made available to all users or just the user who installed it. If you're not sure what values to use, just select both boxes.

6   The last step allows you to review all of your selections. If you want to revise any of your choices, press the Back button until you reach the appropriate step. Otherwise, press the Finish button to create the new project.

> **Tip**   **Developing Add-Ins That Span Multiple Office Applications**
>
> It's possible to develop an add-in that can be used with multiple Office applications. This can be very useful if you want to write a general-purpose add-in such as an image browser or a file locator. By using the application object passed to the add-in *OnConnection* method, you can determine which application called the add-in and make the appropriate modifications to the menus or information contained in the application.

Modifying the Template

Even though you selected Excel when you ran the wizard, you still need to explicitly add a reference to the Excel TypeLib in your Visual Basic .NET program. You can do this by choosing Project, Add Reference from the main menu. In the Add Reference dialog box, choose the COM tab and then select Microsoft Excel 11.0 Object Library. Finally, press the Select button and then OK to add the reference to your project.

Because the code skeleton created with the Shared Add-In Wizard merely constructs a minimal *IDTExtensibility2* interface, you'll need to add your own code to make the add-in do something useful.

In this case, we need to declare a module-level variable that contains information about the button to be added on the toolbar. The following statement defines the *MyButton* object. Notice that the *WithEvents* keyword is included. When the button is pressed in Excel, the *Click* event associated with the *MyButton* object will be fired.

```
Dim WithEvents MyButton As CommandBarButton
```

The *OnConnection* routine is called by the host application to initialize the add-in. As you saw earlier in this chapter, the only real work required by this routine is to save an object reference to the application object. All the following code is automatically generated by the wizard. The *applicationObject* variable is also defined by the wizard as a module-level variable and is used to access the resources owned by the application hosting the add-in.

```
Public Sub OnConnection(ByVal application As Object, _
    ByVal connectMode As Extensibility.ext_ConnectMode, _
    ByVal addInInst As Object, ByRef custom As System.Array) _
    Implements Extensibility.IDTExtensibility2.OnConnection

    applicationObject = application
    addInInstance = addInInst

End Sub
```

> **Note** The *Implements* keyword indicates that this routine implements a routine found in a particular interface. In this case, you can see that the *IDTExtensibility2.OnConnection* routine is being referenced.

The *OnStartupComplete* routine is called after the add-in has been initialized, but before the user can start using the application. This is the best place to modify menus or make any other changes to Excel.

You can add a button to a toolbar with this code. First you create a new instance of the *MyButton* object by using the *Add* method associated with the *Controls* collection on a particular toolbar. Next set the *Caption* property to hold the name to be displayed on the button and set the *Style* property so that the caption is displayed on the button rather than on an icon.

```
Public Sub OnStartupComplete(ByRef custom As System.Array) _
    Implements Extensibility.IDTExtensibility2.OnStartupComplete

    MyButton = applicationObject.CommandBars("Standard").Controls.Add(1)
    MyButton.Caption = "My Button"
    MyButton.Style = MsoButtonStyle.msoButtonCaption
    MyButton.Tag = "My Button"
    MyButton.OnAction = "!<MyCOMAddin.Connect>"

    MsgBox("Startup complete")

End Sub
```

You should then set the *Tag* property to indicate the name of the button, along with defining the *OnAction* property so that it points to this component.

> Refer to Chapter 18, "Manipulating Menus and Toolbars," for more information on how to create and manipulate menus and toolbars.

When the application is ready to end, you need to properly remove the button using code like the *OnBeginShutdown* routine. The button's *Delete* method is used to actually remove the button from the toolbar. Then the resources associated with the button object are destroyed by setting the *MyButton* object to *Nothing*.

```
Public Sub OnBeginShutdown(ByRef custom As System.Array) _
    Implements Extensibility.IDTExtensibility2.OnBeginShutdown

    MyButton.Delete()
    MyButton = Nothing

End Sub
```

Finally, the code associated with the button's click event is called whenever My Button is pressed on the toolbar. As you can see in this example, the *MyButton_Click* routine merely calls the *MsgBox* routine to display a simple message on the screen. However, in a more complex add-in, routines like this will handle the interactions associated with the add-in for the user.

```
Private Sub MyButton_Click(ByVal Ctrl As _
    Microsoft.Office.Core.CommandBarButton, _
    ByRef CancelDefault As Boolean) Handles MyButton.Click

    MsgBox("My button was clicked")

End Sub
```

Installing the Add-In

To install the add-in, you must first build it. Then you must build the installation program and finally run the installation program.

1. Choose Build, Build Solution from the Visual Studio .NET main menu. This will compile your add-in.

2. The next step is to build the installation program. This is done by right-clicking the Setup project in the Solution Explorer and choosing build from the context menu.

> **Note** The installation package created by the add-in wizard does not include the .NET Framework, which must be installed prior to installing your add-in. If you already have Visual Studio .NET installed on your computer, you also have installed the .NET Framework.

3. Once the build is complete, right-click the Setup project again and choose Install from the popup menu. This will run the MyCOMAddinSetup Setup Wizard, which will guide the user through the steps required to install the add-in on the user's computer.

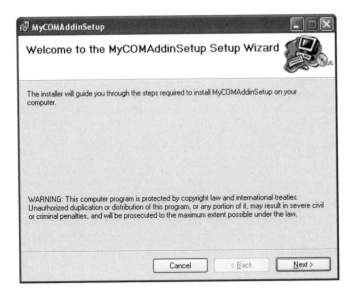

You can verify that the add-in is properly installed by starting Excel. When the add-in runs, you'll see a message box informing you that the add-in's startup is complete. Then you should notice the My Button button on the Standard toolbar along with other buttons such as the New, Open, and Save buttons.

Pressing the My Button button results in a simple message box that indicates that the My Button button was clicked.

In this chapter, you learned about add-ins and how you can incorporate them into an Excel application. Then you learned how to use the Add-Ins dialog box to incorporate an add-in into Excel. Finally you learned three different techniques to build an add-in: creating a workbook with a series of Excel macros and saving it as an .xla file; creating an automation add-in using Visual Basic 6; and creating a COM add-in using Visual Basic .NET. Each of these techniques has its strengths and weaknesses depending on how you plan to incorporate it into your application.

Understanding and Using Events

Enabling and Disabling Events 266   Worksheet Events 273
Workbook Events 267   Application Events 276

Within Microsoft Excel, any actions that occur, such as opening a workbook, saving the file or recalculating a worksheet, are referred to as *events*. Some events are triggered by the application and some by the user, but no matter how the event is initiated, by assigning procedures to these events you can enhance how the user interacts with your Excel application.

When a trigger occurs, Excel will look for an event procedure named *Object_EventName*, in which *Object* is the object that generates and contains the event, and *EventName* is the name of the specific trigger. For example, when the user changes the selection, either by clicking a cell in the workbook or by using the navigation keys, Excel generates a *SelectionChange* event and will execute any code in a procedure named *Object_SelectionChange*. Similarly, changing a cell's value, either by typing a new value into the cell or by changing the *Value* property from a Visual Basic for Applications (VBA) procedure, will cause Excel to trigger a *Change* event and execute the *Object_Change* event procedure.

In this chapter, you will learn how to enable and disable events and use *Workbook*, *Worksheet*, and *Application* events effectively.

> For information on *Chart* events, refer to Chapter 15, "Charts," and for information on *UserForm* events, refer to Chapter 19, "Creating User Forms."

Excel can monitor many different events that occur. These events are grouped into the following categories:

- *Workbook* events   Events that occur for a particular workbook. Some examples are the *Open*, *Activate*, and *NewSheet* events.
- *Worksheet* events   Events that occur for a particular worksheet. Some common examples used at the worksheet level are the *Calculate*, *Change*, and *BeforeRightClick* events.
- *Chart* Events   Events that occur for a particular chart. Some examples are the *Select*, *Activate*, and *SeriesChange* events.
- *Application* Events   Events that occur for the application, Excel. Several examples would be the *SheetChange*, *NewWorkbook*, and *WorkbookBeforeClose* events.
- *UserForm* Events   Events that occur for a particular User Form or an object contained on the User Form. Some commonly used events are *Click* and *Initialize*.

Not all events are defined by all objects. In general, if an object has an event, its parent object will also have the same event. For example, the *Change* event is contained at the "lowest" level by the *Worksheet* object. The *Worksheet* object's parent is the *Workbook* object; it also has the same event called *Workbook_SheetSelectionChange*. The *Workbook* object's parent, the *Application*, also has a *Change* event. The "lower" event does not need to be programmed in order to receive the event at a higher level. For example, the *Workbook_SheetChange* event is triggered regardless of whether you have a *Worksheet_Change* event coded.

When evaluating the results you want to achieve with your event procedure, keep in mind at which level it should occur. A common mistake is programming the event procedure in the wrong location. The Visual Basic Editor window displays all open projects, arranging all components in a collapsible list, as shown in Figure 12-1. Ensure you have the correct object active before programming your event procedure.

Figure 12-1. The components for each VBA Project are displayed in an expandable list.

Enabling and Disabling Events

The Excel *Application* object has an *EnableEvents* property that you can use to enable or disable event triggers. Because VBA code, including event procedures, can cause events to be triggered, you might find situations where you will be required to disable events. For example, changing a cell's value from VBA will trigger the *Change* events in all object levels. If you have code in the *Worksheet_Change* event procedure that modifies another cell, you must disable events to prevent *Worksheet_Change* from calling itself repeatedly. If the procedure continually called itself, Excel would either overflow its *call stack* (an internal record of the pending jobs within Excel) or run out of memory.

By default all events are enabled. To disable all events, add the following line of code to your VBA procedure:

```
Application.EnableEvents = False
```

To enable the events, use this line of code:

```
Application.EnableEvents = True
```

Note This setting is for the entire Excel application, so setting it to *False* will affect all your open workbooks, not just the active workbook containing the code. Also, remember that Excel doesn't restore the setting when your code ends, so be sure to set it back to *True* to reactivate the events.

The primary reason to disable events is to prevent an infinite loop of continuous events. For example, let's say you have developed a timesheet and the maximum number of hours an employee is allowed to work is 40 hours per week. You can write the code to validate the cell contents whenever data is entered into the cell containing the total hours of work for each employee. In this example, you would monitor the *Change* event for the worksheet using a procedure named *Worksheet_Change*. Your procedure would check the user's entry to verify that it is less than 40. If the entry exceeds 40, the procedure will display a message informing the user that he or she has exceeded the allowed hours of work and then clear the entry in the cell. The problem with this scenario is that when the cell contents are cleared, the VBA code generates a new *Change* event, so the event is executed again. This is not what you want to happen, so you need to disable events before you clear the cell, and then reactivate the events so that you can monitor the next user entry. The following *Worksheet_Change* event displays the required code to validate the users input in a range named *Hours*. For this example you can replace the range name Hours with a specific cell address to test this code in any workbook. Because this Event procedure refers to the worksheet level, the code needs to be added to the module of the worksheet that you want to trigger the *Change* event.

```
Private Sub Worksheet_Change(ByVal Target As Excel.Range)
    Dim VRange As Range
    Set VRange = Range("Hours")
    If Intersect(Target, VRange).Value > 40 Then
        MsgBox "The weekly hours cannot exceed 40."
        Application.EnableEvents = False
        ActiveCell.Value = ""
        Application.EnableEvents = True
    End If
End Sub
```

Note `Application.EnableEvents = False` will affect all open workbooks; however, it does not affect events outside of the Excel Object Model. Events associated with ActiveX controls and User Forms will continue to occur.

Workbook Events

Events for the *Workbook* object occur within a particular workbook. The *Workbook* events are activated by default, but as mentioned in the previous section, they can be disabled by setting the *EnableEvents* property to *False*. To display the event procedures for a workbook, start by opening the Visual Basic Editor. Expand the desired project in the project window and double-click the *ThisWorkBook* object to active it. All event procedures in the workbook will be displayed in the code window on the right side of the screen.

To create a new *Workbook* event procedure, follow these steps:

1 Double-click the *ThisWorkbook* object to activate it.

2 Click the Object drop-down list, and select the Workbook option.

3 Click the Procedure drop-down list, and select the desired event.

In Figure 12-2, the Visual Basic Editor displays the Procedure drop-down list while creating a new *Workbook* event procedure.

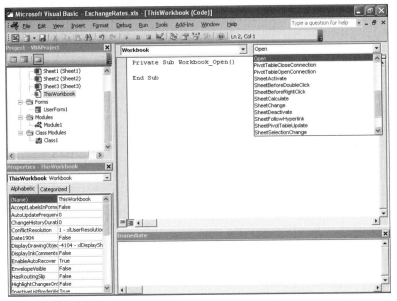

Figure 12-2. The VB Editor is the best way to create a new event procedure.

After you have created the new event procedure, you'll notice the `Private Sub Workbook_Event` and `End Sub` lines have been added to the code window. Now that you've created the event procedure's framework, you can to add the code to be executed when the event is triggered. Table 12-1 describes the commonly used events that can be attached to the *Workbook* object.

Table 12-1. Commonly Used *Workbook* Events

Workbook Event	Action That Triggers the Event
Open	Monitors the *Open* event for a workbook. The event is triggered when the workbook or add-in is opened and executes the *Workbook_Open* procedure.
Activate	Monitors the *Activate* event for a workbook. The event is triggered whenever the workbook is activated.

Table 12-1. Commonly Used *Workbook* Events

Workbook Event	Action That Triggers the Event
SheetActivate	Monitors the *SheetActivate* event for the workbook. The event is triggered when any sheet within the workbook is activated.
NewSheet	Monitors the *NewSheet* event for the workbook. The event is triggered whenever a new sheet is added to the workbook. Because a new sheet can be a worksheet or a chart sheet, this procedure would be executed regardless of the type of sheet added.
BeforeSave	Monitors the *BeforeSave* event for the workbook. The event is triggered whenever the user saves the workbook and is executed before the save action.
Deactivate	Monitors the *Deactivate* event. The event is triggered when the workbook is deactivated, such as by closing the workbook or by opening a new workbook.
BeforePrint	Monitors the *BeforePrint* event. The event is triggered when the user uses the Print Preview feature or tries to print the workbook. The event will occur before the preview window or print request is executed.
BeforeClose	Monitors the *BeforeClose* event for the workbook. The event is triggered when the user closes the workbook but is executed before the workbook is closed.

Open Event

The *Open* event is one of the most commonly monitored events. This event is triggered each time a workbook or add-in is opened. The *Workbook_Open* event can accomplish a large variety of tasks, such as if you want to generate a log file as to who used the workbook and when. You can create a User Form that's opened using this event. The User Form would require the user to select their name from a drop-down list and type a password before gaining entry to the file. After the user's name and password have been accepted as an authorized user, the user's name can be recorded in a log file with a time/date stamp. Some additional practical applications for the *Open* event include the following:

- Activating a particular worksheet or cell.
- Setting the workbook's window state to normal, minimize, or maximize.
- Opening additional workbooks.

To create the new event procedure, you can use the steps discussed earlier in the chapter in "*Workbook* Events" or type the following:

```
Private Sub Workbook_Open()
```

The following event procedure will ensure that the Excel application window is maximized and displays a message box reminding the user of the current date:

```
Private Sub Workbook_Open()
    Application.WindowState = xlMaximized
    Msgbox "The date is:" & Date
End Sub
```

> **Note** If you hold down the Shift key when you start Excel or when you open a workbook, you will prevent the *Workbook_Open* procedure from executing.

Activate Event

The *Activate* event is triggered when the workbook is activated, such as when it is initially opened, when switching to the Excel window after viewing another program, or when switching between open workbooks. For example, if you want to ensure that the workbook is maximized when working in the file, you can add the following event procedure to the *ThisWorkbook* object:

```
Private Sub Workbook_Activate()
    ActiveWindow.WindowState = xlMaximized
End Sub
```

SheetActivate Event

The *SheetActivate* event is executed when any sheet is activated within the workbook. The event will occur regardless of the type of sheet activated, *Worksheet* or *Chart*. It's important to verify which type of sheet is activated. An *If…Then…Else* statement can be used to determine which code will execute for each type of sheet. For example, you could select cell A1 on the worksheet to assist the users who work with the file. The following event procedure will verify the type of sheet and then activate cell A1:

```
Private Sub Workbook_SheetActivate(ByVal Sh As Object)
    If TypeName(Sh) = "Worksheet" Then Range("A1").Select
End Sub
```

NewSheet Event

The *NewSheet* event is executed when a new sheet is added to the workbook. The sheet is passed to the event as an argument so you can manipulate the created sheet. The following procedure moves the new sheet to the end of the workbook:

```
Private Sub Workbook_NewSheet(ByVal Sh as Object)
    Sh.Move After:=Sheets(Sheets.Count)
End Sub
```

The *NewSheet* event procedure is often used to assist users by automating their work. For example, The Garden Company's accountant has asked her assistant to document when new worksheets have been added to the Income Statement.xls file. They decided to input the date that the worksheet was created in cell A1. To ensure that the creation date is added to new worksheets, the following *NewSheet* procedure was created:

```
Private Sub Workbook_NewSheet(ByVal Sh as Object)
    If TypeName(Sh) = "Worksheet" Then _
        Range("A1") = "Worksheet created on " & Now()
End Sub
```

BeforeSave Event

The *BeforeSave* event procedure is executed before the workbook is saved. This procedure uses two arguments, the *SaveAsUI* and *Cancel*. The *SaveAsUI* argument is used to identify if the Save As dialog box will be displayed, and the *Cancel* argument can be used to cancel the save operation. For example, the following event procedure will prompt users before they save the workbook to verify that they want to save the changes made:

```
Private Sub Workbook_BeforeSave(ByVal SaveAsUI As Boolean, Cancel as Boolean)
    a = MsgBox ("Do you want to save the changes to this workbook?", vbYesNo)
    If a = vbNo Then Cancel = True
End Sub
```

When the user saves the workbook, the *Workbook_BeforeSave* procedure is executed. If the save operation brings up Excel's Save As dialog box, the *SaveAsUI* variable is *True*. If the *BeforeSave* procedure sets the *Cancel* argument to *True*, the file will not be saved.

Deactivate Event

The *Deactivate* event occurs when the workbook is deselected. The following procedure arranges all open windows when the workbook is deactivated:

```
Private Sub Workbook_Deactivate()
    Application.Windows.Arrange xlArrangeStyleTiled
End Sub
```

Caution The *Deactivate* event occurs when a workbook is deselected; however, it's also triggered when a new workbook is opened or when the workbook is closed. Be careful when using this event; thoroughly test your procedure to ensure you are achieving the required result.

BeforePrint Event

The *BeforePrint* event is executed when the user tries to print the workbook or uses Print Preview. The request is transferred to the event procedure as a *Cancel* argument, which can be used to cancel the print request if set to *True*. Unfortunately, there is a limitation with this event procedure: it can't determine whether it is a print request or if the user is trying to preview the workbook.

The following event procedure recalculates the entire workbook before the active workbook is printed:

```
Private Sub Workbook_BeforePrint(Cancel As Boolean)
    For Each wk in Worksheets
        wk.Calculate
    Next
End Sub
```

> **Note** When testing the *BeforePrint* event procedure you can save time and paper by using the Print Preview option rather than printing the workbook.

The *BeforePrint* event procedure can be used to ensure that certain formats have been applied to the workbook. For example, you could adjust the page margins, set the print area, set headings and columns that are to repeat on every page, or simply set the worksheet to print to a single page. If there are a series of formats that are required before you print your workbook, an event procedure including the correct page layout can be used to eliminate the time spent reprinting workbooks with improper formatting.

BeforeClose Event

The *BeforeClose* event procedure is executed before the workbook is closed. This event is often used with the *Workbook_Open* event procedure. For example, the *Workbook_Open* procedure might open a custom menu for the workbook, and the *Workbook_BeforeClose* procedure would then close the custom menu. In this scenario, the custom menu would only be visible when the workbook is open. The following event procedures demonstrate how to use the *Workbook_Open* and *Workbook_BeforeClose* events to accomplish opening and closing the custom menu:

```
Private Sub Workbook_Open
    Call OpenCustomMenu
End Sub

Private Sub Workbook_BeforeClose (Cancel as Boolean)
    Call CloseCustomMenu
End Sub
```

However, there is a problem with this scenario because Excel's "Do you want to save changes you made to 'workbookname.xls'?" prompt occurs *after* the *Workbook_BeforeClose* event procedure is executed. If the user clicks Cancel, the workbook remains open, but the custom menu has already been closed. To avoid this problem, you can add your own code to prompt the user to save the workbook. The following event procedure will demonstrate the modifications required for the *BeforeClose* procedure:

```
Private Sub Workbook_BeforeClose(Cancel as Boolean)
    Dim Msg as String
    If Me.Saved Then
        Call DeleteMenu
        Exit Sub
    Else
        Msg = "Do you want to save the changes you made to " & Me.Name & "?"
        Ans = MsgBox (Msg, vbQuestion + vbYesNoCancel)
        Select Case Ans
        Case vbYes
            Me.Save
            Call DeleteMenu
        Case vbNo
            Me.Save = True
            Call DeleteMenu
        Case vbCancel
            Cancel = True
        End Select
    End If
End Sub
```

This event procedure checks the *Saved* property of the *Workbook* object to determine if the workbook has been saved. If the workbook has been saved, the *DeleteMenu* procedure is executed and the workbook is closed. However, if the workbook has not been saved, the procedure will display the normal Excel warning. If the user selects Yes, the workbook is saved, the menu is deleted, and the workbook is closed. If the user selects No, the workbook is not saved but the *Saved* property is set to *True*, the procedure deletes the menu and closes the workbook. If the user clicks Cancel, the *BeforeClose* event is canceled and the procedure ends without deleting the menu.

Worksheet Events

The events for the *Worksheet* object are some of the most useful events at your disposal in the world of Microsoft Excel. As you will see, the events for the *Worksheet* object occur when the worksheet is activated or the user changes the content of a cell. The *Worksheet* events are also activated by default, but as mentioned in the "Enabling and Disabling Events" section earlier, you can disable or deactivate the events.

To display the event procedures for a worksheet, use the Visual Basic Editor. Expand the desired project in the project window and double-click the worksheet to activate it. All event procedures associated with the worksheet will be displayed in the code window on the right side of the window.

To create a new *Worksheet* event procedure, follow these steps:

1 Double-click the *Worksheet* object named *Sheet1 (Sheet1)* to activate it.
2 Click the Object drop-down list, and select the Worksheet option.
3 Click the Procedure drop-down list, and select the desired event.

In Figure 12-3, you can see how to create a new *Worksheet* event procedure.

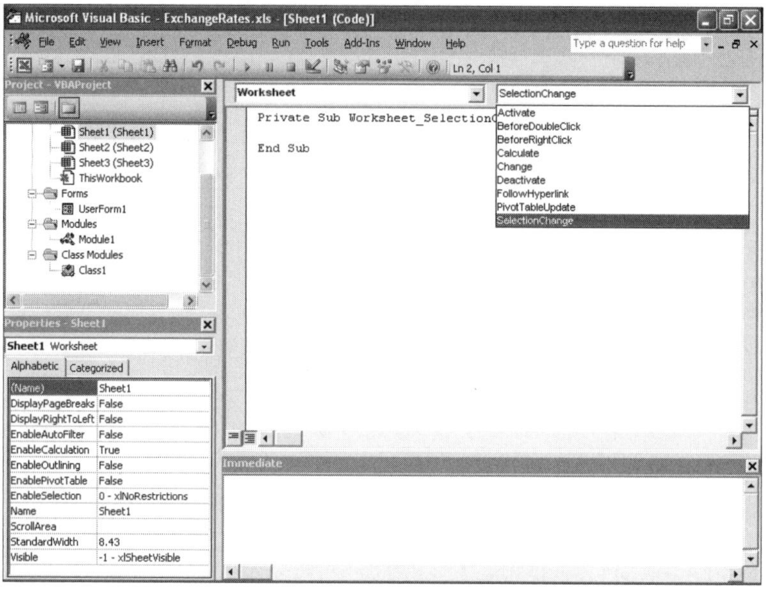

Figure 12-3. This is how to create a new *Worksheet* event procedure.

After you have created the new event procedure, you'll notice the `Private Sub` `Worksheet_Event` and `End Sub` code has been added to the code window. Table 12-2 describes the commonly used *Worksheet* events.

Table 12-2. Commonly Used *Worksheet* Events

Worksheet Event	Action That Triggers Event
Change	Monitors the *Change* event for the worksheet. The event is triggered when the cells of the worksheet are changed by the user or by an external link.
Selection Change	Monitors the *SelectionChange* event for the worksheet. The event is triggered when the user chooses a new selection on the worksheet.
BeforeRightClick	Monitors the *BeforeRightClick* event for the worksheet. The event is triggered when the user right-clicks the worksheet.

Note To navigate to the event procedures in a worksheet, you can right-click the sheet tab in the Excel program window and select View Code.

Change Event

The *Change* event occurs when any cell in a worksheet is changed by the user, by VBA code, or by an external link. The *Change* event is not triggered when a calculation generates a different value for a formula, or when an object is added to the worksheet.

> **Note** The *Change* event does not occur when cells change during recalculation. Use the *Calculate* event to trap a sheet recalculation.

When the *Worksheet_Change* procedure is executed, it receives a *Range* object as its *Target* argument. This *Range* object represents the changed cell or range that triggered the event. The following event procedure displays the address of the *Target* range:

```
Private Sub Worksheet_Change (ByVal Target As Excel.Range)
    MsgBox "Range " & Target.Address & " was changed."
End Sub
```

Inside Out

The Quirky *Change* Event

To get a better grasp of what causes the *Change* event to trigger, type the previous procedure into a code module and start modifying your worksheet. Every time the *Change* event occurs, you will see the address of the range that was modified.

There are some quirks associated with the *Change* event that you should be aware of, such as actions that should trigger the *Change* event but don't, as well as actions that do trigger the *Change* event when they should not. The following list highlights some of these quirks:

- Changing the format of the cell does not trigger the *Change* event, but using the **Clear Formats** command from the Edit menu does trigger the event.
- Inserting, editing, or deleting a cell comment does not trigger the *Change* event.
- Pressing the Delete or Backspace key and then pressing the Enter key triggers the *Change* event, even if the cell is empty.
- Cells that are changed by using Excel commands might or might not trigger a change event. For example, adding new records to a Data Form or sorting data does not trigger the *Change* event. However, if you have made any spelling changes in your worksheet, using the Excel Spell checking feature or using the Replace feature will generate a *Change* event.

As you can see by the inconsistencies with the preceding list, it isn't a good idea to rely on the *Change* event to detect all cell changes. However, you can work around these problems if you are aware of them. For example, if you know that the cell contents are required to have a specific format or value, you can use the *BeforeSave* event procedure to verify that the *Change* event did not miss an invalid entry.

SelectionChange Event

The *SelectionChange* event procedure is executed each time the user selects a new cell or range of cells on the worksheet. This procedure is commonly used to assist the user in navigating through large files. For example, the event procedure could shade the row and column of the intersecting cell that is active. When a new selection is made you can turn off the current shading and then reapply the shading for the new row and column intersection.

The following event procedure was created to help the employees at The Garden Company navigate through the Productlist.xls file. The procedure scrolls through the workbook window until the current selection is in the upper-left corner of the window.

```
Private Sub Worksheet_SelectionChange(ByVal Target As Range)
    With ActiveWindow
        ScrollRow = Target.Row
        ScrollColumn = Target.Column
    End With
End Sub
```

BeforeRightClick Event

The *BeforeRightClick* event is triggered when the user right-clicks the worksheet. If you would like to disable the shortcut menu from being displayed when the user right-clicks the worksheet, you can trap the *RightClick* event and set the *Cancel* argument to *True*.

> **Note** The *BeforeRightClick* event does not occur if the pointer is on a shape, a toolbar, or a menu bar.

The following procedure will prevent the user from accessing the shortcut menus in a worksheet:

```
Private Sub Worksheet_BeforeRightClick(ByVal Target As Excel.Range, Cancel _
    As Boolean)
    Cancel = True
    MsgBox "The shortcut menu is unavailable for " & Cells.Worksheet.Name
End Sub
```

Application Events

The events for the *Application* occur when any workbook is created, opened, or changed. If you need to write an event procedure at the *Application* level, you need to create a new object in a class module. After the new class module is created, you can attach macros with a variety of events, such as *NewWorkbook*, *SheetActivate*, or *WorkbookOpen*.

Table 12-3 describes the commonly used *Application* events that can be programmed in your workbooks.

Table 12-3. Commonly Monitored Events by the *Application* Object

Event	Action That Triggers the Event
NewWorkbook	Monitors the *NewWorkbook* event for the Excel application. The event is triggered when a new workbook is created.
SheetActivate	Monitors the *SheetActivate* event for the entire Excel program. The event is triggered when any sheet is activated within the program.
WorkbookOpen	Monitors the *WorkbookOpen* event for the Excel application. The event is triggered when any workbook is opened within the Excel window.

Inside Out

Locate Events Using the Object Browser

The Object Browser is a useful tool that can help you learn about objects, their properties, and their methods. The Object Browser is also useful when trying to find which objects are supported by a particular event. For example, say you would like to find out which objects support the *Change* event. Activate the Visual Basic Editor, and press F2 to display the Object Browser window. Make sure <All Libraries> is selected, and then type **Change** and click the binoculars icon, as shown in the following graphic.

continued

The Object Browser displays a list of matching items. Events are indicated with a small yellow lightning bolt. From this list, you can see which objects support the *Change* event.

Notice how the list is divided into three columns: *Library*, *Class*, and *Member*. The match for the item you are searching for might appear in any of these columns. The name of an event or term belonging to one library or class might be the same as that for another belonging to a different library or class, although they probably don't share the same functionality. When clicking each item in the Object Browser list, check the status bar at the bottom of the list for the syntax. You might find that one class or library treats an event differently than another.

Turning on *Application* Event Monitoring

In the previous sections, we discussed how to create *Worksheet* events and *Workbook* events. Those events are for a particular workbook. If you need to monitor events for the entire Excel application, use *Application*-level events. To use Application events, you must enable event monitoring. Follow these steps to activate *Application* event monitoring:

1. Create a new class module.

2. Set a name for the class module in the Properties window under Name. For example: **AppEventClass**.

3. In the class module, declare a public *Application* object using the *WithEvents* keyword. For example:

```
Public WithEvents Appl As Application
```

4. To test the application event procedure, enter the following examples in the new class module after the public variable:

```
Private Sub Appl_NewWorkbook(ByVal Wb As Workbook)
    MsgBox "You created a new workbook."
End Sub

Private Sub Appl_WorkbookBeforeClose(ByVal Wb As Workbook, Cancel As Boolean)
    MsgBox "You closed the workbook."
End Sub

Private Sub Appl_WorkbookBeforePrint(ByVal Wb As Workbook, Cancel As Boolean)
    MsgBox "You are printing the workbook."
End Sub

Private Sub Appl_WorkbookBeforeSave(ByVal Wb As Workbook, ByVal _
    SaveAsUI As Boolean, Cancel As Boolean)
    MsgBox "You saved your workbook."
End Sub

Private Sub Appl_WorkbookOpen(ByVal Wb As Workbook)
    MsgBox "You opened a workbook."
End Sub
```

5 Create a variable that you can use to refer to the declared *Application* object in the class module. This should be a module-level object variable, declared in a regular VBA module or in the *ThisWorkbook* object. For example:

```
Dim ApplicationClass As New AppEventClass
```

6 Connect the declared object with the *Application* object. This is often done in a *Workbook_Open* procedure. For example:

```
Private Sub Workbook_Open()
    Set ApplicationClass.App1 = Application
End Sub
```

After you save the workbook, close it, and reopen it to trigger the *Workbook_Open* event procedure, the events attached to the *Application* object will be activated.

Understanding how the events are triggered, as well as the sequence in which they are executed, is crucial when designing your Excel applications. Use the preceding example to play with your application and test the firing sequence. Taking time and effort in the planning stages of your event sequences will save a lot of time and frustration in the development of your current and future projects.

Detecting When a Workbook Is Opened

Because Excel only allows one copy of a workbook to be open, it's important to determine if the workbook is currently open or needs to be opened. If you do not verify the status of the file, you will receive an error and your event will stop.

For example, The Garden Company uses a file named Invoice.xls that's dependent on the ProductList.xls file. The Invoice.xls file uses a lookup to input the correct product name on the invoice. It's crucial for the ProductList.xls file to be open for the Invoice.xls file to operate properly. To avoid lookup errors, the following function, named *WorkbookOpen*, was created to test whether the ProductList.xls file is currently open. The function will return the answer *True* if the workbook is open.

```
Function WorkbookOpen(WorkBookName As String) As Boolean
    WorkbookOpen = False
    On Error GoTo WorkBookNotOpen
    If Len(Application.WorkBooks(WorkBookName).Name) > 0 Then
        WorkbookOpen = True
        Exit Function
    End If
WorkBookNotOpen:
End Function
```

Once the function has been added to the *ThisWorkbook* object within the Invoice.xls file, you can use the function to evaluate whether the desired workbook is open. The following *If...Then...Else* statement, which you could use as a subroutine within a larger procedure, ensures the ProductList.xls workbook will be open when you need to use it in a procedure.

Chapter 12

```
If Not WorkbookOpen("ProductList.xls") Then
    Workbooks.Open "ProductList.xls"
End If
```

This chapter has exposed you to three layers of events: application, workbook, and worksheet. When analyzing the needs of your workbook, it's important to remember your final goals for your project. When you have a list of event procedures that are required, the next step is to determine at which level the procedures should be stored. Remember that the most common error while programming event procedures is coding the events for the wrong object.

Keep in mind as you are programming the required event procedures that some triggers actually cause several events to run. The best way to get a feel for event procedures is to thoroughly test them. You might go through several drafts before you finalize how you want to set up your event handlers.

Chapter 13

Manipulating Files

Locating External Files 281
Writing to an External File 295
Reading from an External File 296
Searching a File for a Value 298

Many applications that you develop for Microsoft Excel require working with multiple files. For example, you might need to get a listing of files in a directory, delete files, or rename files. Excel, of course, can import and export several types of text files. In many cases, however, Excel's built-in text file handling is not sufficient. For example, you might need to import a text file that contains more than 256 columns of data, which is Excel's limit, or the file might use a nonstandard delimiter such as a backward slash (\).

In this chapter, you'll learn how to locate, write to, and read from external files. You'll also learn to narrow your search using wildcards, as well as to search files for specific values.

Locating External Files

The Office Object Model is made available to all Microsoft Office applications, as discussed in previous chapters. It contains objects that are used by all Office applications, such as the *CommandBars* object, which is discussed in Chapter 17. You'll learn how to utilize two objects contained in the Office Object Model that you use to search for files: *FileSearch* and *FileDialog*. You'll also evaluate the following objects associated with each object.

The following files are associated with the *FileSearch* object:

- *FoundFiles*
- *FileTypes*
- *SearchScopes*
- *ScopeFolders*
- *SearchFolders*

The following files are associated with the *FileDialog* object:

- *FileDialogFilters*
- *FileDialogSelectedItems*

The *FileSearch* object allows you to search for files with a wide range of search criteria. You are able to search by file type, file size, file location, and date of last modification. The *FileSearch* object places the names of the files it finds in the *FoundFiles* collection.

You can use the *FileSearch* object instead of the VBA *Dir* function for a range of file operations. *FileSearch* is useful for maintenance of files. For example, you can locate files of a certain age and delete them or move them to an archive directory. The *FileSearch* object is also useful when you need to retrieve data from a number of related files. For example, you can find all the Excel files in a certain directory that pertain to a new marketing initiative for The Garden Supply Company, before you consolidate the information into a summary file.

The *FileDialog* object was introduced in Office XP and enhanced with Office 2003. You are able to display the *File Open* and *File Save As* dialog boxes as well as a subdirectory browser. *FileDialog* is a more powerful version of the *GetOpenFileName* and *GetSaveAsFileName* methods of the Excel *Application* object, which are available in previous versions of Excel, but have not been available to other Office applications. *FileDialog*, being an Office object, is available to all Office applications.

Returning All Files

The *FileSearch* property is used to located file names based on your search criteria. It places the file names returned from the search in the *FoundFiles* collection. This object gives your code the functionality of the File Search feature available in the Excel application. For example, you can search for all Excel files by the file extension or search for files containing specific text. Table 13-1 lists some of the properties and methods used in the *FileSearch* object.

Table 13-1. List of Properties and Methods of the *FileSearch* Object

Property or Method	Result
FileName	Searches for the name of the file specified. Wildcards can be used in the search criteria.
FoundFiles	Returns an object that contains the names of the files found.
LookIn	Specifies the directory to be searched.
SearchSubFolders	Sets the search to look in subfolders if *True*, or to ignore subfolders if set to *False*.
Execute	Initiates the search.
NewSearch	Clears previous results in the *FileSearch* object from previous searches.

Consider the following example, in which the object variable *FS* is declared as part of the *Office.FileSearch* object. The *Office* prefix is not required, but this prefix makes it clear that the *FileSearch* object is an object in the Office library. In the code, the *FileSearch* property of the Excel *Application* object returns a reference to the *FileSearch* object and assigns it to the *FS* variable. Values are then assigned to a number of *FileSearch* properties. The *LookIn* property tells *FileSearch* which subdirectory to search. *NewSearch* is a method that clears all the *FileSearch* properties except *LookIn*. Because these properties are retained while Excel is open, it's a good idea to execute *NewSearch* each time you use the *FileSearch* method. The *SearchSubFolders* property controls whether you look in subdirectories below the *LookIn* subdirectory.

> **Note**   Be sure to clear your previous search settings by executing the *NewSearch* method each time the *FileSearch* method is used. The *FileSearch* properties are retained in the Excel application during your current session in Excel.

```
Sub FindAccountingExcelFiles()
    Dim FS As Office.FileSearch
    Dim strPath As String
    Dim vaFileName As Variant
    Dim strMessage As String
    Dim i As Long
    Dim iCount As Long

    Set FS = Application.FileSearch
    strPath = "C:\GSC\Accounting"

    With FS
        .NewSearch
        .LookIn = strPath
        .SearchSubFolders = True
        .FileType = msoFileTypeExcelWorkbooks
        .LastModified = msoLastModifiedAnyTime
        iCount = .Execute

        strMessage = Format(iCount, "0 ""Files Found""")

        For Each vaFileName In .FoundFiles
            strMessage = strMessage & vbCr & vaFileName
        Next vaFileName

        MsgBox strMessage
    End With
End Sub
```

The *FileType* property determines which file extensions will be included in the search criteria. The *msoFileTypeExcelWorkbooks* constant directs the search to include all the Excel file extensions: .xls, .xlt, .xlm, .xlc, and .xla. Table 13-2 lists the other constants available.

Table 13-2. List of File Types and Their Values

msoFileType Constants	Value
msoFileTypeAllFiles	1
msoFileTypeOfficeFiles	2
msoFileTypeWordDocuments	3
msoFileTypeExcelWorkbooks	4
msoFileTypePowerPointPresentations	5
msoFileTypeBinders	6
msoFileTypeDatabases	7

continued

283

Table 13-2. List of File Types and Their Values *(continued)*

msoFileType Constants	Value
msoFileTypeTemplates	8
msoFileTypeOutlookItems	9
msoFileTypeMailItem	10
msoFileTypeCalendarItem	11
msoFileTypeContactItem	12
msoFileTypeNoteItem	13
msoFileTypeJournalItem	14
msoFileTypeTaskItem	15
msoFileTypePhotoDrawFiles	16
msoFileTypeDataConnectionFiles	17
msoFileTypePublisherFiles	18
msoFileTypeProjectFiles	19
msoFileTypeDocumentImagingFiles	20
msoFileTypeVisioFiles	21
msoFileTypeDesignerFiles	22
msoFileTypeWebPages	23

The *LastModified* property can use the following constants listed in Table 13-3.

Table 13-3. List of *LastModified* Properties and Their Values

msoLastModified Constants	Value
msoLastModifiedYesterday	1
msoLastModifiedToday	2
msoLastModifiedLastWeek	3
msoLastModifiedThisWeek	4
msoLastModifiedLastMonth	5
msoLastModifiedThisMonth	6
msoLastModifiedAnyTime	7

Instead of using the *FileType* property, you can specify the *FileName* property.

```
.FileName = "*.xls"
```

The *FileName* property allows you to narrow your search more than the *FileType* constant. If you use both *FileType* and *FileName*, the *FileName* property overrides the *FileType* property. You can also search the text contained in the properties of a file or in the body of the file itself by assigning the text to the *TextOrProperty* property of the *FileSearch* object.

The *Execute* method of the *FileSearch* object carries out the search and adds an object representing each file to the *FoundFiles* collection. The *Execute* method also returns a value that is the number of files found.

You use the *FoundFiles* collection to access the names, including the path, of the files found. The code from the previous example uses a *For Each…Next* loop to process the list, adding each name to *strMessage*, separated by a carriage return.

Limiting the File Search

There are times when you need to reopen a file from several months ago, but you don't remember its exact location. We have all run into this problem at one time or another. The File Search feature in Excel can accomplish this task. However, you can use the *PropertyTests* collection in your VBA procedure to automate the search process.

For example, the Garden Supply Company has decided to reorganize their historical files. All files created in the previous year will be moved to an Archive folder on the company's file server. The following procedure was designed to search for files that were modified in the previous month:

```
Sub FindLastMonthFiles()
    Dim FS As Office.FileSearch
    Dim vaFileName As Variant
    Dim strMessage As String
    Dim i As Long
    Dim iCount As Long

    Set FS = Application.FileSearch
    strPath = "C:\GSC\Accounting"

    With FS
        .NewSearch
        .LookIn = strPath
        .SearchSubFolders = True

        With .PropertyTests
            For i = .Count To 1 Step -1
                .Remove i
            Next i

        .Add Name:="Files of Type", _
            Condition:=msoConditionFileTypeExcelWorkbooks
        End With
```

```
        .LastModified = msoLastModifiedLastMonth
        iCount = .Execute
        strMessage = Format(iCount, "0 ""Files Found""")

        For Each vaFileName In .FoundFiles
            strMessage = strMessage & vbCr & vaFileName
        Next vaFileName

        MsgBox strMessage
    End With
End Sub
```

The *PropertyTests* collection operates independently of any settings in the File Search task pane. This collection doesn't recognize any conditions in the task pane and it doesn't change the settings. If you add tests to the *PropertyTests* collection, they are retained until a *NewSearch* is executed.

The *Add* method of the *PropertyTests* collection adds the new tests, which are specified by assigning a string to the *Name* parameter that is identical to the string that appears in the Property combo box in the File Search task pane.

The *FileType* property for *FileSearch* can be used to limit your search to a specific file type or multiple file types. The *FileTypes* collection allows you to specify multiple file types. The following example will return all Microsoft Word and Excel files in the specified folders:

```
Sub FindWordandExcelFiles()
    Dim FS As Office.FileSearch
    Dim vaFileName As Variant
    Dim stMessage As String
    Dim i As Long
    Dim iCount As Long

    Set FS = Application.FileSearch
    strPath = "C:\GSC\Accounting"

    With FS
        .NewSearch
        .FileType = msoFileTypeExcelWorkbooks
        .FileTypes.Add msoFileTypeWordDocuments
        .LookIn = strPath
        .SearchSubFolders = True
        .LastModified = msoLastModifiedAnyTime
        iCount = .Execute
        stMessage = Format(iCount, "0 ""Files Found""")

        For Each vaFileName In .FoundFiles
            stMessage = stMessage & vbCr & vaFileName
        Next vaFileName

        MsgBox stMessage
    End With
End Sub
```

The *FileTypes* collection is retained until you execute *NewSearch*, which clears the collection and places the value of *msoFileTypeOfficeFiles* in the collection. However, there's no need to empty the *FileTypes* collection before adding new entries. If you assign an entry to the *FileType* parameter, any existing entries in the *FileTypes* collection are destroyed and the new entry becomes the first and only entry in the collection. You can then use the *Add* method of the collection to add more entries. You can use the same type constants that were listed earlier in the chapter.

All the code that we have evaluated so far in this section assumes that you know the directory organization of the computer you are searching and can specify the subdirectories that you want to search. If you do not know the structure and need to map it yourself, a utility must be designed to search for files on any computer.

The *SearchScopes* collection provides a mechanism for carrying out the directory mapping process. The following example examines each member of the collection; each member is a *SearchScope* object.

```
Sub ListSearchScopeOptions()
    Dim SS As SearchScope
    Dim strMessage As String

    For Each SS In Application.FileSearch.SearchScopes
        strMessage = strMessage & SS.ScopeFolder.Name & vbTab
        strMessage = strMessage & " Type=" & SS.Type & vbCr
    Next SS

    MsgBox strMessage
End Sub
```

The *SearchScope* objects represent the structures you can examine. The *Type* property identifies the category of each structure. The presence of My Computer and Network Places is no surprise. However, notice that Microsoft Outlook is given as another location. Your code should result in a dialog box similar to the one shown in Figure 13-1.

Figure 13-1. The *ListSearchScopeOptions* procedure result. Your result might vary slightly depending on how your computer is configured.

There are four *SearchIn* constants available. Table 13-4 lists the constants available.

Table 13-4. List of *msoSearchIn* Properties and Their Values

msoSearchIn Constants	Value
msoSearchInMyComputer	0
msoSearchInOutlook	1
msoSearchInMyNetworkPlaces	2
msoSearchInCustom	3

The *ScopeFolder* property is available for each *SearchScope* object and references a *ScopeFolder* object. The *ScopeFolder* represents the top of the structure in the *ScopeFolders* collection that contains more *ScopeFolder* objects. The following example displays the *Name* and *Path* properties of the *ScopeFolders* under the top-level *ScopeFolder* of each structure:

```
Sub ListScopeFolderObjects()
    Dim SS As SearchScope
    Dim SF As ScopeFolder
    Dim strMessage As String

    Application.FileSearch.RefreshScopes

    For Each SS In Application.FileSearch.SearchScopes
        Select Case SS.Type

        Case msoSearchInMyComputer
            strMessage = SS.ScopeFolder.Name & vbCr
            For Each SF In SS.ScopeFolder.ScopeFolders
                strMessage = strMessage & SF.Name & vbTab & vbTab
                strMessage = strMessage & "Path = " & SF.Path & vbCr
            Next SF

        Case msoSearchInMyNetworkPlaces
            strMessage = strMessage & vbCr & SS.ScopeFolder.Name & vbCr
            For Each SF In SS.ScopeFolder.ScopeFolders
                strMessage = strMessage & SF.Name & vbTab
                strMessage = strMessage & "Path = " & SF.Path & vbCr
            Next SF

        Case msoSearchInOutlook
            strMessage = strMessage & vbCr & SS.ScopeFolder.Name & vbCr
            For Each SF In SS.ScopeFolder.ScopeFolders
                strMessage = strMessage & SF.Name & vbTab & vbTab
                strMessage = strMessage & "Path = " & SF.Path & vbCr
            Next SF

        Case Else
            strMessage = strMessage & vbCr & "Unknown SearchScope object"
```

```
        End Select
    Next SS

    MsgBox strMessage

End Sub
```

The code will return a result similar to Figure 13-2.

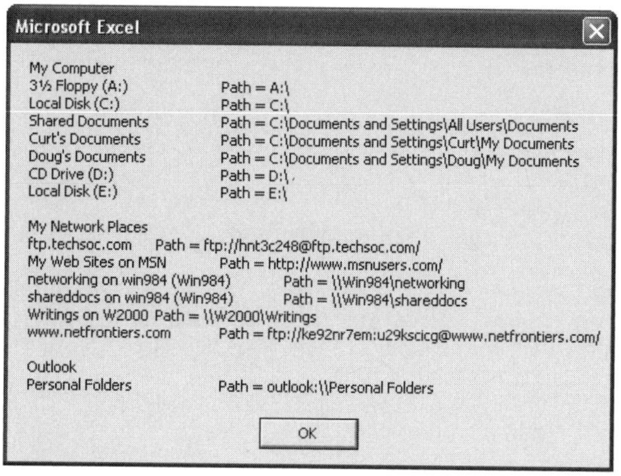

Figure 13-2. Here is the *ListScopeFolderObjects* procedure result. Your result might vary depending on how your computer is configured.

The *Select Case* statements were used to isolate and examine each of the top-level structures. Each top-level *ScopeFolders* collection contains *ScopeFolder* objects that represent the root directories of the file structures available to it. Each of these *ScopeFolder* objects contains another *ScopeFolders* collection that represents the subdirectories under it. This provides a way to navigate through the directory trees.

The *SearchFolders* collection defines additional directory paths to be searched by adding *ScopeFolder* objects to the collection. *SearchFolders* is not like the *FileTypes* collection that is recreated when you assign a value to the *FileType* property. *SearchFolders* isn't affected when you assign a value to the *LookIn* property or when you execute *NewSearch*. The *LookIn* value is additional to the *SearchFolders* entries.

The *SearchFolders* collection is also retained in the current Excel session, so empty the collection before executing a new search. Remember to empty the *SearchFolders* collection by looping through each *ScopeFolder* object and removing it. Review the following example to get a better understanding of how to search through all subdirectories in the root directory of the C drive. When it finds a directory starting with the characters *Product*, it will add the directory to the *SearchFolders* collection.

```
Sub SetupSearchFoldersCollection()
    Dim FS As FileSearch
    Dim SS As SearchScope
    Dim SF As ScopeFolder
    Dim sfSubFolder As ScopeFolder
    Dim strMessage As String
    Dim i As Long

    Set FS = Application.FileSearch

    For i = FS.SearchFolders.Count To 1 Step -1
        FS.SearchFolders.Remove i
    Next i

    For Each SS In FS.SearchScopes
        Select Case SS.Type
        Case msoSearchInMyComputer
            For Each SF In SS.ScopeFolder.ScopeFolders
                Select Case SF.Path
                    Case "C:\"
                        For Each sfSubFolder In SF.ScopeFolders
                            If UCase(Left(sfSubFolder.Name, 6)) = _
                                "PRODUCT" Then
                                sfSubFolder.AddToSearchFolders
                            End If
                        Next sfSubFolder
                        Exit For
                End Select
            Next SF
            Exit For
        End Select
    Next SS
    Search_SearchFolders
End Sub
```

The example empties the *SearchFolders* collection and then searches through the *SearchScopes* and *ScopeFolders* collections to locate the C drive. The code then evaluates the *Name* property of each *ScopeFolder* in the root directory of the C drive to determine if the name begins with *Product*. Since the comparison of text is case sensitive, the *Name* property is converted to uppercase.

The previous example is dependent on the *Search_SearchFolders* procedure. When the code finds a matching directory, it uses the *AddToSearchFolders* method of the *ScopeFolder* object to add the object to the *SearchFolders* collection. The *Search_SearchFolders* routine is listed here:

```
Sub Search_SearchFolders()
    Dim FS As Office.FileSearch
    Dim vaFileName As Variant
    Dim strMessage As String
    Dim iCount As Long
```

```
        Set FS = Application.FileSearch

        With FS
            .NewSearch
            .LookIn = "c:\"
            .SearchSubFolders = True
            .Filename = "*.xls"
            .LastModified = msoLastModifiedAnyTime
            iCount = .Execute
            strMessage = Format(iCount, "0 ""Files Found""")
            For Each vaFileName In .FoundFiles
                strMessage = strMessage & vbCr & vaFileName
            Next vaFileName
            MsgBox strMessage
        End With
End Sub
```

The *Search_SearchFolders* collection sets the *LookIn* property of *FileSearch* to the C drive to ensure that it doesn't contain any directory references from previous *FileSearch* operations.

Inside Out

Determining if a File Exists Using *FileSearch*

There might be times when your procedure won't run successfully without a particular file. You can simply use a function to determine if that file exists. For example, the following function was written to verify whether a file and its path are valid. The function will return *True* if the file exists and *False* if it was not found.

```
Function FileExists(path, fname) As Boolean
    With Application.FileSearch
        .NewSearch
        .filename = fname
        .LookIn = path
        .Execute
        If .FoundFiles.Count = 1 Then
            FileExists = True
        Else
            FileExists = False
        End If
    End With
End Function
```

Finding Files with the FileDialog Dialog Box

The *FileDialog* object allows you to display the *Open* and *Save As* dialog boxes using VBA code. The *GetOpenFileName* and *GetSaveAsFileName* methods of the *Application* object achieve similar results and can be used for backward compatibility. However, the *FileDialog* object is available to all Office applications and is a familiar interface to the users.

In the following example, The Garden Supply Company has a list of pictures used in their spring catalog. You have been asked to create a worksheet that allows the user to choose the images and insert a preview into the worksheet.

> **Important**   The following two procedures assume there is a worksheet named *ImagePreview* in the active workbook.

```
Private Sub cmdGetFile_Click()
    Dim FD As FileDialog
    Dim FFs As FileDialogFilters
    Dim strFileName As String

    On Error GoTo Problem

    Set FD = Application.FileDialog(msoFileDialogOpen)

    With FD
        Set FFs = .Filters

        With FFs
            .Clear
            .Add "Pictures", "*.jpg"
        End With

        If .Show = False Then Exit Sub

        Worksheets("ImagePreview").Pictures.Insert (.SelectedItems(1))

    End With

    Exit Sub

Problem:
    MsgBox "You have not selected a valid picture."

End Sub
```

The *FileDialog* property of the *Application* object returns a reference to the Office *FileDialogs* object. Table 13-5 lists the *msofileDialogType* constants available to specify the type of dialog.

Table 13-5. List of Dialog Types and Their Values

msoFileDialog Constants	Value
msoFileDialogOpen	1
msoFileDialogSaveAs	2
msoFileDialogFilePicker	3
msoFileDialogFolderPicker	4

The *Filters* property of the *FileDialog* object returns a reference to the *FileDialogFilters* collection for the *FileDialog*. The filters control the types of files that are displayed. By default, there are 24 preset filters that the user can select from the drop-down list at the bottom of the File Open dialog box. The *Clear* method of the *FileDialogFilters* collection removes the preset filters, and we add our own filter that shows only .jpg files.

The *Show* method of the *FileDialog* object displays the dialog box. When the user clicks the Open button, the *Show* method returns a value of *True*. If the user clicks the Cancel button, the *Show* method returns *False* and you'll exit the procedure.

The *Show* method does not actually open the selected file, but instead places the file name and path into the *FileDialogSelectedItems* collection. It's possible to set this property to allow users to select multiple files. By default, the name of the file is returned from the first item in the *FileDialogSelectedItems* collection, which is referred to by the *SelectedItems* property of the *FileDialog* object.

There are few differences between the four possible dialog types apart from the heading on the title bar. The file picker and folder picker types show Browse in the title bar, and the others show File Open and File Save As, as appropriate. All the dialogs show the folders and files except the folder picker dialog, which shows only folders.

As you have seen, the *Show* method displays the *FileDialog*, and the items chosen are placed in the *FileDialogSelectedItems* object without any attempt to open or save any files. The following example shows how you can use the *Execute* method with the File Open and Save As dialogs to carry out the required Open or Save As operations immediately when the user clicks the Open or Save button.

```
With Application.FileDialog(xlDialogOpen)
    If .Show Then .Execute
End With
```

Consider the following example. The *cmdShowProductImage_Click* procedure has been modified to allow the user to select multiple files by holding down the Shift or Ctrl keys while clicking on the file names. The file names are then loaded into the List box named lstFileList, allowing the user to display the files by selecting the file name.

```
Private Sub cmdShowProductImage_Click()
    Dim FD As FileDialog
    Dim FFs As FileDialogFilters
    Dim strFileName As String
    Dim vaItem
    Dim intCounter As Integer

    On Error GoTo Problem

    Set FD = Application.FileDialog(msoFileDialogOpen)

    With FD
        Set FFs = .Filters
```

```
With FFs
    .Clear
    .Add "Pictures", "*.jpg"
End With

.AllowMultiSelect = True

If .Show = False Then Exit Sub

 intCounter = 1

For Each vaItem In .SelectedItems
    Worksheets("ImagePreview").Pictures.Insert _
        (.SelectedItems(intCounter))
    intCounter = intCounter + 1
Next vaItem

End With

Exit Sub

Problem:
    MsgBox "You have not selected a valid picture."

End Sub
```

The *AllowMultiSelect* property is set to *True*, allowing the user to select multiple files. The list box is cleared of any previous entries, and the *For...Each Loop* adds the items into the *FileDialogSelectedItems* collection. The *ListIndex* property is set to 0 each time the user selects a new file, and then the *Change* event procedure is executed loading the new image.

Inside Out

Determining if a File Exists Using *FileDialog*

Previously in this chapter, you saw how to determine if a file existed using the *FileSearch* object. Now that you have reviewed the *FileDialog* object, review the following function. The same results are returned, but a different method is used to achieve the same results. The function will return *True* if the file exists and *False* if it isn't found.

```
Function FileExists2(fname) As Boolean
    Set FileSys = CreateObject("Scripting.FileSystemObject")
    FileExists2 = FileSys.FileExists(fname)
End Function
```

The function created an instance of the *FileSystemObject* object. The *FileSystemObject* gives you access to the computer's file system. Once access is granted to the computer's file system, the function uses the *FileExists* property of the *FileSys* object to determine if the file exists. The code is much simpler and more elegant than the earlier example.

Writing to an External File

VBA contains a number of statements that allow file manipulation. These *Input/Output* statements give you more control over files than Excel's normal text file import and export options.

The standard procedure for writing to a text file is listed here:

1 Open or create the file using the *Open* statement.

2 Specify the position in the file using the *Seek* function, which is optional.

3 Write the data to the file using the *Write #* or the *Print #* statement.

4 Close the file using the *Close* statement.

> **Note** Do not confuse the VBA *Open* statement with the *Open* method for the *Application* object. VBA's *Open* statement is used to open a file for reading or writing whereas the *Open* method for the *Application* object actually opens the file.

Inside Out

Opening a Text File

Before you are able to read or write to a file, you must open it. The *Open* statement is quite versatile, and the syntax can be a challenge.

```
Open pathname For mode [Access access] [lock] As [#]filenumber _
[Len=reclength]
```

- **pathname**   A required element that contains the name and path of the file to be opened.

- **mode**   A required element that specifies which mode the file will be using, such as *Append*, *Input*, *Output*, *Binary*, or *Random*.

> **Note** The VBA Help file for the mode parameter says that it's required but that if you leave it out, Excel will assume the mode is Random. We weren't able to resolve the contradiction, so the authors' advice is to always set the parameter.

- **access**   Specifies the file operation as *Read*, *Write*, or *Read Write*.

- **lock**   Specifies the file status as *Shared*, *Lock Read*, *Lock Write*, or *Lock Read Write*.

- **filenumber**   A required element that sets the file number ranging from 1 to 511. The *FreeFile* function can be used to assign the next available number.

- **reclength**   Sets the record length for random access files or the buffer size for sequential access files.

The following example exports data from a specified range to a CSV text file. Notice that the procedure uses two *Write #* statements. The first statement ends with a semicolon, so a carriage return/linefeed sequence is not written. For the last cell in a row, however, the second *Write #* statement does not use a semicolon, which causes the next output to appear on a new line.

```
Sub ExportSelectedRange()
    Dim FileName As String
    Dim NumRows As Long
    Dim NumCols As Integer
    Dim r As Long
    Dim c As Integer
    Dim Data
    Dim ExpRng As Range

    Set ExpRng = Selection
    NumCols = ExpRng.Columns.Count
    NumRows = ExpRng.Rows.Count
    FileName = "C:\textfile.txt"
    Open FileName For Output As #1
        For r = 1 To NumRows
            For c = 1 To NumCols
                Data = ExpRng.Cells(r, c).Value
                If IsNumeric(Data) Then Data = Val(Data)
                If IsEmpty(ExpRng.Cells(r, c)) Then Data = ""
                If c <> NumCols Then
                    Write #1, Data;
                Else
                    Write #1, Data
                End If
            Next c
        Next r
    Close #1
End Sub
```

The variable named *Data* stores the contents of each cell. If the cell is numeric, the variable is converted to a value. This step ensures that numeric data will not be stored with quotation marks. If a cell is empty, its *Value* property returns 0. Therefore, the code also checks for a blank cell using the *IsEmpty* function and substitutes an empty string instead of a zero. It's also important to remember that a date is actually a value that's formatted to appear in a common date format. Remember that if the information in the variable *Data* contains a date, the value is what will actually be stored in this variable.

Reading from an External File

The procedure to read a file is quite similar to the procedure used to write to a file. The steps required to read a text file using VBA are listed here:

1   Open the file using the *Open* statement.

2   Specify the position in the file using the *Seek* function, which is optional.

3 Read the data from the file using the *Input, Input #,* or *Line Input #* statement.

4 Close the file using the *Close* statement.

The following example reads the text file that was created in the previous example and stores the values beginning in the active cell. The code reads each character and separates the line of data, ignoring quote characters and looking for commas to deliminate the columns.

```vba
Sub ImportRange()
    Dim ImpRng As Range
    Dim FileName As String
    Dim r As Long
    Dim c As Integer
    Dim txt As String
    Dim Char As String * 1
    Dim Data
    Dim i As Integer

    Set ImpRng = ActiveCell
    On Error Resume Next
    FileName = "C:\textfile.txt"
    Open FileName For Input As #1
    If Err <> 0 Then
        MsgBox "Not found: " & FileName, vbCritical, "ERROR"
        Exit Sub
    End If
    r = 0
    c = 0
    txt = ""
    Do Until EOF(1)
        Line Input #1, Data
        For i = 1 To Len(Data)
            Char = Mid(Data, i, 1)
            If Char = "," Then
                ActiveCell.Offset(r, c) = txt
                c = c + 1
                txt = ""
            ElseIf i = Len(Data) Then
                If Char <> Chr(34) Then txt = txt & Char
                ActiveCell.Offset(r, c) = txt
                txt = ""
            ElseIf Char <> Chr(34) Then
                txt = txt & Char
            End If
        Next i
        c = 0
        r = r + 1
    Loop
    Close #1
End Sub
```

> **Note** The procedure is a starting point. It doesn't take into account how to handle data that might contain commas or a quote character. You'll also notice that if a date is imported, number signs appear around the date.

Searching a File for a Value

There will be times when you do not require the entire text file contents to be copied. You can specify your search to determine which text you are looking for. When the text is found, you can then determine which actions to take.

The following procedure uses two text files at the same time. The FilterFile procedure reads the text from textfile.txt and copies only rows that contain a specific text string to a second output.txt file.

```
Sub FilterFile()
    Open "c:\textfile.txt" For Input As #1
    Open "c:\output.txt" For Output As #2
    TextToFind = "January"
    Do Until EOF(1)
        Line Input #1, Data
        If InStr(1, Data, TextToFind) Then
            Print #2, Data
        End If
    Loop
    Close
End Sub
```

The *FileSearch* and *FileDialog* objects provide useful tools when programming VBA procedures. Because these objects are part of the *Office* object model, they have the advantage of being available to all Office VBA applications.

The *FileSearch* object is used to locate files with common characteristics, such as file names or similar locations, so that they can be processed in subsequent code. The *FileDialog* object is used to display the File Open and File Save As dialog boxes to allow the user to browse the folders. It provides a more powerful tool than the *GetOpenFileName* and *GetSaveAsFileName* functions used in previous versions of Excel.

The file search capabilities reviewed in this chapter can enhance the projects that you work with. Limit your searches using the criteria discussed, such as a specific file extension or a value within the file. These search techniques can be incorporated in your future projects to enhance your results. Once the desired files have been located, remember that you can read the contents of the file and then write the contents into new files when appropriate.

Developing Class Modules

Introducing Class Modules 300

Properties, Methods, and Events 303

Building a Class 305

Practical Class Design 312

This chapter introduces the concept of *classes*. In this chapter, you'll learn about classes, objects and why they aren't the same thing. You'll also learn how to construct classes in Microsoft Visual Basic for Applications (VBA), including defining their properties, methods, and events.

What Is an Object?

An *object* is a logical representation of a thing. The thing can be a physical entity such as a person, a flower, a machine, or a place. The thing can also be a logical entity such as a report, an order, or a transaction. The thing can also represent something on the computer such as a button, a cell, a worksheet, or a form.

What Is a Class?

A *class* is a template from which an object is created. This template includes both variables and code that are wrapped together in a single entity. An object represents a single instance of a class that can be manipulated by your program.

Confused? Think of a class as a data type such as *Integer* or *String*. Before you can use an *Integer* or a *String*, you must declare a variable of that type. Just as you can have multiple variables defined as *Integers* or *Strings*, you can have multiple variables defined as instances of a single class.

Classes are implemented in Visual Basic for Applications through the *class module*. Each class module holds exactly one class and includes all the properties, methods, and events associated with the class's interface, along with any other local variables, functions, and subroutines needed to make the class work properly.

What Are Properties?

Properties are attributes of the thing an object represents. For example, a flower will have attributes such as its name, its color, its size, and so on. A person's attributes include name, address, ID number, and birth date.

An object can also contain references to other objects. An order might have a reference to a customer, or a form might contain a button. For purposes of this discussion, these object references may also be characterized as properties.

An object can also represent a collection of similar things. For example the *Employees* object could contain a collection of individual *Employee* objects.

> **Tip** Adjectives Describe Nouns
>
> You can think of objects as nouns and properties as adjectives, that is, the red flower or the six-foot-tall person. This concept isn't perfect because some attributes are relatively specific, such as the truck with 55,230 miles, but this idea might be helpful as you begin working with objects.

What Are Methods?

Methods are actions that are performed by the object. For example, a report object might include a print method that sends the report to a printer. Another way of thinking about methods is that methods describe the operations performed with the information contained in the properties of the object.

> **Tip** Verbs Describe Actions
>
> You can characterize methods as a verb that performs an operation or a task with the properties in the object.

What Are Events?

Although not strictly a part of the object programming model, *events* are a useful tool that allow an object to communicate information with the program that created the object. Simply put, an event is a subroutine residing in the program that created the object that's called by the object, which is called from within the object.

An event is a useful technique that obviates the need for a program to constantly monitor an object for changes. Instead, the object calls the event to inform the calling program of a change in the object's state.

Introducing Class Modules

Class modules are among the most important tools in a VBA programmer's tool chest. A *class module* allows you to create your own objects, which you can manipulate just like objects already supplied with Microsoft Excel. And just like the objects available in Excel, a class module can have properties, methods, and events.

Accessing Objects

There's one big difference between a simple variable and an object variable. The object variable is merely a pointer in memory. You must explicitly create the object and save its location in the object variable. This process is known as *creating a new instance* of an object or *instantiating* an object.

Because objects are different from variables, Visual Basic for Applications uses a special statement called the *Set* statement. The *Set* statement has two forms. Here's the first form:

```
Set ObjectVariable = New ClassName
```

In this form, the *Set* statement creates a new object based on *ClassName*. This means that Visual Basic will allocate memory for the object and save the memory location in the *ObjectVariable* class.

```
Set ObjectVariable = ObjectExpression
```

In the second form, the *Set* statement does two things. The statement first releases the object that it was pointing to, and then it saves a pointer to an already existing object in *ObjectVariable*.

When Are Objects Really Created?

The *New* keyword in a *Dim*, a *Public*, or a *Private* statement doesn't create a new instance of an object. Instead, Visual Basic adds code in front of every reference to the object to see if a new instance of the class has been created. If a new instance of the class hasn't been created, the object will automatically be created before it's used.

For the most part it really doesn't matter if you use a *Dim* statement or a *Set* statement to create a new instance of the class. However, using the *Set New* statement is slightly more efficient than using a *Dim New* statement because Visual Basic doesn't generate the extra code to verify that a new instance of the class has been created.

Using a *Set New* statement instead of a *Dim New* statement also prevents some debugging problems. Suppose you have a situation where you believe that you have created a new instance of a class, but for some reason the object wasn't created. With the *Dim New* approach, the object will automatically be created and your program might try to use the object expecting it to hold certain information, but it won't because the object was just created.

Creating the object with the *Set New* statement means that the object couldn't be created on the fly, and your program would get some run-time error if it tried to access an object that hasn't been created yet. Although the run-time error wouldn't be pretty, it would let you know that there's a problem somewhere in your code. Otherwise, you might not even realize there was a bug.

Declaring Objects

You can declare an object using a *Dim*, a *Public*, or a *Private* statement using two different forms. Here's the first form:

```
Dim ObjectVariable As ClassName
```

This statement simply reserves space for *ObjectVariable* and the variable now has a type of *ClassName*.

```
Dim ObjectVariable As New ClassName
```

This second form does everything the previous form did, but will automatically create a new object the first time *ObjectVariable* is referenced.

Objects and *Nothing*

Visual Basic for Applications includes a special value called *Nothing*. You can use this value only with objects. *Nothing* is the value associated with an object variable that doesn't currently point to an instance of a class. An object variable declared with a *Dim* statement will initially be set to *Nothing*.

You can determine if a new instance of a class has been created by using *Is Nothing* in an *If* statement like this:

```
If ObjectVariable Is Nothing Then
```

> **Warning**   Although the expression *ObjectVariable Is Not Nothing* might make perfect sense in English, Visual Basic for Applications doesn't understand it. If you need to verify that an object variable refers to an instance of an object, you should use the expression *Not ObjectVariable Is Nothing*.

The *Is Nothing* test results in a *Boolean* value and can be used anywhere you can use a Boolean expression.

You can use the following statement to destroy an object:

```
Set ObjectVariable = Nothing
```

This statement will release the reference to the object and set the object variable to its uninitialized state. Assuming that there was only one object variable that pointed to the object, this statement will also destroy the object and release all the resources associated with it.

However, if multiple object variables point to this object, all of them must be set to *Nothing* before the object is destroyed. For example, in the following code fragment, the object created from *MyClass* continues to exist, even though *ObjectVariable1* was set to *Nothing*.

```
Set ObjectVariable1 = New MyClass
Set ObjectVariable2 = ObjectVariable1
Set ObjectVariable1 = Nothing
```

Objects with Multiple Object Variables

It's important to keep in mind that an object is not the same thing as an object variable. For example, the following code creates an object, which has two variables pointing to it:

```
Set ObjectA = New MyClass
Set ObjectB = ObjectA
```

The first *Set* statement creates a new instance of *MyClass*, whereas the second *Set* statement merely creates a second pointer to the same object created by the first statement.

This means that the following statements will do the same thing because both *ObjectA* and *ObjectB* point to the same object:

```
ObjectA.Name = "Roses"
ObjectB.Name = "Roses"
```

If this isn't confusing enough, executing the following statement will not destroy the object.

```
Set ObjectA = Nothing
```

Because *ObjectB* still points to the object, it will remain in memory until *ObjectB* is also set to *Nothing*.

Properties, Methods, and Events

Associated with every object is a collection of properties, methods, and events, which are used to communicate information between the object and the routine that created the object.

Public vs. *Private* Properties, Methods, and Events

The individual parts of a class can be labeled as either *Public* or *Private*. Anything marked as *Public* is visible to anyone using the class, whereas anything marked as *Private* can be accessed only from the code within the class.

Tip Don't Rely on Defaults

Always explicitly mark everything within a class as either *Public* or *Private*, so you never have to worry about whether something defaulted to *Public* or *Private*.

Properties

Within a class, you'll find a number of different things. You can define class-level variables, which can be accessed from anywhere in the class. If a class-level variable is marked as *Public*, it becomes available to anyone using the class and is then known as a *Property* of the class.

In addition to public class-level variables, properties might also have code associated with them. Each property where you want to use code is organized into two routines, which return the value to the calling program or change the value in the class. The *Get* routine returns a value to the caller, whereas the *Let* or the *Set* routine allows the caller to assign a value to the property.

Remember that you can define a property with only a *Get* routine or a *Let* or *Set* routine. If you use only a *Get* routine, the property becomes read-only and it's value can't be changed by the program using the object. Likewise, if you include only a *Let* or a *Set* routine, the property becomes write-only, and its value can't be viewed by the calling program.

Methods

Along with class-level variables and property routines, a class can also contain a series of regular subroutines and functions. If a function or a subroutine is marked as *Public*, it's known as a *method*. Methods can be invoked from code residing inside or outside of the class.

Events

Events are subroutines that exist outside the code associated with the class that can be called from statements within the class. Events provide a way for a class to interrupt the program that created an instance of the object from the class, thereby allowing the program to perform its own processing in response to a situation encountered by the object. Remember that the code associated with an event actually resides outside the class. The only information stored within the class is the event's definition, including the parameters that will be passed to the external program.

> **Note** Classes containing events require the *WithEvents* keyword to be placed in the object's declaration. If the declaration doesn't include this keyword, any events that occur will be ignored by the external program.

Together these public properties, methods, and events of a class provide the *interface* to the object. The interface isolates the code inside the class from the code that uses the objects created from this class. This isolation is highly desirable for several reasons. First, it allows you to test the class independently of the rest of the application. Once you are satisfied that the class is stable, you can treat it as a black box that simply works. Second, it makes it easier for multiple people to work on a single application. One person can work on the class, while others work on code that use the class. Third, it's possible to modify the code inside the class without necessarily impacting applications that use the class. This way you can implement new algorithms or add new features to the class without changing the programs that use the class.

Building a Class

The class module contains all of the properties, methods, and events associated with the class's interface, along with any local variables, functions, and subroutines used by the class.

Creating a Class Module

You can add a class module to your VBA program by choosing Insert, Class Module from Visual Basic's main menu. The initial name of the class is formed by appending a unique number to the word *Class*. Thus, the first class you create will be *Class1*, and the second will be *Class2*.

Because a name like *Class1* isn't very descriptive, you should always give the class a more meaningful name. To change the name of a class, select the class in the Project Explorer, and then go to the Properties window and change the *Name* property associated with this class. (See Figure 14-1.)

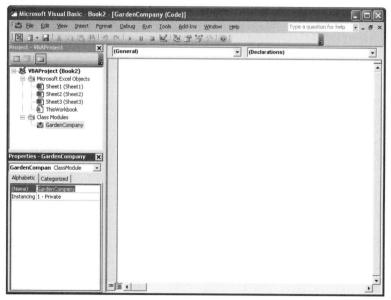

Figure 14-1. Use the Properties Window to change the *Name* property associated with the class.

Defining Simple Properties

There are two different types of properties: public class-level variables and property routines. Class-level variables must be defined before any subroutines, functions, or property routines are defined. In practical terms, this means that all of your class-level variables should be located at the start of the class module.

For example, the following line defines a simple property:

```
Public ProductId As Long
```

> **Warning**   Simple properties can't be used to return an array, a fixed-length string, a constant, or a complex structure created with a *Type* statement. If you need a property that returns any of these things, create the appropriate private class-level variable and then create a property routine that performs the same action. For example, you can create a property routine that accepts a series of parameters that allow the routine to look like an array. Likewise, you can create a property routine that accepts and returns fixed-length strings or complex structures.

Defining Property Routines

There are three different property routines: *Get*, *Set*, and *Let*. The *Property Get* routine always returns a value. Here's a simple example that references a private class-level variable named *TheProductName*.

```
Public Property Get ProductName As String

ProductName = TheProductName

End Property
```

The *Property Let* and *Property Set* routines are called to save a value into the property. The *Property Let* statement is used when the property is a normal variable, whereas the *Property Set* statement is used when the property is an object.

The corresponding *Property Let* routine for the *ProductName* property would look like this:

```
Public Property Let ProductName(value As String)

TheProductName = value

End Property
```

> **Note**   The only difference between a *Property Set* statement and a *Property Let* statement is that you use a *Property Set* statement whenever you are dealing with objects, whereas you would normally assign values using the *Set* statement. Likewise, you would use the *Property Let* statement whenever you are returning any other value.

Property routines may also have one or more parameters. Typically, you would use parameters with a property routine if you wanted to simulate an array. For example the following code fragment declares a private class-level variable named *MyNames*, which is an array of 100 *Strings*. The code fragment also includes two property routines that make the property appear as an array.

```
Private MyNames (99) As String

Public Property Get NameArray(index As Long) As String

NameArray = MyNames(index)

End Property

Public Property Let NameArray (index As Long, value as String)

MyNames = value

End Property
```

> **Note** You can specify as many parameters as you wish for the property routines. However, they must be identical between the *Get* and *Let/Set* routines, except for the very last parameter in the *Let/Set* routine, which contains the value for the property.

Someone using the class might access the property like this:

```
MyObject.NameArray (10) = "Item 10 in the array"
```

Or like this:

```
MyVar = MyObject.NameArray (10)
```

> **Tip** Property Routines and Parameters
> Although you can specify a list of parameters for a property routine, you should limit the use of the parameters in a property routine to those parameters that make the property routine look like an array. If you need to use parameters other than subscripts, you should consider creating one or more methods with the parameters you need.

Using Property Statements with User Defined Types

If you have defined a set of property routines to manipulate a complex structure created with a *Type* statement, you might run into problems when you attempt to assign a value directly to one of the elements in the structure in a single statement. Suppose you have the following statements in your class:

```
Public Type MapCoordinateType
    Latitude As Single
    Longitude As Single
End Type

Private MyMapCoordinate As MapCoordinateType

Public Property Get MapCoordinate As MapCoordinateType

MapCoordinate = MyMapCoordinate

End Property

Public Property Let MapCoordinate (value as MapCoordinateType)

MapCoordinate = value

End Property
```

Now, assuming that you instantiated the class as *MicrosoftWay*, you can reference the *Lattitude* value like this:

```
TempLatitude = MicrosoftWay.MapCoordinate.Latitude
```

Because this works, you might be tempted to use the following statements:

```
MicrosoftWay.MapCoordinate.Latitude = 47.63
MicrosoftWay.MapCoordinate.Longitude = 122.13
```

However, if you use them, you'll find that the *MicrosoftWay.MapCoordinate.Latitude* is zero!

Although this seems like a bug in Visual Basic, it really isn't. Visual Basic is working properly. When you reference the *Latitude* element in the first statement, Visual Basic creates a temporary *MapCoordinateType* variable and sets the *Latitude* value to 47.63. Because the temporary variable is filled with zeros when it's allocated and a value isn't explicitly assigned to *Longitude*, it contains a value of zero. Thus, when the *MapCoordinate Let* routine is called, with the temporary variable that Visual Basic created, *Latitude* element will be set to 47.63 and *Longitude* element will be set to zero.

The same situation occurs when you execute the second statement. Because a value wasn't assigned to *Latitude* in the temporary variable, the previous value of 47.63 is over-written by zero, which undoes the change made in the first statement.

There are a couple of ways to avoid this problem. The first and probably best way is to create a class rather than use a *Type* statement. However, if you really want to use the *Type* statement, you should create a temporary variable of your own, assign the values to the structure, and then assign the structure to the property like this:

```
Dim TempVar As MapCoordinateType
TempVar.Latitude = 47.63
TempVar.Longitude = 122.13
MicrosoftWay.MapCoordinate = TempVar
```

Defining Methods

Methods are simply public functions and subroutines. They are free to accept any set of parameters and return any type of value. They can also access any class-level variable whether it's public or private, along with any property routine.

For example, assume that the class held information about a particular product from the Garden Company. You might create a function that computes the discounted price like this:

```
Public Function DiscountedPrice (Discount As Currency) As Currency

If Discount >= 0 and Discount < 1.0 Then
    DiscountedPrice = MyListPrice * (1 - Discount)

Else
    DiscountedPrice = MyListPrice

End If

End Function
```

This routine verifies that the input parameter is valid by making sure that it's in the range of 0 to 1 and then computes the discount price accordingly. If the discount value is illegal, the list price of the item is returned.

Tip Saving Cycles
If you have a choice between using a property routine or a private class-level variable in a method, use the private class-level variable. Doing that avoids the extra processor cycles and memory required by the property routine and helps to speed up your application.

Defining Events

Events can be very useful in a class, but you can't assume that everyone that uses your class will actually use the events. Therefore, if you decide to use events in your class, you need to ensure that the class will continue to function if the user doesn't respond to any of the events.

The *Event* statement is used to define an event. For all practical purposes, this is effectively a subroutine statement minus the code. This definition is necessary because it identifies the parameters that will be passed to the event. The event definition is used by the by the Visual Basic compiler to ensure that the number of parameters and the type of the parameters match the definition.

> **Note** Although you can specify nearly any type of parameter you can use in a subroutine, events can't have named arguments, optional parameters, or *ParamArray* arguments.

A sample event definition might look like this:

```
Event DiscountError (value As Currency, Msg As String)
```

Within the class, you would use a *RaiseEvent* statement to trigger an event in the user program. Following the *RaiseEvent* statement name is the name of the event, followed by a list of values that will be passed to the user program. For example, this statement passes two values back to the calling program.

```
RaiseEvent DiscountError(discount, "Illegal discount amount. ")
```

To use events in an application, the *WithEvents* keyword must be included when the object is defined. Without the *WithEvents* keyword, all events will be ignored. The following statement shows how you would declare an object with events:

```
Dim WithEvents MyObject As GardenCompany
```

Defining Private Variables, Subroutines, and Functions

Although you need not mark your subroutines or functions as *Private* in a class, you should note that without the *Private* keyword, any subroutine or function will default to *Public*. In many situations, this might not be a serious problem, especially if you are the one person using the class. However, if you plan to share your class with others, you might find them relying on a routine where you accidentally omitted the *Private* keyword, which means you can't change the definition of the routine without impacting all the programs that use it.

Special Events for Classes

VBA defines two special events for all classes, the *Initialize* event and the *Terminate* event.

The *Class_Initialize* event contains code that will be run when an object is created based on this class. This event is useful for initializing class-level variables including executing any *Set New* statements needed to create any objects that are needed by this object.

```
Set ObjectVar = New MyClass
```

The *Class_Terminate* event contains code that will be run just before an object is destroyed. This event is an ideal place to destroy any objects that are local to the class by setting them to *Nothing* using code like this:

```
Set ObjectVar = Nothing
```

> **Note** The *Class_Initialize* and *Class_Terminate* events are fired only when the actual object is created or destroyed. Merely setting one object variable to another will not trigger the *Class_Initialize* event. If two or more object variables point to the same object, merely setting one object variable to *Nothing* will not trigger the *Class_Terminate* event.

Resolving References

Sometimes you'll find yourself in a situation where you have a local variable and a class-level variable with the same name. This frequently happens when you want to give a parameter in a method the same name as a property. To differentiate between a class-level variable and a local variable or parameter, you can prefix the class level variable with *Me.* as in the following example:

```
If Me.Name <> Name Then
```

In this statement, the variable *Me.Name* refers to a class-level variable, whereas the unqualified variable *Name* refers to a local variable or parameter.

> **Tip** Identifying Things That Belong to *Me*
> The keyword *Me* can also be used to qualify any public or private element of a class from the code within that class, including class-level variables, subroutines, functions, and property routines.

Practical Class Design

Now that you know what a class is and the mechanics of building one, it's worth briefly covering some practical tips for building classes.

A Simple Class

It's quite reasonable to create a class that simply contains only properties and no methods. (See Figure 14-2.)

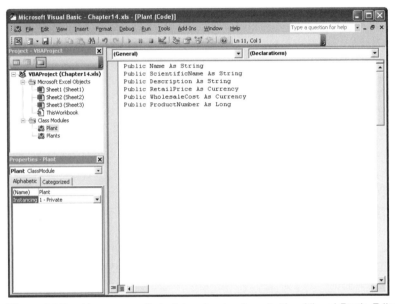

Figure 14-2. You can easily build a simple class in the Visual Basic Editor.

You can create this class by following these steps:

1 Select Insert, Class Module from the VBA main menu.

2 Select the new class in the Project Explorer, and change the Name property in the Properties window to Plant.

3 Enter the following statements into the Edit Window:

```
Public CommonName As String
Public ScientificName As String
Public Description As String
Public RetailPrice As Currency
Public WholesaleCost As Currency
Public ProductNumber As Long
```

Extending a Simple Class

One of the advantages of using a class to hold related data is that you can easily extend the class using several different techniques. For example, you can easily add a synonym for an existing property with a pair of property routines like this:

```
Public Property Get CommonName() As String

CommonName = Name

End Property

Public Property Let CommonName(value As String)

Name = value

End Property
```

These routines are used to return and modify a public class-level variable, thus allowing the user to manipulate the same value by using two different names.

Another useful technique is to add a method that allows you to initialize all the properties of the class with a single call. Notice that the following routine takes advantage of the *Me* keyword so that anyone using this method would know which parameter affects which property:

```
Public Sub Init(Name As String, _
    ScientificName As String, _
    Description As String, _
    RetailPrice As Currency, _
    WholesaleCost As Currency, _
    ProductNumber As Long)

Me.Name = Name
Me.ScientificName = ScientificName
Me.Description = Description
Me.RetailPrice = RetailPrice
Me.WholesaleCost = WholesaleCost
Me.ProductNumber = ProductNumber

End Sub
```

A *Collection* Class

It's often useful to create a collection class to hold a group of objects. This task is made a lot easier by using the Visual Basic *Collection* object to store your data. The following code declares a *Collection* object variable that's local to the class. When the class is first instantiated, the *Collection* object is created, and when the object is destroyed, the *Collection* object will also be destroyed.

Chapter 14

```
Private MyPlants As Collection

Private Sub Class_Initialize()

Set MyPlants = New Collection

End Sub

Private Sub Class_Terminate()

Set MyPlants = Nothing

End Sub
```

An object is added to the collection using the following code. The code assumes that the object being added has a *Name* property whose type is *String*. The routine begins by using the *On Error Resume Next* statement to disable error trapping. Any errors will simply force Visual Basic to execute the next statement. To detect that an error occurred, the *Err* object is used.

```
Public Sub Add(Item As Plant)

Dim i As Long
Dim s As String

On Error Resume Next

i = 0
s = Item.Name
MyPlants.Add Item, s
Do While Err.Number <> 0
    i = i + 1
    Item.Name = s & "(" & FormatNumber(i, 0) & ")"
    Err.Clear
    MyPlants.Add Item, Item.Name

Loop

End Sub
```

The counter *i* is initially set to zero, and the name of the new object is saved in the temporary variable *s*. Then the *Collection* object's *Add* method is used to try to add the new object to the *Collection* object.

If an error occurs in the *Add* method, the counter *i* is incremented. A new *Name* for the object is constructed by using the original name followed by an open parenthesis, the number from the counter *i*, and a close parenthesis. Then the routine attempts to add the new object to the collection again. If the *Add* method fails again, the loop is repeated until the name of the object is unique.

An item is removed from the collection by calling the *Remove* method and specifying either the relative position of the object or the value of the *Name* property. In either case, the *Remove* method from the *Collection* object is used to remove the item from the underlying collection.

```
Public Sub Remove(key As Variant)

MyPlants.Remove key

End Sub
```

In the same fashion, the *Count* method returns the number of items in the collection by calling the underlying *Count* method associated with the *Collection* object.

```
Public Function Count() As Long

Count = MyPlants.Count

End Function
```

The *Clear* method is useful if you want to delete all the objects in the collection. This routine just destroys the underlying *Collection* object and then creates a new instance of the *Collection* object.

```
Public Sub Clear()

Set MyPlants = Nothing
Set MyPlants = New Collection

End Sub
```

The *Item* method returns a single item from the collection. Like the *Remove* and *Count* methods, this item simply calls the *Collection* object's *Item* method.

```
Public Function Item(key As Variant) As Plant

Set Item = MyPlants.Item(key)

End Function
```

The following routine is a macro that iterates through the collection class that was just created. The macro begins by creating a new *Plants* object named *MyPlants*, which contains a collection of *Plant* objects. Then the code calls the *SampleData* method, which simply adds some sample objects to the collection.

```
Sub Test()

Dim MyPlants As Plants
Dim p As Plant
Dim i As Long

Set MyPlants = New Plants
MyPlants.SampleData

For i = 1 To MyPlants.Count
    Set p = MyPlants.Item(i)
    MsgBox p.Name

Next i

Set p = Nothing
Set MyPlants = Nothing

End Sub
```

Next it uses a *For Next* loop to iterate through each item in the collection. The object variable *p* is set to the current item from the collection, and the *Name* property is displayed in a message box.

Notice that the first item in the collection begins with *1*, and the number of items in the collection is retrieved from the collection's *Count* property.

Where Do I Get My Data?

Classes are an ideal way to hold data from an external source. By holding the data in a collection class, you can allow your program to access the data independently of how the data is physically stored.

This way if you change the way the data is stored, you don't have to change the way that the data is accessed. By providing a method named *LoadData*, anyone using the class can load the data from the data source. Then if you migrate the data from a worksheet to an Access database, only the load method will change. The code accessing the collection class won't change, unless you change the parameters to the *LoadData* method.

Likewise, you could provide a standard method called *SaveData*, which would update the data wherever it's stored. With a little work, you could even make the method intelligent enough so that it updates only the objects that were updated, instead of having to update all the data whether it was updated by the user or not.

A Class with Business Rules

You can also extend a class by adding basic business rules. For example, the following method validates the information in a *Plant* object. This code merely checks each property in the class with potential error conditions and returns *True* if no errors are found and *False* if they are.

```
Public Function IsValid() As Boolean

If Len(Name) = 0 Then
    IsValid = False

ElseIf Len(ScientificName) = 0 Then
    IsValid = False

ElseIf WholesaleCost < 0 Then
    IsValid = False

ElseIf RetailPrice < WholesaleCost Then
    IsValid = False

ElseIf ProductNumber < 0 Then
    IsValid = False

Else
    IsValid = True

End If

End Function
```

The *IsValid* procedure could be modified to return a text error message or even a *String* array containing a list of errors found within the data.

Another way to detect errors is to use property routines. For instance, you could create a *Property Let* routine like this one.

```
Public Property Let RetailPrice(value As Currency)

If value > WholesaleCost Then
    MyRetailPrice = value

Else
    RaiseEvent PlantError(1, "Retail price lower than the wholesale cost.")

End If

End Property
```

Chapter 14

The class includes a private class-level variable named *MyRetailPrice* that holds the value for the *RetailPrice* property. If the new value for *RetailPrice* is greater than the *WholesaleCost*, the new retail price will be saved in the *MyRetailPrice* variable.

However, if someone attempts to set the retail price lower than the wholesale cost, the *Plant-Error* event will be fired passing the details of the error to the program that owns the object.

In this chapter, you learned how a class is different from an object. In addition, you learned how to create your own custom classes, including how to define properties, property routines, methods, and events. Some design tips on how to recognize objects, properties, and methods were also discussed. Finally, you learned how to design several different types of classes, including a simple class and a collection class, along with how to extend your classes to include initializing a class and implementing business rules.

Part 5

Manipulating Excel Objects

15	Charts	321
16	PivotTables and PivotCharts	341
17	Command Bars	365
18	Customizing Dialog Boxes	383
19	Creating User Forms	395
20	Creating Advanced User Forms	419

Charts

Introducing Charts 321
Manipulating Charts 327

Final Thoughts on
Programming Charts 339

Microsoft Excel's charting feature is an impressive tool. A *chart* allows the user to graphically display almost any type of data stored in a worksheet. There are times when a chart is more meaningful than a list of numbers. For example, a user might have a better grasp of the increase and decrease of monthly sales if shown using a line or bar chart. To write the same kind of information in simple text would take many paragraphs and not flow all that well.

When creating charts, there are more than 100 types to choose from. With the many objects contained within the charts, such as the *Legend*, the x-axis and the y-axis, and the *Chart Titles*, the end result will differ greatly from chart to chart depending on your formatting requirements.

The *Chart* object itself and the objects contained within the chart can be modified directly by the user or with a Visual Basic for Applications (VBA) macro.

In this chapter, you'll learn about the key concepts required to write the VBA code that generates and manipulates charts. The code is designed to show you how to create and gain access to the *ChartObjects* collection within the workbook. You'll also learn how to modify existing charts, their data series, and their formats, as well as how to use descriptive chart labels that refer to cell references.

Introducing Charts

The chart itself is considered an object within the Excel workbook; the *ChartObject* object acts as a container for the items located within it. These items include the source data plotted on the *Chart Area*, the *Legend*, and the *Chart Titles*. Each object within the chart contains its own properties and methods. Because of the complexity of the *chart* Object Model, manipulating charts with VBA code can be a challenge. A good understanding of the *Chart* model is vital when programming *Chart* objects to ensure that you are using the correct object and property.

> **Note** Refer to the "Defining the Chart Object Model" section located later in this chapter to review how the Chart Object Model is structured.

Before diving into *Chart* properties, methods and events, it'll pay to review the individual components used to generate the chart. Table 15-1 explains the objects located within a chart that will be used throughout this chapter.

Table 15-1. Components Contained Within the Chart

Object	Description
Chart Titles	Describes the information that is being plotted. They include the actual title for the chart as well as the x-axis and the y-axis titles.
Data Series	Stores numerically the data in the ranges that define the chart and determines how the information is displayed in the Plot Area. A chart can contain a minimum of one plotted data series.
Legend	Provides the visual explanation of how data is plotted. The series name is listed with the corresponding color.
Plot Area	Displays the data series information graphically. It's the background, or container, that surrounds the plot area.
X-Axis and Y-Axis	Determines where the information will be grouped and plotted on the chart.

Creating Embedded Charts or Chart Sheets

As you are aware, you can create a chart using the Excel Chart Wizard. The wizard guides you through the selection of all available chart options, including *Chart Type*, *Data Range*, and *Location*. There are two locations in which a chart can be inserted: within a worksheet as an embedded object or on its own chart sheet.

Which destination you choose depends on the effect you are trying to accomplish. If you want the user of the workbook to be able to compare several charts side by side, insert the charts within the same worksheet. However, you should probably choose to insert a chart on its own sheet when working with a large, complex chart with many data series. There are other times you'll use individual chart sheets for preference reasons as well. Remember that you can always embed a chart later using a simple location change.

You aren't limited to using the Chart wizard to create a chart. They can also be created using VBA code. The *Add* property for the *Charts* object can be used to insert the new chart.

```
Charts.Add
```

The following example displays a basic macro that creates a chart as an object variable. The macro defines the *Chart Type*, *Data Source*, and *Chart Titles*.

```
Sub AddChartSheet()
    Dim Chrt As Chart

    Set Chrt = Charts.Add
    With Chrt
        .ChartType = xlColumnClustered
        .SetSourceData Source:=Sheets("Sheet1").Range("A4:D7"), _
            PlotBy:=xlRows
        .HasTitle = True
    End With
End Sub
```

> **Note**   When creating charts in your workbook, create the chart as an object variable. It's easier to reference the *Chart* object and manipulate the chart when using this technique. The remaining examples in this chapter will use this method to create charts.

By default, if the chart *Location* property has not been set in the macro, the chart is placed on its own sheet, rather than as an embedded object. To set the chart location, you must use the *Location* property. Table 15-2 defines the three location options available.

Table 15-2. Chart Location Properties

Property	Location
xlLocationAsNewSheet	The chart is placed on a new chart sheet.
xlLocationAsObject	The chart is placed as an embedded chart object within the specified worksheet.
xlLocationAutomatic	The chart is placed as an embedded chart object within the active worksheet.

The following example sets the chart as an embedded object in "*Sheet1*":

```
Variable = ChartObject.Location(xlLocationAsObject,"Sheet1")
```

When working with embedded charts, it's a good idea to name the *ChartObject* object so that you can easily reference the chart in later code. To rename an existing chart manually, hold down the Ctrl key and click the chart. This will select the *ChartObject* object, rather than activate the chart. Click the Name Box, and type the new name. You are also able to name the *ChartObject* object within the macro by setting the *Name* property of the object.

As displayed in Figure 15-1, notice that the chart handles are unfilled circles to help you distinguish whether the chart is selected or has been activated. The Name Box currently displays Chart1 as the name of the *ChartObject* object.

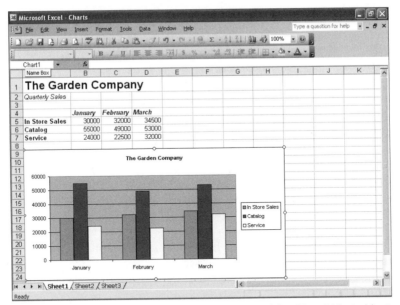

Figure 15-1. The Name Box displays the name of the *ChartObject* object when it's selected, rather than active on the screen.

> **Note** If the chart has been activated, the chart handles are displayed as black boxes. However, if the *ChartObject* object is selected, the handles appear as unfilled circles.

The following example creates an embedded chart named *GSCProductChart*. The macro starts by deleting any existing embedded charts on the active worksheet. It then creates the new chart and uses the *Parent* property to identify the *ChartObject* object. The code proceeds to set the object variable *Chrt* to refer to the *ChartObject* object. Because the default is to create a chart sheet, the *Location* method is used to define the chart as an embedded object.

```
Sub AddEmbeddedChart()
    Dim Chrt As Chart

    ActiveSheet.ChartObjects.Delete
    Set Chrt = Charts.Add
    Set Chrt = Chrt.Location(where:=xlLocationAsObject, Name:="Sheet1")
    With Chrt
        .ChartType = xlColumnClustered
        .SetSourceData Source:=Sheets("Sheet1").Range("A4:D7"), _
            PlotBy:=xlRows
        .HasTitle = True
        .ChartTitle.Text = "=Sheet1!R1C1"
        With .Parent
            .Top = Range("A9").Top
            .Left = Range("A1").Left
            .Name = "GSCProductChart"
```

```
            End With
        End With
    End Sub
```

> **Note** Remember the default location is a chart sheet. So when the *Location* method of the *Chart* object is used, the *Chart* object is re-created and any reference to the original *Chart* object, which is the chart sheet, is destroyed. It's necessary to assign the return value of the *Location* method to the *Chrt* object variable so that it refers to the new *Chart* object. To test this, step through your code and view the workbook. You'll notice that the chart sheet is initially created and then removed after the *Location* has been set to *xlLocationAsObject*.

As you can see, the event procedure *AddEmbeddedChart* has introduced some additional settings. The *ChartTitle* is assigned to a formula referring to cell A1. The location of the embedded chart on the worksheet was set using the *Top* and *Left* properties of cell A9. The *Parent* property of the *Chart* object was used to refer to the *ChartObject* object, and it was set by defining the *Top* and *Left* properties of the *ChartObject* object to be the same as the *Top* property of cell A9 and the *Left* property of cell A1. The chart is aligned with the top of cell A9, but the chart will align with the left edge of cell A1. The *AddEmbeddedChart* macro finally assigns the new name to the *ChartObject* object so that it can easily be referenced in the future.

> **Note** When defining the chart title as a formula, you must use the R1C1 addressing method, not the A1 addressing method.

Inside Out

The Recorded Macro and Creating Charts

The recorded macro generates code that is reasonably efficient. However, manipulating the chart is easier if the chart is created as an object. The following example displays the recorded macro, which uses the *Add* method to create a new chart. The macro defines the *ChartType* property and then uses the *SetSourceData* method to define the ranges plotted on the chart. The *Location* property defines the chart as a chart sheet and assigns the name *Product Sales* to the sheet. Then the macro sets the *HasTitle* property to *True* so that it can define the *ChartTitle* property. Finally, the code sets the *HasTitle* property of the axes back to *False*, which is an unnecessary step.

```
Charts.Add
ActiveChart.ChartType = xlColumnClustered
ActiveChart.SetSourceData Source:=Sheets("Sheet1").Range("A3:D7"), _
    PlotBy:= xlRows

ActiveChart.Location Where:=xlLocationAsNewSheet, Name:="Product Sales"
```

continued

```
With ActiveChart
    .HasTitle = True
    .ChartTitle.Characters.Text = "Product Sales"
    .Axes(xlCategory, xlPrimary).HasTitle = False
    .Axes(xlValue, xlPrimary).HasTitle = False
End With
```

The recorded macro will create the chart; however, you'll see that there are additional and redundant lines of code added to the macro. Be sure to remove unnecessary lines of code within a recorded macro.

Defining the Chart Object Model

The Chart Object Model at times can be overwhelming due to the layering effect. However, use the Object Browser in the Visual Basic Editor to help you get your bearings as you begin the task of coding procedures involving charts.

The hierarchy of a chart is determined by its location. For example, when working with an embedded chart, if you would like to modify the text contained within the *ChartTitle* you'll need to review the object levels. The top-level object is the *Application*. The *Application* object contains the *Workbook* object, and the *Workbook* object contains a *Worksheet* object. The *Worksheet* object contains a *ChartObject* object, which contains a *Chart* object. The *Chart* object has a *ChartTitle* object, and the *ChartTitle* object contains a *Characters* object. The *Text* property of the *Characters* object stores the text that is displayed as the chart's title. To summarize how each object is connected, refer to the following list:

```
Application
    Workbook
        Worksheet
            ChartObject
                Chart
                    ChartTitle
                        Characters
```

However, when working with a chart that is located on its own sheet you'll see that the hierarchy is simplified. A chart sheet is technically at the same level as the worksheet because it's simply a different type of sheet. Review the levels as indicated here, and notice that two levels have been removed.

```
Application
    Workbook
        Chart
            ChartTitle
                Characters
```

The *Charts* collection holds the collection of chart sheets in a workbook. The *Workbook* object is always the parent of the *Charts* collection. The *Charts* collection holds only the chart sheets. Because individual charts can also be embedded in worksheets and dialog sheets, the *Chart* objects in the *Charts* collection can be accessed using the *Item* property. Either the name of the chart can be specified as a parameter to the *Item's* parameter or it can be an index number describing the position of the chart in the workbook from left to right.

The *Chart* object allows access to all of the attributes of a specific chart in Excel. This includes chart formatting, chart types, and chart-positioning properties. The *Chart* object also exposes events that can be used programmatically.

> Event procedures are executed when the appropriate trigger is initiated. Specific events can also be monitored at the *Chart* level. For more information, review the side bar, "To Use or Not to Use *Chart* Events." For a review of event procedures at the Application, Workbook, and Worksheet levels, refer to Chapter 12, "Understanding and Using Events."

The *ChartObjects* collection represents all the *ChartObject* objects on a specified chart sheet or worksheet. The *ChartObject* object acts as a container for a *Chart* object. Properties and methods for the *ChartObject* object determine the appearance and the size of the embedded chart on the worksheet. The *ChartObject* object is a member of the *ChartObjects* collection. The *ChartObjects* collection contains all the embedded charts on a single sheet.

Use *ChartObjects(index)*, where index is the embedded chart index number or name, to return a single *ChartObject* object. In the following example, the chart name has been set to *SampleChart* in an embedded chart on the worksheet named "*Sheet1*."

```
Worksheets("Sheet1").ChartObjects("Chart 1").Name = "SampleChart"
```

The embedded chart name is shown in the Name box when the embedded chart is selected. Use the *Name* property to set or return the name of the *ChartObject* object. The following example puts rounded corners on the embedded chart named "*SampleChart*" on the worksheet named "*Sheet1*."

```
Worksheets("Sheet1").ChartObjects("SampleChart").RoundedCorners = True
```

Manipulating Charts

A procedure can be used to create a chart; however, you'll commonly create macros that will modify existing charts. For example, a procedure can be used to streamline the formatting of all the embedded charts within a workbook for the Garden Company. The procedure might include resizing all charts to a standard size, specifying the chart location within a worksheet, or even adding the company name in a label using the company colors.

Activating a Chart

A chart is activated when a user selects a chart, regardless of its location. Using VBA code, you can activate an embedded chart using the *Activate* method.

```
ActiveSheet.ChartObjects("Chart1").Activate
```

Microsoft Office Excel 2003 Programming Inside Out

To activate a chart on an individual chart sheet, you can use the following statement:

```
Sheets("Chart1").Activate
```

When a chart is activated, you can refer to it in your code as *ActiveChart*. This is a great way to simply your code. For troubleshooting purposes, you can verify which chart has been activated by adding a message box to display the chart name. Once you have verified that the correct chart has been activated, you can add a single quote at the beginning of the line that calls the message box to make the line a comment. Making the line a comment means the line won't be executed. You can, of course, delete the code after you have completed testing the procedure.

```
MsgBox ActiveChart.Name
```

When creating a procedure that modifies a chart, you are not required to activate it, but this is an easy way to refer to the chart in your code. The following examples modify the chart type and return the same results, but the first procedure activates the chart sheet and the second procedure accesses an embedded chart:

```
Sub ModifyChart1()
    ActiveSheet.ChartObjects("Chart1").Activate
    ActiveChart.Type = xlLine
    ActiveChart.Deselect
End Sub

Sub ModifyChart2()
    ActiveSheet.ChartObjects("Chart1").Chart.Type = xlLine
End Sub
```

Keep in mind when creating your macro that if the procedure is written so that it's dependent on the chart being activated, an error will occur if the user hasn't activated the chart. The following example displays several different formats that can be changed. Try executing the macro with the chart active, as well as with cell A1 selected.

```
Sub ModifyActiveChart()
    With ActiveChart
        .Type = xlArea
        .ChartArea.Font.Name = "Tahoma"
        .ChartArea.Font.FontStyle = "Regular"
        .ChartArea.Font.Size = 8
        .PlotArea.Interior.ColorIndex = xlNone
        .Axes(xlValue).TickLabels.Font.Bold = True
        .HasLegend = True
        .Legend.Position = xlLegendPositionBottom
    End With
End Sub
```

Notice that run-time error '91': *Object variable or With block variable not set* occurs when you execute the *ModifyActiveChart* procedure and the chart is not selected. To solve this problem, specify which chart to modify when the procedure is executed. Modify the previous procedure to include the chart reference.

```
Sub ModifySpecificChart()
    With Sheets("Sheet1").ChartObjects("Chart1").Chart
        .Type = xlArea
        .ChartArea.Font.Name = "Tahoma"
        .ChartArea.Font.FontStyle = "Regular"
        .ChartArea.Font.Size = 8
        .PlotArea.Interior.ColorIndex = xlNone
        .Axes(xlValue).TickLabels.Font.Bold = True
        .HasLegend = True
        .Legend.Position = xlLegendPositionBottom
    End With
End Sub
```

Inside Out

To Use or Not to Use *Chart* Events

An event is used to monitor an object. Your chart is considered an object regardless of its location. So if you have a specific event that in turn requires a specific action, you should use *Chart* events.

Some of the triggers available for a *Chart* object are *Activate*, *MouseDown*, *MouseMove*, and *SeriesChange*. To write an event procedure for an embedded chart, you must create a new object using the *WithEvents* keyword in a class module and declare an object of type *Chart* with events.

Consider the following example. Assume a new class module is created and named *EventClassModule*. The new class module contains the following *WithEvents* statement:

```
Public WithEvents myChartClass As Chart
```

After the new object has been declared with events, it appears in the *Object* drop-down list in the class module. You can now create an event procedure for this object. However, before the procedure will run, you must connect the declared object with the embedded chart. The following code can be used in any module to achieve the required result:

```
Dim myClassModule As New EventClassModule

Sub InitializeChart()
    Set myClassModule.myChartClass = Worksheets(1).ChartObjects(1).Chart
End Sub
```

After the InitializeChart procedure has been executed, the *myChartClass* object in the class module points to the first embedded chart on the first worksheet in the workbook. All event procedures in the class module for the object will now be evaluated as the triggers occur.

Deactivating a Chart

When a macro is created using the recorder, you'll find the recorder generates a statement, such as

```
ActiveWindow.Visible = False
```

This statement deactivates the chart, but it's not clear as to why the chart is deactivated. When writing a macro that involves charts, try using the *Deselect* method.

```
ActiveChart.Deselect
```

These two statements have slightly different results. Setting the *Visible* property of the *ActivateWindow* object to *False* causes the embedded chart to be selected but no longer activated. The *Deselect* method will deactivate and deselect the chart.

Modify the *AddEmbeddedChart* event procedure that was created in the "Creating Embedded Charts or Chart Sheets" section earlier in the chapter by setting the *ActiveWindow* object to *False* to deactivate the chart.

```
Sub AddEmbeddedChart()
    Dim Chrt As Chart

    ActiveSheet.ChartObjects.Delete
    Set Chrt = Charts.Add
    Set Chrt = Chrt.Location(where:=xlLocationAsObject, Name:="Sheet1")
    With Chrt
        .ChartType = xlColumnClustered
        .SetSourceData Source:=Sheets("Sheet1").Range("A4:D7"), _
            PlotBy:=xlRows
        .HasTitle = True
        .ChartTitle.Text = "=Sheet1!R1C1"
        With .Parent
            .Top = Range("A9").Top
            .Left = Range("A1").Left
            .Name = "GSCProductChart"
        End With
    End With
ActiveWindow.Visible = False
End Sub
```

Now that you have tested the *ActiveWindow* method to deactivate the chart, use the deselect method. Replace the `ActiveWindow.Visible = False` line with *ActiveChart.Deselect*.

For each procedure you create, you can evaluate which method of deactivation will achieve the required results for your current scenario.

Chapter 15

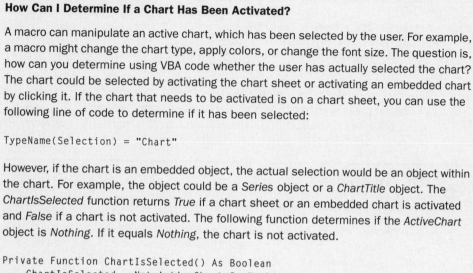

Troubleshooting

How Can I Determine If a Chart Has Been Activated?

A macro can manipulate an active chart, which has been selected by the user. For example, a macro might change the chart type, apply colors, or change the font size. The question is, how can you determine using VBA code whether the user has actually selected the chart? The chart could be selected by activating the chart sheet or activating an embedded chart by clicking it. If the chart that needs to be activated is on a chart sheet, you can use the following line of code to determine if it has been selected:

```
TypeName(Selection) = "Chart"
```

However, if the chart is an embedded object, the actual selection would be an object within the chart. For example, the object could be a *Series* object or a *ChartTitle* object. The *ChartIsSelected* function returns *True* if a chart sheet or an embedded chart is activated and *False* if a chart is not activated. The following function determines if the *ActiveChart* object is *Nothing*. If it equals *Nothing*, the chart is not activated.

```
Private Function ChartIsSelected() As Boolean
    ChartIsSelected = Not ActiveChart Is Nothing
End Function
```

Modifying a Chart's Data Series

A chart consists of any number of series, and the data used in each series is determined by the range references in its SERIES formula. When a series is selected in the chart, the SERIES formula is displayed in the formula bar. In some cases, using range names in the SERIES formulas in a chart can simplify things when you need to change the chart's source data. For example, consider the following SERIES formula:

```
=SERIES(,Sheet1!$A$1:$A$6,Sheet1!$B$1:$B$6,1)
```

You can define range names for the ranges and then edit the SERIES formula so that it uses the range names instead of the range references. For example, if you have two ranges that are named *Categories* and *Data* you can modify the formula to

```
=SERIES(,Sheet1!Categories,Sheet1!Data,1)
```

> **Note** This formula might change when you type it in the formula bar. For example, *Sheet1* might evaluate to the name of the workbook, producing an argument such as *Products.xls!Categories*.

When the names have been defined and the SERIES formula has been edited, your VBA code can work with the names, and the changes will be reflected in the chart. For example, the following statement redefines the range as *Data*:

```
Range("B1:B12").Name = "Data"
```

After executing the *Name* statement, the chart will update itself and use the new definition of *Data*.

Now that you understand what the SERIES formula is responsible for, how do you modify it? The easiest method is to redefine the chart data using the *SetSourceData* method of the *Chart* object. However, you can manipulate individual series using the *Series* object. The *Series* object is a member of the chart's *SeriesCollection* object.

Inside Out

How the Chart SERIES Formula Works

The data used in each series in a chart is determined by its SERIES formula. When you select a data series in a chart, the SERIES formula appears in the formula bar. The SERIES formula is not a formula that you are able to enter into a worksheet as a traditional formula. Basically, you can't use it in a cell, nor can you use a function or formula within a SERIES formula. It's possible, however, to edit the SERIES formula.

The Catalog Sales series is currently selected on the chart, indicated by the handles on the Catalog plotted points. Notice the formula bar contains the SERIES formula for the Catalog series.

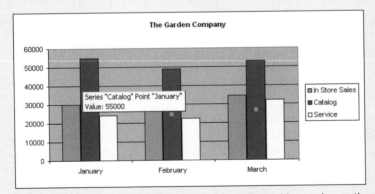

Figure 15-2. The selected data series is indicated by marks on the corresponding chart elements.

A SERIES formula uses the following syntax:

```
=SERIES(name,category_labels,values,order)
```

- **name (Optional)**   The name used in the legend. If the chart has only one series, the name argument is used as the title.
- **category_labels (Optional)**   The range that contains the labels for the category axis. If omitted, Excel uses consecutive integers beginning with 1.
- **values**   The range that contains the values.
- **order**   An integer that specifies the plotting order of the series (relevant only if the chart has more than one series).

Range references in a SERIES formula are always absolute, and they always include the sheet name, as in the following example:

```
=SERIES(,Sheet1!$B$1,Sheet1!$B$2:$B$7,1)
```

A range reference can consist of a noncontiguous range. If so, each range is separated by a comma, and the argument is enclosed in parentheses. In the following SERIES formula, the values' ranges consist of B2:B3 and B5:B7:

```
=SERIES(,,(Sheet1!$B$2,Sheet1!$B$5:$B$7),1)
```

You can substitute range names for the range references. If you do so, Excel changes the reference in the SERIES formula to include the workbook, as in the following example:

```
=SERIES(Sheet1$B$1,,budget.xls!MyData,1)
```

Modifying a Chart to Use Data from Arrays

A chart series can be defined by assigning a VBA array to its *Values* property. This is useful if you need to generate a chart that is not linked to the original data. The chart can be distributed in a separate workbook that's independent of the source data.

Figure 15-3 displays the Garden Company Product Sales Chart with the *Catalog* series selected. Notice the difference between this graphic and the graphic located within the Inside Out: "How the Chart SERIES Formula Works" that displayed the *Catalog* series using information from *Sheet1*. You can see the definition of the first data series in the formula bar above the worksheet. The values on the y-axis are defined by an Excel array. The category names have been assigned as text to the series names.

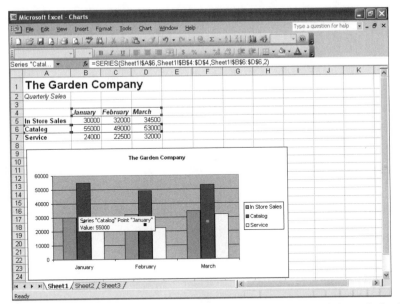

Figure 15-3. The Catalog series is displayed with the SERIES formula in the Formula Bar.

Note The array is limited to approximately 250 characters. This limits the number of data points that can be plotted using an array.

You can easily convert an existing chart to use arrays instead of cell references. This will make the chart independent of the original data it was based on. The following code shows how to achieve this effect:

```
Sub ConvertSeriesValuesToArrays()
    Dim Ser As Series
    Dim Chrt As Chart

    On Error GoTo Failure

    Set Chrt = ActiveSheet.ChartObjects(1).Chart
    For Each Ser In Chrt.SeriesCollection
        Ser.XValues = Ser.Values
        Ser.Name = Ser.Name
    Next Ser

    Exit Sub
Failure:
    MsgBox "The data exceeds the array limits."
End Sub
```

Charts

For each series in the chart, the *XValues* and *Name* properties are set equal to themselves. Although these properties can be assigned range references, they always return an array of values when they are referenced. This behavior can be used to convert the cell references to arrays.

Keep in mind that the number of data points that can be contained in an array reference is limited to approximately 250 characters. The code will fail if the limits are exceeded, so use an error trap to cover this possibility.

Defining a Chart's Labels

Adding data labels to a chart is easy, as long as the labels are based on the data series values or x-axis values. These options are available using the Chart menu and Chart Options.

You can also enter your own text or formula into each label, but this involves a lot of manual work. You would need to add standard labels to the series and then individually select each one and either replace it with your own text or click in the formula bar and enter a formula. To save time and effort, you can write a macro to achieve the same results.

Figure 15-4 displays the Garden Product Sales Chart with the Monthly Sales and the top selling product. The labels have been defined by formulas linked to row 4 of the worksheet, and as you can see, Fertilizer was the top-selling product in April. The formula in the formula bar points to cell E4.

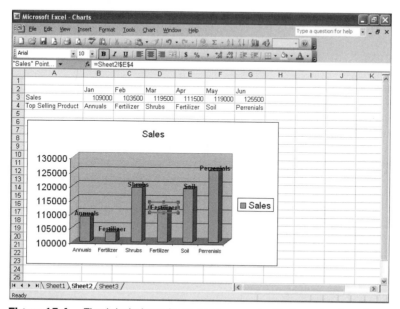

Figure 15-4. The labels have been programmed with formulas to point to a cell in the worksheet.

For example, set up a line chart similar to Figure 15-4. Add the following macro to add the chart labels that correspond to the top-selling products in row 4:

```
Sub AddDataLabels()
    Dim seSales As Series
    Dim Pts As Points
    Dim pt As Point
    Dim rng As Range
    Dim i As Integer

    Set rng = Range("B4:G4")
    Set seSales = ActiveSheet.ChartObjects(1).Chart.SeriesCollection(1)
    seSales.HasDataLabels = True
    Set Pts = seSales.Points
    For Each pt In Pts
        i = i + 1
        pt.DataLabel.Text = "=" & rng.Cells(i).Address(RowAbsolute:=True, _
            ColumnAbsolute:=True, ReferenceStyle:=xlR1C1, External:=True)
        pt.DataLabel.Font.Bold = True
        pt.DataLabel.Position = xlLabelPositionCenter
    Next pt
End Sub
```

The object variable *rng* is assigned a reference to B4:G4. The *seSales* series is assigned a reference to the first and only series in the embedded chart, and the *HasDataLabels* property of the series is set to *True*. The *For Each…Next* loop processes each point in the data series. For each point, the code assigns a formula to the *Text* property of the point's data label. The formula refers to the worksheet cell as an external reference in the *R1C1* format. The data label is also boldfaced, and the label positioned above the data point.

Formatting a Chart

Chart formatting is a broad category. You are able to format the *ChartObject* itself, as well as all the objects contained within the chart. For example, you may modify the *ChartObject Location*, such as changing an embedded chart to its own chart sheet. You may also classify modifying the color selection for the data series as chart formatting. There are more than 60 chart properties available; Table 15-3 lists the commonly used *Chart* property names and the results returned.

Table 15-3. *Chart* Properties

Name	Returns	Description
ChartType	xlChartType	Used to set the chart type or return the current chart type.
HasDataTable	Boolean	Used to set whether the associated data table will be displayed on the chart. The default is set to *False*, so the data table is not included if this property is not set.
HasLegend	Boolean	Used to set whether the legend will be displayed.

Table 15-3. *Chart* Properties

Name	Returns	Description
HasTitle	Boolean	Used to set whether the chart will display a chart title.
PlotBy	xlRowCol	Used to set whether columns in the original data are used as individual data series (xlColumns) or if the rows in the original data are used as the data series (xlRows).

Table 15-4 lists the commonly used *ChartObject* property names and their results.

Table 15-4. *ChartObject* Properties

Name	Returns	Description
BottomRightCell	Range	Returns the single cell range located under the lower right corner of the embedded *ChartObject*.
Chart	Chart	Returns the actual chart associated with the *ChartObject*.
Height	Double	Sets the height of the embedded chart.
Left	Double	Sets the distance from the left edge of the margin to the left edge of the *ChartObject*.
Name	String	Sets the name of the *ChartObject*.
PrintObject	Boolean	Sets whether the embedded object will be printed when the worksheet is printed.
RoundedCorners	Boolean	Sets whether the embedded chart will have rounded corners. By default, the property is set to *False*, which displays right-angled corners.
Shadow	Boolean	Sets whether a shadow will appear around the embedded chart.
Top	Double	Sets the distance of the *Top* edge of the *ChartObject* to the top of the worksheet.
Visible	Boolean	Sets whether the *ChartObject* is visible.
Width	Double	Sets the width of the embedded chart.

Each object within the chart has a series of properties as well. For example, the *ChartTitle* object can have a navy blue 2 point border or no border with a shadow. The *ChartTitle* can be set using the position properties, such as *Left* and *Top*. In fact, the orientation can also be set. When it comes to formatting a chart by enhancing the cosmetic appearance, the possibilities are almost endless. Before programming the macro, modify an existing chart and document the changes you have made to the chart. Now based on the sample chart and your documentation, add the appropriate lines of code to your procedure.

Chapter 15

Consider this scenario. The Garden Company has a Product Sales chart that is created monthly. Each month several modifications need to be applied after the chart has been created. To ensure consistency to the charts, you decide to create a procedure that applies the required formats. Figure 15-5 shows the desired end result. Notice that the chart type is set to 3D Clustered Bar, the Data Table is visible, and the Legend has been removed.

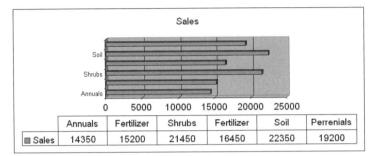

	Annuals	Fertilizer	Shrubs	Fertilizer	Soil	Perrenials
■ Sales	14350	15200	21450	16450	22350	19200

Figure 15-5. The sample formatting for the Garden Supply Company Monthly Sales Chart.

The following procedure will modify the chart shown in Figure 15-5 to include the formatting that was determined necessary:

```
Sub FormatChart()
    Dim chrt As Chart
    Set chrt = ActiveSheet.ChartObjects(1).Chart
    chrt.ChartType = xl3DBarClustered
    ActiveChart.HasLegend = False
    ActiveChart.HasDataTable = True
    ActiveChart.DataTable.ShowLegendKey = True
End Sub
```

Modifying All Charts in a Workbook

There will be times where you want to establish consistency throughout your workbook by applying the same formats to all charts. You can specify whether to apply the formats to all *ChartObjects* or just to a specific *ChartObject* type, such as embedded charts or chart sheets. To achieve this result, use a *For...Next* loop to cycle through each object in the *ChartObjects* collection, and then accesses the *Chart* object in each and change its *ChartType* property. The following example changes all charts on the active worksheet to an Area chart:

```
Sub ChangeChartType()
    Dim chtobj as ChartObject
    For Each chtobj In ActiveSheet.ChartObjects
        chtobj.Chart.ChartType = xlArea
    Next chtobj
End Sub
```

Printing Charts

When printing a chart sheet, by default it will print on its own page. However, when working with embedded charts, you need to determine if the chart should be printed on its own page or with the worksheet. For a user to print an embedded chart on its own page, they are required to first select the chart and then choose File, Print. This will allow the embedded chart to be printed as if it were on a chart sheet.

The following procedure demonstrates how to preview all embedded charts in a worksheet as full pages. To send the charts to the default printer, change the *PrintPreview* method to *PrintOut*.

```
Sub PrintEmbeddedCharts()
    For Each chtObj In ActiveSheet.ChartObjects
        chtObj.Chart.PrintPreview
    Next chtObj
End Sub
```

In contrast, if you would like to print the embedded chart as an object with the contents of the worksheet, you can simply print the worksheet and the chart will be included automatically. However, there might be situations where you want to exclude the chart when printing the worksheet. To accomplish this task successfully, you must set the *PrintObject* property for the *ChartObject* to *False*. By default, the *ChartObject* is included when printing a worksheet, so the only time you need to set the *PrintObject* property is when you need to exclude the embedded charts from the print job.

The following procedure prints the active worksheet and excludes all chart objects. Substitute the *PrintPreview* property to *PrintOut* to send the print job to the default printer.

```
Sub PrintWorksheetOnly()
    For Each chtObj In ActiveSheet.ChartObjects
        chtObj.PrintObject = False
    Next chtObj
    ActiveSheet.PrintPreview
End Sub
```

Final Thoughts on Programming Charts

After reviewing the variety of options available when creating and modifying charts in a procedure, you'll see that creating a programmatic reference to a chart on a chart sheet is easy. The *Chart* object is a member of the *Charts* collection of the workbook. The challenge is setting the reference to an embedded chart. You must be aware that the embedded *Chart* object is contained in a *ChartObject* object that belongs to the *ChartObjects* collection of the worksheet. Remember, the Object Browser can be your greatest asset when troubleshooting your VBA code.

Chapter 15

You can move or resize an embedded chart by changing the *Top*, *Left*, *Width*, and *Height* properties of the *ChartObject* object. If you already have a reference to the *Chart* object, you can get a reference to the *ChartObject* object through the *Parent* property of the *Chart* object.

Individual series in a chart are *Series* objects and belong to the *SeriesCollection* object of the chart. The *Delete* method of the *Series* object is used to delete a series from a chart. You use the *NewSeries* method of the *SeriesCollection* object to add a new series to a chart.

You can assign a VBA array, rather than the more commonly used *Range* object, to the *Values* property of a *Series* object. This creates a chart that is independent of worksheet data and can be distributed without a supporting worksheet.

The *Values* and *XValues* properties return data values, not the range references used in a chart. You can determine the ranges referenced by a chart by examining the SERIES function in the *Formula* property of each series.

Keep in mind the complexity of the Chart Model as you create procedures that reference charts. Use some of the recommended tips provided to simplify how to reference the chart and produce cleaner code, such as assigning the chart an object variable.

In the next chapter, you will learn how to setup your workbook so you can use PivotTables and PivotCharts.

PivotTables and PivotCharts

PivotTables and PivotCharts 341
PivotTable Objects. 348
Programming PivotTables. 356

Manipulating PivotTables
Programmatically. 359

This chapter discusses how to create and manipulate PivotTables and PivotCharts using Microsoft Visual Basic for Applications (VBA). In this chapter, you will learn about the objects associated with PivotTables and PivotCharts and how to manipulate PivotTables and associated objects programmatically.

PivotTables and PivotCharts

Worksheets are a useful tool when you are dealing with two-dimensional data that can be organized into rows and columns. However, there are many situations where your data can be viewed in multiple ways. Although you could build multiple worksheets and charts based on the data from the original worksheet, creating a new worksheet or chart for every different aspect of your data that you want to emphasize can quickly spin out of control. Fortunately, Microsoft Excel includes a feature that gives you a powerful tool to deal with this problem.

PivotTables and PivotCharts provide useful ways to look at your data from multiple perspectives. Often you can find hidden relationships between two or more fields that you might have otherwise ignored.

Introducing PivotTables

A *PivotTable* is a tool that lets you deal with *multidimensional* reports. Figure 16-1 contains a simple two-dimensional report—also known as a *cross tabulation* report—where you have a predefined collection of columns and rows indexing summary data.

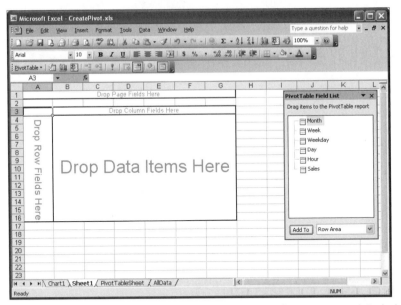

Figure 16-1. A simple two-dimensional report contains summary data indexed by two fields.

If you want to represent a report with three fields, you need to envision a cube where the intersection of any row, column, and depth variable will produce a single summary value. To make a three-dimensional report easier to deal with, you can "flatten" the report by cutting the cube into multiple slices along the depth axis and representing the third dimension at the top of each page of the report, as is often done when you create reports in Microsoft Access.

Visualizing a report with more than three variables is something that many humans aren't capable of doing, but it's easy to flatten a report with any number of variables. Simply choose the fields for the rows and columns for the flattened report, and display the values of the other fields at the top of each page.

The data that you would use for a PivotTable is typically organized as a series of rows known as *facts*, which consists of a collection of *keys* and *measures*. A measure is a numeric value such as the number of sales or the total dollar value of the sales. A key, which can be composed of one or more columns, characterizes a corresponding measure and usually answers questions such as when the sales were made or to whom the sales were made. A *key field* (or collection of fields) always contains a unique value for each row in a table, allowing Excel to identify the corresponding measure. In the following table, the Month, Week, Weekday, Day, and Hour fields comprise the key, while the Sales field contains a measure.

Month	Week	Weekday	Day	Hour	Sales
January	1	Mon	1	9	147
January	1	Tue	2	9	161
January	1	Wed	3	9	182
January	1	Thu	4	9	201

Chapter 16

January	1	Fri	5	9	158
January	1	Sat	6	9	190
January	1	Sun	7	9	243
January	2	Mon	8	9	147
January	2	Tue	9	9	161
January	2	Wed	10	9	182
January	2	Thu	11	9	201
January	2	Fri	12	9	685

Excel uses individual transactions such as these to create the facts that are displayed in the PivotTable. This process involves two steps: extracting the keys from the information in the transactions and identifying the corresponding measure.

A PivotTable implements multidimensional reports by combining the facts in different ways. You can drag and drop key fields from the PivotTable Field List to the page area to determine which specific page is displayed. You can also drag and drop key fields onto the column and row areas to determine which column and rows will be displayed. Measures should be dragged only into the Data area because these values will be computed based on the other fields. These actions result in a PivotTable that looks like Figure 16-2.

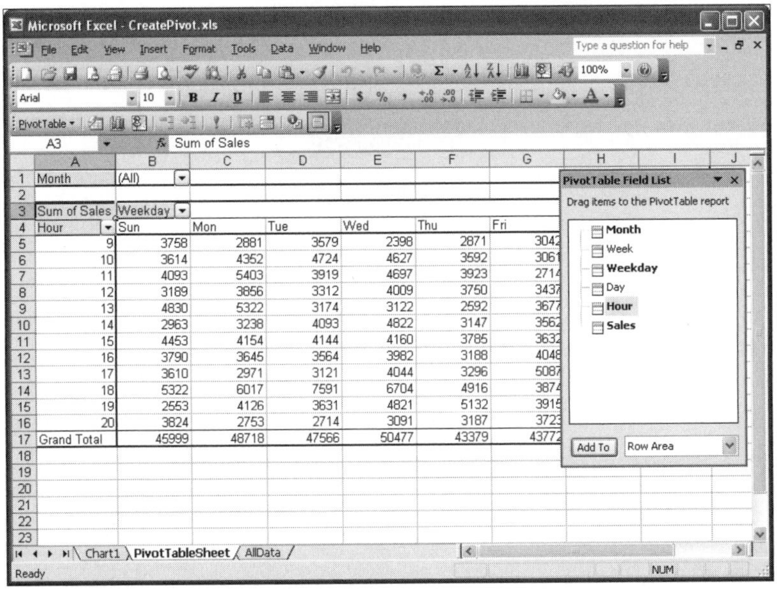

Figure 16-2. A PivotTable allows a user to combine facts in many different ways.

Creating a PivotTable with the PivotTable Wizard

Although you can manually create a PivotTable, the PivotTable wizard really simplifies the process. To create a PivotTable with the PivotTable wizard, follow these steps:

1 Choose Data, PivotTable and PivotChart Report from the Excel main menu.

2 On the first step of the wizard, choose the location of your data and then select PivotTable.

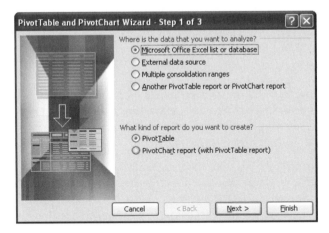

3 The second step of the wizard prompts you to select the source data for the PivotTable. You can either enter a range in the Range box or press the button at the end of the box to collapse the dialog box, allowing you to select a range in any of the currently open workbooks. You can press the Browse button if you want to open a new workbook.

4 In the last step of the wizard, you choose the location where the wizard will place the PivotTable. You can select a location on the current worksheet, or the wizard will create a new worksheet for you. Pressing the Layout button displays a dialog box that allows you drag and drop the various fields for the PivotTable's initial configuration.

5 If you press the Options button in the last step of the wizard, the wizard will display the PivotTable Options dialog box. You can select from a wide range of options, as shown here.

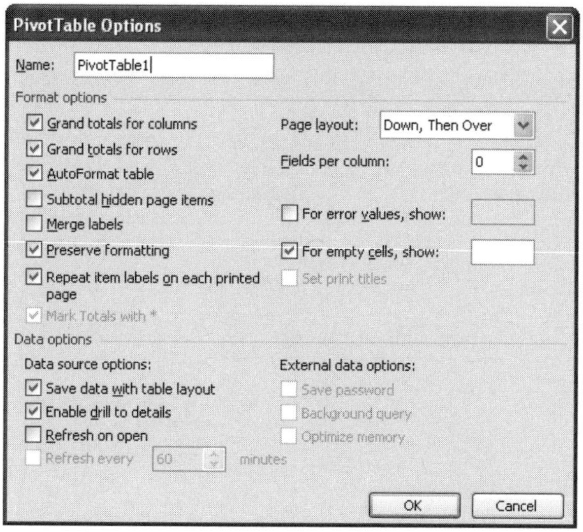

6 Press the Finish button to create the PivotTable.

When the wizard is finished, you'll see a PivotTable similar to the one shown in Figure 16-3.

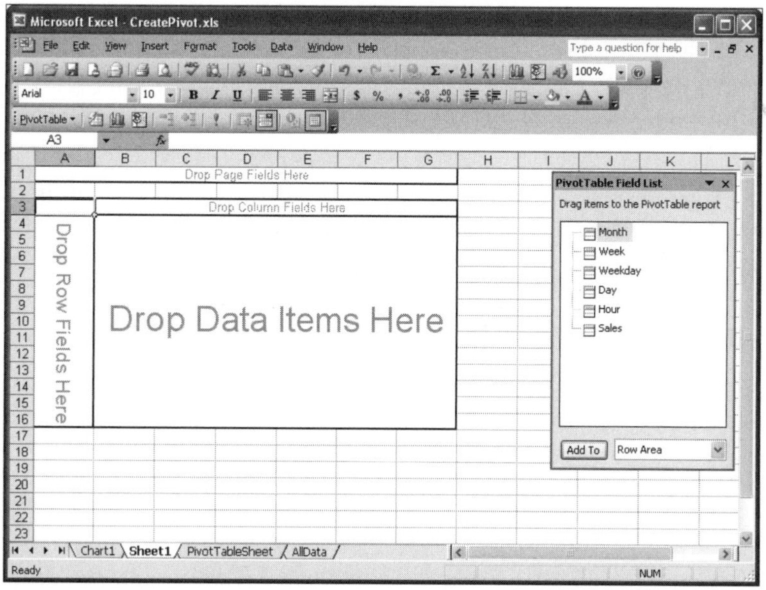

Figure 16-3. A PivotTable contains summary information based on the underlying data supplied.

Introducing PivotCharts

A PivotChart is simply a graphical representation of a PivotTable. (See Figure 16-4.) In fact, a PivotChart is generally created from the data of an existing PivotTable. Just as with a Pivot-Table, you can drag fields into the appropriate areas of a PivotChart.

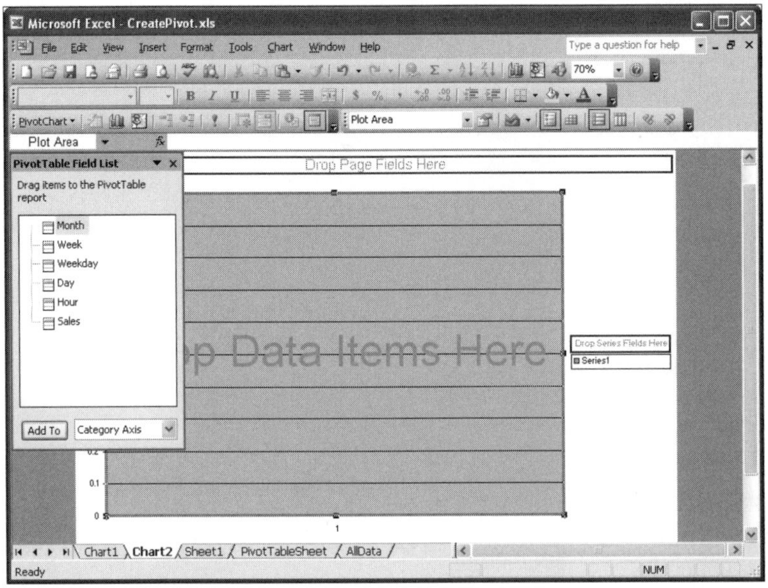

Figure 16-4. A PivotChart contains drag and drop areas similar to a PivotTable.

The chart's x-axis and y-axis correspond to the row and column areas in the PivotTable, whereas the page area is located near the top of the chart. More technically, these areas are known as the *category* and *series* areas. The page area and the data area are carried over directly from the PivotTable.

After you drag and drop the fields into the various parts of the PivotChart, you can change the type of chart by choosing Chart, Chart Type from the Excel main menu. You can also use most of Excel's chart-formatting tools to customize the chart to fit your needs.

Creating a PivotChart with the PivotTable Wizard

The same wizard you use to create a PivotTable can also create a PivotChart. Under the covers, the wizard creates a new PivotTable and then uses that PivotTable to create a PivotChart. If you already have a PivotTable, simply select any cell within the one you wish to use and choose Insert, Chart from the Excel main menu. A resulting chart is shown in Figure 16-5.

PivotTables and PivotCharts

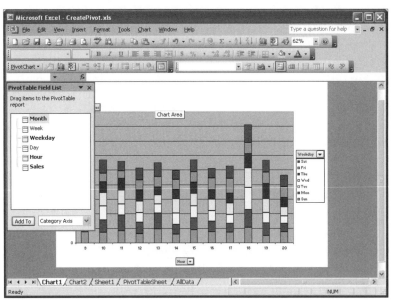

Figure 16-5. A PivotChart is a graphical representation of a PivotTable.

Online Analytical Processing (OLAP) Issues

PivotTable data can come from a number of sources besides a worksheet. Typically, the data is imported into Excel, while the information necessary to get a fresh copy is also preserved. This arrangement allows the PivotTable user to refresh the data easily.

The one big limitation is that an Excel PivotTable isn't capable of managing large volumes of data directly. This limitation should be expected when you consider that a worksheet is limited to 65,536 rows. However, Excel has a facility that lets a PivotTable work with a special type of external database server known as an Online Analytical Processing (OLAP) server.

> **Note** SQL Server Standard Edition and Enterprise Edition include a tool called Analysis Services, which provides the OLAP database facilities that can be accessed from Excel.

With an OLAP database, much of the processing required to summarize data is shifted from the local computer to the OLAP server. An OLAP server is capable of dealing with large volumes of data and is designed to provide summaries of its data quickly and efficiently by pre-computing many useful values.

> **Note** Because Excel relies on the OLAP server to precompute the data, each time you change the layout of a PivotTable, Excel will request a fresh copy of the data from the OLAP server. This could cause unexpected delays as the data is transmitted from the OLAP server to Excel.

Chapter 16

347

Microsoft Office Excel 2003 Programming Inside Out

Because Excel uses the summary data directly, you can't change the summary functions for data fields. Another side effect of using the summary data is that you might not be able to access the detail data. This information is determined by the design of the OLAP database.

> **Warning** PivotTables based on OLAP data sources behave somewhat differently than those created using non-OLAP data sources. This is due to the fact that OLAP servers return data that's already summarized, so different objects are used internally to store the summary data and to interact with the OLAP server. The rest of this chapter assumes that you are working with non-OLAP data sources.

PivotTable Objects

Each Excel worksheet can hold multiple PivotTables. To access a particular *PivotTable* object, you start with the *Worksheet* object that represents the worksheet containing the PivotTable that you want to manipulate. Then you use the *PivotTables* collection to reach the specific *PivotTable* object that you want to manipulate.

Each *PivotTable* object contains several key objects that represent the various pieces of a PivotTable. (See Figure 16-6.)

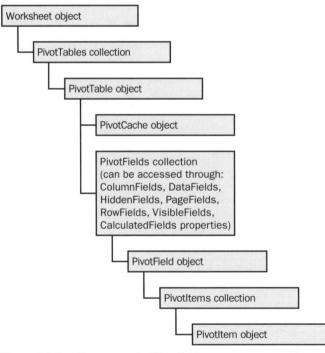

Figure 16-6. The parts of a PivotTable are represented by a collection of different types of objects.

PivotTables Collection

The *PivotTables* collection contains the set of all PivotTables in a particular worksheet. Table 16-1 lists the key properties and methods for the *PivotTables* collection. You can access the *PivotTables* property from a *Worksheet* object using the following code:

```
ActiveSheet.PivotTables(1)
```

Table 16-1. Key Properties and Methods of the *PivotTables* Collection

Property/Method	Description
Add(PivotCache, TableDestination, TableName, ReadData, DefaultVersion)	Method: adds a new PivotTable to the collection. *PivotCache* refers to the data that will be displayed in the PivotTable; *TableDestination* passes a *Range* object whose upper-left corner marks the location of the PivotTable in the worksheet; *TableName* contains the name of the PivotTable (optional); *ReadData*, when *True*, caches all records from an external database in *PivotCache*; *DefaultVersion* specifies the version of Excel that created the PivotTable.
Count	Property (read-only): returns the number of items in the *PivotTables* collection.
Item(index)	Method: returns the *PivotTable* object reference associated with *index*. *Index* may refer to the PivotTable by either its name or its relative position in the collection.

PivotTable Object

The *PivotTable* object represents a single PivotTable. You can use this object to access an existing PivotTable on a worksheet, or you can use the *Add* method from the *PivotTables* collection to add a new one. You can even use the *PivotTableWizard* method from the *Worksheet* object to create a new PivotTable.

Table 16-2 contains a list of the key properties and methods associated with the *PivotTable* object.

Chapter 16

Table 16-2. Key Properties and Methods of the *PivotTable* Object

Property/Method	Description
AddDataField(Field, Caption, Function)	Method: This routine adds a data field to a PivotTable. *Field* is a *PivotField* object associated with the PivotTable. *Caption* contains a value that will be used to label the specified *PivotField* (optional). *Function* specifies the summary function performed on the data field.
CalculatedFields	Method: returns a *CalculatedFields* collection, which contains the set of *PivotField* objects, which are computed based on other fields in the PivotTable.
ColumnFields	Property (read-only): returns either a *PivotField* object or a *PivotFields* collection containing the fields that are currently displayed as column fields.
ColumnGrand	Property: when *True*, the PivotTable report displays grand totals for each column in the *PivotTable* object.
DataFields	Property (read-only): returns either a *PivotField* object or a *PivotFields* collection containing the fields that are currently displayed as data fields.
DisplayErrorString	Property: when *True*, any cells with errors will display the text in the *ErrorString* property.
DisplayNullString	Property: when *True*, any cells with null values will display the text in the *NullString* property.
ErrorString	Property: contains the text that will be displayed in cells with errors, if the *DisplayErrorString* property is *True*.
Format (format)	Method: sets the PivotTable's format to one of the formats specified in *XlPivotFormatType*. Valid formats are *xlPTClassic*, *xlPTNone*, *xlPTReport1* to *xlPTReport10*, and *xlPTTable1* to *xlPTTable10*.
HiddenFields	Property (read-only): returns either a *PivotField* object or a *PivotFields* collection containing the fields that are not currently displayed as row, column, page, or data fields.
Name	Property: contains the name of the PivotTable.
NullString	Property: contains the text that will be displayed in cells with null values when the *DisplayNullString* property is *True*.
PageFields	Property (read-only): returns either a *PivotField* object or a *PivotFields* collection containing the fields that are currently displayed as page fields.

Table 16-2. Key Properties and Methods of the *PivotTable* Object

Property/Method	Description
PivotCache	Method: returns an object reference to the *PivotCache* object associated with the PivotTable.
PivotFields (index)	Method: returns either the *PivotField* object specified by the *index* parameter, or returns the collection of all *PivotFields* if *index* is omitted.
PivotTableWizard (SourceType, SourceData, TableDestination, TableName, RowGrand, ColumnGrand, SaveData, HasAutoFormat, AutoPage, Reserved, BackgroundQuery, OptimizeCache, PageFieldOrder, PageFieldWrapCount, ReadData, Connection)	Method: constructs a PivotTable named *TableName* using data from *SourceData* and places the result at *TableDestination*.
RefreshTable	Method: refreshes the data displayed in the PivotTable based on the data in the associated data source.
RowFields	Property (read-only): returns either a *PivotField* object or a *PivotFields* collection containing the fields that are currently displayed as row fields.
RowGrand	Property: when *True*, displays grand totals for each row in the PivotTable.
VisibleFields	Property (read-only): returns either a *PivotField* object or a *PivotFields* collection containing the fields that are currently displayed in the PivotTable.

> **Tip** **Refresh Your Data**
>
> Use the *RefreshTable* method to update the information displayed in the PivotTable if the source data changes.

PivotCaches Collection

The *PivotCaches* collection contains the set of all *PivotCache* objects (see Table 16-3). Because *PivotCache* objects are stored at the workbook level, they can be easily used to create PivotTables and PivotCharts anywhere in the workbook.

Chapter 16

Table 16-3. Key Properties and Methods of the *PivotCaches* Collection

Property/Method	Description
Add(SourceType, SourceData)	Method: adds a new *PivotCache* object to the collection. *SourceType* identifies where the data is coming from. Can be *xlConsolidation*, *xlDatabase*, *xlExternal*, *xlPivotTable*, or *xlScenario*. *SourceData* specifies additional information about the source of the data. Typically, this source is a *Range* object, although in the case of an external database it's a two-element string array, where the first element contains the connection string and the second element contains the SQL query that retrieves the data.
Count	Property (read-only): returns the number of items in the *PivotCaches* collection.
Item(index)	Method: returns the *PivotCache* object reference associated with index. *Index* may refer to the PivotTable by either its name or its relative position in the collection.

PivotCache Object

The data displayed in a PivotTable is stored in the *PivotCache* object. You can reference the *PivotCache* through the *PivotCache* method associated with the *PivotTable* object or through the *PivotCache* collection associated with the *Workbook* object. Multiple PivotTables can share the same *PivotCache* object.

Table 16-4 contains a list of the key properties and methods associated with the *PivotCache* object.

Table 16-4. Key Properties and Methods of the *PivotCache* Object

Property/Method	Description
CommandText	Property: contains a database command string used to retrieve data from an external database.
CommandType	Property: identifies the type of data stored in *CommandText* using a constant found in the *XlCmdType* enumeration. Valid command types are *xlCmdCube*, *xlCmdDefault*, *xlCmdList*, *xlCmdSql*, and *xlCmdTable*.
Connection	Property: contains an OLE DB or ODBC connection string used to access an external database; may also contain a URL to connect a Web data source or the fully qualified name of a text file or Access database. Use the *Refresh* method to update the data contained in the data source.

Table 16-4. Key Properties and Methods of the *PivotCache* Object

Property/Method	Description
CreatePivotTable (TableDestination, TableName, ReadData, DefaultVersion)	Method: creates a *PivotTable* object based on the current *PivotCache* object.
Index	Property (read-only): returns the index number of the *PivotCache* within the *PivotCaches* collection.
IsConnected	Property (read-only): when *True*, means that the *PivotCache* is currently connected to a data source.
MakeConnection	Method: opens a connection between the *PivotCache* and the data source specified in the *Connection* property.
MemoryUsed	Property (read-only): returns the number of bytes used by the current *PivotCache* object.
OLAP	Property (read-only): returns *True* when the cache is connected to an OLAP server.
QueryType	Property (read-only): returns the type of query as enumerated in *XlQueryType* that is used to populate the cache. Value query types are *xlADORecordset*, *xlDAORecordset*, *xlDDBCQuery*, *xlOLEDBQuery*, *xlTextImport*, and *xlWebQuery*.
RecordCount	Property (read-only): returns the number of records in the cache.
Recordset	Property: contains the *Recordset* object that will be used to populate the cache.
Refresh	Method: updates the information in the *PivotCache* object and the associated *PivotTable* object.
RefreshDate	Property (read-only): returns the date when the cache was last refreshed.
RefreshPeriod	Property: contains the number of minutes between refreshes. Setting this property to zero disables automatic refreshes.

PivotField Objects

The *PivotField* object represents one of the fields in a PivotTable. This object contains a lot of useful information that describes the field, including its *Name*, *MemoryUsed*, and *NumberFormat*. However, the most important properties are the *Orientation* and *Position* properties. The *Orientation* property determines the area on the *PivotTable* where the field is located, and the *Position* property determines the order of the field within a particular area.

The *PivotItems* method returns a collection of *PivotItem* objects. Each *PivotItem* object represents a specific value within the *PivotField* object.

You can access a *PivotField* object through these properties associated with the *PivotTable* object. These properties provide a shortcut to commonly used subsets of the data.

- The *PivotFields* collection contains the complete set of all *PivotField* objects associated with the PivotTable.
- The *HiddenFields* property returns the set of *PivotField* objects that are not currently displayed on the PivotTable or the PivotChart.
- The *VisibleFields* property returns the set of *PivotField* objects that are currently displayed on the PivotTable or the PivotChart.
- The *ColumnFields* property returns the set of *PivotField* objects that are displayed as columns in a PivotTable or a PivotChart.
- The *RowFields* property returns the set of *PivotField* objects that are displayed as rows in a PivotTable or a PivotChart.
- The *PageFields* property returns the set of *PivotField* objects that are displayed in the page area of a PivotTable or a PivotChart.
- The *DataFields* property returns the set of *PivotField* objects that are displayed in the data area of a PivotTable or a PivotChart.
- The *CalculatedFields* collection contains the set of *PivotField* objects that are computed from other fields in the PivotTable.

> **Note** If there is only one *PivotField* in a collection, the associated property from the *PivotTable* object will point directly to the *PivotField* object rather than to a *PivotFields* collection.

Table 16-5 contains a list of the key properties and methods associated with the *PivotField* object.

Table 16-5. Key Properties and Methods of the PivotField Object

Property/Method	Description
Caption	Property (read-only): returns the label text for the field.
CurrentPage	Property: contains the current page for a page field.
DataRange	Property (read-only): returns a *Range* object with the data contained in the field.
DataType	Property (read-only): returns the type of data from the *XlPivotFieldDataType* enumeration (*xlDate*, *xlNumber*, or *xlText*) that represents the field.

Table 16-5. Key Properties and Methods of the PivotField Object

Property/Method	Description
DragToColumn	Property: when *False*, means that the field cannot be dragged to the column area in the PivotTable.
DragToData	Property: when *False*, means that the field can't be dragged to the data area in the PivotTable.
DragToHide	Property: when *False*, means that the field can't be dragged away from the PivotTable.
DragToPage	Property: when *False*, means that the field can't be dragged to the page area of the PivotTable.
DragToRow	Property: when *False*, means that the field cannot be dragged to the row area in the PivotTable.
LayoutForm	Property: contains the way that PivotTable items appear. *xlTabular* implies table format; *xlOutline* specifies outline format.
MemoryUsed	Property (read-only): returns the number of bytes used by the current *PivotField* object.
Name	Property: contains the name of the *PivotField* object.
NumberFormat	Property: contains the formatting specifications that will be used to display the information from the *PivotField* object. Applies only to fields used in the data area of the PivotTable.
Orientation	Property: contains the location of the field in a PivotTable as specified by the *XlPivotFieldOrientation* type (*xlColumnField*, *xlDataField*, *xlHidden*, *xlPageField*, or *xlRowField*).
PivotItems	Method: returns the collection of *PivotItems* representing the individual items within a particular field.
Position	Property: contains the relative position of the field within its orientation.
ShowAllItems	Property: when *True*, means that all items in the PivotTable report will be displayed even if they don't contain summary data.
Value	Property: contains the name of the specified field in the PivotTable report.

Chapter 16

PivotItem Object

The *PivotItem* object represents a single, specific value for a particular *PivotField* object. Table 16-6 contains a list of the key properties and methods associated with the *PivotItem* object.

Table 16-6. Key Properties and Methods of the *PivotItem* Object

Property/Method	Description
Caption	Property (read-only): returns the label text for the field.
DataRange	Property (read-only): returns a *Range* object with the data contained in the field.
Formula	Property: contains the formula associated with the item in A1-style notation. If the cell is empty, an empty string will be returned. If the cell contains a constant, the constant will be returned.
LabelRange	Property (read-only): returns the *Range* object representing the cells in the PivotTable report that contain the item.
Name	Property: contains the name of the *PivotItem* object.
Position	Property: contains the relative position of the field within its orientation.
RecordCount	Property (read-only): returns the number of records in the *PivotCache* containing the specified item.
Value	Property: contains the name of the specified item in the PivotTable field.
Visible	Property: when *True*, means that the item is visible.

Programming PivotTables

Programming PivotTables involves creating the appropriate *PivotCache* object and then using the *PivotCache* object to create a *PivotTable* object. Once the *PivotTable* object is available, you can modify its properties to view the data from different positions.

> **Tip Make Things Easy on Yourself**
> Creating PivotTables can be difficult, so you might want to fall back on the standard macro writer's trick: record a new macro using the commands necessary to perform the task you wish to program, and then use the recorded code as the basis of your new program. This trick is extremely useful when dealing with complex object models such as those used by Excel to manipulate PivotTables.

Creating a PivotTable

The code to create a simple PivotTable is shown the following listing. The routine begins by declaring temporary objects to hold references to the *PivotCache* and the *PivotTable* objects, plus a temporary variable that will be used to delete the worksheet containing the PivotTable.

```
Sub CreatePivotTable()

Dim pc As PivotCache
Dim ws As Worksheet
Dim pt As PivotTable

For Each ws In ActiveWorkbook.Worksheets
    If ws.Name = "PivotTableSheet" Then
        ws.Delete

    End If

Next ws

Set ws = ActiveWorkbook.Worksheets.Add()
ws.Name = "PivotTableSheet"

Set pc = ActiveWorkbook.PivotCaches.Add(xlDatabase, "AllData!R1C1:R1117C6")

Set pt = pc.CreatePivotTable("PivotTableSheet!R1C1", "My Pivot Table")

pt.PivotFields("Month").Orientation = xlRowField
pt.PivotFields("Month").Position = 1

pt.PivotFields("Hour").Orientation = xlColumnField
pt.PivotFields("Hour").Position = 1

pt.AddDataField pt.PivotFields("Sales"), "Sum of Sales", xlSum

End Sub
```

A simple *For Each* loop is used to scan through the collection of *Worksheet* objects associated with the active workbook, looking for a worksheet named *PivotTableSheet*. If the worksheet is found, the worksheet is deleted. After the worksheet is deleted, a new worksheet with the same name is added to the *Worksheets* collection. This code ensures that the worksheet is empty before the PivotTable is added.

Next a *PivotCache* object is created using the *PivotCaches.Add* method. The *xlDatabase* argument indicates that the data is formatted as a series of rows and columns, while the second parameter indicates that the data is located on the *AllData* worksheet in columns 1 to 6 and rows 1 to 1117.

Once the *PivotCache* object has been created, a *PivotTable* object can be created by using the *PivotCache* object's *CreatePivotTable* method. The *CreatePivotTable* method takes two arguments, the location of the upper-left corner of the PivotTable and the name of the PivotTable.

By default, the PivotTable is empty, so you need to define the row fields, the column fields, and the data fields. Defining the rows and the columns involves using the *PivotTable* object's *PivotFields* collection and setting the *Orientation* property. The *Position* property is also set to 1, to allow you to add additional row and column fields.

Finally, the *AddDataField* method is used to define which fields are included in the data area of the PivotTable. This routine takes three arguments, the *PivotField* object that should be added to the data area, the title for the field, and the function used to combine the data fields together.

Running the *CreatePivotTable* routine creates the PivotTable shown in Figure 16-7.

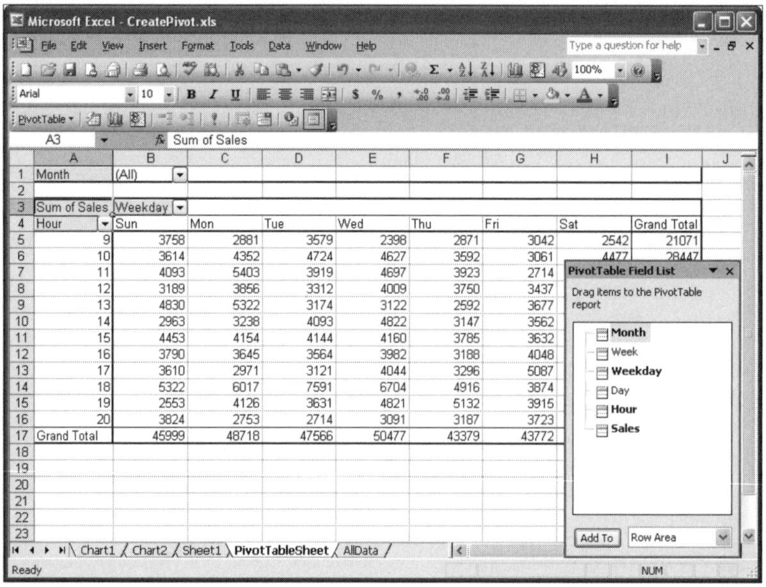

Figure 16-7. This PivotTable is the result of running the subroutine shown on page 358.

Creating a PivotChart

Once you've created a PivotTable, creating a PivotChart is very easy. Simply create a new *Chart* object and use the PivotTable as the data source using the following code:

```
Charts.Add
ActiveChart.SetSourceData Sheets("PivotTableSheet").Range("A1")
ActiveChart.Location xlLocationAsNewSheet, "Pivot Chart"
```

The *Charts.Add* method creates a new *Chart* object. Then *SetSourceData* method specifies the PivotTable located on *PivotTableSheet* starting at cell A1. Finally, the *Location* method is used to create a new sheet to hold the PivotChart and to give it the title *Pivot Chart*.

Manipulating PivotTables Programmatically

Pivoting a PivotTable by hand is a straightforward operation…you just drag the field header to the desired location in the PivotTable layout. One common complaint from PivotTable users, however, is that they often forget the exact configuration they need to emphasize a certain point. When you have a relatively simple PivotTable, such as the six-field table used as the example in this chapter, you probably won't have too many difficulties remembering what goes where. However, if your PivotTable has more than six fields, or if you're working with unfamiliar data, you might need to use some macro helpers to get you through your presentation. This section contains four macros that you can use to build your own solutions.

Pivoting a PivotTable Programmatically

The first procedure shows you how to change the position of a field within a PivotTable. In this case, you start with the PivotTable found on the PivotTable sheet of the EditPivot.xls workbook, arranged in the layout shown in Figure 16-8.

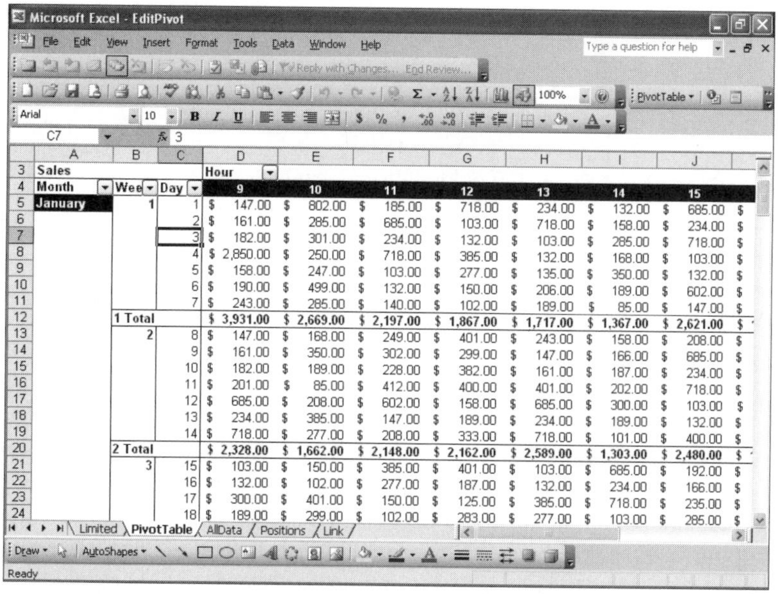

Sales			Hour						
Month	Wee	Day	9	10	11	12	13	14	15
January	1	1	$ 147.00	$ 802.00	$ 185.00	$ 718.00	$ 234.00	$ 132.00	$ 685.00
		2	$ 161.00	$ 285.00	$ 685.00	$ 103.00	$ 718.00	$ 158.00	$ 234.00
		3	$ 182.00	$ 301.00	$ 234.00	$ 132.00	$ 103.00	$ 285.00	$ 718.00
		4	$ 2,850.00	$ 250.00	$ 718.00	$ 385.00	$ 132.00	$ 168.00	$ 103.00
		5	$ 158.00	$ 247.00	$ 103.00	$ 277.00	$ 135.00	$ 350.00	$ 132.00
		6	$ 190.00	$ 499.00	$ 132.00	$ 150.00	$ 206.00	$ 189.00	$ 602.00
		7	$ 243.00	$ 285.00	$ 140.00	$ 102.00	$ 189.00	$ 85.00	$ 147.00
	1 Total		$ 3,931.00	$ 2,669.00	$ 2,197.00	$ 1,867.00	$ 1,717.00	$ 1,367.00	$ 2,621.00
	2	8	$ 147.00	$ 168.00	$ 249.00	$ 401.00	$ 243.00	$ 158.00	$ 208.00
		9	$ 161.00	$ 350.00	$ 302.00	$ 299.00	$ 147.00	$ 166.00	$ 685.00
		10	$ 182.00	$ 189.00	$ 228.00	$ 382.00	$ 161.00	$ 187.00	$ 234.00
		11	$ 201.00	$ 85.00	$ 412.00	$ 400.00	$ 401.00	$ 202.00	$ 718.00
		12	$ 685.00	$ 208.00	$ 602.00	$ 158.00	$ 685.00	$ 300.00	$ 103.00
		13	$ 234.00	$ 385.00	$ 147.00	$ 189.00	$ 234.00	$ 189.00	$ 132.00
		14	$ 718.00	$ 277.00	$ 208.00	$ 333.00	$ 718.00	$ 101.00	$ 400.00
	2 Total		$ 2,328.00	$ 1,662.00	$ 2,148.00	$ 2,162.00	$ 2,589.00	$ 1,303.00	$ 2,480.00
	3	15	$ 103.00	$ 150.00	$ 385.00	$ 401.00	$ 103.00	$ 685.00	$ 192.00
		16	$ 132.00	$ 102.00	$ 277.00	$ 187.00	$ 132.00	$ 234.00	$ 166.00
		17	$ 300.00	$ 401.00	$ 150.00	$ 125.00	$ 385.00	$ 718.00	$ 235.00
		18	$ 189.00	$ 299.00	$ 102.00	$ 283.00	$ 277.00	$ 103.00	$ 285.00

Figure 16-8. This is the starting layout for your PivotTable manipulations.

There are three fields (Month, Week, and Day) in the Row area, and there is one field (Hour) in the Column area. You could pivot the PivotTable to create a single column of results by pivoting the Hour field to the fourth position in the Row area. The following procedure does just that, generating the results shown in Figure 16-9:

```
Sub PivotHourTo4()
On Error Goto NotEnough
    With ActiveSheet.PivotTables("PivotTable8").PivotFields("Hour")
        .Orientation = xlRowField
        .Position = 4
    End With
NotEnough: MsgBox ("There are fewer than three fields in the Row area.")
End Sub
```

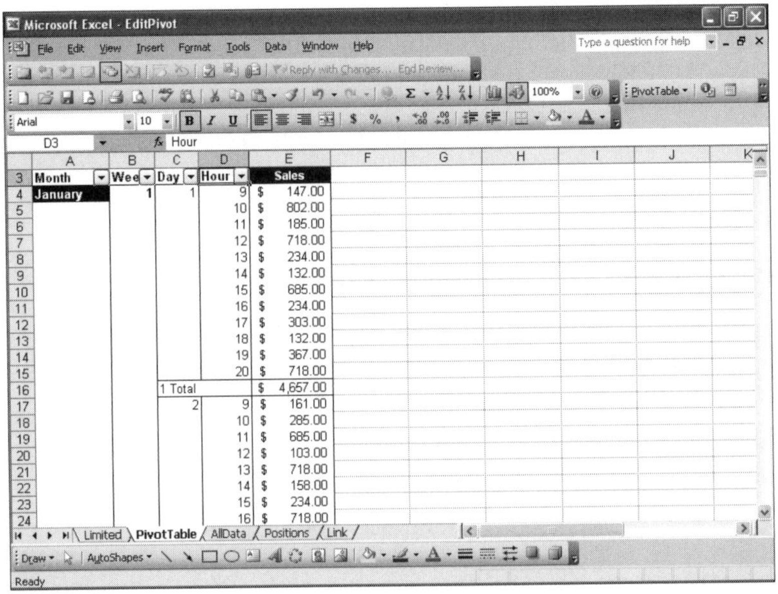

Figure 16-9. Putting the Hour field in the fourth position in the Row area generates this result.

Inside Out

An Interesting Occurrence

For this macro to work correctly, there must be three fields in the Row area. The order of the fields matters in that it affects data presentation, but the order doesn't matter when it comes to the procedure functioning properly. The presence or absence of the *On Error* statement, however, makes an interesting difference in how Excel handles the result of the instruction to place the Hour field at the fourth position in the Row area. If you leave out the *On Error* statement and there are fewer than three fields in the Row area, Excel won't be able to find the fourth position in the Row area, and you'll get this error: "Run-time error '1004': Unable to set the *Position* property of the *PivotField* class." However, if you include the *On Error* statement, which directs the program to jump to the line with the *NotEnough:* label if an error occurs, Excel will interpret the instruction to move the Hour field to the fourth position in the Row area as an instruction to move the Hour field to the last position in the Row area. Maybe this is a reward for good programming behavior.

Resetting a PivotTable to Its Original Position

After you've manipulated a PivotTable for a while during a presentation, it's very easy to forget the original arrangement of fields in the PivotTable. If you want to reset a PivotTable to its original condition, all you need to do is re-order the fields. Doing it by hand might be problematic when you're trying to concentrate on your message, so it makes sense to write a macro that re-creates the original layout. The next procedure sets the PivotTable in Edit-Pivot.xls to the layout shown in Figure 16-8.

```
Sub ResetPivotTable()

With ActiveSheet.PivotTables("PivotTable8").PivotFields("Month")
    .Orientation = xlRowField
    .Position = 1
End With

With ActiveSheet.PivotTables("PivotTable8").PivotFields("Week")
    .Orientation = xlRowField
    .Position = 2
End With

With ActiveSheet.PivotTables("PivotTable8").PivotFields("Day")
    .Orientation = xlRowField
    .Position = 3
End With

With ActiveSheet.PivotTables("PivotTable8").PivotFields("Hour")
    .Orientation = xlColumnField
    .Position = 1
End With

End Sub
```

Note Notice that the code moves the fields into position in order, so that the field in the Row area's position 1 goes in before the field in position 2.

Recording and Restoring Arbitrary PivotTable Positions

Specifying the exact location of each field in a PivotTable is great if you know the desired layout of your PivotTable, but how do you remember when you're playing around with a PivotTable and you happen upon an arrangement you love? The old way to remember the layout was to write down the order, keep the paper handy, and reconstruct the PivotTable by hand. The new way is to use the *RecordPosition* macro to write the field order to a group of cells in the active worksheet. Again, the macro is specific to the PivotTable on the EditPivot.xls workbook's PivotTable worksheet.

Chapter 16

> **Note** You need to make sure the active cell is in a location where there will be room to paste the position data this macro creates. To that end, it's a good idea to create a new worksheet, perhaps named *RecordedPositions*, to save these layouts.

```
Sub RecordPosition()

Dim pvtMyField As PivotField
Dim i As Integer

i = 1

ActiveCell.Value = "Field Name"
ActiveCell.Offset(0, 1).Value = "Orientation"
ActiveCell.Offset(0, 2).Value = "Position"

With Worksheets("PivotTable").PivotTables("PivotTable8")
    For Each pvtMyField In .PivotFields

        ActiveCell.Offset(i, 0) = pvtMyField.Name
        ActiveCell.Offset(i, 1) = pvtMyField.Orientation
        ActiveCell.Offset(i, 2) = pvtMyField.Position

        i = i + 1
    Next
End With

End Sub
```

Figure 16-10 shows the results of running the *RecordPosition* macro against the default arrangement of the PivotTable in EditPivot.xls.

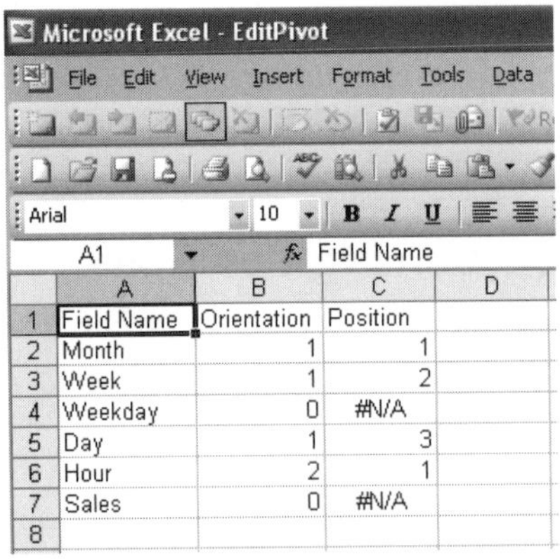

Figure 16-10. Excel records your PivotTable position for future use.

It's important to realize that the values assigned to the *Position* property are represented internally as numbers, not the Excel constants in the *XlPivotFieldOrientation* group. Table 16-7 lists the *XlPivotFieldOrientation* constants and their corresponding numerical values.

Table 16-7. Numerical Values of *XlPivotFieldOrientation* Constants

Constant	Numerical Value
xlColumnField	2
xlDataField	0
xlHidden	0
xlPageField	3
xlRowField	1

Caution   When you write the values representing a PivotTable's layout to a worksheet, you'll need to be sure there's a blank row below the last entry to ensure the restore macro will run correctly.

Now comes the moment of truth. You've recorded the PivotTable layout using the *RecordPosition* procedure, but it's time to see if you can use that data to re-create the layout you recorded. To test the restoration procedure, change the layout of the PivotTable on the PivotTable worksheet of EditPivot.xls and run the *ResetFromRecorded* macro.

Important   For this macro to run correctly, the active cell needs to be on the worksheet that contains the recorded position data. This macro also assumes you're using the PivotTable in the EditPivot.xls workbook. If you want to use it on another PivotTable, you'll need to change the *With* statement so it reflects the worksheet name (PivotTable in the example) and identifier of the PivotTable (PivotTable8 in the example).

```
Sub ResetFromRecorded()

Dim myRange As Range
On Error Resume Next

Set myRange = Application.InputBox(Prompt:="Please click the cell _
that contains the Field Name column heading.", Type:=8)
myRange.Select

Do While ActiveCell.Offset(1, 0).Value <> ""
    ActiveCell.Offset(1, 0).Select
        With Worksheets("PivotTable").PivotTables("PivotTable8") _
    .PivotFields(ActiveCell.Value)
            .Orientation = ActiveCell.Offset(0, 1).Value
            .Position = ActiveCell.Offset(0, 2).Value

        End With

Loop

End Sub
```

This procedure starts with the cell that contains the Field Name label, verifies that the next cell in the field name column isn't blank, and then moves through the *Do...While* loop, assigning fields to the listed orientation and position, until it finds a blank cell in the list of field names.

> **Tip** **Make Each One Special**
>
> You should make a version of the *ResetFromRecorded* procedure for each stored position you want to use. In doing so, you would be able to specify the starting cell in the macro code and attach the macro to a menu item, toolbar button, or other object so that the macro can be run with a single click.

In this chapter, you've explored PivotTables and PivotCharts, learning how to create them programmatically and through the Excel user interface. After the discussion of how to create PivotTables, you learned some valuable techniques for manipulating them programmatically. The procedures at the end of the chapter are valuable tools for anyone who wants to use data to tell a story, instead of fumbling for words while trying to find a particular PivotTable layout.

Chapter 17

Command Bars

Identifying Parts of the Menu System . 365   Command Bar Controls 371

The ability to manipulate menus in Microsoft Excel is very important when creating custom add-ins. By trapping the appropriate events in an add-in, the add-in can automatically add the appropriate menu items, making the add-in appear to be a standard part of Excel. In this chapter, you'll learn about the various objects associated with menus and toolbars and how to add new menu items, modify existing menu items, and undo the changes your application made, to restore Excel to its unmodified state.

Identifying Parts of the Menu System

Microsoft has developed a very flexible object model that combines menus, command buttons, combo boxes, and pop-up menus into a single extendable system. (See Figure 17-1.) This system separates the visual presentation of the choices to the user from the underlying hierarchical structure menus and buttons, which simplifies the development process.

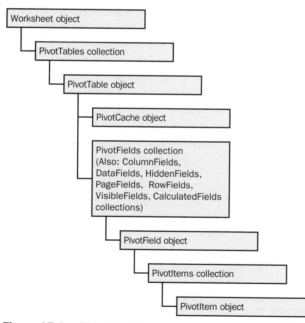

Figure 17-1. The *CommandBar* set of objects gives VBA programmers a lot of flexibility to integrate their applications into Excel.

CommandBars **Collection**

The *CommandBars* collection contains all the command bars defined in Excel. For the most part, the *CommandBars* collection is just a normal collection with properties and methods such as *Item*, *Count*, and *Add*. However, it also has some properties that determine how the command bars operate, including enabling or disabling features such as adaptive menus, menu customization, and menu animation.

Table 17-1 contains a list of the key properties and methods of the *CommandBars* collection.

Table 17-1. Key Properties and Methods of the *CommandBars* Collection

Property/Method	Description
AdaptiveMenus	Property: when *True*, means that adaptive menus will be used in Excel.
Add(Name, Position, MenuBar, Temporary)	Method: creates a new command bar object and adds it to *CommandBars*. *Name* is the name of the new command bar, *Position* specifies where the command bar is located, *MenuBar*, when *True*, means that the command bar replaces the currently active menu bar. *Temporary*, when *True*, means that the command bar will be automatically deleted when Excel ends.
Count	Property (read-only): returns the number of *CommandBars* in the collection.
DisableCustomize	Property: when *True*, means that command bars may not be customized by the user.
FindControl(Type, Id, Tag, Visible, Recursive)	Method: returns an object reference to the *CommandBarControl* object that matches the specified criteria. *Type* specifies the type of control using the *MsoControlType* enumeration. *Id* specifies the name of the control. *Tag* searches for matches using the control's *Tag* property. *Visible*, when *True*, limits the search to only those controls that are visible; *Recursive*, when *True*, searches through the current *CommandBar* object and all of its pop-up subtoolbars.
Item(Index)	Property: returns the command bar object specified by *Index*.
LargeButtons	Property: when *True*, means that toolbar buttons will be displayed larger than normal.
MenuAnimationStyle	Property: specifies how the command bar is animated. Can specify one of the following: *msoMenuAnimationNone*, *msnMenuAnimationRandom*, *msoMenuAnimationSlide*, or *msoMenuAnimationUnfold*.

The *Add* method creates an empty command bar object with the specified properties, and the *FindControl* method searches through all the command bars looking for a control with the specified criteria.

CommandBar Objects

CommandBar objects represent containers in which the individual menu items or icons can be placed. A *CommandBar* object is referenced through the *CommandBars* collection. This collection exists for the *Application* object, as well as other *CommandBarControls* that can contain other controls, such as a menu control having a submenu. Table 17-2 lists the key properties and methods for the *CommandBar* object.

Table 17-2. Key Properties and Methods of the *CommandBar* Object

Property/Method	Description
AdaptiveMenus	Property: when *True*, means that adaptive menus will be used with this command bar.
BuiltIn	Property (read-only): returns *True* if the command bar is a part of Excel.
Controls	Property (read-only): returns an object reference to a *CommandBarControls* collection containing all the controls on the command bar.
Delete	Method: removes this command bar from the *CommandBars* collection.
Enabled	Property: when *True*, means that the *CommandBar* object will be displayed in the list of available command bars.
FindControl(Type, Id, Tag, Visible, Recursive)	Method: returns an object reference to the *CommandBarControl* object that matches the specified criteria. *Type* specifies the type of control using the *MsoControlType* enumeration. (See Table 17-4 for a complete list of the enumeration.) *Id* specifies the name of the control. *Tag* searches for matches using the control's *Tag* property. *Visible*, when *True*, limits the search to only those controls that are visible. *Recursive*, when *True*, searches through the current *CommandBar* object and all of its pop-up sub-toolbars.
Height	Property: contains the height of the command bar in pixels.
Index	Property (read-only): returns the relative position of the command bar in the *CommandBars* collection.

continued

Table 17-2. Key Properties and Methods of the *CommandBar* Object *(continued)*

Property/Method	Description
Left	Property: contains the distance between the left edge of the screen and the command bar in pixels.
Name	Property: name of the command bar.
Position	Property: contains the position of the command bar. Can be any of these values: *msoBarBottom*, *msoBarFloating*, *msoBarLeft*, *msoBarMenuBar*, *msoBarPopup*, *msoBarRight*, or *msoBarTop*.
RowIndex	Property: contains the relative position of a command bar in a docking area.
ShowPopup(x, y)	Method: displays a *CommandBar* as a shortcut menu at the specified location. If *x* and *y* are omitted, the current x and y coordinates from the pointer are used.
Top	Property: contains the distance between the top edge of the *CommandBar* and the top edge of the screen.
Type	Property (read-only): indicates the command bar's type. *msoBarTypeMenuBar* means that the command bar contains menu buttons; *msoBarTypeNormal* means that the command bar displays icons; *msoBarTypePopup* means that the command bar is a shortcut menu.
Visible	Property: *True* when the command bar is displayed on the screen. Remember that the *Enabled* property must be *True* before you can set this property to *True*.
Width	Property: contains the width of the command bar in pixels.

Each *CommandBar* object represents a collection of menu items and toolbar icons that can be displayed on screen. The exact type is identified by the *Type* property. The *Controls* collection contains the set of command bar control objects that are present in the command bar.

The *Enabled* and *Visible* properties determine if the command bar is seen by the user and available for use. Right-clicking while the mouse pointer is hovering over any toolbar will list all the command bars that can be displayed. To be included on this list, the command bar must be enabled. If the *Visible* property is *True*, the command bar name will be preceded by a check mark on the shortcut menu, indicating that it is visible, too.

You can determine if the command bar was originally included in Excel by checking to see if the *BuiltIn* property is set to *True*.

The *FindControl* method locates a specific control based on the some of the control's property values. This can be extremely useful if the user has moved the control from its original location onto a different *CommandBar* object.

Listing *CommandBar* Objects

Excel maintains a large collection of built-in command bars, which you can list using the following routine. (See Figure 17-2.) This routine begins by making the *ListCommandBars* sheet active and then it uses a *For Each* loop to scan through the *CommandBars* collection. (You can change this to "Sheet3" or any other existing sheet name you specify.) Using the *CommandBar* object from the *For Each* statement, the *Index*, *Enabled*, *Visible*, *Type*, and *Name* properties are copied to the worksheet beginning in row 4.

```
Sub ListCommandBars()
Dim c As CommandBar
Dim i As Long

Sheets.Item("ListCommandBars").Activate

i = 3
For Each c In Application.CommandBars
    i = i + 1
    ActiveSheet.Cells(i, 1) = c.Index
    ActiveSheet.Cells(i, 2) = c.Enabled
    ActiveSheet.Cells(i, 3) = c.Visible
    ActiveSheet.Cells(i, 4) = c.Type
    ActiveSheet.Cells(i, 5) = c.Name

Next c
End Sub
```

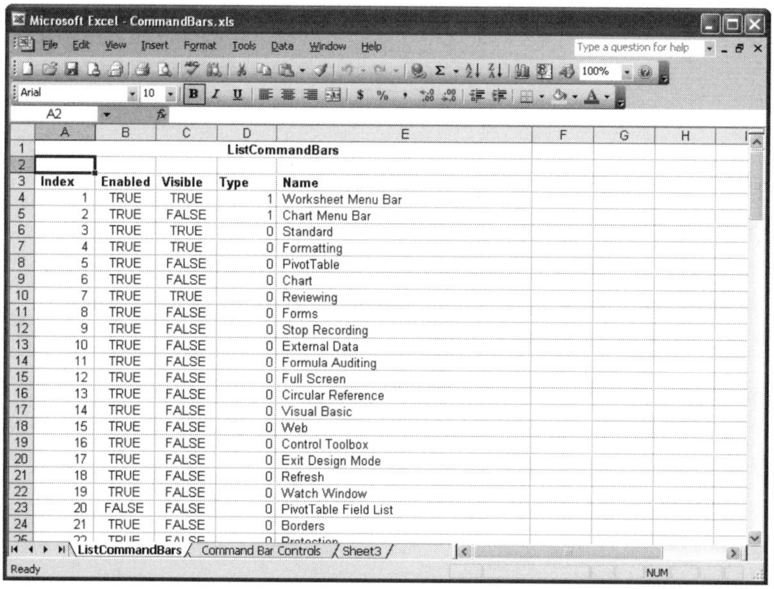

Index	Enabled	Visible	Type	Name
1	TRUE	TRUE	1	Worksheet Menu Bar
2	TRUE	FALSE	1	Chart Menu Bar
3	TRUE	TRUE	0	Standard
4	TRUE	TRUE	0	Formatting
5	TRUE	FALSE	0	PivotTable
6	TRUE	FALSE	0	Chart
7	TRUE	TRUE	0	Reviewing
8	TRUE	FALSE	0	Forms
9	TRUE	FALSE	0	Stop Recording
10	TRUE	FALSE	0	External Data
11	TRUE	FALSE	0	Formula Auditing
12	TRUE	FALSE	0	Full Screen
13	TRUE	FALSE	0	Circular Reference
14	TRUE	FALSE	0	Visual Basic
15	TRUE	FALSE	0	Web
16	TRUE	FALSE	0	Control Toolbox
17	TRUE	FALSE	0	Exit Design Mode
18	TRUE	FALSE	0	Refresh
19	TRUE	FALSE	0	Watch Window
20	FALSE	FALSE	0	PivotTable Field List
21	TRUE	FALSE	0	Borders

Figure 17-2. The *Index*, *Enabled*, *Visible*, *Type*, and *Name* properties for each *CommandBar* object are copied to an Excel worksheet.

Adding a Floating Command Bar

You can add a floating command bar (shown in Figure 17-3) to Excel with the following routine. Notice that the *Add* method uses the name *Excel2k3 VBA*, which has embedded spaces. The *msoBarFloating* value specifies that the bar should not be docked with the other command bars, but instead should be displayed in a separate window that can be moved around by the user.

```
Sub FloatingCommandBar()
Dim c As CommandBar

Set c = Application.CommandBars.Add("Excel2k3 VBA", _
    msoBarFloating, False, True)
c.Enabled = True
c.Visible = True
End Sub
```

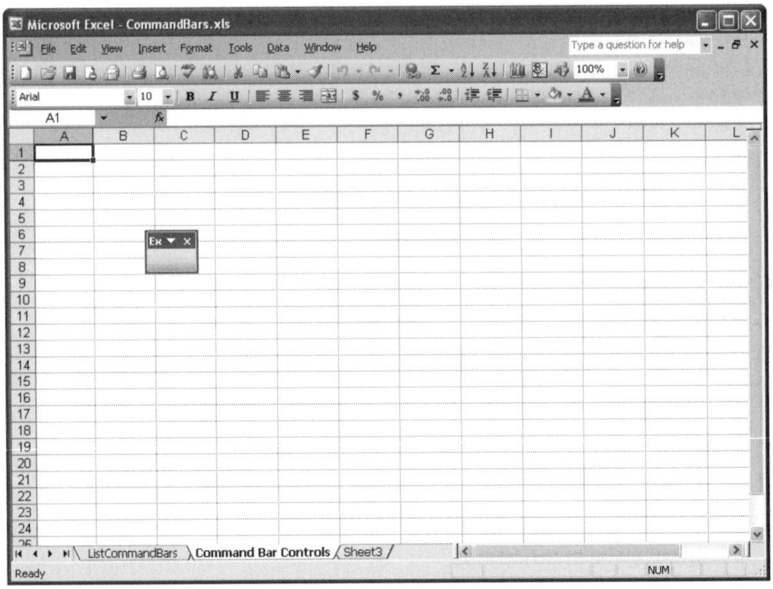

Figure 17-3. A floating command bar is not docked with the other command bars.

Setting the third parameter of the *Add* method to *False* means that the command bar will simply be added to the collection. A value of *True* means that this bar will replace the standard menu bar in the Excel application.

The final parameter in the *Add* method is set to *True*, indicating that this command bar is temporary and will automatically be deleted when the user exits Excel.

By default, the command bar is neither enabled nor visible, so to display the command bar it's necessary to *Enable* it and then make it *Visible*. It must be done in this order because the bar must be enabled before you can set *Visible* to *True*.

> **Note**   You can also specify that the command bar is a pop-up menu by specifying *msoBarPopup* as the second parameter to the *Add* method.

Deleting a Command Bar

Deleting a command bar is merely a matter of locating the command bar by name and calling the *Delete* method like this:

```
Sub DeleteBar()
Application.CommandBars("Excel2k3 VBA").Delete
End Sub
```

> **Tip**   Clean Up Before You Leave
> When building an add-in that includes its own command bars, you should ensure that the command bars are deleted when the add-in is removed. As a general precaution, you might want to specify that the command bar is temporary so that it is removed when Excel ends. However, if you do this, you will need to verify that the command bar doesn't exist when the add-in starts and then explicitly add the command bar if it's missing.

Command Bar Controls

You can add a wide range of command bar controls to a command bar. All these controls have a common set of properties and methods, which are found in the *CommandBarControl* object. In addition to the *CommandBarControl* object, there are three other types of control objects: *CommandBarButton*, *CommandBarComboBox*, and *CommandBarPopup*.

CommandBarControls Collection

The *CommandBarControls* collection contains the set of command bar controls displayed in a command bar. Unlike the *CommandBars* collection, which had a number of special properties that governed how command bars work in Excel, *CommandBarControls* is a relatively simple collection object. (See Table 17-3.)

Chapter 17

Table 17-3. Key Properties and Methods of the *CommandBarControls* Collection

Property/Method	Description
Add(Type, Id, Parameter, Before, Temporary)	Method: creates a new command bar object and adds it to the *CommandBarControls* collection. *Type* specifies the general type of control that should be added. It can be one of the following: *msoControlButton*, *msoControlEdit*, *msoControlDropDown*, *msoControlComboBox*, or *msoControlPopup*; *Id* is an integer value that specifies a built-in control. A value of 1 or omitting this parameter will add a custom control; *Parameter* contains programmer-defined information that can be used by the control's *OnAction* routine to determine how to process this instance of the control; and *Before* contains the position of the new control in the collection. If omitted, the control will be added at the end of the collection; *Temporary*, when *True*, means that the control will be automatically deleted when Excel ends.
Count	Property (read-only): returns the number of *CommandBars* in the collection.
Item(Index)	Property: returns the command bar object specified by *Index*.

Although there are many different types of controls (listed in Table 17-4), they can be loosely grouped into four major categories: Normal, Button, Combo Box, and Pop-up. Normal controls have all the properties and methods associated with the *CommandBarControl* object, whereas Buttons, Combo Boxes, and Pop-ups have additional properties and methods.

Table 17-4. Command Bar Control Types

Constant	Description
msoControlActiveX	Normal
msoControlAutoCompleteCombo	Normal
msoControlButton	Contains a single menu item, an icon button, a menu item with an icon, or an icon with text below the image
msoControlButtonDropdown	Combo Box
msoControlButtonPopup	Pop-up
msoControlComboBox	Combo Box
msoControlCustom	Button
msoControlDropdown	Combo Box
msoControlEdit	Combo Box
msoControlExpandingGrid	Normal
msoControlGauge	Normal

Table 17-4. Command Bar Control Types

Constant	Description
msoControlGenericDropdown	Normal
msoControlGraphicCombo	Combo Box
msoControlGraphicDropdown	Combo Box
msoControlGraphicPopup	Pop-up
msoControlGrid	Normal
msoControlLabel	Normal
msoControlLabelEx	Normal
msoControlOCXDropdown	Combo Box
msoControlPane	Normal
msoControlPopup	Pop-up
msoControlSpinner	Normal
msoControlSplitButtonMRUPopup	Pop-up
msoControlSplitButtonPopup	Pop-up
msoControlSplitDropdown	Combo Box
msoControlSplitExpandingGrid	Normal
msoControlWorkPane	Normal

CommandBarControl Object

CommandBarControl objects represent the individual choices that a user can make. These choices take the form of command buttons, drop-down lists, combo boxes, and many other items. Table 17-5 lists the key properties and methods for the *CommandBarControl* object.

Table 17-5. Key Properties and Methods of the *CommandBarControl* Object

Property/Method	Description
BeginGroup	Property: when *True*, means this control marks the beginning of a group of controls on a control bar.
BuiltIn	Property (read-only): returns *True* if the command bar is a part of Excel.
Caption	Property: contains the text associated with a command bar control.
Copy (Bar, Before)	Method: creates a copy of the current command bar control to the specified command bar before the specified control. If *Bar* is not specified, the current bar is assumed. If *Before* is not specified, the copy will be placed at the end of the command bar.

continued

Table 17-5. Key Properties and Methods of the *CommandBarControl* Object *(continued)*

Property/Method	Description
Delete(temporary)	Method: removes this command bar from the *CommandBarControls* collection associated with a command bar. *Temporary*, when *True*, means that the control will be automatically deleted when Excel ends.
Enabled	Property: when *False*, means that the control is disabled.
Execute	Method: runs the procedure specified in the *OnAction* property.
Height	Property: contains the height of the command bar control in pixels.
HelpContextId	Property: contains the help context ID number associated with the command bar control. Remember that the *HelpFile* property must also be specified for the help subsystem to work properly.
HelpFile	Property: contains the name of the help file associated with the command bar control.
Id	Property: determines the built-in action for a control. Remember that *Id* is set to 1 for all custom controls.
Index	Property (read-only): returns the relative position of the command bar control in the *CommandBarControls* collection.
Left	Property (read-only): returns the distance between the left side of the docking area and the command bar control.
Move (Bar, Before)	Method: moves the current command bar control to the specified command bar before the specified control. If *Bar* is not specified, the current bar is assumed. If *Before* is not specified, the copy will be placed at the end of the command bar.
OnAction	Property: contains the name of a subroutine that will be run when the user invokes the command bar control. You may also specify a COM add-in by creating a string using the following syntax: "!<***add-in-name***>", where *add-in-name* is the name of the COM add-in that should be used.
Parameter	Property: contains extra information that can be used by the code associated with the control to modify the default behavior of the control.
Priority	Property: specifies the relative priority of a command bar control so that if there isn't space available in the docking area to fit all the controls, controls with a value of 1 can't be dropped. Valid values range from 0 to 7.

**Table 17-5. Key Properties and Methods of the *CommandBarControl*
Object** *(continued)*

Property/Method	Description
Tag	Property: contains programmer-defined information. This property can be used with the *CommandBar.FindControl* method to help locate a particular control.
TooltipText	Property: contains text that will be displayed if the user hovers the mouse pointer over the control. By default, the value from the *Caption* property will be displayed.
Top	Property: contains the distance between the top edge of the command bar control and the top edge of the screen.
Type	Property (read-only): indicates type of the command bar control.
Visible	Property: *True* when the *CommandBarControl* is displayed on the screen. Remember that the *Enabled* property must be *True* before you can set this property to *True*.
Width	Property: contains the width of the command bar control in pixels.

When the user clicks or selects a command bar control, the subroutine specified in the *OnAction* property is fired. You also have the option to execute the routine associated with the command bar control by using the *Execute* method.

The *Parameter* and *Tag* properties are simply areas in which you can store additional information about the specific instance of the control. The *Tag* property can be useful if you want to locate a specific control based on its *Tag* value with the *FindControl* method. You could create a common *OnAction* routine that performs various actions based on the specific value in the *Parameter* property for each control.

The *Copy* and *Move* methods allow you to relocate controls from one command bar to another, and the *Delete* method will remove the control from the command bar and the application.

Button Controls

There is only one specific type of button control, which is *msoControlButton*. This object is useful in situations where you wish to execute a subroutine in response to the user pressing a button or selecting a menu item. Table 17-6 lists the unique properties and methods for the *CommandBarButton* object when compared with the base *CommandBarControl* object.

Table 17-6. **Unique Properties and Methods of the *CommandBarButton* Object**

Property/Method	Description
BuiltInFace	Property: *True* if the face of a command bar button is the original face for the button. Setting this value to *True* will restore the built-in face.
CopyFace	Method: copies the current face to the clipboard.
FaceId	Property: contains the *Id* value for a particular face that will be displayed on the button. A *FaceId* value of zero means that the command bar button has a custom face.
PasteFace	Method: pastes the face from the clipboard to the command bar button.
ShortcutText	Property: contains text displayed to the caption that represents a shortcut. Remember that this property works only for command bar buttons that have a valid *OnAction* macro.
State	Property: indicates the visual state of the button. Can be one of the following values: *msoButtonDown*, *msoButtonMixed*, or *msoButtonUp*.
Style	Property: contains the way the button is displayed. *msoButtonAutomatic* chooses the appropriate style based on the values set in the properties; *msoButtonCaption* displays the caption as text on the button; *msoButtonIcon* displays the icon identified by *FaceId* on the button; *msoButtonIconAndCaption* displays the caption to the right of the icon; *msoButtonIcon-AndCaptionBelow* displays the caption below the icon; *msoButtonIconAndWrapCaption* displays the complete caption to the right of the button even if it has to wrap the text to fit; *msoButtonIconAndWrapCaptionBelow* displays the text below the icon, wrapping as needed; and *msoButtonWrapCaption* displays the complete text from the caption, wrapping the text as necessary.

The *Style* property dictates the way the control will be drawn on the screen. Basically, you can choose to display the text from the *Caption* property or the icon specified by the *FaceId* property or both. If you choose both, you can position the caption to the right of the icon or below the icon.

You can choose to display a custom button in any of three different states (up, down, and mixed) using the *State* property. This is useful if you want to use the button to indicate the status of your code in the same way as the Bold button works. Although the up and down states are self-explanatory, the *mixed state* is not. This state is useful to reflect a situation where the button should be both up and down, which might occur when you select a range of cells that includes text that is both normal and bold.

Creating Toolbars

A toolbar is a collection of buttons arranged horizontally. You can mix and match various types of buttons together in a single toolbar. (See Figure 17-4.)

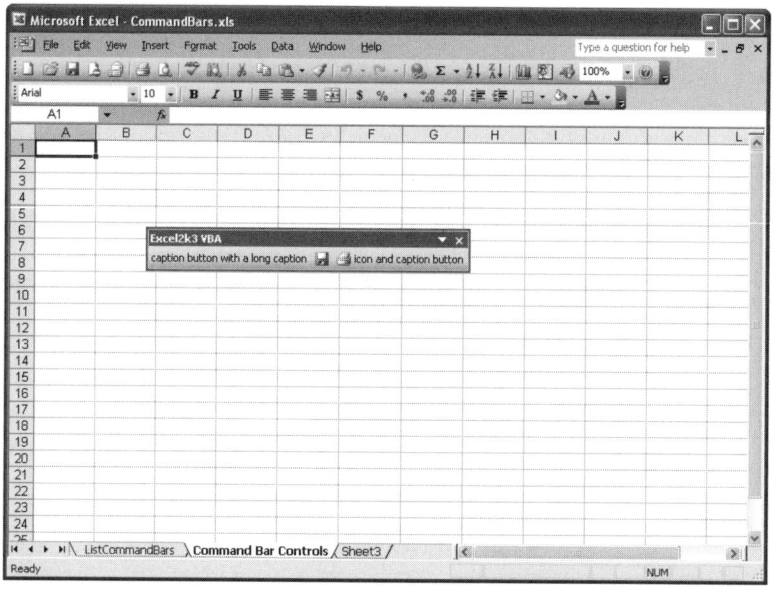

Figure 17-4. You can combine multiple types of buttons into a single command bar to create a toolbar.

The following routine was used to create the toolbar shown in Figure 17-4. The code begins by locating the command bar that will hold the controls by using the *CommandBars* collection and specifying the desired name. Then the routine uses the *Add* method of the *Controls* collection to create a new button. The button's *Style* property is set the proper style for the button, while the *Caption* property contains text that might or might not be displayed depending on the type of button.

```
Sub CreateBar()
Dim c As CommandBar
Dim cb As CommandBarButton

Set c = Application.CommandBars("Excel2k3 VBA")

Set cb = c.Controls.Add(msoControlButton, 2)
cb.Style = msoButtonCaption
cb.Caption = "caption button with a long caption"

Set cb = c.Controls.Add(msoControlButton, 3)
cb.Style = msoButtonIcon
cb.Caption = "icon button"
```

```
Set cb = c.Controls.Add(msoControlButton, 4)
cb.Style = msoButtonIconAndCaption
cb.Caption = "icon and caption button"
End Sub
```

Combo Box Controls

There are a number of different variations of the combo box control that you can choose from. (See Table 17-4.) All these variations have one thing in common: the user is allowed to choose from a list of items. All but one of the extra properties and methods are devoted to managing the list of items. (See Table 17-7.)

Table 17-7. Unique Properties and Methods of the *CommandBarComboBox* Object

Property/Method	Description
AddItem(Text, Index)	Method: adds the value contained in *Text* to the list at the specified *Index* position. If *Index* is omitted, the item is added to the end of the list.
Clear	Method: removes all the list items from the list associated with the combo box.
DropDownLines	Property: contains the number of lines displayed in a drop-down list box or a combo box.
List(Index)	Property: returns a string value representing the item in the list position specified by *Index*. Remember that the first item in the list has an *Index* value of 1.
ListCount	Property (read-only): returns the number of items in the list.
ListHeaderCount	Property: contains the number of list items that appear above the separator line.
ListIndex	Property: contains the item number of the currently selected item in the list portion of the combo box control. A value of zero means that nothing is selected.
RemoveItem(Index)	Method: removes the item from the list at the position specified by *Index*.
Style	Property: specifies the appearance of the control. Can be either *msoComboLabel* or *msoComboNormal*.

The list of items that appears in a combo box is essentially a string array. You can retrieve or change an element though the *List* property by specifying the item's relative location in the list. The *ListIndex* property points to the currently selected item in the list, whereas the *ListCount* contains the total number of items in the list.

Chapter 17

Items are added to the list using the *Add* method. You can optionally specify the relative position of the item to be added. All items, starting with the item at the specified location, will be moved one position toward the end of the list. Items are removed from the list by using the *RemoveItem* method and specifying the relative position of the item to be removed. All subsequent items will be moved one position closer to the start of the list.

Using a Combo Box

Combo boxes and drop-down lists are great ways to allow a user to quickly select from a list of values. The following routine creates a new drop-down list control with three items. The *Parameter* property is used to identify this particular control, and the *OnAction* property specifies a macro that will be processed when a value from the drop-down list is selected.

```
Sub AddCommandCombo()

Dim c As CommandBar
Dim cb As CommandBarComboBox

Set c = Application.CommandBars("Excel2k3 VBA")

Set cb = c.Controls.Add(msoControlDropdown)
cb.Style = msoComboNormal
cb.AddItem "Item 1"
cb.AddItem "Item 2"
cb.AddItem "Item 3"
cb.Parameter = "Dropdown Box #1"
cb.OnAction = "ThisWorkbook.TestControl"

End Sub
```

The *OnAction* routine shown here is called whenever the user selects an item from the drop-down list. The *With* statement is used to simplify the reference to the active control that triggered the macro, which is referred to by the *CommandBars.ActionControl* property. Remember that you have to run both the *AddFloatingCommandBar* routine and the *AddCommandCombo* routines in order to test the *OnAction* event.

```
Public Sub TestControl()

With Application.CommandBars.ActionControl
    If .Parameter = "Dropdown Box #1" Then
        MsgBox .List(.ListIndex)

    End If

End With

End Sub
```

Inside the routine, the *Parameter* property associated with the control is examined to see if it was the drop-down list that was created earlier. If it was, the index of currently selected item is used to extract the appropriate item from the list.

Pop-Up Controls

Pop-up controls are used to display hierarchical information, such as a drop-down menu or list of icons. Unlike the other types of command bar controls in Excel, pop-up controls include two unique properties. (See Table 17-8.)

Table 17-8. Unique Properties of the *CommandBarPopup* Object

Property/Method	Description
CommandBar	Property (read-only): returns an object reference to a *CommandBar* object representing the menu for the pop-up.
Controls	Property (read-only): returns an object reference to a *CommandBarControls* object containing the command bar controls for a pop-up menu.

Displaying a Pop-Up

Displaying pop-up menus is a useful task for many VBA programs. The following routine shows how to create and display a pop-up menu. This routine begins by disabling error trapping by using the *On Error Resume Next* statement. Then the routine tries to get an object reference to the *Excel2k2 VBA Popup* command bar. If the command bar object doesn't exist, the variable *c* will be set to *Nothing*. Without the *On Error* statement, any attempt to reference a nonexistent command bar would trigger a run-time error.

```
Sub ShowCommandPopup()

Dim c As CommandBar
Dim cb As CommandBarButton
Dim cp As CommandBarPopup

On Error Resume Next
Set c = Application.CommandBars("Excel2k3 VBA Popup")
If c Is Nothing Then
    Set c = Application.CommandBars.Add("Excel2k3 VBA Popup", _
        msoBarPopup, False, True)
    c.Enabled = True
    c.Visible = True

    Set cb = c.Controls.Add(msoControlButton)
    cb.Style = msoButtonIconAndCaption
    cb.Caption = "Menu button #1"
    cb.Parameter = "Menu #1"
    cb.OnAction = "ThisWorkbook.TestPopup"
```

```
Set cb = c.Controls.Add(msoControlButton)
cb.Style = msoButtonIconAndCaption
cb.Caption = "Menu button #2"
cb.Parameter = "Menu #2"
cb.OnAction = "ThisWorkbook.TestPopup"

Set cp = c.Controls.Add(msoControlPopup)
cp.Parameter = "Popup #1"
cp.Caption = "Submenu choices"

Set cb = cp.Controls.Add(msoControlButton)
cb.Style = msoButtonIconAndCaption
cb.Caption = "Submenu button #1"
cb.Parameter = "Sub menu #1"
cb.OnAction = "ThisWorkbook.TestPopup"

Set cb = cp.Controls.Add(msoControlButton)
cb.Style = msoButtonIconAndCaption
cb.Caption = "Submenu button #2"
cb.Parameter = "Submenu #2"
cb.OnAction = "ThisWorkbook.TestPopup"

End If

c.ShowPopup

End Sub
```

To create the pop-up menu, a new command bar object of type *msoBarPopup* must be created. Then the individual controls can be added to the pop-up menu.

Simply adding *msoControlButton* objects creates the traditional list of menu items. If you wish to display submenu items, you need to add an *msoControlPopup* item. This item adds an item to the menu with an arrow indicating that there are submenus available. It also acts as a container for the submenu items, which can be added using the same technique as was used for the pop-up bar.

Finally, once the command bar has been initialized, it may be shown using the *ShowPopup* method. Remember that you need to execute this method each time you want to display the pop-up menu because once the user selects an item from the menu, the menu will disappear. Typically, you display a pop-up menu in response to a user action such as running a particular macro, handling a particular condition with a larger Excel application, or in responding to a key sequence.

Adding Items to an Existing Menu

You can integrate your application into Excel's normal menu structures by adding your own menu items to the standard Excel menu items. For example, the following routine adds an About menu item for a custom VBA application:

```
Sub AddMenuItem()

Dim c As CommandBar
Dim cb As CommandBarButton
Dim cp As CommandBarPopup

On Error Resume Next
Set c = Application.CommandBars("Worksheet Menu Bar")
If Not c Is Nothing Then
    Set cp = c.Controls("&Help")

    If Not cp Is Nothing Then
        Set cb = cp.Controls.Add(msoControlButton)
        cb.Style = msoButtonCaption
        cb.Caption = "About My VBA App"
        cb.OnAction = "ThisWorkbook.TestMenu"

    End If

End If
End Sub
```

The first step is to locate the command bar where you want to add the new menu item. Because all menu items in Excel are located in the Worksheet menu bar, the easiest way to begin is to locate this command bar. Then within this command bar, an object reference to the *&Help* pop-up control is located.

Finally, using the *&Help* pop-up control's *Controls* collection, a new control button can be added to the end of the list for your application's About message. The *OnAction* property specifies the routine that will be called to display the about message.

In this chapter, you learned that command bars combine the functions of menu items and toolbars into a single unified system. You learned about the *CommandBar* object (which can represent a menu or a toolbar) and the *CommandBars* collection, which contains references to all of the *CommandBar* objects in your workbook. Then you learned how to add various command bar controls, such as pop-up menus, buttons, and combo boxes to your command bars. Finally, you learned how to define a routine that will respond to an event fired by a command bar control, giving you application an opportunity to perform the task associated with the command bar control. These facilities allow you to create macros and add-ins that appear as if they were part of Excel itself.

Customizing Dialog Boxes

Displaying Existing Dialog Boxes 384   Planning with Dialog Boxes 394
Modifying Existing Dialog Boxes 388

You don't have to invent everything on your own when you can use features that already exist. Microsoft Excel gives you access to most of the built-in dialogs within Excel and the other applications in the Microsoft Office System 2003 Edition.

It's true that your worksheet can be modified using the properties and methods supplied by Visual Basic for Applications (VBA) code. However, if you have variables that the user wants to be able to select while the macro is running, what options do you have? Your first option is to design a User Form, as discussed in Chapter 19. The User Form can have the available options listed, and the user could then select the appropriate settings. From the user's selections, you can then apply her choices to the appropriate ranges within your workbook. Sure, some of us delight in creating our own User Forms and using them whenever we can. However, typically there is training involved to have the user execute the macro to achieve the results she has requested. User Forms require you to create everything from scratch, anticipating and programming every option you want to give to your users.

Your second option is to prompt the user for variable information using built-in dialog boxes. For example, you can open the Border dialog box and apply the user's selections to the ranges you specify in your code. You can follow the same pattern with any dialog box that is presented to the user. If the options the user has selected are applied to a blank workbook, you can then extract the properties using VBA code and then apply those properties to the appropriate ranges.

In general, when user intervention is required, your best option is to provide a dialog box that users are already familiar with. You will find the training time is minimal when using built-in dialog boxes.

The example macro provided in this chapter is specific to format changes; however, it certainly works with other variable changes, too. For example, if you want to prompt the user to navigate to the folder where the workbook is saved, you can display the built-in dialog Save As, using the following code:

```
Sub ShowSaveAs()
    Application.Dialogs(xlDialogSaveAs).Show
End Sub
```

In this chapter, you will learn how to display built-in dialog boxes and manipulate them by passing arguments to them and setting the dialog box properties.

Displaying Existing Dialog Boxes

The procedures that you write in VBA can execute Excel's menu commands, and if those commands lead to a dialog box, your code can apply settings to the dialog box. You can also access Excel's built-in dialog boxes using the *Dialog* object. An interesting and very useful fact about working with dialog boxes is that you can execute your dialog box routines completely behind the scenes; the dialog box doesn't need to be in view to apply the settings.

The *Dialogs* collection represents the list of dialog boxes that are built into Excel. The *xlBuiltinDialog* constant is used to access an individual *Dialog* object in the *Dialogs* collection. Use the syntax *Dialogs(xlDialogObjectName)*, where *xlDialogObjectName* is the built-in constant identifying the dialog box you want to open. The following example displays the built-in File Open dialog box:

```
Sub ShowOpen()
    Result = Application.Dialogs(xlDialogOpen).Show
End Sub
```

The *Result* variable lets you determine if the user clicked the OK button or if the action was cancelled by pressing the Esc key or by the user clicking the Cancel button. You can then use the value assigned to the variable to specify the next action that should occur based on the user's input.

The Excel Object Library includes intrinsic constants for many of the built-in dialog boxes. Each constant is formed from the prefix *xlDialog* followed by the name of the dialog box. For example, the Data Validation dialog box constant is *xlDialogDataValidation*, and the Define Name dialog box constant is *xlDialogDefineName*. These constants are examples of the type of members found in the *xlBuiltinDialog* property.

> For more information about, and a complete list of, the available *xlDialog* constants, type **built-in dialog boxes** in the Visual Basic Editor Ask a Question box and click the Built-in Dialog Box Argument Lists help topic.

A *Dialog* object represents a single built-in Excel dialog box. Each *Dialog* object will have additional custom properties depending on what type of *Dialog* object it is. Besides the typical collection attributes, the *Dialogs* collection also has a *Count* property that returns the number of *Dialog* objects in the collection.

For example, the following VBA statement is equivalent to clicking Edit, Go To, and specifying the range A1:C3 and clicking OK. However, when you use the VBA code, the Go To dialog box does not need to appear, so the action is seamless to the user.

```
Sub GotoRange()
Application.Goto Reference:=Range("A1:C3")
End Sub
```

In some cases, however, you might want to display one of Excel's built-in dialog boxes so the user can make the choices. There are two ways to do this:

- Access the *Dialogs* collection of the *Application* object.
- Execute a menu item directly.

The *Dialogs* collection of the *Application* object represents most of Excel's built-in dialog boxes. The *Dialogs* collection has predefined constants to make it easy to specify the dialog box that you need. For example, Excel's Go To dialog box is represented by the constant *xlDialogFormulaGoto*.

Use the *Show* method to actually display the dialog box. Here is an example that displays the Go To dialog box, with the results shown in Figure 18-1.

```
Sub ShowGoto()
Application.Dialogs(xlDialogFormulaGoto).Show
End Sub
```

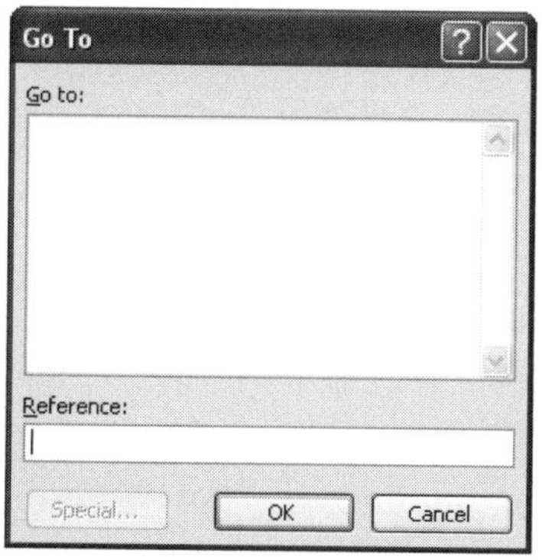

Figure 18-1. The Go To dialog box appears when called using the xlDialogFormulaGoto intrinsic constant.

When the Go To dialog box is shown, the user can specify a named range or enter a cell address to go to. The dialog box displayed using the *xlDialogFormulaGoto* constant is the same one that appears when you choose the Go To command from the Edit menu.

You can also write code that uses a variable to determine how the user dismissed the dialog box. In the following statement, the *Result* variable will be *True* if the user clicked OK, and *False* if the user clicked Cancel or pressed the Esc key.

```
Sub ShowGoto2()
Result = Application.Dialogs(xlDialogFormulaGoto).Show
End Sub
```

Contrary to what you might expect, the *Result* variable does not hold the range that was specified in the Go To dialog box. Instead, as stated, the variable holds a Boolean value that reflects how the dialog box was dismissed.

It's important to understand that built-in dialog boxes are not documented very well. The online help is very sketchy, and the files do not mention the fact that displaying one of Excel's dialog boxes using VBA code might not always work exactly the same as using a menu command to display the dialog box. Consequently, you might have to do some experimentation to make sure your code performs as it should.

In the case of the Go To dialog box, you will notice that the Special button is grayed out when the dialog is shown using a VBA statement. This button normally displays the Go To Special dialog box. To display the Go To Special dialog box using the VBA code, you need to use the intrinsic constant for that dialog box, *xlDialogSelectSpecial*. The results are shown in Figure 18-2.

```
Sub ShowGotoSpecial()
Application.Dialogs(xlDialogSelectSpecial).Show
End Sub
```

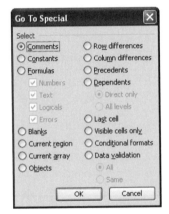

Figure 18-2. Displaying the Go To Special dialog box requires you to use the intrinsic constant for that dialog box.

Another potential problem you might encounter when you work with the built-in dialog boxes is that you are not able to display some tabbed dialog boxes as they appear when you display them using the menu system. For example, there's no way to show the Format Cells dialog box with the tabs. Rather, you can only show one tab at a time. The following statement displays the Alignment tab of the Format Cells dialog box (with the results shown in Figure 18-3).

```
Sub ShowAlignmentTab()
Application.Dialogs(xlDialogAlignment).Show
End Sub
```

To show other tabs in the Format Cells dialog box, use any of these constants: *xlDialogFormatNumber*, *xlDialogBorder*, *xlDialogCellProtection*, *xlDialogPatterns*, or *xlDialogFontProperties*. Notice that there is no consistency in the naming of these constants.

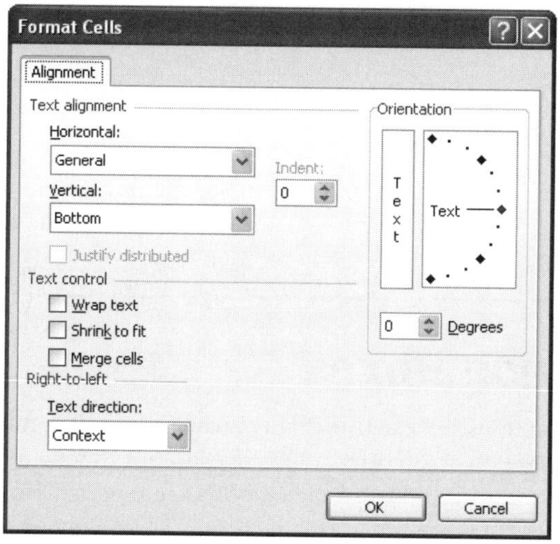

Figure 18-3. You can display the Format Cells dialog box, albeit one tab page at a time.

Inside Out

Return Variables or Execute?

When a dialog box is opened several options are available. If you execute the dialog box, the desired actions of the dialog box will occur. If you are only trying to gather information such as a filename, you should choose another method, such as *GetOpenFilename* or *GetSaveAsFilename*. Both methods display their respective dialogs but don't actually open or save the files when the user confirms the dialog box. The methods instead return the complete filename as a variable for use in later code.

The following example uses the *GetOpenFilename* and *GetSaveAsFilename* methods to return the name of the selected file:

```
Sub GetFileName()
FullFileName = Application.GetOpenFilename("Excel files (*.xl*), *.xl*", _
    1, "Custom Dialog Title", , False)
FullFileName = Application.GetSaveAsFilename("DefaultFilename.xls", _
    "Excel files (*.xl*), *.xl*, 1, "Custom Dialog Title")
End Sub
```

Once the filename has been passed to the variable, it can be used in whichever method you choose. For example, with the filename it would be simple to open the file using the *Open* method.

```
Workbooks.Open FullFileName
```

continued

You can also save the workbook with the new file name using the following line of code:

```
Workbooks.SaveAs FullFileName
```

When the users have confirmed the FileOpen dialog or the FileSaveAs dialog, they might have changed the active or current folder. Using the FileOpen and FileSaveAs dialog boxes lets the users choose the current folder and navigate the drives of their computers. This is the easiest method to let users choose the destination for their files.

Modifying Existing Dialog Boxes

There will be times when you want to use an existing dialog box; however, you might want to set the default choices within the dialog box. For example, if you want to set a default directory where a workbook will be saved, you can use a dialog box's arguments to modify the default selections, but you'll be heading into uncharted territory. The following section explains how to access the *Dialogs* collection and pass arguments to the dialog box.

Most of the built-in dialog boxes also accept arguments, which typically correspond to the controls on the dialog box. For example, the Cell Protection dialog box, which is executed by the *xlDialogCellProtection* constant, has two arguments associated with it: *locked* and *hidden*. If you want to display that dialog box with both of these options checked, you would use the following statement to set both of the arguments to *True*. The results are shown in Figure 18-4.

```
Sub ProtectionArgs()
    Application.Dialogs(xlDialogCellProtection).Show True, True
End Sub
```

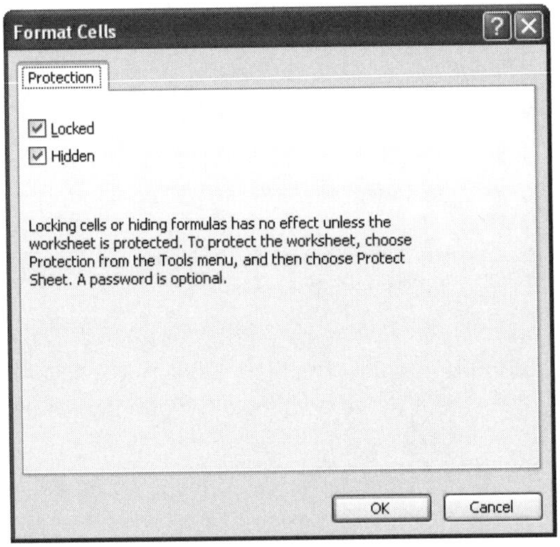

Figure 18-4. Both check boxes in the Cell Protection dialog box can be selected by default using the proper VBA code.

> **Note** The arguments for each of the built-in dialog boxes are listed in online help. To locate the help topic, search for Built-In Dialog Box Argument Lists. Unfortunately, the help topic provides no explanation of what the arguments are used for.

According to the help file, the Go To dialog box executed by the *xlDialogFormulaGoto* constant uses two arguments: *Reference* and *Corner*. The *Reference* argument provides a default range that appears in the Reference box. The *Corner* argument is a value you set to either *True* or *False* to specify whether to display the target cell so that it appears in the upper-left corner of the window. The following example uses both of these arguments:

```
Sub GotoArguments()
    Application.Dialogs(xlDialogFormulaGoto).Show Range("Z100"), True
End Sub
```

As you work through the dialog boxes, you will find that some trial and error is required to successfully use the *Dialogs* collection.

Exploring the *Dialogs* Collection

The *Dialogs* collection of the *Application* object consists of more than 250 members that represent most of Excel's built-in dialog boxes. Each *Dialog* object has a predefined constant to make it easy to specify the dialog box that you need.

To get a complete list of the dialog box constants available, use the Object Browser. Follow these steps to display the members of the *Dialogs* collection in the Object Browser.

1   Open a VBA module.

2   Press F2 to open the Object Browser.

3   Type **xlDialog** into the search text box.

4   Click the find button to execute the search.

Chapter 18

Figure 18-5 displays the result after the search.

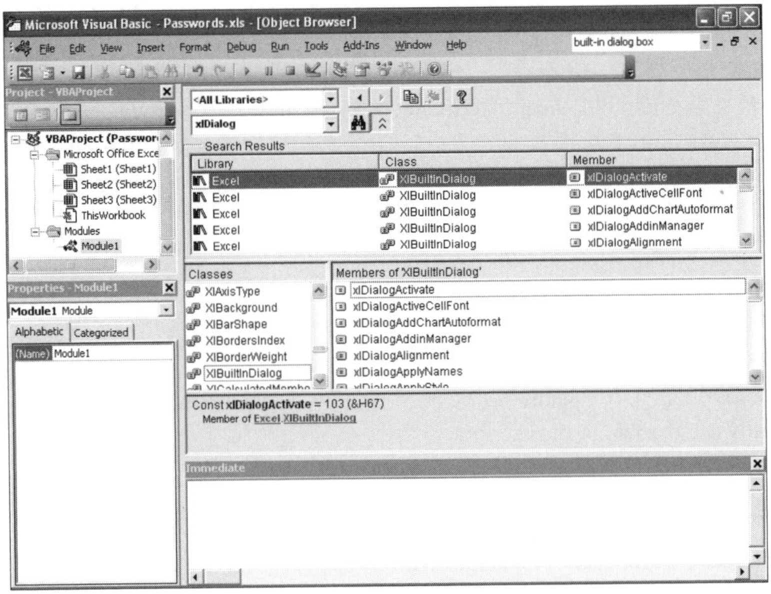

Figure 18-5. The Object Browser displays the search results for the built-in dialog boxes available in Excel.

There are more than 250 dialog boxes you can call using the *xlDialog* intrinsic constants, but some of them are more useful than others. The following three tables list dialog boxes used to format cells, modify charts, and perform other miscellaneous but useful tasks.

Tip   **Check Your Work Against the interface**
The arguments for each dialog box aren't spelled out well in the online help files or in any other available literature, but in many cases an argument will correspond to a check box, an option button, or another control that appears somewhere in the dialog box. For example, the *xlDialogFont* constant calls the Fonts dialog box. You select the Tahoma font and a size of 12 by default using the code.

Note   `Application.Dialogs(xlDialogFont).Show "Tahoma", 12.`

To display the default font, you would leave the first argument blank, as in the statement `Application.Dialogs(xlDialogFont).Show, 12.`

Table 18-1 lists some of the common dialog boxes used to format cells in the workbook.

Table 18-1. *xlDialog* **Boxes Used to Format Cells**

xlDialog Box	Description
xlDialogActiveCellFont	font, font_style, size, strikethrough, superscript, subscript, outline, shadow, underline, color, normal, background, start_char, char_count
xlDialogAlignment	horiz_align, wrap, vert_align, orientation, add_indent
xlDialogBorder	outline, left, right, top, bottom, shade, outline_color, left_color, right_color, top_color, bottom_color
xlDialogCellProtection	locked, hidden
xlDialogFont	name_text, size_num
xlDialogFontProperties	font, font_style, size, strikethrough, superscript, subscript, outline, shadow, underline, color, normal, background, start_char, char_count
xlDialogFormatFont	name_text, size_num, bold, italic, underline, strike, color, outline, shadow
xlDialogPatterns	apattern, afore, aback, newui

Table 18-2 lists some of the common dialog boxes used to insert or modify charts in a workbook.

Table 18-2. *xlDialog* **Boxes Used to Modify Charts**

xlDialog Box	Description
xlDialogAddChartAutoformat	name_text, desc_text
xlDialogAxes	x_primary, y_primary, x_secondary, y_secondary
xlDialogChartAddData	ref, rowcol, titles, categories, replace, series
xlDialogChartWizard	long, ref, gallery_num, type_num, plot_by, categories, ser_titles, legend, title, x_title, y_title, z_title, number_cats, number_titles
xlDialogDataLabel	show_option, auto_text, show_key
xlDialogDataSeries	rowcol, type_num, date_num, step_value, stop_value, trend
xlDialogEditSeries	series_num, name_ref, x_ref, y_ref, z_ref, plot_order
xlDialogFormatChart	layer_num, view, overlap, angle, gap_width, gap_depth, chart_depth, doughnut_size, axis_num, drop, hilo, up_down, series_line, labels, vary

continued

Chapter 18

Table 18-2. *xlDialog* **Boxes Used to Modify Charts**   *(continued)*

xlDialog Box	Description
xlDialogFormatCharttype	apply_to, group_num, dimension, type_num
xlDialogFormatLegend	position_num
xlDialogGallery3dBar	type_num
xlDialogGallery3dColumn	type_num
xlDialogGallery3dLine	type_num
xlDialogGallery3dPie	type_num
xlDialogGalleryDoughnut	type_num, delete_overlay
xlDialogGalleryLine	type_num, delete_overlay
xlDialogGalleryPie	type_num, delete_overlay
xlDialogMainChartType	type_num

Table 18-3 lists some of the common dialog boxes used to access a variety of options available using Excel's menu structure.

Table 18-3. *xlDialog* **Boxes Found in Excel's Menu Structure**

xlDialog Box	Description
xlDialogApplyNames	name_array, ignore, use_rowcol, omit_col, omit_row, order_num, append_last
xlDialogAutoCorrect	correct_initial_caps, capitalize_days
xlDialogColorPalette	file_text
xlDialogColumnWidth	width_num, reference, standard, type_num, standard_num
xlDialogCreateNames	top, left, bottom, right
xlDialogDefineName	name_text, refers_to, macro_type, shortcut_text, hidden, category, local
xlDialogDefineStyle	style_text, number, font, alignment, border, pattern, protection
xlDialogFilterAdvanced	operation, list_ref, criteria_ref, copy_ref, unique
xlDialogGoalSeek	target_cell, target_value, variable_cell
xlDialogInsertObject	object_class, file_name, link_logical, display_icon_logical, icon_file, icon_number, icon_label
xlDialogOpen	file_text, update_links, read_only, format, prot_pwd, write_res_pwd, ignore_rorec, file_origin, custom_delimit, add_logical, editable, file_access, notify_logical, converter

Table 18-3. *xlDialog* Boxes Found in Excel's Menu Structure

xlDialog Box	Description
xlDialogPageSetup	head, foot, left, right, top, bot, hdng, grid, h_cntr, v_cntr, orient, paper_size, scale, pg_num, pg_order, bw_cells, quality, head_margin, foot_margin, notes, draft
xlDialogSaveAs	document_text, type_num, prot_pwd, backup, write_res_pwd, read_only_rec
xlDialogSendMail	recipients, subject, return_receipt
xlDialogShowToolbar	bar_id, visible, dock, x_pos, y_pos, width, protect, tool_tips, large_buttons, color_buttons
xlDialogZoom	magnification

There are many other built-in dialog boxes available. To locate all the arguments available to the built-in dialog boxes, search the MSDN Web site and online help.

Passing Arguments to Existing Dialog Boxes

At times, a dialog box is your solution; the dialog box will allow the user to interact with a familiar dialog box when the *Show* property is set to *True*. Keep in mind that you are not limited to how the dialog box displays by default. You are able to modify the default settings by passing arguments to the dialog box.

> **Note** It's not very efficient to use a *Dialog* object to return or change a value for a dialog box when you can return or change it using a property or method. Keep in mind that when VBA code is used in place of accessing the *Dialog* object, the code is simpler and shorter.

Prior to returning or changing a dialog box setting using the *Dialog* object, you need to identify the individual dialog box, which is done using the *Dialogs* property with an *xlDialog* constant. After you have initiated a *Dialog* object, you can return or set options in the dialog box.

For example, if you want the user to be able to verify the settings that will be applied to a range of cells but you also want to minimize the user's interaction, you can pass the settings to the dialog box so that they are automatically selected. To display the Alignment dialog box such that it is ready to format the selected text centered top and bottom with word wrap turned on, you can use the following code:

```
Sub VerifyAlignment()
    Application.Dialogs(xlDialogAlignment).Show 3, 1, 2
End Sub
```

Chapter 18

Figure 18-6 displays the Alignment dialog box with the arguments set as indicated by the preceding procedure.

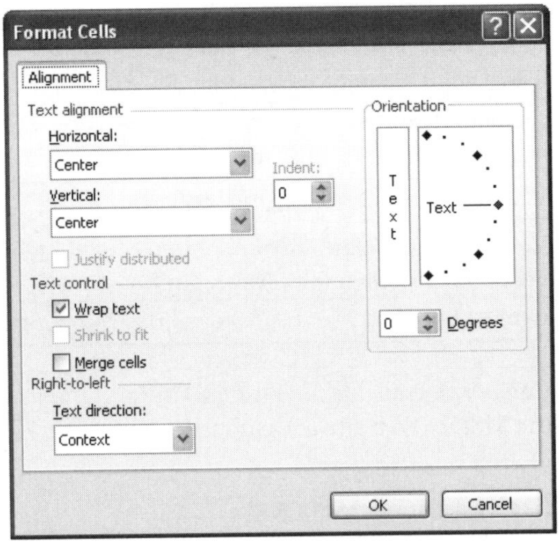

Figure 18-6. The Alignment dialog box with the Horizontal and Vertical alignment set to centered, as well as Wrap Text set to true.

Planning with Dialog Boxes

Throughout this chapter, you have learned how to access and pass arguments to built-in dialog boxes. Through proper use of the built-in dialog boxes, you can save yourself time and minimize your coding efforts. Simple and effective working is the goal of a good procedure. Keep this in mind as you tackle your next project.

Creating User Forms

Creating a *UserForm* 395   *UserForm* Controls 401

User forms give Microsoft Excel programmers the opportunity to provide a different way for users to interact with their applications. In this chapter, you'll learn how to create a form and populate it with the standard controls supplied by Microsoft Visual Basic for Applications (VBA). Then you'll learn how to display and close forms from your own routines. Finally, you'll learn how to interact with the form from your VBA application.

Creating a *UserForm*

Visual Basic for Applications includes a special object known as a *UserForm*. A *UserForm* object provides a visible surface on which you can place graphical controls, such as buttons, images, and text areas.

Adding a *UserForm*

You can add a *UserForm* to your project by choosing Insert, UserForm from the Visual Basic Editor. (See Figure 19-1.) The user form consists of mockup of a window, including a title bar complete with the title *UserForm1* and a Close button, plus a drawing surface filled with dots.

In addition to displaying the user form, the Visual Basic Editor also displays a floating toolbar called the *Toolbox*. The Toolbox contains various controls that can be placed on the drawing surface of the user form.

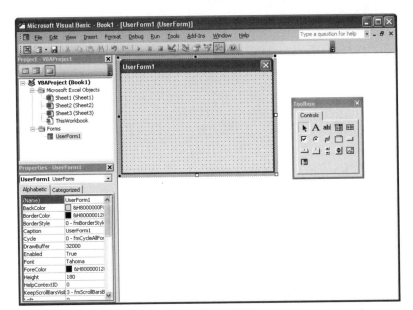

Figure 19-1. A *UserForm* object allows a VBA programmer to design a graphical interface to his application.

Designing a *UserForm*

Designing a *UserForm* involves selecting controls from the Toolbox and dragging them onto the drawing surface. Once they are on the form, you modify how they look by selecting the control and then working with it graphically or by going to the Properties window and modifying the control's properties.

To walk through a simple example of how this process works, just follow these steps:

1 Create a new *UserForm* by choosing Insert, UserForm from the Visual Basic Editor's main menu.

2 Move the mouse pointer over the *Label* control in the toolbox.

3 Click and hold the mouse button down.

4 Move the mouse pointer onto the drawing surface and release the mouse button. This will add the *Label* control to the form.

5   The text displayed in the *Label* control reflects the control's name, which in this case is *Label1*. You can change this value by changing the *Caption* property in the Properties window or by clicking the control and typing the new caption directly on the form.

6   You can test your new user form at any time by choosing Run, Run Sub/UserForm from the Visual Basic Editor's main menu. This will result in the Excel window being displayed with your new form displayed on top.

7   Click the Close box to close the user form and return to the Visual Basic Editor.

Modifying a *UserForm*

To modify a *UserForm*, you must first select it. You can select the user form by clicking any-place on the form that doesn't have a control. You can also select the form by selecting it from the drop-down menu in the Properties window. When the form is selected, it will be dis-played with a border of dots and squares.

Once you've selected the form, you can adjust its size by dragging its borders. Move the mouse pointer over one of the squares on the border, and the mouse pointer will change to a double arrow. Click and hold the mouse button while moving the mouse to adjust the size of the form.

You can also adjust the form's size in the Properties window. The height of the form is controlled by the *Height* property, and its width is controlled by the *Width* property. These values are measured in points.

Properties of a *UserForm*

The *UserForm* contains a wide range of properties that control how it looks and works. Table 19-1 lists some of the key properties.

Table 19-1. Key Properties of the *UserForm* Object

Property	Description
BackColor	Contains the color of the background of the form.
Caption	Contains the value displayed in the form's title.
Enabled	When *True*, means that the form is available for use.
Height	Specifies the height of the form in points.
Left	Specifies the distance between the left edge of the form and the left edge of the screen.
Name	Contains the name of the form.
Picture	Displays the specified picture as the background of the form.
ScrollBars	Specifies which scroll bars appear on the form. Can be: *fmScrollBarsNone*, *fmScrollBarsHorizontal*, *fmScrollBarsVertical*, or *fmScrollBarsBoth*.
StartUpPosition	Determines where the form is displayed on the screen. A value of 0 means that the *Top* and *Left* properties are used to position the form. A value of 1 means that the form will be displayed on the center of the Excel application. A value of 2 means that the form will be displayed in the center of the screen. A value of 3 means that the form will be displayed in the upper-left corner of the screen.
Top	Specifies the distance between the top of the form and the top edge of the screen.
Width	Specifies the width of the form in points.

The *Name* property contains the name of the user form. Remember that this property actually appears at the top of the list of properties rather than in alphabetical order like the rest of the properties are listed.

Adjusting the height and the width of the form graphically will automatically update the *Height* and *Width* properties. The *Top* and *Left* properties control the location of the form on the screen when the *StartUpPosition* property is set to 0.

The *BackColor* property allows you to change the color of the background of the form, whereas the *Picture* property lets you display a picture in the background. By default, these properties are set to use the settings from Windows. So if the user has a particular Windows theme installed, the form will use those colors.

Displaying a *UserForm*

User forms are just another object in Visual Basic, so they can be manipulated in code by setting properties, calling methods, and responding to events. You can easily create a macro that will display a form on the screen, and you can include code with the form that will be executed in response to various events (in programmer-speak this is called *trapping* events).

Displaying a form in VBA is a two-step process. First the form must be loaded, and then it must be shown. Loading a form allocates memory and initializes the form in preparation for showing it. Showing a form merely creates the graphical window that contains the form and makes it visible to the user.

You can load a form by calling the form's *Load* method, and you can display a form by calling the form's *Show* method. If the form isn't loaded when you call the *Show* method, it will be loaded for you automatically.

The opposite of *Show* is *Hide*, and the opposite of *Load* is *Unload*. So by calling the *Hide* method, you can remove a form from display without releasing its resources. Likewise, calling the *Unload* method will release all the resources associated with a form. Calling *Unload* while the form is visible on the screen will automatically remove the form from the display before releasing its resources.

> **Tip** **Faster Forms**
> Loading a user form can take a lot of resources. The more complex the form, the more resources it will take to load. If you plan to display the form quickly, you might want to hide the form, rather than unload it, to make your program run a little quicker. On the other hand, if you don't use a form very often, unloading it will save system resources that might be better used elsewhere.

There are two ways you can display a form: *modal* and *modeless*. When you display a modal form, all processing in the associated application stops until the form is closed. A message box is a good example of a modal form.

You can show a modeless form with the following statement:

```
UserForm1.Show vbModeless
```

You can show a modal form with the following statement:

```
UserForm1.Show vbModal
```

However, if you call the *Show* method without specifying a mode, the form will be displayed as modal.

Tip   Forms and Command Bar Controls

You might want to use the subroutine associated with the *OnAction* routine to call the *Show* method for a *UserForm*. This is a great way to start wizards or allow the user to input data into your application.

A modeless form does not block the application while the form is active. The application continues to operate as if the form were not present. This approach can be useful for many applications, but you should use modeless forms with care because they don't appear in the task bar, nor do they appear in the window tab order. This means that your users might lose a modeless form when they switch to another application or another window in the current application.

Associated with the life cycle of a form are three key events. The *Activate* event is triggered just before the form becomes the active window. The *Deactivate* event is triggered when the form is no longer the active window. The *Terminate* event is fired when the form is unloaded.

Remember that the *Activate* and *Deactivate* events are fired only as you move around in the VBA application. Switching to another application or switching from another application to Excel and your VBA program will not fire these events.

Inside Out

Built-in vs. Custom Dialog

You are probably wondering why you would want to use a dialog box to modify your worksheet when you can use the methods and properties supplied in VBA code. Well, there are times when you want the user to make the choice as to which color fill should be used or which font size is appropriate. This is the perfect example of when a dialog box should be used. It's much easier to show a built-in dialog box and allow users to select a color using a dialog box they are familiar with. After the color has been chosen, you can take their selections and apply them to the ranges you choose.

Using the built-in dialog box allows the user to interact with your code and still provide productivity. You can use an *If Then...Else* statement to apply a default color in case the user selects the Cancel button or has pressed the Esc key.

Remember, your code should work with the user. Your code should provide easy-to-use solutions that require little or no training to use. Using the built-in dialog boxes allows you to use an interface that the user is already comfortable with, so the user should require no training.

Before you create a custom dialog box, stop and evaluate if creating a dialog box is actually necessary. Is there a dialog box that exists that will save you the trouble? If so, try using the built-in dialog boxes and see if you are able to achieve your desired results.

UserForm Controls

The toolbox contains a useful assortment of controls that can be placed on a form. Some, like the *Label* control, are static and merely modify how the form appears. Other controls, such as the *TextBox* and the *CommandButton*, interact with the user to edit information and trigger tasks.

Programming Controls

In addition to displaying the form, the Visual Basic Editor also displays a floating toolbar called the *toolbox*. The toolbox contains the list of controls that can be placed on a form.

To add a control to the form, select the control from the toolbox, drag it onto the form, and drop it where you want the control. You can adjust the size and placement of the control graphically by selecting the control and dragging the control around or by dragging the box that surrounds the control. (See Figure 19-2.)

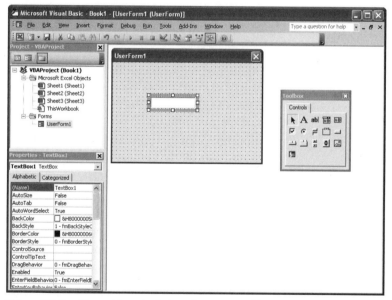

Figure 19-2. You add controls to a form control by selecting a control and dragging and dropping it on the form.

All of the code associated with the form and its controls are stored in the form module. This is an independent element much like a regular module or a class module. Double-clicking a control will switch you from the graphical view of the form to the code view of the form and automatically insert the subroutine definition for the default event for that control.

Common Properties, Methods, and Events

Because *UserForm* controls are objects like the other objects you have already seen, they have a rich collection of properties, methods, and events. Table 19-2 contains a list of the key properties, methods, and events that are common to many of the form controls.

Table 19-2. Key Properties, Methods, and Events of the *UserForm* Controls

Property/Method	Description
BackColor	Property: controls the color of the background of the control.
Caption	Property: contains text that's displayed on the control, but can't be changed by the user.
Change	Event: called when the *Value* property changes.
Click	Event: called when the user clicks the control using the mouse.
ControlTipText	Property: contains text that is displayed when the user hovers the mouse pointer over the control for a moment.
DblClick	Event: called when the user double-clicks the control with the mouse.
Enabled	Property: when *True*, means that the control can receive the focus and will respond to user input.
Enter	Event: called just before the control receives the focus from another control on the same form.
Exit	Event: called just before the control loses the focus to another control on the same form.
Font	Property: contains an object reference to a *Font* object, which defines the characteristics of the text displayed on the control.
ForeColor	Property: contains the color used to draw the foreground of the control.
Height	Property: contains the height of the control in points.
Left	Property: contains the distance between the left edge of the control and the left edge of the form on which the control resides.
Locked	Property: when *True*, the user is not permitted to change the value of the control.
Name	Property: contains the name of the control.
SpecialEffect	Property: specifies how the control is drawn.
TabIndex	Property: specifies the control's relative position in the tab sequence.
TabStop	Property: when *True*, means that the control will accept the focus when the user tabs to it.
Top	Property: contains the distance between the top edge of the control and the top edge of the form on which the control resides.
Value	Property: describes the state or content of a control.

Creating User Forms

Table 19-2. Key Properties, Methods, and Events of the *UserForm* Controls

Property/Method	Description
Visible	Property: when *True*, means that the control is displayed on the form.
Width	Property: contains the width of the control in points.
ZOrder (zPosition)	Method: moves the control to the front (*fmTop*) or the bottom (*fmBottom*) of the z-order.

The *Height*, *Width*, *Top*, and *Left* properties dictate the physical size and placement of the control on the form. The *Enabled* property determines if the control can receive the focus, whereas the *Visible* control determines whether the control will be drawn. When the *Locked* property is *True*, the user can manipulate the contents of the control but will be unable to change its value. For instance, setting the *Locked* property to *True* means that the user could scroll through a large, multi-line text box to see all of the data. If the *Enabled* property were set to *False*, the text box control would still be visible, but the user would be unable to scroll to see any text that isn't currently visible on screen.

When two controls overlap, the *ZOrder* method controls which one is completely visible and which one is partially or totally hidden. Moving a control to the top of the z-order means that it will be displayed last—thus ensuring that the control will be visible even if it overlaps any other controls. Likewise, using *ZOrder* to move a control to the bottom means that it will be rendered first, and any other control that is rendered later might hide this control from view.

TabIndex identifies the order in which the focus will shift from one control to the next when the user presses the Tab key, and *TabStop* determines whether the control will accept the focus or the focus should shift to the control with the next higher *TabIndex* value. The *Enter* and *Exit* events are fired as the focus shifts from one control to the next on the form. The *Exit* routine contains a single argument called *Cancel*, which you can set to *True* to prevent the user from switching to a different control.

Tip Checking Information

Because the code in the *Exit* event is only executed when the user switches to another control, it's an excellent time to examine the contents of the control to determine if the value is correct. For example, you can verify that the contents of the control are numeric, and if the user entered an invalid value, you can notify the user using a message box and then set the *Cancel* argument to *True*, thus preventing the user from switching to a new control on the same form.

The exact meaning of the *Value* property depends on the control, but in general it contains the value associated with the control. When this value changes, the *Change* event is fired. Remember that the *Value* property is different from the *Caption* property in that the *Caption* property usually represents a block of text that can be changed only by the program, whereas the *Value* property usually contains information that can be changed by the user interacting with the form.

The *Click* and *DblClick* events occur when the user clicks or double-clicks the mouse. In some cases, the *Change* event might also fire if clicking or double-clicking the control affects the control's *Value*.

The *Label* Control

The *Label* control allows your program to display text on the form that the user can't modify. Typically, the *Label* control is used to describe the contents of other controls, such as the *TextBox* control.

Although the user cannot change the value of a *Label* control, your program can, by assigning a value to the *Caption* property. Unlike many other controls, the *Label* control doesn't have a *Value* property because there's nothing the user can change. However, the *Label* control will respond to mouse clicks, triggering either the *Click* or the *DblClick* event.

The *CommandButton* Control

The *CommandButton* control displays a button that, when clicked, triggers the *Click* event associated with the control. Another way to trigger a command button is to use the Tab key to shift the focus to the command button and then press the Enter key or the Spacebar.

The following routine changes the text displayed on the button each time the button is clicked. So if the *Caption* property reads "Off", the routine will reset the value to "On"; otherwise, the *Caption* property will be set to "Off".

```
Private Sub CommandButton1_Click()

If CommandButton1.Caption = "Off" Then
    CommandButton1.Caption = "On"

Else
    CommandButton1.Caption = "Off"

End If

End Sub
```

> **Tip** A Push of a Button
>
> Use the command button when you want to call a subroutine to process the information on the form.

The *TextBox* Control

The *TextBox* control is the primary control that's used to accept text from the user. Text boxes come in two main flavors: *single-line* and *multi-line*. This is controlled by the *Multiline* property. When *Multiline* is *True*, the control will display multiple lines of text in the box; otherwise, the text box will display only a single line of text.

> **Tip** Taking a Break
>
> You can force the text to start on a new line by embedding the constant *vbCrLf* (carriage-return, line-feed) before the first character of the next line. This white space can be helpful if you wish to break a long block of text into paragraphs.

If you have more text than can be displayed in either a single-line or multi-line text box, you have the option to include scroll bars so that the user can scroll to see the hidden text. You can set the *ScrollBars* property to *fmScrollBarsHorizontal* to display a scroll bar on a single-line text box, or you can set the *ScrollBars* property to *fmScrollBarsHorizontal*, *fmScrollBarsVertical*, or *fmScrollBarsBoth* to display a horizontal or vertical scroll bar, or both in a multi-line text box. Set this property to *fmScrollBarsNone* for either type of text box if you don't want to display any scroll bars.

Another useful property for multi-line text boxes is the *WordWrap* property. When *WordWrap* is set to *True*, any lines that are too long to be completely displayed in the horizontal space available will be wrapped to the next line on a word boundary so as not to split a word between lines. However, in this case, you will not be able to display a horizontal scroll bar.

The *LineCount* property returns the number of lines in a multi-line text box.

The characters displayed in a text box control are available in both the *Text* and *Value* properties, and you can change what is displayed in the text box by changing either property. However, it's customary to use the *Text* property instead of the *Value* property. The *Change* event will be fired if a value is assigned to either property.

> **Note** The *Change* event is fired for each character entered by a user into the text box. This event can be used to validate the information entered into the text box one character at a time. However, if you wish to validate the entire text box after the user has finished entering data, use the *Exit* event (which is fired automatically when the focus leaves the text box) instead of the *Change* event.

You can hide the characters entered into a text box by specifying a value for the *PasswordChar* property. This property is typically used to hide password information. Typically, an asterisk (*) is used for this property. Set this property to the empty string to display the actual characters entered.

The *MaxLength* property specifies the maximum number of characters that can be entered into the *TextBox*, and the *TextLength* property returns the total length of the text. Notice that *TextLength* will include carriage return and linefeed characters in the count when they are present in a multi-line text box. If the *AutoTab* property is *True*, the focus will be shifted to the next control in the tab sequence when the maximum number of characters have been entered into the control.

The *CheckBox* Control

The *CheckBox* control provides the user a way to chose between two values, such as Yes and No, True and False, and Enabled or Disabled. The text in the *Caption* property is displayed next to the check box.

The *Click* and *Change* events in this control accomplish the same thing because to change the check box's value, the user simply clicks anywhere over the control, including the caption. You can display the value of the *CheckBox* control by using code like this in the check box's *Click* event:

```
Private Sub CheckBox1_Change()

MsgBox "Value of checkbox is " & CheckBox1.Value

End Sub
```

The *ToggleButton* Control

The *ToggleButton* control is similar to a *CheckBox* control in that it gives the user a way to choose between two values. The only real difference is that the *ToggleButton* control appears to be "up" when the *Value* property is set to *False* and "down" when *Value* is set to *True*.

The *SpinButton* Control

The *SpinButton* control makes it easy for the user to choose from a range of numeric values. The *Value* property holds the current value of the control. Pressing the Up Arrow button increases the value, and pressing the Down Arrow button decreases the value.

The *Min* and *Max* properties specify the smallest and the largest values for the control. The *SmallChange* property specifies the number that will be added or subtracted each time the Up Arrow button or the Down Arrow button is pressed. By default, this value is 1.

Each time the *Value* property is changed in this control, the *Change* event is fired. If the Up Arrow button is pressed, the *SpinUp* event will also be fired. If the Down Arrow button is pressed, the *SpinDown* event is triggered.

The *Delay* property specifies the amount of time between *Change* events when the user clicks and holds the mouse down on the Up Arrow or the Down Arrow button. The default is 50 milliseconds. The delay between the first call and the second call is five times the *Delay* value to make it easier for a user to press the button once. After the second call, the *Change* event will be called after the amount of time specified in *Delay* has elapsed.

Typically, you will want to include a *TextBox* or a *Label* control beside the *SpinButton* control to display the current value. This value is displayed by using code like the following:

```
Private Sub SpinButton1_Change()

    TextBox1.Text = SpinButton1.Value

End Sub
```

The *Frame* Control

The *Frame* control provides a way to group together a series of controls. Technically, this control is known as a *container* because it's the only control in Visual Basic form controls that can hold other controls. The controls contained in a frame are also known as *child controls*.

Tip   From Frame to Form

You can't drag an existing control onto a frame, nor can you drag a control from the frame to the *UserForm*. Instead, if you wish to move a control from a frame to the form or from the form to the frame, you need to use a cut-and-paste operation. Select the control, and select Edit, Cut from the main menu. Then select the desired container (either the frame or the form), and select Edit, Paste from the main menu. Once the control is on the form or frame, you can drag it around to place it exactly where you want it.

Frames are also useful if you want to draw visual attention to a group of controls. The *Caption* property is displayed on the border of the *Frame* control.

Tip   Moving Frames

Resizing and/or moving a frame around on a form also moves all the controls that it contains. The same relative position between the child controls and the upper-left corner of the frame will remain constant.

Frame [X]

Frame1

    Inside Frame1

Frame2

    Inside Frame2

The *OptionButton* Control

The *OptionButton* control provides a way to choose exactly one item from a group of items. Each option button works like a check box in that the option button control has two states, either selected or not selected. However, only a single option button on a form may be selected. When the user clicks on a different option button, the currently selected option button is unselected before the new option button is selected. This means that if your form has 20 option button controls on it, only one will be selected at a time.

If you need to display more than one group of option buttons on a form, you need to place each group of option buttons in its own *Frame* control. This means that the group of option buttons can affect only the values of the other option buttons in the same frame. Any option buttons outside a frame will not be affected, nor will any option buttons stored in any other frame.

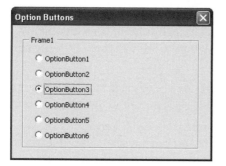

> **Warning** Use extreme caution when deleting a *Frame* control. Deleting the *Frame* control will also delete any controls that it contains. If you want to preserve these controls, you should cut or copy them to the clipboard, and then delete the *Frame* control itself. When the *Frame* control is gone, you can paste those controls directly onto the form or wherever else you want to place them.

The *Image* Control

The *Image* control is a relatively simple control that allows you to display a picture on a form. It supports only these file formats: BMP, CUR, GIF, ICO, JPG, and WMF.

The *Picture* property contains the actual binary picture image that will be displayed in the control. In the Visual Basic Editor, you can enter the name of a file and it will automatically load the image for you. However, if you want to load an image while the program is running, you will need to use the *LoadPicture* function like this, where *<pathname>* contains the file name and path.

```
Image1.Picture = LoadPicture(<pathname>)
```

By default, when a picture is loaded into the control, either initially in the Visual Basic Editor or in your application, the picture will be displayed at its normal size. This means that you will see the complete picture only if the image control is the same size as the image. If the control is smaller than the image, you will see only the upper-left corner of the image, but if the control is larger than the image, you'll see the entire image, plus the background of the control.

The *PictureAlignment* property controls how the image is placed in the control. By default, the picture is aligned such that the upper-left corner of the picture is placed in the upper-left corner of the control (*fmPictureAlignmentTopLeft*). However, you can set this property to these values as well: *fmPictureAlignmentTopRight*, *fmPictureAlignmentCenter*, *fmPictureAlignmentBottomLeft*, and *fmPictureAlignmentBottomRight*.

You can use the *PictureSizeMode* property to automatically resize the image to see the entire picture. A value of *fmPictureSizeModeStretch* resizes the image to fill the entire space of the control. However, you might need to adjust the *Height* and *Width* properties to prevent the image from being distorted. Setting this property to *fmPictureSizeModeZoom* will enlarge or shrink the picture to fit the box, but it won't change its height-to-width ratio. A value of *fmPictureSizeModeClip* displays the image at normal size and chops off any part of the image that will not fit into the control.

When the *PictureTiling* property is *True*, the image is repeated as many times as necessary to fill up the area available in the image control. The first copy of the image is placed according to the *PictureAlignment* property.

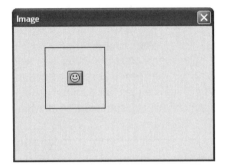

The *ScrollBar* Control

The *ScrollBar* control allows you to add a classic Windows scroll bar to your application. Depending on the value of the *Orientation* property, your scroll bar will appear to be horizontal (*fmOrientaionHorizontal*) or vertical (*fmOrientationVertical*).

> **Note** By default, the *Orientation* property is set to *fmOrientationAuto*, meaning that the Visual Basic Editor will automatically select the control's orientation based on whether the control is wider than tall (horizontal) or taller than wide (vertical).

Moving the scroll box along the scroll bar changes the *Value* property of the control. The *Min* and *Max* properties specify the minimum and maximum numbers that will be returned through the *Value* property. The *Min* value will be returned when the scroll box is at the top of a vertical scroll bar or at the left side of a horizontal scroll bar. The *Max* property will be returned when the scroll box is at the bottom of a vertical scroll bar or at the right of a horizontal scroll bar.

The *LargeChange* property specifies how much the scroll box will be moved when the user clicks in between the scroll box arrow buttons, whereas the *SmallChange* property specifies how much the scroll box will be moved when the user clicks the arrow buttons on each end of the scroll bar.

The *Scroll* event is fired whenever the scroll box is moved on the scroll bar, but the *Change* event is fired whenever the value changes. For all practical purposes, these two events are the same. The only difference between the two events is that the *Scroll* event will be triggered multiple times while the user moves the scroll box around on the scroll bar. The *Change* event will be fired only after the user has released the scroll box.

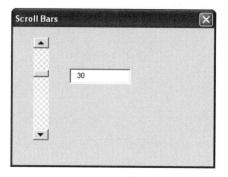

The *ListBox* Control

The *ListBox* control displays a list of information to the user, from which the user can select one or more entries. The list of items that can be selected are arranged into a series of rows and columns. The number of columns is controlled by the *ColumnCount* property. This value contains the number of columns that are available. By default, this property is set to 1, meaning that a single column will be displayed. If you set this property to -1, all available columns will be displayed (up to a total of 10).

When the *ColumnHeads* property is *True*, the first row in the list is used as the header for the column. Notice that this row can't be selected. The *ColumnWidths* property specifies the size of each column. The sizes for all column widths are contained in a single string formatted as a set of numbers separated by semicolons (;). Each number specifies the width of the column in points. You may also specify widths in centimeters (*cm*) and inches (*in*). Decimal points are allowed. Specifying a value of zero as the width of a particular column means that that particular column won't be displayed.

The *ListCount* property contains the number of rows in the list. The *List* property accesses the list of items and takes two parameters, the row number and the column number. Both parameters start with zero and have a maximum value of one less than the *ColumnCount* or *ListCount* properties. If you reference the *List* property without any arguments, you can copy a two-dimensional array of values to the property in a single statement.

The following routine shows how you might use the *List* and *ColumnCount* properties to initialize a list box control:

```
Private Sub UserForm_Initialize()

Dim MyList(10, 2) As String
Dim i As Long

MyList(0, 0) = "Line"
MyList(0, 1) = "Column A"
MyList(0, 2) = "Column B"

For i = 1 To 10
    MyList(i, 0) = "#" & FormatNumber(i, 0)
    MyList(i, 1) = "A" & FormatNumber(i, 0)
    MyList(i, 2) = "B" & FormatNumber(i, 0)

Next i

ListBox1.ColumnCount = 3
ListBox1.List = MyList

End Sub
```

The *Column* property can be used to reference a particular column or row and column value. If only one argument is supplied to the *Column* property, you can assign values to the specified column in the list. Notice that the arguments are column number and row number, which is the reverse order of the *List* property.

The *AddItem* method is typically used to add a new item to the list. You may optionally specify the row where the new row should be placed. (Rows are numbered starting with row 0.) The *RemoveItem* method removes the specified row from the list. The *Clear* method removes all items from the list.

The *TopIndex* property contains the index of the first visible row in the list. The *ListIndex* property contains the index of the currently selected row. It might also have a value of -1, meaning that no row is currently selected. The *Click* event is called when the user clicks the control. This routine displays the currently selected item in the list when the user clicks the item.

```
Private Sub ListBox1_Click()

MsgBox ListBox1.ListIndex

End Sub
```

When the *MultiSelect* property is set to *fmMultiSelectMulti*, the user may select more than one item in the list by pressing the spacebar or clicking the desired item. A value of *fmMultiSelectExtended* allows the user to use the Shift and Ctrl keys to aid in the selection process. Holding the Shift key while moving the mouse pointer adds all the items between the last selected item and the item currently under the mouse pointer. The Ctrl key allows users to click and select multiple nonadjacent items. However, if the user releases both the Shift and Ctrl keys, clicking on a single item will clear the list and mark only the newly selected item.

When your program allows multiple items to be selected, you should use the *Selected* property along with the row number to determine the status of each row. A value of *True* means that the row is currently selected.

Setting the *ListStyle* property to *fmListStylePlain* means that the list of items are displayed as a normal list. Selected items are highlighted by changing the item's background color. However, a value of *fmListStyleOption* means that option buttons (*MultiSelect=False*) or check boxes (*MultiSelect=True*) will be displayed in front of each row to simplify the selection process.

The *Text* property contains the currently selected value from the list. If the list has more than one column, the *TextColumn* property identifies which column will be saved into the *Text* property.

The *MatchEntry* property determines how the *ListBox* can be searched. A value of *fmMatchEntryFirstLetter* means that when the user types a letter, the list is searched for the first row that has a matching character in the first position. Pressing the same character again will locate the second occurrence of the letter as the first character. A value of *fmMatchEntryComplete* allows the user to select the row by typing the prefix of characters that match the desired entry. A value of *fmMatchEntryNone* disables the match function.

The *ComboBox* Control

The *ComboBox* control is perhaps one of the most complicated controls in Visual Basic. It combines the functions of both a *ListBox* control and a *TextBox* control. All the properties and methods discussed in the previous section, "The *ListBox* Control," also apply to the *ComboBox* control.

The only feature of the *ListBox* control not supported by the *ComboBox* is the ability to select multiple items from the list. Therefore, the *MultiSelect* and *Selected* properties are not available in this control. Also, any of the features related to multi-line text boxes aren't present in the *ComboBox* control.

By default, a *ComboBox* consists of a text field in which the user can enter characters followed by a drop-down button, which when pressed will display a *ListBox* containing a list of values that can be selected. By setting the *Style* property to *fmStyleDropDownList*, the user may not type a value, but instead must choose one of the values displayed in the drop-down list. The currently selected value is displayed in the text box field.

You can also specify when the drop-down button is displayed at the end of the text field by setting the *ShowDropButtonWhen* property. Possible values include: *fmShowDropButton-WhenNever*, which hides the drop-down button; *fmShowDropButtonWhenFocus*, which shows the button only when the control has the focus; and *fmShowDropButtonWhenAlways*, which means that the button is always displayed.

You can also modify the symbol displayed on the drop-down button using the *DropButtonStyle* property. By default, a down arrow is displayed in the button (*fmDropButtonStyleArrow*). However, you can also display an ellipsis (…) by using the *fmDropButtonStyleEllipsis* or display an underscore (_) by specifying *fmDropButtonStyleReduce*. Finally, you can leave the button blank by choosing *fmDropButtonStylePlain*.

When *AutoSize* is *True*, the control will automatically be expanded to accommodate the longest line; otherwise, the drop-down list will be truncated at the edge of the control. If you merely want to control the width of the drop-down list, you can use the *ListWidth* property. Be sure to allow sufficient space for a vertical scroll bar when specifying a value for *ListWidth*.

The *MatchFound* property is *True* when the value displayed in the text box portion of the control matches one of the items in the list. If *MatchRequired* property is *True*, the user will not be allowed to leave the control until a matching entry is selected.

The *RefEdit* Control

The *RefEdit* control makes it easy to select a range of cells from a workbook. The user has the option to enter the text value of the range in the text box part of the control. However, pressing the button located to the right of the control will collapse the current form so that only the *RefEdit* control is visible and then transfer control back to Excel. There the user can select the range of cells that will appear in the text box. Pressing the button a second time will restore the original form with the newly selected range reference inserted in the *RefEdit* box.

The *TabStrip* Control

By providing a series of control containers such as the *Frame* control, plus a mechanism for selecting a container, the *TabStrip* control provides a simple way to fit more controls onto a form than otherwise would fit.

Each tab on the tab strip is an independent object within the *TabStrip* control. The *Tabs* collection returns a collection of *Tab* objects. Methods are included in the collection to *Add* a new *Tab* object, *Remove* an existing *Tab* object, or to *Clear* the collection. The currently selected tab can be referenced directly through the *TabStrip* control's *SelectedItem* property.

Each tab object contains unique *Name* and *Index* values, which are used to locate the tab from within the collection. The *Caption* property contains the text that will be displayed on the tab.

The *Style* property allows you to choose the way the tab information is displayed. By default, *fmTabStyleTabs* is selected. However, you can specify *fmTabStyleButtons* to display buttons instead of tabs. Finally, you can choose *fmTabStyleNone* so that no tab information is displayed on the control.

When the *MultiRow* property is *True*, the tab strip can have more than one row of tabs. The *TabOrientation* property specifies where the tabs are located. Valid choices for *TabOrientation* include: *fmTabOrientationTop*, *fmTabOrientationBottom*, *fmTabOrientationLeft*, and *fmTabOrientationRight*.

The size of the tabs are specified using the *TabFixedHeight* and *TabFixedWidth* properties. If these properties are assigned a value of zero, the tab sizes are automatically adjusted to fit the contents; otherwise, the value specifies the point size that will be used for each tab.

Typically, you'll use this control at design time and drag controls onto the various tab surfaces as you design your application. At run time, the user merely clicks the appropriate tab button to switch to the desired tab. You can add and remove forms within the *TabStrip* control by right-clicking the control and choosing the appropriate option from the pop-up menu.

Tip **No Programming Required**
This control typically needs no programming. The only time you might want to write any code for a *TabStrip* control is when you want to automatically shift the user from one tab to another as a result of interacting with a control on one of the tabs.

The *MultiPage* Control

The *MultiPage* control is similar to the *TabStrip* control. It has a collection of *Page* objects, which correspond directly to the *Tab* objects. The primary difference between the *TabStrip* control and the *MultiPage* control is that the individual *Page* objects with the *MultiPage* control include a richer collection of properties and methods. In fact, the *MultiPage* control contains most of the properties and methods available on the *UserForm* object, such as the ability to display scroll bars and use pictures as the background.

The *TransactionEffect* property associated with the *Page* object controls the visual representation of one page moving to another. With this property, you can instruct the new page to move over the old page horizontally, vertically, or diagonally; or you can specify that the new page will "push" the old page off the screen either horizontally or vertically. The *Transition-Period* property defines the milliseconds that the transaction effect will last.

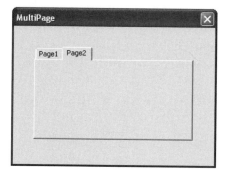

In this chapter, you learned about user forms and the controls you can add to them. User forms are useful when you need to prompt the user to enter information or display a result to the user. The most common controls are the *label* control, the *text box* control, and the *command button* control. The *label* control provides a way to display information to the user. The *text box* control provides a way for the user to accept information from the user, while the *command button* control provides a convenient way for the user to request the application to perform a specific task. The other controls available for a user form provide alternate ways to present information to a user or accept information from a user.

Chapter 20

Creating Advanced User Forms

Capturing Information. 419   Building a Multi-Step Wizard 431

User forms are a critical part of Microsoft Excel programming in that they provide a surface that is totally under your control with which you can interact with a user. This makes it possible to build more complex Excel applications. Forms can also be used to collect and verify information from a user before it's entered into a worksheet. They can also be used as part of an add-in to display options and control execution of a particular task. In this chapter, you'll learn how to build a user form that allows a user to input data into the worksheet, plus how to build an add-in that invokes a multi-step wizard that creates a chart based on selections made by a user.

Capturing Information

Entering information into a worksheet can be painful sometimes. It's difficult to ensure that the data is valid and is properly formatted. It can also be difficult to ensure that the data is added at the proper location. In this example, you'll learn how to construct a simple form that accepts data from the user and stores it in a worksheet.

Form Application Overview

The Excel worksheet used in this sample application merely records six pieces of information about a customer at The Garden Company: CustomerId, Name, City, State, ZipCode, and DateAdded. (See Figure 20-1.)

This form is started by running a macro and remains up until the user explicitly closes the form. Buttons on the form control which row of the worksheet is displayed through the form, and the form itself allows the user to enter or edit any data stored in a particular row.

 On the CD   The complete source code for this example is found on the Companion CD for this book in FormApp.xls. Rather than entering each code listing found in this chapter, you should load the sample file, which includes some sample data you can use for testing.

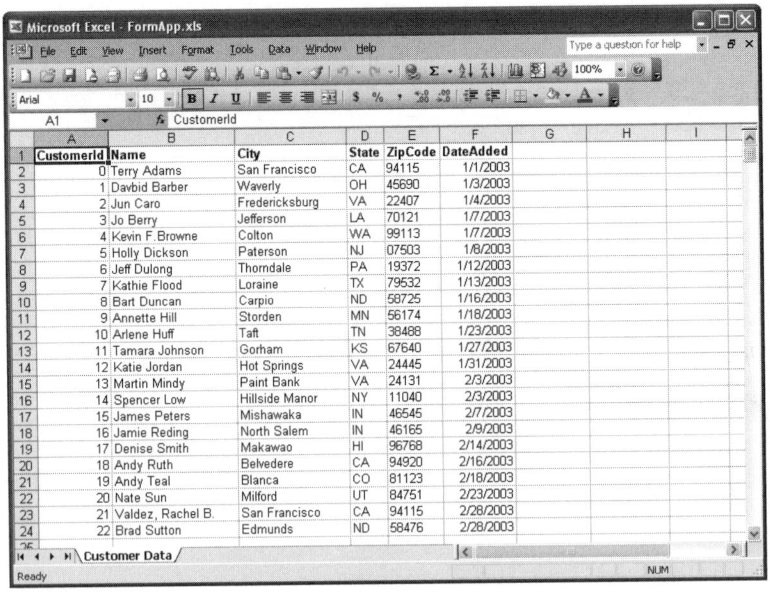

CustomerId	Name	City	State	ZipCode	DateAdded
0	Terry Adams	San Francisco	CA	94115	1/1/2003
1	Davbid Barber	Waverly	OH	45690	1/3/2003
2	Jun Caro	Fredericksburg	VA	22407	1/4/2003
3	Jo Berry	Jefferson	LA	70121	1/7/2003
4	Kevin F.Browne	Colton	WA	99113	1/7/2003
5	Holly Dickson	Paterson	NJ	07503	1/8/2003
6	Jeff Dulong	Thorndale	PA	19372	1/12/2003
7	Kathie Flood	Loraine	TX	79532	1/13/2003
8	Bart Duncan	Carpio	ND	58725	1/16/2003
9	Annette Hill	Storden	MN	56174	1/18/2003
10	Arlene Huff	Taft	TN	38488	1/23/2003
11	Tamara Johnson	Gorham	KS	67640	1/27/2003
12	Katie Jordan	Hot Springs	VA	24445	1/31/2003
13	Martin Mindy	Paint Bank	VA	24131	2/3/2003
14	Spencer Low	Hillside Manor	NY	11040	2/3/2003
15	James Peters	Mishawaka	IN	46545	2/7/2003
16	Jamie Reding	North Salem	IN	46165	2/9/2003
17	Denise Smith	Makawao	HI	96768	2/14/2003
18	Andy Ruth	Belvedere	CA	94920	2/16/2003
19	Andy Teal	Blanca	CO	81123	2/18/2003
20	Nate Sun	Milford	UT	84751	2/23/2003
21	Valdez, Rachel B.	San Francisco	CA	94115	2/28/2003
22	Brad Sutton	Edmunds	ND	58476	2/28/2003

Figure 20-1. A simple worksheet tracks customer information such as name and address and the date the customer was added.

Designing a Form

For most data-driven forms, you should place the fields in a single column with labels next to each field. This arrangement makes it easy for the user to find information on the form. However, with some fields, such as those that are part of an address, you might find it better to arrange the fields more intuitively, such as placing the City, State, and ZipCode fields on the same line.

It's important to note that the placement of the fields on the form is completely independent of the code that accesses it. If you wished to arrange all of the fields in a circle, it wouldn't make a bit of difference to your code. While this fact is something that might seem obvious, it was the revolutionary concept that started the Microsoft Visual Basic revolution.

> **Tip** **Work with What Works**
> When designing user forms, take a look at the various windows and dialog boxes built into Excel and other applications for design ideas.

Follow these steps to create a form that will interact with the user:

1. Start the Visual Basic Editor, and choose Insert, UserForm from the main menu. This will create a new *UserForm* object in your application.
2. From the Toolbox, drag a *TextBox* control and a *Label* control for each column in the worksheet. Drag a *ComboBox* control to hold the list of states. You might have to adjust the size of the user form to accommodate the controls.

Tip **Double-Click to Save Time**

If you wish add multiple copies of the same control to a user form, double-click the control in the toolbox. The mouse pointer will change to reflect the selected control. You may then draw multiple controls on the user form. When you're finished adding that particular control, you may double-click another control in the toolbox to add multiple copies of that control or click the arrow in the toolbox to return the mouse pointer to normal.

3 Use the Properties window to change the *Name* property of each text box to reflect the database fields (**CustomerId, CustomerName, City, ZipCode,** and **DateAdded**). Change the *Name* property of the combo box control to **State**. Also change the *Caption* property for each *Label* control to something more descriptive. (See Figure 20-2.)

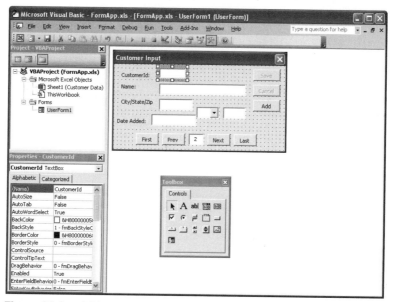

Figure 20-2. Add *TextBox* and *Label* controls for each column in the worksheet and their properties as directed.

4 Add *CommandButton* controls to the user form that will allow the user to scroll through the rows. Change the *Caption* property to read **First, Previous, Next,** and **Last.** Leave a space between the *Previous* and *Next* controls.

Tip **Controls Have Freedom of Movement**

Once a control is on the form, you can select it and move it anywhere on the form you wish. You can also do the same thing with multiple controls by clicking the form and dragging to select the group of controls you want to move. Then you can drag the selected group around on the form.

5 Add a *TextBox* control in between the *Previous* and *Next* controls. Change the *Name* property to **RowNumber.** Set the *Text* property to **2.**

6 Add three more *CommandButton* controls. Change the *Caption* property of the first one to **Save**, the second one to **Cancel**, and the last one to **Add**.

7 Change the *Enabled* property on the *Save* and *Cancel CommandButton* controls to **False**.

8 Once all of the controls have been added, you can tweak their sizes and exact placement on the form until you find a pleasing arrangement. (See Figure 20-3.)

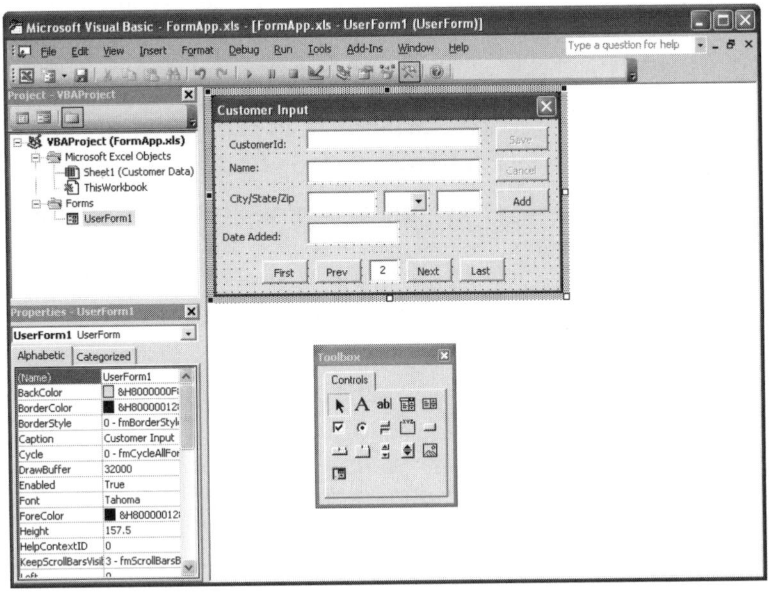

Figure 20-3.   Finishing the form layout.

Displaying Data

With the form constructed, it's time to copy data from the worksheet to the form. The RowNumber text box contains the number of the row that should be displayed on the form, so the real trick is to convert the value in the *RowNumber* text box into a value that can be used to extract the data from the worksheet using the *Cells* method.

The following program listing shows the *GetData* routine, which is located in the module associated with the user form. *GetData* copies the data from the currently active worksheet to the user form. After declaring a temporary variable *r* to hold the current row, the routine verifies that the value in the *RowNumber* control is numeric. This step is important because the user could type any value into this field.

```
Private Sub GetData()

Dim r As Long

If IsNumeric(RowNumber.Text) Then
    r = CLng(RowNumber.Text)
```

```
Else
    ClearData
    MsgBox "Illegal row number"
    Exit Sub

End If

If r > 1 And r <= LastRow Then
    CustomerId.Text = FormatNumber(Cells(r, 1), 0)
    CustomerName.Text = Cells(r, 2)
    City.Text = Cells(r, 3)
    State.Text = Cells(r, 4)
    Zip.Text = Cells(r, 5)
    DateAdded.Text = FormatDateTime(Cells(r, 6), vbShortDate)

    DisableSave

ElseIf r = 1 Then
    ClearData

Else
    ClearData
    MsgBox "Invalid row number"

End If

End Sub
```

Knowing that *RowNumber* contains a numeric value, the *CLng* function is used to convert the value in *RowNumber* into the variable *r*. The rest of the code merely uses *r* to extract the information from the proper row and copy it to the correct field. Otherwise, a message box will be displayed to the user indicating that the row number value is invalid. The *ClearData* routine simply assigns an empty string to each field on the form to clear out any values that might have already been displayed on the form. (Remember that the *ComboBox* control can't be set to an empty string and should be set to a valid state value.)

```
Private Sub ClearData()

CustomerId.Text = ""
CustomerName.Text = ""
City.Text = ""
State.Text = "AK"
Zip.Text = ""
DateAdded.Text = ""

End Sub
```

Simply because the row number is numeric doesn't mean that it's safe to pass the number to the *Cells* method. You can add the constant *LastRow* to the start of the user form module like this while testing this routine. (Later in this chapter, you'll see how to determine the real last row of data in the worksheet, and you'll convert this constant to a module level variable.)

```
Const LastRow = 20
```

Using this value, you can verify that the row number is always in the range of *2* to *LastRow*, thus ensuring that the value in *r* always points to a valid row on the worksheet.

Remember that we have to handle the value of 1 as a special case because it's possible that the user has entered a 1 into the RowNumber text box as part of entering a number beginning with 1, such as 12 or 123. The easiest way to handle this issue is to simply clear the form by calling *ClearData* without issuing an error message.

Notice that the *FormatNumber* routine is used to convert the value in the first column to a number rather than simply assigning the value directly to the text box control. This technique ensures that the value is properly formatted in the field.

The same argument applies to the date data from the sixth column. The *FormatDateTime* function ensures that the data is properly formatted. While the function isn't specifically needed, it serves to remind you that you aren't dealing with text data.

Once the data is loaded onto the form, the Save and Cancel buttons are disabled by calling the *DisableSave* routine. These buttons are enabled only when the user changes a piece of information on the form.

```
Private Sub DisableSave()

CommandButton5.Enabled = False
CommandButton6.Enabled = False

End Sub
```

To hook the *GetData* routine into the form, switch from the code view of the user form to the object view showing the graphical representation of the form. Double-clicking the *RowNumber* control will take you back to the code view, but with one minor exception: the cursor will be placed in the middle of a new routine named *RowNumber_Change*.

Inside the new event, add a call to the *GetData* routine. This means that any time the data in the *RowNumber* control changes, the data shown in the form will be updated.

```
Private Sub RowNumber_Change()

GetData

End Sub
```

To test the routine, choose Run, Run Sub/UserForm from the main menu or press the F5 key. Then enter a row number into the *RowNumber* control. You will notice that the data from the appropriate row will be displayed. Also notice that it's impossible to enter a bad value for the row without generating an error message.

Chapter 20

Navigating The Worksheet

Clicking any of the four navigation buttons should automatically adjust the value in the *RowNumber* text box. Then, because the value in *RowNumber* has been changed, the *RowNumber_Change* event will be fired and the currently displayed row will be updated.

Each of the four buttons represents a slightly different situation. The code for the First button is the simplest in that only a simple assignment statement is necessary to set *RowNumber* to *2*. As with the *RowNumber* text box, the easiest way to edit the code for the appropriate event is to double-click the graphical control. The Visual Basic Editor will automatically add the event, and you can enter this line of code to complete it.

```
RowNumber.Text = "2"
```

> **Tip** **Test As You Go**
>
> As you create the code for each button, take time to run the program and see the results. One of the strengths of Visual Basic is that you can quickly test your programs. It's far easier to debug 5 or 10 lines of code that you just added than to wait until you've added a few hundred lines of code.

The Prev and Next buttons are a little more complicated because you need to compute the value of the previous or next row based on the value of the current row. Like the *GetData* routine, this routine (shown in the following listing) begins by verifying that the value contained in *RowNumber* is numeric.

```
Private Sub CommandButton2_Click()

Dim r As Long

If IsNumeric(RowNumber.Text) Then
    r = CLng(RowNumber.Text)

    r = r - 1
    If r > 1 And r <= LastRow Then
        RowNumber.Text = FormatNumber(r, 0)

    End If

End If

End Sub
```

Once the routine has a numeric value, it computes the new position by subtracting *1* (or adding *1* to find the next row). Finally, if the resulting row number is in the range of *2* to *LastRow* −*1*, the value is saved into the RowNumber text box. The assignment will trigger the *Change* event for the *RowNumber* control, and the new information will be loaded.

Jumping to the last row is a bit more difficult because the concept of the last row is somewhat nebulous. After all, just because a worksheet can handle 65,536 rows of data doesn't mean that the user of that application wants to view rows that far down. Instead, it makes sense to look through the worksheet to find the last row with a value in the first column and treat that as the last row.

To make the last row dynamic, a few changes need to be made to the program. First the *LastRow* constant needs to be switched to a variable like this:

```
Public LastRow As Long
```

Then the constant needs to be assigned an initial value when the user form is initially loaded. There are two ways to do this. The easiest way is just to assign it a valid row number such as 3 and then call *GetData* to load the initial values into the form. So, use the following code to create the *UserForm_Initialize* event.

```
Private Sub UserForm_Initialize()

GetData

End Sub
```

If users want to see the last line in the form, they will need to press the Last button. There are several ways to locate the last row in response to the user clicking the Last button. One way would be to scan through all of the data looking for the first empty cell in column one each time the Last button was clicked.

A better way would be to scan through the worksheet and locate the first blank cell in column 1 and assign the value to *LastRow*, which is what the routine shown in the following listing does. This routine is located in the user form module.

```
Private Function FindLastRow()

Dim r As Long

r = 2
Do While r < 65536 And Len(Cells(r, 1).Text) > 0
    r = r + 1

Loop

FindLastRow = r

End Function
```

The *FindLastRow* function scans through the worksheet to find the first cell that doesn't have a value. A simple *While* loop iterates through each cell in column one of the worksheet, and the length of the return value is tested to see if the length is zero. If the length is zero, the loop will end and *r* will point to the last row in the worksheet, which is the first blank row following the data in the worksheet.

Chapter 20

Then you can set the *LastRow* variable by adding the following line to the *UserForm_Initialize* event.

```
LastRow = FindLastRow
```

The *FindLastRow* function can also be used in the event associated with the Last button to update the *LastRow* variable as well as set the value for the *RowNumber* control.

```
Private Sub CommandButton4_Click()

LastRow = FindLastRow - 1
RowNumber.Text = FormatNumber(LastRow, 0)

End Sub
```

Editing Data

At this point, you can view any row of data in the worksheet, but any changes you make in the data displayed on the form aren't saved in the worksheet. There are a lot of different techniques you can use, but here's one that should work well for you.

In this approach, the data displayed on the form is kept separate from the cells on the worksheet until the user explicitly presses either the Save or the Cancel button. Pressing the Save button should copy the data from the form to the worksheet, whereas pressing Cancel should reload the data from the worksheet, overwriting any changes in the user form that may have been made by the user. Both the Save and Cancel buttons should be disabled until the data on the form is actually changed.

The easiest way to disable these buttons is to set their *Enabled* property to *False*. Then change the *Enabled* property to *True* once one of the values in the field changes. You can reduce the amount of work by creating two subroutines, one named *EnableSave* and one named *DisableSave*, which enable and disable the command buttons associated with Save and Cancel, respectively. Then, in the *Change* event associated with the text boxes that contain data, add a call to the *EnableSave* subroutine. This setting means that any change to the data will mark the entire form as *dirty*, meaning that the data in the form is different from the data on the worksheet.

Because loading the data directly from the source means that the data is clean, the Save and Cancel buttons should call the *DisableSave* routine. This call should be placed only after the data is loaded onto the form because it's possible that the user might not have entered a valid row number and *GetData* might not actually reload any data.

The *PutData* routine found in the user form module (shown in the following listing) is similar to the *GetData* routine in that all the validations used to ensure that the value in *RowNumber* is valid are included. The main difference between the two routines is that the *GetData* routine copies information *from* the worksheet, whereas the *PutData* routine copies data *to* the worksheet.

```
Private Sub PutData()

Dim r As Long

If IsNumeric(RowNumber.Text) Then
        r = CLng(RowNumber.Text)

Else
        MsgBox "Illegal row number"
        Exit Sub

End If

If r > 1 And r < LastRow Then
        Cells(r, 1) = CustomerId.Text
        Cells(r, 2) = CustomerName.Text
        Cells(r, 3) = City.Text
        Cells(r, 4) = State.Text
        Cells(r, 5) = Zip.Text
        Cells(r, 6) = DateAdded.Text

        DisableSave

Else
        MsgBox "Invalid row number"

End If

End Sub
```

The error checking isn't absolutely necessary, but it probably is a good idea just in case someone put an invalid value in the *RowNumber* text box, jumped to another application, and then came back. In that scenario, it's possible to enter a different value in the RowNumber text box without retrieving any data.

Notice that after the data is saved to the worksheet, *DisableSave* routine is called. This is necessary because the data on the user form now represents the same data stored on the worksheet.

Adding Data

Pressing the Add button calls the *CommandButton7_Click* event, which displays the first blank row at the end of the worksheet. Because the *LastRow* variable points to this row, it's merely a matter of setting the *Text* property of the *RowNumber* control to this value using code like this:

```
Private Sub CommandButton7_Click()

RowNumber.Text = FormatNumber(LastRow, 0)

End Sub
```

Validating Data

At this point, the form is fully capable of capturing data from the user and inserting it into the worksheet. The form also allows the user to edit the values already stored in the worksheet. The only limitation is that none of the data is validated for correctness.

For instance, it's possible to enter an invalid date as part of the *DateAdded* field. Also, there are no checks to ensure that the *CustomerId* value is numeric. Finally, it's possible to enter the wrong two-character state code. Here are some techniques that you can use to ensure that the data is valid before it reaches your worksheet.

The first technique involves using the *KeyPress* event to ensure that the user can enter only a particular type of information. For example, you could ensure that the user can only enter numbers into the *CustomerId* control using this code:

```
Private Sub CustomerId_KeyPress(ByVal KeyAscii As MSForms.ReturnInteger)

If KeyAscii < Asc("0") Or KeyAscii > Asc("9") Then
    KeyAscii = 0

End If

End Sub
```

> **Tip   Defining Events**
>
> Double-clicking the *CustomerId* control on the user form will automatically take you to the *CustomerId_Change* event. If the event doesn't exist, it will automatically be created. If you want to handle a different event, simply choose the name of the event from the drop-down list at the top of the code window and the Visual Basic Editor will automatically create a blank event with the appropriate parameters.

Another approach involves using the *Exit* event. In the *Exit* event associated with a particular control on the user form, you can determine if the user made an error and highlight the background to give the user a visual clue. You can also display a message box that contains a description of the error using code like this:

```
Private Sub DateAdded_Exit(ByVal Cancel As MSForms.ReturnBoolean)

If Not IsDate(DateAdded.Text) Then
    DateAdded.BackColor = &HFF&
    MsgBox "Illegal date value"
    Cancel = True

Else
    DateAdded.BackColor = &H80000005

End If

End Sub
```

Chapter 20

429

One nice feature of the *Exit* event is that if you set the *Cancel* argument to *True*, the user will be unable to switch the focus to a different control until the text box contains a proper date.

Remember that you also need to set the background color to Window Background (&H80000005) if there isn't an error, to reset any previous error conditions. This is handled by the *Else* clause.

The final technique used in this application prevents errors by substituting a combo box control in place the text box control for *State*. Because the user is limited to choosing one value from the provided list of values, it becomes impossible to enter invalid data.

By setting the *MatchRequired* property of the combo box control to *True*, the user will be prevented from leaving the control until the input matches one of the values in the *List*. Another way to ensure that only a valid value is selected is to set the *Style* property of the combo box control to *fmStyleDropDownList*, which forces the control to operate as a list box, where the user can only choose a value from the specified list of values in the drop-down list instead of typing a value that might not be on the list.

In either case, a routine like the following *AddStates* routine is necessary to initialize the combo box control. This routine would typically be called from the user form's *Initialize* event.

 On the CD   The full list of the states can be found in the *AddStates* routine in the sample program.

```
Private Sub AddStates()

State.AddItem "AK"
State.AddItem "AL"
State.AddItem "AR"
State.AddItem "AZ"

End Sub
```

For more information on validating data, see "Getting Data Entry Right the First Time" on page 187.

Displaying the User Form

The final step in this process is to create a simple macro that displays the user form. In this case, adding the following subroutine to the *ThisWorkbook* object in the Visual Basic Editor is all that's required to show the form. Any time the user wants to use this form, he simply has to run this macro.

```
Public Sub ShowForm()

UserForm1.Show vbModal

End Sub
```

Chapter 20

Creating Advanced User Forms

As the *vbModal* value implies, once the form is displayed, it remains on the screen, preventing the user from accessing any part of the Excel worksheet underneath it. If it's important to provide this level of access, you can switch the *vbModal* value to *vbModeless*. Then the user will be able to switch between the form and the worksheet. (See Figure 20-4.)

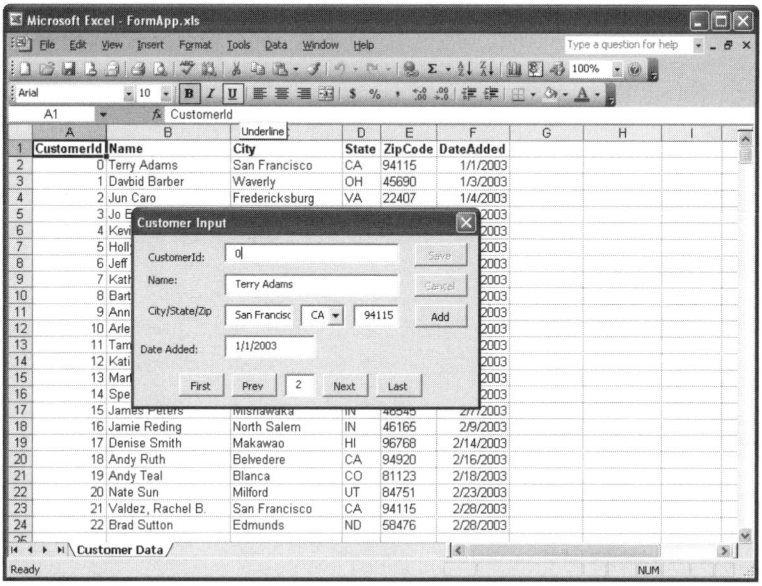

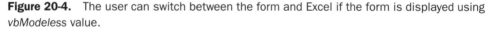

Figure 20-4. The user can switch between the form and Excel if the form is displayed using *vbModeless* value.

> **Warning** Use the *vbModeless* value with care. In this example, allowing the user to access the underlying worksheet also permits the user to change the data that's currently displayed on the user form. If this happens and the user presses the Save button, any changes that the user might have made directly to the row will be lost.

Building a Multi-Step Wizard

The other example in this chapter shows you how to build a multi-step wizard that's invoked from Excel's menus. This example gives you the framework with which to develop your own wizards.

Wizard Application Overview

The wizard in this example merely collects information over several steps and summarizes the information in the final step. Step 1 of the wizard (shown in Figure 20-5) presents the user a choice of four different options using *OptionButton* controls that are nested inside a single frame control. Notice that the Prev button is disabled because this is the first step of the wizard.

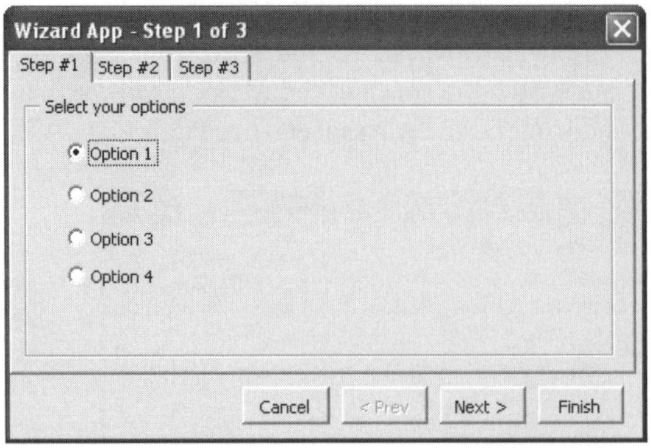

Microsoft Office Excel 2003 Programming Inside Out

Figure 20-5. Step 1 of the wizard allows the user to select from multiple options using the *OptionButton* controls.

Step 2 of the wizard allows the user to enter values into two distinct text box controls. (See Figure 20-6.) Again, a frame control is used to provide instructions to the user.

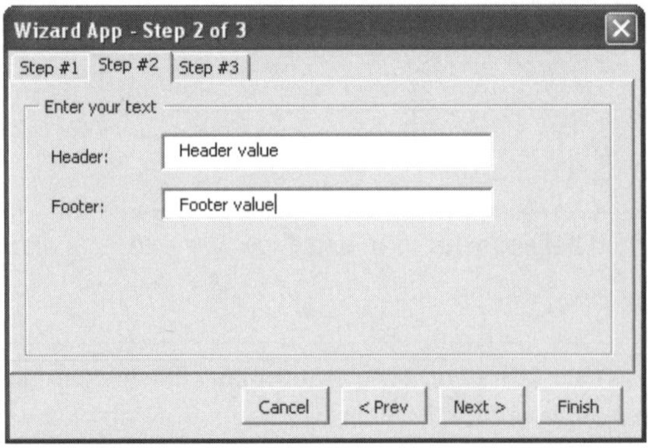

Figure 20-6. The user can enter information into multiple text boxes in step 2 of the wizard.

In the final step of the wizard, the user is given a chance to review the information entered in the previous steps of the wizard. (See Figure 20-7.) The Next button is disabled because there are no subsequent steps. To end the wizard, the user can press either the Cancel or the Finish button.

On the CD The complete source code for this example is found on the CD in WizardApp.xls.

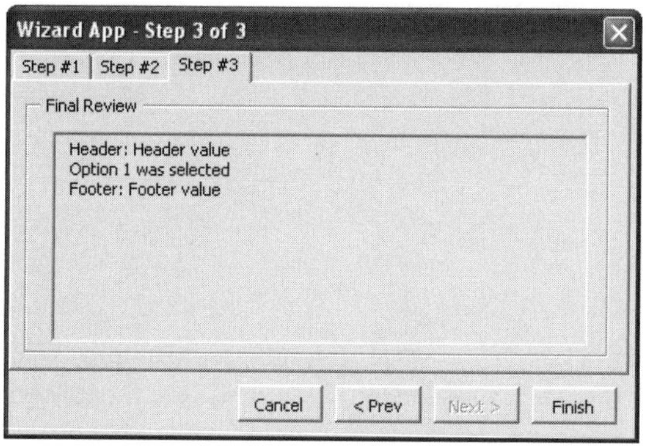

Figure 20-7. Step 3 of the wizard lets the user review all of her choices before clicking Finish.

Handling Menus

The first step in building the wizard application is to trap the workbook's *Open* event to add the necessary menu button. This also means that the *BeforeClose* event should also remove the menu button.

In the *Workbook_Open* event in the *ThisWorkbook* module (see the following listing), a command bar button is added to the Tools menu. The first step is to locate the Worksheet Menu Bar through the *Application.CommandBars* collection. Once the proper command bar is located, then the specific popup control for the Tools menu is located. Finally, a new command button is added to the end of the popup control.

```
Private Sub Workbook_Open()

Dim c As CommandBar
Dim cb As CommandBarButton
Dim cp As CommandBarPopup

On Error Resume Next
Set c = Application.CommandBars("Worksheet Menu Bar")
If Not c Is Nothing Then
    Set cp = c.Controls("&Tools")

    If Not cp Is Nothing Then
        Set cb = cp.Controls.Add(msoControlButton)
        cb.Tag = "Excel 2k3 WizardApp"
        cb.Style = msoButtonCaption
        cb.Caption = "Excel 2k3 Wizard"
        cb.OnAction = "ThisWorkbook.RunWizard"

    End If

End If

End Sub
```

The new command button will fire the *ThisWorkbook.RunWizard* subroutine when the new button is clicked. The only thing that the *RunWizard* routine does is show the wizard's user form using one line of code.

```
Public Sub RunWizard

UserForm1.Show vbModal

End Sub
```

Notice that the *Tag* property in the *Workbook_Open* routine is set to a unique value, to make it easy to remove the button in the *Workbook_BeforeClose* event. (See the following listing.)

```
Private Sub Workbook_BeforeClose(Cancel As Boolean)

Dim c As CommandBar
Dim cb As CommandBarButton

On Error Resume Next
Set c = Application.CommandBars("Worksheet Menu Bar")
If Not c Is Nothing Then
    Set cb = c.FindControl(, , "Excel 2k3 WizardApp", , True)
    Do While Not cb Is Nothing
        cb.Delete
        Set cb = c.FindControl(, , "Excel 2k3 WizardApp", , True)

    Loop

End If

End Sub
```

The code for the *Workbook_BeforeClose* event is probably more complex than is really needed, but it also ensures that any buttons associated with the wizard application are deleted. The code merely locates the first control that contains Excel 2k3 Wizard App in the tag property using the *FindControl* method. Then the code enters a *While* loop that will delete this specific control and then search for the next control with the same *Tag* value.

Building the UserForm

Because the wizard displays several forms' worth of information, it's natural to use the *MultiPage* control. The *MultiPage* control has several properties that make it very useful for this particular situation. First, the *MultiPage* control contains a number of individual *Page* objects.

> For more information about the *MultiPage* control and the *Page* objects, see Chapter 19, "Creating User Forms."

Each *Page* object is a control container, which means that you can drag multiple controls onto each page and access them as if they were placed directly on the form. The real strength of the *MultiPage* control is its ability to switch from one page to another by merely updating the *Value* property. This means that you can prepare a *Page* object for each step of the wizard and then display the *Page* object that corresponds to the appropriate step of the wizard.

To maneuver through the steps of the wizard, you need to add four command button controls at the bottom of the form. Since these buttons are outside of the *MultiPage* control, they will always appear on each step of the wizard. Set the captions for these buttons to **Cancel**, **< Prev**, **Next >**, and **Finish**.

Because this wizard has three steps, you need to add a third page. Right-click over the tab area, and select New Page from the popup menu. This will add a new *Page* object to the *MultiPage* control. (See Figure 20-8.) Then change the caption property for each page to **Step 1**, **Step 2**, and **Step 3**.

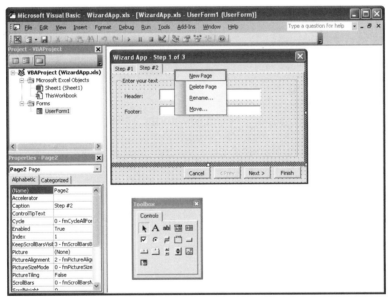

Figure 20-8.   Right-click over the tab area, and select New Page from the popup menu to add a new Page to the *MultiPage* control.

Navigating the Pages

The four buttons at the bottom of the page are the primary tool for navigation in the wizard. Pressing the Cancel button triggers the *CommandButton1_Click* event, which runs the *End* statement to stop the program. Pressing the Prev or Next buttons moves the wizard to the previous or next step, respectively. The Finish button is the only way to trigger the final execution of the wizard.

```
Private Sub CommandButton1_Click()

End

End Sub
```

When the user presses the Prev button, the event associated with the control in the user form module in the following listing is executed. This code computes the new page to be displayed by subtracting 1 from the current page using the *Value* property. If the new page number is greater than or equal to zero, then the new page number is assigned to the *Value* property; otherwise, the click is just ignored.

```
Private Sub CommandButton2_Click()

Dim i As Long

i = MultiPage1.Value - 1

If i >= 0 Then
    MultiPage1.Value = i

End If

End Sub
```

The Next button uses similar code, but increments the *MultiPage* control's *Value* property and verifies that it is less than *MultiPage1.Pages.Count*.

```
Private Sub CommandButton3_Click()

Dim i As Long

i = MultiPage1.Value + 1

If i < MultiPage1.Pages.Count Then
    MultiPage1.Value = i

End If

End Sub
```

In addition to using the Prev and Next buttons, the user can directly select one of the wizard's steps from the tabs at the top of the *MultiPage* control. You can easily hide the tabs by setting the multi-page control's *Style* property to *fmTabStyleNone*.

Tip   **Finding Hidden Controls**

If a control is hidden on the form and you want to change one of its properties, simply select the desired control from the drop-down list of controls at the top of the Properties window.

Any time the *Value* property of the *MultiPage* control is changed, the control's *Change* event is fired. The *MultiPage1_Change* event found in the user form module is the real heart of the wizard's control. Each possible page value is tested and the code appropriate for that page is executed.

```
Private Sub MultiPage1_Change()

If MultiPage1.Value = 0 Then
    CommandButton2.Enabled = False
    CommandButton3.Enabled = True
    UserForm1.Caption = "Wizard App - Step 1 of 3"

ElseIf MultiPage1.Value = 1 Then
    CommandButton2.Enabled = True
    CommandButton3.Enabled = True
    UserForm1.Caption = "Wizard App - Step 2 of 3"

ElseIf MultiPage1.Value = 2 Then
    CommandButton2.Enabled = True
    CommandButton3.Enabled = False
    UserForm1.Caption = "Wizard App - Step 3 of 3"
    GenerateOptions

Else
    MsgBox "Error: invalid page value"

End If

End Sub
```

For the first page (*Value = 0*), the Prev button is disabled, the Next button is enabled, and the user form's *Caption* property is updated to reflect that this is the first step of the wizard. The Prev button is disabled because it's impossible to move before the first step in the wizard. If the user wants to end the wizard, the Cancel button can be pressed.

On the second page (*Value = 1*), both the Prev and Next buttons are enabled because the user can choose to press either button. The user form's *Caption* property is also updated.

On the last page (*Value = 2*), the Next button is disabled because there are no other steps in the wizard. Unlike the other steps in this wizard, there's an extra line of code that prepares the information on the form before the form is displayed to the user. A call to *GenerateOptions* handles the necessary work.

If the *Value* property doesn't match any of the pages associated with the steps of the wizard, a message box displays an error message. In theory, you should never see this message. In practice, it can be very useful when debugging the navigation logic.

Collecting Options for the Wizard

Now that the framework for running the wizard is in place, it's time to show how you might collect some information from the user. These steps demonstrate some of the ways you might collect information. You'll need to determine what information your wizard really needs to collect to perform the task assigned to the wizard.

In step 1 of the wizard, a *Frame* control surrounds a set of four *OptionButton* controls. (See Figure 20-9.) This allows the user to choose any one of four different options without any programming.

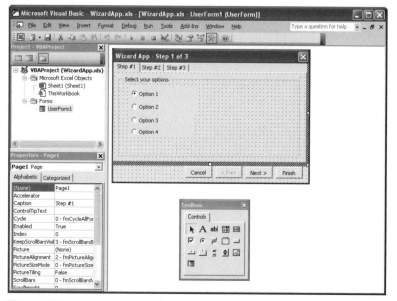

Figure 20-9. A *Frame* control surrounds a set of *OptionButtons*.

In step 2 of the wizard, another *Frame* control is used to provide a consistent look and feel with step 1. Within the frame, two label and text box controls are displayed to capture other information. (See Figure 20-10.) The text box controls are named *Header* and *Footer* to match the *Captions* displayed on the label controls beside them.

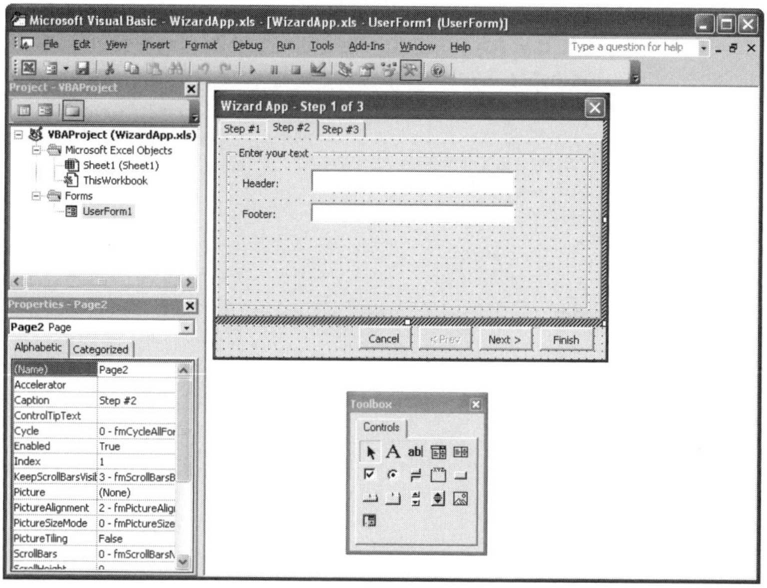

Figure 20-10. A *Frame* control surrounds a collection of label and text box controls.

In the final step of the wizard, shown in Figure 20-11, yet another *Frame* control provides a container for a text box control called *Review*. This text box has the *MultiLine* property set to *True* and the *BackColor* property set to &H8000000F, which is the same color as the background of the form. This indicates to the user that the data contained in the text box can't be changed.

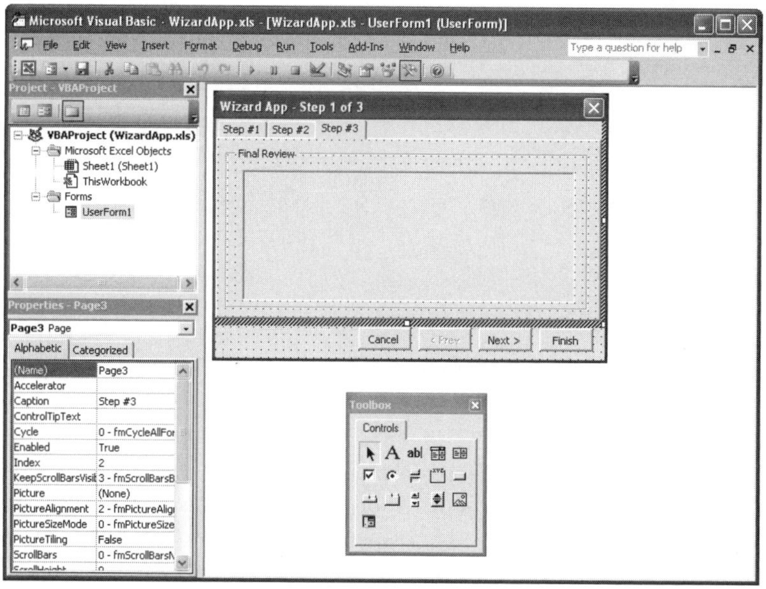

Figure 20-11. A summary of the options selected is displayed in the *Review* text box.

To prevent the user from changing the information in the *Review* text box, the *Review_KeyPress* event is used to suppress any character typed. Setting the *KeyAscii* argument to zero means that the character the user pressed will not be added to the text box.

```
Private Sub Review_KeyPress(ByVal KeyAscii As MSForms.ReturnInteger)

KeyAscii = 0

End Sub
```

Summarizing the Options

The *GenerateOptions* routine (shown in the following listing) combines the information collected in the previous steps of the wizard and displays it for the user's review. This routine is located in the user form module. Remember that this routine accesses the controls that were placed on the other pages of the *MultiPage* control as if they were directly on the user form itself.

```
Private Sub GenerateOptions()

Review.Text = "Header: " & Header.Text & vbCrLf

If OptionButton1.Value Then
    Review.Text = Review.Text & "Option 1 was selected"

ElseIf OptionButton2.Value Then
Review.Text = Review.Text & "Option 2 was selected"

ElseIf OptionButton3.Value Then
    Review.Text = Review.Text & "Option 3 was selected"

ElseIf OptionButton4.Value Then
    Review.Text = Review.Text & "Option 4 was selected"

Else
    Review.Text = Review.Text & "No options were selected"

End If

Review.Text = Review.Text & vbCrLf

Review.Text = Review.Text & "Footer: " & Footer.Text

End Sub
```

This routine uses a multi-line text box control on which the various choices made by the user are displayed. In this example, the information from the various controls is copied to the multi-line text box. Notice that a *vbCrLf* is appended to the *Text* property after each line of information is generated. This forces the next line to be displayed starting at the left edge of the control.

Running the Wizard

Pressing the Finish button actually runs the wizard. In this example, the wizard's execution consists of displaying a message box and then ending the program. In a real wizard, the *MsgBox* statement would be replaced with a call to a subroutine that takes the information collected through the various steps of the wizard and performs whatever task the wizard was designed to perform.

```
Private Sub CommandButton4_Click()

MsgBox "Ending the wizard"

End

End Sub
```

More typically, this routine would collect information collected from the various controls on the user form and then execute whatever function that the wizard was supposed to perform.

It's important to remember that the user may choose to press the Finish button at any time while the wizard is active. Therefore, it might be desirable to give each control on the wizard a meaningful default value so that pressing the Finish button will produce a useful result.

If you choose not to give each control a meaningful value, you should examine the information stored in the controls to determine if there is sufficient information to produce a useful result. If a user hasn't given the wizard enough information to produce a useful result, your verification routine should display the wizard step where the user can supply the information.

In this chapter, you saw how to build two different applications that rely on user forms. In the first application, you saw how you can easily build a user form that allows someone to edit the data contained in a worksheet. By providing a user form, you can insure that the data that's entered into the worksheet is both valid and properly formatted. In the second application, you saw how to build a multi-step wizard with a single a user form and *MultiPage* control. Each *Page* in the *MultiPage* control allows you to create a custom appearance for each step of the wizard, and using a single user form simplifies the development process.

Chapter 20

Part 6

Excel and the Outside World: Collaborating Made Easy

21	Excel and Other Office Applications	445
22	Excel and the Structured Query Language	467
23	Introducing ADO	481
24	Excel Query Program	497
25	Excel and the Web	519
26	Excel and the Extensible Markup Language (XML)	539

Excel and Other Office Applications

Starting Another Application. 445
Activating Another Application 449
Binding 449

Interacting with Other
Office Applications 455
Working with Multiple Applications
to Get the Job Done 465

In the early days of personal computing, communication between multiple applications was rare. The idea of sharing data between two applications meant retyping the information required. However, with today's technologies, communication between applications occurs with most software, although the user usually is unaware of the communication. Thank goodness sharing data between two applications has become as simple as a drag and drop operation.

The Microsoft Office application programs, Microsoft Excel, Word, PowerPoint, Outlook, and Access, all use the same Microsoft Visual Basic for Applications (VBA) language. Once you understand the VBA syntax in Excel, you'll know how to use VBA in all the other applications. Where the Office applications differ is in their individual object models.

The significant advantage about the common VBA language is that all Office applications are able to expose their objects to each other, and you can program interaction between all the applications from any one of them. To work with Word objects from Excel, for example, you only need to establish a link to Word, and then you have access to its objects as if you were programming with VBA in Word itself.

In this chapter, you'll learn how to start and activate another application from Excel. In addition, you'll be examining how to interact with other Office files, such as using late binding and early binding, opening a document in Word, accessing an active Word document, and creating a new Word document. Finally, to finish the chapter, you'll examine how to control Excel from other Office applications.

Starting Another Application

There are times when you need to start another application from Excel. Later in this chapter, you'll review how to interact with other Office applications, but right now you'll review how to open an application that falls outside the Office application scope.

There are a variety of reasons why you might need to interact with an additional application. For example, you might want to use the Calculator, Character Map, or even a DOS batch file from Excel. In fact, you can execute a Control Panel application, if necessary. To accomplish these tasks using VBA code, use the *Shell* function. The following procedure starts the Calculator application using the *Shell* function:

```
Sub RunCalculator()
    On Error Resume Next
    Program = "calc.exe"
    TaskID = Shell(Program, vbNormalFocus)
    If Err <> 0 Then
        MsgBox "Unable to start " & Program, vbCritical, "Error"
    End If
End Sub
```

The *Shell* function returns the task identification number for the application. The task identification number can be used in later code to activate the task. The second argument for the *Shell* function determines the window state of the application, such as minimized, maximized, hidden, or normal. If the function generates an error, the *On Error* statement will display a message indicating that the file can't be found.

> **Note** Remember that if you have subsequent code following the *Shell* function, the code will be executed immediately. If an instruction requires user intervention, Excel's title bar flashes to notify the user while the other application is active.

An alternate method used to start an application is using the **Start** command. The **Start** command can be executed from the Run dialog box or directly from a DOS window. This command is available in most versions of Microsoft Windows. The **Start** command is used to start a Windows-based application from a DOS window. Using the **Start** command doesn't require the code to open the program associated with the document; the command uses the program associated with the filename to open the application as well as the file. You are required to enter the full path to the file and extension for this command to execute properly. Figure 21-1 shows an example of how to open the Fall Initiative.ppt file using the **Start** command.

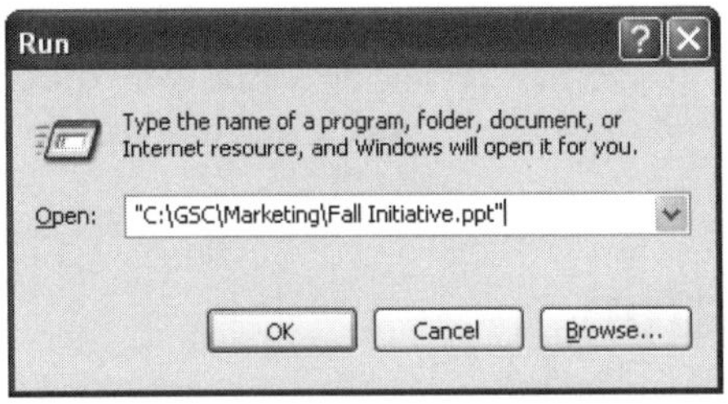

Figure 21-1. You can use a **Start** command in the Run dialog box to open a presentation file.

Excel and Other Office Applications

You're able to achieve the same results using the **Start** command within your VBA code. For example, a sales representative from The Garden Company can launch PowerPoint and open a Marketing presentation file from Excel. Review the code that follows to see how to achieve these results.

> **Note** The following example will work if you are using an operating system previous to Microsoft Windows NT. If you have Microsoft Windows NT or later, you will need to use the *ShellExecute* function to achieve the same results. The *ShellExecute* function is explained in the next example. Although you need Microsoft Windows 2000 or Windows XP (or later) to run Excel 2003, this procedure will work if you're trying to run Excel 2003 code in an older version of Excel. There might, of course, be other incompatibilities.

```
Sub OpenPresentation()
    Filename = "C:\Garden Supply Company\Marketing\Fall Initiative.ppt"
    Shell "Start " & Filename
End Sub
```

> **Tip** **Automating Mail**
> To send an e-mail message using VBA code, the **Start** command is an effective way to start the message. Use `Shell "Start info@thegardencompany.com"` to start the default mail client. If you are using Windows NT or later, you will need to replace the **Shell** command with the *ShellExecute* function.

Because the **Start** command isn't available with Windows NT or later operating systems, you need to use the *ShellExecute* function to achieve similar results. The following example uses the *ShellExecute* function to open Microsoft's home page:

```
Private Declare Function ShellExecute Lib "shell32.dll" Alias "ShellExecuteA" _
    (ByVal hWnd As Long, ByVal lpOperations As String, ByVal lpfile As String, _
    ByVal lpParameters As String, ByVal lpDirectory As String, ByVal nShowCmd _
    As Long) As Long

Sub OpenFile()
    File = "http://www.microsoft.com"
    Call ShellExecute(0&, vbNullString, file, vbNullString, vbNullString, _
        vbNormalFocus)
End Sub
```

Inside Out

Simulate a Pause in VBA code

There might be times when you are required to launch an application; however, you'll want to pause your VBA code until the application is closed. For example, the application launched is creating a file that is required later in your procedure. Because you're unable to pause your code, you can work around this situation by programming a loop that monitors the applications status. The following procedure was designed to display a message box when the application launched by the *Shell* function is no longer active:

```
Declare Function OpenProcess Lib "kernel32"
(ByVal dwDesiredAccess As Long, ByVal bInheritHandle As Long, ByVal _
dwProcessId As Long) As Long

Declare Function GetExitCodeProcess Lib "kernel32"
(ByVal hProcess As Long, lpExitCode As Long) As Long

Sub RunCharMap()
    Dim TaskID As Long
    Dim hProc As Long
    Dim lExitCode As Long

    ACESS_TYPE = &H400
    STILL_ACTIVE = &H103

    Program = "Charmap.exe"
    On Error Resume Next

    TaskID = Shell(Program, vbNormalFocus)
    hProc = OpenProcess(ACCESS_TYPE, False, TaskID)

    If Err <> 0 Then
        MsgBox "Unable to start " & Program, vbCritical, "Error"
        Exit Sub
    End If

    Do
        GetExitCodeProcess hProc, lExitCode
        DoEvents
    Loop While lExitCode = STILL_ACTIVE

    MsgBox Program & " is no longer the active application"
End Sub
```

While the launched program is active, the procedure continues to loop until the *lExitCode* returns a different value. When the loop ends, the VBA code will resume.

Chapter 21

Activating Another Application

You might be wondering what steps to take if the application you want to use is already open. Using the *Shell* function would create a second instance of the program taking up valuable memory. In most cases, you should activate the program that's running, rather than creating a new instance of the program.

Consider the following example, in which the *ActivateCalculator* procedure uses the *AppActivate* statement to activate the application if the application is already running. The argument for the *AppActivate* statement is the caption of the application's title bar. If the *AppActivate* statement generates an error, it means the Calculator isn't running, so the procedure will start the application.

```
Sub ActivateCalculator()
    AppFile = "Calc.exe"
    On Error Resume Next
    AppActivate "Calculator"
    If Err <> 0 Then
        CalcTaskID = Shell(AppFile, vbNormalFocus)
        If Err = 0 Then MsgBox "Unable to start the Calculator"
    End If
End Sub
```

Binding

You can write an Excel macro to control the most important component of Microsoft Word, its *automation server*. In such a macro, Excel would act as the client application and Word would act as the server application. You can also write a VB application to control Excel. The process of one application controlling another is referred to as *Automation*, formerly *OLE Automation*.

Automation allows you to develop complex macros that have the ability to control objects from a variety of applications. This is an incredibly powerful tool when creating application files. Automation allows the user to interact with multiple applications, such as Access, and not even realize the interaction is occurring. Automation allows a single seamless interface for the end user.

As you are aware, you can use the Insert menu to add a variety of Objects into your workbook. You can alternatively use Excel VBA to create the same types of objects. When you create the object, you'll have full access to the object's properties and methods available from its host application. This automation method is preferable for developers, rather than using the **Object** command from the Insert menu. When the object is embedded, the user must know how to use the *Automation* object's application. However, when you use VBA to manipulate the object, you can program the object so that the user can manipulate it by clicking the object.

Before you work with the external object, you must create an instance of the object. This can be done using one of the two types of binding, early or late. *Binding* refers to matching the function calls to the actual code that implements the function.

449

Late Binding

In *late binding*, the matching process between the object variable and the object takes place when the application is run. The result is slower performance compared to *early binding*, in which the binding takes place when the application is compiled.

With late binding, you need to declare general object variables because the Object Library belonging to the foreign application is not activated. It is more challenging to program the foreign objects because the properties, methods, and events won't automatically appear while programming your procedure in regard to the foreign object. However, late binding lets you create an *Application* object regardless of the version installed on the user's system. This is the preferred method of binding when the file will be distributed to users that might have different versions of the software. Therefore, your procedure would open Microsoft Word regardless of the version installed.

You use the *CreateObject* function to create the object or the *GetObject* function to create the instance of the application. The object is then declared as a generic *Object* type, and its object reference is resolved at run time. The following procedure displays how to use late binding with the Word application:

```
Sub UsingLateBinding()
    Dim oApp As Object
    Dim oDoc As Object
    On Error Resume Next
    Set oApp = GetObject(, "Word.Application")

    If oApp Is Nothing Then
        Set oApp = CreateObject("Word.Application")
    End If
    On Error GoTo 0
    If oApp Is Nothing Then
        MsgBox "The application is not available!", vbExclamation
    End If
    With oApp
        .Visible = True
        Set oDoc = _
            .Documents.Open("C:\GSC\Employee Info\Health Benefits.doc")
        oDoc.Close True
        .Quit
    End With
    Set oDoc = Nothing
    Set oApp = Nothing
End Sub
```

This additional sample procedure also uses late binding but shows you how to create an entry in the Outlook Calendar.

```
Sub MakeOutlookAppointmentLateBinding()
    Dim olApp As Object
    Dim olAppointment As Object
    Const olAppointmentItem = 1

    Set olApp = CreateObject("Outlook.Application")
    Set olAppointment = olApp.CreateItem(olAppointmentItem)

    With olAppointment
        .Subject = "Spring Sales Initiative Meeting"
        .Location = "Radisson: Meeting Room A"
        .Start = DateSerial(2005, 3, 7) + TimeSerial(9, 30, 0)
        .End = DateSerial(2005, 3, 7) + TimeSerial(11, 30, 0)
        .ReminderPlaySound = True
        .Save
    End With
    olApp.Quit
    Set olApp = Nothing
End Sub
```

The basic technique in programming another application is to create an object variable referring to that application. The object variable in this case is *olApp*. You then use the *olApp* variable to refer to objects in the external application's object model. In this example, the *CreateItem* method of Outlook's *Application* object is used to create a reference to a new *AppointmentItem* object.

Because Outlook's constants are not available when late binding is used, you must define your own constants, such as *olAppointmentItem* in this example, or substitute the value of the constant as the parameter value. The properties and methods of the *Appointment* object in the *With…End With* structure modify the new object that was created.

When declaring the *olApp* and *olAppointment* as generic Object types, late binding is forced on the VBA procedure. All the links to Outlook can't be established until the procedure executes the *CreateObject* function. The *CreateObject* input argument defines the application name and class of object to be created. *Outlook* is the name of the application and *Application* is the class. Many applications allow you to create objects at different levels in the object model. For example, Excel allows you to create *WorkSheet* or *Chart* objects from other applications, using *Excel.WorkSheet* or *Excel.Chart* as the input parameter of the *CreateObject* function.

Tip **Save Your Memory**

It's good programming practice to close the external application when you are finished with it and set the object variable to *Nothing*. This releases the memory used by the link and the application.

If you execute this macro in Excel, it appears as though nothing has happened. However, if you open Outlook and navigate to March 7, 2005, you'll see the appointment has been added to the Calendar. Figure 21-2, displays the appointment created in the Calendar on March 7, 2005.

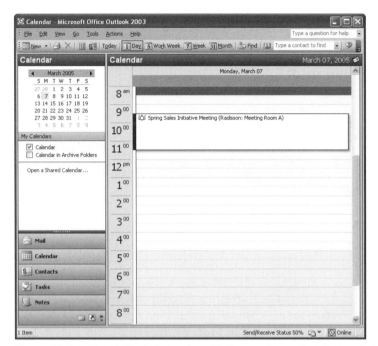

Figure 21-2. The Outlook Calendar with the newly created Spring Sales Initiative Meeting on the morning of March 7, 2005.

Early Binding

In early binding, the binding between the object variable and the object occurs when the application is compiled. The end result is better performance compared to late binding. You can add an Object Library using the **References** command from the Tools menu in the Visual Basic Editor. When the reference has been added to the VBA Project, you are able to declare specific object variables. This is an easier method of programming foreign objects because the Visual Basic Editor will display the same programming help regarding the foreign object that it would display for the object belonging to the application you are working from.

Before programming the procedure, add the appropriate reference. Follow these steps to add a reference to Microsoft Outlook.

1 Open the Visual Basic Editor.

2 Select the References option from the Tools menu.

3 Scroll through the available references until you find the Microsoft Outlook Object Library.

4 Check the box beside the reference.

5 Click OK to close the References dialog box.

Figure 21-3, displays the References dialog box with the Outlook Object Library selected.

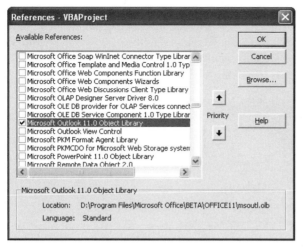

Figure 21-3. The References dialog box displays all available references. To activate a library file, select the reference and click OK.

Now that the reference has been added to the Visual Basic Editor, you'll have the available assistance with objects created using this library file. VBA will search through the type libraries, in the order shown from top down, to find the references to object types. If the same object type is present in more than one library, VBA will use the first one found. You can select a library and click the Priority buttons to move it up and down the list to change the order in which libraries are searched. There's no need to depend on priority; you can reference the object with the application object. For example, instead of using *AddressList*, use *Outlook.AddressList*.

Review the following example to see how early binding is used. The procedure lists all the names in the Outlook Contacts folder, placing them in column A of the active worksheet. Make sure that you have added a reference to the Outlook Object Library before executing this procedure.

```
Sub DisplayOutlookContactNamesEarlyBinding()
    Dim olApp As Outlook.Application
    Dim olNameSpace As Outlook.Namespace
    Dim olAddresslist As AddressList
    Dim olEntry As AddressEntry
    Dim i As Long

    Set olApp = New Outlook.Application
    Set olNameSpace = olApp.GetNamespace("Mapi")
    Set olAddresslist = olNameSpace.AddressLists("Contacts")
    For Each olEntry In olAddresslist.AddressEntries
        i = i + 1
        Cells(i, 1).Value = olEntry.Name
    Next

    olApp.Quit
    Set olApp = Nothing
End Sub
```

You probably noticed that while this code was executed, you received a warning similar to the one in Figure 21-4. The security against viruses has increased dramatically since the release of Office XP. The trend has continued with the release of Office 2003. Any attempt by programs trying to access e-mail addresses will execute a warning message. You'll also receive a warning each time an e-mail message is sent using VBA code.

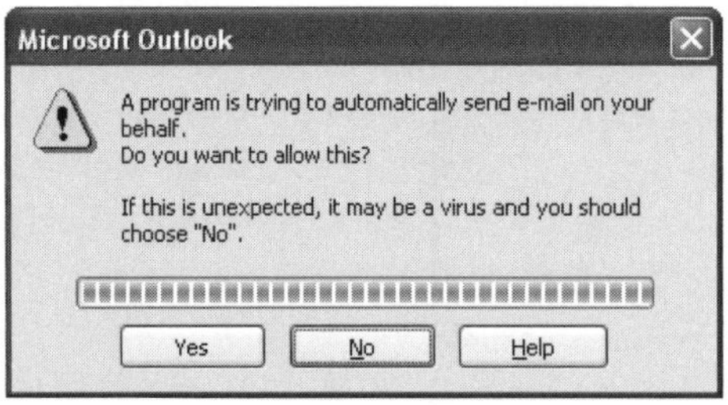

Microsoft Outlook

A program is trying to automatically send e-mail on your behalf.
Do you want to allow this?

If this is unexpected, it may be a virus and you should choose "No".

Yes   No   Help

Figure 21-4.   Warning message you get when executing code that interrogates your Contacts folder in Outlook.

Inside Out

Early Binding vs. Late Binding

Both early binding and late binding have advantages and disadvantages. Late binding is slower than early binding because the binding occurs during run time. When you complete the work in design time, the code will run faster. When you are writing code using late binding, you lose some conveniences. Specifically, you aren't able to use the IntelliSense that displays the available properties and methods available for the objects that you're using. The Object Browser also won't list the objects for the application objects that you're programming. Another disadvantage is that the convenience of built-in constants isn't available when using late binding.

It would appear that a strong case has been made to use early binding; however, there's one strong advantage to late binding that shouldn't be overlooked. When late binding is used, it doesn't matter which version of the application is installed. The application object will search for the version installed on your system and choose the correct object mode to reference. In early binding, you'll choose the application's Object Library from the References list. The References list will contain only installed object libraries. If you choose to share your procedure with others, the list will be coded specifically to the version of the software that's installed on your system.

The moral of the story is to write your code initially using early binding, but before distributing the file you should modify the code to use late binding. It would be a good idea to modify your personal projects to late binding as well, so a problem won't arise when your software is upgraded in the future.

Chapter 21

In the *DisplayOutlookContactNamesEarlyBinding* procedure, you declared *olApp* to be an *Outlook.Application* type. The other *Dim* statements also declare object variables of the type that you required to complete the objectives. If the same object name is used in more than one Object Library, you can precede the object name by the name of the application, rather than depend on the priority of the type library. You'll notice this technique was used with the Outlook *NameSpace* property. The *New* keyword is used when assigning a reference to *Outlook.Application* to *olApp* to create a new instance of Outlook.

Because the variable types were declared, the VBA procedure is forced to use early binding. You could use the *CreateObject* function to create the *olApp* object variable, instead of the *New* keyword, without affecting the early binding. But it's more efficient to use the *New* keyword.

Interacting with Other Office Applications

Using VBA to access other Microsoft Office applications is similar to using code to work with objects within the code's host application. To begin, you create an object variable that points to the *Application* object representing the Office application that contains the objects you want to work with. It's preferable to use an early bound object variable by using the *New* keyword. Alternatively, you can choose to use the *CreateObject* function or the *GetObject* function to create an object variable.

When VBA code manipulates objects within the same application, the reference to the *Application* object is implicit. However, when you are automating another application, the reference to the *Application* object must be explicit.

Review the following examples to see the difference between how the *Application* object is referenced, implicitly and explicitly. The first procedure demonstrates how to create a new Excel workbook and how to reference the *Application* object implicitly. The second procedure demonstrates how to refer to the Microsoft Word application explicitly and to create a new document. For the second procedure to be executed successfully, the reference to the Microsoft Word Object Library must first be added to the Excel application using the Tools, References command in the Visual Basic Editor.

```
Sub CreateNewWorkbookFromExcel()
    Dim xlNew As Excel.Workbook

    Set xlNew = Workbooks.Add
    ActiveCell.Value = "Created " & Date
End Sub

Sub CreateWordDocumentFromExcel()
    Dim wdApp As Word.Application
    Dim docNew As Word.Document
```

```
    Set wdApp = New Word.Application
    Set docNew = wdApp.Documents.Add
    wdApp.Selection.TypeText "This file was created " & Date
        With docNew
        MsgBox "'" & .Name & "' was created " & Date & "."
        .Close wdDoNotSaveChanges
    End With
    wdApp.Quit
    Set wdApp = Nothing
End Sub
```

Typically, you'll create an object variable that refers to the *Application* object representing the application you want to access through automation. When the *Application* object has been referenced, you can include additional references to the object's *child objects* to navigate to the object or method you want to manipulate. Use the *Set* statement to assign object variables to child objects.

> **Note** The top-level object is the *Application* object. The *Application* object contains other objects that you can only access if the *Application* object exists. The objects dependent on the *Application* objects, are often referred to as the *child objects*. The child objects may also have children of their own. For example, the Excel *Workbook* object is the child object to the Excel *Application* object, and the *Worksheets* object is the child object of the Excel *Workbook* object.

However, Microsoft Excel and Word make it possible to create a top-level reference to some child objects of the *Application* objects. Knowing this fact, you can rewrite the code for the *CreateWordDocumentFromExcel* procedure to start from a reference to a Word *Document* object.

```
Sub CreateWordDocumentFromExcel2()
    Dim docNew As Word.Document

    Set docNew = New Word.Document
    Set docNew = Documents.Add
    docNew.Application.Selection.TypeText "This file was created " & Date
    With docNew
        MsgBox "'" & .Name & "' was created " & Date & "."
        .Close wdDoNotSaveChanges
    End With
    Set docNew = Nothing
End Sub
```

You can use the same theory in Excel using the *Workbook* object as your top-level reference. You can do this by using the *Excel.Sheet* class name to create the workbook or by using the *Excel.Chart* class name to create a workbook that contains a worksheet with an embedded *Chart* object and a worksheet that contains a default data set for the chart.

To create a *Workbook* object, you use the *CreateObject* function because the *Excel.Sheet* and *Excel.Chart* class names don't support the *New* keyword. The following example automates Excel, starting with a *Workbook* object that contains a single worksheet:

```
Dim wbkSheet As Excel.Workbook
Set wbkSheet = CreateObject("Excel.Sheet")
```

To automate Excel starting with the *Workbook* object that contains a worksheet with a chart and another worksheet, use the following code.

```
Dim wbkChart As Excel.Workbook
Set wbkChart = CreateObject("Excel.Chart")
```

When automating Excel starting from a *Workbook* object or automating Word starting from a *Document* object, an implicit reference is created to the *Application* object. If you need to access properties and methods of the *Application* object, use the appropriate *Application* property of the *Document* or *Workbook* objects. Using the *Document* or *Workbook* objects as top-level objects reduces the amount of code you have to write. In most cases your code will be easier to follow and more consistent than when you reference the *Application* object. Table 21-1 lists all the top-level *Office* objects that can be referenced and their class names.

Table 21-1. Top-Level Office Objects and Their Associated Class Names

Top-Level *Office* Object	Class Name
Access Application object	*Access.Application*
Excel Application object	*Excel.Application*
Excel Workbook object	*Excel.Sheet*
	Excel.Chart
FrontPage Application object	*FrontPage.Application*
Outlook Application object	*Outlook.Application*
PowerPoint Application object	*PowerPoint.Application*
Word Application object	*Word.Application*
Word Document object	*Word.Document*

Opening a Document in Word

If you want to open a file created using a different Office application than you are currently using, use the *GetObject* function to directly open the file. However, it's just as easy to open an instance of the application and open the file from the application.

The following code copies a range in Excel to the clipboard. It then starts a new instance of Word, opens an existing Word document and pastes the range at the end of the document. Because the code uses early binding, be sure to set up the reference to the Word Object Library first.

> **Note** In the example that follows, be sure to replace the worksheet name and the file-name to reference a file located on your computer. If you are referencing files that don't exist, an error will occur when you test this procedure.

457

```
Sub CopyFromExcelToWord()
    Dim wdApp As Word.Application

    ThisWorkbook.Sheets("Table").Range("A1:B6").Copy
    Set wdApp = New Word.Application

    With wdApp.Application
        .Documents.Open Filename:="C:\test.doc"
        With .Selection
            .EndKey unit:=wdStory
            .TypeParagraph
            .Paste
        End With
        .ActiveDocument.Save
        .Quit
    End With
    Set wdApp = Nothing
End Sub
```

> **Tip**   **Debugging with Hidden Application Objects**
>
> When a procedure includes applications that aren't visible, you might run into memory issues when debugging your code. When a procedure opens a hidden copy of an application and the code is stopped before the *Quit* method has been executed, an instance of the application will continue to run in the background until it has been forced to close. Each time the procedure is run and stopped before the *Quit* method is executed, an additional copy of the application will be in memory. This can cause serious memory errors with your system, so be sure to force the hidden application to close by using the Task Manager.

The *New* keyword creates a new instance of Word, even if it is already open. The *Open* method of the *Documents* collection is used to open an existing file. The code then selects the end of the document, enters a new empty paragraph, and pastes the range. The document is then saved, and the new instance of Word is closed.

Now that you can open an existing Word document and place Excel data into Word, consider the following scenario. The Garden Supply Company has the promotional schedule outlined in a document named Spring Promotion.doc. You need to enter the same information into Excel. The following procedure will open the Word document and will place a copy of the file contents into a new Excel workbook:

```
Sub CopyWordToExcel()
Dim wrdApp As Word.Application
Dim wrdDoc As Word.Document
Dim tString As String
Dim tRange As Word.Range
Dim i As Long
Dim r As Long
```

```
        Workbooks.Add
        r = 3
        Set wrdApp = CreateObject("Word.Application")
        Set wrdDoc = GetObject("C:\GSC\Correspondence\Spring Promotion.doc")
        With wrdDoc
            For i = 1 To .Paragraphs.Count
                Set tRange = .Range(Start:=.Paragraphs(i).Range.Start, _
                    End:=.Paragraphs(i).Range.End)
                tString = tRange.Text
                tString = Left(tString, Len(tString) - 1)
                ActiveSheet.Range("A" & r).Formula = tString
                r = r + 1
            Next i
        End With
        With Range("A1")
            .Formula = "File Contents of: " & wrdDoc.Name
            .Font.Italic = True
            .Font.Size = 18
        End With
        wrdDoc.Close
        wrdApp.Quit
        Set wrdDoc = Nothing
        Set wrdApp = Nothing
        ActiveWorkbook.Saved = True
    End Sub
```

Inside Out

GetObject vs. CreateObject

The *GetObject* and the *CreateObject* functions both return references to an object, so how do you choose which one to use?

The *CreateObject* function is used to create a new instance of the application. Use this function if the application you need to reference is not currently open. If an instance is already running, a second instance of the application will be initiated. Consider the following example. The Garden Supply Company has an Excel Workbook that copies data into a Microsoft Word document for the monthly sales reports. To create a new instance of Microsoft Word, you should use the following code:

```
Set xlApp = CreateObject("Word.Application")
```

The *GetObject* function is used with an application that is already running or to start an application with a file already loaded. The following example starts Excel and opens Myfile.xls:

```
Set XLBook = GetObject("C:\Myfile.xls")
```

The object returned in *XLBook* is a reference to the *Workbook* object.

Accessing an Active Word Document

Now that you can open an Office application, what if you simply need to access a program that is already open? If you have a current instance of an application running, you don't need to create a new instance and use additional resources. You can activate the running application by using the *GetObject* function.

The following example uses early binding and the *GetObject* function to copy a table to an open Word document:

> **Note** This function requires Microsoft Word to be open for the information to be pasted into the active document.

```
Sub CopyFromExcelToOpenWordDocument()
    Dim wdApp As Word.Application

    ThisWorkbook.Sheets("Table").Range("A1:B6").Copy

    Set wdApp = GetObject(, "Word.Application")
    With wdApp.Selection
        .EndKey unit:=wdStory
        .TypeParagraph
        .Paste
    End With
    Set wdApp = Nothing
End Sub
```

The *GetObject* function has two input parameters, both of which are optional. The first parameter specifies a file to be opened. The second parameter specifies the application used to open the file. If you don't specify the first parameter, the *GetObject* function assumes you want to access a currently open instance of Word. If you specify a zero-length string as the first parameter, *GetObject* assumes you want to open a new instance of Word.

You can use the *GetObject* function, to access a current instance of Word that's in memory. But if there is no current instance of Word running, the *GetObject* function with no first parameter causes a run-time error.

> **Note** When any program is opened, it creates an instance of the application in the computer's memory. If the same application is opened multiple times, you will see multiple entries for the application in the Task Manager. For the best performance, it's preferable to use an open instance of an application, rather than creating a new instance.

The following example accomplishes the same task. However, the Word window is visible, and the text is inserted at the insertion point:

```
Sub AccessActivateApp()
    Application.ActivateMicrosoftApp xlMicrosoftWord
    Dim appWord As Word.Application
    Dim doc As Word.Document
```

```
    Set appWord = GetObject(, "Word.Application")

    appWord.Visible = True
    appWord.Activate

    Set doc = appWord.ActiveDocument

    appWord.ShowMe

    With doc
        doc.Activate
        doc.Application.Selection.TypeText "This file was created " & Date
    End With
End Sub
```

Creating a New Word Document

There will be times when you want to create a new file instead of working with an existing Word document. To accomplish this task, you need to have an open instance of Word and then you'll create a new document.

The following example uses early binding, so the code to create a new document is the same as if you were creating a new document from Word. Before you test this procedure, add the Word Object Library to your procedure.

```
Sub CopyFromExcelToNewWordDocument()
    Dim wdApp As Word.Application

    ThisWorkbook.Sheets("Table").Range("A1:B6").Copy

    On Error Resume Next
    Set wdApp = GetObject(, "Word.Application")

    If wdApp Is Nothing Then
        Set wdApp = GetObject("", "Word.Application")
    End If
    On Error GoTo 0

    With wdApp
        .Documents.Add
        .Visible = True
    End With

    With wdApp.Selection
        .EndKey unit:=wdStory
        .TypeParagraph
        .Paste
    End With

    Set wdApp = Nothing
End Sub
```

If there isn't a current instance of Word, using the *GetObject* function with no first argument causes a run-time error. The On Error Resume Next line will allow the code to continue and use the value in the *wdApp* variable to determine if a new instance of the application will be opened. If the Word application is not loaded into memory, the code then uses the *GetObject* function with a zero-length string as the first argument, which opens a new instance of Word. Once the instance of Word has been identified, the procedure creates a new document. The code also makes the new instance of Word visible, unlike our previous examples, where the work was done behind the scenes without showing the Word window. The copied data is then pasted at the end of the Word document. At the end of the procedure, the object variable *wdApp* is released, but the Word window is accessible on the screen so that you can view the result.

The *CreateNewWordDoc* procedure demonstrates how to create a new document, but rather than paste contents into the document the procedure enters the creation date of the file. The program window is also closed, and the file is saved as NewWordDoc.doc.

```
Sub CreateNewWordDoc()
    Dim wrdApp As Word.Application
    Dim wrdDoc As Word.Document
    Dim i As Integer
    Set wrdApp = CreateObject("Word.Application")
    wrdApp.Visible = True
    Set wrdDoc = wrdApp.Documents.Add
    With wrdDoc
        .Content.InsertAfter "This document was created " & Date & " " & _
            Time & "."
        .Content.InsertParagraphAfter
        .Content.InsertParagraphAfter
        If Dir("C:\NewWordDoc.doc") <> "" Then
            Kill "C:\NewWordDoc.doc"
        End If
        .SaveAs ("C:\NewWordDoc.doc")
        .Close
    End With
    wrdApp.Quit
    Set wrdDoc = Nothing
    Set wrdApp = Nothing
End Sub
```

Controlling Excel from Other Office Applications

Now to go full circle, you should know how to reference the Excel *Application* object from other Office applications. The same concepts apply; you must start by adding the Excel Object Library to the procedure of the host application, if using early binding. Then you must create an Excel object as outlined in Table 21-2.

Table 21-2. Excel Objects and Their Functions

Top-Level *Office* Object	Class Name
Application object	CreateObject("Excel.Application")
Workbook object	CreateObject("Excel.Sheet")
Chart object	CreateObject("Excel.Chart")

The following procedure was created in Word 2003. A reference was included to reference the Excel Object Library. To execute this procedure, you must add the Excel reference, enter the procedure into Word, and then create a new workbook in the root directory of your C: drive named *NewExcelWbk.xls*.

```
Sub OpenWriteExcelWbkContents()

Dim xlApp As Excel.Application
Dim xlWbk As Excel.Workbook
Dim tString As String, r As Long
    Documents.Add
    Set xlApp = CreateObject("Excel.Application")
    Set xlWbk = Excel.Workbooks.Open("C:\NewExcelWbk.xls")
    r = 1
    With xlWbk.Worksheets(1)
        While .Cells(r, 1).Formula <> ""
            tString = Cells(r, 1).Formula
            With ActiveDocument.Content
                .InsertAfter "Contents of file: " & xlWbk.Name
                .InsertParagraphAfter
                .InsertParagraphAfter
                .InsertAfter tString
                .InsertParagraphAfter
            End With
            r = r + 1
        Wend
    End With
    xlWbk.Close
    xlApp.Quit
    Set xlWbk = Nothing
    Set xlApp = Nothing
End Sub
```

The previous example created a basic Excel workbook. Now that you can create a basic workbook, you can copy data and a chart into a Word document. One such workbook is shown in Figure 21-5.

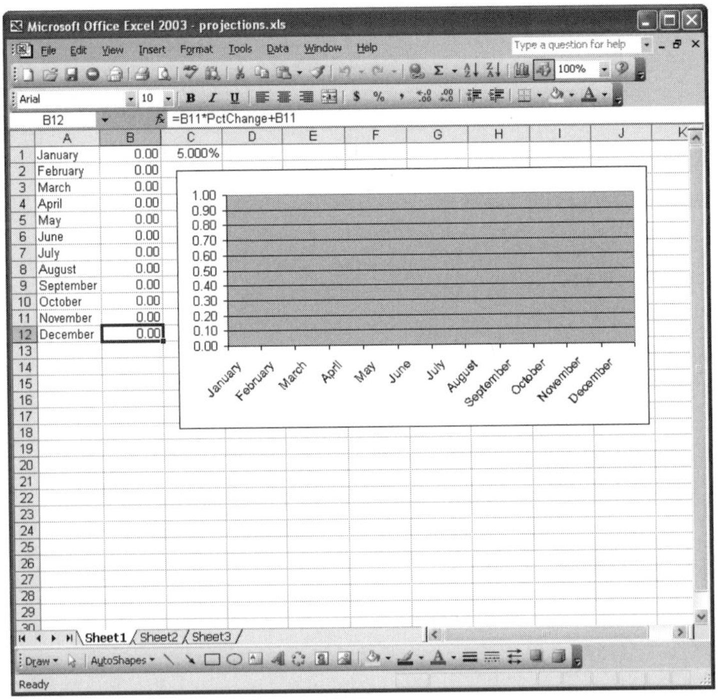

Figure 21-5. Here's a sample workbook, displaying the basic setup of data used to create the chart.

> **Tip** Setup Requirements
>
> The workbook requires some basic setup to run the procedure effectively. The procedure references the filename projection.xls; if you choose to use a different filename, modify your code to reflect the filename you've chosen. You need to define the range names: *StartingValue* and *PctChange*. Each month is calculated based on the previous month multiplied by the *PctChange* value. These values won't be saved in the Excel workbook before it's closed. The information used to create the chart has also been assigned the range name *Data*. Finally, create an embedded chart to see the full scope of this procedure.

The *CreateExcelChart* procedure prompts the user for two values and inserts the values into the worksheet. When the new data is entered into the worksheet the chart is automatically updated.

```
Sub CreateExcelChart()
    Dim XLSheet As Object

    Documents.Add

    StartVal = InputBox("Starting Value?")
```

Chapter 21

```
PctChange = InputBox("Percent Change?")

WBook = "C:\GSC\Financial\projections.xls"
Set XLSheet = GetObject(WBook, "Excel.Sheet").ActiveSheet

XLSheet.Range("StartingValue") = StartVal
XLSheet.Range("PctChange") = PctChange
XLSheet.Calculate

With Selection
    .Font.Size = 14
    .Font.Bold = True
    .TypeText "Monthly Increment: " & Format(PctChange, "0.0%")
    .TypeParagraph
    .TypeParagraph
End With

XLSheet.Range("data").Copy
Selection.Paste

XLSheet.ChartObjects(1).Copy
Selection.PasteSpecial link:=False, DataType:=wdPasteMetafilePicture, _
    Placement:=wdInLine, DisplayAsIcon:=False
Set XLSheet = Nothing
End Sub
```

Working with Multiple Applications to Get the Job Done

There are times when simply working within Excel is too restrictive. That's the main reason you bind your workbook to additional applications.

Throughout this chapter, you learned how to access different applications. The *Shell* function can be used to open programs that fall outside of Microsoft Office Suite. However, when working within the Microsoft Office Suite you need to access the different *Application* objects. It's possible to reference a new *Application* object using late binding; however, it's recommended that you use early binding when programming your procedures.

To automate the objects in another application, you create an object variable referring to the target application or an object in the application. You can use early binding or late binding to establish the link between VBA and the other application's objects. Early binding requires that you establish a reference to the target application's object library, and you must declare any object variables that refer to the target objects using their correct type. If you declare the object variables as the generic *Object* type, VBA uses late binding.

Early binding produces code that executes faster than late binding, and you can get information on the target application's objects using the Object Browser and the shortcut tips that automatically appear as you type your code. Syntax checking and type checking is also performed as you code, so you are less likely to get errors when the code executes than with late binding.

You must use the *CreateObject* or the *GetObject* function to create an object variable reference to the target application when using late binding. You can use the same functions when early binding, but it's more efficient to use the *New* keyword. However, if you want to test for an open instance of another application at run time, *GetObject* can be used with early binding as well.

The techniques presented in this chapter allow you to create powerful programs that tap into the unique abilities of different products. The user remains in a familiar environment such as Excel, while the code ranges across any product that has a type library and exposes its objects to VBA.

Excel and the Structured Query Language

Comparing Spreadsheets
and Databases 467
Manipulating Databases with SQL 471
The *Select* Statement 471
The *Insert* Statement 478
The *Update* Statement 479
The *Delete* Statement 479

One of the many useful features of Microsoft Excel is its ability to access information in databases. You can copy information from a database table to a worksheet or from a worksheet to a database table. You can even combine information from a Microsoft Access database or a Microsoft SQL Server database with a user form.

This chapter serves as a brief introduction to using databases such as Microsoft Access and Microsoft SQL Server with Microsoft Excel. Because designing an effective database is beyond the scope of this book, design is not discussed at all. But there are a number of good books that cover Microsoft Visual Basic and database programming. However, in the context of programming Excel 2003, you should look for a book that covers database programming for Visual Basic 6, not for Visual Basic .NET. Visual Basic .NET is not compatible with the Visual Basic for Applications (VBA) facilities included with Excel. On the other hand, Visual Basic 6 is fairly close to VBA, and it uses the same tools (specifically ADO) to access a database. So the database programming techniques for Visual Basic 6 can be carried over to Excel and VBA without change.

Comparing Spreadsheets and Databases

In many respects, a *worksheet*, consisting of a series of rows and columns, is very much like a table in a relational database. This similarity can make a worksheet a powerful tool for manipulating database information.

Fundamental Database Concepts

A *relational database* consists of a series of tables. Each table roughly corresponds to a single worksheet. A table is structured as a series of rows and columns of data, as shown in Figure 22-1.

Customer ID	Company Name	Contact Name	Contact Title
ALFKI	Alfreds Futterkiste	Maria Anders	Sales Representative
ANATR	Ana Trujillo Emparedados y helados	Ana Trujillo	Owner
ANTON	Antonio Moreno Taquería	Antonio Moreno	Owner
AROUT	Around the Horn	Thomas Hardy	Sales Representative
BERGS	Berglunds snabbköp	Christina Berglund	Order Administrator
BLAUS	Blauer See Delikatessen	Hanna Moos	Sales Representative
BLONP	Blondel père et fils	Frédérique Citeaux	Marketing Manager
BOLID	Bólido Comidas preparadas	Martín Sommer	Owner
BONAP	Bon app'	Laurence Lebihan	Owner
BOTTM	Bottom-Dollar Markets	Elizabeth Lincoln	Accounting Manager
BSBEV	B's Beverages	Victoria Ashworth	Sales Representative
CACTU	Cactus Comidas para llevar	Patricio Simpson	Sales Agent
CENTC	Centro comercial Moctezuma	Francisco Chang	Marketing Manager
CHOPS	Chop-suey Chinese	Yang Wang	Owner
COMMI	Comércio Mineiro	Pedro Afonso	Sales Associate
CONSH	Consolidated Holdings	Elizabeth Brown	Sales Representative
DRACD	Drachenblut Delikatessen	Sven Ottlieb	Order Administrator
DUMON	Du monde entier	Janine Labrune	Owner
EASTC	Eastern Connection	Ann Devon	Sales Agent
ERNSH	Ernst Handel	Roland Mendel	Sales Manager
FAMIA	Familia Arquibaldo	Aria Cruz	Marketing Assistant

Figure 22-1. A database table is constructed as a series of rows and columns.

A database table doesn't rely on row numbers, like a worksheet. Also, columns don't have arbitrary column names such as A, B, or C. Instead, tables rely on *set theory*, which means that you deal with groups of rows, not the individual columns. A set of rows extracted from one or more tables can be thought of as a *virtual table* or a *view*. The tables used to create a view are known as *base tables*. A view can be created from one or more base tables or other views in the database. Views are important because many operations in a relational database create or return virtual tables.

Unlike worksheets, whose cells can store any type of data, relational databases require that each column must have a single data type. Typically, this data type can be a binary number, a string of characters, a *Boolean* value, a date/time value, or an unformatted binary value. In addition to having a data type associated with each column, a column in a particular row may contain a *Null* value. *Null* means that a value has not been assigned to the column. Notice that an empty string isn't the same thing as a *Null* value; an empty string is a string that contains zero characters, whereas *Null* simply means that the column doesn't have a value.

> **Note** It's possible to create tables where *Null* values are not acceptable for a particular column or columns. See your database documentation for more information about how *Null* values are handled.

Because of the rigid structure imposed on tables, data is typically separated into multiple tables, with each table containing information about a single entity. Thus, you might have one table containing information about customers, another containing information about products, and a third table containing information about the orders the customers place. Fortunately, you can manipulate this complex arrangement of data using a language called the Structured Query Language (SQL). SQL statements make it possible to retrieve and update information stored in tables.

> **Note** Depending on whom you talk to, you'll hear the acronym SQL pronounced either as the word *sequel* or as a series of letters (*S-Q-L*). Both pronunciations are correct, but the first came about because the Structured Query Language used to be known as the Structured *English* Query Language.

Inside Out

Database Design and Administration

Designing and using databases can be a complex task. Most organizations have one or more individuals that are responsible for the database system. This is especially true if you are using a high-performance database such as Microsoft SQL Server, Oracle, or DB2. If you are not sure how these databases work in your organization, look for the individual called the *database administrator*. The database administrator should be able to answer many questions that apply to your specific environment.

In situations where you are dealing with simple database systems such as Access, you might not have a database administrator. In these cases, you might want to talk to the person who wrote the programs for the database. This individual should be able to provide you information, such as connection strings, that you need to open the database from Excel.

If you want to design your own database, keep in mind the following: KISS (Keep It Simple Stupid) and SMILE (Simple Makes It Lots Easier). If you have only a few hundred pieces of data, consider keeping all the data in a set of Excel worksheets. You might find it easier to maintain than building a real database.

If you really believe that you need a database, take some time and read some books that provide a good introduction to databases such as *Microsoft Office Access Inside Out* by John L. Viescas (Microsoft Press, 2003). Just keep in mind that it's very easy to design a database that's so complex to use that it really doesn't address your original needs.

Database Keys

A database *key* is a way to identify a set of rows in a table. The *primary key* for a table is a way to uniquely identify a particular row in the table. Often the primary key is a single column, such as *CustomerId* or *EmployeeId*, which could uniquely identify a row in the Customers or Employees tables. However, it's desirable that the primary key for a table can span multiple columns. In other words, the combination of *OrderNumber* and *ItemNumber* uniquely identifies a particular item purchased within an order.

A *secondary key* is different from the primary key in that it need not uniquely identify a single row. In fact, secondary keys are useful for locating groups of rows that have something in common, such as all the customers in a particular city or all the orders that were placed on the same date.

A *foreign key* is merely a secondary key in one table that is also the primary key in another table. Foreign keys are useful for identifying a group of data that is related, such as the collection of orders that was placed by a particular customer or the item numbers that comprise a single order.

Tip   Indexes Save Time

Primary keys and foreign keys are often used to optimize database access. Database designers use the keys to create indexes on the tables, which can significantly speed up access to a particular set of rows. Whenever possible, you should use indexes as part of the search criteria when retrieving data from a database.

Some databases, including Microsoft Access, allow you to define an *identity column*. An identity column (called an *AutoNumber* column in Access) automatically generates a new value when a row is inserted into the table. This type of column is extremely useful as the primary key for a table because the database guarantees that the value is always unique.

Accessing Databases from Excel

Databases are typically organized around the client/server concept. (See Figure 22-2.) This model assumes that the database server is separate from the database program that accesses the server. A database program uses a particular application programming interface (API), which in turn, communicates with the database server.

Client

Server

Figure 22-2.   Databases are typically organized as a database client talking to a database server.

Excel relies on an API called Active Data Objects (ADO) to access databases. ADO is a standard component in Microsoft Windows, so it's always available to your program. Using ADO, you can connect to a variety of different databases, including Access, SQL Server, Oracle, and others.

Note   Although Access doesn't rely on the traditional client/server model, you still use the ADO interface to connect to an Access database.

Once you've established a connection with a database server with ADO, you can execute SQL statements to return data to your application or to make changes to the data stored in a table.

Chapter 22

Manipulating Databases with SQL

SQL provides a rich collection of statements for manipulating data in a relational database. In practice, most of these statements apply to creating or modifying tables or other database objects stored in the database, which leaves only four main statements that the average programmer really needs to understand in order to write database programs.

- The *Select* statement specifies the rows of data you want to retrieve from the database.
- The *Delete* statement specifies the rows of data you want to remove from the database.
- The *Insert* statement specifies the rows of data that you want to add to the database.
- The *Update* statement specifies how to change existing rows of data in the database.

For instance, here's a *Select* statement that retrieves some rows of customer information:

```
Select CustomerId, Name, City, State
From Customers
Where State = 'WA'
```

This *Select* statement returns a set of rows that contains four columns, CustomerId, *Name*, *City*, and *State*, all from the Customers table. However, instead of returning every row in the table, only the rows where the State column contains the string 'WA' are returned. The other statements are equally easy to use. The statements have a number of common clauses, which means that if you know how to use one of the statements, learning how to use the others will be a straightforward process.

> **Note** Although the SQL language is an international standard, each database vendor is free to add extensions to the language. What this generally means is that the exact syntax of the SQL language will vary from one database to another. For the most part, these differences aren't important, especially if you stick to the core syntax.

The *Select* Statement

The *Select* statement is used to retrieve a set of rows from one or more tables and is probably the most commonly used statement in the SQL language. Here is its syntax:

```
Select <selectexpression> [,<selectexpression>]…
From <tableref> [,<tableref>]…
[Where <expression>]
[Order By <expression> [Asc|Desc] [, <expression> [Asc|Desc] ] …
Where
<selectexpression> ::= * |
    <selectitem> [ [As] <alias> ]
<selectitem> ::= <column> |
    <table>.<column> |
    <tablealias>.<column> |
    <expression> |
    <function> ( <expression> )
```

```
<function> ::= Count |
    Max |
    Min |
    Sum
<tableref> ::= <table> |
    <table> <tablealias>
```

Where *<alias>* is an alternate name of a column, *<tablealias>* is an alternate name of a table and, *<expression>* is a valid expression.

> **Note** The *Select* statement is the most complicated statement in the SQL language. Although the syntax in the preceding code might seem intimidating, keep in mind that it represents only a small part of the full syntax for a *Select* statement. However, the syntax listed here is generally supported by all database vendors, so you can use it with most applications.

Simple *Select* Statements

Rather than spend a lot of time trying to learn the syntax rules for the *Select* statement, you're going to see a series of examples for common situations that illustrate how use the *Select* statement.

Retrieving Everything

The following *Select* statement retrieves all the columns and rows from the Customers table:

```
Select *
From Customers
```

The asterisk (*) indicates that all the columns in the table should be retrieved, and the *From* clause indicates that the command should pull the records from the Customers table.

Retrieving a List of Columns

Suppose that you don't want to retrieve all the columns from a table. You can use this *Select* statement to retrieve only the columns that you are planning to use. This query retrieves only the CustomerId and *Name* columns from the Customers table.

```
Select CustomerId, Name
From Customers
```

> **Tip** Only Take What You Really Need
>
> Although using an * to retrieve columns makes your SQL statement easier to type, it can cause problems. The more data you retrieve from a database, the longer the query will take to process and the more additional memory will be required to hold the results. Granted, the extra time and space might be negligible for many queries, but it's still a good programming practice to request only the resources you really need.

Retrieving Rows

Both of the prior examples retrieve all the rows of data from the database. Although doing so can be useful in many situations, it can also cause significant problems, too. Imagine that you're working for a large company whose tables contain millions of rows of data. Retrieving all that data would overwhelm any computer. Instead of returning every row from a table, if all you really want to do is to retrieve the rows associated with a particular customer or for a particular Zip code, you can use the *Where* clause to pick just the rows you want.

> **Important**   If your *Select* statement doesn't contain a *Where* clause, you should probably ask if you really need all the data or if you just need some of the rows. Although it can be appropriate to retrieve all the rows from a table (for example, when you want to copy a table to a worksheet), in most cases it isn't necessary and could have a negative impact on your database server's performance.

Using Simple Search Expressions

Using the *Where* clause entails creating an expression that identifies the rows you want to retrieve. If the expression is *True*, the row will be returned; otherwise, it'll be ignored.

For example, the following *Select* statement retrieves only the rows where the *CustomerId* is 101. Because the *CustomerId* column is the primary key for this table, this statement will always return a single row from the table.

```
Select *
From Customers
Where CustomerId = 101
```

Notice that you can use other comparison operators in the *Where* clause. In addition to the equals sign (=), you can use the less than sign (<), the greater than sign (>), the less than or equal to sign (<=), the greater than or equal to sign (>=), or the not equal to sign (<>).

Using Complex Search Expressions

You can also use other operators such as *And*, *Or*, and *Not* to create more complex expressions. This query chooses every customer that was added during 2003.

```
Select *
From Customers
Where DateAdded >= '01-Jan-2003' And DateAdded <= '31-Dec-2003'
```

> **Note**   The SQL syntax requires that non-numeric values such as character strings and dates should be enclosed in single quotes ('). Double quotes (") are used to specify column and table names which contain spaces.

Using *Null*

You can determine if a column doesn't have a value in a particular field by using the *Is Null* expression. In this example, only the rows where the DateAdded field contains a *Null* value will be returned.

```
Select *
From Customers
Where DateAdded Is Null
```

Using the *Like* Operator

The *Like* operator is a very powerful tool that lets you search for values in a column using wildcard characters. For instance, the following *Select* statement matches every customer where the value in the Name column starts with the letters *Free*:

```
Select *
From Customers
Where Name Like 'Free*'
```

Table 22-1 contains a list of wildcard characters that you can use with the Access database. Remember that these characters can be used in any combination, as in the following *Select* statement, which retrieves all customers whose names begin with *D*, *E*, or *F*:

```
Select *
From Customers
Where Name Like '[D-F]*'
```

Table 22-1. Wildcard Characters in Access

Character	Meaning	Examples
*	Matches zero or more characters.	A*
		True: A, AA, AB, ACC
		False: B, BA
		A*A
		True: AA, AAA, ABA, ACCA
		False: AB, AAB
		A
		True: A, AB, CAC,
		DADD
		False: B, BB, CCC
?	Matches a single character.	A?
		True: AA, AB, AC
		False: AAA, BA

474

Table 22-1. **Wildcard Characters in Access**

Character	Meaning	Examples
#	Matches a single digit.	A#
		True: A0, A9
		False: AA, A00
[]	Matches the character or range of characters specified inside the brackets. Remember that using an exclamation point (!) means that the characters outside the range will match the value.	A[*]A
		True: A*A
		False: AAA
		A[D-F]A
		True: ADA, AFA
		False: AAA, ADAA
		A[!0-9]
		True: AA, AB
		False: A0, A9

When possible, try to limit the use of the *Like* operators to those columns that are part of an index. Without the index, the database might have to examine each and every row to find the rows that match. And, even with an index, you'll get the best performance if you use the wildcard characters at the end of the search string.

> **Note** Every database system has its own unique set of wildcard characters. For instance, the * used by Access is the % in SQL Server. Be sure to make sure that you're using the proper wildcard characters in your program.

Sorting Rows

One of the architectural quirks of a relational database is that the database server is free to return rows in any order. However, you can use the *Order By* clause to force the database server to return in the order you specify. For example, the following *Select* statement retrieves all the customers from the database in Zip code order:

```
Select Name, Street, City, State, Zip
From Customers
Order By ZipCode
```

This *Select* statement will sort the rows first by Zip code and then within each Zip code by customer's name.

```
Select Name, Street, City, State, Zip
From Customers
Order By ZipCode, Name
```

Finally, you could use the *Desc* (short for *descending*) keyword to reverse the order of the sort in the *Select* statement. Thus, although the rows will be stored in ascending order by Zip code, within each Zip code, the customer names will be ordered from Z to A (descending order) instead of A to Z (ascending order).

```
Select Name, Street, City, State, Zip
From Customers
Order By ZipCode, Name Desc
```

Using Multiple Tables

Thus far, you've seen how to use the *Select* statement with a single table. It's possible to retrieve rows from multiple tables to create a single virtual table. This is called a *join opera-tion*. Adding a *From* clause to a *Select* statement lets you specify more than one table name. However, joining two tables can be very tricky, and you might not necessarily get the results you would expect.

The Wrong Way to Join Two Tables

If you assume that joining two tables would result in a combination of all the columns from both tables, you would be correct. However, if you assume that the rows are combined intel-ligently, you would be wrong.

Simply specifying two table names in a *Select* statement means that the database will combine the first row in the first table with each row in the second table. Then the database will take the second row in the first table and combine it with each row in the second table. This pro-cess repeats for each row in the first table, which means that if the first table has 100 rows, and the second table has 200 rows, simply joining the two tables together will return a table con-taining 20,000 rows.

The Right Way to Join Two Tables

Rather than blindly joining all the rows in the first table with those in the second, you can use the *Where* clause to identify how the two tables will be joined. Typically, you will join two tables together when a particular value in one table is the same as a value in another table. For example, consider two tables. One table contains customers, whereas the second contains orders placed by customers. Typically, each customer in the Customers table would have a field that uniquely identifies the customer, such as *CustomerId*.

Likewise, the Orders table would also contain a field that indicates which customer placed the order. Let's assume that this field is also named *CustomerId*. Now suppose you want to create a list of all the customers and the orders they placed. You want to join the Customers table with the Orders table, but only when the *CustomerId* in each table is identical so that you will only join a customer's information and the customer's orders.

Resolving Column Names

If you tried to code the preceding example as a *Select* statement, you would run into a problem because both tables have a *CustomerID* column. Fortunately, the *Select* statement lets you use *dot notation* to combine a table name with a column name to uniquely identify a column when dealing with multiple tables. The form is *<tablename>.<columnname>*, so in the case of the previous example, you would refer to the columns as `Customers.CustomerId` and `Orders.CustomerId`. The resulting *Select* statement would look like this:

```
Select *
From Customers, Orders
Where Customers.CustomerId = Orders.CustomerId
```

Using Aliases

Just as Excel lets you create names you can use to refer to groups of cells, SQL lets you define aliases for a table name. An *alias* is merely a short name that can be used in place of the table's name. To define an alias, you follow the name of the table with its alias when you refer to the table in the *From* clause.

```
Select *
From Customers c, Orders o
Where c.CustomerId = o.CustomerId
```

Using Functions

The *Select* statement lets you perform summary operations over the entire set of rows that would normally be returned. Just as summary operations in Excel (such as SUM, COUNT, or COUNTBLANK) return a single value, the SQL summary functions return a single row containing the result of the function. For example, you can count the number of records a *Select* statement might return by using the COUNT function to count the number of *CustomerId* values retrieved.

```
Select Count(CustomerId)
From Customers
```

Other functions available include: MIN, MAX, and AVERAGE. You should be aware that while the COUNT function merely counts each individual row, the other functions work with the value contained in each individual column. Thus, MAX and MIN will return the largest and smallest values found in that column, respectively. The AVERAGE function totals all the values found in that column and then divides by the number of rows. If you apply the AVERAGE function to a column that doesn't contain numeric values, you will get an error.

The *Insert* Statement

The *Insert* statement adds a new row to a table. Here is its syntax:

```
Insert [Into] <table> [(<column> [, <column> ]…)]
[Values (<value> [, <value> ]…)]
```

Where *<table>* is the name of the table where the new row will be added,*<column>* is the name of a column in the table, and *<value>* is the value for the corresponding column.

> **Note**   Like the *Select* statement, the syntax presented here covers only part of the full syntax for the *Insert* statement. However, the information presented here will work on nearly any database server. Check your database vendor's documentation for the complete set of options for the *Insert* statement.

Using the *Insert* Statement

You must specify the name of the table where the row will be added with the *Insert* statement; following the table name is an optional list of column names and a list of values to be inserted into the database. The position of each value in the list of values corresponds to the position of the column in the list of columns. If you don't specify all the columns in the *Insert* statement, columns not listed will be set to *Null*.

Although the list of column names is optional, you probably should list them anyway. Otherwise, you have to ensure that your values are listed in the same order that the columns are listed in the database. Although this isn't hard to verify, if you do make a mistake or, more importantly, if the database is changed, the order of the columns might change.

> **Caution**   If your table contains an Identity column, you should not include it in the list of columns when you execute an *Insert* statement. The database will generally return an error if you explicitly attempt to insert a value into the Identity column. There are techniques that might permit you to insert a value instead of relying on the database to automatically generate one. See your database system's documentation for more information.

The following statement shows how to insert a new row of data into the Customers table. The value *12345* is stored in the CustomerId column, *a customer* is stored in the *Name* column, and so forth. Any columns not specified in this list will contain *Null*.

```
Insert Into Customers (CustomerId, Name, Street, City, State, ZipCode)
Values (12345, 'A customer', 'on a street', 'Tacoma, 'WA', 98422)
```

The *Update* Statement

The *Update* statement changes the values for one or more columns in the table. Here is its syntax:

```
Update <table>
Set <column> = <value> [, <column> = <value>]…
[Where <expression>]
```

Where *<table>* is the name of the table that you wish to update, *<column>* is the name of the column in the table, *<value>* is the new value that will be stored in the column, and *<expression>* is true for all the rows that should be updated.

The *Update* statement provides a method that permits you to change the value of one or more columns in the table. You must explicitly specify each column that you wish to change, along with the column's new value. Also remember that the *Update* statement can include a *Where* clause. This *Where* clause is identical to the one you use in the *Select* statement and it works just like you would expect. Only the rows that match the expression in the *Where* clause will be updated—the other rows will remain unchanged.

Tip   Limit Your Exposure

If your *Update* statement doesn't have a *Where* clause, ask yourself "Do I really want to change all the rows in the table?" If your answer is no, you had better double-check the statement before you try to execute it.

In this example, the *Where* clause is used to identify all the rows that contain a *Null* value in the *DateUpdated* field. The *DateUpdated* column is then set to '*01-Jan-2003*'.

```
Update Customers
Set DateUpdated = '01-Jan-2003'
Where DateUpdated Is Null
```

The *Delete* Statement

The *Delete* statement removes rows from a table. Here is its syntax.

```
Delete From <table>
[Where <expression>]
```

Where *<table>* is the name of the table that you wish to update, and *<expression>* is true for all the rows that should be updated.

You can use the *Delete* statement to remove one or more rows from a table. Simply specifying *Delete From Customers* will delete every row from the Customers table. However, this isn't a good idea unless you really want an empty table. Using the same *Where* clause in the *Select* statement lets you limit the number of rows deleted.

Caution If you accidentally delete all the rows from your table, you might be in trouble. Once the rows are deleted, they can't be undeleted. There isn't really an Undo function for a database like you find in Excel. Pressing Ctrl+Z will not undo your changes. There are techniques (for example, using transactions) that an advanced database programmer can use to allow you to recover from this type of error, but in general once the rows are deleted, it's best to assume they're gone.

This example deletes all the rows that have a *DateUpdated* value that is earlier than 31 December 2002.

```
Delete From Customers
Where DateUpdated <= '31-Dec-2002'
```

In this chapter, you learned a little bit about how relational databases such as Microsoft Access and Microsoft SQL Server work. You also learned about the Structured Query Language more commonly referred to as *SQL*. This language defines statements that allow you to retrieve data from a database (*Select*), add data to a database (*Insert*), change data in the database (*Update*), and remove data from the database (*Delete*).

Introducing ADO

The ADO Object Model 482   The *Command* Object. 487
The *Connection* Object 483   The *Recordset* Object. 491

ActiveX Data Objects (ADO) lets you use Excel VBA to access a database. ADO relies on a Data Provider/Data Consumer model. (See Figure 23-1.) This model is similar in concept to the client/server model, except that the client/server model generally assumes that your database operates as an independent server. This restriction doesn't apply to ADO.

Figure 23-1.   A data consumer makes requests to a data provider, which returns a response about the request to the data consumer.

Instead, ADO requires only that the data provider supply data upon request of the Data Consumer. The actual protocol used between the data provider and data consumer is known as OLE DB, which means that as long as a program has an OLE DB–compliant data provision routine, it can appear to an application program as a database. The net result is that a wide variety of programs that might not be considered database providers can be used as data sources for Microsoft Excel Visual Basic for Applications (VBA), in addition to Excel.

Note   Besides ADO, you can use other programming interfaces such as RDO (Remote Database Objects) and DAO (Data Access Objects) to manipulate your database. Both of these programming application program interfaces (APIs) have a lot of limitations when compared with ADO, which is why they aren't covered in this book. ADO is more flexible and better supported than RDO, whereas DAO is specifically optimized for Microsoft Access databases. Unless you have a specific requirement to use either of these APIs, you'll be better off using ADO.

The ADO Object Model

There are three main objects in the ADO object model. (See Figure 23-2.) The *Connection* object represents the information needed to establish the connection between the data consumer and the data provider. The *Command* object contains information about an SQL statement or other database command that will be executed by the database server. The *Recordset* object contains the rows from the virtual table that was created by the *Command* object.

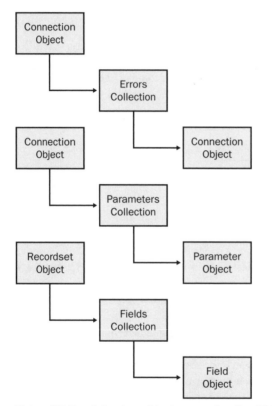

Figure 23-2. A few key objects comprise the ADO object model.

In addition to these objects, there are also a few other objects that support these main objects. Those supporting objects are the *Error* object, which contains information about any errors that occur, and the *Parameter* object, which contains information about any parameters associated with the *Command* object. The *Field* object contains information about a column returned in the *Recordset* object.

Using the ADO Object Model

There are two basic scenarios for using ADO depending on the type of command you want to execute. If the command doesn't return any rows, the following scenario works well.

1 Create a *Connection* object to connect to the desired database.

2 Open the *Connection* object.

3 Prepare a *Command* object that contains the database command to be executed.

4 Add any necessary *Parameter* objects to the *Command* object, including the values to be passed to the command. Remember that not all commands require parameters.

5 Set the *ActiveConnection* property to the *Connection* object.

6 Execute the *Command* object.

7 Close the *Connection* object.

If the command returns rows from the database, you should use this approach:

1 Create a *Connection* object to connect to the desired database.

2 Open the *Connection* object.

3 Prepare a *Command* object that contains the database command to be executed.

4 Add any necessary *Parameter* objects to the *Command* object, if the *Command* object has parameters.

5 Set the *ActiveConnection* property to the *Connection* object.

6 Create a new *Recordset* object with all the options that you plan to use.

7 Set the *ActiveCommand* property in the *Recordset* to the *Command* object that you created.

8 Open the *Recordset* object.

9 Retrieve the rows from the *Recordset* object.

10 Close the *Recordset* object.

11 Close the *Connection* object.

The *Connection* Object

The *Connection* object describes the connection between the application program and the database server. Coupled with the *Errors* collection and the *Error* object, the *Connection* object controls the logical connection to the database.

Chapter 23

483

Key Properties and Methods of the *Connection* Object

Table 23-1 lists some of the key properties and methods associated with the *Connection* object.

Table 23-1. Key Properties and Methods of the *Connection* Object

Property/Method	Description
Close	Method: closes the connection to the database.
ConnectionString	Property: defines how to connect to the database.
CursorLocation	Property: specifies where the current record pointer is maintained. Can be: *adUseClient* or *adUseServer*.
Errors	Property: pointer to an *Errors* collection object containing the list of individual *Error* objects that describe the most recent error encountered on the connection.
Mode	Property: determines how the database is opened. Can be *adModeRead*, *adModeWrite*, *adModeReadWrite*, *adModeShareDenyRead*, *adModeShareDenyWrite*, *adModeShareExclusive*, or *adModeShareDenyNone*.
Open ConnectionString, UserId, Password	Method: establishes a connection to the database using the optionally supplied *ConnectionString*, *UserId*, and *Password* values.
State	Property: describes the state of the connection. Can be *adStateClosed* or *adStateOpen*.

The *Open* method opens a connection to the database using the optional information. If not supplied, the information from the *ConnectionString* property will be used. The *Close* method terminates an open connection to the database server. The *State* property allows you to determine if the connection is open or closed to the database.

The *CursorLocation* property determines where the cursor is kept. Typically, you'll set this property to *adUseServer* to simplify the programming involved, especially if you're using Access. However, if you're using SQL Server, Oracle, DB2, or some other shared database server, you might want to check with your database administrator to determine what value is appropriate.

The *Mode* property determines what level of data access you require. Specifying *adModeRead* means that your program only reads data from the database and that your program can coexist with other applications that specified *adModeRead*. If you plan only to write to the database (which isn't very common), you can use the *adModeWrite* value. However, if you plan to read and write information from the database, you should choose the *adModeReadWrite* value.

The *adModeShareDenyRead*, *adModeShareDenyWrite*, and *adModeShareExclusive* properties all control how other programs will share the database with yours. In general, if you have multiple users sharing the same database, see your database administrator for the appropriate values for the *Mode* property.

Connecting to Different Database Management Systems

The *ConnectionString* property is the most important property in the *Connection* object. The exact information in the connection string varies depending on the type of database you want to use.

Connection strings are composed of a series of keywords and values separated by semicolons that provide the information necessary to locate the data provider and the database, along with any security information that might be required.

Connecting to Access Databases

Access databases rarely require little more than the name of the provider and the location of the database file in a connection string, like this:

```
Provider=Microsoft.Jet.OLEDB.4.0;Data Source=C:\Excel2k3\Customer.mdb
```

The *Provider* keyword selects the data provider for Access. For Access 2000 and newer databases, you should use the Microsoft.Jet.OLEDB.4.0 provider. Older Access databases might require this provider: Microsoft.Jet.OLEDB.3.51.

> **Note** The database engine typically used to power an Access database is known as *Microsoft Jet*. In addition to Access, several other products rely on the Jet database engine. However, because most people access Jet only through Access, it's common to refer to the database engine as Access as well.

The *Data Source* keyword points to the location of the database on disk. Typically, this is a file path as shown in the earlier example, although it can reference a file using a file share format (\\athena\d\Excel2k3\Customer.mdb).

Connecting to SQL Server Databases

Connecting to SQL Server databases involves a somewhat more complicated connection string, although it's not as bad as you might expect.

```
Provider=SQLOLEDB.1;Data Source=athena.justpc.com;
    Initial Catalog=Music;User ID=Wayne;Password=TopSecret
```

The *Provider* keyword references SQLOLEDB.1, which is the SQL Server data provider.

The *Data Source* keyword points to the database server that you want to access, and the *Initial Catalog* keyword indicates the name of the database on the particular database server that you want to open.

Finally, the *User ID* and *Password* keywords present authentication information to the database server. If you wish to use your Windows authentication information—the User ID that you gave when you logged onto Windows—you can replace the *User Id* and *Password* keywords with the *Integrated Security* keyword, as in the following connection string:

```
Provider=SQLOLEDB.1;Data Source=athena.justpc.com;
    Initial Catalog=Music;Integrated Security=SSPI
```

Connecting to Other Databases

As long as you can find the proper data provider you can connect to many different types of databases. The main requirement is that the database supports OLE DB. Some of these databases and their providers are listed in Table 23-2.

Table 23-2. Other OLE DB Data Providers

Database	Data Provider(s)
DB2	IBM OLE DB Provider for DB2
Oracle	Microsoft OLE DB Provider for Oracle Oracle Provider for OLE DB

In case the database you wish to use doesn't support OLE DB, but supports only ODBC, Microsoft includes a special data provider named Microsoft OLE DB Provider for ODBC drivers, which translates OLE DB calls into ODBC. However, you should use this provider only if you can't find an OLE DB provider because performance will suffer.

Using the *Errors* Collection

The *Errors* collection contains information about the errors that occur while executing a database command. Because it's quite possible that one error might trigger several others when executing a command, you can't always rely on the VBA *Err* object to reveal the true cause of the error. Therefore, the ADO *Errors* collection contains the full set of errors that occur while executing a command. (See Table 23-3.)

Table 23-3. Key Properties and Methods of the *Errors* Collection

Property/Method	Description
Clear	Method: Removes all the items from the collection.
Count	Property: Returns the number of items in the collection.
Item(index)	Property: returns the *Error* object at the location specified by *index*.

> **Tip** **Clearing the Err**
> Even though you can't rely on the *Err* object for all the details about an error, you can rely on the *Err* object to identify that an error has occurred. Just remember to use the *Clear* method to remove any previous information in the *Err* object before you execute your database request.

The *Errors* collection object is a typical collection object containing a *Count* property and an *Item* property that returns an *Error* object. You can use a *For…Each* loop to process all the items in the collection, and then use the *Clear* method to erase all the *Error* objects in the collection.

> **Note** The *Errors* collection is populated only when an error occurs. Use the *Clear* method before you execute a command to avoid detecting an error that has already been handled.

Using the *Error* Object

The *Error* object contains a number of properties that describe a specific error condition. (See Table 23-4.) For the most part, these properties provide information about the error from several different perspectives, which might be necessary depending on the exact cause of the error.

Table 23-4. Key Properties of the *Error* Object

Property	Description
Description	Contains a short text description of the error.
NativeError	Contains a provider-specific error code.
Number	Contains the OLE DB error code.
SQLState	Contains the standard five-character ANSI SQL error code.

The *Command* Object

The *Command* object contains information about the task that the database will run. Depending on the type of command you want to execute, you might also have to use the *Parameter* object and the *Parameters* collection to execute a stored procedure.

Chapter 23

Key Properties and Methods of the *Command* Object

Table 23-5 lists some of the key properties and methods associated with the *Command* object.

Table 23-5. Key Properties and Methods of the *Command* Object

Property/Method	Description
ActiveConnection	Property: points to an open *Connection* object that will be used to execute the command or that contains a connection string that will be used to connect to the database.
CommandText	Property: the command that will be executed on the database.
CommandType	Property: specifies the type of command in *CommandText*. Can be *adCmdText*, *adCmdTable*, or *adCmdStoredProc*.
CreateParameter(Name, Type, Direction, Size, Value) As Parameter	Method: creates a *Parameter* object using the specified type information.
Execute(RecordsAffected, Parameters, Options) As Recordset	Method: executes the command and optionally returns a *Recordset* object containing any rows retrieved from the database.
Name	Property: contains the name of the command.
Parameters	Property: pointer to a *Parameters* collection object containing the parameter values that will be substituted into the command when it's executed.

The *CommandText* property contains the command that you want to execute, whereas the *CommandType* property describes the type of command stored in the *CommandText* property. There are three basic types of commands you can create: SQL statements, table names, and stored procedures.

> For more information on SQL syntax, see Chapter 22, "Excel and the Structured Query Language".

The *ActiveConnection* property contains either an object reference to an open *Connection* object, or it contains a connection string that will be used to dynamically create a connection to the database when the *Execute* method is called.

The *CreateParameter* method creates a new *Parameter* object using the specified information about the data type. Once you've created the new Parameter object, you must add it to the *Parameters* collection using the *Parameters.Append* method.

Inside Out

Stored Procedures

Stored procedures are merely precompiled routines available on the database server that someone can execute to perform a database task. Although Access doesn't support stored procedures, many other database systems, such as SQL Server, Oracle, and DB2, all support stored procedures.

Typically, stored procedures are written using SQL statements connected together with other statements, such as *If* statements, looping statements, *Print* statements, and so on. Each vendor has its own syntax for these statements, so stored procedures aren't portable from one database system to another. However, stored procedures are much faster than simply executing an SQL statement. When stored procedures are created on the database server, they are stored in a precompiled form, which saves a lot of resources because the SQL statements need not be compiled each time you execute a database command.

Stored procedures are in many ways like subroutines. You can create stored procedures with a list of parameters and pass values for each parameter when you run the command. Again, this has a big impact on speed and throughput, both of which are a big concern to most database administrators. Finally, stored procedures offer another way to secure access to the database. In these days when computer hackers commonly attack all kinds of computers, many people consider security even more important than performance.

Using the *Parameters* Collection

The *Parameters* collection contains information about the parameters associated with a *Command* object. (See Table 23-6.)

Table 23-6. Properties and Methods of the *Parameters* Collection

Property/Method	Description
Append(Parameter)	Method: appends the specified *Parameter* object to the collection.
Count	Property: returns the number of items in the collection.
Delete(index)	Method: removes the *Parameter* object with the specified *index*.
Item(index)	Property: returns the *Parameter* object at the location specified by *index*.
Refresh	Method: connects to the database and retrieves a copy of the parameter information for the stored procedure specified in *CommandText*.

The *Parameters* collection is essentially a normal collection object with two differences. The *Append* method is used to add a new *Parameter* object to the end of the collection. Depending on how the parameters are defined in the command, the order can be very important.

The *Refresh* method populates the *Parameters* collection using the name of the stored procedure from the *CommandText* property. This can be a useful shortcut that avoids the extra code to define all the parameters manually.

> **Note** Although you can use the *Refresh* method to get a copy of the parameters for a stored procedure directly from the database, you might not want to do this each time you call the stored procedure. There's a fair amount of overhead associated with retrieving the parameters from the database, which could add up if you're calling the stored procedure from within a loop.

Using the *Parameter* Object

The *Parameter* object contains a number of properties that describe a specific parameter that is passed to a parameterized query or a stored procedure. (See Table 23-7.)

Table 23-7. Key Properties of the *Parameter* Object

Property	Description
Direction	Indicates whether the parameter is an input (*adParamInput*), output (*adParamOutput*), or input/output (*adParamInputOutput*) parameter to the stored procedure.
Name	Contains the name of the parameter.
NumericScale	Contains the number of digits to the right of the decimal point for a numeric field.
Precision	Contains the total number of digits in a numeric field.
Type	Contains the data type associated with the parameter. Some common values are *adSmallInt*, *adInteger*, *asSingle*, *adDouble*, *adCurrency*, *adDate*, *adBSTR*, *adBoolean*, *adDecimal*, *adBigInt*, *adBinary*, *adChar*, *adWChar*, *adNumeric*, *adDBDate*, *adDBTime*, *adVarNumeric*, *adVarChar*, *adLongVarChar*, *adVarWChar*, *adLongVarWChar*, *adVarBinary*, and *asLongVarBinary*.
Value	Contains the value of the parameter. For input parameters and input/output parameters, this value will be passed to the stored procedure. For input/output and output parameters, this value is set after the stored procedure is executed.

Each *Parameter* object describes a single parameter to a stored procedure. The *Name* property must match the parameter name defined in the stored procedure. You must specify the database type associated with the parameter, along with which direction the value is passed.

The *Value* property contains the value that's passed and/or returned from the stored procedure. Typically, you define a *Command* object with all its associated parameters only once. Then you modify the set of *Value* properties so that you pass the appropriate information to the stored procedure.

Chapter 23

The *Recordset* Object

When a database request returns rows to your program, they are made available through the *Recordset* object.

Key Properties and Methods of the *Recordset* Object

Table 23-8 lists some of the key properties and methods associated with the *Recordset* object.

Table 23-8. Key Properties and Methods of the *Recordset* Object

Property/Method	Description
ActiveConnection	Property: points to an open *Connection* object that will be used to execute the command or contains a connection string that will be used to connect to the database.
AddNew	Method: adds a new row to the end of the *Recordset*.
BOF	Property: returns *True* when the current record pointer is before the first record in the recordset.
CancelUpdate	Method: restores the current row in the *Recordset* to its original values.
Close	Method: closes an open *Recordset* object and releases all its resources.
Delete	Method: deletes the current record.
EditMode	Property: describes the edit status of the current record. Can be *adEditNone* (current record is unchanged), *adEditInProgress* (current record has been changed, but not saved), *adEditAdd* (the *AddNew* method created a new, empty record, which hasn't been saved yet), or *adEditDelete* (the current record is deleted).
EOF	Property: returns *True* when the current record pointer is past the last row in the recordset.
Fields	Property: returns a *Fields* collection containing the set of fields associated with the current record.
Filter	Property: can be a string containing an expression similar to an SQL *Where* clause.
Move(NumRecords)	Method: moves the current record pointer forward (positive value) or backward (negative value) the specified number of rows.
MoveFirst	Method: moves the current record pointer to the first row in the *Recordset*.
MoveLast	Method: moves the current record pointer to the last row in the *Recordset*.

continued

Chapter 23

Table 23-8. Key Properties and Methods of the *Recordset* Object *(continued)*

Property/Method	Description
MoveNext	Method: moves the current record pointer to the next row in the recordset.
MovePrevious	Method: moves the current record pointer to the previous row in the recordset.
Open	Method: gains access to the data in the *Recordset*.
RecordCount	Property: contains the total number of rows retrieved from the database.
Sort	Property: contains the list of column names on which the results should be sorted.
Source	Property: contains either an object reference to a *Command* object or a string with an SQL statement.
Update	Method: saves any changes you might have made to the current row to the database.

The *ActiveConnection* property points either to the *Connection* object associated with *Recordset*, or it contains a connection string value. If the property contains a connection string, a connection to the database will be automatically opened when the *Recordset* object is opened.

The *Source* property contains either an object reference to a *Command* object or a string containing the name of a table, a stored procedure or an SQL statement. If you assign a *Command* object to the source property, reading the source property will return the *CommandText* value from the *Command* object rather than an object reference.

Once you've set up all the information that you need to retrieve data from the database, use the *Open* method to gain access to the information in the *Recordset* object. When you are through with the data, use the *Close* method to release all the resources associated with the *Recordset* object.

The *Recordset* object exposes the returned records from the database one row at a time. Internally, the *Recordset* object maintains a pointer referred to as the *current record pointer*, which points to the current record.

Because only one record is available at a time, you must use the move methods (*MoveFirst*, *MovePrevious*, *MoveNext*, and *MoveLast*) to navigate your way through the records in the *Recordset*. The *Move* method allows you to jump forward or backward in the record the specified number of rows.

As you move through the records in the *Recordset*, the *BOF* and *EOF* properties will automatically be set as the current record pointer changes. *BOF* stands for *Beginning Of File*, and *EOF* stands for *End Of File*. The best way to think of these two properties is that they represent locations before the first row in the *Recordset* (*BOF*) and after the last row in the *Recordset* (*EOF*).

When you initially open the *Recordset* object, the current record pointer will point to the first row. Calling the *MoveNext* method will move the current record pointer through each of the rows, up to and including the last row. If the current record pointer is on the last row, calling *MoveNext* will set the *EOF* property to *True*. If you call *MoveNext* a second time, although the *EOF* property is *True*, you'll get an error.

Tip   **The Ends of the Earth**

Never call the *MoveNext* method when the *EOF* property is *True*, and never call the *MovePrevious* method when the *BOF* property is *True*. Calling either of these methods will result in an error because it's impossible to move the current record pointer before the beginning of the *Recordset* (*MovePrevious*) or move the current record pointer after the end of the *Recordset* (*MoveNext*).

The *RecordCount* property contains the total number of rows retrieved from the database. Remember that this property may have a value of *-1*, meaning that the total isn't known at the current time. If this happens, use the *MoveLast* method to move to the end of the *Recordset*. Using the *MoveLast* method will also update the *RecordCount* property.

The *Filter* property can be used for several different purposes. The most useful is when you assign it a string value containing an expression similar to one you'd use in an SQL *Where* clause. This technique can be useful if you wish to restrict the *Recordset* to only a subset of the data you just retrieved.

Tip   **Only Take What You Need**

Although you can use the *Filter* property to view a subset of the rows returned from the database, it's always better to retrieve only those rows you really want to process from the database.

The *Sort* property is essentially the same as the SQL *Select* statement's *Order By* clause. Simply assign a list of column names followed by an optional *Asc* keyword or a *Desc* keyword and then a comma, and ADO will sort the rows in the *Recordset* and return them to your program in the desired order.

You can access each individual column through the *Fields* collection. You can extract the current value for the column through a *Field* object as well as by saving a new value into the column in the current row. Changing any of the values forces the *EditMode* property to change from *adEditNone* to *adEditInProgress*. Once you are finished making changes, you should call the *Update* method to save the changes to the database.

The first step in writing data to a table is to make sure the *EditMode* property is set to *adEditAdd*. Then you can use the *AddNew* method to insert a blank row at the end of the recordset, into which you can write each column's value using the values in the *Fields* collection. Finally, you use the *Update* method to save the changes to the database.

Chapter 23

493

The *Delete* method deletes the current row and sets the *EditMode* property to *adEditDelete*. Again, you need to use the *Update* method to make the changes final.

One nice feature of the *Recordset* object is the *CancelUpdate* method. If you have made any changes to the current row and call *CancelUpdate*, all the changes will be discarded and the original values would be restored. If you had added a new row using the *AddNew* method, the new row will be discarded and the current record pointer will be reset to point to the row it was pointing to prior to calling *AddNew*.

Using the *Fields* Collection

The *Fields* collection contains information about the columns in the current row of the *Recordset* object. (See Table 23-9.)

Table 23-9. Key Properties of the *Fields* Collection

Property/Method	Description
Count	Property: returns the number of items in the collection.
Item(index)	Property: returns the *Field* object at the location specified by *index*.

For the most part, you'll use the *Fields* collection simply to access the various *Field* objects associated with the current row. The other properties and methods in the *Fields* collection exist to add and remove *Field* objects from the collection and aren't critical to the average database programmer.

Using the *Field* Object

The *Field* object contains information about a single column associated with the current row of the *Recordset* object. Some of the most useful properties are listed in Table 23-10.

Table 23-10. Key Properties of the *Field* Object

Property	Description
Name	Contains the name of the database column.
OriginalValue	Contains the original value of the field from the database.
Type	Contains the OLE DB data type of the column. Some common values are adSmallInt, adInteger, asSingle, adDouble, adCurrency, adDate, adBSTR, adBoolean, adDecimal, adBigInt, adBinary, adChar, adWChar, adNumeric, adDBDate, adDBTime, adVarNumeric, adVarChar, adLongVarChar, adVarWChar, adLongVarWChar, adVarBinary, and asLongVarBinary.
UnderlyingValue	Contain the current value of the column as found in the database.
Value	Contain the current value of the field.

The *Name* property contains the name of the column as it was defined in the database or the *Select* statement that returned the rows. The *Type* property describes the OLE DB type of the column.

There are several different properties containing the value of the column in the *Field* object. The *Value* property represents the current value of the column as seen by the application program. If your program doesn't explicitly change the *Value* property, it will have the same value as found in the *OriginalValue* property. The *OriginalValue* property always contains the value of the column when it was originally retrieved from the database.

On the other hand, the *UnderlyingValue* property contains the most recent value of the column stored in the database. Because it's possible that the database has been updated since the original *Recordset* object was created, you can use the *UnderlyingValue* property to go back to the database to get a fresh copy of the column.

> **Note**   Use the *UnderlyingValue* property carefully; it forces ADO to go back to the database to get the most current value. Although it's OK to do this every now and then, performing this action repetitively can have an adverse impact on your application's performance.

In this chapter, you learned about the key objects that comprise the ADO architecture. Each of three main objects performs a specific task. The *Connection* object contains the information necessary for your application to communicate with a database server. The *Connection* object also contains the *Errors* collection, which describes the most recent error encountered while using ADO. The *Command* object describes an SQL statement that will be executed, including the collection of *Parameter* objects that will be passed to the command for execution. Finally, the *Recordset* object provides access to data that may be returned by executing a *Command* object, with the individual values associated with each returned row being exposed through the *Fields* collection and each individual column being exposed through the *Field* object.

Excel Query Program

Connecting to a Database 501

Editing a Query 505

Executing a Database Query 508

Using the Excel Query Program 515

The Excel Query program developed for this book is a practical application of many of the tools and techniques that you learned elsewhere in this book. The program can easily be packaged as an add-in or work as a stand-alone workbook template, plus it combines various forms and toolbar elements into a cohesive program.

Excel Query Program Overview

The Excel Query program is implemented as an add-in to Microsoft Excel. This add-in lets you perform database queries and return the results as part of a worksheet. The interface to the program is through a new command bar, named *Excel2k3 VBA Query*, and it has four main components: a drop-down list containing the queries that have been executed, a button to edit a query, a button to run the query, and a button to configure the database connection. (See Figure 24-1.)

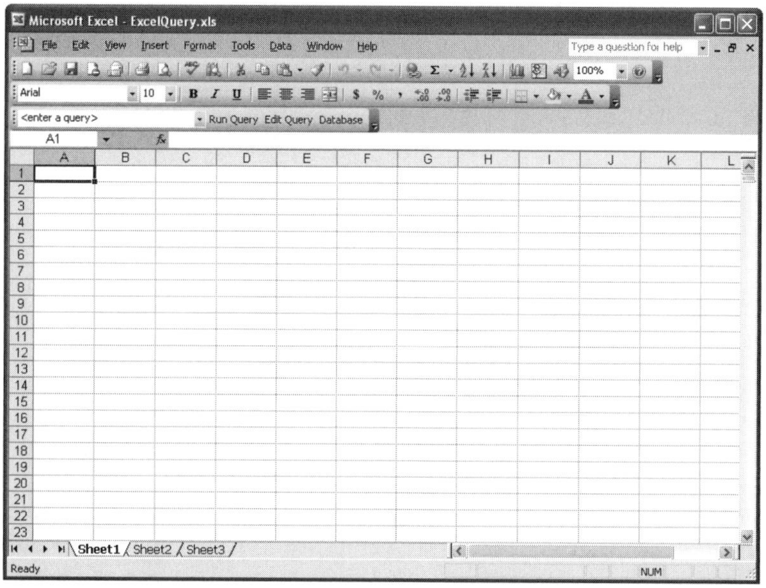

Figure 24-1. The user interface to the query program is through a new command bar added to Excel.

> **On the CD**   The complete source code for the Excel Query program can be found on the Companion CD in ExcelQuery.xls.

Setting Up the Project

Most of the code for this project is stored in the ThisWorkbook module. Two user forms are also used, DBInfo and DBQuery. The ThisWorkbook module is automatically created when the workbook is created. The user forms can be added to the project by choosing Insert, UserForm from the main menu and modifying the name of the user form in the Properties pane.

At the beginning of each module, you should add the following lines of code. The first statement forces you to declare variables before you use them, which helps to prevent typing errors. The second statement instructs Visual Basic to perform all string comparisons in a case-insensitive manner, which reduces the amount of code you need to write when comparing strings.

```
Option Explicit
Option Compare Text
```

To execute any of the database code, the ADO database library needs to be added to the project. Choose Tools, References from the main menu and place a check mark in the box for the Microsoft ActiveX Data Objects 2.7 library. (See Figure 24-2.) Then press OK to close the dialog box and make the library available for use in your application.

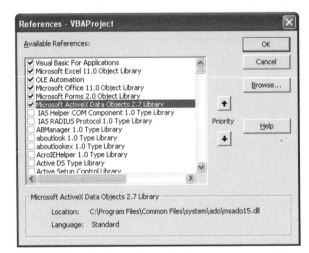

Figure 24-2.   Use the References dialog box to add a reference to the ADO database library.

Initializing the Program

When the Excel Query program first starts, it uses the *Workbook_Open* event in the This-Workbook module to call the *AddCommandBar* routine that adds the Excel2k3 VBA Query command bar to Excel.

```
Private Sub Workbook_Open()

AddCommandBar

End Sub
```

The *AddCommandBar* routine begins by disabling error checking with the *On Error Resume Next* statement. Then the routine tries to create an object reference to the Excel 2k3 VBA Query command bar by referencing its name in the *CommandBars* collection.

```
Private Sub AddCommandBar()

Dim c As CommandBar
Dim cc As CommandBarComboBox
Dim cb As CommandBarButton

On Error Resume Next
Set c = Application.CommandBars("Excel2k3 VBA Query")
If Not c Is Nothing Then
    Application.CommandBars("Excel2k3 VBA Query").Delete

End If

Set c = Application.CommandBars.Add("Excel2k3 VBA Query", _
    msoBarFloating, False, True)
c.Enabled = True
c.Visible = True

Set cc = c.Controls.Add(msoControlComboBox, 1)
cc.Tag = "Excel2k3 VBA Query Statement"
cc.Text = "<enter a query>"
cc.Width = 200
cc.OnAction = "ThisWorkbook.EnterDatabaseQuery"

Set cb = c.Controls.Add(msoControlButton, 1)
cb.Tag = "Excel2k3 VBA Query Run"
cb.Style = msoButtonCaption
cb.Caption = "Run Query"
cb.OnAction = "ThisWorkbook.RunDatabaseQuery"
```

Chapter 24

499

```
Set cb = c.Controls.Add(msoControlButton, 1)
cb.Tag = "Excel2k3 VBA Query Edit"
cb.Style = msoButtonCaption
cb.Caption = "Edit Query"
cb.OnAction = "ThisWorkbook.EditDatabaseQuery"

Set cb = c.Controls.Add(msoControlButton, 1)
cb.Tag = "Excel2k3 VBA Query Database"
cb.Style = msoButtonCaption
cb.Caption = "Database"
cb.OnAction = "ThisWorkbook.ShowDatabaseInfo"

End Sub
```

Normally, if this command bar doesn't exist, the program will generate an error. However, with error checking disabled, the temporary object *c* will remain, set to *Nothing*. If *c* is *Nothing*, the command bar doesn't exist and will be deleted. This step ensures that the command bar is always created with the proper controls.

Once the program is certain that the command bar doesn't exist, it creates a new floating bar, which can be docked with the other command bars, as shown in Figure 24-1. The remaining statements in the *AddCommandBar* routine merely add the combo box control, along with the three control button controls used to manage the application.

Two of the actions associated with the command bar controls open user forms. The *ShowDatabaseInfo* routine shown below opens the DBInfo user form as a modal form.

```
Private Sub ShowDatabaseInfo()

DBInfo.Show vbModal

End Sub
```

The *EditDatabaseQuery* routine does the same thing with the DBQuery form.

```
Private Sub EditDatabaseQuery()

DBQuery.Show vbModal

End Sub
```

Ending the Program

The *Workbook_BeforeClose* event calls the *DeleteCommandBar* routine to ensure that all the changes it made to Excel's menus are removed prior to Excel shutting down.

```
Private Sub Workbook_BeforeClose(Cancel As Boolean)

DeleteCommandBar

End Sub
```

The logic in the *DeleteCommandBar* routine is similar to the logic in the *AddCommandBar* routine that ensures that the command bar doesn't exist before creating a new one. Error checking is disabled, and a temporary object reference to the *CommandBar* object is created from the *CommandBars* collection. If the temporary object reference is valid, the *Delete* method is used to remove the entire command bar with all its command bar controls from Excel.

```
Sub DeleteCommandBar()

Dim c As CommandBar

On Error Resume Next
Set c = Application.CommandBars("Excel2k3 VBA Query")
If Not c Is Nothing Then
    Application.CommandBars("Excel2k3 VBA Query").Delete

End If

End Sub
```

Connecting to a Database

To execute a database query, you need to create a connection to the database. However, because you need different connection information for each database, it makes sense to use a user form to collect this information. (See Figure 24-3.)

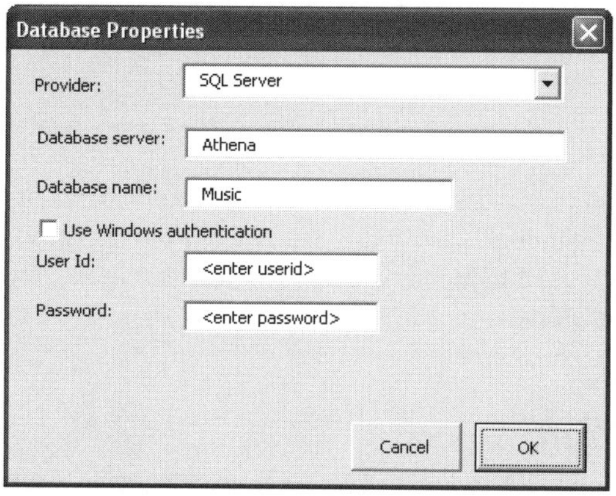

Figure 24-3. The user supplies the database connection information through the Database Properties dialog box.

The program stores the connection information in the Microsoft Windows registry so the program will remember the last value that the user selected.

Because each database system needs different connection information, a hidden *MultiPage* control contains a unique *Page* object for each supported database. A *ComboBox* control at the top of the user form selects which page is visible. This arrangement is more clearly illustrated in the Visual Basic Editor, as shown in Figure 24-4.

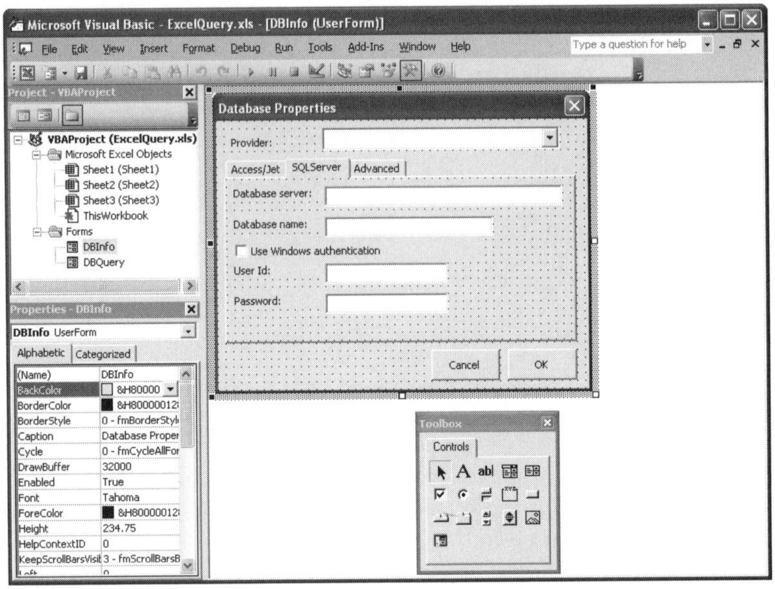

Figure 24-4. Each page in the *MultiPage* control contains connection information unique to each particular database.

Tip Keep an Eye on Your Tabs

When you are developing applications with the *MultiPage* control, you might want to leave the tabs visible in design mode even though you want to hide them from the user. Doing so lets you quickly switch to the tab you want to modify while in development mode. Then, when you load the form, just set the *Style* property to: `MultiPage1.Style = fmTabStyleNone`.

Initializing the DBInfo *UserForm*

When the DBInfo form, which generates the Database Properties dialog box, is loaded, the *UserForm_Initialize* event shown in the following code is fired. The first step is to populate the *Provider ComboBox* control with the list of supported databases. For this example, only the Microsoft Access and SQL Server databases have their own pages; however, an Advanced page was added that allows the user to input any connection string value.

```
Private Sub UserForm_Initialize()

Provider.AddItem "Access (Jet)"
Provider.AddItem "SQL Server"
Provider.AddItem "Advanced"

DBProperties.Style = fmTabStyleNone

DBName.Text = GetSetting("Excel2k3 VBA", "Query", "DBName", _
    "<enter database name>")
DBPassword.Text = GetSetting("Excel2k3 VBA", "Query", "DBPassword", _
    "<enter password>")
DBPath.Text = GetSetting("Excel2k3 VBA", "Query", "DBPath", _
    "<enter path to database file>")
DBServer.Text = GetSetting("Excel2k3 VBA", "Query", "DBServer", _
    "<enter database server>")
DBWindowsAuth.Value = GetSetting("Excel2k3 VBA", "Query", _
    "DBWindowsAuth", True)
DBUserId.Text = GetSetting("Excel2k3 VBA", "Query", "DBUserId", _
    "<enter userid>")
ConnectionString.Text = GetSetting("Excel2k3 VBA", "Query", _
    "ConnectionString", "<enter connection string>")

Provider.ListIndex = GetSetting("Excel2k3 VBA", "Query", "DBType", 0)

End Sub
```

The tabs on the *MultiPage* control are hidden by setting the *Style* property to *fmTabStyleNone*.

The *GetSetting* function is used to extract the values for each field on the form from the registry. The *GetSetting* function takes four parameters. The first three parameters represent a key that is used to identify the value, while the fourth parameter provides a default value in case the value isn't currently stored in the registry.

At the bottom of the listing, the last *GetSetting* function is used to choose the selected database and set the *ComboBox* control accordingly. Note that setting the *ListIndex* property will also fire the *Change* event associated with the control.

Changing Database Providers

The *Provider_Change* event in the *DBInfo* user form is fired any time the user selects a new database from the drop-down box or the *ListIndex* property changes. All this routine does is to select the appropriate page to display in the *MultiPage* control by setting its *Value* property like this:

```
Private Sub Provider_Change

DBProperties.Value = Provider.ListIndex

End Sub
```

Selecting Windows Authentication

A check box on the SQL Server page allows the user to select Windows authentication. When the Windows authentication information is used, there is no need to display the userid and passwords fields to the user.

The following code handles the *Click* associated with the check box and hides the userid and password fields when the value of the control is *True* and displays them when the value is *False*.

```
Private Sub DBWindowsAuth_Click()

If DBWindowsAuth.Value Then
    DBUserId.Visible = False
    DBPassword.Visible = False
    DBUserIdLabel.Visible = False
    DBPasswordLabel.Visible = False

Else
    DBUserId.Visible = True
    DBPassword.Visible = True
    DBUserIdLabel.Visible = True
    DBPasswordLabel.Visible = True

End If

End Sub
```

Saving the Database Info

When the user clicks the OK button, the code that follows is executed. The procedure calls the *SaveSetting* routine to save the values input by the user into the Windows registry.

```
Private Sub CommandButton1_Click()

SaveSetting "Excel2k3 VBA", "Query", "DBName", DBName.Text
SaveSetting "Excel2k3 VBA", "Query", "DBPassword", DBPassword.Text
SaveSetting "Excel2k3 VBA", "Query", "DBPath", DBPath.Text
SaveSetting "Excel2k3 VBA", "Query", "DBServer", DBServer.Text
SaveSetting "Excel2k3 VBA", "Query", "DBWindowsAuth", DBWindowsAuth.Value
SaveSetting "Excel2k3 VBA", "Query", "DBUserId", DBUserId.Text
SaveSetting "Excel2k3 VBA", "Query", "ConnectionString", _
    ConnectionString.Text
SaveSetting "Excel2k3 VBA", "Query", "DBType", Provider.ListIndex

Unload Me

End Sub
```

Once the values have been saved to the Windows registry, the *Unload* routine is called to close the current form. Notice that the Cancel button's *Click* event merely calls the *Unload* routine to unload the form. Any changes made to the fields on the form are discarded.

> **Tip   I Am Me**
>
> *UserForm* modules are like regular class modules, so you can refer to the current instance of the object by using the keyword *Me*. This can be extremely useful with some statements, such as the *Unload* statement, where you have to supply an object reference to the *UserForm* object you wish to unload.

When the user clicks the Cancel button, the *CommandButton2* event is called. Because the user has chosen not to change the connection information stored in the registry, the only step necessary is to unload the current form.

```
Private Sub CommandButton2_Click()

Unload Me

End Sub
```

Editing a Query

The query values are stored in the *ComboBox* control on the Excel2k3 VBA Query command bar. Each query has its own entry, which can be selected by choosing the appropriate entry from the drop-down list. Pressing the Edit Query button on the command bar loads the DBQuery *UserForm* (shown in Figure 24-5) with the currently selected query from the *ComboBox* control on the command bar.

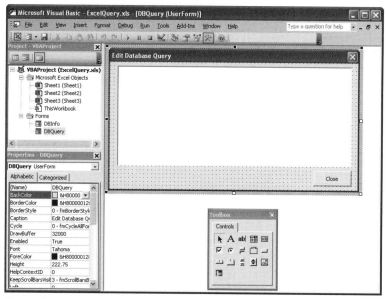

Figure 24-5. The DBQuery form is essentially a large textbox that allows the user to enter his query.

The following code is executed when the *UserForm* is loaded. After locating the proper command bar, the *FindControl* method is used to get an object pointer to the *Command barComboBox* control by searching for the proper *Tag* property value. Then, assuming that the control exists, the *Text* property of the combo box control is copied to the large, multi-line textbox control on the *UserForm*.

```
Private Sub UserForm_Initialize()

Dim c As CommandBar
Dim cc As CommandBarComboBox

On Error Resume Next
Set c = Application.CommandBars("Excel2k3 VBA Query")
Set cc = c.FindControl(, , "Excel2k3 VBA Query Statement")
If Not cc Is Nothing Then
    Query.Text = cc.Text

End If

End Sub
```

Once the user has made the desired changes to the query, pressing the Close button closes the user form.

```
Private Sub CommandButton1_Click()

Unload Me

End Sub
```

When the user form is closed, the *SaveData* routine is called from the *UserForm_Terminate* event to insure that the query is always saved when the form is closed. By placing the call to *SaveData* here, the query is saved no matter how the form is closed.

```
Private Sub UserForm_Terminate()

SaveData

End Sub
```

The *SaveData* routine copies the query statement to the *Text* property of the *CommandBar-ComboBox* control using the same basic technique that was used to load the query.

```
Sub SaveData()

Dim c As CommandBar
Dim cc As CommandBarComboBox
```

```
On Error Resume Next
Set c = Application.CommandBars("Excel2k3 VBA Query")

Set cc = c.FindControl( , , "Excel2k3 VBA Query Statement")
If Not cc Is Nothing Then
    cc.Text = Query.Text

End If

End Sub
```

Notice that saving the query in this fashion triggers the *OnAction* event associated with this control, which is the *EnterDatabaseQuery* routine located in the ThisWorkbook module, which is shown here. This routine scans the list of queries stored in the control and appends the new query to the end if it isn't found, letting users rerun a particular query quickly.

```
Sub EnterDatabaseQuery()

Dim c As CommandBar
Dim cc As CommandBarComboBox
Dim q As String
Dim i As Long

On Error Resume Next
Set c = Application.CommandBars("Excel2k3 VBA Query")
Set cc = c.FindControl( , , "Excel2k3 VBA Query Statement")
If Not cc Is Nothing Then
    q = cc.Text
    i = 1
    Do While i <= cc.ListCount
        If q = cc.List(i) Then
            Exit Sub

        End If

        i = i + 1

    Loop

    cc.AddItem cc.Text

End If
```

This routine begins by locating the *CommandBarComboBox* control, and then saves the value from the *Text* property into a temporary variable named *q*. Next the routine uses a *Do…While* loop to scan through the list of queries stored in the drop-down list. If a match is found, the *Exit Sub* statement ends the routine without action. If no match is found, the *AddItem* method is used to add the query to the end of the list of drop-down items.

> **Note**   One limitation of this approach is that the queries are lost when the user exits Excel. The program shouldn't take up a lot of space in the Windows registry just to store the history of queries, and, while this version of the program doesn't use an external file that would need to be loaded and saved each time Excel starts, it would be straightforward to add a Save/Load set of dialog boxes to this form that would let you save an individual query to disk.

Executing a Database Query

Clicking the Run Query button on the Excel2k3 VBA Query command bar runs the query currently selected in the *ComboBox* on the command bar.

Getting the Information to Run the Query

In the ThisWorkbook module, the *RunDatabaseQuery* routine, shown here, builds a connection string using the *BuildConnectionString* function and gets the query string from the combo box on the command bar using the *GetDBQuery* routine. The *Trim* function is used to delete any unnecessary blanks as the beginning and the end of the strings.

> For more information on using text functions to clean up your data, see Chapter 9, "Manipulating Data with VBA".

```
Sub RunDatabaseQuery()

Dim c As String
Dim q As String

c = Trim(BuildConnectionString)
q = Trim(GetDBQuery)

If Len(c) = 0 Then
    DBInfo.Show vbModal

ElseIf Len(q) = 0 Then
    DBQuery.Show vbModal

Else
    RunQuery c, q

End If

End Sub
```

The length of each temporary variable holding the connection string and the query is verified to be non-zero. If the length is zero, the appropriate form is displayed to the user to fill in the necessary information. When the form is closed, the user must hit the Run Query button to try the query again.

Assuming that there is information in the connection string and the query string, the *RunQuery* routine is called to execute the query with both the connection string and the query string passed as parameters.

Building a Connection String

The following *BuildConnectionString* routine creates a connection string from information previously stored in the Windows registry. The routine, which is located in the ThisWorkbook module, begins by declaring a number of temporary variables that will hold the information extracted from the registry, along with another temporary variable *c* that will hold final return value from the function.

```
Function BuildConnectionString() As String

Dim c As String

Dim DBName As String
Dim DBPassword As String
Dim DBPath As String
Dim DBServer As String
Dim DBType As Long
Dim DBUserId As String
Dim DBWindowsAuth As Boolean

c = ""

DBType = GetSetting("Excel2k3 VBA", "Query", "DBType", 0)

Select Case DBType
Case 0
    DBPath = GetRegistryValue("DBPath", "<enter path to database file>")

    If Len(DBPath) <> 0 Then
        c = "Provider=Microsoft.Jet.OLEDB.4.0"
        c = c & ";Data Source=" & DBPath

    End If

Case 1
    DBWindowsAuth = GetSetting("Excel2k3 VBA", "Query", _
        "DBWindowsAuth", True)
```

```
DBName = GetRegistryValue("DBName", "<enter database name>")
DBPassword = GetRegistryValue("DBPassword", "<enter password>")
DBServer = GetRegistryValue("DBServer", "<enter database server>")
DBUserId = GetRegistryValue("DBUserId", "<enter userid>")

If Len(DBServer) = 0 Then
    DBServer = "localhost"

End If

If Len(DBName) <> 0 Then
    c = "Provider=SQLOLEDB.1"
    c = c & ";Data Source=" & DBServer
    c = c & ";Initial Catalog=" & DBName

    If DBWindowsAuth Then
        c = c & ";Integrated Security=SSPI"

    ElseIf Len(DBUserId) <> 0 And Len(DBPassword) <> 0 Then
        c = c & ";User ID=" & DBUserId
        c = c & ";Password=" & DBPassword

    Else
        c = ""

    End If

End If

Case 2
    c = GetRegistryValue("ConnectionString", "<enter connection string>")

End Select

BuildConnectionString = c

End Function
```

After setting *c* to an empty string, the routine grabs the type of database from the registry and stores it in *DBType*. This variable is then incorporated into a *Select Case* statement, which builds different connection strings depending on the type of database being used.

If an Access (Jet) database is being used, the *DBPath* value is extracted from the Windows registry using the *GetRegistryValue* helper function. This function takes two parameters, the key and the default value. If the value extracted from the registry is different than the default value, an empty string will be returned.

If *GetRegistryValue* returned an empty string (len = 0), *c* remains an empty string. Otherwise, the appropriate connection string is created for an Access database using the value extracted from the registry.

The same approach is used for SQL Server databases (DBType = 1). The value for *DBWindowsAuth* is extracted directly from the registry because its default value is not a string, whereas the values for *DBName*, *DBPassword*, *DBServer*, and *DBUserId* are extracted from the registry using the *GetRegistryValue* routine.

Unlike Access connection strings, the routine attempts to substitute intelligent values in case the user hasn't supplied a default value. For instance, if the length of *DBServer* is zero, the program assumes that the user is running the query against the local computer. If the length of *DBName* isn't zero, the program attempts to build a partial connection string using *DBName* and *DBServer*. Then, if Windows authentication is used, Integrated Security=SSPI is appended to the connection string and the information in *DBUserId* and *DBPassword* is ignored.

If *DBWindowsAuth* is *False*, the *DBUserId* and *DBPassword* are checked to see if they contain a value. If both contain information, these fields are appended to the connection string. If one of these fields doesn't have any information, *c* is set to the empty string, destroying the partial connection string that already exists.

If the user selected Advanced on the *DBInfo* form, the *ConnectionString* value is extracted from the registry using the *GetRegistryValue* helper function. No further checking is required here because *GetRegistryValue* ensures that an empty string is returned if the default value is retrieved from the registry.

Finally, the routine ends by returning the temporary variable *c* as the value of the function.

The *GetRegistryValue* helper function calls the *GetSetting* function to retrieve the desired key from the registry. If the return value is the same as the supplied default value, the return value is set to the empty string.

```
Function GetRegistryValue(key As String, default As String) As String

Dim r As String

r = GetSetting("Excel2k3 VBA", "Query", key, default)

If r = default Then
    r = ""

End If

GetRegistryValue = r

End Function
```

Getting the Query

Getting the query string from the combo box on the command bar follows the same basic approach discussed elsewhere in this chapter. After locating the appropriate command bar, the *FindControl* method is used to search for the specific control containing the combo box. The following function is also located in the ThisWorkbook module:

```
Function GetDBQuery() As String

Dim c As CommandBar
Dim cc As CommandBarComboBox

On Error Resume Next
Set c = Application.CommandBars("Excel2k3 VBA Query")

Set cc = c.FindControl(, , "Excel2k3 VBA Query Statement")
If Not cc Is Nothing Then
    GetDBQuery = cc.Text

ElseIf cc.Text = "<enter a query>" Then
    GetDBQuery = ""

Else
    GetDBQuery = ""

End If

End Function
```

The main benefit of this routine is that the query string is compared to the default value that was loaded when the program began. If it is, the function will return an empty string, indicating that the user should be prompted to enter a query.

Running a Query

Once the user has supplied values for the connection string and the query string, which have passed some simple edit checks, the *RunQuery* routine, located in the ThisWorkbook module, is called to get the information from the database.

```
Sub RunQuery(c As String, q As String)

Dim cn As ADODB.Connection
Dim cmd As ADODB.Command
Dim rs As ADODB.Recordset

On Error Resume Next

Set cn = New ADODB.Connection
cn.ConnectionString = c
cn.Open
If Err.Number <> 0 Then
```

```
    MsgBox "Connection error: " & Err.Description
    Exit Sub

End If

Set cmd = New ADODB.Command
Set cmd.ActiveConnection = cn
cmd.CommandText = q
cmd.CommandType = adCmdText

Set rs = New ADODB.Recordset
Set rs.Source = cmd

cn.Errors.Clear
rs.Open

If Err.Number = 0 Then
    CopyRows rs

Else
    MsgBox "Query error: " & Err.Description

End If

rs.Close
cn.Close

End Sub
```

To execute the query, this routine uses three ActiveX Data Object (ADO) database objects: a *Connection* object, a *Command* object, and a *Recordset* object. Each is declared at the start of this routine. Next, error checking is disabled by using the *On Error Resume Next* statement because the routine checks for errors after any critical statement.

The first step in retrieving rows from a database is to establish a connection to the database. A new instance of the *ADODB.Connection* object is created, and the connection string value that's passed to this routine is assigned to the *Connection* object's *ConnectionString* property. After instantiating the *Connection* object, the *Open* method is used to open a connection to the database.

Tip Out with the New

Never use the *New* keyword when defining an object using a *Dim*, a *Private*, or a *Public* statement. Visual Basic for Applications (VBA) includes extra code around each object reference to determine whether the object has been instantiated. If the object hasn't been instantiated, the code will automatically create a new instance of the object for you. Although this extra code doesn't add a lot of overhead, you will be better off controlling exactly when a new object is instantiated.

If there was a problem opening the connection, an error message is displayed to the user and the *Exit Sub* statement is used to leave the subroutine with any further processing.

Next a new instance of the *ADODB.Command* object is created. The newly opened *Connection* object is assigned to the *ActiveConnection* property, and the query is assigned to the *CommandText* property. Finally, the *CommandType* property is set to *adCmdText*, meaning that the *Command* object contains an SQL statement.

A new *ADODB.Recordset* object is created, and the *Source* property is set to the *Command* object that was just initialized. The *Connection* object's *Errors* collection is explicitly cleared, and then the *Recordset* object's *Open* method is called.

Any errors that occur while opening the *Recordset* are trapped, and an error message is displayed to the user. Otherwise, the *CopyRows* subroutine is called to copy the rows from the *Recordset* object to the current worksheet.

Finally, the *Recordset* object and the *Connection* object are closed (in that order). These steps release any resources held by those objects back to the operating system.

> **Tip   Close Your Connections**
> For the best database server performance, always minimize the amount of time that a connection is open. Closing unneeded connections reduces the resources required to run the database server, which in turn lets the database server handle more connections and perform more work.

Copying Rows

Once you have a *Recordset* that contains rows from the database, the only step left is to copy the rows to your worksheet one row at a time. The *CopyRows* routine in the ThisWorkbook module relies on three local variables: *i* and *j*, which contain pointers to the current cell row and the column on the worksheet, and *f*, which contains a field from the *Recordset* object.

```
Sub CopyRows(rs As ADODB.Recordset)

Dim i As Long
Dim j As Long
Dim f As ADODB.Field

Cells.Select
Selection.ClearContents

i = 1
Do While Not rs.EOF
    j = 1
    For Each f In rs.Fields
        Cells(i, j) = f.Value
        j = j + 1
```

```
    Next f

    rs.MoveNext
    i = i + 1

Loop

End Sub
```

After the space for the variables has been reserved, the entire worksheet is cleared by selecting all the cells on the worksheet (*Cells.Select*) and then clearing the selection with the *ClearContents* method. Then the variable *i* is set to 1, which points at the first row in the worksheet.

Next a loop is set up that iterates through each row in the *Recordset* object. This loop continues until the *EOF* method returns *True*, meaning that the current record pointer has moved beyond the last row contained in the *Recordset*.

Inside the loop, *j* is set to 1, which points to the first column in the worksheet. A *For...Each* loop is used with the variable *f* to retrieve each *Field* object from the recordset's *Fields* collection. The value of the field is copied directly from the *Value* property to the appropriate cell pointed by *i* and *j*. After a field is copied, *j* is incremented to point to the next column.

Once all the fields for a particular row have been copied, the *MoveNext* method is used to reposition the current record pointer to the next record. Also *i* is incremented to point to the new row in the worksheet.

Using the Excel Query Program

Here's a short example that uses the Excel Query Program to retrieve a list of customers from the Northwind sample database that is installed with Microsoft Access. This database is usually kept in the OFFICE11\SAMPLES directory, which might look like the following path if you installed Microsoft Office in its default location:

```
c:\Program Files\Microsoft Office\OFFICE11\SAMPLES\Northwind.mdb
```

> **Note** If you can't find the Northwind sample database in the Microsoft Office\OFFICE11 \SAMPLES directory, verify that you installed the sample databases for Access by rerunning the Office 11 Setup program.

Chapter 24

Configure the Connection Information

After loading the sample workbook, press the Database button and select Access (Jet) in the drop-down box at the top of the Database Properties window. (See Figure 24-6.) Then enter the full path to the file containing the database and press OK.

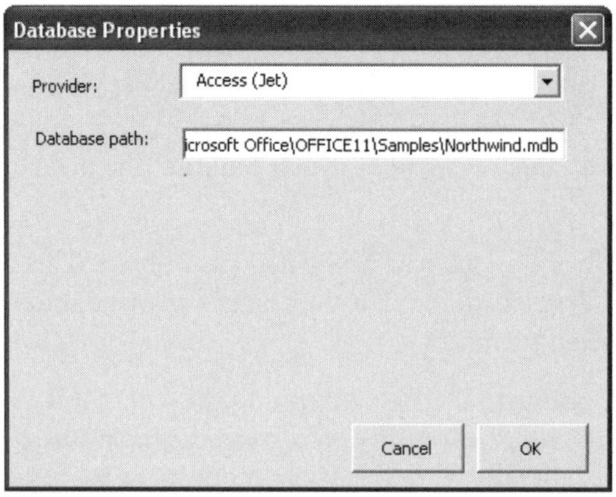

Figure 24-6. Choose Access (Jet) in the drop-down box, and then enter the path in the database.

Enter a Query

Next press the Edit Query button, enter the following query (shown in Figure 24-7), and press the Close button.

```
Select *
From Customers
Order By CustomerId
```

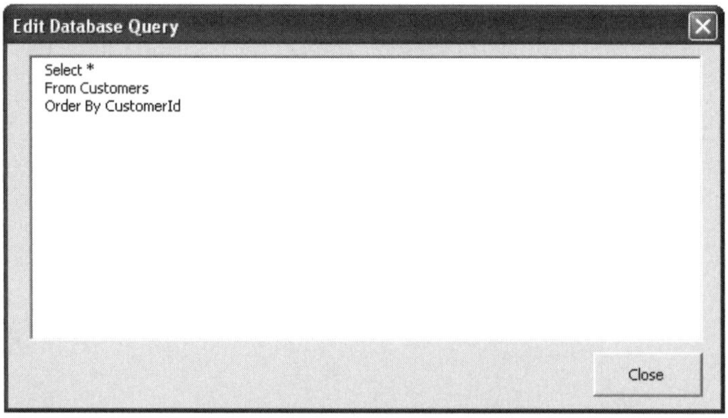

Figure 24-7. Enter the query you want to run.

Run the Query

Press the Run Query button to retrieve the information from the database and display it in the current worksheet (see Figure 24-8).

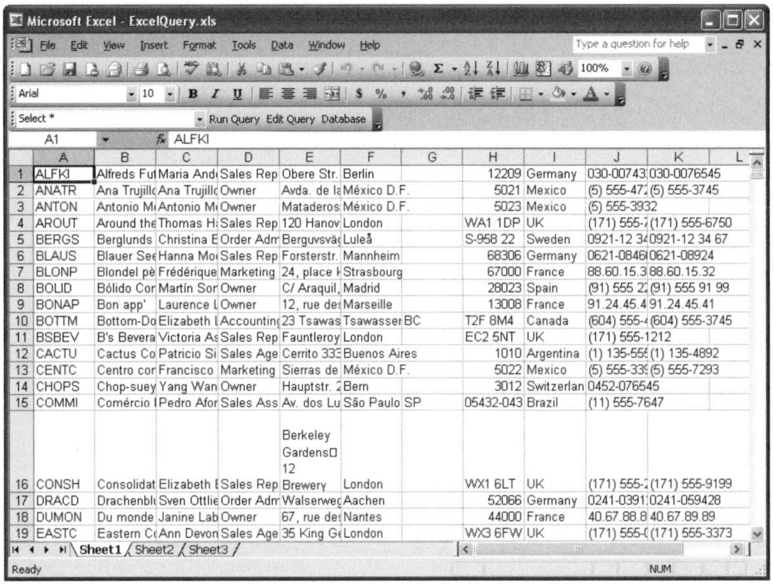

Figure 24-8. View the results from the database query as a normal worksheet.

In this chapter, you learned how to combine database programming with user forms and command bars to create a useful application that runs in Excel. The program began by loading a command bar containing the controls that operate the application. Pressing the Database button displays a form where the user can enter the information necessary to connect to the database. Pressing the Edit Query button displays another user form that displays the current database query and allows the user to change it. Finally, pressing the Run Query button runs the query using calls to ADO and displays the results in the currently active worksheet.

Excel and the Web

HTML. 520

Using the Internet as a Data Source. . . 527

Using the Internet to Publish Results. . .533

Using Internet Solutions with Excel 537

Back in the day, a typical Microsoft Excel–based application was almost entirely contained within Excel itself; the only external interaction would be with the user. The user would provide the data and then present the results. If you needed to store the data, you would use separate worksheets and try to simulate a relational database as best you could.

As data access technologies developed from Open Database Connectivity (ODBC) drivers, through Data Access Objects (DAO) to the current versions of ActiveX Data Objects (ADO), it became more commonplace to store data in external databases and even retrieve data from and update data in other systems across the network. It's now quite common to see Excel used as a front-end querying and analysis tool for large corporate databases, using QueryTables and PivotTables to retrieve the data. The data available to your Excel applications was limited to data available on the company network, and to those databases that you could get permission to access.

Starting with the release of Microsoft Office 97, Microsoft has slowly extended Excel's reach to include the Internet and associated technologies. Excel has added Web functionality directly into Excel, such as Web Queries, as well as ensuring that Excel developers can easily use standard external objects, such as the Internet Transfer Control, the Web Browser control, and the MSXML parser. These objects are included within the Office installation.

Excel provides you with sufficient functionality to reconsider your approach to developing Excel applications. You can start to think outside of the pure Excel/ADO environment in terms of obtaining data, publishing results, monitoring your applications, and sharing data outside of the corporate network.

This chapter introduces the functionality available to you in Excel and demonstrates how to interact with the Internet in your applications. You'll learn how to save a worksheet as a Web page, publish a worksheet to the Web, make the worksheet interactive, and update the worksheet programmatically. Once you can save the worksheet as a Web page, you'll learn how to use existing Web pages as a data source. You'll start with opening a Web page in Excel, create and use Web Queries, and parse Web pages for specific information. To finish off the chapter, you'll evaluate how to set up and communicate with a Web server.

HTML

The Hypertext Markup Language (HTML) is the standard markup language used for documents on the World Wide Web. HTML uses *tags* to indicate how Web browsers should display page elements such as text and graphics and how to respond to user actions.

The concept of publishing Excel spreadsheet data on the World Wide Web makes a lot of sense, both from the standpoint of the worksheet's tabular layout and the worksheet's calculated contents. Anyone who has coded an HTML table can tell you that this is a tedious task. Even creating the simplest HTML table is time consuming because you have to use <TH> and </TH> tags to set up the column headings in the table, along with <TR> and </TR> tags to set up the rows of the table, and <TD> and </TD> tags to define the number and width of the columns, as well as what data goes in each cell of the table.

Saving a Worksheet as a Web Page

Saving a Worksheet as a Web page is a simple task in Excel. You can set up your worksheet with the appropriate data, charts, and PivotTables. Once the setup is complete, you can save your worksheet as a Web page.

Excel enables you to create Web pages that display your worksheet data either in a static, "look but do not touch" mode, or in an interactive, "have some fun" mode. When you create a Web page with static worksheet data, your users can view the Excel data only with their Web browsers. However, when you create a Web page with interactive worksheet data, your users can continue to play around with the data by editing and formatting its values. Depending upon the nature of the spreadsheet, your users can even continue to perform calculations and, in cases of data lists, manipulate the data by sorting and filtering it.

There are many considerations before you save your workbook or worksheet as a Web page. For example, you'll need to decide if you plan to save a portion of a workbook or a part of a worksheet. When you decide to save a part of a worksheet, you should select the cells before you start the save process. You aren't limited to saving a range of cells—you can save a chart as a Web page, as well.

When choosing the location to place the Web page, you should consider whether it will be stored on your local hard drive or network drive, or whether you want to post the Web page directly on your company's Internet or intranet Web site. To save the new page on a File Transfer Protocol (FTP) site, select FTP Locations from the Save In drop-down list box and then open the FTP folder in which you want the page saved. The Web folders or FTP locations must be set up before you can save your worksheet Web pages to these locations. You can also add a title, which appears centered at the top of the page before any of the data or charts. This isn't the only time you can specify your Web page title; you can add or edit the Web page title after the page is created.

To create a static Web page, you follow these general steps:

1 Open the workbook with the data to be saved as a Web page.

2 Click the File menu and select the Save as Web Page option, as shown in Figure 25-1.

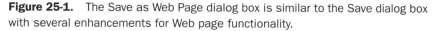

Figure 25-1. The Save as Web Page dialog box is similar to the Save dialog box with several enhancements for Web page functionality.

Tip **Select What to Save**

If you know that you want to save a particular chart or particular range of cells of a worksheet in the new Web page, you should select the chart to be saved before you open the Save As dialog box. By selecting a particular chart or a range of cells, you will be able to save only the required information to your Web page. Selecting the chart ahead of time changes the Selection: Sheet option button to the Selection: Chart option button. In the case of a cell range selection, the Selection: Sheet option button changes to a Selection: option button, followed by the address of the cells selected.

---

3 Specify the location where the Web page is to be saved.

4 Indicate which part of the workbook is to be saved in the new Web page. To save the contents of all sheets in the workbook, make sure that the Entire Workbook option button is selected. To save only the data in the current worksheet, choose the Selection: Sheet option button instead. Remember, if you clicked the chart in the worksheet that you intend to convert into a Web page graphic before opening the Save As dialog box, you need to choose the Selection: Chart option button, which replaces the Selection: Sheet button. If you selected a cell range, you need to choose the Selection: option button, followed by the address of the selected cell range. If you want to save the contents of a worksheet other than the one currently selected, you can specify this later.

5 Type the name for the new Web page in the File Name text box.

Caution Notice that Excel appends the filename extension *.htm* to whichever filename you enter in this text box. This is the standard extension for a HyperText Markup text file. If you plan to publish the Web page on a UNIX Web server, keep in mind that this operating system is sensitive to uppercase and lowercase letters in the filename. The Macintosh and Windows operating system are both case blind when it comes to filenames.

6 Specify a title for the Web page; click the Change Title button in the Save As dialog box. Type the text for the title in the Set Page Title dialog box, and click OK.

Tip **The Procedure Depends on You**
To save a chart that wasn't selected prior to opening the Save As dialog box, click the Publish button and then select the chart, identified by its description from the Choose drop-down list. To save a specific range of cells that you didn't select prior to opening the Save As dialog box, click the Publish button. Then select Range of Cells from the Choose drop-down list before you type the range address in the text box immediately below, or enter the range by selecting the range of cells by highlighting them in the worksheet.

While saving your worksheet data in the new Web page, Excel automatically creates a new folder with the same name as the .htm file that contains all the supporting files, including the graphics files and charts among the numerical data. So if you move the Web page from a local drive to a Web server, you need to copy the supporting files folder, as well as its Web page file, to ensure that the user's browser can successfully open the entire contents of the page.

If you don't want Excel to create a separate folder with the supporting files, change the setting in the Web Options dialog box. To open the Web Options dialog box, select the Tools menu from Microsoft Excel and then select Options. Select the General Tab, and click the Web Options button. In the Web Options dialog box, select the Files tab. Remove the check mark from the Organize Supporting Files in a Folder check box on the Files tab.

Note Keep in mind that when you save an entire workbook containing worksheet data and charts on separate worksheets, Internet Explorer preserves the original Excel sheet arrangement in the resultant static Web page by adding sheet tabs at the bottom of the Internet Explorer window.

Alternatively you can save your worksheet as a Web page using Microsoft Visual Basic for Applications (VBA) code. Review the following simple procedure to save your active worksheet as a Web page:

```
Sub SaveAsWebPage()

    With ActiveWorkbook.PublishObjects.Add(xlSourceSheet, _
        "C:\Page.mht", "Sheet1", "", xlHtmlStatic, _
        "ProductSales_18739", "My Web")
        .Publish (False)
        .AutoRepublish = False
    End With
End Sub
```

This procedure simply saves the active worksheet as a Web page. Remember that thorough testing should be included whenever a new Web page is created. Testing will alleviate end user problems before your page is published on the Web.

Publishing a Worksheet to the Web

After the Web page has been saved, you are required to publish the page to the Web before you can share it with the world. The following steps review how to post your Web page on the Internet:

1 Click File, Save as Web Page to open the Save As Web Page dialog box. Select the Entire Workbook option. Then click the Publish button. The Publish as Web Page dialog box opens, as shown in Figure 25-2.

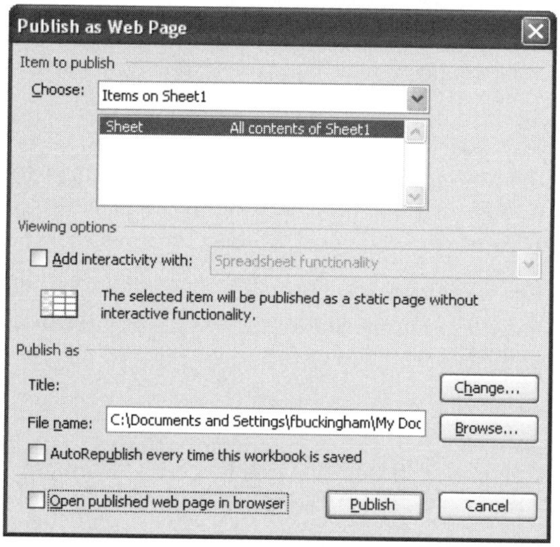

Figure 25-2. The Publish as a Web Page dialog box displays the options available before the save operation is complete. You can set up the location, file name, and other options from this dialog box.

2 Click the Browse button to select the location for the Web page to be stored.

3 If you have already set up a Web folder, navigate to the appropriate folder and skip forward to step 10; otherwise, follow these steps.

4   To create a new Network Place, click My Network Places in the Save In list and click Add a Network Place. The Add Network Place Wizard window opens, as shown in Figure 25-3.

Figure 25-3.   The Add Network Place wizard will guide you through creating a new network location for your Web page.

> **Note**   You can return to Excel when you have completed the setup of the new network location.

5   Click the Next button to accept the default, Create a Shortcut to an Existing Network Place. Then type your network location in the Location field, such as **http://mytestdomain.com/userid**. Click the Finish button to complete the wizard.

6   Enter your username and password so the Web server can authenticate you.

7   Type the file name, and click OK. You'll be returned to the Publish as Web Page dialog box.

8   Click the Publish button.

> **Note**   Remember the URL displayed in the Filename text box.

9   Open the Web Page in your Web Browser.

When you have completed the publication of your Web page, make sure that you test the functionality of the file. The testing phase should be thorough to avoid any complications when users begin to interact with the file. It's good practice to test all links and interactivity to ensure you have obtained the functionality you were striving for.

Now that you understand the Web publishing process, it's quite simple to add the publication step to the procedure you created earlier. The following procedure has been modified so that the Web page is published after it has been created:

```
Sub SaveAsWebPage()

    With ActiveWorkbook.PublishObjects.Add(xlSourceSheet, _
        "C:\My Webs\MyPage.mht", "Sheet1", "", xlHtmlStatic, _
        "ProductSales_18739", "My Web")
        .Publish (True)
        .AutoRepublish = False
    End With

End Sub
```

Inside Out

Web Page Style and Publication

Keep in mind that whether you are positing your data so that it's available to your intranet or to the world on the Internet, you are sharing information. This information should be presented on the screen in an easy-to-read format. Displaying a table of information is great, but a chart might be easier for the audience to quickly digest.

There are also several general rules of thumb to follow when you create your Web site. For example, I am sure that you've visited a Web site that was difficult to read because of the color selection. If a site has a dark background and a dark font color, it might be too frustrating for the audience to stay long enough to read your information. The page layout is also important, in addition to using appropriate, user-friendly navigational tools. Remember that users will become frustrated if you have your information laid out well but it's inconvenient to return to previous pages or the top of the current page.

Finally, before you publish your Web page, you should make sure it's ready by checking for broken hyperlinks, verifying that the pages look the way you want them to, and testing the Web to make sure that everything works. A good way to ensure your Web is ready is to preview it in more than one Web browser.

Making Web-Based Worksheets Interactive

Interactive components allow people to manipulate your data on the Web page in the browser. For example, you can publish an interactive spreadsheet that calculates loan information. A user can browse through the page and enter financial information such as the loan amount and interest rate to calculate his monthly payment.

The interactive components used in the HTML file can't be opened and modified in Excel, so you should maintain a master copy of the Excel workbook from which you published, so that you can make changes to it and republish the workbook if necessary.

When a Web page is published with interactivity, users can manipulate data. You create an interactive Excel Web page by saving the data with *spreadsheet functionality*. When you publish interactively with spreadsheet functionality, users can do the following:

- Enter data
- Format data
- Calculate data
- Analyze data
- Sort and filter

There are several types of interactivity available to your worksheet. Table 25-1 outlines the available options.

Table 25-1. Interactivity Options

Interactivity	Description
Spreadsheet functionality	Users can modify the data by changing the values in the cells. The formulas are then automatically updated to reflect the changes. This option also allows you to filter lists on the Web page.
PivotTable functionality	Users can change the layout of rows and columns to see different summaries of the source data if using a PivotTable report. Using PivotTable also allows the user to update the external data range.
Chart functionality	Provides the user with interactive options with the chart on the Web page.

> **Note** The browser used to display the interactive components must be Microsoft Internet Explorer 4.1 or later and have an appropriate Microsoft Office license to work with spreadsheets, charts, or PivotTable lists published interactively from Excel.

The steps below outline how to add interactivity on your Web page.

1. Select the File menu, and then select the Save as Web page menu option.
2. Type the filename in the Filename text box.
3. Place a check mark in the Add Interactivity check box.
4. Click the Publish button.
5. Select the type of interactivity you want from the Add Interactivity With list. The type of interactivity that's available is limited to the types of objects in your worksheet.
6. Click the Publish button.

> **Note** You will be able to open and use interactive Web pages in your Web browser. However, if you need to modify the data on the Web site, you won't be able to open and modify interactive Web pages in Excel. You should store a backup copy of the original workbook you published, in case you need to modify the data. If changes are made to the original spreadsheet, you'll need to republish and set up the interactivity with the new Web page.

Using the Internet as a Data Source

The Excel application has two commonly known sources of data: databases on any given network, and the user. Traditionally, if an item of data wasn't available in a database, the user was required to type it in and maintain it. To enable this, the application had to include a number of sheets and dialog boxes to store the information and provide a mechanism for the data entry.

A typical example of this would be maintaining exchange rate information in a financial model. It's usually the user's responsibility to obtain the latest rates and type them into the model. You can add value to the application by automating the retrieval of up-to-date exchange rate information from one of many Web sites.

The following sections demonstrate different techniques for retrieving information from the Web, using the USD exchange rate available from *http://www.fms.treas.gov/intn.html#rates* as an example. The Web page should look similar to Figure 25-4.

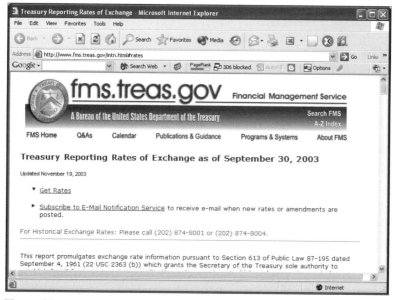

Figure 25-4. The U.S. Treasury site shows sample data laid out in a table format. This information will be evaluated in the next sections.

Opening Web Pages as Workbooks

The simplest solution is to open the entire Web page as if it were a workbook, and then scan the sheet for the required information, such as the USD/Canadian exchange rate. However, the problem with this approach is that the entire Web page is loaded. The Web page usually includes graphics, banners, and information that aren't required. The additional data will slow down the performance of the speed of data retrieval. Later in this chapter, you'll review using Web Queries to improve performance.

In the meantime, review the following procedure that opens the U.S. Treasury Web site within Excel:

```
Sub OpenUSDRatesPage()

    Dim webBk As Workbook
    Dim webRng As Range

    Set webBk = Workbooks.Open("http://www.fms.treas.gov/intn.html#rates")
    Set webRng = webBk.Worksheets(1).Cells.Find("CANADA - DOLLAR")

    MsgBox "The USD/Canadian exchange rate is " & webRng.Offset(0, 1).Value

End Sub
```

This procedure uses the *Open* method to open an existing Web page rather than a Web browser. When the Web page appears, it then searches for the specified type of currency and displays the current exchange rate in a message box. This procedure can be used with other Web pages that display information in a table format. Simply enter the appropriate label in the Find criteria. Remember that if you are actively searching the Internet for updated information, you'll require an active Internet connection.

 ## Troubleshooting

Web Page Frames

There might be times when a Web page is opened in Excel, but nothing is there. Don't worry, you did open the page correctly, but Excel can't open Web pages that contain frames.

A frames page allows a single Web page to be divided into sections that each displays a separate Web page. Each of these sections is called a *frame*. The frames page is the container that hosts the group of frames. Excel can't open a Web page that contains a frames page.

If you know how to work with HTML source code, you can use an HTML editor to copy the information you want, without the frames page code, to a new file. When the new file has been created, you can open it in Excel.

Using Web Queries

Web Queries were introduced in Excel 97 and have been enhanced with each subsequent version of Excel. They allow you to retrieve a single table of information from a Web page, with options to automatically refresh the data each time the workbook is opened, or at specific intervals.

One of the problems with Web Queries is that Excel uses the thousands and decimal separators specified in the Windows Regional Settings when attempting to recognize numbers in the page. If, for example, an exchange rate Web page is retrieved from one of many European countries, the period is treated as a thousands separator, not a decimal separator, resulting in exchange rates that are many times too large. Therefore, Web Queries couldn't be reliably used in versions prior to Excel 2002 in countries that used non-U.S. format decimal and thousand separators. However, now there's a workaround for this problem.

There are three properties to the *Application* object to temporarily override the settings used when recognizing numbers. The following properties are available:

- *Application.DecimalSeparator*
- *Application.ThousandsSeparator*
- *Application.UseSystemsSeparators*

Using these properties, you can set Excel's separators to match those on the Web page, perform the query, and then set them back again. If you want to use the Web Query's automatic refreshing options, you have to set these separators in the *BeforeRefresh* event and set them back in the *AfterRefresh* event. To capture these events, class modules need to be set up.

The following procedure demonstrates how to retrieve the table of exchange rates using a Web Query created within the procedure.

> **Note** The *RetrieveWebQueryData* procedure imports the table of exchange rates into the Excel workbook. If you don't see the Exchange Rates in the workbook, verify which table you need to import. The sidebar "That Was Table Number 2?", on p. 531, explains this scenario.

```
Sub RetrieveWebQueryData()

    ActiveWorkbook.Worksheets.Add
    With ActiveSheet.QueryTables.Add(Connection:= _
        "URL;http://www.fms.treas.gov/intn.html", Destination:=Range("A1"))
        .Name = "USD"
        .FieldNames = True
        .RowNumbers = False
        .FillAdjacentFormulas = False
        .PreserveFormatting = True
        .RefreshOnFileOpen = False
        .BackgroundQuery = True
        .RefreshStyle = xlInsertDeleteCells
```

```
        .SavePassword = False
        .SaveData = True
        .AdjustColumnWidth = True
        .RefreshPeriod = 0
        .WebSelectionType = xlSpecifiedTables
        .WebFormatting = xlWebFormattingNone
        .WebTables = "2"
        .WebPreFormattedTextToColumns = True
        .WebConsecutiveDelimitersAsOne = True
        .WebSingleBlockTextImport = False
        .WebDisableDateRecognition = False
        .WebDisableRedirections = False
        .Refresh BackgroundQuery:=False
    End With

End Sub
```

The .WebTables = 2 line in the preceding example tells Excel that you want the third table on the page. Literally, this is the third occurrence of a <TABLE> tag in the source HTML for the page.

With Excel, you have the ability to incorporate data that you locate from the Web into your spreadsheets. It's not necessary to know how the page was created or how to create a query file. You can select the data you want, and once the information is imported into the spreadsheet, you can refresh the data with a single click of the mouse. Alternatively, the data can be refreshed when the workbook is opened, or at specific time intervals.

You can alternatively create a new Web Query using the Import External Data feature within Excel. Follow these steps outlined to review how to navigate through the dialog box.

1 Click Data, Import External Data, and then New Web Query.

2 Type the Web page URL in the Address text box.

3 Click the Go button to show the Web page within the New Web Query dialog box. Notice the arrows that appear on the Web page. The arrows when selected will outline the entire table to be imported into your worksheet.

4 Select the table to import. When the table is selected, the arrow changes to a check mark as displayed in Figure 25-5.

5 Click the Import button.

6 Two options are available to place the contents of the Web query. Select Existing Worksheet if you want to display the data in the active worksheet, or select New Worksheet if you want the data to be placed in a new sheet.

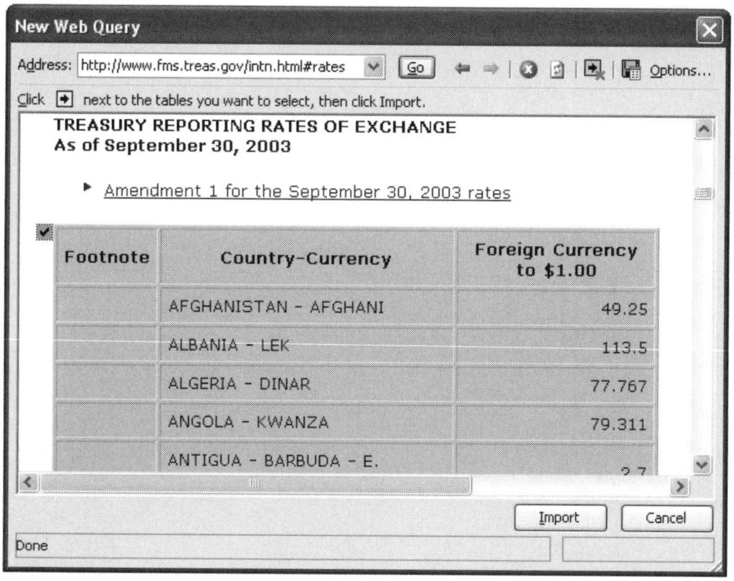

Figure 25-5. The New Web Query dialog box shows the table of exchange rates ready to be imported into the Excel spreadsheet.

Inside Out

That Was Table Number 2?

There are times when you view a Web page that contains many tables. Web sites that contain many tables can make it difficult to determine the number of the *WebTables* property. It might be difficult to determine the table number, but there are ways to verify the number.

A quick way to verify the number of a table within the Web site is to record a macro and set up a Web Query. The Web Query should import the table you need to work with in a new sheet to avoid complications. After the Web Query has been created, stop recording the macro.

Review the recorded macro code until you find the *WebTables* property. The value assigned to the *WebTables* property will be the table number you were searching for.

There are times when recording macros can assist in finding values and properties that are otherwise tedious to locate. Sometimes when working through new properties and new object models, recording simple macros and reviewing their code will show you properties and methods you didn't know existed. Keep in mind that any recorded macros should be cleaned up, however. There are always additional lines of code that are unnecessary.

Parsing Web Pages for Specific Information

Web Queries are an excellent way of retrieving tables of information from Web pages, but they're a little cumbersome if you're only interested in one or two items of information. Another way is to read the page using a hidden instance of Internet Explorer, search within the page for the required information, and then return the result. The following code requires you to click the Tools, References command and select the Microsoft Internet Controls object library:

```
Sub GetUSDtoCanadian()

    Dim webIE As SHDocVw.InternetExplorer
    Dim strPage As String
    Dim lngCanadian As Long
    Dim lngDec As Long
    Dim lngStart As Long
    Dim lngEnd As Long
    Dim dblRate As Double

    Set webIE = New SHDocVw.InternetExplorer
    webIE.Navigate "http://www.fms.treas.gov/intn.html#rates"

    Do Until webIE.ReadyState = READYSTATE_COMPLETE
        DoEvents
    Loop

    strPage = webIE.Document.body.innerHTML

    lngCanadian = InStr(1, strPage, "CANADA - DOLLAR")
    lngDec = InStr(lngCanadian, strPage, ".")

    lngStart = InStrRev(strPage, ">", lngDec) + 1
    lngEnd = InStr(lngDec, strPage, "<")

    dblRate = Val(Mid$(strPage, lngStart, lngEnd - lngStart))

    MsgBox "The USD/Canadian exchange rate is " & dblRate

End Sub
```

In determining whether to use a Web Query or parse a Web page, the most appropriate method to use will depend on the precise circumstances and how much data is required. For single items, it's probably easier to search the Web page for the required information. However, for more than a few items it'll be easier to use a Web Query to read the page or table into a workbook and then find the required items on the sheet.

Using the Internet to Publish Results

A Web server can be used as a repository of information, storing your application's results and presenting them to a wider audience than can be achieved with printed reports. By presenting results as Web pages, the reader of those pages can easily use the results as sources of data for his own analysis and easily pass those results to other interested parties.

Setting Up a Web Server

There are entire books written on this subject. Consider this section a brief overview of how to set up a Web server. You can find more information about setting up a Web server in Windows 2003 Server in *Microsoft Windows Server 2003 Administrator's Companion*, from Microsoft Press. For information on setting up a Web server in Windows XP Professional, see *Microsoft Windows XP Networking Inside Out* (also from Microsoft Press).

The examples that you'll review in the following sections will require write access to a Web server. To host Web pages, you must first install Internet Information Server (IIS). This can be done using the Add or Remove Programs applet found in the Control Panel. Once IIS is installed, the Management Console can be found within the Administrative Tools folder in the Control Panel. Using the Console, you can manage various aspects of your Web server.

The Home Directory is used to store your Web page. To configure the properties of your Web Servers Home Directory, Open IIS, and right-click the Default Web Site node. Select Properties, and click the Home Directory tab. You'll be presented with various configuration options for the default Web site. Make sure that the Read and Write check boxes are selected, and click OK. See Figure 25-6. This ensures that you are able to post new content to the folder.

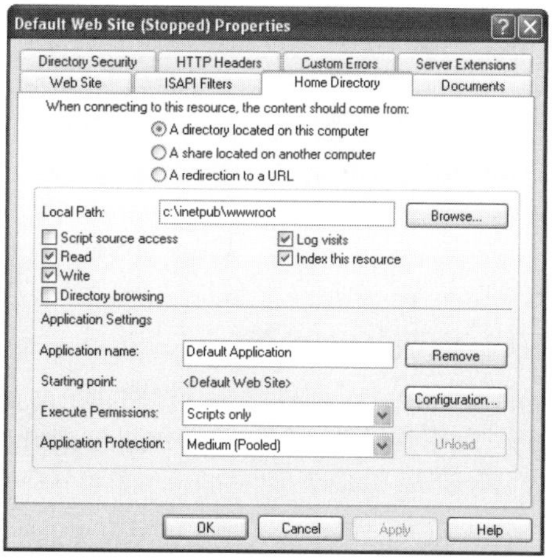

Figure 25-6. The Default Web Site Properties dialog box is used to configure IIS. To post Web pages to your Web server, ensure a check mark is placed in the Read and Write check boxes.

Notice the Local Path box. This is where the root of your Web server is located. By default, the path is C:\inetpub\wwwroot. Any Web pages placed in this directory are published at the following URL: *http://localhost/PageName.html*.

Saving Worksheets as Web Pages

To help save time and effort, it's best if a template is created for updating the latest information to your Web site. The template provides the easiest way to present your results on a Web page. The template workbook contains all the formatting and links that are required. When your application produces its results, it's a simple task to copy the relevant numbers into the template, and then save the template directly to the Web server.

The following example uses a template file to post the new results directly to the Web server:

> **Tip** **Customize the Procedure**
> The following procedure will need to be customized using a folder you have created on your computer. Keep in mind that to run this procedure you'll need to modify filenames, range references, references to charts, and PivotTables.

```
Sub PublishResultsToWeb()

    Dim webBk As Workbook
    Dim webSht As Worksheet

    Set webBk = Workbooks.Add("C:\WebTemplate.xls")
    Set webSht = webBk.Worksheets(1)

    webSht.Range("Profits").Value = Workbooks("Results.xls") _
        .Worksheets("Financials").Range("Profits").Value

    webSht.SaveAs "http://localhost/resultsjuly2001.htm", xlHtml

    webBk.Close False

End Sub
```

Adding Interactivity with the Web Components

The previous example saved a static rendition of the worksheet in HTML format to the Web server. However, Office Web Components can create interactive Web pages. When saving a worksheet in interactive form, several conversions occur:

● Worksheet or ranges on the sheet are converted to Spreadsheet Web Components

● Selected Charts are converted to Chart Web Components

● PivotTables are converted to PivotTable Web Components

These components are ActiveX controls that are embedded in the HTML page, designed to provide similar interaction as in Excel but from the browser.

It's beyond the scope of this book to document the Web Components, but the following code can be used to save a workbook as an interactive Web page, where the workbook contains a range of data to be published in a specified range, a PivotTable, and an embedded chart.

Tip **Customize Your Procedure**

Keep in mind that to run this procedure you'll need to customize the *PublishInteractivePage* procedure to reference your Web server, the correct filenames, and the worksheet name you have set up for this example.

```
Sub PublishInteractivePage()

    With ActiveWorkbook.PublishObjects
        .Delete
        .Add(xlSourcePivotTable, "http://localhost/page.htm", "Sheet1", _
            "PivotTable1", xlHtmlList).Publish True
        .Add(xlSourceRange, "http://localhost/page.htm", "Sheet1", _
            "A1:C30", xlHtmlCalc).Publish False
        .Add(xlSourceChart, "http://localhost/page.htm", "Sheet1", _
            "Chart 1", xlHtmlChart).Publish False
    End With

End Sub
```

Tip **Expanding Your Web Page**

To publish workbook components to individual Web pages, save the individual objects to a new page.

The resulting Web page is quite simple because only placeholders for the various Web Components are added. Now that the page has been created and contains the Web Components, modify this page so that it's presentation quality.

Microsoft Office Web Components provide the means to make it possible for you to publish Office documents to the Web while preserving the interactivity the documents have when they are viewed in their native applications. The Office Web Components are a collection of ActiveX controls. When Microsoft Office users view a Web page that contains an Office Web Component, they can interact with the data displayed in that document right in Microsoft Internet Explorer. Users can sort, filter, add, or change data, expand and collapse detail views, work with PivotTable lists, and chart the results of their changes. In addition, the Office Web Components are fully programmable, which makes it possible for you create rich, interactive content for Web-based applications.

Note Office Web Components only work in Internet Explorer 4.01 or later, and the Microsoft Access data access pages work only in Internet Explorer 5 or later. In addition, you get the most complete functionality with all the Office Web Component controls in Internet Explorer 5 or later.

Communicating with a Web Server

Within a corporate network, nearly all data transfer takes place using proprietary binary formats, ranging from transferring files to performing remote database queries. Due primarily to security considerations, communication across the Internet has evolved to use textual formats, the simplest being a URL, such as http://mysite.com/mywebpage.html.

To communicate with an application running on a Web server, you need to be able to perform some processing on the server and pass information to and receive information from that application.

The *Workbook* object's *FollowHyperlink* method can be used to communicate with a Web server. There are a few problems with using this method, including the following:

- If an error occurs during the connection, Excel will freeze.
- Any data returned from the hyperlink is automatically displayed as a new workbook.
- You have very little control over the communication.

There are more flexible alternatives provided by the Microsoft Internet Transfer Control, *msinet.ocx*. This ActiveX control, often referred to as the ITC, is an easy-to-use wrapper for the wininet.dll file, which provides low-level Internet-related services for the Microsoft Windows platform.

There are two mechanisms that can be used to send information to a Web server. You can either include the information as part of the URL string, or you can send it as a separate section of the HTTP request.

URL Encoding uses parameters included with the URL string by appending them to the end of the URL. You've probably noticed as you surf through Web pages that after you type the address, the address bar automatically updates to the destination URL with question marks and equal signs, with several letters thrown into the mix. Next time, pay attention to the character string. Upon closer examination, you'll see that after the URL there's a question mark followed by *param1=value&param2=value*. For example, when you navigate to the MSN Hotmail Web page, you type in the address, *www.hotmail.com*. However, after you press Enter, the following result appears in the address bar:

```
http://loginnet.passport.com/login.srf?id=2&svc=mail&cbid=24325&msppjph=1&tw=0&
fs=1&fsa=1&fsat=1296000&lc=1033&_lang=EN
```

That is certainly different from what was initially typed in, but somehow you reach the destination Web site.

One advantage to including the parameters as part of the URL is that the URL with the parameters can be stored as part of the user's favorites. However, a URL is limited to 2083 characters in Internet Explorer, which in turn restricts the amount of information that can be passed using this method.

If you choose to send information as a separate section of the HTTP request, you will be using the POST field to transfer the information. POSTing data uses the POST field to send information to the Web server. Because there's almost no limit to the amount of data that can be put in a POST field, it's the preferred way of transferring information to the server.

How do you return information to the client? The data can be presented to the client as a Web page that can be read using the same techniques described throughout this chapter.

Using Internet Solutions with Excel

Microsoft has enabled the Excel developer to use the Internet as an integral part of an application solution. For example, workbooks can be opened from and saved to Web servers, Excel can open HTML pages as though they were workbooks, and Web Queries can be used to extract tables of data from Web pages. The Internet Explorer object library can also be automated to retrieve individual items of data from a Web page, without the overhead of using a workbook.

Besides the ability to utilize and extract data from the World Wide Web, you can also save Excel workbooks as content-rich Web pages. Interactive Web pages can easily be produced, providing Excel-like interaction within the Web browser.

All these tools discussed in this chapter enable you to develop new types of business solutions where Excel is one key part of a larger business process. This process is not limited to a single organization; rather, your solutions can span multiple organizations and geographical locations.

After reviewing this chapter, you might need to rethink your strategy on developing Excel application solutions. The Internet is a valuable resource and can be easily used. Not only can you use the information found on the Internet, but Excel has added Internet functionality to assist you in sharing data with the world. While developing your solutions, you might need to think outside the typical box to achieve the desired results.

Excel and the Extensible Markup Language (XML)

Introducing Data Lists. 539
Creating XML Schemas. 546
Creating XML Data Files 549
Adding XML to a Workbook Manually . . 550
Adding XML to a Worksheet
Programmatically. 553

Support for XML, including the ability to save files as XML documents, was introduced in Microsoft Office XP, but the technology is one of the focal points of Office 2003. If you work in an enterprise that exchanges data with other organizations in the form of purchase orders, parts data, financial data, or product catalogs, you can use XML to transfer the data among your colleagues and suppliers regardless of the program used to create the data.

In this chapter, you'll learn how to:

- Create data lists manually and programmatically
- Create XML schemas and data files
- Associate XML schemas with workbooks
- Import and export XML data manually and programmatically
- Associate schema elements with columns
- Associate schemas with existing data lists

Introducing Data Lists

In Microsoft Excel Version 2002 and earlier versions, you needed to create a *data list* to use certain functions such as sorting and filtering data or creating a PivotTable. Though the concept of a data list was only loosely defined in the help system, the bottom line was that you needed to have a series of columns, with headers, and a series of rows with values for the columns. Figure 26-1 shows a data list of suppliers derived from the Suppliers table in the Northwind sample database (included with Microsoft Access).

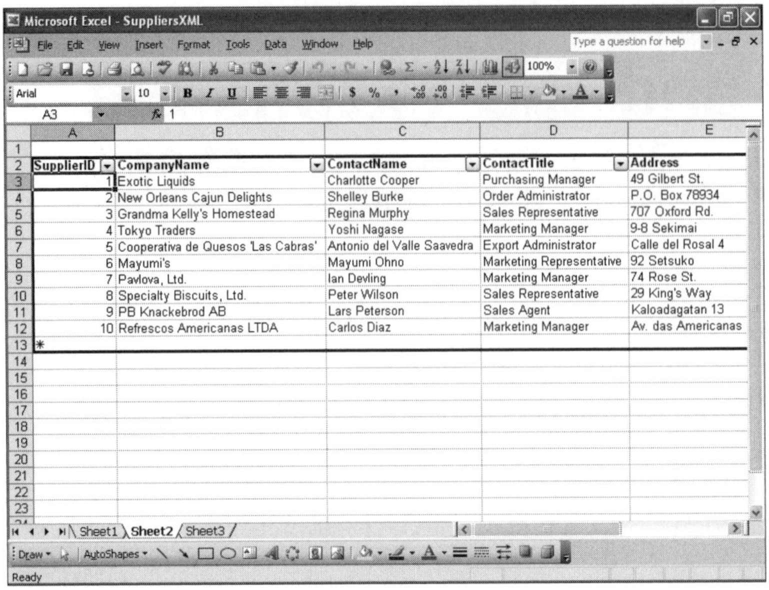

Figure 26-1. A data list has column headers and rows of data, with each row representing a complete set of column values.

One of the advances of Microsoft Office Excel 2003 is that the concept of data lists has been codified into a coherent whole, implementing the new vision in a manner very like an Access table or a data form (not to be confused with a user form).

To create a data list using the Excel interface, follow these steps:

1 Type the names in the cells that will become the top row of the list.

2 Click Data, List, Create List to display the Create List dialog box (shown in Figure 26-2).

3 Select the cells to be part of the list.

4 Select the My List Has Headers check box if the top row you selected contains the column headings.

5 Click OK.

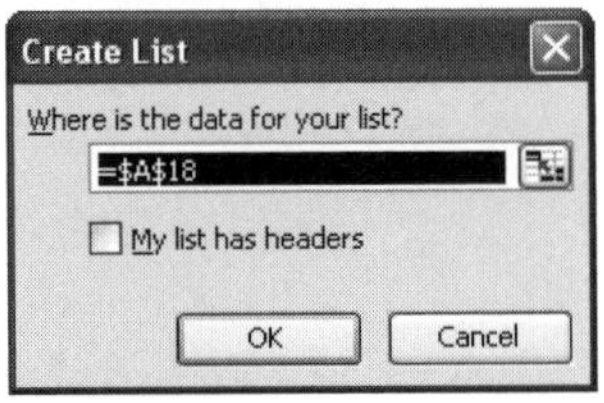

Figure 26-2. The Create List dialog box lets you determine the structure of your data list.

After you've created your list, you can begin typing data into the *insert row*, where the left-most cell contains an asterisk. Pressing the Tab key moves you to the next column, whereas pressing the Enter key creates a new row in the list. Once you have data in the list, you can use the down arrow buttons in the first row (usually the header row) to filter the values in your list as if you had created an Advanced Filter. You can add a total row to the list by clicking any cell in the list and then clicking Data, List, Total Row. Clicking a cell in the total row displays a down arrow button that you can click to select the function you want to use in each total cell.

> **Note** If you no longer want to use the list functionality but do want to retain the data in the list, click any cell in the list and then click Data, List, Convert to Range.

Creating Data Lists Programmatically

Individual data lists are represented in the Excel object model by the *ListObject* object, which has a variety of properties and methods that you can use to manipulate your lists using Microsoft Visual Basic for Applications (VBA). Table 26-1 summarizes the *ListObject* object's properties and methods.

Table 26-1. Properties and Methods of the Object

Property or Method	Description
Property	
Active	This property returns a Boolean value that is *True* if the active cell is within the body of the *ListObject*.
DataBodyRange	This property returns a read-only *Range* object that refers to the list's cells between the header row and the insert row.
DisplayRightToLeft	This read-only property returns *True* if the worksheet, the list, or the window is displayed in a language that displays characters from right to left.
HeaderRowRange	This property returns a read-only *Range* object that refers to the cells in the header row of the *ListObject*.
InsertRowRange	This property returns a read-only *Range* object that refers to the cells in the insert row of the *ListObject*.
ListColumns	This property returns a *ListColumns* collection that contains all the columns in the *ListObject*.
ListRows	This property returns a *ListRows* collection that contains all the rows in the *ListObject*.
Name	A property used to identify the *ListObject* as a unique member of the *ListObjects* collection. The *Name* property can only be set and read using VBA; you can't affect it using the Excel interface.

continued

Table 26-1. Properties and Methods of the Object *(continued)*

Property or Method	Description
Property	
QueryTable	A property used to create a link to a table providing data to the ListObject.
Range	This property returns a read-only Range object that refers to all the cells in the ListObject.
SharePointUrl	This read-only property returns a string that contains the URL of the Microsoft SharePoint list for a given ListObject object.
ShowAutoFilter	A Boolean value that, when set to True, displays the results of the active AutoFilter on the contents of the ListObject. The default value is False.
ShowTotals	A Boolean value that, when set to True, displays a Totals row for the ListObject. The default value is False.
SourceType	A read-only constant that reflects the type of source providing data to the ListObject. The available data sources are xlSrcExternal (an external data source such as a Web page), xlSrcRange (a range of cells in an Excel workbook), and xlSrcXml (an XML data file).
TotalsRowRange	This property returns a read-only Range object that refers to the cells in the totals row of the ListObject.
XmlMap	This read-only property returns an XmlMap object representing the schema mapped to the specified list.
Method	
Delete	This method deletes the active ListObject and deletes all cell data associated with it.
Publish(Target(Url, ListName, Description), LinkSource)	This method publishes a LinkObject to a SharePoint Services site. The Target argument contains an array of three values: the URL of the SharePoint server, the list name, and an optional description. The LinkSource argument is a required Boolean value that, when set to True, links the current LinkObject to the published LinkObject. Setting the LinkSource argument to False means the two objects won't be linked (and that any updates to the LinkObject that called the Publish method won't be reflected in the LinkObject on the SharePoint site).
Refresh	This method updates the data and schema for a ListObject that draws its data from a SharePoint site.

Table 26-1. Properties and Methods of the Object *(continued)*

Property or Method	Description
Method	
Resize(Range)	This method lets you change the range of cells associated with the list. If the list draws its data from a source on a SharePoint site, you can only add rows, not columns. The method doesn't delete any existing data.
Unlink	This method breaks the link between the *ListObject* and a source on a SharePoint site. No data is deleted.
Unlist	This method removes data list functionality from the list. The cells in the *ListObject* become regular cells and retain their data.
UpdateChanges (XlListConflict)	This method updates the list on a SharePoint site with the changes made to the list in the worksheet. The optional *XlListConflict* constant can be any of these intrinsic constants: *xlListConflictDialog* (the default, which displays the Conflict dialog box), *xlListConflictRetryAllConflicts* (which attempts to update the data again), *xlListConflictDiscardAllConflicts* (which ignores any changes that conflict with other users' changes), and *xlListConflictError* (which indicates an error and halts the update).

All the data lists in a worksheet have a place in the *Worksheet* object's *ListObjects* collection. The collection starts out empty, but you can use the collection's *Add* method to create a new *ListObject* in the worksheet that calls the method.

The *ListObjects.Add* method has the following syntax:

```
expression.Add(SourceType, Source, LinkSource, HasHeaders, <;$RD>
    Destination).Name=namestring
```

Table 26-2 details the *Add* method's arguments.

Table 26-2. Arguments of the *ListObjects* Collection's *Add* Method

Argument	Required or Optional	Description
expression	Required	An expression that returns a *ListObject* object.
SourceType	Optional	One of two *XlListObjectSourceType* constants: *xlSrcExternal*, which indicates an external data source, or *xlSrcRange* (the default), which indicates the data source is a range in a workbook.

continued

Table 26-2. Arguments of the *ListObjects* Collection's *Add* Method *(continued)*

Argument	Required or Optional	Description
Source	Optional if *SourceType* is set to *xlSrcRange*; required if *SourceType* is set to *xlSrcExternal*	When *SourceType* is set to *xlSrcRange*, this argument refers to the range used to create the *ListObject*. When *SourceType* is set to *xlSrcExternal*, this argument must contain an array of three strings (a URL to a page on a SharePoint site, a list name, and a value representing the view to be applied to the list). There's no list of these values in the Visual Basic Editor Help system, so you should leave the third element of the array blank unless you are, or can get the correct values from, a SharePoint administrator.
LinkSource	Optional	A Boolean value that indicates whether to link the list to an external data source. The default value is *True* if the *SourceType* argument is set to *xlSrcExternal*. Setting the argument to either *True* or *False* when the *SourceType* argument is set to *xlSrcRange* creates an error.
HasHeaders	Optional	A variant value that indicates whether the *ListObject* has an existing set of column labels. The argument can be set to *xlGuess*, *xlNo*, or *xlYes*. If the source data doesn't contain column labels, or if Excel can't detect them, the method will create headers.
Destination	Required if the *SourceType* argument is set to *xlSrcExternal*; ignored if the *SourceType* argument is set to *xlSrcRange*	A *Range* object that identifies the cell at the top left corner of the new list object. The destination must be on the worksheet that called the *Add* method.
namestring	Required	A string that contains a unique name for the list.

Note The *Add* method inserts new columns to the right of the cell identified in the *Destination* argument to ensure that there's room for the new list; existing data won't be overwritten.

Chapter 26

Inside Out

A Better Way to Create Lists

If you check the Visual Basic Editor Help file for the *ListObjects* collection's *Add* method, you won't see the `.Name = namestring` bit at the end. The example in the Help system requires you to create a new object and use a much longer statement to generate the same result. Also, if you use the *Add* method in the manner described in the Help system, you'll get error messages because the *ListObject* you create has no name. The *Add* statement in the example might seem a bit confusing, but you can think of it as a form of the following statement:

```
ListObjects(0).Name = namestring
```

You're creating the member of the *ListObjects* collection in the same statement where you name it, but all is well because the *ListObject* exists when the Visual Basic Editor encounters the *Name* method.

As an example of how to use the *ListObjects* collection's *Add* method, consider the worksheet shown in Figure 26-3, which has a series of cells that contain values to be used as column labels.

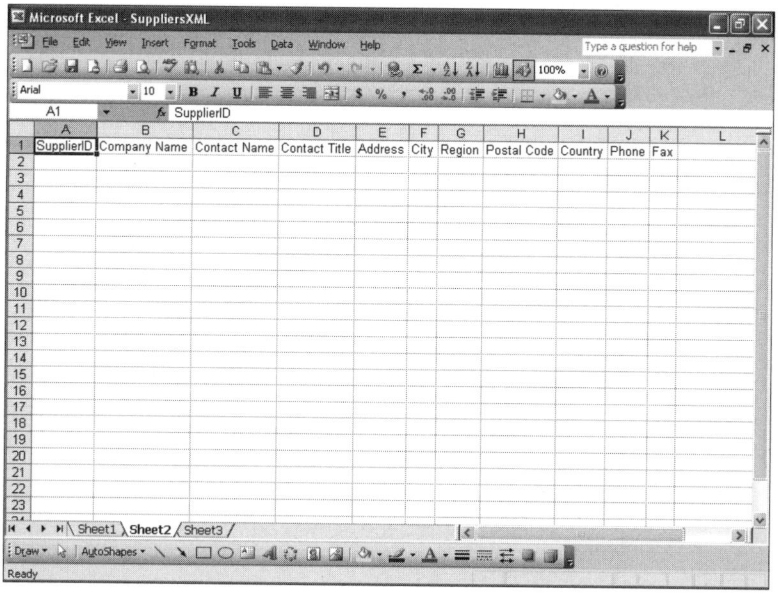

Figure 26-3. This worksheet has existing column labels and is ready for a list.

You could create a list based on that set of column labels using this procedure (which you would add to a code module):

```
Sub CreateListObject()
    ActiveSheet.ListObjects.Add(xlSrcRange, Range("$A$1:$K$1"), , xlYes)<;$RD>
    .Name = "Suppliers1"
End Sub
```

Lists are a terrific addition to your battery of Excel tools, but they're even more powerful when you combine them with XML data. The next section of this chapter introduces the basics of the Extensible Markup Language and how Excel uses it to facilitate data handling.

Creating XML Schemas

At the heart of XML-based data interchange is the *schema*, which is a document that defines the structure of a set of XML files. You can create a custom schema in an XML editor, write the XML code yourself in a simple text editor such as Notepad, or you can have Excel do it for you when you save a workbook as an XML document. The following listing, which was created using Notepad, shows the schema used in the examples throughout this chapter:

```xml
<?xml version="1.0" encoding="utf-8" ?>
<schema xmlns="http://www.w3.org/2001/XMLSchema">
 <element name="Root">
  <complexType>
   <sequence>
      <element name="Supplier" maxOccurs="unbounded">
          <complexType>
            <sequence>
              <element name="SupplierID" type="positiveInteger"/>
              <element name="CompanyName" type="string"/>
              <element name="ContactName" type="string"/>
              <element name="ContactTitle" type="string"/>
              <element name="MailingAddress">
                <complexType>
                  <sequence>
                    <element name="Address" type="string"/>
                    <element name="City" type="string"/>
                    <element name="Region" type="string"/>
                    <element name="PostalCode" type="string"/>
                    <element name="Country" type="string"/>
                  </sequence>
                </complexType>
              </element>
             <element name="Phone" type="string"/>
             <element name="Fax" type="string"/>
            </sequence>
          </complexType>
        </element>
      </sequence>
    </complexType>
  </element>
 </schema>
```

Don't let the long set of closing tags at the bottom of the list fool you—the structure of the data objects depicted in the schema isn't that complex. Figure 26-4 depicts the schema's structure graphically instead of textually.

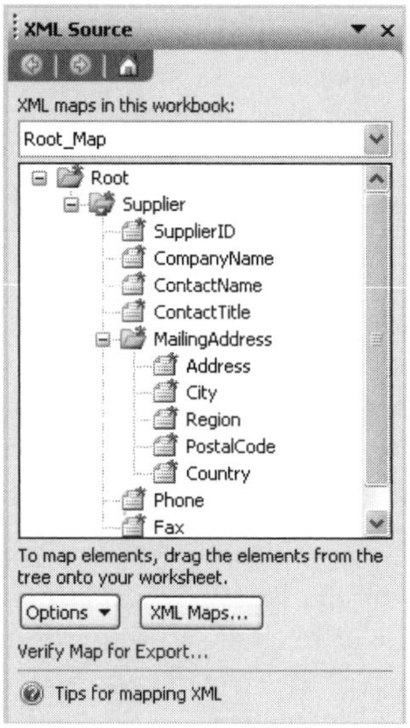

Figure 26-4. XML schemas are detailed, but not overly complicated.

> **Note** You can display the XML Source task pane, which displays any schemas assigned to a workbook, by clicking Data, XML, XML Source.

The first two lines of the listing are housekeeping details that tell the XML interpreter which version of XML is used, which character encoding standard the data conforms to, and a reference to the schema standards document online at the World Wide Web Consortium's Web site.

```
<?xml version="1.0" encoding="utf-8" ?>
<schema xmlns="http://www.w3.org/2001/XMLSchema">
```

Inside Out

Watch Your Language

The *utf-8* encoding scheme is used to represent relatively simple character sets such as that used in American English. American English employs few accents (and then only on borrowed words), which means computers can represent the entire character set (including numbers, capital letters, punctuation, and certain special characters such as spaces, tabs, and so on) using only eight bits of data. For other languages that have differing basic characters or use accents, you need to use another eight bits to represent all the possible characters. The encoding scheme for most of those languages is *utf-16*.

The next several lines of code identify the basic element in the schema (often named *Root*) and indicate what structure the data will take.

```
<element name="Root">
  <complexType>
   <sequence>
     <element name="Supplier" maxOccurs="unbounded">
       ...
     </element>
   </sequence>
  </complexType>
</element>
```

The *<complexType>* tag in this XML schema code indicates that the *Root* element is *complex*, meaning it's allowed to contain multiple subelements. If you refer back to Figure 26-4, you can see that the *Root* element does indeed have subelements, the first of which is *Supplier*. The *<sequence>* tag indicates that the subelements will always appear in the same order, which is to be expected when you generate an XML data file from a spreadsheet or database table.

There is something new in the *Supplier* element declaration: the maxOccurs="unbounded" parameter setting. This parameter tells the XML interpreter that there can be more than one *Supplier* element in any XML data file that follows this schema. If you leave this parameter out, the interpreter knows to expect a single occurrence of the element, which is handy if you want to add information regarding the document author, the department, or the project code at the beginning of the data file.

You should think of XML elements as being similar to objects with properties. For example, the following abbreviated code sample shows some of the properties associated with a supplier:

```
<element name="SupplierID" type="positiveInteger"/>
<element name="MailingAddress">
  <complexType>
    <sequence>
      <element name="Address" type="string"/>
      <element name="City" type="string"/>
      <element name="Region" type="string"/>
      <element name="PostalCode" type="string"/>
      <element name="Country" type="string"/>
    </sequence>
  </complexType>
</element>
```

You should remember that any simple element (that is, an element with a single value associated with it) is enclosed within a single tag that ends with />. In addition to the name of the element, the element tag also contains a *type* parameter, which indicates the data type the element must contain. The two types used in the sample are *positiveInteger* and *string*, which are self-explanatory.

To save your schema as an XML schema file, follow these steps in Notepad:

1 Click File, Save.

2 Click the Save As Type down arrow and click All Files.

3 Type the name of the file in the File Name box. For example, if the name of the file you want to save as an XML schema file is MySuppliers, you would type **MySuppliers.xsd**.

For more information on XML data types, visit the World Wide Web Consortium's reference page at *http://www.w3.org/* and type **xml data types** into the search box.

Creating XML Data Files

A schema is only one half of what you need to work with XML data; the other half of the equation is the data itself. After you have created a schema that reflects the structure of your data, you can write your data into a file with tags corresponding to the outline in your schema file. The following listing, which you can type into a Notepad file, contains the data for the first two suppliers in the MySuppliers.xml file included on the CD-ROM:

```xml
<?xml version="1.0" encoding="UTF-8" ?>
<Root xmlns:xsi="http://www.w3.org/2001/XMLSchema-instance"
<;$RD> xsi:noNamespaceSchemaLocation="MySuppliers.xsd">

<Supplier>
 <SupplierID>1</SupplierID>
 <CompanyName>Exotic Liquids</CompanyName>
 <ContactName>Charlotte Cooper</ContactName>
 <ContactTitle>Purchasing Manager</ContactTitle>
 <MailingAddress>
  <Address>49 Gilbert St.</Address>
  <City>London</City>
  <Region></Region>
  <PostalCode>EC1 4SD</PostalCode>
  <Country>UK</Country>
 </MailingAddress>
 <Phone>(171) 555-2222</Phone>
 <Fax></Fax>
</Supplier>

<Supplier>
 <SupplierID>2</SupplierID>
 <CompanyName>New Orleans Cajun Delights</CompanyName>
 <ContactName>Shelley Burke</ContactName>
 <ContactTitle>Order Administrator</ContactTitle>
 <MailingAddress>
  <Address>P.O. Box 78934</Address>
  <City>New Orleans</City>
  <Region>LA</Region>
  <PostalCode>70117</PostalCode>
  <Country>USA</Country>
 </MailingAddress>
 <Phone>(100) 555-4822</Phone>
 <Fax></Fax>
</Supplier>
</Root>
```

To save your data as an XML file, follow these steps in Notepad:

1 Click File, Save.

2 Click the Save As Type down arrow and click All Files.

3 Type the name of the file in the File Name box. For example, if the name of the file you want to save as an XML file is MySuppliers.xml, you would type **MySuppliers.xml**.

There are several aspects of the data in the MySuppliers.xml file that you should notice. For example, the first two lines of the data file provide information similar to the first two lines in the schema file.

```
<?xml version="1.0" encoding="UTF-8" ?>
<Root xmlns:xsi="http://www.w3.org/2001/XMLSchema-instance"
<;$RD> xsi:noNamespaceSchemaLocation="MySuppliers.xsd">
```

The first line indicates the XML version and the text-encoding scheme used in the file, and the second line indicates the base element in the schema (*Root*), the URL indicating the standards document to which the data file conforms, and the name of the schema file (MySuppliers.xsd).

> **Note** You can use the first two lines of the sample MySuppliers.xml file in your own XML files. All you need to do is open the MySuppliers.xml file in a text editor, copy the lines, paste them into your other XML file, and replace MySuppliers.xsd with the name of your schema file.

The next section of the file contains the data used to populate your worksheet; it's no surprise that the structure of the data in MySuppliers.xml conforms exactly to the structure of the schema presented in MySuppliers.xsd (which you can find on the companion CD-ROM). For example, the schema file has the *CompanyName* element defined in the following line:

```
<element name="CompanyName" type="string"/>
```

And the data file has a corresponding line in each set of supplier data:

```
<CompanyName>New Orleans Cajun Delights</CompanyName>
```

Not every element has to contain data, but every element does need to occur within each repetition of the *Supplier* element. For example, the *Fax* element in both of the sample data sets contains no value, but the tags do have to occur in the XML data file so that the sequence of elements occurs exactly as defined in the schema file.

Adding XML to a Workbook Manually

Once you have created an XML schema and an associated XML data file, you need to add the structure of the schema to a worksheet. To do so, you establish a *data map*, or pattern of data represented in a file, in your worksheet.

> **Note** The words *map* and *schema* are often used interchangeably.

To associate a data map with a worksheet, follow these steps:

1 Click Data, XML, XML Source to display the XML Source task pane.
2 Click the XML Maps button to display the XML Maps dialog box.
3 Click Add to display the Select XML Source dialog box.
4 Navigate to the folder that contains the schema (a file with an .xsd extension) you want to map to the worksheet.
5 Click the file, and then click Open to add an outline of the schema to the XML Source task pane.

You can now drag individual elements from the map to the worksheet cells where you want the data to appear. After you drag an element to the worksheet, an AutoFilter down arrow will appear at the right edge of the cell. Click the down arrow, and select where you want the element label (the element's name, such as *CompanyName*) to appear.

> **Note** The names of elements you have mapped to a cell in a worksheet appear in bold type in the XML Source task pane.

If you want to add an entire element with all its subelements, you can do so by dragging the main element to a cell in the worksheet. Figure 26-5 shows the result of dragging the *Supplier* element from the MySuppliers.xsd schema to cell A1.

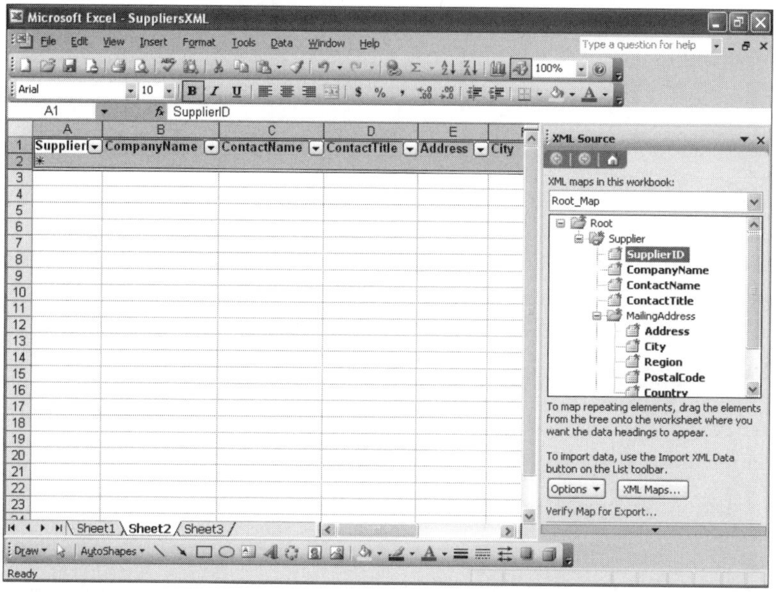

Figure 26-5. You can map an entire element (with all its subelements) to a worksheet at once.

> **Note** When you add a complex element (an element with subelements) to a worksheet, Excel treats the element as a single list, not a series of lists, which occurs when you drag simple elements to the worksheet individually.

After you've added the desired elements to your workbook, you can delete them as you would delete any other workbook contents. You can also remove an element from a worksheet by right-clicking the element in the XML Source task pane and clicking Remove Element on the shortcut menu.

If you want to change how the XML data is inserted into your worksheet, click the Options button in the XML Source task pane. You can use the options to preview your data in the task pane, hide help messages in the task pane, and let Excel know you have already added data labels so that it won't ask every time you insert a field. You can also change how Excel imports XML data by opening the Data menu, pointing to XML, and clicking XML Map Properties. You can use the controls in the XML Map Properties dialog box, shown in Figure 26-6, to change whether Excel resizes the columns to reflect the size of the data, preserves number formatting, and validates XML data against the associated schema before importing or exporting that data.

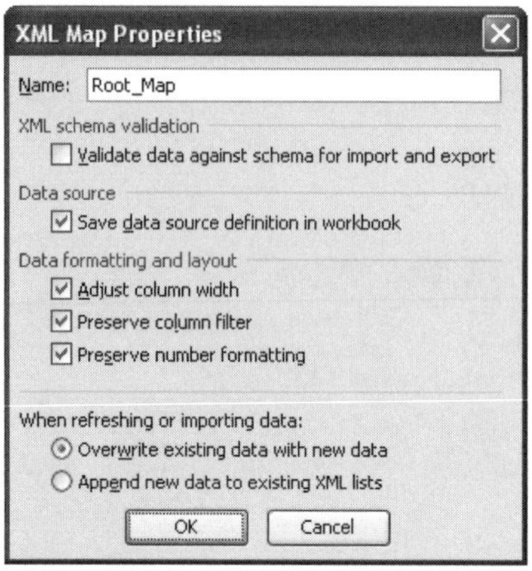

XML Map Properties

Name: Root_Map

XML schema validation
☐ Validate data against schema for import and export

Data source
☑ Save data source definition in workbook

Data formatting and layout
☑ Adjust column width
☑ Preserve column filter
☑ Preserve number formatting

When refreshing or importing data:
◉ Overwrite existing data with new data
○ Append new data to existing XML lists

[OK] [Cancel]

Figure 26-6. The XML Map Properties dialog box gives you more tools to control your XML data.

Importing XML Data Manually

Once you have assigned the schema elements to worksheet cells, you can import data into the worksheet from the XML data file that matches the structure of the schema.

To import data into an existing XML schema, follow these steps:

1 Click Data, XML, Import.
2 In the Import XML dialog box, navigate to the folder that contains the XML data file, click it, and click Import.

> **Note** You don't need to map every element of a schema to a worksheet for the data import to work correctly.

Adding XML to a Worksheet Programmatically

As you might expect, every XML-related action you can take using the Excel interface has its counterpart in the Excel object, although there are times when you have to dig a bit to find out how to do something in VBA that takes a simple and intuitive action when going through the interface. One example of that phenomenon is the series of actions you need to take to create a single data list (rather than a series of lists) from an XML schema.

Mapping a Schema to a Worksheet Programmatically

When you map an XML schema to a worksheet in VBA, you do so by creating a variable that contains a reference to an *XmlMap* object, which is the object used to represent a schema contained in an .xsd file. Table 26-3 lists the *XmlMap* object's properties and methods.

Table 26-3. **Selected Properties and Methods of the *XmlMap* Object**

Property or Method	Description
Property	
AdjustColumnWidth	A Boolean value that, when set to *True* (the default), causes Excel to change the column width to fit the data imported into that column. Setting the property to *False* causes the columns to retain their width at the time of the import.
AppendOnImport	A Boolean value that, when set to *False* (the default), causes data imported into a schema to overwrite the existing values. Setting this property to *True* causes newly imported data to be appended to an existing list.
IsExportable	A Boolean value that returns *True* if Excel can use the *XPath* objects in the specified schema map to export XML data and if all XML lists mapped to the specified schema map can be exported.
Name	A string that contains the name of an XML map. The string must be unique within the workbook and cannot exceed 255 characters.
PreserveColumnFilter	A Boolean value that, when set to *True* (the default), causes any list filter to be retained when the map is refreshed.

continued

Chapter 26

Table 26-3. Selected Properties and Methods of the XmlMap Object *(continued)*

Property or Method	Description
Property	
PreserveNumberFormatting	A Boolean value that, when set to *True*, retains any number formatting changes when the XML map is refreshed. The default value is *False*.
RootElementName	A read-only string that contains the name of the root element of the mapped schema.
SaveDataSourceDefinition	A Boolean value that, when set to *True* (the default value), causes Excel to save the data source definition of the mapped schema with the workbook.
Schemas	A property that returns an *XmlSchemas* collection that contains each schema mapped to the active workbook.
ShowImportExportValidationErrors	A Boolean value that, when set to *True*, causes Excel to display a dialog box that details any schema-validation errors that occur when data is imported or exported through the specified XML schema. The default value is *False*.
Method	
Delete	The *Delete* method removes the named schema from a workbook.
Export(Url, Overwrite)	The *Export* method writes the contents of cells mapped to the specified *XmlMap* object to an XML data file. The *Url* argument is a string that contains the full path of the file to which you want to write the XML data. The *Overwrite* argument, when set to *True*, replaces any existing file with the same name. (The default value is *False*.) The *Export* method returns one of two constants: *xlXmlExportSuccess*, which indicates the export happened without error, or *xlXmlExportValidationFailed*, which indicates the data did not match the *XmlMap* schema.
ExportXml(Data)	The *ExportXml* method writes the contents of cells mapped to the specified *XmlMap* object to the string named in the *Data* argument. The method returns one of two constants: *xlXmlExportSuccess*, which indicates the export happened without error, or *xlXmlExportValidationFailed*, which indicates the data did not match the *XmlMap* schema.

continued

**Table 26-3. Selected Properties and Methods of the
XmlMap Object** *(continued)*

Property or Method	Description
Method	
Import(Url, Overwrite)	The *Import* method writes data from the file at the specified URL to cells mapped with the *XMLMap* that called the method. The *Url* argument holds a file path or Web address. The *Overwrite* argument is a variant that, when set to *False* (the default), appends the imported data after any existing data, or when set to *True* overwrites any existing data. The *Import* method returns one of three constants: *xlXmlImportElementsTruncated*, which indicates that the contents of the specified XML data file have been truncated because the XML data file is too large for a cell; *xlXmlImportSuccess*, which indicates the import was successful; and *xlXmlImportValidationFailed*, which indicates that the contents of the XML data file don't match the specified schema.
ImportXml(XmlData, Overwrite)	The *ImportXml* method writes data from a string variable (specified in the *XmlData* argument) to cells mapped with the *XmlMap* that called the method. The *Overwrite* argument is a variant that, when set to *False* (the default), appends the imported data after any existing data, or when set to *True* overwrites any existing data. The method returns one of three constants: *xlXmlImportElementsTruncated*, which indicates that the contents of the specified XML data file have been truncated because the XML data file is too large for a cell; *xlXmlImportSuccess*, which indicates the import was successful; and *xlXmlImportValidationFailed*, which indicates that the contents of the XML data file don't match the specified schema.

All the schemas assigned to a workbook are stored in the *Workbook* object's *XmlMaps* collection. You can refer to individual members of the collection by noting their names, as in the following statement:

```
ActiveWorkbook.XmlMaps("Root_Map")
```

Although most of the properties and methods you'll need to work with XML maps are contained in the *XmlMap* object, the *XmlMaps* collection does contain the vital *Add* method, which you use to assign a schema to a workbook. The *Add* method has this syntax:

```
Add(Schema, RootElementName)
```

The *Schema* argument is a string variable that contains the full path of the schema to add to the workbook, and the *RootElementName* argument contains the name of the root element in the schema. The following procedure adds the MySuppliers.xsd schema to the active workbook:

```
Sub ApplySchema()
    Dim myMap As XmlMap
    Dim xSchemaFile As String

    xSchemaFile = "C:\MySuppliers.xsd"
    Set myMap = ActiveWorkbook.XmlMaps.Add(xSchemaFile, "Root")
End Sub
```

This procedure defines an object variable (*myMap*) to hold the reference to the *XmlMap*. After you assign the schema file path to the *xSchemaFile* variable, you use the *Set* command to assign the named schema file to the active workbook's *XmlMaps* collection.

When you attach a map to a workbook, the map is assigned the name of the root element followed by an underscore and the word *Map*. The map you just added, which has a root element named Root, would be assigned the name *Root_Map*.

To delete the *XmlMap* you just added to your workbook, you would run the following procedure:

```
Sub RemoveMap()
    ActiveWorkbook.XmlMaps("Root_Map").Delete
End Sub
```

Note If a map has been attached to a workbook and you attempt to assign the map to the workbook again, Excel will add a number to the end of the map name. For example, adding the *Root_Map* map to a workbook additional times would result in the map being named *Root_Map2*, *Root_Map3*, and so on.

If you wanted to write the data currently within the cells assigned to the *Root_Map* schema to a file named SuppliersBackup.xml, you could use the following procedure:

```
Sub BackupXML()
    ActiveWorkbook.XmlMaps("Root_Map").Export _
        Url:= "C:\SuppliersBackup.xml", Overwrite:=True
    If Err.Number = 0 Then
        MsgBox "Data exported to SuppliersBackup.xml successfully."
    Else
        MsgBox "There was a problem exporting to SuppliersBackup.xml."
        Exit Sub
    End If
End Sub
```

Warning Because the *Overwrite* argument is set to *True*, this procedure will delete any existing data in the SuppliersBackup.xml file. Also, if the data list is empty, the procedure will generate an error.

Mapping Schema Elements to Cells Using XPath

After you have mapped a schema to a workbook, you need to map every element you want to appear in the worksheet to a range of cells so that you have a place for the associated XML data to reside. You don't need to assign every element in a schema to a cell or range; Excel will skip any unused elements when it imports the data from your XML file.

You identify which element in a schema file to map to a cell using the XML Path language (XPath). Although the full XPath specification is long and involved, it boils down to a system of positively identifying the schema element to be mapped. In fact, XPath notation is very similar to the notation you use to identify the path of a Microsoft Windows file. For example, the path of a file might be C:\ExcelProg\MySuppliers.xml, which indicates that the MySuppliers.xml file is in the ExcelProg directory on the C drive. The difference between the XPath language and the Windows file path notation system is that you need to specify the location of an element with a schema. As an example, consider the schema displayed in Figure 26-4 on page 547. The root element is named *Root*, which has the subelement *Supplier*, which in turn has the subelement *SupplierID*. The XPath notation for the *SupplierID* subelement is as follows:

```
/Root/Supplier/SupplierID
```

The Excel object model contains an *XPath* object with the properties and methods that Excel needs to use XPath data in its operations. Table 26-4 lists the *XPath* object's properties and methods.

Table 26-4. The *XPath* Object's Properties and Methods

Name	Description
Property	
Map	A read-only property that returns the *XmlMap* object that represents the schema assigned to the *XPath* object.
Repeating	A read-only Boolean value that returns *True* if the *XPath* object is assigned to a list, or returns *False* if the object is assigned to a single cell.
Value	Returns a string that represents the *XPath* for the object.
Method	
Clear	Clears the schema mapping from the cell or cells mapped to the specified *XPath*.
SetValue(Map, XPath, SelectionNamespace, Repeating)	The *Map* argument (required) is an *XmlMap* variable representing the schema map into which you'll import your XML data; *XPath* (required) is a valid XPath statement; *SelectionNamespace* (an optional variant) specifies any namespace prefixes (you can leave this argument out if you put the full XPath in the *XPath* argument); *Repeating* (an optional Boolean) indicates whether the *XPath* object should be mapped to a single cell (*False*) or to a column in the list (*True*).

> For more (and very technical) information on the XML Path language, visit the official XPath Web site at *http://www.w3.org/TR/xpath*.

The *XPath* object's *SetValue* method is the most important method in the bunch—it lets you map a schema element directly to a cell or range. The following procedure defines the data file that contains the XML data, assigns the schema to be used in the *SetValue* method calls to the *myMap* object variable, and maps the elements to specific ranges. The result of the procedure is shown in Figure 26-7.

> **Warning**   This procedure will only run correctly if you have previously mapped the MySuppliers.xsd schema to the active workbook. You can do so by running the *ApplySchema* procedure from the "Mapping a Schema to a Worksheet Programmatically" section found earlier in this chapter or by mapping the schema to your workbook manually.

```
Sub AssignElementsToRanges()
    Dim myMap As XmlMap
    Dim strXPath As String
    Dim strSelNS As String
    Dim xMapName As String
    Dim xDataFile As String
```

```vba
On Error Resume Next

xDataFile = "C:\MySuppliers.xml"

Set myMap = ActiveWorkbook.XmlMaps("Root_Map")

strXPath = "/Root/Supplier/SupplierID"
Range("B2:B10").XPath.SetValue myMap, strXPath
Range("B2").Value = "Supplier ID"

strXPath = "/Root/Supplier/CompanyName"
Range("C2:C10").XPath.SetValue myMap, strXPath
Range("C2").Value = "Company Name"

strXPath = "/Root/Supplier/ContactName"
Range("D2:D10").XPath.SetValue myMap, strXPath
Range("D2").Value = "Contact Name"

strXPath = "/Root/Supplier/ContactTitle"
Range("E2:E10").XPath.SetValue myMap, strXPath
Range("E2").Value = "Contact Title"

strXPath = "/Root/Supplier/MailingAddress/Address"
Range("F2:F10").XPath.SetValue myMap, strXPath
Range("F2").Value = "Address"

strXPath = "/Root/Supplier/MailingAddress/City"
Range("G2:G10").XPath.SetValue myMap, strXPath
Range("G2").Value = "City"

strXPath = "/Root/Supplier/MailingAddress/Region"
Range("H2:H10").XPath.SetValue myMap, strXPath
Range("H2").Value = "Region"

strXPath = "/Root/Supplier/MailingAddress/PostalCode"
Range("I2:I10").XPath.SetValue myMap, strXPath
Range("I2").Value = "Postal Code"

strXPath = "/Root/Supplier/MailingAddress/Country"
Range("J2:J10").XPath.SetValue myMap, strXPath
Range("J2").Value = "Country"

strXPath = "/Root/Supplier/Phone"
Range("K2:K10").XPath.SetValue myMap, strXPath
Range("K2").Value = "Phone"

strXPath = "/Root/Supplier/Fax"
Range("L2:L10").XPath.SetValue myMap, strXPath
Range("L2").Value = "Fax"

ThisWorkbook.XmlMaps("Root_Map").Import xDataFile
If Err.Number = 0 Then
    MsgBox "Data from " & xDataFile & " was imported into " & _
        "the " & xMapName & " map."
Else
    MsgBox "There was a problem importing from " & xDataFile
    Exit Sub
End If

End Sub
```

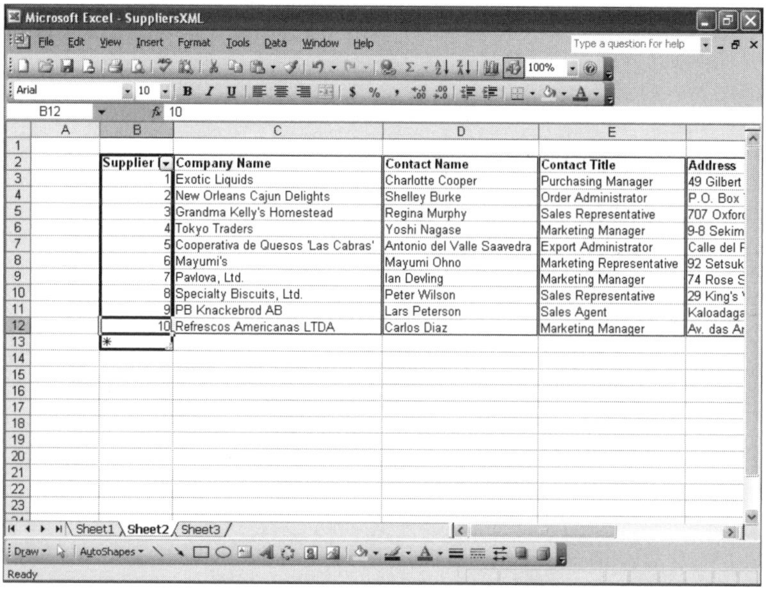

Figure 26-7. The *AssignElementsToRanges* procedure maps schema elements to cell ranges on your worksheet, creating lists.

The AssignElementsToRanges procedure creates a list for each element in the MySuppliers.xsd schema, but creating individual lists poses a problem: when you type a new data element into a list (for example, the SupplierID list) and press Tab, you're taken to a new row in the same list, not to what is logically the next cell in the list. You can tell that the procedure created a series of lists, not a single list, by the presence of blue lines on the borders of the columns. If you were to map the same schema to your worksheet by dragging the Supplier element from the XML Source task pane to cell B2, you would create a single list. The good news, however, is that if you filter a list by clicking the down arrow at the right edge of a column heading and selecting a filter criteria, you still filter all the lists. But how do you create a list that lets you tab from one column to another?

Inside Out

Mapping a Schema to a Single List

When you create a multi-column list, you create a seamless object into which you can type data. But creating a series of lists, as in this chapter's *AssignElementsToRanges* procedure, doesn't let you use the Tab key to move from one column to the next in the collection of lists. So how do you map a series of schema elements in such a way that you get full list functionality? By creating a list on your worksheet and mapping the schema elements to the list's column headers. The following procedure creates just such a list for the MySuppliers.xsd and MySuppliers.xml files, with the results shown in Figure 26-8.

Chapter 26

> **Caution** This procedure assumes the worksheet that you're manipulating is blank and that you haven't mapped the MySuppliers.xsd schema to the active workbook. In fact, it's best if you run this procedure on a new workbook.

```vba
Sub CreateOneList()

    Dim myMap, myMap2 As XmlMap
    Dim xSchemaFile, strXPath, strSelNS, xMapName, xDataFile As String

    Range("A2").Value = "SupplierID"
    Range("B2").Value = "CompanyName"
    Range("C2").Value = "ContactName"
    Range("D2").Value = "ContactTitle"
    Range("E2").Value = "Address"
    Range("F2").Value = "City"
    Range("G2").Value = "Region"
    Range("H2").Value = "Postal Code"
    Range("I2").Value = "Country"
    Range("J2").Value = "Phone"
    Range("K2").Value = "Fax"

    xSchemaFile = "C:\MySuppliers.xsd"
    Set myMap = ActiveWorkbook.XmlMaps.Add(xSchemaFile, "Root")

    ActiveSheet.ListObjects.Add(xlSrcRange, Range("A2:K2"), , xlYes).Name = _
        "List1"
     Range("A3").Select

    On Error Resume Next

    xDataFile = "C:\MySuppliers.xml"

    Set myMap2 = ActiveWorkbook.XmlMaps("Root_Map")

    strXPath = "/Root/Supplier/SupplierID"
    Range("B2").XPath.SetValue myMap, strXPath
    Range("B2").Value = "Supplier ID"

    strXPath = "/Root/Supplier/CompanyName"
    Range("C2").XPath.SetValue myMap, strXPath

    strXPath = "/Root/Supplier/ContactName"
    Range("D2").XPath.SetValue myMap, strXPath

    strXPath = "/Root/Supplier/ContactTitle"
    Range("E2").XPath.SetValue myMap, strXPath

    strXPath = "/Root/Supplier/MailingAddress/Address"
    Range("F2").XPath.SetValue myMap, strXPath

    strXPath = "/Root/Supplier/MailingAddress/City"
    Range("G2").XPath.SetValue myMap, strXPath
```

```
strXPath = "/Root/Supplier/MailingAddress/Region"
Range("H2").XPath.SetValue myMap, strXPath

strXPath = "/Root/Supplier/MailingAddress/PostalCode"
Range("I2").XPath.SetValue myMap, strXPath

strXPath = "/Root/Supplier/MailingAddress/Country"
Range("J2").XPath.SetValue myMap, strXPath

strXPath = "/Root/Supplier/Phone"
Range("K2").XPath.SetValue myMap, strXPath

strXPath = "/Root/Supplier/Fax"
Range("L2").XPath.SetValue myMap, strXPath

ActiveWorkbook.XmlMaps("Root_Map").Import URL:="C:\MySuppliers.xml"

End Sub
```

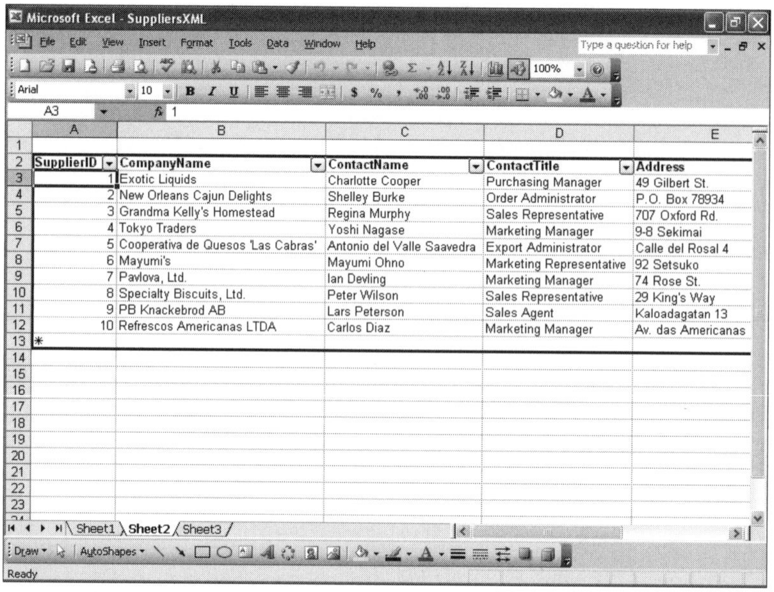

Figure 26-8. Assigning schema elements to column headers in an existing data list gives you full list functionality and a data map.

In this chapter, you've learned how to use the new XML capabilities in Excel 2003. Although the ability to save files as XML workbooks has been around since Excel Version 2002, you now have greater access to the XML object model and can import, export, and manipulate data within your workbooks programmatically. The tools at your disposal make it possible to transport data across a wide variety of platforms, making it easier for you to work with customers, suppliers, and colleagues regardless of the spreadsheet application they use.

Index

Symbols and Numerics

= (assignment operator), 64
<> (brackets) around markers, 203
^ (caret) key code for Ctrl, 127
: (colon) in line labels, 82
, (comma) as separator, 132
& (concatenation) operator, 198–200
... (ellipsis), displaying, 414
= (equals) comparison operator, 75
(error value), 124
! (exclamation point) as separator, 181
> (greater than) comparison operator, 75
>= (greater than or equal to) comparison operator, 75
< (less than) comparison operator, 75
<= (less than or equal to) comparison operator, 75
- (minus sign), 134
<> (not equal) operator, 75
<> (not equal to sign), 473
=NOW formula, 213
(number signs), 60
% (percent sign) key code for Alt, 127
. (period), referencing subelements of data types, 73
+ (plus sign) key code for Shift, 127
(pound signs), enclosing date in DateDiff, 216
[] (square brackets) in time formats, 217
~ (tilde) in SEARCH function, 203
_ (underscore), displaying on drop-down buttons, 414
* (wildcard character), 203, 474
# (wildcard character), 475
? (wildcard character), 203, 474
24 hours, times exceeding, 217
56 colors tracked in Excel color palette, 221
256 intensities for each primary color, 220

A

A1 notation, 180
A1 style of rotation, 179
Abort, Retry, Ignore buttons, displaying, 68
About menu item, adding, 382
Absolute constant, 180
absolute references, 30
   in SERIES formula, 333
   specifying for cells, 166
abstract data types, 26
Access, 467
   connecting to, 485
   connection strings, 511
   wildcard characters used with, 474–75
AccessActivateApp procedure, 460
AccessMode parameter, 136
actions
   informing users of, 67
   performed by objects, 119, 300
Activate event, 268, 270, 400
Activate method
   activating embedded charts, 327
   compared to Select method, 159
   of target worksheet, 27
   of Workbook object, 145
   of Workbooks collection, 137
ActivateCalculator procedure, 449
active cell, 110
   changing font color, 88
   checking contents, 88
   compared to selected, 161
   reference to, 109
active charts, 331
active code module, 87
Active Data Objects.
      See ADO (Active Data Objects)
Active property, 541
active range, finding, 161
active sheet, deleting, 152
active sheet tabs, 231
active Word documents, accessing, 460–61
active workbook, 19
   changing, 137
   switching to, 45
active worksheet, 27
   calculating, 120
   referencing ranges on, 166

ActiveCell property, 109
ActiveCell.Value property, 101
ActiveChart, 328
ActiveChart property, 111, 139
ActiveConnection property
   of Command object, 488, 514
   of Recordset object, 491, 492
ActivePrinter parameter, 148
ActiveSheet property, 112, 152
ActiveWindow property, 113–15
ActiveWorkbook object, 137
ActiveWorkbook property
   of Application object, 115
   compared to ThisWorkbook, 119
   referring to different workbook, 145
ActiveX controls, 535
adaptive menu system, 18
AdaptiveMenus property, 366, 367
Add Interactivity check box, 526
Add method, 177, 189
   of AddIns collection, 244
   of Charts collection, 359
   of Collection object, 314
   of CommandBarControls collection, 372
   of CommandBars collection, 366, 367
   of Controls collection, 377
   of ListObjects collection, 543–46
   of PivotCaches collection, 352, 357
   of PivotTables collection, 349
   of PropertyTests collection, 286
   of Sheets collection, 150–51
   of Validation object, 189
   of Workbooks collection, 129
   of XmlMaps collection, 556
Add Network Place Wizard window, 524
Add Procedure dialog box
   creating a Function procedure, 100
   displaying, 45, 87
   opening, 54
Add property for the Charts object, 322
Add Reference dialog box, 96, 259

Add Watch dialog box, 47
Add Watch item on the Debug
menu, 47
AddChartSheet macro, 322
AddCommandBar routine,
499–500
AddCommandCombo routine, 379
AddDataField method, 350, 358
AddDataLabels macro, 336
AddEmbeddedChart event
procedure, 330
AddEmbeddedChart macro, 324
Add-in Manager, 240
displaying, 254
installing add-ins, 241, 243
AddIn object, 245–46
AddIn project template, 252
add-in projects, naming, 253
add-in workbook, adding, 244
AddInDesigner, 252
AddinInstall event, 245
add-ins, 239
creating, 241
installed with Excel, 240
installing, 241, 243, 261
loading dynamically, 249
locating, 241
opening Excel 4, 131
reasons for using, 239
saving, 242
spanning multiple Office
applications, 259
specifying titles for, 242
stored in external files, 247
system resources and, 239
trapping events in, 365
types of, 239
unloading, 241
AddIns collection, 244, 246
AddinUninstall event, 245
AddItem method
of CommandBarComboBox
object, 378
of ListBox control, 413
Additional Controls dialog box, 48
Additional Controls item on the
Tools menu, 48
additive color system, 220
AddMenuItem routine, 382
AddNew method, 491, 493
Address parameter of
FollowHyperlink method, 146
AddStates routine, 430
AddToFavorites method, 145

AddToMru parameter of
ThisWorkbook.SaveAs method,
136
AddToMRU parameter of
Workbooks.Open method, 131
AddToSearchFolders method of
ScopeFolder object, 290
adjectives, characterizing
properties as, 300
AdjustColumnWidth property, 553
ADO (Active Data Objects), 470
Data Provider/Data Consumer
model, 481
database library, 498
database objects, 513
object model, 482–83
ADODB.Command object, 514
ADODB.Connection object, 513
ADODB.Recordset object, 514
After parameter
of Add method, 150
of Move and Copy methods, 153
AfterRefresh event, setting
separators, 529
alert boxes, turning off, 152
alerts, 116
AlertStyle property, 188
algorithm, 25
aliases, 477
Align item on the Format menu, 46
Align submenu, 46
Alignment dialog box, 393
Alignment tab of Format Cells
dialog box, 386
All Open Workbooks in Macro
dialog box, 31
AllowDeletingColumns parameter,
158
AllowDeletingRows parameter, 158
AllowFiltering parameter, 158
AllowFormattingCells parameter,
158
AllowFormattingColumns
parameter, 158
AllowFormattingRows parameter,
158
AllowInsertingColumns parameter,
158
AllowInsertingHyperlinks
parameter, 158
AllowInsertingRows parameter,
158
AllowMultiSelect property, 294
AllowSorting parameter, 158

AllowUsingPivotTables parameter,
158
ALT key
combining with key codes, 126
key codes for, 127
ALT+F8, 41
ALT+F11, 41
Always Show Full Menus option, 18
Always Trust Macros from this
Publisher check box, 40
Ambiguous name detected error,
95
American dollars, converting into
Swedish krona, 94
American English character set,
547
Analysis Services tool, 347
Analysis ToolPak add-in, 240
And operator, 199, 473
animation for command bars, 366
API (application programming
interface), 470, 481
AppActivate statement, 449
Append method, 489
AppendOnImport property, 553
Application event monitoring, 278
application event procedures, 278
Application events, 265, 276–80
application modal, marking a
message box as, 69
Application object, 107, 108, 456
accessing from other Office
applications, 462
commonly monitored events,
277
creating, 450
overriding settings used to
recognize numbers, 529
passing to the add-in
OnConnection method, 259
properties of, 108
referencing, 455
application programming interface
(API), 470, 481
Application property
of AddIn object, 245
of AddIns collection, 244
applications
activating, 449
adding scroll bars to, 411
closing external, 451
creating instances of, 459
decision-making ability of, 74–77
graphical interfaces to, 396
making changes to, 249

multiple, 465–66
sending key strokes to, 127
sharing data between, 445
starting from Excel, 445–48
window states of, 446
ApplyBorders procedure, 109
ApplySchema procedure, 556
Appointment object, 451
arglist element
  of Function procedure, 99
  of Sub procedure, 86
arguments, 102
  accepted by built-in dialog boxes, 388
  for dialog boxes, 390
  passing to existing dialog boxes, 393
  passing to procedures, 101
arithmetic average (mean) of a data set, 206
Arrange Buttons item on the Format menu, 46
arrays, 64
  boundaries, 64
  creating, 65, 66
  data points plotted with, 334
  decreasing the size, 66
  determining the size, 185
  dynamic, 66
  fixed, 66
  lower and upper boundaries, 185
  modifying charts to use data from, 333–35
  returned by the InputBox method, 123
  in Sheets collection, 153
  simulating for property routines, 307
  sizing to match ranges, 186
  variant variable required for loops, 79
ascending order, 476
Ask A Question box, 19
Assign Macro dialog box, 34, 171
AssignElementsToRanges procedure, 558–60
assignment (=) operator, 64
asterisk (*), retrieving all columns from a table, 472
asterisk (*) wildcard character, 203, 474
attributes, 299. See also properties
Auto Data Tips, 50
Auto Indent code formatting option, 50
Auto List Members check box, 50

Auto Quick Info, 50
auto routines, 246
Auto Syntax Check option, 50
Auto_Activate macro, 246
Auto_Add macro, 246
Auto_Close macro, 246
Auto_Deactivate macro, 246
AutoFilter controls, 9
AutoFit method, 173, 174
AutoFormats, 233
automatic refreshes, disabling, 353
Automation, 449, 456
automation add-ins, 239
  building, 250–56
  creating DLL files for, 254
  defining, 247
  designing, 250–56
  IDTExtensibility2 interface and, 248
  uses of, 247
Automation button, 254
automation servers
  displaying list of, 254
  writing Excel macros to control, 449
AutoNumber column, 470
Auto_Open macro, 31, 36, 246
Auto_Remove macro, 246
Auto_reserved names, 182
AutoSize property, 414
AutoTab property, 406
AVERAGE function, 206, 477
average sales, calculating, 173

B

BackColor property
  of text box, 439
  of user form control, 402
  of UserForm object, 398, 399
background
  setting, 430
  for UserForm object, 399
Background Compile option, 52
Background property of Font object, 232
Backspace key, 126
BackupXML procedure, 556
.bas (Basic) file, importing, 45
base object. See root object
base tables, 468
Basic file (.bas) file, 45
Before parameter
  of Add method, 150
  of Move and Copy methods, 153

BeforeClose event for a workbook, 269
BeforeClose event procedure, 272–73
BeforePrint event, 269, 271
BeforeRefresh event, 529
BeforeRightClick event, 274, 276
BeforeSave event, 269, 271
BeginGroup property, 373
binding, 449
BINOMDIST function, 4
bite-sized procedures, 104
black boxes, chart handles displayed as, 324
black VBA color constant, 219
BlackAndWhite property of PageSetup object, 154
blank cells
  allowing, 188
  checking for, 296
  counting, 206
blue VBA color constant, 219
BlueBorder procedure, 236
BOF property of Recordset object, 491, 492
Bold property of Font object, 232
BorderAround method, 237
borders, formatting, 236–37
Borders object, 236
Borders property, 236–37
BottomMargin property, 154
BottomRightCell property, 337
boundaries of arrays, 64
brackets <> around markers, 203
Break in Class Module option, 52
Break item on the Run menu, 48
Break key, 126
Break mode, placing code in, 48
Break on All Errors option, 52
Break on Unhandled Errors option, 52
breakpoints, 35
  clearing, 35, 47
  creating in code, 47
  inserting in macro code, 35
Browse button in Add-in Manager, 241
browsers
  displaying interactive components, 526
  interpreting names of colors, 226
  interpreting RGB color values, 226
BuildConnectionString function, 508

BuildConnectionString routine, 509–11
built-in command bars, 9
built-in constants
    not available with late binding, 454
    in VBA, 59
Built-in Dialog Box Argument Lists help topic, 384
built-in dialog boxes
    arguments accepted by, 388
    vs. constant, 400
    documentation for, 386
BuiltIn property
    of CommandBar object, 367, 368
    of CommandBarControl object, 373
BuiltInFace property, 376
business rules, 317–18
button controls, 375
button objects
    arranging on a user form, 46
    defining, 259
button options for message boxes, 68–69
buttons
    adding to toolbars, 260
    combining into a single command bar, 377
    removing from toolbars, 261
    specifying in a message box, 68
    visual state of, 376
    ways of displaying, 376
Byte data type, 58, 61
ByVal keyword, 103

C

C drive, searching through subdirectories in, 289
Calculate event, 275
Calculate method
    of Application object, 119, 156
    calling, 27
    of Worksheet object, 156
CalculateBeforeSave property, 157
CalculatedFields collection, 350, 354
CalculatedFields method, 350
CalculateFull method, 120
Calculate_Table macro, 170
Calculate_Table routine, 167–69
calculations, limiting, 120
Calculator application, starting, 446

Call keyword, running a Sub procedure, 94
call stack, 48, 266
Call Stack dialog box, 45
Cancel argument
    of BeforeSave event procedure, 271
    of Exit event, 403
Cancel button
    adding to a user form, 427
    adding to a wizard application, 435
    disabling, 424
CancelUpdate method, 491, 494
Caps Lock key, 126
Caption property
    of CheckBox control, 406
    of CommandBarButton object, 376
    of CommandBarControl object, 373
    of CommandButton control, 404
    of Frame control, 408
    of Label control, 404, 421
    of PivotField object, 354
    of PivotItem object, 356
    of TabStrip control, 416
    updating for a user form, 437
    of user form control, 402, 403
    of UserForm object, 398
    of Window object, 113
case sensitivity of FIND function, 203
Case statements, 89–90
Categories pane of Customize dialog box, 33
category area in a PivotChart, 346
CBool() conversion function, 61
CByte() conversion function, 61
CCur() conversion function, 61
CD. See Companion CD for this book
CDate() conversion function, 61
CDbl() conversion function, 61
CDec() conversion function, 61
cell edit mode, 249
Cell object, 107
Cell Protection dialog box, 388
CellBorder procedure, 109
cells, 14, 15, 161. See also active cell; blank cells; empty cells
    allowing users to format, 158
    allowing users to leave blank, 188
    changing comments, 275
    copying to an array first, 186

counting the number in a range, 206
default size for, 172
detecting empty, 176–77
determining if text, 193
determining if within a specific range, 125
displaying values in bold type, 161
formatting, 16, 233–35
limiting user selection of, 159
manipulating groups of, 172–77
mapping schema elements to, 557–62
measuring the dimensions of, 174
number of digits visible in, 175
protecting data, 103
range of, 521, 522
reading or writing to multiple, 185
recalculating, 119
recalculating formulas for, 120
referencing, 167–69, 172
researching the contents of, 8
resizing programmatically, 172
sections of, 233
selecting a range of, 162–64
selecting discontiguous groups of, 17
selecting for a formula, 16
specifying the character separating, 131
xlDialog boxes used to format, 391
Cells method, 172, 179, 422
Cells property, 172
Center in Form item on the Format menu, 46
CenterHorizontally property, 154
CenterVertically property, 154
Change event, 265
    of Application object, 266
    of CheckBox control, 406
    of MultiPage control, 437
    quirks associated with, 275
    of RowNumber control, 425
    of ScrollBar control, 411
    of SpinButton control, 407, 408
    of TextBox control, 405
    of user form control, 402, 403, 404
    for worksheet, 274, 275
    of Worksheet object, 266
ChangeChartType procedure, 338
ChangePattern procedure, 235

changing cells, maximum number,
15
character string, 214
characters, 197, 199, 200–202
Characters object, 326
Characters property, 233
Chart Area. *See* Plot Area object
Chart events, 265, 329
chart functionality, 526
chart handles, 323
Chart object, 321
   allowing access to all attributes,
     327
   creating, 358
   exposing events, 327
   properties of, 336
   triggers available for, 329
Chart Object Model, 321, 326
Chart property, 337
chart sheets, 13, 149, 322
   activating charts on, 328
   printing, 339
   programmatic reference to a
     chart on, 339
   at the same level as worksheets,
     326
chart title, defining as a formula,
325
Chart Titles object, 322
Chart Web Components, 534
Chart wizard, 322
ChartIsSelected function, 331
ChartObject object, 321, 327
   contained in a Worksheet object,
     326
   getting a reference to, 340
   naming, 323
   properties of, 337
ChartObjects collection, 321, 327,
338
charts, 321. *See also* embedded
   charts; PivotCharts
   activating, 327–29
   adding series to, 340
   building three-dimensional
     columns, 111
   changing the type of all, 338
   converting to use arrays, 334
   creating, 118, 322
   creating macros to modify
     existing, 327
   deactivating, 330
   defining the labels of, 335
   deleting series from, 340

   determining if activated, 331
   displaying information about,
     139
   distributing independently of the
     source data, 333
   formatting, 336–38
   hierarchy of, 326
   locations for, 322
   manipulating, 111, 327–39
   modifying all in a workbook, 338
   modifying data series of, 331
   modifying formats in, 328
   modifying to use date from
     arrays, 333–35
   printing, 339
   programming, 339
   renaming existing, 323
   saving to a Web page, 522
   selecting to save in a Web page,
     521
   types of, 321
   xlDialog boxes used to modify,
     391
Charts collection, 326
ChartTitle object, 337
ChartTitle property, 325
ChartType property, 325, 336
CheckBox control, 406
CHIINV function, 4
child controls, 408
child objects, 456
Chrt object variable, 324
CInt() conversion function, 62
class (.cls) file, 45
class modules, 42, 299, 300
   creating, 305
   inserting into current projects,
     45
Class Modules folder, 42
classes, 299
   adding business rules, 317–18
   building, 305–11, 312–18
   calling external code, 304
   changing the name of, 305
   creating simple, 312
   defining events for, 310
   designing, 312–18
   determining if new instances
     created, 302
   extending, 313
   marking as Public or Private, 303
   modifying, 304
   special events for, 311
   testing independently, 304

Class_Initialize event, 311
class-level variables
   defining, 305
   differentiating from local
     variables or parameters, 311
   initializing, 311
   marking as Public, 304
   prefixing with Me, 311
Class_Terminate event, 311
CLEAN function, 195
Clear All Breakpoints item on the
   Debug menu, 47
Clear Formats command, 275
Clear key, 126
Clear method
   of Collection object, 315
   of CommandBarComboBox
     object, 378
   of Errors collection, 486
   of FileDialogFilters collection,
     293
   of ListBox control, 413
   of XPath object, 558
ClearContents method, 515
ClearData routine, 423
Click event
   of CheckBox control, 406
   of ListBox control, 413
   of user form control, 402, 404
client. *See* database client
client/server concept, 470
Clip Art task pane, 20
Clipboard task pane, 20
CLng function, 62, 423
Close button, 19
Close method
   of Connection object, 484
   of Recordset object, 491
   of ThisWorkbook, 138
Close window button, 53
.cls (class) file, importing, 45
CLSID property, 245
cmdShowProductImage_Click
   procedure, 293
code
   adding to a project, 53
   associated with properties, 304
   branching to another section of,
     82
   compiling for the currently
     selected project, 47
   digitally signing, 48
   executing remaining, 47
   isolating inside a class, 304

code, *continued*
jumping to the next line of, 47
making readable, 54
placing in Break mode, 48
running up to the cursor, 47
setting the next line of, 47
stepping through one line at a
time, 47
code formatting options, 50
Code item on the View menu, 44
code modules
adding a procedure to, 86
creating a Function procedure in,
100
declarations section of, 92
naming, 95
Code Settings options, 50
Code window
displaying for the currently
selected item, 44
in Visual Basic Editor, 43
code windows. *See also* **windows**
customizing, 51
handling, 53
managing, 53–55
minimizing or resizing, 53
navigating, 53
switching among open, 53
**Collapse Proj. Hides Windows
option, 52**
Collate parameter, 148
Collection class, 313–16
Collection object, 315
Collection object variable, 313
collections, 28, 108
finding the number of objects in,
28
of objects, 79
removing items from, 315
returning a single item from, 315
colon (:) in a line label, 82
**Color argument of BorderAround
method, 237**
Color Model list box, 224
color palette. *See* **Excel color
palette**
Color property
of Borders object, 236
compared to PatternColor, 235
of Font object, 232
of Interior object, 234
of Worksheet object, 230
color systems, 220
**Color tab in Options dialog box,
224, 226**

color wheel, 220
**ColorIndex argument of
BorderAround method, 237**
ColorIndex property
of Borders object, 236
compared to PatternColorIndex,
235
of Font object, 232
of Interior object, 234
of Worksheet object, 230
colors
creating on a computer, 220
displaying, 223
in graphics, 225
represented by VBA constants,
88
in worksheets, 219–31
Colors property
of Workbook object, 223
of Workbooks collection, 225
column fields for a PivotTable, 358
column format for a text file, 133
column names
listing, 478
resolving, 477
Column property, 413
ColumnCount property, 412
ColumnFields property, 350, 354
ColumnGrand property, 350
ColumnHeads property, 412
columns
allowing users to delete, 158
allowing users to format, 158
allowing users to insert into, 158
changing in tables, 479
in a database table, 468
maximum number of, 14
maximum width of, 14
referencing, 172
retrieving, 472
Columns property of Select, 172
**ColumnWidths property of ListBox
control, 412**
COM add-ins, 239
building, 256
creating, 248–50
IDTExtensibility2 interface and,
248
providing entries in Windows
registry, 250
typical uses of, 247
COM Add-Ins button, 248
COM Add-ins dialog box, 247
**COM tab in Add Reference dialog
box, 259**

combo box controls, 378–79, 430
combo boxes, 379
ComboBox control, 414, 505
comma (,), as a separator, 132
Comma parameter, 133
comma-delimited data, 132
command bar button, 433
**command bar controls, 371,
372–73**
command bars
adding floating, 370
deleting, 371
displaying, 371
in Excel window, 19
positioning, 368
types of, 368
command button controls, 435
command buttons, triggering, 404
Command object
in ADO object model, 482,
487–90
in RunQuery routine, 513
**CommandBar objects, 367–68,
369**
CommandBar property, 380
**CommandBarButton object,
375–76**
**CommandBarComboBox object,
378–79**
**CommandBarControl objects,
373–75**
**CommandBarControls collection,
371–73**
CommandBarPopup object, 380
CommandBars collection, 366–67
**CommandButton controls, 401,
404, 421, 425–27**
CommandButton2_Click event, 425
CommandButton7_Click event, 428
**CommandLineSafe registry entry,
250**
**Commands tab in Customize dialog
box, 32, 33, 146**
CommandText property
of Command object, 488
of PivotCache object, 352
CommandType property
of Command object, 488, 514
of PivotCache object, 352
comments in VBA code, 328
**communication across the Internet,
536**
Companion CD for this book
Excel Query program, 498
FormApp.xls, 419

MySuppliers.xml file, 549
MySuppliers.xsd, 550
WizardApp.xls, 432
comparison operators in the Where clause, 473
comparisonoperator argument in a Select Case statement, 76
Compile item on Debug menu, 47
Compile on Demand option, 52
complex element, 552
complex Root element, 548
complexType statement in an XML schema, 11
concatenation (&) operator, 198–200
condition statements, 74
conditional criteria, validating, 198
conditional formats
creating, 89, 232
pitfalls of, 89–90
Conditional Sum Wizard add-in, 240
CONFIDENCE function, 4
Conflict dialog box, 543
conflict-resolution dialog box, 136
connection information, configuring, 516
Connection object
in ADO object model, 482, 483–86
in RunQuery routine, 513
Connection property of PivotCache object, 352
connection string, building, 509–11
ConnectionString property, 484, 485, 513
Consecutive Delimiter parameter, 133
Consolidate_Area reserved name, 182
constants, 57
defining, 59
scope and lifetime of, 62
specifying, 59
Contacts folder, 454
containers, 53, 104, 408
Contents parameter of Protect method, 158
context-sensitive help
for an input box, 72
for a message box, 68
Continue command, 48
control characters, 195
control objects, types of
CommandBar, 371

controls. See also user form controls
adding to a command bar, 371
finding hidden, 436
Controls property
of CommandBar object, 367
of CommandBarPopup object, 380
ControlTipText property, 402
conversion functions for data types, 61
converters, 131
ConvertFormula function, 123
ConvertFormula method, 179, 180
ConvertSeriesValuesToArrays procedure, 334
cookies, text of, 205
Copies parameter of PrintOut method, 148
Copy Colors From down arrow, 226
Copy method
of CommandBarControl object, 373, 375
of Sheets collection, 153
CopyFace method, 376
CopyFromExcelToNewWord-Document procedure, 461
CopyFromExcelToOpenWord-Document procedure, 460
CopyFromExcelToWord procedure, 457
CopyRows routine, 514
CopyWordToExcel procedure, 458
Corner argument, 389
corners, rounded vs. right-angled, 337
corporate profiles, 8
CorruptLoad parameter, 131
COUNT function, 206, 477
Count method, 315
Count parameter, 151
Count property
of AddIns collection, 244
of a collection, 316
of CommandBarControls collection, 372
of CommandBars collection, 366
of Dialogs collection, 384
of Errors collection, 486
of Fields collection, 494
of Parameters collection, 489
of PivotCaches collection, 352
of PivotTables collection, 349
of Sheets collection, 149
of Worksheets collection, 149

COUNTA function, 206
COUNTBLANK function, 206
counter variable in a For...Next loop, 77
COUNTIF function, 206
Create List dialog box, 9, 540
CreateBackup parameter, 136
CreateExcelChart procedure, 463
CreateItem method, 451
CreateNames sample macro, 178
CreateNewWordDoc procedure, 462
CreateObject function, 450, 451, 456, 459
CreateOneList procedure, 560–62
CreateParameter method, 488
CreatePivotTable method, 353, 358
CreateWordDocumentFromExcel procedure, 456
Creator property
of AddIn object, 245
of AddIns collection, 244
CRITBINOM function, 4
criterion operators for validation, 188
critical icon in a message box, 70
cross tabulation report, 341
CSng() conversion function, 62
CSV text file, 296
CTRL key
aiding in selection process, 413
combining with key codes, 126
key codes for, 127
CTRL+F4, 53
CTRL+F6, 53
CTRL+F8, 35
CTRL+F9, 35
CTRL+SHIFT+F8, 35
CTRL+SHIFT+F9, 35
cube, envisioning for a report, 342
Currency data type, 58, 61, 102
currency quotes on the Web, 94
current date, returning, 214
current record pointer, 492
current time, returning, 214
CurrentPage property, 354
CurrentRegion property, 162
cursor, returning to the last line of code edited, 45
CursorLocation property, 484
custom add-ins, 365
custom colors, substituting, 224
custom data formats, 217
custom data types, 72

custom dialog boxes vs. built-in, 400
custom macro toolbar, 32
Custom Menu Item command, 33
custom menus
  creating for macros, 33
  opening and closing, 272
Custom number formats, 195
Custom tab in Options dialog box, 224
CustomColors procedure, 225
Customize dialog box
  Categories pane, 33
  Commands tab, 32, 33
  displaying, 49
  Toolbars tab page, 32
CVar() conversion function, 62
cyan VBA color constant, 219
CycleGridlines procedure, 230

D

DAO (Data Access Objects), 481
data
  in a collection class, 316
  copying, 185–87, 422–24, 427–28
  displaying graphically, 321
  managing large volumes, 347
  manipulating, 193–217
  from multiple perspectives, 341
  validating, 429–30
data area
  in PivotChart, 346
  in PivotTable, 358
Data Consumer, 481
data entry, 187–89
data fields
  adding to PivotTables, 350
  defining for PivotTables, 358
data files
  creating XML, 549–50
  importing into an XML schema, 552
data form, 540
data labels. See labels
data lists, 539–41
  creating, 540
  creating programmatically, 541–46
data map, 550, 551
Data Provider/Data Consumer model, 481
data providers for Access, 485

data series, modifying a chart's, 331
Data Series object, 322
Data Source keyword, 485
data sources
  for Excel VBA, 481
  for a ListObject object, 542
  using the Internet as, 527–32
data types
  associated with parameters, 490
  available for validation, 188
  conversion functions for, 61
  creating custom, 72
  defining, 58–59
  for elements, 548
  in relational databases, 468
  returned by a Function procedure, 99
data validation code, 82
database client, 470
database info, saving, 504
database keys, 469. See also keys
database management systems, connecting to, 485–86
Database Properties dialog box, 501
Database Properties window, 516
database providers, changing, 503
database queries. See queries
database server, 470
database tables. See tables
databases
  accessing from Excel, 470
  comparing to spreadsheets, 467–70
  connecting to, 501–5
  designing and administering, 469
  fundamental concepts, 467–69
  manipulating with SQL, 471
  retrieving rows from, 513
  using with Excel, 467
databases administrator, 469
DataBodyRange property, 541
DataFields property, 350, 354
Data_Form reserved name, 182
DataRange property
  of PivotField object, 354
  of PivotItem object, 356
DataType parameter, 133
DataType property, 354
date and time functions, 213–16

Date arguments of DateDiff function, 216
Date data type, 60
Date format, default, 214
Date function, 214
date serial numbers, 213
Date variables, 60
DateAdd function, 214, 215
DateDiff function, 215
dates
  difference between two, 215
  handling, 60
  manipulating, 213–17
  prior to January 1, 1900, 213
DateSerial function, 214, 215
Date/Time data type, 61
DateValue function, 214
Day function, 214
days, number between events, 213
DB2 databases, 486
DBInfo user form, 498
  initializing, 502–3
  opening, 500
DblClick event, 402, 404
DBPath value, 510–11
DBQuery user form, 498
  loading, 505
  opening, 500
DBType variable, 510
DBWindowsAuth value, 511
Deactivate event
  with user form, 400
  for workbook, 269, 271
Debug menu, 46–47
debugging, 34
  converting to, 61
  the execution of procedures, 46
  with hidden application objects, 458
  macros, 34–36
Decimal data type, 58
DecimalSeparator parameter, 134
DecimalSeparator property, 529
decisions, made by applications, 74–77
declarations, avoiding errors through, 50
declarations section
  declaring module variables in, 63
  displaying for a code module, 92
  entering using the keyboard, 93
default buttons in a message box, 69
default Date format, 214

default docked location, 49
Default to Full Module View, 51
Default Web Site Properties dialog box, 533
Define Name dialog, 182
Define Names dialog box, 17
Definition item on the View menu, 44
Delay property of SpinButton control, 407
Delete key, 127
Delete method
    of a button, 261
    of Charts collection, 152
    of CommandBar object, 367
    of CommandBarControl object, 374, 375
    deleting a command bar, 371
    invoking, 152
    of ListObject object, 542
    of Parameters collection, 489
    of Recordset object, 491, 494
    removing the entire command bar, 501
    of Series object, 340
    of Sheets collection, 152–53
    of Validation object, 189
    of Worksheets collection, 152
    of XmlMap object, 554
Delete statement, 471, 479
DeleteCommandBar routine, 500
DeleteMenu procedure, 273
Delimiter parameter, 131
delimiters
    for cells, 132
    defining non-standard, 134
    other than commas, 132
    treating consecutive, 133
Desc (descending) keyword, 476
Description property
    of Err object, 83
    of Error object, 487
Description subkey for COM add-in, 250
descriptive names, 55
Deselect method, 330
Design mode, toggling, 48
Design Mode item on Run menu, 48
DetermineAllInterest procedure, 210
DetermineInterest procedure, 209
dialog boxes
    customizing, 383–94

displaying existing, 384–88
documentation for, 386
formatting cells, 391
inserting or modifying charts, 391
modifying default settings in, 393
modifying existing, 388–94
passing arguments to existing, 393
setting default choices within, 388
Dialog object, 384
dialog sheets, 13
dialog types, 293
Dialogs collection, 384, 385, 389–93
Dialogs property, 393
dictionaries, 20
dictionary words, avoiding for passwords, 144
digital certificates, 38, 39
digital signatures, 37, 39
Digital Signatures dialog box, 48
digits, number visible in a cell, 175
Dim New statement, 301
Dim (dimension) statement
    declaring objects, 302
    declaring strings, 60
    declaring variables, 58
Dir function, 282
Direction property of Parameter object, 490
directory organization for a computer, 287
dirty user forms, 427
Disable Macros, 37
DisableCustomize property, 366
DisableSave routine
    in GetData routine, 424
    in PutData routine, 428
DisableSave subroutine, 427
DiscountedPrice function, 255
DiscountPrice function, 250
DisplayAlerts property, 116, 152
DisplayDrawingObjects method, 139
DisplayErrorString property, 350
DisplayNullString property, 350
DisplayOutlookContactNamesEarly Binding procedure, 453
DisplayPalette procedure, 223, 225
DisplayRightToLeft property, 541
#DIV/0! error value, 124

divide by zero error, 50
DLL components, 248
DLL file, creating, 254
Do Until...Loop, 79–80
Do While...Loop, 79–80
dockable windows, specifying, 52
docked location for windows, 49
Document object, 457
Document Recovery task pane, 20
Document Updates task pane, 20
document workspaces, 6
documents, Word, 457–62
Do...Loop Until loop, 80–81
Do...Loop While loop, 80–81
DOS window, starting Windows-based applications from, 446
dot notation
    calling methods, 27
    placing the name of a module, 94
    referring to properties in VBA, 26
    with Select statement, 477
dots in a pixel, 220
Double data type, 59, 61
double quotation marks, 60, 473
Down Arrow key, 127
Drag-and-Drop-Text option, 51
DragToColumn property, 355
DragToData property, 355
DragToHide property, 355
DragToPage property, 355
DragToRow property, 355
drawing objects, 139
DrawingObjects parameter, 157
DropButtonStyle property, 414
drop-down button, hiding, 414
drop-down lists, 379
DropDownLines property, 378
DSTDEV function, 4
DSTDEVP function, 4
duplicate colors in color palettes, 225
DVAR function, 4
DVARP function, 4
dynamic arrays, 66

E

early binding, 450, 452–54, 465
Edit Query button
    in Excel Query program, 516
    on Excel2k3 VBA Query command bar, 505
Edit Watch dialog box, 47

Edit Watch item on Debug menu, 47
Editable parameter of Open method, 131
EditDatabaseQuery routine, 500
EditMode property, 491, 493
Editor Format tab page, 51
Editor tab in Options dialog box, 50
element definition statements, 11
elements
  mapping to a worksheet, 551
  simple, 548
eLibrary, 8
ellipsis (...), displaying, 414
Elself, 74
e-mail messages, sending, 447
embedded charts, 322
  activating, 327
  creating, 324
  creating a programmatic reference to, 339
  determining if activated, 331
  excluding from a print job, 339
  moving or resizing, 340
  naming the ChartObject object, 323
  previewing all, 339
  printing, 339
  writing event procedures for, 329
empty cells
  detecting, 176–77
  referring to, 194
empty string, 60
  compared to a Null value, 468
  setting a parameter to, 126
Enable Macros, 37
EnableChanges parameter, 148
Enabled property, 403
  for buttons, 427
  of CommandBar object, 367, 368
  of CommandBarControl object, 374
  of a user form control, 402, 403
  of UserForm object, 398
EnableEvents property, 266
EnableSave subroutine for command buttons, 427
EnableSelection property, 159
encapsulation within objects, 26
encryption algorithm, 144
END key, 127, 163
End method, 163, 164
Enter event of a user form control, 402, 403

ENTER key, 17, 127
EnterDatabaseQuery routine, 507
EntireColumn method, 164
EntireRow method, 164
EOF property, 491, 492
equals (=) comparison operator, 75
equals sign (=), 64, 473
Err object, 486
  detecting errors, 314, 487
  properties of, 83
error 1004 run-time error message, 135
error conditions, informing users of, 67
error handling, 82–84
Error object, 482, 487
error trapping, 82
  disabling, 380
  General tab page options for, 52
  when turning off screen updates, 118
error values
  cell, 124
  referring to, 194
  returned by InputBox method, 123
ErrorHandler label, branching to, 83
ErrorMessage property, 188
errors, avoiding through declarations, 50
Errors collection, 486
Errors property, 484
ErrorString property, 350
ErrorTitle property, 188
ESC key, 69
Euro Currency Tools add-in, 240
EUROCONVERT function, 240
event handlers, 27
event procedures
  displaying, 267, 273
  executing, 327
  level of occurrence, 266
  navigating in a worksheet, 274
  writing, 276, 329
Event statement, 310
event triggers, 266
event-driven language, VBA as, 73
events, 27, 265, 300, 304, 329
  categories of, 265
  in charts, 329
  defining, 310, 429
  enabling and disabling, 266–67
  monitoring, 278
  number of days between, 213
  primary reason to disable, 267

trapping, 399
  of user form controls, 402–4
  for the Worksheet object, 273
Excel
  add-ins, 239, 240, 241–43
  automating from a Workbook object, 457
  blocking from behaving normally, 125
  color display limitation of, 221
  controlling from other Office applications, 462–65
  extending, 239
  improvements in, 3
  interface, 18–21, 304
  Internet solutions with, 537
  mapping data to XML schemas, 10
  monitoring events, 278
  other Office applications and, 445–66
  starting another application from, 445–48
  treating dates and times as numbers, 213
  window, 18
  working with older files, 13
Excel 4.0, macro sheets, 13, 149
Excel 5.0, dialog sheets, 13
Excel Chart Wizard, 322
Excel color palette
  56 colors tracked in, 221
  assigning a color to a gridline from, 230
  assigning colors to worksheet elements, 223
  assigning new colors to slots in, 224
  changing back to the default, 226
  compared to the main program palette, 223
  copying from another workbook, 225
  displaying the colors in, 223
  displaying the default colors of, 230
  duplicate colors in the standard, 225
  matching colors to the Web, 229
  RGB values assigned to entries in, 221–23
  standard HTML colors, 229
  on the Web, 226–29
Excel lists. See lists, creating

Excel Object Library, 384, 462
Excel object model, 107, 108
Excel objects. *See* objects
Excel Query program, 497
    building a connection string,
        509–11
    changing database providers,
        503
    configuring connection
        information, 516
    connecting to a database,
        501–5
    copying rows, 514–15
    editing queries, 505–8
    ending, 500
    entering a query, 516
    getting the query, 512
    initializing, 499–500
    initializing the DBInfo user form,
        502–3
    retrieving a list of customers,
        515–17
    running a query, 512–14, 517
    saving database information,
        504
    selecting Windows
        authentication, 504
    setting up, 498
Excel template, 131
Excel TypeLib, referencing, 259
Excel VBA. *See* VBA (Visual Basic for
    Applications)
Excel worksheets. *See* worksheets
Excel2k3 VBA Query command bar,
    497, 499
exchange rates
    in a financial model, 527
    retrieving using a Web Query,
        529
exclamation icon in a message box,
    70
exclamation point (!) as a separator,
    181
exclusive mode for a file, 136
EXE components, compared to DLL,
    248
Execute As Recordset method, 488
Execute method
    of CommandBarControl object,
        374, 375
    with File Open and Save As
        dialog, 293
    of FileSearch object, 282
Exit Do statement, 80

Exit event
    of TextBox control, 405
    of a user form control, 402, 403
    using to validate data, 429
Exit For statement
    in For Each...Next loop, 79
    in For...Next loop, 77
expired certificates, signing macros
    with, 39
Export File dialog box, saving
    deleted code in a text file, 56
Export method, 554
ExportSelectedRange procedure,
    296
ExportXml method, 554
Expression parameter
    of FollowHyperlink method, 146
    of PrintOut method, 148
    of Protect method, 157
expressionlist argument in a Select
    Case statement, 76
expressions, 47
extended XML capabilities, 8
Extensibility Projects, 257
Extensible Markup Language. *See*
    XML
extensions to SQL, 471
external add-ins, 247
external data sources, 141
external files
    locating, 281–82
    reading from, 296
    writing to, 295–96
Extract reserved name, 182

F

F-test, 4
F1 through F15 keys, 127
F5 macro keyboard shortcut, 35
F8 key, 34
F8 macro keyboard shortcut, 35
F9 key, 119
F9 macro keyboard shortcut, 35
FaceId property, 376
FACT function, 97
factorial of a number, 97
facts, 342, 343
Favorites list, 145
Favorites toolbar button, 146
Field object, 482, 494–95
FieldInfo parameter, 133
fields
    changing within PivotTables, 359
    placing on user forms, 420
Fields collection, 493, 494

Fields property, 491
file extensions, 283
file format constants, 136
File item on Insert menu, 45
File Open dialog box, 45, 384
file picker dialog, 293
File Search feature, 282
file searches, limiting, 285
file settings, managing, 140–41
File Transfer Protocol site, 520
file types, specifying for a search,
    286
FileDialog dialog box, 291–94
FileDialog object, 281, 298
    determining if a file exists, 294
    displaying the Open and Save As
        dialog boxes, 291
    enhanced with Office 2003, 282
FileDialog property, 292
FileDialogFilters collection, 293
FileDialogFilters file, 281
FileDialogSelectedItems collection,
    293, 294
FileDialogSelectedItems file, 281
FileExists function, 291
FileExists property, 294
FileExists2 function, 294
FileFormat parameter, 136
FileName parameter
    of Open method, 130
    of OpenText method, 133
    of SaveAs method, 136
FileName property, 282, 284
FileOpen dialog box, 388
files
    adding the list of most recently
        used, 136
    determining the existence of,
        291, 294
    finding, 291–94
    locating, 120, 281–82
    maintaining, 282
    manipulating, 281
    navigating through large, 276
    opening existing in Word, 458
    reading from external, 296
    retrieving data from, 282
    returning all, 282–85
    returning the name of selected,
        387
    searching for a value, 298
    searching for all modified, 285
    testing for open, 279
    text format, 131
    writing to external, 295–96

files folder for a Web page, 522
Files tab in Web Options dialog box, 522
FileSaveAs dialog box, 388
FileSearch object, 281, 298
FileSearch property, 282, 291
FileSystemObject object, 294
FileType property, 283, 286
FileTypes file, 281
fill color of a cell, 233, 234
fill patterns, 234, 235
Filter property, 491, 493
FilterFile procedure, 298
filters, setting, 158
Filters property, 293
financial calculations, 208–12
FIND function, 203–5
Find Printer button, 147
FindControl method
  of CommandBar object, 367, 368
  of CommandBarControl object, 375
  of CommandBars collection, 366
  getting an object pointer, 506
FindEmptyCells procedure, 176
FindFile method, 120
FindLastMonthFiles procedure, 285
FindLastRow function, 426
FindWordandExcelFiles procedure, 286
Finish button, 441
FINV function, 4
First button, 425
firstdayofweek argument, 216
FirstPageNumber property, 154
firstweekofyear argument, 216
FitToPagesTall property, 154
FitToPagesWide property, 154
fixed arrays, 66
fixed-length strings, 60
flattened reports, 342
floating command bar, 370
folder picker dialog, 293
folders within projects, 42
FollowHyperlink method, 146–47, 536
font color, changing, 88
Font object, 231
Font property, 233, 402
font style for displaying code, 51
fonts, formatting, 231–33
Fonts dialog box, 390
FontStyle property, 232
FooterMargin property, 154

For Each...Next loops, 28, 78
  deleting all but one sheet, 152
  exiting prematurely, 79
  moving through the Workbooks collection, 129
  saving every open workbook, 137
FORECAST function, 4
ForeColor property, 402
foreign keys, 470
Form Editor, 43
Form Grid Settings option, 51
FormApp.xls, 419
Format Cells dialog box, 16
  custom data formats in, 217
  custom number formats available in, 195
  displaying with tabs, 386
Format menu, 46
Format method, 350
Format parameter, 131
FormatChart procedure, 338
FormatDateTime function, 424
FormatNumber routine, 424
formatting
  cells, 233–38
  charts, 338
  worksheet elements, 230–31
Formatting toolbar, 16
forms. See user forms
Forms folder, 42
Formula Auditing toolbar, 16
formula bar, 19
Formula properties of Validation object, 188
Formula property, 356
FormulaLocal property, 123, 124
formulas, 21
  defining chart titles as, 325
  displaying in cells, 15
  recalculating in worksheets, 156
  returning as text strings, 123
  storing names of ranges as, 181
For...Next loops, 28, 77–78
  adding around periodic interest calculations, 210
  exiting prematurely, 77
  iterating through each item in collections, 316
  nesting inside one another, 78
  syntax of, 77
FoundFiles collection, 281, 285
FoundFiles file, 281
FoundFiles property, 282
four-digit year, including, 60

Frame control, 408
  deleting, 409
  placing a group of option buttons in, 409
  surrounding a collection of label and text box controls, 439
  surrounding OptionButton controls, 438
frames, 408, 528
From clause, 476
From parameter of PrintOut method, 148
FTP site, 520
full name of a workbook, 140
FullName property, 245
Function procedures
  calling, 101
  compared to Sub procedures, 85
  creating, 100
  defining, 98–104
  elements of, 99
  in formulas, 101
  running, 101
  syntax of, 99
functions
  built into VBA, 196
  converting values, 61
  defaulting to Public, 310
  finding all or part of a date or time, 214
  IS family of, 194
  listing all available, 22
  marking as Public, 304
  public, 309
  with the Select statement, 477
  statistical, 3–5
  for summary calculations, 206
  values returned by, 98
fv (future value) argument
  of PMT function, 208
  of PV function, 212
  of RATE function, 211

G

GAMMAINV function, 4
garbage in, garbage out, 176
General object, 43
General tab page, 51
GenerateOptions routine, 440
Get property routine, 306
Get routine, 304
GetData routine, 422–24
GetDBQuery function, 512
GetDBQuery routine, 508

GetObject function, 450, 459
GetOpenFileName method, 282, 291, 387
GetRegistryValue helper function, 510–11
GetSaveAsFileName method, 282, 291, 387
GetSetting function, 503, 511
Getting Started task pane, 20
Go To dialog box, 385, 389
Got To Special dialog box, 386
GoTo statement, 82
grand totals in PivotTable report, 350
graphical interface, designing, 396
graphical representation of a PivotTable, 346
graphics, colors in, 225
greater than (>) comparison operator, 75
greater than or equal to (>=) comparison operator, 75
greater than or equal to sign (>=), 473
greater than sign (>), 473
greedy searches, 165
green VBA color constant, 219
grid dots, 51
GridlineColor property, 230
GridlineColorIndex property, 230
gridlines, 230
Group item on the Format menu, 46
groups of cells, manipulating, 172–77
GROWTH function, 4
GSCProductChart embedded chart, 324
Guess argument of RATE function, 211

H

HasDataLabels property, 336
HasDataTable property, 336
HasLegend property, 336
HasTitle property, 337
HeaderMargin property, 154
HeaderRowRange property, 541
height of a cell, 174
Height property
  of ChartObject object, 337
  of CommandBar object, 367
  of CommandBarControl object, 374

of Row object, 172
of a user form, 398
of a user form control, 402
of UserForm object, 398, 399
Help button, adding to a message box, 69
help context ID number, 374
Help context number, 68, 72
Help key, 127
Help task pane, 20
hidden application objects, 458
hidden argument of Cell Protection dialog box, 388
hidden controls, finding, 436
HiddenFields property of PivotTable object, 350, 354
Hide method, 399
hierarchical information, displaying, 380
High macro security level, 39, 40
historical events, number of days between, 213
Home Directory tab, 533
Home key, 127
horizontal pages, setting, 154
Horizontal Spacing item on the Format menu, 46
hot keys, 125, 126
Hour function, 214
.htm filename extension, 522
HTML, 520
  coding a table, 520
  colors, 226–29
  compared to XML, 8
HTTP request, 537
Hungarian notation, 55
hyperlinks, 146, 158
Hypertext Markup Language. See HTML
HyperText Markup text file, 522
HYPGEOMDIST function, 4

I

icons in message boxes, 68, 70
Id property, 374
identity column, 470, 478
IDTExtensibility2 interface, 248–49, 250, 259
If...Then statements, 90
If...Then...Else statements, 74–75
  determining which code will execute, 270
  inside a Select Case statement, 77

for validation, 198
IgnoreBlank property, 188
IgnoreReadOnly Recommended parameter, 130
IIS (Internet Information Server), 533
Image control, 410
Immediate window, 45, 140
Implements keyword, 260
Import External Data feature, 530
Import method, 555
Import XML dialog box, 552
imported data, storing, 150
ImportRange procedure, 297
ImportXml method, 555
inactive sheet tabs, 231
inactive worksheet, referencing, 167
InCellDropdown property, 188
InchesToPoints method, 155
index number of an array element, 64, 66
Index property
  of CommandBar object, 367
  of CommandBarControl object, 20
  of PivotCache object, 353
indexes on database tables, 470
infinite loop, preventing, 267
information, entering, 419–31
information box, displaying, 188
information icon in a message box, 70
Information Rights Management (IRM) capabilities, 7
Initial Catalog keyword, 485
Initial Load Behavior drop-down box, 253
Initialize event, 311
InitializeChart procedure, 329
in-process components, 248
input boxes, 71–72
InputBox function, 71, 121
InputBox method, 121–23
InputMessage property, 188
input/output parameter to a stored procedure, 490
Input/Output statements, 295
InputTitle property, 188
Ins key, 127
Insert button, 53
Insert Function dialog box, 21
Insert key, 127

Insert menu, 45
Insert Procedure dialog box, 100
insert row, 9, 541
Insert statement, 471, 478
InsertRowRange property, 541
installation program, building, 261
Installed property of AddIn object, 245
instantiating an object, 301
INSTR function, 204
integer, month corresponding to, 214
Integer data type, 59, 62
Integrated Security keyword, 486
IntelliSense, 50, 454
interactive Web pages, 534–35
interactive Web-based worksheets, 525–27
interactive worksheet data on a Web page, 520
interactivity
    adding with Web Components, 534–35
    options for worksheets, 526
INTERCEPT function, 4
interest rate, 210
interface, 18–21, 304
Interior object, 234
interior of a cell, 233
Interior property
    of a cell, 234
    of Range object, 236
International Standard Book Numbers (ISBNs), 197
Internet
    as a data source, 527–32
    interacting with, 519
    publishing results, 533–37
Internet Assistant VBA add-in, 240
Internet Explorer, hidden instance of, 532
Internet Information Server (IIS), 533
Internet solutions, 537
Intersect method, 124
intersection of two ranges, 124
Interval argument of DateDiff function, 216
intrinsic constants, 59
invalid data message, displaying, 188
investments, 211, 212
IPMT worksheet function, 209
IRM (Information Rights Management), 7

IS family of functions, 194
Is Nothing test, 302
Is Null expression, 474
ISBLANK function, 194
ISBNs (International Standard Book Numbers), 197
IsConnected property, 353
IsEmpty function, 296
ISERR function, 194
ISERROR function, 194
IsExportable property, 553
ISLOGICAL function, 194
ISNA function, 194
ISNONTEXT function, 194
ISNUMBER function, 194
isolation feature of an EXE component, 248
ISREF function, 194
ISTEXT function, 193, 194
IsValid procedure, 317
Italic property, 232
ITC (Microsoft Internet Transfer Control), 536
Item method
    of Collection object, 315
    of PivotCaches collection, 352
    of PivotTables collection, 349
Item property
    accessing Chart objects in Charts collection, 327
    of AddIns collection, 244
    of CommandBarControls collection, 372
    of CommandBars collection, 366
    of Errors collection, 486
    of Fields collection, 494
    of Parameters collection, 489
items, selecting, 409, 413
iteration loops, 77–79

J

Jet database engine, 485
join operation, 476

K

key buffer, 128
key codes, 126
key fields, 342, 343
key modifiers, 126
key sequence, assigning a macro to, 31
key server, 38
keyboard, entering a declarations section, 93

keyboard buffer, sending key strokes to, 127
keyboard shortcuts, assigning to macros, 31
KeyPress event, 429
keys, 342. See also database keys
    for a digital signature, 37

L

Label control, 401, 404
    adding to a user form, 396
    beside a SpinButton control, 408
LabelRange property, 356
labels, 335
landscape mode, 154
landscape orientation, changing, 73
language in regional settings, 124
large files, navigating, 276
LargeButtons property, 366
LargeChange property, 411
Last button, 426
Last Position item on the View menu, 45
LastModified property, 284
LastRow constant, 423, 426
LastRow variable, 427
late binding, 450–52, 454, 465
layering effect of Chart Object Model, 326
Layout button, 344
LayoutForm property, 355
lazy searches, 165
LBound function, 185
leap years, 76
Left Arrow key, 127
Left function, 200
Left property
    of ChartObject object, 337
    of CommandBar object, 368
    of CommandBarControl object, 374
    of a user form control, 402
    of UserForm object, 398, 399
LeftMargin property, 154
Legend object, 322
LEN function, 197
less than (<) comparison operator, 75
less than or equal to (<=) comparison operator, 75
less than or equal to sign (<=), 473
less than sign (<), 473
Let property routine, 306

Let routine, 304
lifetime of variables, 62
light, creating colors using, 220
lightning bolt, indicating events, 278
Like operator, 474–75
line breaks in a message box, 67
line labels, 82
line numbers for GoTo statements, 82
LineCount property, 405
LINEST function, 4
LineStyle argument, 237
LineStyle property, 236
LinkObject, 542
links
    to external data sources, 141
    to other workbooks, 130
list box, combo box control operating as, 430
list box controls, initializing, 412
List property
    of CommandBarComboBox object, 378
    of ListBox control, 412
List toolbar, 9
ListBox control, 412
ListColumns property, 541
ListCount property
    of CommandBarComboBox object, 378
    of ListBox control, 412
ListHeaderCount property, 378
ListIndex property
    of CommandBarComboBox object, 378
    of ListBox control, 413
ListObject object, 541–44
ListObjects collection, 543
ListRows property, 541
lists, creating, 9
ListScopeFolderObjects procedure, 288
ListSearchScopeOptions procedure, 287
ListStyle property, 413
ListWidth property, 414
Load method of a user form, 399
LoadBehavior subkey, 250
LoadData method, 316
LoadPicture function, 410
Loan Calculation workbook, 170–71
loan payments, 208, 209

Local parameter
    of Open method, 131
    of OpenText method, 134
    of SaveAs method, 136
Locals window, 45
Locals Window item on View menu, 45
location
    for a chart, 323–25
    for a PivotTable, 344
Location method, 324, 325, 359
Location property, 323, 325
locked argument, 388
locked cells, protecting, 158
Locked property, 402, 403
log file, generating, 269
LOGEST function, 4
logical loops, 79–81
logical (And) operator, 199
logical value
    referring to, 194
    returned by the InputBox method, 123
LOGINV function, 4
LOGNORMDIST function, 4
Long data type, 59
Long Integer data type, 62
LookIn property, 282, 291
Lookup Wizard add-in, 240
loops, 77–81
Low macro security setting, 36
lower boundary for an array, 64, 65

M

macro code, 34, 35
Macro dialog box, opening, 41, 91
macro helpers for PivotTable presentations, 359
Macro Name box, 29
macro security settings, 36
macro toolbar buttons, 32
macro viruses, 36
macro writer's trick, 356
macros, 29
    adding weekday and date, 113
    assigning to key sequences, 31
    assigning to menu items, 33
    assigning to toolbar buttons, 32
    breaking up into several procedures, 54
    building a new quarterly workbook, 115
    calculating the active sheet, 120
    creating charts as object variables, 322
    creating new sheets, 112

debugging, 34–36
digitally signing, 39
displaying alerts while running, 116
editing or viewing, 41
executing the next step in, 35
implementing security for, 36–40
increasing the Zoom level, 114
intersection of two ranges, 124
iterating through a collection class, 315
locating the ProductList.xls file, 120
monthly totals, 122
one-click access to zoom, 114
pausing, 117
recalculating all open workbooks, 119, 120
recording, 29, 356, 531
removing all unused worksheets, 116
running, 31–34, 93
saving every open workbook, 137
signing with expired certificates, 39
skipping a step in, 35
storing, 55
viewing VBA code for, 29
Macros dialog box, 48
magenta VBA color constant, 219
magnification level, 154
mail. See e-mail messages, sending
Main procedure, 104
main program feature of an EXE component, 248
Make Same Size item on the Format menu, 46
MakeConnection method, 353
MakeOutlookAppointment-LateBinding procedure, 450–52
malware, 36
manual page breaks, 155
Map property, 558
Margin Indicator Bar, 51
marker sequences, 203
MatchEntry property, 413
MatchFound property, 415
MatchRequired property, 415, 430
MAX function, 206, 477
Max property
    of ScrollBar control, 411
    of SpinButton control, 407
Maximize button, 19
MaxLength property, 406

maxOccurs=unbounded parameter setting, 548
Me keyword, 311, 313, 505
measures, 342, 343
MEDIAN function, 206
median value, 206
Medium macro security level, 37
member of a collection, 108
MemoryUsed property
  of PivotCache object, 353
  of PivotField object, 355
menu item, assigning a macro to, 33
menu structure, dialog boxes accessing options, 392
menu system, parts of, 365–71
MenuAnimationStyle property, 366
menus
  adding items to existing, 382
  manipulating for custom add-ins, 365
  in Visual Basic Editor, 44–48
message box statement, 67
message boxes
  button options for, 68–69
  creating, 67–70, 104
  displaying, 69, 119
  displaying error descriptions, 429
  displaying information about charts, 139
  with a welcome or information message, 70
messages on the status bar, 67–70, 117
metadata, 6
methods, 27, 107, 119, 300
  adding to allow initialization of all properties of a class, 313
  characterizing as verbs, 300
  of a class, 304
  of Command object, 488
  of CommandBar object, 367–68
  of CommandBarComboBox object, 378–79
  of CommandBarControl object, 373–76
  of CommandBars collection, 366–67
  of Connection object, 484
  defining, 309
  of Errors collection, 486
  of ListObject object, 542–44
  of Recordset object, 491–94
  for taking action in workbooks, 145–47
  of user form controls, 402–4

of Validation object, 187
of XmlMap object, 554–56
of XPath object, 557
Microsoft Access. See Access
Microsoft ActiveX Data Objects 2.7 library, 498
Microsoft Excel. See Excel
Microsoft Excel 11.0 Object Library, 254
Microsoft Excel Object Model, 107, 108
Microsoft Internet Controls object library, 532
Microsoft Internet Transfer Control, 536
Microsoft Jet, 485
Microsoft Office applications. See Office applications
Microsoft Office Excel 2003. See Excel
Microsoft Office Excel Add-in, 239
Microsoft Office Excel item on the View menu, 45
Microsoft Office Excel Objects folder, 42
Microsoft Office Web Components. See Web Components
Microsoft Office Web site, 239
Microsoft OLE DB Provider for ODBC Drivers, 486
Microsoft Outlook. See entries under Outlook
Microsoft SQL Server. See SQL Server
Microsoft Visual Studio .NET. See Visual Studio .NET
Microsoft Windows SharePoint Services. See SharePoint Services
MID function, 202, 204
MIN function, 206, 477
Min property
  of ScrollBar control, 411
  of SpinButton control, 407
Minimize button, 19
minus sign (-), 134
Minute function, 214
mixed state for a button, 376
modal form, displaying, 399
modality for a message box, 69
MODE function, 206
mode parameter of Open statement, 295
Mode property of Connection object, 484
modeless forms, 399, 400
Modify method, 189

ModifyActiveChart procedure, 328
ModifyChart procedures, 328
ModifySpecificChart procedure, 329
Module item on the Insert menu, 45
module windows, 51
module-level variables
  declaring, 63, 259
  resetting, 48
modules, 42. See also code modules
  adding, 53
  copying between projects, 57
  creating, 55
  deleting, 56
  exporting, 56
  inserting into current projects, 45
  opening, 53
  separating code by task, 53
Modules folder, 42
month, weekday and date for the upcoming, 113
Month function, 214
monthly payment on a loan, 208
MonthlyPayment function, 209
MonthName function, 214
Move method
  of CommandBarControl object, 374, 375
  of Recordset object, 491
  of Sheets collection, 153
MoveFirst method, 491
MoveLast method, 491, 493
MoveNext method
  in CopyRows routine, 515
  of Recordset object, 492, 493
MovePrevious method, 492, 493
MsgBox (message box) function, 67, 68–69
MsgBox procedure, 104
msinet.ocx, 536
msoBarFloating value, 370
msoControlActiveX constant, 372
msoControlAutoCompleteCombo constant, 372
msoControlButton constant, 372
msoControlButton objects, 375, 380
msoControlButtonDropdown constant, 372
msoControlButtonPopup constant, 372
msoControlComboBox constant, 372
msoControlCustom constant, 372

msoControlDropdown constant, 372
msoControlEdit constant, 372
msoControlExpandingGrid constant, 372
msoControlGauge constant, 372
msoControlGenericDropdown constant, 373
msoControlGraphicCombo constant, 373
msoControlGraphicDropdown constant, 373
msoControlGraphicPopup constant, 373
msoControlGrid constant, 373
msoControlLabel constant, 373
msoControlLabelEx constant, 373
msoControlOCXDropdown constant, 373
msoControlPane constant, 373
msoControlPopup constant, 373
msoControlPopup item, 380
msoControlSpinner constant, 373
msoControlSplitButtonMRUPopup constant, 373
msoControlSplitButtonPopup constant, 373
msoControlSplitDropdown constant, 373
msoControlSplitExpandingGrid constant, 373
MsoControlType enumeration, 366, 367
msoControlWorkPane constant, 373
msoFileDialog constants, 292
msoFileType constants, 283
msoFileTypeExcelWorkbooks constant, 283
msoLastModified constants, 284
msoSearchIn constants, 288
multidimensional arrays, 65, 186
multidimensional reports, 341
multi-line If...Then...Else statements, 74
MultiLine property of a text box, 439
Multiline property of TextBox control, 405
multi-line text box control, 440
multi-line text boxes, 405
MultiPage control, 417
    containing connection information, 502
    hiding tabs, 503

incrementing the Value property, 436
leaving tabs visible in design mode, 502
Page objects contained in, 434
tabs at the top of, 436
MultiPage1_Change event, 437
multiple applications, 465–66
multiple cells, transferring, 185
multiple file types for a search, 286
multiple items, selecting, 413
multiple object variables, 303
MultiRow property, 416
MultiSelect property, 413
multi-step wizard, 431–41
My List Has Headers check box, 540
MyCOMAddinSetup Wizard, 261
MySuppliers.xml file, 549–50
MySuppliers.xsd schema, 558, 560

N

#N/A error value, 124, 194
Name Box
    displaying the name of ChartObject object, 324
    drop-down list provided in, 177
    in the Excel window, 19
name element
    of Function procedure, 99
    of Sub procedure, 86
Name property
    of AddIn object, 245
    associated with a class, 305
    of ChartObject object, 323, 327, 337
    of a code module, 95
    of a combo box control, 421
    of Command object, 488
    of CommandBar object, 368
    of Field object, 494
    of Font object, 232
    of ListObject object, 541
    for modules and worksheets, 42
    for objects in Excel, 26
    of Parameter object, 490
    of PivotField object, 355
    of PivotItem object, 356
    of PivotTable object, 350
    for a project, 97
    of ScopeFolder, 290
    of Sheets collection, 149
    of a text box, 421

of a user form control, 402
of UserForm object, 398
of XmlMap object, 553
#NAME? error value, 124
named arguments, 104
    not allowed in events, 310
    passing, 103
named colors, 226
named ranges, 177
    creating, 17
    defining, 177
    managing, 17
    shrinking or expanding, 186
names
    choosing concise, 55
    creating, 178
    expanding using relative references, 181
    specifying, 181
Names collection, 177
Names list box, 182
naming convention, 55
naming rules for VBA objects, 43
NativeError property, 487
navigation buttons in RowNumber text box, 425
NEGBINOMDIST function, 4
.NET Framework, installing, 261
net present value, 212
new instance of an object, 301
New keyword
    creating a new instance of Word, 458
    creating an object variable, 455
    in a Dim, Public, or Private statement, 301
    extra code included by VBA, 513
New Project, creating, 257
New Projects dialog box, 252
New Web Query dialog box, 530
New Workbook task pane, 20
NewSearch method
    clearing the FileTypes collection, 287
    of FileSearch object, 282
NewSeries method, 340
NewSheet event for a workbook, 269, 270
NewSheet event procedure, 271
NewWindow parameter of FollowHyperlink method, 146
NewWorkbook event, 277
Next button
    adding to a user form, 425
    adding to a wizard application, 436

Next counter statement, 77
no changes mode for a file, 136
non-blank cells, counting, 206
non-contiguous groups of cells, 172
noncontiguous ranges, 333
non-OLAP data sources, 348
nonprinting characters, stripping,
    195
non-standard delimiter character,
    134
nontext item, referring to, 194
NORMDIST function, 5
NORMINV function, 5
NORMSDIST function, 5
NORMSINV function, 5
Northwind sample database, 515
not equal (<>) comparison
    operator, 75
not equal to sign (<>), 473
Not ObjectVariable Is Nothing
    expression, 302
Not operator, 473
notation styles, 179–80
Nothing value
    returned by the ActiveWorkbook
        property, 115
    using with objects, 302
Notify Before State Loss option, 52
Notify parameter, 131
nouns, characterizing objects as,
    300
=NOW formula, 213
Now function, 101, 214
nper argument
    of PMT function, 208
    of PV function, 212
    of RATE function, 211
NPV function, 212
Null value
    in a database column, 468
    selecting rows containing, 474
#NULL! error value, 124
NullString property, 350
#NUM error value, 124
Num Lock key, 127
number format, changing to text,
    195
Number property
    of Err object, 83
    of Error object, 487
number signs (#), assigning values
    to date variables, 60
NumberFormat property
    of PivotField object, 355
    of Range object, 195

numbers
    factorials of, 97
    manipulating, 206–12
    referring to, 194
    returned by the InputBox
        method, 123
    validating the entry of, 429
numeric data types, 58–59
numerical error code, 83
NumericScale property, 490

O

Object box in Code window, 43
Object Browser, 326
    listing dialog box constants, 389
    locating events, 277
Object Browser window, 44, 45
object collections, 79
object levels in a chart, 326
object model, 107, 108
object references, characterizing as
    properties, 300
object variables, 301
    creating, 455
    creating charts as, 323
    declaring, 72
    defining, 72
    objects with multiple, 303
    referring to applications, 451
    setting to uninitialized state, 302
Object_Change event procedure,
    265
object-oriented programming,
    25–28
objects, 26, 42, 299
    accessing, 301
    actions performed by, 119
    adding to a collection class, 314
    adjusting vertical spacing
        among, 46
    aspects of, 26–28
    automating, 465
    centering on a form, 46
    containing, 107
    creating, 300, 301
    declaring, 302
    deleting all in a collection, 315
    destroying, 302, 311
    exposing common directly,
        108
    formatting, 219–37
    grouping selected, 46
    instantiating, 301
    interface to, 304
    lining up along a common border,
        46

monitoring the state of, 300
    with multiple object variables,
        303
    naming, 43
    Nothing value and, 302
    as nouns, 300
    removing groupings, 46
    representing a collection of
        similar things, 300
    resizing, 46
    supported by particular events,
        277
    used to control Excel, 107
    validating information in, 317
    working with, 107
Objects folder, 42
Object_SelectionChange event
    procedure, 265
ObjectVariable Is Not Nothing
    expression, 302
ODBC
    connection string, 352
    data provider for, 486
Office applications, 445
    add-ins spanning multiple, 259
    interacting with, 455–60
Office Clipboard, 20
Office documents, publishing to the
    Web, 535
Office Marketplace, 8
Office Object Model, 281
Office objects, 457
Office Web Components. See Web
    Components
Offset property, 167–69
OK button, 68
OLAP database, 347, 348
OLAP property of PivotCache
    object, 353
OLAP server, 347
OLE Automation. See Automation
OLE DB call, translating, 486
OLE DB connection string, 352
OLE DB data type, 494
OLE DB protocol, 481
On Error command, 82
On Error Resume Next statement,
    314, 380, 513
On Error statement, 360
OnAction event, testing, 379
OnAction property, 374, 375
OnAction routine, 400
OnAddInsUpdate method, 248, 249
OnBeginShutdown method of
    IDTExtensibility2 interface,
    248, 249

OnBeginShutdown routine, 261
OnConnection method, 252
  of IDTExtensibility2 interface,
    248
  passing the application object to,
    259
OnConnection routine, 260
OnDisconnection method, 249, 252
OnKey method, 125–27
OnLine Analytical Processing
    server, 347
OnStartupComplete method, 249
OnStartupComplete routine, 260
Open dialog box, 120, 291
Open event, 268, 269, 433
open files, checking for, 134
Open method
  of Application object, 295
  of Connection object, 484
  of Documents collection, 458
  opening a connection to a
    database, 513
  opening existing Web pages, 528
  of Recordset object, 492, 514
  of Workbooks collection, 130–31
Open statement of VBA, 295
OpenText method of Workbooks,
    132–34
OpenWriteExcelWbkContents
    procedure, 463
operating system
  for a text file, 133
  for a workbook, 130
Operator property, 188
Option Base statement, 64
Option Explicit statement, 254
Option Private Module statement,
    91
Option Private statement, 86, 99
optional parameters, not allowed in
    events, 310
OptionButton controls, 409, 431
Options dialog box, 50–52
  Color tab, 224, 226
  Custom tab, 224
  displaying, 48
options for a wizard, 438–40
Or operator, 473
Oracle databases, connecting to,
    486
Order By clause, 475, 493
Order item on the Format menu, 46
Organize Supporting Files in a
    Folder check box, 522

Orientation property
  of PageSetup object, 154
  of PivotField object, 353, 355
  of ScrollBar control, 411
Origin parameter
  of Open method, 130
  of OpenText method, 133
OriginalValue property, 494
Other parameter, 134
OtherChar parameter, 134
outline format, specifying, 355
Outlook, adding a reference to, 452
Outlook Calendar, 450, 452
Outlook Contacts folder, 453
Outlook Object Library, 452
out-of-process components, 248
output parameter to a stored
    procedure, 490
OverWrite alert, 116

P

page area in a PivotChart, 346
page breaks, 14, 155
Page Down key, 127
Page objects, 417, 434
Page Up key, 127
PageFields property, 350, 354
pages, navigating in a wizard
    application, 435–37
PageSetup object, 154
ParamArray arguments, not
    allowed in events, 310
Parameter object, 482, 488, 490
Parameter property, 374, 375
parameters
  of FollowHyperlink method, 146
  for the Open method of
    Workbooks, 130
  of property routines, 307
  of ThisWorkbook.SaveAs, 135
  with the Workbooks.OpenText
    method, 134
  of Worksheet.Protect method,
    157–58
Parameters collection, 489
Parameters property, 488
Parent property
  of AddIn object, 245
  of AddIns collection, 244
  of Chart object, 325, 340
parse information, 133
Password keyword, accessing a SQL
    Server database, 486

Password parameter
  of Open method, 130
  of Protect method, 157
  of SaveAs method, 136
PasswordChar property, 406
passwords
  entering before opening
    workbooks, 157
  guaranteeing a minimum length
    for, 197
  hard-to-guess, 144
  hiding information, 406
  requiring to open workbooks,
    141–42
  verifying, 142
PasteFace method, 376
path of a workbook, 140
Path property of AddIn object, 245
Pattern property, 234
PatternColor property, 234
PatternColorIndex property, 234
patterns
  filling the interior of a cell, 234
  viewing available, 235
pause, simulating in VBA code, 448
pausing macros, 117
PEARSON function, 5
per argument in IPMT function, 209
period (.), referencing subelements
    of a data type, 73
Picture property
  of Image control, 410
  of UserForm object, 398, 399
PictureAlignment property, 410
pictures, displaying, 410
PictureSizeMode property, 410
PictureTiling property, 410
pigments, 220
PivotCache method, 351, 352
PivotCache object, 352–53, 356,
    357
PivotCaches collection, 351, 352
PivotCharts, 346, 358
PivotField object, 353
  properties and methods of,
    354–55
  returning, 350
PivotFields collection, 350, 354,
    358
PivotFields (index) method, 351
PivotItem objects, 354, 356
PivotItems method, 354, 355
PivotTable Field List, 343
PivotTable functionality, 526
PivotTable objects, 348, 349–51,
    353, 354, 358

PivotTable Options dialog box, 345
PivotTable Web Components, 534
PivotTable wizard
  creating PivotCharts, 346
  creating PivotTables, 343
PivotTables, 341
  based on OLAP data sources, 348
  creating, 343, 357–58
  graphical representation of, 346
  managing large volumes of data, 347
  manipulating programmatically, 359–64
  pivoting programmatically, 359
  programming, 356–59
  recording and restoring arbitrary positions, 361–64
  resetting to original position, 361
  sources of data for, 347
  updating information displayed in, 351
  using on protected worksheets, 158
PivotTables collection, 348, 349
PivotTableWizard method
  of PivotTable object, 351
  from the Worksheet object, 349
pixels, 220
Plot Area object, 322
PlotBy property of Chart object, 337
pmt argument
  of PV function, 212
  of RATE function, 211
PMT function, 208
points, 155, 174
POISSON function, 5
pop-up controls, 380
pop-up menus
  creating, 381
  displaying, 380–81
  specifying command bars as, 371
portrait mode, 154
portrait orientation, changing, 73
Position property
  of CommandBar object, 368
  of PivotField object, 353, 355
  of PivotItem object, 356
POST field, 537
pound signs (##) in DateDiff, 216

PPMT function, 210
Precision property of Parameter object, 490
present value. See PV (present value)
presentation file, opening, 446
Preserve keyword, 66
PreserveColumnFilter property, 553
PreserveNumberFormatting property, 554
preset filters, 293
Prev button
  adding to a user form, 425
  adding to a wizard application, 436
Preview parameter, 148
primary colors, 220
primary key, 469
principal, 210
Print dialog box, controls in, 147
Print Preview
  BeforePrint event triggered by, 271
  displaying a workbook in, 148
  event triggered by, 269
  taking a user directly to, 148
  testing BeforePrint, 272
PrintArea property, 182
Print_Area range, 183
Print_Area reserved name, 182
PrintEmbeddedCharts procedure, 339
PrintObject property, 337, 339
PrintOut method, 147, 339
PrintPreview method, 148, 339
Print_Titles reserved name, 182
PrintToFile parameter, 148
PrintWorksheetOnly procedure, 339
Priority property of CommandBarControl object, 374
private class-level variables, 306, 309
Private declaration, 90
Private element
  of Function procedure, 99
  of Sub procedure, 86
private key, 38
Private keyword, 310
Private parts of a class, 303
Private statement, 302
procedural pitfalls, 97
procedural programming languages, 25
Procedure box in Code window, 43

procedure calls, 97–98
Procedure item on Insert menu, 45
Procedure Separator option, 51
procedures
  adding to modules or class modules, 54
  assigning to events, 265
  calculating average sales, 173
  calling from other modules, 94
  calling from within the same, 97
  changing the scope from Public to Private, 93
  error-handling abilities of, 82
  executing, 47, 48
  hiding all in a module from view, 92
  keeping as short as possible, 54
  passing arguments to, 101
  resuming execution of, 84
  returning a value, 85
  running Sub procedures from within, 93–97
  with the same name, 95
  stopping the execution of, 48
  storing, 55
  toggle Design mode for selected, 48
  types of, 85
  using a copy of the original data, 103
  writing bite-sized, 104
processor cycles, saving, 309
ProgId property of AddIn object, 245
program flow, controlling, 73–82
program window controls, 19
programming style, 54
programs
  adding class modules to, 305
  basing on recorded code, 356
  testing in Visual Basic, 425
Project Explorer
  compared to Windows Explorer, 53
  developing projects, 55–57
Project Explorer item on the View menu, 45
Project Explorer window
  copying modules from within, 57
  displaying, 45
  selecting a macro, 41
Project Properties dialog box, 48
projects, 41
  adding code to, 53
  copying modules between, 57

properties

developing with Project Explorer, 55–57
displaying all open, 266
elements utilized by, 42
folders within, 42
renaming, 97
setting properties for, 48
properties, 26, 107, 299
  of AddIn object, 245–46
  adding synonyms for existing, 313
  of AddIns collection, 244
  as adjectives, 300
  of Application object, 108
  of Borders object, 236
  of Chart object, 336
  of ChartObject object, 337
  of ChartTitle object, 337
  of a class, 304
  of Command object, 488
  of CommandBar object, 367–68
  of CommandBarComboBox object, 378–79
  of CommandBarControl object, 373–76
  of CommandBarPopup object, 380
  of CommandBars collection, 366–67
  of Connection object, 484
  defining, 304, 305
  of Errors collection, 486
  of Field object, 494–95
  of Fields collection, 494
  of Font object, 231
  of Interior object, 234
  of ListObject object, 541–42
  of Recordset object, 491–94
  types of, 305
  of user form controls, 402–4
  of user forms, 399
  of Validation object, 187
  of workbooks, 138–44
  of XmlMap object, 553–54
  of XPath object, 557
Properties button in Print dialog box, 147
Properties item on Tools menu, 48
Properties window, 42
  changing the Name property, 305
  displaying, 45
  sizing user forms, 398
Property Get statement, 306
Property Let routines, 317
Property Let statement, 306

property routines
  compared to private class-level variables, 309
  defining, 306
  parameters of, 307
  using to detect errors, 317
Property Set statement, 306
property statements with user defined types, 308
PropertyTests collection, 285, 286
Protect method
  of Sheet and Worksheet object, 157
  of Workbook object, 142, 157
  of Worksheet object, 156, 157–59
protection, removing from workbooks, 144
ProtectStructure property, 143
ProtectWindow property, 143
Provider ComboBox control, 502
Provider keyword, 485
Provider_Change event in DBInfo user form, 503
PrToFileName parameter, 148
public class-level variables, 304
  defining, 305
  returning and modifying, 313
Public declaration, 90
Public element
  of a Function procedure, 99
  of a Sub procedure, 86
public functions, 309
public key, 38
Public keyword, 100
Public modifier, 63
Public parts of a class, 303
Public statement, 302
public subroutines, 309
public-key encryption, 38
Publish as Web Page dialog box, 523
Publish button
  in Publish as Web Page dialog box, 524
  in Save as Web Page dialog box, 522
Publish method, 542
PublishInteractivePage procedure, 535
PublishResultsToWeb procedure, 534
PutData routine, 427–28

PV (present value), 211, 212
pv argument
  of PMT function, 208
  of RATE function, 211

Q

queries
  editing, 505–8
  executing, 508–15
  running, 512–14
query string, getting from a combo box, 512
query types, valid, 353
QueryTable property, 542
QueryType property, 353
question icon in a message box, 70
question mark (?) wildcard character, 203, 474
Quick Watch dialog box, 47

R

R1C1 notation, 179
Raiseevent statement, 310
Range box in PivotTable wizard, 344
range names
  reserved, 182
  in SERIES formulas, 331
  substituting for range references, 333
Range object, 161
  methods available to, 164
  received by Worksheet_Change, 275
  returned by ActiveCell property, 109
  returned by RangeSelection property, 116
  specifying cells for recalculation, 120
range of cells, 521, 522
Range property, 166, 167, 542
range references, 331, 333
ranges. *See also* named ranges
  arithmetic sum of, 206
  comparing two or more, 124
  defining on a chart, 325
  defining using the Cells property, 172
  drawing outlines around, 237
  extending, 165
  joining together, 173–74
  largest value in, 206
  manipulations of, 161

ranges, *continued*
most common value in, 206
named, 177
naming guidelines, 178
not necessary to first select, 166
referring to, 166–69
returning multi-dimensional
arrays, 185
selecting, 162–64
separating for tracking purposes,
173
separating with commas, 172
smallest value in, 206
standard deviation, 206
RangeSelection property, 116
Range(<cell>).Value property, 101
rate argument
of PMT function, 208
of PV function, 212
RATE function, 211
RDO (Remote Database Objects),
481
readability of code, 54
ReadOnly parameter, 130
read-only property, 304
Read-Only Recommended option,
130
ReadOnlyRecommended
parameter, 136
reads and writes, reducing to a
worksheet, 185
read-write mode, 131
recalculation, 275
Record Macro dialog box, 29
record pointer, 484
RecordCount property
of PivotCache object, 353
of PivotItem object, 356
of Recordset object, 492, 493
recorded macros, 325
RecordPosition macro, 361–64
RecordSet object
in ADO object model, 482,
491–94
in RunQuery routine, 513
Recordset property of PivotCache
object, 353
recursive procedures, 97
red VBA color constant, 219
RedBorder procedure, 237
ReDim statement, 66
#REF! error value, 124
RefEdit control, 415
Reference argument, 389
reference materials, 7

references
to procedures, 96
referring to, 194
resolving, 311
References command, 452
References dialog box
displaying, 48, 96
referencing the ADO database
library, 498
in Visual Basic Editor, 453
Refresh method
of ListObject object, 542
of Parameters collection, 489
of PivotCache object, 353
updating data, 352
RefreshDate property, 353
RefreshPeriod property, 353
RefreshTable method, 351
RegEdit program, 250, 256
regional settings, language
specified in, 124
registry. *See* Windows registry
registry entries, 250
relational database, 467
relative references, 30
expanding names, 181
specifying for cells, 166
Relative References button, 30
Remove method, 315
RemoveItem method
of CommandBarComboBox
object, 378
of ListBox control, 413
RemoveMap procedure, 556
Repeating property of XPath object,
558
reports, 342
REPT function, 199
Require Variable Declaration
option, 50
Research task pane, 7, 20
research tools, updating, 8
reserved range names, 182
Reset item on the Run menu, 48
ResetAllPageBreaks method of
Worksheets, 155
ResetColors method, 226
ResetFromRecorded macro, 363
ResetPivotTable macro, 361
Resize method, 186, 543
Restore button, 19
Result variable, 385
results, publishing on the Internet,
533–37
Resume command, 84

Resume Next statement, 84
RetrieveWebQueryData procedure,
529
Retry and Cancel buttons, 68
Return key, 127
Review text box, 439
Review_KeyPress event, 440
RGB color combinations, 221
RGB color values, 226–29
RGB function of Visual Basic, 220
RGB values
of colors, 221–23
setting gridline colors to, 230
of VBA color constants, 220
Right Arrow key, 127
Right function, 200
right-angled corners, 337
RightMargin property, 154
root directories of file structures,
289
Root element in a schema, 548
root object, 42
RootElementName property, 554
rounded corners, 327
RoundedCorners property, 337
row fields for a PivotTable, 358
row height, measured in points,
174
RowFields property, 351, 354
RowGrand property, 351
RowIndex property, 368
RowNumber text box, 422, 425
RowNumber_Change event, 425
rows
adding to tables, 478
allowing users to delete, 158
allowing users to format, 158
allowing users to insert into, 158
computing the previous, 425
copying to a worksheet, 514
in a database table, 468
maximum height of, 14
maximum number of, 14
referencing, 172
removing from tables, 479
retrieving all from a table, 472
retrieving from a database, 513
retrieving from one or more
database tables, 471
retrieving selected, 473–75
sorting, 475
specifying for new items, 413
Rows property of Select, 172
RSQ function, 5
Run Macro dialog box, 48

Run menu, 48
Run method, 94, 95
Run Query button, 508, 517
Run Sub/UserForm item on the Run
    menu, 48
Run to Cursor item on the Debug
    menu, 47
RunCharMap procedure, 448
RunDatabaseQuery routine, 508
running total feature, 21
RunQuery routine
    in Excel Query program, 509
    in ThisWorkbook module,
        512–14
Run-time error 1004, 360
RunWizard routine, 434

S

Save As built-in dialog, 383
Save As dialog box, 242, 291
Save as Web Page dialog box, 521
Save button, 424, 427
Save method, 135
SaveAs method
    of ThisWorkbook property,
        135–36
    for workbooks, 116
    of Worksheet method, 159
    of Worksheet object, 156, 159
SaveAsUI argument, 271
SaveAsWebPage procedure, 525
SaveCopyAs method, 137
Saved property, 273
SaveData method, 316
SaveData routine, 506
SaveDataSourceDefinition property,
    554
SaveLinkValues property, 141
SaveSetting routine, 504
Scenario Manager dialog box, 15
scenarios, 15
Scenarios parameter, 158
schema standards document, 547
schemas, 10, 546
    adding to active workbooks, 556
    creating custom, 546–49
    importing data into, 552
    mapping elements to cells,
        557–62
    mapping Excel data to, 10
    mapping to single lists, 560
    mapping to worksheets
        programmatically, 553–57
    saving as XML schema files, 548

Schemas property of XmlMap
    object, 554
schema-validation errors, 554
scope of variables, 62
ScopeFolder object, 288
ScopeFolders collection, 289
ScopeFolders file, 281
screen flashing, minimizing, 118
screen updates, disabling, 118
ScreenUpdating property, 118
scroll bars
    adding to applications, 411
    including the TextBox control,
        405
Scroll event of ScrollBar control,
    411
Scroll Lock key, 127
scrollable window, 51
ScrollBar control, 411
ScrollBars property
    of TextBox control, 405
    of UserForm object, 398
ScrollColumn property, 114
ScrollRow property, 114
search expressions with a Select
    statement, 473
Search For box in the Research task
    pane, 7
SEARCH function, 203–5
Search Results task pane, 20
searches, limiting, 286
SearchFolders collection, 289
SearchFolders file, 281
SearchIn constants, 288
SearchScope object, 287
SearchScopes collection, 287
SearchScopes file, 281
Search_SearchFolders collection,
    291
Search_SearchFolders routine, 290
SearchSubFolders property, 282
Second function, 214
secondary keys, 469
seconds, number since midnight,
    214
sections of cells, 233
security for macros, 36–40
Security Warning box, 40
Select All button, 19
Select Case statements, 75–77
    creating effective, 90
    definitive rules in, 89
    generating an incorrect result, 88
    in ListScopeFolderObjects
        procedure, 289

setting to the number of days in
    each month, 76
    syntax of, 75
Select Certificate dialog box, 39
Select method
    of Range object, 162
    of Worksheet object, 156, 159
Select statement, 471–77
    examples using, 472
    Where clause, 473
Select XML Source dialog box, 551
selected cell, compared to active,
    161
Selected property, 413
SelectedItem property (TabStrip
    control), 415
SelectedItems property (FileDialog
    object), 293
Selection Change event, 274
Selection object, 161
selection process, SHIFT and CTRL
    keys aiding in, 413
Selection property
    of Application object, 117
    compared to ActiveCell, 110
selection statements, 74–77
SelectionChange event, 265
SelectionChange event procedure,
    276
SelectPrint routine, 183
Semicolon parameter, 133
SendKeys method, 127
sequence statement in an XML
    schema, 11
sequence tag for subelements, 548
series, 340
series area in a PivotChart, 346
SERIES formula
    in a chart, 331, 332
    editing, 332
    modifying, 332
    syntax of, 333
Series objects, 332, 340
server, 470. See also automation
    servers; Web server
Set command, 72
Set New statement, 301
Set Next Statement item on the
    Debug menu, 47
Set Page Title dialog box, 522
Set property routine, 306
Set routine, 304
Set statement, 122, 301, 456
set theory, 468

SetSourceData method, 325, 332, 359
SetupSearchFoldersCollection procedure, 289
SetValue method, 558
Shadow property, 337
Shared Add-in template, 257
Shared Add-in Wizard, 257
shared file, 136
shared workbooks, conflicting changes in, 136
Shared Workspace task pane, 7, 20
SharePoint Services, 6
  lists and, 10
  support for, 20
SharepointUrl property, 542
sheet tabs, 14, 21, 230
SheetActivate event
  for Application object, 277
  for a workbook, 269, 270
sheets. *See also* worksheets
  adding to the end of workbooks, 151
  copying or moving to a new workbook, 153
  deleting by name instead of position, 152
  displaying on the sheet tab, 150
  forcing to be printed in black and white, 154
  repositioning in workbooks, 153
  types of, 13, 149
Sheets collection
  index value beginning with 1, 151
  methods, 150–55
  properties in common with Worksheets, 149–50
  specifying an array in, 153
Sheets In New Workbook box, 13
SheetSelectionChange event, 266
Shell function, 446
ShellExecute function, 447
SHIFT key
  aiding in the selection process, 413
  combining with key codes, 126
  key codes for, 127
  preventing the Workbook_Open procedure from executing, 270
SHIFT+CTRL+F6, 53
SHIFT+F8, 35
SHIFT+F9, 35, 157
shortcut key, assigning to a macro, 31

shortcut menus, disabling, 276
ShortcutText property, 376
Show method
  displaying a dialog box, 385
  of FileDialog object, 293
  modal form as the default, 400
  of a user form, 399
Show Next Statement item, 47
ShowAllItems property, 355
ShowAutoFilter property, 542
ShowCommandPopup routine, 380
ShowDatabaseInfo routine, 500
ShowDropButtonWhen property, 414
ShowError property, 188
ShowForm subroutine, 430
ShowImportExportValidationErrors property, 554
ShowInput property, 188
ShowPopup method, 368, 380
ShowTotals property, 542
Simonyi, Dr. Charles, 55
simple properties, 306
simple variable, compared to an object variable, 301
simultaneous scrolling of windows, 7
Single data type, 59, 62
single procedure view, 51
single quotes in SQL, 473
single-line If...Then...Else statements, 74
single-line text boxes, 405
single-precision floating-point number, 59
Size property of Font object, 232
Size To Fit item on the Format menu, 46
Size to Grid item on the Format menu, 46
SLOPE function, 5
SmallBags function, 101
SmallChange property
  of ScrollBar control, 411
  of SpinButton control, 407
smart documents, 6
Solver Add-in, 240
Sort property, 492, 493
sorting on protected worksheets, 158
source data for a PivotTable, 344
Source property, 492, 514
SourceType property, 542
Space parameter, 133
SpecialCells methods, 164, 176

SpecialEffect property, 402
Spell checking feature, 275
SpinButton control, 407, 408
SpinDown event, 407
SpinUp event, 407
Split command, 53
spreadsheet functionality, 526
Spreadsheet Web Components, 534
spreadsheets
  comparing to databases, 467–70
  publishing with Web components, 11
SQL (Structured Query Language), 468
  extensions to, 471
  manipulating databases, 471–80
SQL Server, 467
  connection strings, 511
  databases, 485
SQLState property of Error object, 487
square brackets ([]) in a time format, 217
Start command, 446
Start Searching button, 7
StartRow parameter, 133
StartUpPosition property, 398
State property
  of CommandBarButton object, 376
  of Connection object, 484
statements, provided in SQL, 471
statements element
  of Function procedure, 99
  of Sub procedure, 86
static controls, 401
Static element
  of Function procedure, 99
  of Sub procedure, 86
Static keyword, 97, 98
static procedures, 98
Static statement, 62
static variables, 62
static Web page, 521
static worksheet data, 520
statistical functions, 3–5
status bar, 21, 117
status messages, 67–70
StatusBar property, 117
STDEV function, 5, 206
STDEVA function, 5
STDEVP function, 5

STDEVPA function, 5
Step Into item, 47
Step Out item, 47
Step Over item, 47
step value in a For...Next loop, 77
STEYX function, 5
stop box, displaying during
    validation, 188
Stop Recording toolbar, 29, 30
storage requirements for data
    types, 58
stored procedures, 489, 490
STR function, 194
Strikethrough property, 232
string array, 65
string data, 194, 195
String data type, 59
string description of an error, 83
string expressions in conversion
    functions, 61
string variables in message boxes,
    70
strings
    adding characters to the
        beginning or end of, 199
    comparing, 498
    declaring, 60
    determining the number of
        characters in, 197
    empty, 60, 126, 468
    finding within another string,
        202–5
    handling, 59
    returning characters from,
        200–202
    types of, 59
structure of a workbook, 143
Structured Query Language. See
    SQL (Structured Query
    Language)
Style property
    of ComboBox control,
        414, 430
    of CommandBarButton object,
        376
    of CommandBarComboBox
        object, 378
    of MultiPage control, 436, 503
    of TabStrip control, 416
Sub procedures
    adding to a code module, 86
    compared to Function
        procedures, 85
    constructing a series of, 54
    defining, 85–97

defining the scope of, 90–93
elements of, 86
running from within procedures,
    93–97
syntax of, 86
SubAddress parameter of
    FollowHyperlink method, 146
subelements of Root element, 548
subroutines
    called from within objects, 300
    calling to process information on
        user forms, 405
    defaulting to Public, 310
    marking as Public, 304
    public, 309
Subscript property, 232
subscription services, 8
subtractive color system, 220
SUM function, 98, 206
SUMIF function, 206
Summarize procedure, 206–8
summary calculations, 206–8
summary functions in SQL, 477
summary operation for cell data,
    21
Superscript property, 232
Swedish krona, 94
syntax errors, 50
system model, 69

T

tab bar
    in the Excel interface, 21
    on the Excel window, 14
TAB key
    key codes for, 127
    shifting the focus to the
        command button, 404
Tab Order dialog box, 45
Tab Order item on the View menu,
    45
Tab parameter, 133
Tab Width code formatting option,
    50
TabFixedHeight property, 416
TabFixedWidth property, 416
TabIndex property, 402, 403
table format, specifying for
    PivotTable items, 355
table numbers, determining from
    Web sites, 531
tables
    adding rows to, 478

changing the value of columns
    in, 479
compared to worksheets, 467
copying to open Word
    documents, 460
joining, 476
removing rows from, 479
retrieving all rows and columns
    from, 472
retrieving rows from multiple,
    476–77
TabOrientation property, 416
Tabs collection, 415
tabs in Options dialog box, 50–52
TabStop property, 402, 403
TabStrip control, 415
Tag property
    of CommandBarControl object,
        375
    in Workbook_Open routine, 434
tags, 520
Taiwanese era dates, 133
Target range, 275
task identification number, 446
Task Manager, forcing hidden
    applications to close, 458
task panes, 20
tasks, informing users about, 67
template add-ins, included in Visual
    Basic 6, 250
Template parameter of Workbooks
    Add method, 129
templates
    classes as, 299
    creating, 14, 534
    for creating add-ins, 256
    modifying, 259–61
temporary variable, 309
Terminate event, 311, 400
testcondition argument, 76
TestControl routine, 379
TestPlants procedure, 125
tests, 286
text
    accepting from users, 405
    aligning in a message box, 69
    concatenating, 198–200
    determining if a cell is, 193–95
    manipulating, 193–205
    in a message box, 67
    reading and copying, 298
    referring to, 194
    returned by the InputBox
        method, 123

text boxes
  hiding characters entered into,
    406
  validating entire, 405
text files
  importing, 45
  importing modules from, 55
  opening, 134, 295
  reading using VBA, 296
  representing spreadsheet data,
    132
  saving deleted code in, 56
  standard procedure for writing to,
    295
text format of files, 131
Text Import Wizard, 132
Text property
  of Characters object, 326
  of ListBox control, 413
  of TextBox control, 405
text responses, accepting from
    users, 71
TextBox control, 401, 405, 408
TextCodePage parameter, 136
TextColumn property, 413
TextLength property, 406
TextOrProperty property, 285
TextQualifier parameter, 133
textual formats for communication
    across the Internet, 536
TextVisualLayout parameter
  of OpenText method, 133
  of SaveAs method, 136
Thawte Consulting, 38
thesauruses in the Research task
    pane, 20
ThisWorkbook module, 498
ThisWorkBook object, 267
ThisWorkbook property
  of Application object, 119, 135
  Close method, 138
  FullName method, 140
  Path method, 140
  referring to a different workbook,
    145
  RunWizard subroutine, 434
  Save method, 135
  SaveAs method, 135–36
Thomson Profiles collection, 8
ThousandsSeparator parameter,
    134
ThousandsSeparator property, 529
three-dimensional reports, 342
tilde (~) in the SEARCH function,
    203

time and date serial numbers, 213
time entries, searching for all in one
    month, 163
time formats, square brackets ([])
    in, 217
time functions, 213–16
time period, adding to a date or a
    time, 214
time serials, 216
time units, 215
Timer function, 214
times
  exceeding 24 hours, 217
  handling, 60
  manipulating, 213–17
TimeSerial function, 214, 215
TimeValue function, 214
TINV function, 5
title bar
  in Excel window, 19
  of a message box, 68
titles
  specifying for add-ins, 242
  specifying for Web pages, 522
To parameter of PrintOut method,
    148
toggle, 19
Toggle Breakpoint item on the
    Debug menu, 47
Toggle Total Row button, 9
ToggleButton control, 407
tool tips
  controlling the display of,
    50, 51
  displaying expected formula
    parameters, 21
toolbar button, assigning a macro
    to, 32
Toolbar Name box, 32
Toolbar Options button, 49
toolbars
  adding buttons to, 260
  compared to menus for custom
    macros, 33
  creating, 32, 377
  customizing, 49
  moving, 49
  removing buttons from, 261
  showing or hiding available,
    49
Toolbars item on the View menu, 45
Toolbars tab page, 32
Toolbox
  adding more controls to, 48
  displaying objects, 45

toolbox floating toolbar, 401
Toolbox toolbar, 395
Tools menu, 48, 433
ToolTips, turning on and off for
    toolbars, 51
TooltipText property, 375
Top property
  of ChartObject object, 337
  of CommandBar object, 368
  of CommandBarControl object,
    375
  of a user form control, 402
  of UserForm object, 398
TopIndex property, 413
top-level Office objects, 457
TopMargin property, 154
total row, displaying, 9
TotalsRowRange property, 542
TrailingMinusNumbers parameter,
    134
TransactionEffect property, 417
TransitionPeriod property, 417
translation utility, 20
trapping
  events, 399
  VBA errors, 82
tree view, presenting projects in, 41
TREND function, 5
triggers for a Chart object, 329
TRIM function, 196
Trim function in GetDBQuery
    routine, 508
trusted source, adding, 40
twip, 71
two-digit years in VBA, 60
two-dimensional report, 342
.txt (text) file. See text files
type, as a reserved word in VBA,
    209
type argument
  of PMT function, 208
  of PV function, 212
  of RATE function, 211
type element of a Function
    procedure, 99
Type parameter
  of Add method, 151
  of an element tag, 548
  setting to xlValidateTextLength,
    198
Type property
  of CommandBar object, 8
  of CommandBarControl object,
    22

of Field object, 494
of Parameter object, 490
of Validation object, 188
Type statement
creating a temporary variable for, 309
defining a new data type, 73
defining property routines, 308

U

UBound function, 185, 186
Underline property, 232
UnderlyingValue property, 494
underscore (_), displaying on a drop-down button, 414
Undo function, not available for databases, 480
unfilled circles, chart handles displayed as, 323
Ungroup item on the Format menu, 46
Unhide dialog box, 150
Union method, 173
Unlink method, 543
Unlist method, 543
Unload method, 399
Unload routine, 504
Unprotect method
of ActiveWorkbook, 144
of ActiveWorksheet, 159
unsaved changes, tracked by Excel, 141
untrapped errors, entering Break mode on, 52
unused worksheets, removing, 116
Up Arrow key, 127
Update method, 492, 493
update procedures, placing in a module, 97
Update statement, 471, 479
UpdateChanges method, 543
UpdateLinks parameter, 130
upper boundary for an array, 65
URL
to connect a Web data source, 352
encoding, 536
including the parameters as part of, 536
of the SharePoint list for a ListObject object, 542
U.S. Treasury Web site, 527

user form controls, 401–17
accepting the focus, 403
adding to user forms, 401, 421
examining the contents of, 403
placing on user forms, 421
properties, controls, methods and events of, 402–4
user form module, validating data in, 429–30
user forms, 42, 419
adding, 395
constructing, 419–31
creating, 395–400, 420
creating advanced, 419–41
designing, 51, 383, 396, 420–22
displaying, 399–400, 430
executing, 48
inserting into current projects, 45
life cycle of, 400
loading, 399
marking as dirty, 427
modifying, 397
moving controls to frames, 408
moving to the last line in, 426
placing on the screen, 398
properties of, 399
selecting, 397
testing, 397
typing data into, 187
User Id keyword, 486
UserForm events, 265
UserForm item on the Insert menu, 45
UserForm object, 395
adding to a project, 395
building for a wizard application, 434
creating, 396, 398, 420
UserForm_Initialize event, 502
creating, 426
in Excel Query program, 506
setting the LastRow variable in, 427
UserForm_Terminate event, 506
UserInterfaceOnly parameter, 158
user-level permissions, 7
users
accepting input from, 67, 71–72
accepting text responses from, 71
allowing to select multiple files, 294

allowing to unprotect worksheets, 159
choosing from a range of numeric values, 407
code prompting to save workbooks, 272
displaying a list to, 412
interfacing with, 400
performing selective validation of input, 121
presenting with messages, 67
preventing from accessing shortcut menus, 276
prompting for values, 122
selecting a range of cells from a workbook, 415
UseSystemsSeparators property, 529
UsingLateBinding procedure, 450
utf-8 encoding scheme, 547
utf-16 encoding scheme, 547
utility, designing to search for files, 287

V

validation
of the length of data strings, 197
rules, 187, 189
setting criteria for cells, 189
Validation object, 187, 189
Validation property, 187, 198
Value property
of Field object, 494
of MultiPage control, 436
of Parameter object, 490
of PivotField object, 355
of PivotItem object, 356
of ScrollBar control, 411
of SpinButton control, 407
of TextBox control, 405
of a user form control, 402, 403
of Validation object, 188
of XPath object, 558
#VALUE! error value, 102, 124
values
assigning to date variables, 60
assigning to string variables, 60
assigning to variables, 64
checking for the most restrictive set first, 90
retaining between procedure calls, 97–98
retrieving from arrays, 66
returned by message boxes, 69

VAR function, 5
VARA function, 5
variable-length strings, 60
variables, 57
    assigning a specific instance of
        an object to, 122
    assigning the value of one to
        another, 64
    assigning values to, 64
    declaring, 58, 63
    determining if text, 193
    displaying the value of, 47
    lifetime of, 62
    local and class-level, 311
    in procedural programming, 25
    scope of, 62
    setting to the days in each
        month, 76
    simple compared to object, 301
    visibility of, 62
variant arrays, 185
Variant data type, 61
    converting to, 62
    declaring a Decimal data type,
        58
Variant Date, 62
Variant Double, 62
variant variable, 185
variants, 61
VARP function, 5
VARPA function, 5
VB Editor, 268
VB runtime error 1004, 116
VBA (Visual Basic for Applications),
    41, 445
    adding class modules to
        programs, 305
    automatic data type conversions
        by, 61
    color constants, 219, 220, 230
    creating procedures, 85
    data types available in, 58
    displaying user forms in, 399
    Excel as a series of objects, 25
    functions available for dates and
        times, 214
    macros as interpreted code, 247
    manipulating data with,
        193–217
    minimizing reads or writes to a
        worksheet, 185
    modules, 55, 56
    naming rules, 43
    objects used by, 107
    range references in, 166

selecting a delimiter, 132
statements allowing file
    manipulation, 295
trapping errors, 82
two-digit years, 60
VBA array, 340
VBA code
    containers for, 104
    generating and manipulating
        charts, 321
    in place of accessing the Dialog
        object, 393
    saving a worksheet as a Web
        page, 522
    simulating a pause in, 448
VBA projects. See projects
vbAbort constant, 69
vbAbortRetryIgnore constant, 68
vbApplicationModal constant, 69
VBAProject references, 97
vbBlack constant, 219, 220
vbBlue constant, 219, 220
vbCancel constant, 69
vbCr constant, 67
vbCritical constant, 68
vbCrLf (carriage-return, line-feed)
    constant, 67, 405, 440
vbCyan constant, 219, 221
vbDefaultButton constants, 69
vbExclamation constant, 68
vbFirstFourDays constant, 216
vbFirstFullWeek constant, 216
vbFirstJan1 constant, 216
vbFriday constant, 216
vbGreen constant, 219, 220
vbIgnore constant, 69
vbInformation constant, 68
vbLf constant, 67
vbMagenta constant, 219, 221
vbModal value, 431
vbModeless value, 431
vbMonday constant, 216
vbMsgBoxHelpButton constant, 69
vbMsgBoxRight constant, 69
vbMsgBoxRtlReading constant, 69
vbMsgBoxSetForeground constant,
    69
vbNo constant, 69
vbOk constant, 69
vbOkCancel constant, 68
vbOkOnly constant, 68
vbQuestion constant, 68
vbRed constant, 219, 220
vbRetry constant, 69
vbRetryCancel constant, 68

vbSaturday constant, 216
vbSunday constant, 216
vbSystemModal constant, 69
vbThursday constant, 216
vbTuesday constant, 216
vbUseSystem constant, 216
vbWednesday constant, 216
vbWhite constant, 219, 221
vbYellow constant, 219, 220
vbYes constant, 69
vbYesNo constant, 68
vbYesNoCancel constant, 68
Vehicle Identification Numbers
    (VINs), 202
verbs, characterizing methods as,
    300
VeriSign, 38
vertical pages for a worksheet
    printout, 154
Vertical Spacing item, 46
View Code icon, 254
View menu, 44–45
views, 468
VINs (Vehicle Identification
    Numbers), 202
virtual tables, 468
viruses, 36
visibility of variables, 62
Visible control, 403
Visible parameter of Add method,
    178
Visible property
    of ActivateWindow object, 330
    of ChartObject object, 337
    of CommandBar object, 368
    of CommandBarControl object,
        375
    of PivotItem object, 356
    of a user form control, 403
    in Worksheets and Sheets
        collections, 150
VisibleFields property, 351, 354
Visual Basic
    building automation add-ins, 250
    creating a new add-in in, 252
    RGB function, 220
    testing programs in, 425
Visual Basic Editor
    Ambiguous name detected error,
        95
    building a simple class, 312
    changing displays in, 50
    customizing, 49–52
    displaying, 86, 100
    introduction to, 41–84

Visual Basic Editor Ask a Question box

keyboard shortcuts for executing macro steps, 35
listing expected arguments for a procedure, 103
menus, 44–48
opening, 41
recognizing parts of, 41–48
References dialog box, 96
signing code associated with a workbook, 39
tools for testing macros, 34–36
viewing macro code, 29
Visual Basic Editor Ask a Question box, 384
Visual Basic Editor Code window. *See* Code window
Visual Basic Editor Form Editor, 43
Visual Basic Editor window, 266
Visual Basic for Applications. *See* VBA (Visual Basic for Applications)
Visual Basic modules, 254
Visual Basic .NET
building COM add-ins with, 256
compared to Visual Basic 6, 467
Visual Studio .NET
compiling add-ins, 261
Shared Add-in Wizard, 257

W

Wait method, 117, 128
warning box, during validation, 188
Watch window, 45
Web
currency quotes on, 94
Excel color palette on, 226–29
publishing worksheets to, 523–25
Web Components
adding interactivity with, 534–35
in Office 2003, 11
Web Options dialog box, 522
Web pages
adding interactivity on, 526
containing frames, 528
naming, 521
opening as workbooks, 528
opening in Excel, 528
parsing, 532
posting on the Internet, 523–25
presenting results as, 533–37
publishing to behave like spreadsheets, 11

saving help and informational files as, 146
saving worksheets as, 520–23, 534
specifying titles for, 522
Web Queries, 529–31, 532
Web server. *See also* **server**
communicating with, 536–37
posting new results directory to, 534
sending information to, 536
setting up, 533
Web Servers Home Directory, 533
Web sites, 525, 531
Web-based worksheets, 525–27
WebTables property, 531
Weekday function, 214
Weight argument of BorderAround method, 237
Weight property of Borders object, 236
Where clause
comparison operators in, 473
in Select statement, 473
in Update statement, 479
white space
determining for a worksheet, 154
stripping from a string, 196
white VBA color constant, 219
width of a cell, 174
Width property
of ChartObject object, 337
of Column object, 172
of CommandBar object, 368
of CommandBarControl object, 375
of a user form, 398
of a user form control, 403
of UserForm object, 398
wildcard characters
used with the Access database, 474–75
using with SEARCH, 203
Window menu in Visual Basic Editor, 53
Window Settings options, 51
window state of an application, 446
windows. *See also* **code windows**
arranging all open when a workbook is deactivated, 271
controlling the zoom level of, 114
layout preventing users from changing, 143
moving, 49

Workbook_BeforeClose event

moving to display a particular cell, 114
returning the currently selected, 113
returning to a docked position, 49
simultaneous scrolling of two, 7
specifying dockable, 52
undocking, 49
Windows authentication, 504
Windows Explorer, 53
Windows program controls, 19
Windows registry
manually changing, 250
verifying entries in, 256
Windows-based applications, starting from a DOS window, 446
wininet.dll file, wrapper for, 536
With...End With command, 73
WithEvents keyword, 278, 304, 310
WizardApp.xls, 432
wizards
building multi-step, 431–41
collecting options for, 438–40
navigating pages in, 435–37
running, 441
summarizing options in, 440
Word application, late binding with, 450
Word documents, 457–59, 460–62
WordWrap property, 405
Workbook event procedures, 268
Workbook events, 265, 267–73
Workbook object, 107
calling the Save method, 135
contained in an Application object, 326
creating, 456
events attached to, 268
events for, 267
as the parent of the Charts collection, 326
returned by ActiveWorkbook, 115
as the top-level object, 457
workbook window
controls, 19
scrolling through, 276
Workbook_Activate event, 246
Workbook_AddinInstall event, 245
Workbook_AddinUninstall event, 245
Workbook_BeforeClose event, 434, 500

Workbook_BeforeSave procedure, 271

Workbook_Close event, 246

Workbook_Deactivate event, 246

Workbook_Open event, 246, 269
in Application object, 277
in Excel Query program, 499
in ThisWorkbook module, 433

Workbook_Open event procedure, 268, 269, 272, 279

WorkbookOpen function, 279

workbooks, 13, 129
activating, 137, 145
adding sheets to the end of, 151
adding XML to manually, 550–53
building new quarterly, 115
changing every open, 129
changing the active, 137
changing the position of sheets in, 153
checking for write-protected, 142
checking to see if open, 134
closing, 138
comparing side by side, 7
copying color palettes from, 225
creating, 129, 151, 241–43
detecting when opened, 279
digitally signing, 39
displaying in Print Preview mode, 148
displaying macros in, 31
forcing to recalculate, 120
of macro currently running, 119
making backup copies of, 137
maximizing, 270
maximum number of colors, 14
methods, 145–47
modifying all charts in, 338
opening, 130–35
opening Web pages as, 528
printing and previewing, 147–48
properties of, 138–44
protecting from changes, 142–43
providing hot keys specific to, 126
recalculating, 119, 120, 272
referencing the currently selected, 115
removing protection from, 144
requiring passwords to open, 141–42, 157
saving, 135–37, 138, 141, 242
selecting a range of cells from, 415

signing VBA code associated with, 39
write-protected, 142

Workbooks collection, 129–48

worksheet elements
assigning colors to, 223
formatting, 230–31

Worksheet events, 265, 273–76

worksheet functions, 197

Worksheet object
contained in Workbook object, 326
containing a PivotTable, 348
events for, 273

Worksheet_Change procedure, 230
calling itself repeatedly, 266
executing, 275
monitoring the Change event, 267

WorksheetFunction object
calling the PMT function, 209
calling the SEARCH and FIND functions, 204
calling worksheet functions as properties of, 197
need for, 196

worksheets, 13, 14
alternative data sets for, 15
centering vertically on the printed page, 154
changing the name of, 149
changing the tabs of, 230
code ensuring an empty, 357
colors in, 219–31
compared to tables, 467
computing the previous row in, 425
creating with new PivotTables, 357–58
data limits of, 14
dealing with two-dimensional data, 341
entering information into, 419–31
event triggered when right-clicking, 274
forcing to print on a specified number of pages, 155
methods, 156–60
navigating among, 14
navigating event procedures in, 274
number of default, 13
printing on a specified number of pages, 154

proving two at a time, 159
publishing to the Web, 523–25
recalculating all formulas in, 156
reducing read and writes to, 185
reformatting the elements of, 219–37
removing unused from a workbook, 116
retrieving currently selected, 112
right-clicking, 276
saving as Web pages, 520–23, 534
selecting, 160
shrinking for printing, 154
typing data into, 187

Worksheets collection, 149–50, 151

Write# statements, 296

write-only property, 304

write-protected workbooks, 142

WriteReserved property, 142

write-reserved workbook, 130

WriteResPassword parameter, 130, 136

X

x-axis on a PivotChart, 346
x-axis title in a chart, 322
.xla file extension, 283
XLA file type, 239, 242
xlA1 constant, 180
xlAbsrowRelColumn constant, 180
xlBackgroundAutomatic constant, 232
xlBackgroundTransparent constant, 232
xlBetween constant, 188
XlBordersIndex constants, 236
XlBorderWeight constants, 236
xlBuiltinDialog constant, 384
xlBuiltinDialog property, 384
.xlc file extension, 283
XlCalculate constants, 156
xlCalculationAutomatic constant, 157
xlCalculationManual constant, 157
xlCalculationSemiautomatic constant, 157
xlCellType constants, 176
xlChart constant, 151
XlCmdType enumeration, 352
xlColorIndexAutomatic constant, 230, 236
xlColorIndexNone constant, 236

xlColumnDataType constants, 133
xlColumnField constant, 363
xlContinuous constant, 236
xlDash constant, 236
xlDashDot constant, 236
xlDashDotDot constant, 236
xlDatabase argument, 357
xlDataField constant, 363
xlDelimited constant, 133
xlDiagonalDown constant, 236
xlDiagonalUp constant, 236
xlDialog constants, 384
xlDialog intrinsic constants, 390
xlDialogActiveCellFont constant, 391
xlDialogAddChartAutoformat constant, 391
xlDialogAlignment constant, 391
xlDialogApplyNames constant, 392
xlDialogAutoCorrect constant, 392
xlDialogAxes constant, 391
xlDialogBorder constant, 386, 391
xlDialogCellProtection constant, 386, 388, 391
xlDialogChartAddData constant, 391
xlDialogChartWizard constant, 391
xlDialogColorPalette constant, 392
xlDialogColumnWidth constant, 392
xlDialogCreateNames constant, 392
xlDialogDataLabel constant, 391
xlDialogDataSeries constant, 391
xlDialogDefineName constant, 392
xlDialogDefineStyle constant, 392
xlDialogEditSeries constant, 391
xlDialogFilterAdvanced constant, 392
xlDialogFont constant, 390, 391
xlDialogFontProperties constant, 386, 391
xlDialogFormatChart constant, 391
xlDialogFormatCharttype constant, 392
xlDialogFormatFont constant, 391
xlDialogFormatLegend constant, 392
xlDialogFormatNumber intrinsic constant, 386
xlDialogFormulaGoTo constant, 385, 389
xlDialogGallery3dBar constant, 392
xlDialogGallery3dColumn constant, 392

xlDialogGallery3dLine constant, 392
xlDialogGallery3dPie constant, 392
xlDialogGalleryDoughnut constant, 392
xlDialogGalleryLine constant, 392
xlDialogGalleryPie constant, 392
xlDialogGoalSeek constant, 392
xlDialogInsertObject constant, 392
xlDialogMainChartType constant, 392
xlDialogOpen constant, 392
xlDialogPageSetup constant, 393
xlDialogPatterns constant, 386, 391
xlDialogSaveAs constant, 393
xlDialogSelectSpecial intrinsic constant, 386
xlDialogSendMail constant, 393
xlDialogShowToolbar constant, 393
xlDialogZoom constant, 393
xlDisplayShapes constant, 140
xlDMYFormat constant, 133
xlDot constant, 236
xlDot intrinsic constant, 59
xlDouble constant, 236
xlDYMFormat constant, 133
xlEdgeBottom constant, 236
xlEdgeLeft constant, 236
xlEdgeRight constant, 236
xlEdgeTop constant, 236
xlEMDFormat constant, 133
xlEqual constant, 188
xlErrors constant, 176
xlExcel4IntMacroSheet constant, 151
xlExcel4MacroSheet constant, 151
xlExclusive constant, 136
xlFileFormat constants, 136
xlFixedWidth constant, 133
xlGeneralFormat constant, 133
xlGreater constant, 188
xlGreaterEqual constant, 188
xlHairline constant, 236
xlHidden constant, 363
xlHide constant, 140
xlInputOnly validation type, 189
xlLess constant, 188
xlLessEqual constant, 188
xlLineStyle constants, 236
xlLineStyleNone constant, 236
xlListConflict constants, 543
xlListObjectSourceType constants, 543

xlLocalSessionChanges constant, 136
xlLocationAsNewSheet option, 323
xlLocationAsObject option, 323
xlLocationAutomatic option, 323
xlLogical constant, 176
.xlm file extension, 283
xlMDYFormat constant, 133
xlMedium constant, 236
xlNoChange constant, 136
xlNone constant, 155
xlNoRestrictions constant, 159
xlNoSelection constant, 159
xlNotBetween constant, 188
xlNotEqual constant, 188
xlNumbers constant, 176
xlOtherSessionChanges constant, 136
xlPageBreakManual constant, 155
xlPageBreakNone constant, 155
xlPageField constant, 363
XlPattern constants, 234
xlPatternAutomatic constant, 234
xlPatternChecker constant, 234
xlPatternCrissCross constant, 234
xlPatternDown constant, 234
xlPatternGray constants, 234
xlPatternGrid constant, 234
xlPatternHorizontal constant, 234
xlPatternLightDown constant, 234
xlPatternLightHorizontal constant, 234
xlPatternLightUp constant, 234
xlPatternLightVertical constant, 234
xlPatternNone constant, 234
xlPatternSemiGray75 constant, 234
xlPatternSolid constant, 234
xlPatternUp constant, 234
xlPatternVertical constant, 234
XlPivotFieldDataType enumeration, 354
XlPivotFieldOrientation constants, 362
XlPivotFieldOrientation types, 355
XlPivotFormatType formats, 350
xlPlaceHolders constant, 140
XlQueryType enumeration, 353
xlR1C1 constant, 180
xlReferenceStyle constants, 180
xlReferenceType constants, 180
xlRelative constant, 180
xlRelRowAbsColumn constant, 180
xlRowField constant, 363

.xls file extension, 135, 283
XLSaveConflictResolution constants, 136
xlShared constant, 136
xlSheetHidden constant, 150
xlSheetVeryHidden constant, 150
xlSheetVisible constant, 150
xlSkipColumn, 133
xlSlantDashDot constant, 236
xlSpecialCellsValues constants, 176
*.xlt file, opening for editing, 131
.xlt file extension, 283
xlTextFormat constant, 133
XlTextParsingType constants, 133
XlTextQualifer constant, 133
xlTextQualifierDoubleQuote constant, 133
xlTextQualifierSingleQuote constant, 133
xlTextValues constant, 176
xlThick constant, 236
xlThin constant, 236
xlUnderlineStyleDouble constant, 232
xlUnderlineStyleDoubleAccounting constant, 232
xlUnderlineStyleNone constant, 232
xlUnderlineStyleSingle constant, 232
xlUnderlineStyleSingleAccounting constant, 232
xlUnlockedCells constant, 159
xlUserResolution constant, 136
xlValidAlertInformation constant, 188
xlValidAlertStop constant, 188
xlValidAlertWarning constant, 188
xlValidateCustom validation type, 188, 189

xlValidateDate validation type, 188, 189
xlValidateDecimal validation type, 188, 189
xlValidateInputOnly validation type, 188
xlValidateList validation type, 188, 189
xlValidateTextLength validation type, 188, 189, 198
xlValidateTime validation type, 188, 189
xlValidateWholeNumber validation type, 188, 189
xlWorksheet constant, 151
xlXmlExportSuccess constant, 554
xlXmlExportValidationFailed constant, 554
xlXmlImportElementsTruncated constant, 555
xlXmlImportSuccess constant, 555
xlXmlImportValidationFailed constant, 555
xlYDMFormat constant, 133
xlYMDFormat constant, 133
XML, 3
    adding to a workbook manually, 550–53
    adding to a worksheet programmatically, 553–62
    capabilities extended, 8, 9
    elements, 548
    files, 13, 550
    map, 553
    schema files, 548
    support for, 539
XML data. See data files
XML Map Properties dialog box, 552
XML Maps dialog box, 551

XML Path language. See XPath
XML schemas. See schemas
XML Source task pane, 20
    displaying, 547, 551
    Options button, 552
XML Spreadsheet Schema, 9
XmlMap object, 553–56
XmlMap property, 542
XmlMaps collection, 555
XmlSchemas collection, 554
XPath, 557–62
xpos argument for an input box, 71
.xsd file, 10

Y

y-axis on a PivotChart, 346
y-axis title in a chart, 322
Year function, 214
years
    leap, 76
    two-digit in VBA, 60
yellow lightning bolt, 278
yellow VBA color constant, 219
Yes, No, and Cancel buttons in a message box, 68
ypos argument for an input box, 71

Z

z-order, 403
zeros, adding to the beginning of a cell value, 200
zoom level
    of a window, 114
    of a worksheet, 175
Zoom property
    of ActiveWindow, 114
    of PageSetup object, 154
ZOrder method, 403
ZTEST function, 5

About the Authors

Curtis Frye is the author of *Microsoft Office Excel 2003 Step by Step, Microsoft Excel Version 2002 Plain & Simple, Faster Smarter Home Networking* (all from Microsoft Press), several books on Microsoft Access, and numerous online training courses.

Wayne S. Freeze, a computer consultant and author with more than a dozen books and 50+ articles to his credit, specializes in programming for Microsoft Office, Microsoft SQL Server, and Microsoft DirectX.

Felicia K. Buckingham, an expert on Excel and VBA programming, is the principal of FKB Consulting, based in Manitoba, Canada.